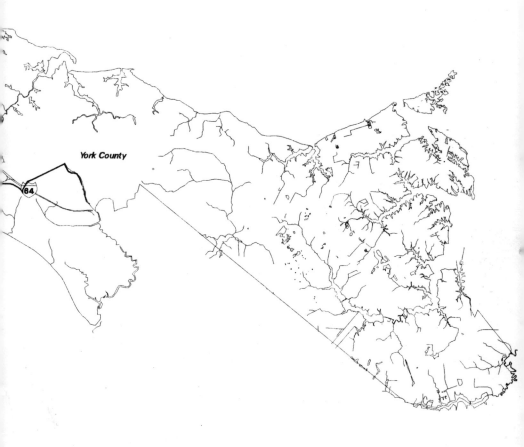

York County

64

JAMES CITY COUNTY
KEYSTONE OF THE COMMONWEALTH

Detail from Captain John Smith's map, "Virginia Discovered and Discribed [sic]," 1612. Library of Congress. See enlarged map, page 2.

JAMES CITY COUNTY
KEYSTONE OF THE COMMONWEALTH

by Martha W. McCartney

James City County
Board of Supervisors
James City County, Virginia, 1997

THE
DONNING COMPANY
PUBLISHERS

Dedicated to the people of James City County, especially my daughter, Cathleen Leigh McCartney.

James City County Board of Supervisors, 1997
David L. Sisk, Chairman, Roberts District
Perry M. De Pue, Powhatan District
Jack D. Edwards, Berkeley District
Robert A. Magoon, Jamestown District
Stewart U. Taylor, Stonehouse District

Sanford B. Wanner, County Administrator

Copyright © 1997 by James City County Board of Supervisors
James City County, Virginia

The Donning Company/Publishers
184 Business Park Drive, Suite 106
Virginia Beach, Virginia 23462

Steve Mull, General Manager
B. L. Walton, Jr., Project Director
Lisa Arnold, Project Research Coordinator
Dawn Kofroth, Assistant General Manager
Elizabeth B. Bobbitt, Executive Editor
Joseph C. Schnellmann, Graphic Designer
Tony Lillis, Director of Marketing
Teri S. Arnold, Marketing Coordinator

Library of Congress Cataloging-in-Publication Data

McCartney, Martha W.
     James City County: keystone of the commonwealth / by Martha W. McCartney.
         p.   cm.
     Includes bibliographical references (p.) and index.
     ISBN 0-89865-999-X (hardcover: alk. paper)
     1. James City County (Va.)—History. 2. Afro-Americans—Virginia—James City County—History. I. Title.
F232.J15M38   1997
975.5'4251—dc21
                                        97-3113
                                        CIP

Printed in the United States of America

Table of Contents

Foreword

The place now called James City County is a remarkable place to live, and has been so for many thousands of years. Martha McCartney's important study, JAMES CITY COUNTY: KEYSTONE OF THE COMMONWEALTH covers with extraordinary breadth and depth this complex entity, once part of the domain of Powhatan, then site of the earliest colonial settlement in English North America, and now home to a burgeoning intellectual, cultural, and economic center.

Martha McCartney brings to this study her formidable experience as an historian and author. Her career, which has encompassed many positions of importance, has centered around the careful sifting and analysis of many pieces of seemingly unrelated information, to form larger pictures of historic settlement and social history. Her memory for facts, her tireless pursuit of elusive materials, and her ability to synthesize these into a coherent picture of earlier ways of life is well-known among professionals and interested laypersons alike. In the present volume, McCartney reviews with unprecedented depth the social and landscape history of James City County, each chapter containing much new information based on McCartney's years of experience researching in archives both in Virginia and in England. Arranged chronologically, this volume represents a coherent historical narrative, marked by more detailed discussions of specific topics such as the founding of Jamestown and surrounding plantations, the Revolutionary War, Reconstruction, and the crucial inter-war years of the twentieth century. Ms. McCartney also includes three chapters dealing with Black history, education, and belief systems.

Although destined to become an indispensable source for scholars, this volume is sure to be a welcome addition to every library. McCartney's readable style, her insight into the most significant of historical events and issues, and her enthusiasm for her subject will be apparent to all. This volume marks the beginning of a new era in James City County history, while celebrating the contributions of the old.

KATHLEEN BRAGDON, PH.D.
College of William and Mary
Department of Anthropology

Acknowledgments

I am especially grateful to the James City County Board of Supervisors and the County Administrator's staff who made possible the publication of this manuscript. Special thanks are also due the James City County Historical Commission which initiated its production. Phyllis P. Cody of the James City County satellite office has served as the "sparkplug" of the project. Norman Danuzer, who devoted numerous hours to reviewing local newspapers, and Nan and Ralph Maxwell, the capable photographers whose photos grace this volume deserve special recognition. Deborah L. Wilson and Christina A. Kiddle created the maps that help to link historical events to specific places in the county. David K. Hazzard produced the stunning cover photo that appears on the dust jacket of this volume.

Colleagues at the Colonial Williamsburg Foundation unflaggingly provided assistance and encouragement. Linda Rowe and Robert M. Watson Jr. provided me invaluable insights on black history, whereas Lois Danuzer, Susan Berg, Liz Ackert, John Ingram, Gail Greavy, Catherine Grosfils, and Del Moore dealt patiently with my requests for obscure archival materials. Retired professor Ludwell H. Johnson shared his extensive knowledge of Civil War history and Dennis Blanton of the College of William and Mary's Center for Archaeological Research provided much helpful information on prehistory. The opportunity to conduct extensive research on Jamestown Island's history, undertaken as part of the National Park Service's Jamestown Archaeological Assessment, has made it possible for me to venture into European sources and to share more fully the story of America's best known historic attraction. James Haskett, Jane Sundberg, David Riggs, and Diane Stallings of the National Park Service generously shared their knowledge of local history. Fred Boelt and Margaret N. Weston, two longtime friends with multi-generational ties to James City County, read portions of the manuscript in draft form and shared their knowledge of the area. The constructive comments offered by Kevin Kelly of the Colonial Williamsburg Foundation were invaluable.

Numerous county employees and local citizens generously shared their knowledge, patiently fielded my questions, or helped in countless other ways. Among them are Sanford B. Wanner, Deborah L. Wilson, Donna Temple, Mary Lou Smith, Jody Puckett, Trenton L. Funkhauser, Sylvia Davis, Brenda Grow, Barbra Cook, Mary C. and Howell P. Hazelwood Jr., Kathleen Bragdon, Marley R. Brown III, Hugh Desamper, Joseph Robertson, Marie Sheppard, Roberta Jones, Lou Powers, John Hemphill III, Solomon Ashlock, Margaret Cook, Richard D. Mahone, Warren Smith, Barbara (Babs) Moore, David and Virginia Dare Waltrip, Andy Bradshaw, Caroline W. Dozier, Frances H. McCartney, James Robertson, Nancy S. Bradshaw, Frances H. Hamilton, Dari H. Wahlquist, Cary Carson, and Gregory Brown. Last but not least, my husband, Carl Aschman, offered encouragement and helped in innumerable ways.

MARTHA WALDROP MCCARTNEY
1996

Introduction

A Library of Virginia employee laughed when I said I intended to write a book-length history of James City County and retorted, "It'll be a brief one!" He, like many others, was convinced that the destruction of the county's antebellum court records had left a gap that couldn't be bridged. I hope to prove otherwise, for James City County's history is well documented and as demonstrably rich as it is lengthy.

The records of Virginia's overarching branches of government, both before and after the Civil War, contain a wealth of information on people, places, and events directly associated with our area. These, in combination with historical maps, old photographs, military records, art work, tax rolls, parish registers, insurance policies, land patents, personal narratives and correspondence, newspaper accounts, marriage registers, business records, collections of private papers, and a myriad of other sources are available to help us piece together the past. The amount of material available on the nineteenth and twentieth centuries is almost overwhelming. Information on James City County and its inhabitants is available at the Colonial Williamsburg Foundation Research Archives, the Library of Congress, the National Archives, the Valentine Museum, the Library of Virginia, the Virginia Historical Society, the Museum of the Confederacy, the College of William and Mary's Marshall-Wythe School of Law and the Swem Library, the University of Virginia's Alderman Library, the Mariner's Museum, the National Park Service archives in Jamestown and Yorktown, the U.S. Army Corps of Engineers Archives, the North Carolina Department of Archives and History, and the Virginia Department of Historic Resources. Locally generated documents also are on hand in England at Oxford and Cambridge Universities, at the British Public Records Office, the Staffordshire Record

Office, the British Museum and Library, the Bermuda Archives and Museum, and the Huntington Library in San Marino, California. Archival records on file in the New York Historical Society, the Massachusetts Historical Society, and in the York, Henrico, Surry, Charles City and New Kent County Courthouses shed light upon James City County's history. Cartographic research was done in Ireland and Northern Ireland. Use was made of numerous published and unpublished sources, including archaeological reports, the works of local authors, and the James City County Historical Commission's oral history files. Numerous community service and civic organizations, churches, clubs and institutions responded to queries about their history.

The narrative that follows is structured chronologically. It begins with James City County's first inhabitants, the Native Americans, and ends with the early 1990s. The final three chapters deal with topics that I felt warranted more thorough treatment than could be accomplished artfully within the main narrative. Certain chapters contain mini-histories of local properties, largely drawn from research reports and National Register nominations I've done over the years. At the conclusion are ten appendices.

Throughout this volume are references to people who played a role in the county's history. Readers with a keen interest in family history are encouraged to glance at the footnotes, some of which contain lists of people associated with specific historical events. Detailed annotation has been provided for the sake of credibility and to assist those involved in historic preservation and scholarly research.

C H A P T E R   1

The Prologue To Jamestown

Indigenous Peoples: James City County's First Natives

Literally thousands of years before James City County came into existence, an indigenous population left a faint imprint upon the land. The history of the Indians or Native Americans, though largely unrecorded, is an integral part of our heritage. Much is known to us through archaeology.

The Paleo-Indian (before 6500 B.C.)

North America's earliest inhabitants, the Paleo-Indians, hunted in relatively mobile bands that exploited large game animals. They came on the scene during the late Pleistocene period and followed the roving movements of large game, such as elk, bison, and mastodon. They probably made use of the wide variety of plant foods available in a relatively cool, moist environment. Although evidence of these very early hunters has been discovered on the James-York peninsula, very few fluted projectile points (the Paleo-Indian's "calling-card") have been found within James City and York Counties and nearby Williamsburg.

The Archaic Indian (6500 B.C. to 1000 B.C.)

During the Holocene period, the climate warmed. North America's environment changed and new varieties of game animals and aquatic species became available for human consumption, as did a greater diversity of plant materials. Archaic period Indians foraged for food on a seasonal basis but their movements throughout the countryside were more localized. They began to rely upon local stone materials, such as quartz and quartzite, to fashion their points and tools. Although the James-York peninsula probably was occupied continuously during this period, relatively few Archaic sites have been discovered.

The Woodland Indian (1000 B.C. to 1600 A.D.)

By the Woodland period, the eastern United States was densely forested. Again, the indigenous population responded to the changing environment by modifying its strategy for survival. Between 2000 B.C. and 1000 A.D., the Indians became more sedentary and began making ceramic vessels they could use for cooking and storage. Because they mixed clays with a variety of tempering materials and manufactured ceramic vessels according to specialized techniques, their wares represent different cultural traditions. The Woodland period is divided into three time periods (Early, Middle, and Late) on the basis of cultural evidence.[1]

The Early Woodland Period

Archaeologists believe that pottery-making was introduced into Virginia around 1200 B.C. by people from the coast of what became South Carolina and Georgia. Virginia Indians dug clay from river banks or bluffs, mixed it with water, and added crushed shell or rock that kept the body of their vessels from shrinking or cracking during the drying and firing process. Gradually the Indians learned that they could produce taller vessels by molding their clay into coils they layered, pinched together and then shaped. Later they began smoothing and shaping the outside of their vessels with a paddle wrapped with cord, fabric or net. After the clay pot air-dried, it was placed in an open fire to bake and harden.

The Middle Woodland Period

Native peoples, by the Middle Woodland period, had become much more numerous. They began living as groups in scattered hamlets and small villages situated along Virginia's major streams. They put aside their spears and began using the bow and arrow to hunt wild game. The Indians modified the grooved axe and developed the celt for heavy woodworking. Crafts became increasingly refined and distinctive cultural traditions emerged. The Natives established trade networks for the exchange of goods. In time, certain families' rank or status within their tribal group was enhanced.

The Late Woodland Period

By the Late Woodland period, many important changes had occurred that affected the Native American's way of life. Corn or maize, introduced into the region from Mexico, provided the Indians with better nutrition. This enabled them to thrive and become more populous. Religious ceremonies commemorating the planting and harvesting of corn probably reflect the crop's importance in Native life. Archaeologists surmise that control of the food supply led to the development of a more sophisticated social order in which there were differences in the rank or status of certain individuals.

A surplus of cultivated crops allowed the Indians to store food and remain in one location for longer periods of time. Thus, villages replaced the base camps that characterized earlier periods. But the Indians still followed a seasonal pattern of hunting and gathering. They lived along the banks of tidal waterways

A late sixteenth century Indian village. Theodore De Bry's engraving. Courtesy of Dover Publications.

Theodore De Bry's engraving of John White's illustration. Courtesy of Dover Publications.

during the warm months and in winter, when their gardens were dormant and fishing was less productive, they moved into the interior and relied upon stored food and whatever game they could procure.[2]

Late Woodland Indians, unlike their more nomadic forebears, lived in large, well organized villages that sometimes included hundreds of people. Under the direction of tribal leaders, they worked toward their community's support. In chiefdoms, which had developed by the late 1500s, leaders accepted tribute, which they kept or redistributed at will. Ceremonial life was important and creativity flourished. The Late Woodland Indians created symbolic and ceremonial objects of stone, copper and shell related to their belief system. They preferred the floodplain and low-lying necks of land with rich, sandy soil. Within their villages, which sometimes were surrounded by a palisade, houses were clustered close together or interspersed with fields used for gardening. Beans, squash, and corn were the Late Woodland Indians' principal food crops and as time went on, they began cultivating tobacco. In an Indian village, women and elderly men usually planted the crops, using the slash-and-burn method of clearing the ground in which they set their seeds. The coastal plain offered the Indians a broad variety of fresh and salt-water fish, such as shad and sturgeon, and shell-fish such as oysters and crabs.

By the 1400s, when Europeans began documenting their exploratory visits to the New World, the Late Woodland Indians of Virginia's coastal plain had a well developed social order. They spoke the Algonquian language, a linguistic bond they shared with some of the Native peoples to the north and south.[3] Although European explorers' accounts capture a sense of Native life, at best they project a shallow, distorted image.

The Powhatan Indians of Virginia's Coastal Plain

In 1607, when Virginia's first colonists arrived, Indian villages lined the banks of Tidewater's rivers. Much of the region's population was then under the sway of a paramount chief named Powhatan or Wahunsunacock, who reigned over 32 districts that encompassed more than 150 villages of various sizes. These sub-chiefdoms paid tribute and supported him in times of war. Captain John Smith described Powhatan's style of government as monarchical, for he was an emperor to whom many lesser kings or leaders (called werowances) were subservient.

The first colonists seated themselves upon land that belonged to the Pasbehay Indians, who had a major village at the mouth of the Chickahominy River and two others nearby. Further inland, along the Chickahominy, were numerous sites occupied by the Chickahominy Indians, who were governed by a group of tribal leaders. John Smith's map of Virginia indicates that both Pasbehay and Chickahominy Indian villages were located within James City County. Smith observed that Indian men spent most of their time hunting, fishing and engaging in wars, whereas the women and children made mats, baskets, and pottery and raised the crops upon which their villages depended. He described the Powhatans as generally tall and straight, with black hair and dusky complexions. They were exceptionally strong and agile and could tolerate extremes in weather.

But there were many subtle, more important differences between the Natives and Europeans. The Indians considered land merely a part of the earth, which like the sky, water and the air, was communal and open to all for

Corn was an important staple of the Native diet. A late sixteenth
century Indian village. Theodore De Bry's engraving. Courtesy of
Dover Publications.

Detail from Captain John Smith's
map, "Virginia Discovered and
Discribed [sic]," 1612. Library of
Congress. See enlarged map, page 2.

subsistence. Thus, they couldn't fathom the European concept of *owning* land. The two cultures also had vastly different views of religion. The Powhatans, while open to the idea of a Christian deity, were reluctant to renounce their own gods. Although both cultures viewed accumulated wealth as an emblem of social status, they had a totally different concept of inheritance, for with the Powhatan, it descended through the female rather than the male.[4] In light of the numerous differences between the two cultures and their lack of mutual understanding, they were destined to collide.

Growing Interest in the New World

Explorers began visiting the western hemisphere during the first millennium, nearly 500 years before Christopher Columbus's voyage. In May 1493, Pope Alexander VI declared that Spain was entitled to all lands more than 100 leagues west of the Azores, unless they were in the possession of a Christian kingdom, and that Portugal had a right to all non-Christian lands east of that point. The 1494 Treaty of Tordesillas shifted the dividing line even further west. This concept of territorial rights prevailed in Roman Catholic countries until the late sixteenth century. Even so, in 1496 England sent John Cabot in quest of a westward passage to China. On his second voyage he planted the first English flag on the soil of what became Canada.

During the 1520s European interest in the newly discovered continent quickened. In 1524 Giovanni de Verrazano, a Florentine in the employ of King Francis I of France, sailed along the North American continent, touched land near Cape Fear, and visited the outer banks of North Carolina. He then turned northward, sailing past the Virginia capes and Chesapeake Bay. Verrazano sometimes is credited with naming geographical features within the region, such as the Bahia de Santa Maria or Bahia de Madre Dios, later known as the Chesapeake Bay, and the Rio del Espirita Santo, the James River.

In 1531 the Bristol merchant Robert Thorne urged King Henry VIII to seek a northern route to Cathay. His dictum, "No land uninhabitable nor sea unnavigable," became the byword of Richard Hakluyt, for many years England's most vocal advocate of colonization. Meanwhile, Spain, armed with formidable sea power, laid claim to virtually all of North America from

Florida to the St. Lawrence River. Spanish officials grew increasingly uneasy about French and English interest in western lands. Their concern was not unjustified, for the treasure fleet, when returning from Mexico, rode the northerly-flowing Gulf Stream and passed within 60 miles of the Chesapeake Bay. Thus, the coastline south of the bay's entrance was a potential haven for pirates who could prey upon the heavy-laden treasure ships sailing home.[5]

The Spanish Jesuit Mission

During the late 1550s or early 1560s a Spanish ship visited the Chesapeake and took aboard an Indian lad, reputedly a chief's son. He was transported to Spain, converted to Christianity and given the Spanish name Don Luis de Velasco. Later, he went to Saint Augustine and Cuba, where Jesuit missionaries heard him speak of his homeland, Ajacan, near the Bahia de Santa Maria or Chesapeake Bay. They seized the opportunity to spread the Christian message, using the converted Indian as an intermediary. On

September 10, 1570, a ship bearing Don Luis, eight Jesuits, and a young Cuban boy reached the mouth of the Chesapeake. It entered a broad, navigable river analogous to the James and sailed inland for approximately 40 miles, arriving at a stream comparable to College Creek. The Jesuits and the boy, guided by Don Luis, followed it inland and then portaged overland until they reached another navigable stream, probably Queens Creek. They set out by canoe and when they arrived at a broad river (the York), sought out a suitable place for an encampment.[6]

The Spanish Jesuits' demise. Lewis and Loomie's THE SPANISH JESUIT MISSION IN VIRGINIA, 1570-1572. Library of Congress.

One of the Jesuits dispatched a letter to Cuba via the returning ship.

He said that there had been "six years of famine and death" in Don Luis's land and that due to a severe drought, many Indians had died or left in search of food. Those who remained begged the missionaries to stay in Ajacan, as they wanted to be like Don Luis. The Jesuits requested a shipment of food and said that when relief was expected, they would send two Indians to "the mouth of the arm of the sea along which any ship must sail" (Old Point Comfort) to guide the vessel to the mission.

A few months later a Spanish relief ship, guided by the same pilot who brought the Jesuits to the Chesapeake, sailed into Hampton Roads. Some Indians, upon sighting it, donned the Jesuits' vestments and beckoned the visitors ashore. Meanwhile, warriors in canoes sped toward the ship, discharging a volley of arrows. The Spanish departed without touching land, but not before seizing an Indian who confessed that the missionaries were dead although the Cuban boy was still alive. In 1572 Cuba's governor decided to visit the Chesapeake to learn what happened to the Jesuits. Upon arriving in Hampton Roads, he dispatched a small vessel up the James with a Jesuit, some soldiers and the Indian informant. When they entered College Creek and dropped anchor, some Natives approached and came aboard to trade. The Spaniards, upon noticing that one Indian was wearing a piece of communion silver around his neck, seized the others and weighed anchor. At the entrance to College Creek, some Natives approached, offering to retrieve the Cuban boy. However, when he failed to appear on time, the Spaniards set out down the James, firing a cannon into a crowd of Indians assembled on shore.

When the Spaniards reached the mouth of the James, they found the Cuban youth. He reported that Don Luis, upon reaching his homeland, quickly discarded his mentors and fled to his own people. The Jesuits, abandoned in the wilderness, built a small hut and resigned themselves to great hunger and hardship. As they were anxious to begin their missionary work and needed Don Luis as translator, three Jesuits went to his village to ask for his help. When darkness fell, he and some companions attacked and killed the unsuspecting Jesuits, ransacked their hut, and took whatever they wanted. The Cuban boy, whose life was spared on account of his youth, saw that the Jesuits were buried properly. Later he fled to the territory of a neighboring chief. Cuba's governor, upon hearing the boy's tale, ordered one of his Indian captives to retrieve Don Luis or the others would be executed. As the renegade convert failed to appear, the governor held an inquest, using the boy as translator. Although some of the Indians were deemed innocent and released, the remainder were catechized, baptized, and then hanged from the ship's yardarm. The Spanish then departed, undoubtedly leaving in their wake a legacy of dread and suspicion.[7] The Jesuit mission site, meanwhile, faded into the forest.

England Challenges Spain's Claim

While Spain was attempting to strengthen her claim to land in the western hemisphere, English sea-dogs were growing more bold in challenging her presumed entitlement. Martin Frobisher, when searching for a northwest passage to China, reached the Arctic, Greenland and Baffin Island. His discoveries were eclipsed by Sir Francis Drake's circumnavigation of the world. In June 1578 Sir Humphrey Gilbert obtained a royal patent authorizing him to seek any "remote heathen and barbarous lands . . . not actually possessed of any Christian prince." After Gilbert's untimely death, his half-brother, Walter Raleigh, who became a favorite of Queen Elizabeth, obtained a charter to the western lands between 33 and 40 degrees north. His interest in colonization was fueled by the Hakluyts, who advocated large scale imperial expansion and believed that the new land would surely yield riches.[8]

The Roanoke Colony

In April 1584 Walter Raleigh dispatched two vessels to America to inspect his newly acquired land. Serving as navigator was the Portuguese pilot Simon Fernando. By July the mariners reached the Outer Banks inlet the Indians called "Hatarask." They took formal possession of the region on behalf of their monarch, whose seal they affixed to an upright post. They marveled at the lush vegetation and declared that the soil was "the most plentifull, sweete, fruitfull and wholsome of all the world." Friendly relations were established with the Indians on Roanoke Island and in the mainland. Queen Elizabeth, though unwilling to make Raleigh's colonization venture a national enterprise, provided him with a ship and supplies and allowed him to name the new land Virginia in commemoration of her spinsterhood. Raleigh's patent was confirmed in December 1584 and a month later, he was knighted. Plans immediately were made to send a group of colonists to Virginia. Included were Ralph Lane (a veteran of the attempts to colonize Ireland, who was knowledgeable about fort construction), Portuguese pilot Simon Fernando, artist John White, and Thomas Harriot (the scientist, mathematician, and geographer who schooled Raleigh and his sea captains in the art of navigation). The seven ships that set sail in April 1585 became scattered and straggled to their destination. Wingina, the Roanoke Indians' leader, agreed to allow approximately 100 colonists to establish a settlement on Roanoke Island. The others departed.[9]

By September 1585 Ralph Lane and his fellow adventurers had built a fort and some cottages. During fall and winter they explored the countryside, chronicling their discoveries in reports and sketches prepared for Sir Walter Raleigh. Lane and some others ventured northward by boat and reached the territory of the Chesapeake Indians, who lived near the mouth of the Chesapeake Bay.[10] Lane reported that he intended to spend the summer looking for a better harbor within the territory to the north. John White's exquisite drawings provide a remarkably detailed glimpse of Native life and the coastal plain's fauna and flora. By late May 1586 the growing enmity between the colonists and the Natives culminated in a bloody confrontation. When Sir Francis Drake and his fleet reached the Outer Banks in early June, Lane and his men decided to return to England. Accounts of the colonizing expedition and White's drawings and maps attracted much attention. In January 1587 "The City of Raleigh in Virginia" was incorporated and plans were made to establish a colony in the Chesapeake.

On July 22, 1587, a new group of colonists reached the Outer Banks, intending to pause briefly at Roanoke Island before continuing on to the Chesapeake. But the pilot Simon Fernando abandoned them. In August Governor John White set sail for England to procure some essential supplies. However, sea warfare with Spain and other obstacles delayed his return for three years. In mid-August 1590 when he reached to Roanoke Island, he found that the colonists had built a palisade around their settlement, which was abandoned. Carved upon a large post was the word "CROATAN," the Indian name for Roanoke Island. White, in recounting his search, said that in 1587 when he was preparing to leave for England, the colonists were planning to move 50 miles into the mainland. They agreed to carve upon a tree or door post the name of their destination, using a cross-mark (+) to signify that they were leaving in distress. White resolved to go to Croatan, but rough seas forced his ship's departure. Thus, Roanoke Island's "Lost Colonists" vanished into the wilderness.[11]

Thomas Harriot, in his BRIEF AND TRUE REPORT OF THE NEW FOUND LAND OF VIRGINIA, urged would-be colonists to profit from the Roanoke settlers' experience by preparing for life in a wilderness environment. He cited the need for English victuals, equipment for fishing and hunting, and adequate clothing. He claimed that some colonists "after gold and silver was not so soone found . . . had little or no care for any other thing but to pamper their bellies." Others were miserable because there were no "English cities nor such faire houses nor at their owne wish any of their old accustomed daintie food, nor any soft beds of downe or feathers."[12]

The attempts to plant a colony on Roanoke Island convinced Spain that England intended to establish a military base in the region to prey upon the treasure fleet. In 1588 General Pedro Menendez Marques dispatched men to the Chesapeake to search for "a pirate settlement." They were guided by the Portuguese pilot who had landed the Jesuits there in 1570. Finding no evidence of an English presence, they sailed down the coast and visited the abandoned settlement on Roanoke Island. Surmising that the English had not established a colony, the Spanish turned their attention elsewhere. The defeat of the Armada left them with other concerns.

Sir Walter Raleigh, despite an avowed interest in colonizing Virginia, failed to take up John White's quest for the Roanoke settlers until the mid-1590s. In 1603 his personal fortunes took a dramatic turn for the worse, for he was found guilty of treason, imprisoned, and stripped of his patent, which reverted to King James I.[13]

The New World Beckons

In 1604 Spain and England negotiated a peace treaty despite disagreement over England's insistence upon the right to trade or settle within all untenanted western lands. In 1607 Don Pedro de Zuniga, Spain's ambassador to England, urged his superiors to expel the English from Virginia while they were weak and few in number. He also reminded King James that it was "much against good friendship and brotherliness" to colonize what was part of the Spanish Indies. But James refused to discuss the issue. This impasse endured long after a permanent English colony had been established at Jamestown.[14]

Spain's concern over English colonization of the Chesapeake was not unjustified, for John Pory and others openly called Virginia a promising *sedam belli* or seat of war. But the English generally viewed colonization as a more broadly based economic enterprise. Sir Thomas Smith, an investor in Raleigh's Roanoke ventures and the head of two trading companies, believed that colonizing Virginia would yield great profits. He clung to those views while involved in planting a colony at Jamestown. Merchants in Bristol, Plymouth, and Exeter, participants in the profitable Newfoundland trade, began to consider the potential commercial gain to be derived from Norumbega (New England). Sea captain George Weymouth, who had visited the region in 1605, spoke of its abundance of natural resources and brought back some Indian captives. These and other factors piqued King James' interest in North America. On April 6, 1606, he issued a charter to the Virginia Company, which was headed by a council of royal appointees. Two subunits were created: the Virginia Company of Plymouth, which was responsible for colonizing North Virginia, and the Virginia Company of London, whose territory lay between 34 and 41 degrees north. The London-based group, which land lay at a more temperate latitude, hoped to reap large profits from exporting hides, medicinal substances, dyes, timber products, minerals, and precious metals. They also wanted to produce saleable commodities such as glass, iron, potash, pitch, and tar, making full use of the region's seemingly limitless natural resources. According to Captain John Smith, the two Virginia

Companies controlled approximately 1,500 miles of shore line.[15] Although the Virginia Company of Plymouth attempted to plant a colony at Sagadahoc on the coast of Maine in late 1606, it failed. Thus, the Virginia Company of London's settlement on the James River, in James City County, became America's first permanent English colony.

Notes

1.   Robert R. Hunter Jr., PHASE I ARCHAEOLOGICAL SURVEY OF THE HUNT BROOKS, INC. DEVELOPMENT, JAMES CITY COUNTY, VIRGINIA (Williamsburg, 1988), 6-11; Christopher McDaid et al., A PHASE I CULTURAL RESOURCE SURVEY OF THE UNDERGRADUATE HOUSING PROJECT, COLLEGE OF WILLIAM AND MARY, WILLIAMSBURG (Williamsburg, 1991), 7-8. Located in upper James City County is the Croaker Landing Archaeological Site, which contains evidence of aboriginal occupation that spans approximately 2,500 years. It is on the Virginia Landmarks Register and the National Register of Historic Places.

2.   Keith T. Egloff et al., FIRST PEOPLE: THE EARLY INDIANS OF VIRGINIA (Richmond, 1992), 23-25.

3.   Egloff et al., FIRST PEOPLE, 26, 37; Bruce G. Trigger, ed., HANDBOOK OF NORTH AMERICAN INDIANS: NORTHEAST (Washington, D.C., 1978), 70-74, 240, 253.

4.   Egloff et al., FIRST PEOPLE, 41-43. For example, Powhatan's chiefdom could descend to his next oldest brother or the son of his eldest sister, but not to his own children.

5.   Helen Wallis, RALEIGH AND ROANOKE (Raleigh, 1985), 21; Carl O. Sauer, SIXTEENTH CENTURY NORTH AMERICA (Berkeley, 1975), 51-62, 70, 75; Clifford M. Lewis et al., THE SPANISH JESUIT MISSION (Chapel Hill, 1953), 11; David B. Quinn, NORTH AMERICA FROM EARLIEST DISCOVERY TO FIRST SETTLEMENT, THE NORSE VOYAGES TO 1612 (New York, 1977), 239.

6.   The geographical interpretation made by Lewis and his colleague is accepted by most scholars. The Spanish Jesuit mission site probably was located between Queens and Indian Field Creeks, perhaps on the Cheatham Annex property.

7.   Lewis et al., SPANISH JESUIT, 14, 38, 89-92, 107-109, 121, 118-121, 133-134, 137, 155-156, 185, 191.

8.   Wallis, Raleigh, 29-31, 37, 41; Quinn, NORTH AMERICA, 250.

9.   David B. Quinn, ENGLAND AND THE DISCOVERY OF AMERICA, 1418-1620 (New York, 1973), 2-3, 7; NORTH AMERICA, 327-329.

10.   Lane's account suggests that he and his men went up Currituck Sound to North Landing River and then portaged overland. John White's map suggests that the Chesapeake Indians' village was on the Elizabeth River.

11.   In May 1654 Francis Yeardley of Lynnhaven, a son of the late Virginia governor George Yeardley, paid a visit to "the ruins of Sir Walter Raleigh's fort," shown to him by a local Indian leader. He reportedly "received a sure token of their being there" (Alexander S. Salley, NARRATIVES OF EARLY CAROLINA [New York, 1911], 25-26).

12. Wallis, RALEIGH, 90-91; Quinn, ENGLAND, 110, 113-114, 123, 126; Thomas Harriot, BRIEF AND TRUE REPORT OF THE NEW FOUND LAND OF VIRGINIA (New York, 1972), 49, 74-75. When the Virginia Company of London set out to establish a colony on the James River in 1607, they paid little heed to Harriot's advice.

13. David B. Quinn, ROANOKE VOYAGES, 1584-1590: DOCUMENTS TO ILLUSTRATE THE ENGLISH VOYAGES TO NORTH AMERICA (London, 1955), 772-778; NORTH AMERICA, 430-433; ENGLAND, 447-448.

14. Barbour, JAMESTOWN VOYAGES, I, 118,121-122; Lyon G.Tyler, NARRATIVES OF EARLY VIRGINIA (New York, 1907), 222-224. As late as 1625, colonists near the mouth of the James received detailed instructions on what to do in the event of a Spanish invasion (H. R. McIlwaine, MINUTES OF COUNCIL AND GENERAL COURT, 1622-1632, 1670-1676 [Richmond, 1934], 135).

15. John Pory, JOHN PORY, 1572- 1636, THE LIFE AND LETTERS OF A MAN OF MANY PARTS (Chapel Hill, 1977), 72; Quinn, NORTH AMERICA, 440-444; Barbour, JAMESTOWN VOYAGES, I, 24-34; Captain John Smith, TRAVELS AND WORKS OF CAPTAIN JOHN SMITH, PRESIDENT OF VIRGINIA AND ADMIRAL OF NEW ENGLAND, 1580-1631, (Chapel Hill, 1986), I, 325.

THE CORPORATION OF JAMES CITY'S SETTLEMENTS WITHIN MODERN JAMES CITY COUNTY

(AREAS SETTLED BY 1620)

Map by Deborah L. Wilson.

CHAPTER 2

"Westward Ho" to Virginia
1607–1625

The First Colonists

On Saturday, December 20, 1606, the DISCOVERY, the SUSAN CONSTANT, and the GODSPEED set sail from London, catching the outbound tide. They moved slowly down the Thames and then anchored in the Downs to await favorable winds. Finally, they headed out to sea, carrying their passengers on an adventure that changed the course of history.

Captain Christopher Newport of the SUSAN CONSTANT was in overall command of the fleet. He was a skillful mariner with unrivaled experience in navigating the American coastline. He had sailed with Sir Walter Raleigh's fleet, some of which ships went on to Roanoke Island, and was well known to several members of the Virginia Company. Gabriel Archer and GODSPEED captain Bartholomew Gosnold had sailed to New England in 1602 and were familiar with its Natives and environment. Captain John Smith and others in the group were acquainted with the narratives of Ralph Lane, Thomas Harriot, and John White, which were well known throughout Europe. Thus, some of those who set out to colonize Virginia had an idea of what lay ahead. As Smith and Newport were able to communicate with the Natives, they probably had a minimal working knowledge of the Algonquian language, perhaps derived from the writings of Harriot or from Gosnold's and Archer's experience with the northern Indians.[1]

The SUSAN CONSTANT, GODSPEED and DISCOVERY. Library of Congress.

Captain John Smith. TRAVELS AND WORKS OF CAPTAIN JOHN SMITH, PRESIDENT OF VIRGINIA AND ADMIRAL OF NEW ENGLAND, 1580-1631, Edward Arber, ed. Library of Congress.

When the first colonists left England, they sailed southward along the coasts of Spain and Portugal to the Canary Islands, where they caught the Canary current, which flows in a westerly direction across the Atlantic. Newport's small fleet paused in the West Indies in March 1607 to take on fresh water and perhaps replenish their food supply. As the mariners approached the North American coast, they caught the Gulf current that propelled them northward. When Newport's navigational instruments indicated that he had reached 37 degrees, he would have realized he was near the entrance to the Chesapeake Bay and had his sailors test the depth 15 of the water, which was known to be 80 to 90 fathoms deep, 40 to 50 leagues off shore.[2]

The ships arrived safely in the Chesapeake on April 26, 1607, after more than eighteen weeks at sea. The 104 colonists had endured cramped quarters, seasickness, boredom, a lack of privacy, and food unlike their usual fare. These hardships probably made them ill-tempered and fueled their anxieties about what was yet to come. Nearly half of Virginia's first colonists were gentlemen, scholars, artisans (such as goldsmiths and perfumers) and tradesmen, not the sturdy laborers or yeoman farmers whose practical skills and physical stamina would have been of tremendous value in a wilderness. An exception, however, was John Smith, an experienced explorer and soldier-of-fortune whose survival skills eventually proved invaluable. As soon as Newport reached Virginia, he opened a sealed box that contained the names of the seven men who comprised the colony's highest ranking local officials. The members of this council were to elect a head man or president. The Virginia Company's first charter established the roles of the colony's governing officials, whereas its instructions brought the rudiments of English common law to the New World.[3]

During the first few days in Virginia, Newport and his men went exploring. They found magnificent timber, fields of brilliantly colored flowers, lush vegetation, fertile soil and an abundance of wildfowl, game, and marine life: as one man put it, a veritable paradise on earth. There were beech, oak, cedar, cypress, walnut, and sassafras trees, as well as strawberries, raspberries, mulberries, and fruit and berries that were unfamiliar. The Virginia wilderness also had large meadows that would provide excellent pasturage for cattle. The colonists encountered Natives whose bodies were adorned with brightly

colored furs and jewelry of bone, shell, and copper, and whose hair was orna-
mented with feathers and animal horns. According to John Smith, some of
them welcomed the explorers with food and entertainment. Others discharged
arrows and then fled from retaliatory gunfire.

On May 12th Newport's fleet arrived at a point of land they called
Archer's Hope, which extended from the west side of College Creek's mouth.
The colonists briefly considered building their settlement there, but because
the water was too shallow to moor their ships near the shore, they pressed on
upstream to a marsh-rimmed peninsula which at high tide resembled an
island. There, where the river's channel ran so close to the shore that the
colonists could tie their ships' lines to the trees, they built an outpost they
called *James Cittie* or *Jamestown*, the first permanent English settlement in
North America.[4]

Establishing a Settlement

The first colonists immediately set about fashioning a primitive half-
moon fort from the boughs of trees, for they had seated themselves amidst
Natives viewed as hostile and uncivilized,
within a region Spain considered hers.[5] James
Cittie lay within Pasbehay, the territory of the
Pasbehay Indians, which extended from that
of the Kecoughtans (near the mouth of the
James River) to a point beyond the mouth of
the Chickahominy River.

The so-called ZUNIGA map,
which reached England
prior to September 15, 1608.
Courtesy of Archivo General
de Simancas (Ministerio de
Cultura) and the Library of
Congress.

During the colonists' first night
on Jamestown Island, sentinels sounded an
alarm around midnight, for Indians were seen
approaching in canoes. Finally, the colony's
president decided to build a more substantial
fort that was palisaded and had mounted
ordnance. During the next few weeks, the
colonists worked diligently. They constructed
their fort, prepared ground in which to plant

corn, and fabricated clapboard that could be sent back to England. One early writer described the fort as triangular with a bulwark at each corner, each with four or five pieces of ordnance. A week after the settlers had completed their fort, Newport set sail for England, leaving in his wake quarrelsome men whose food supply was meager. Soon, hunger gnawed at them constantly and infectious diseases took their toll. The colonists obtained their drinking water from the river, which was salty at high tide and slimy and filthy at low, and they were plagued by mosquitoes, ticks, flies, and other insect pests. The marshes around Jamestown Island not only provided mosquitoes with a good breeding ground, the stagnant and contaminated water spread disease, especially during the warmer months. George Percy reported that the men "were destroyed with cruel diseases as swellings, fluxes, [and] burning fevers," but he admitted that "for the most part they died of famine." John Smith added that the colonists were so sick and weak that few among them could stand or move about. Another writer said that a small ladle of barley, ground into meal and made into porridge, comprised a daily ration of food. Although the Indians became more aggressive as they noticed the settlers' waning strength, ultimately they showed mercy and brought food to the fort. It saved the colonists' lives.[6]

The First and Second Supplies of New Settlers

Eight or nine months after Christopher Newport's departure from Virginia, he returned with 120 weak and famished new immigrants, who discovered that neither food nor shelter awaited them. Around 40 of the original settlers were still alive, only ten of whom physically were able to work. Sir Thomas Smith, a Virginia Company officer who accompanied the First Supply, set the newcomers to work digging for gold and felling trees from which masts and clapboard could be made. Thus, more emphasis was placed upon garnering profits for the Virginia Company than assuring the recent arrivals' survival. Again, a large proportion of the immigrants were gentlemen or artisans. John Smith declared that "our drinke was water, our lodgings, castles in the air," a reflection of how poorly the early settlers adapted to primitive living conditions.[7] Another writer recalled that "many famished in holes in the ground," a reference to the rude shelters or pit-houses that some colonists fashioned by digging a cavity six or seven feet deep, lining it with bark or timbers, and then covering it over with spars and bark or sod. Some people built arbor-like cabins by setting closely-spaced wooden poles in the ground, which they arched over and then covered with bark, Indian-style.[8]

In early January 1608, shortly after the First Supply arrived, a devastating fire swept through James Cittie, destroying the colonists' crude dwellings, provisions, and much of the fort. Afterward, Newport and his mariners helped them repair their homes and fortified compound. Two settlers and the Pasbehay Indian king set out into the vast wilderness on the lower side of the James, to search for the "Lost Colonists," rumored to be at Panawixke "beyond Roanoke." Ten days after Newport's April 10th departure, another 40 settlers arrived. They, like the others, were ill-suited to manual labor, but assisted in clearing about four acres of ground and building "a few poore houses." About nine months later, 70 new immigrants landed at Jamestown. Among them were Mrs. Thomas Forrest and her maid, Anne Burras, who married laborer John Laydon. Their union marked the beginning of family life in Virginia. This Second Supply of new colonists included 28 gentlemen, 14 tradesmen, and eight Germans and Poles, who had come to make pitch, tar, pot-ashes or lye, and glass. Within two months, the food supply was exhausted and the colonists were obliged to obtain corn from the Indians.

John Smith, whose experience as an explorer had honed his ability to cope with primitive living conditions, soon emerged as a leader. After he became president in September 1608, he tried to force the colonists to grow food crops, build houses, and strengthen the settlement's defenses.[9] Eventually, however, he was forced to disperse the hungry colonists to live among the Indians. By 1609 Jamestown reportedly was strongly impaled with a 14 to 15 foot high palisade that enclosed a church, storehouse, 40 or 50 houses, and "a faire well of fresh water." The settlers also had planted 100 acres of corn. This, Smith claimed to have accomplished with a carpenter, two blacksmiths, two sailors, a few laborers and a handful of gentlemen, libertines "and such like." In May 1609 the Virginia Company received its second charter, which allowed Company officials to choose a governor to serve as the colony's principal leader. He, in turn, could select the members of his council, his advisors. The governor's might was considerable, for he had "full and absolute power and authority to correct, punish, pardon, governe and rule." Shortly after the second charter became effective, Sir Thomas West, Lord De La Warr, was named governor and captain-general of Virginia. Because he was unable to assume his post at once, Sir Thomas Gates was made interim governor.[10]

The Third Supply

A Third Supply of 500 new settlers set sail for Virginia in May 1609. But the fleet of nine ships got caught in a hurricane and one small catch perished at sea. The flagship SEA-VENTURE, which carried Sir Thomas Gates, Sir George Somers, John Rolfe, and some other notables, was cast upon the rocks of the Bermudas. By mid-August 1609 the seven surviving vessels limped into Jamestown with 200 to 300 famished passengers, including women and children. In three days time they devoured a field of corn, the colony's main food supply. John Smith later claimed that many of the men in the Third Supply were "reckless young fops" hurried off to the colony to "escape evil destinies." Because they found none of the luxuries to which they were accustomed, Virginia was to them "a miserie, a ruine, a death, a hell."

The Specter of Famine

So earnest was the struggle to survive that during the winter of 1609–1610, the infamous "Starving Time," the colonists were divided into three groups, two of which were dispersed abroad. But the Indians harassed them and at the end of six weeks, they were obliged to return to Jamestown. As it was too cold to wade into the water to gather oysters, the colonists were compelled to subsist on roots they dug from the frozen ground and whatever wild and domestic animals they could capture. Some people sought refuge with the Indians, whom they considered mortal enemies. Survivors claimed that cannibalism occurred.[11]

The rigors of the "Starving Time" nearly led to the colony's extinction. In May 1610, when Sir Thomas Gates, Sir George Somers, and a hundred or so new settlers reached Virginia in two ships fashioned from Bermuda's native cedar wood, they found the few surviving colonists "famished and at the point of death." Gates resolved to evacuate them to Newfoundland, where they could recuperate and secure passage to England. Only the timely arrival of Lord De La Warr's three ships, with provisions and 250 new immigrants, averted the abandonment of the colony: when De La Warr entered the mouth of the James in early June, he met Gates' departing fleet. De La Warr, as governor, set about strengthening and refurbishing the colony. He dispatched Somers to Bermuda to bring back naturally-growing foodstuffs and in July he sent Gates to England to secure provisions, supplies and additional settlers. In March 1611, ill health forced De La Warr to withdraw to the West Indies. William Strachey, who arrived in Virginia in May 1610 and departed in 1611, described the Jamestown fort as triangular with a palisade that consisted of sturdy posts and planks set four feet into the ground. The wall facing the river was 420 feet long and the other two were 300 feet in length. A market place, storehouse, corps de guard (guardhouse) and chapel were enveloped by the palisade. Whether Strachey was describing the original fort, the repaired-and-remodeled one or another constructed by De La Warr and Gates is uncertain.

The Establishment of Martial Law

In May 1611 Sir Thomas Dale, who was second in command to Lord De La Warr, arrived in a fleet that carried 300 new settlers plus victuals, supplies, munitions, livestock and seeds to grow vegetable crops. In August he was joined by Gates, who brought 300 more well-supplied people. Dale, a military man, who, like Gates and De La Warr, had extensive experience in the Netherlands, was appalled by the conditions he found at Jamestown where (according to John Smith) the colonists were "at their daily and usuall works, bowling in the streets" while their houses fell into disrepair. In Dale's judgment, they were inadequately defended against the Indians and had even less protection against a foreign foe. Moreover, the settlers were contentious and made little or no effort to provide for themselves. Attributing the colony's woes to the lack of strong leadership, Dale instituted martial law within a month of his arrival. This included a harsh military code of justice that invoked the death penalty for even minor infractions of the law. Many of these measures were termed inhumane and the cruelty of the Dale administration became legendary. But when Sir Thomas Dale left Virginia in May 1616, the colony was on a relatively sound footing and two invaluable lessons had been learned: that the settlers were capable of producing their own food supply and that the colony's success depended upon its inhabitants' being allowed to profit from their own labor.[12]

The Expansion of Settlement

In obedience to the Virginia Company's orders to build the colony's principal town in a healthier, more defensible location than Jamestown Island, Sir Thomas Dale established several new settlements toward the head of the James River. He also saw that a number of new buildings were erected at Jamestown, including shelters for livestock, storehouses for munitions and powder, a blockhouse, and a structure in which sturgeon could be dried. In 1614 he dispatched some colonists to the Eastern Shore to extract salt from seawater, so that fish could be preserved. Dale also introduced several innovative policies that fostered the colony's development. Relations with the Indians improved somewhat during this period, for John Rolfe fell in love with Powhatan's daughter, Pocahontas, and married her on April 5, 1614. Their union ushered in several years of peace, during which the colonists gained a firmer foothold in Virginia.

Agriculture: The Key To Survival

During the Dale administration John Rolfe developed a strain of sweet-scented tobacco that quickly became a highly lucrative money crop. In 1616 he summarized Dale's accomplishments. All farmers were required to defend their own settlements and the colony, perform 31 days public service a year, provide their own households with food and clothing, and contribute 2 1/2 barrels of Indian corn per male household member to the common store. They were prohibited from planting tobacco until they had placed under cultivation two acres of corn per male household member. Having fulfilled that basic obligation, they could raise as much tobacco as they wished. Of the 50 people then living on Jamestown Island, 32 were farmers. Ralph Hamor, another Dale champion, in 1614 said that Jamestown Island had been thickly wooded when the colonists first arrived. Much labor had been expended in converting it into good ground for corn and gardens. Under Dale's skillful leadership the Jamestown settlement had been "reduced into a handsome forme" with "two faire rowes of howses, all of framed Timber, two stories, and an upper Garrett or Corn loft high." As well, there were three large storehouses that together were 120 feet long. Hamor said that "This town hath been newly and strongly impaled" and that "a faire platforme for ordnance" had been built in the west bulwark. Outside of the town, in the island, were "some very pleasant, and beautifull howses, two Blockhouses, to observe and watch lest the Indians at any time should swim over the back river and come into the island, and certain other farme howses." Sir Thomas Dale's policies included giving every new immigrant his first year's corn supply and "a handsome howse of some foure roomes or more, if he have a family, to repose himself in rent free, and 12 English acres of ground adjoining thereto, very strongly impailed, which ground is allotted to him for rents, gardaine hearbs and corn."[13] This statement, though probably an exaggeration, indicates that Dale intended to provide new immigrants with temporary support.

After Dale left Virginia, few of his policies lingered on and according to John Smith, Jamestown soon was in disarray. One writer commented that those who came to the colony during its first 17 years and managed to survive had "grown practiced in a hard way of living." It was not a lifestyle to which gentlemen and urbanites could adapt readily, even if they wanted to. The colonists failed to plant food crops but complained bitterly about hunger and awaited supplies from England. They also bartered with the Indians for corn, but sometimes took it by force, making enemies in the process. One man claimed that after Dale left, "butt one Plough was going in all the Country, wch was the fruite of full 12 years labour." In 1619 John Pory declared that "three things there bee which in a few yeares may bring this colony to perfection: the English plough, vineyards and cattle." He added that the colony's riches lay in tobacco, then a lucrative money crop. He underscored the point by stating that at Jamestown even the cowkeeper strutted about in flaming silk and the wife of a former London collier sported a silk suit and a fine beaver hat. The boom in tobacco prices continued until around 1630, when overproduction glutted the market.[14]

New groups of poorly provisioned immigrants continued to arrive in "pestilent ships" that were "vicutalled with musty bread and stinking beer." They landed sickly and weak, sometimes introducing infectious diseases into the colony. Eventually, Virginia Company officials learned that there was a critical need for laborers and farmers to produce a dependable food supply and that new immigrants required food and shelter while they recovered from their ocean voyage and became acclimated to their new environment. Guesthouses of a proscribed size were to be erected "in due and wholesome places" for "the lodging and entertaining [of] 50 persons in each upon their first arrival." One was built near the mouth of the Chickahominy River.[15]

The Virginia Company's Great Charter

In 1612 the Virginia Company of London received its third and final charter from King James. However, the Company continued to be plagued by financial problems, for the cost of developing and maintaining the colony proved overwhelming. Finally, in 1618 the Company ratified its so-called Great Charter, which paved the way for a number of sweeping changes. One was the establishment of representative government and a system akin to local English law. Virginia's governor and council of state were to be chosen by Company officials in England, but provisions were made for the colonists to elect representatives to a general assembly, the first such group to convene upon North American soil. The Great Charter also ushered in a land policy that enabled the Virginia colonists to acquire real estate and work for personal gain. This, then, was the true beginning of America's free enterprise system. In yet another important move, martial law was abolished.[16] All of these changes were major milestones in the colony's history.

The Corporation of James City

On April 17, 1619, Sir George Yeardley, Virginia's new governor and captain-general, sailed into Jamestown and took the reins of government in hand. In accord with his instructions, he subdivided the colony into four corporations: James City, Charles City, Henrico City, and Kecoughtan (or Elizabeth City). Each was vast in size and spanned both sides of the James River. The corporation of James City extended from Skiffs Creek (on the east), westward to a point just above the mouth of the Chickahominy River, and it reached across the James River, taking in what eventually became Surry County.

The Genesis of Representative Government

Each of Virginia's plantations was invited to send two delegates to Jamestown to formulate the colony's laws. On July 30, 1619, when the members of America's first legislative assembly gathered in the church, present were the governor, six councilors and representatives or burgesses from all but one settlement. Captain William Powell and Ensign William Spence attended on behalf of Jamestown, whereas John Boys (Boise) and John Jackson represented the settlers sent by the Society of Martin's Hundred.[17] Thomas Pawlett and Edward Gouraing appeared on behalf of Argall's Gift, a community just west of Jamestown Island. After the Reverend Richard Buck offered a prayer, Speaker of the Assembly John Pory read aloud from the Virginia Company's Great Charter and reviewed two of the four books of laws sent to the colony. The delegates then separated into two committees to study the remaining books. Their mission wasn't to challenge the basic rules set down for governing the colony, but to petition for any changes they thought necessary. Afterward, the burgesses began drafting some new laws, which were subject to the monarch's approval.

Besides laws that prohibited theft, murder, and other criminal offenses, acts were passed against idleness, gambling, drunkenness, and "excesse in apparel," for which penalties were fixed. Legislation also was enacted making it illegal to trade large hoes, firearms, powder, shot, or English dogs (such as mastiffs, greyhounds, bloodhounds, or spaniels) to the Indians and only small numbers of Natives were permitted to live and work within the settlements. The colonists were required to grow enough corn to feed their own households, putting aside an extra barrel per person for use in times of need. They had to plant vineyards, set out six mulberry trees a year, undertake the cultivation of silk flax, and follow certain procedures when preparing tobacco for market. They could not travel further than 20 miles from home, embark upon a voyage of more than seven days duration, or visit Indian towns. Ministers were to record all Christenings, marriages, and burials and all heads of household were obliged to give the secretary of the colony a list of those under their care. The clergy were to conduct Sunday services and report those suspected of committing moral offenses such as intoxication, fornication, or swearing. In 1622 John Smith reported that courts had been appointed "in convenient places," perhaps a reference to the right of a privately sponsored plantation's local leader to settle disputes among his people. Those who lived in James City brought their problems to the governor's council. By 1624 there were local courts in the corporations of Charles City and Elizabeth City and a year later, on the Eastern Shore. Among the corporation of James City's burgesses between 1619 and 1624 were Ensign William Spence, Richard Kingsmill, Captain William Powell, John Boys, John Jackson, Thomas Pawlett, Edward Gouraing, Edward Blaney, Robert Adams, Richard Stephens, Clement Dilke, John Chew, John Uty, and John Southern. Meanwhile, Jamestown residents such as Sir Francis Wyatt, Sir George Yeardley, George Sandys, Dr. John Pott, John Pountis, Roger Smith, and Ralph Hamor served as members of the governor's council and Wyatt, Yeardley, and Pott held the office of governor at various times.[18]

Virginia's First Black Immigrants

In August 1619 a Dutch frigate, fresh from a plundering expedition in the West Indies, sailed into Hampton Roads bearing 20-some blacks. At Old Point Comfort the vessel's captain conferred with Governor Yeardley and cape merchant Abraham Peirsey, agreeing to exchange his captives for some urgently needed provisions. Shortly thereafter, the newly arrived men and women were brought up to Jamestown and sold into servitude. A ship called the TREASURER also left a black person in Virginia not long after the Dutch frigate's departure. Although the concept of institutionalized slavery did not surface until much later, these individuals, whose distinctive appearance, unfamiliar language, exotic cultural background, and life experience set them apart from the other colonists, were at a decided disadvantage in adapting to the situation at hand.[19]

The Headright System and Indentured Servitude

One of the most important features of the Virginia Company's Great Charter was introduction of the headright system, a land policy that provided prospective immigrants with an incentive to leave overcrowded England to seek their fortunes in Virginia. It also encouraged wealthy investors to underwrite the cost of outfitting and transporting prospective colonists. The opportunity to reap substantial profits from growing tobacco (a commodity so marketable that it gained acceptance as currency) coupled with the prospect of owning land, combined to fuel the spread of settlement. Sometimes, investors pooled their resources to outfit servants and tenants they sent to Virginia to establish so-called "particular plantations." These "Societies of

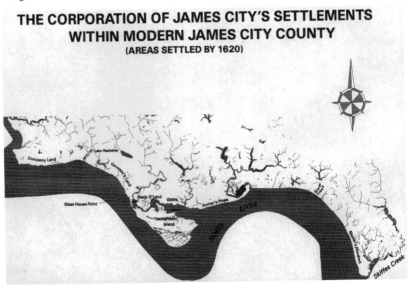

THE CORPORATION OF JAMES CITY'S SETTLEMENTS
WITHIN MODERN JAMES CITY COUNTY
(AREAS SETTLED BY 1620)

Map by Deborah L. Wilson. See enlarged map, page 28.

Adventurers" purchased shares of Virginia Company stock, which entitled them to 100 acres per share. Modern James City County's only "particular plantation" was established by the Society of Martin's Hundred in 1620. The Virginia Company's new land policy stimulated so much development that between 1619 and 1623 a total of 44 grants for particular (or privately sponsored) plantations were made to investors.

Under the headright system, Ancient Planters (men and women who came to Virginia at their own expense and lived in the colony for at least three years prior to Sir Thomas Dale's 1616 departure) were entitled to 100 acres of land. Those who immigrated later, paid the cost of their own transportation and lived in Virginia for three years, were entitled to 50 acres of land. Investors or adventurers who purchased a share of Virginia Company stock were entitled to 100 acres of land as a first dividend, plus another 100 acres when the first tract was planted. An individual also could acquire 50 acres of land by underwriting the cost of another person's transportation. Successful planters, by bringing indentured servants to Virginia to work on their plantations, were able to amass substantial amounts of land while fulfilling their need for labor.

Men and women interested in becoming indentured servants, and the legal guardians of minors, usually signed a contract ("indenture"), agreeing to exchange a certain number of years work for transportation to Virginia. These contracts could be sold to planters needing workers. Many of those who first came to Virginia as indentured servants were respectable citizens who simply lacked the means to cover the cost of their transportation and to outfit themselves for life in the colony. They represented a broad cross-section of society, including the younger sons of prominent families, yeoman farmers, husbandmen, artisans, and laborers. The majority were young males in their late teens or early 20s. Those who owned indentured servants were obliged to provide them with food, clothing, and shelter, and to exact labor under certain conditions. They could discipline their servants, but only within the limits of the law. Indentured servants (especially men and boys) usually worked as field hands during the growing season, dawn to dusk, six days a week. At first, the labor shortage was so critical that employers often worked side by side with their indentured servants. Adult servants usually agreed to work for four years, but those under age 15 might serve seven or more years. Skilled or literate servants often could negotiate shorter terms because they performed more valuable tasks. Once an indentured servant's contract expired, he or she was entitled to "freedom dues," usually defined as a quantity of corn and clothing.[20] Occasionally, indentured servants went to go to court to recover their "freedom dues" from a stingy or financially-strapped master.

Public Land

One of the tasks the Virginia Company assigned to Governor Yeardley was setting aside special tracts of land to be used toward the support of important government officials, reap profits for Company investors, and fulfill specific needs. Each corporation was to have 3,000 acres of Company Land, 1,500 acres of Common Land, and a 100 acre glebe or home farm for its clergyman. In addition, acreage within the corporation of Henrico was set aside for a university and college. In 1620 John Rolfe reported that virtually all of the special parcels had been defined.[21]

Within the corporation of James City was the Governor's Land, a 3,000-acre tract earmarked for the support of the colony's highest ranking official. He had the right to lease portions of the tract to tenants or place his own servants upon it to work on his behalf. The Governor's Land was situated in the mainland, just west of Jamestown Island. It extended west along the banks of the James to Deep Creek (Lake Pasbehay).[22] Between Deep Creek and the mouth of the Chickahominy River was another special parcel: the James City corporation's Company Land.[23] The Virginia Company placed its own indentured servants there to work as sharecroppers, half of whose earnings were sent home to Company investors. Just east of Jamestown Island in the mainland was the glebe of the James City corporation's clergyman. He had the right to occupy the glebe, place his servants upon it, or lease it to others. The location of the corporation's 1,500 acres of Common Land is uncertain.[24] By early 1620 there were four communities of settlers within the boundaries of modern James City County: Jamestown Island, the Company Land, the Governor's Land, and Martin's Hundred. Indentured servants also had been sent to the corporation of James City's Common Land.

Jamestown and Jamestown Island

Although relatively little is known about what Jamestown was like during the early 1620s when it was a fledgling urban community, activities associated with church and state probably took place near the fort, where the market-place, pillory, and whipping post were located. Meanwhile, development was intensified to the east, within the "New Town" west of Orchard Run, where development was encouraged. Almost all of the 1624 patents for New Town lots cite earlier legislation designed "to encourage building."

By 1624 a row of lots had been laid out along a road that traced the river bank. It was here that Sir John Harvey, George Menefie, Ralph Hamor, and Richard Stephens had houses. At the rear of this first tier of lots was the Back Street, which also contained rows of developed lots. Almost all New Town lot owners were wealthy merchants, prominent public officials, or both. One was fort captain William Peirce (John Rolfe's father-in-law) whose dwelling in 1624 served as the collection point for the tobacco levied as taxes. In 1629 Peirce's wife, Joan, "an honest and industrious woman" who had resided in Virginia for nearly 20 years, reportedly had "a garden at Jamestown containing 3 or 4 acres" from which she gathered nearly 100 bushels of excellent figs a year. At the periphery of the New Town's smaller lots were somewhat larger parcels that belonged to notables such as Sir Francis Wyatt, Dr. John Pott, Sir George Yeardley, Secretary of the Colony Richard Kemp, Sir John Harvey, and Captain Roger Smith. An 80-acre farm owned by Richard Kingsmill abutted Back Creek and bordered east and south upon what became known as Kingsmill Creek.[25]

In the eastern end of Jamestown Island were more than a dozen 12-acre parcels, some of which were laid out prior to 1616. Almost all of them had been patented by Ancient Planters. This suggests that the eastern end of the island was purposefully carved up into small farmsteads at a very early date, perhaps between 1611 and 1616 when Virginia was governed by Sir Thomas Dale, who personally owned a 12-acre plot at Goose Hill. In 1619 John Rolfe said that certain Ancient Planters, who had completed their service to the colony, were the first farmers to choose "places to their content, so that now knowing their own land, they strive who should exceed in building and planting." He cited as an example William Spence of Jamestown Island, who claimed and seated a 12-acre tract near Black Point.[26] The presence of Ancient Planters' 12-acre farmsteads in the eastern end of Jamestown Island indicates that colonists' homes were not huddled at its western end, as often is assumed.

By the early 1620s, the masters of all incoming ships were required to open their cargoes at Jamestown before going elsewhere. This policy was in effect through the 1660s and brought a steady stream of commerce and visitors to the island. New Town resident George Menefie served as the corporation of James City's official merchant from 1620 until around 1637. One of his lots was located on the water front. Other prominent merchants who owned (and in most instances, occupied) New Town lots during the 1620s included Richard Stephens (who was married to cape-merchant Abraham Peirsey's daughter), John Chew, William Perry, John Pountis, and Edward Blaney (who wed the widow of Captain William Powell).[27]

Besides merchants and the political elite, Jamestown Island was home to tradesmen and artisans. During the mid-1620s, George Clarke, John Jackson, and John Jefferson were actively employed there as gunsmiths. Thomas Passmore, a carpenter, and John Norton, a smith, owned 12-acre plots in the east-central portion of the island during the 1620s and '30s, as did feather-maker John Radish (Reddish) and joiner Thomas Grubb. During the mid-1620s Thomas Nunn, who was under contract to a group of investors in shipbuilding, constructed vessels at Jamestown, as did boatwright William Bennett. George Menefie had a forge in Jamestown and owned at least two lots in the New Town. As he owned a waterfront lot in the New Town, it may have been located there. In 1624 the Italian glassworkers Vincencio Castillian (Castine) and Bernardo and three others were established at Glass House Point, where "a tryall of glass" had been made earlier on. By 1625 the glassworkers had moved across the river to Treasurer George Sandys' plantation and were clamoring to return home.[28] Archaeologists have discovered that potters, apothecaries, brewers, tobacco pipemakers, and other specialized workers literally set up shop at Jamestown during the 1620s.

The Company Land

On November 4, 1619, a hundred men and boys sent to the colony by the Virginia Company arrived at Jamestown aboard the BONA NOVA. Half of them were dispatched four miles upstream to the Company Land at the mouth of the Chickahominy, where they were placed under the command of Lieutenant Jabez Whittaker. By January they had become well established. When spring came, they were joined by a hundred more. In 1621 Whittaker informed Company officials that he had built a guesthouse to accommodate new immigrants and placed a surgeon there along with an old woman to do laundry and cleaning. The Company servants under Whittaker's command were raising corn and tobacco, but some carpenters, sawyers, smiths, and tailors had been put to work at their trades. Food was in short supply, as was equipment for cooking and serving food.[29]

Theodore De Bry's conjectural rendition of the 1622 Indian uprising. Library of Congress.

The Governor's Land

The 3,000-acre tract known as the Governor's Land, in accord with the Virginia Company's instructions, was "in the best and most convenient place of the territory of Jamestown . . . and next adjoining to the town." Anyone who might have inadvertently seated upon the tract before it was designated public property was allowed to stay on until he recouped the cost of any improvements he had made. Governor Yeardley was told to seat 50 of the Company's indentured servants upon the Governor's Land as his tenants. When he arrived in the colony, he learned that Samuel Argall already had placed a group of people there. Argall, who had come to Virginia in 1609 and stayed on during Sir Thomas Dale's government, left but returned in 1617 as deputy-governor. He and some fellow investors promised to bring a large group of indentured servants to Virginia and on March 30, 1617, secured a patent for 2,400 acres of land. Argall, while in office, seated some people on the Governor's Land who had been sent over by the Society of Martin's Hundred, perhaps intermingling them with his own settlers. Both communities were represented in the colony's first assembly meeting.

At the August 4, 1619, session of the assembly, some "Inhabitants of Paspaheigh, alias Argall's Towne," also known as the "Martins hundred people," asked to be released from their debts to Argall, who claimed a sum for the land they occupied, plus the cost of clearing it and building houses. John Rolfe in January 1620 reported that the Martin's Hundred people, who were still residing upon the Governor's Land, were healthy and had had a good harvest. They left shortly thereafter.[30]

Martin's Hundred

By March 1620 the Society of Martin's Hundred's settlers had relocated to their own patent between Grove and Skiffs Creeks, where they developed a community known as Wolstenholme Towne. The Society sent additional groups of people to Virginia during 1620 and 1621 and a surveyor to lay out its land. Society investors hoped "to buy out the Indians of Chiskiack" on the

York River in order to extend their holdings across the peninsula. Despite these ambitious plans, in late January 1622 Wolstenholme Town reportedly was "weakened and in much confusion." Several Virginia Company officials were members of the Society of Martin's Hundred.[31]

The Population of What Became James City County

By March 1620, there were 928 people living in the Virginia colony: 892 whites, 32 blacks (17 women and 15 men) and four Indians. Of the whites, 677 were men, 119 were women, 39 were "serviceable boys," and 57 were "younger persons." All four Indians and the blacks reportedly were "in ye service of severall planters." Four years later some of the blacks were servants in Jamestown households and one lived in the Neck O'Land. The colonists had 336 cattle (a third of which were on Jamestown Island), ten horses, and 233 goats and kids. For defense, there were 17 pieces of heavy ordnance, 30 barrels of powder, 686 guns, 516 swords, 284 complete suits of armor, plus other protective attire such as shirts of male, head-pieces and breast-plates. There were 222 "habitable houses" in Virginia, exclusive of barns and store-houses, and 39 privately-owned boats and shallops. A year or more later, when a more detailed accounting was made, 117 men, women and children were living on Jamestown Island, making it the largest of the colony's 15 or so settlements. There were 72 people at Martin's Hundred and 15 to 20 men occupying the corporation of James City's Common Land.[32]

The 1622 Indian Uprising

Despite the years of peace that followed Pocahontas' marriage to John Rolfe, after she and Powhatan died in 1617–1618, a more militant attitude emerged on the part of the Natives led by the charismatic paramount chief and war captain, Opechancanough. On Friday, March 22, 1622,[33] the warriors of the Powhatan Chiefdom, threatened by the inroads of expanding settlement, launched a carefully orchestrated attack upon the sparsely inhabited plantations along the James River. It was a vigorous attempt to drive the colonists from their soil. At the end of the day, an estimated 347 men, women and children lay dead, somewhat more than a third of the colony's population. Although no lives were lost at Jamestown, an account purportedly written by an eyewitness states that:

. . . a party of Indians embarked in four boats for Jamestown and the surrounding country, but this hellish plan was frustrated by the disclosure of the project by a converted Indian. . . . Mr. Pace [34] *hastily rowed in a canoe across the river to Jamestown to notify the governor of the impending danger. Hardly had we completed our defensive preparations when the boats bearing the savages hove into sight, but as soon as we opened firre upon them with our muskets they retreated in a cowardly manner.* [35]

Contemporary narratives reveal that outside of Jamestown, the Indians entered the homes of the unsuspecting colonists and then as if on cue, slaughtered them. Near Dancing Point, just west of the Chickahominy River's mouth, several Southampton Hundred colonists lost their lives, as did one man associated with the Company Land. No one perished on the Governor's Land. East of Jamestown Island, in Archers Hope, five men were killed at the home of Ensign William Spence. At Martin's Hundred, the death toll of 73 included 19 women the Pamunkey Indians carried to their village in the upper reaches of the Pamunkey River. One man said that after the Indians' raid, only two houses "and a peece of a church" were left at Martin's Hundred. Even so, John Smith reported that "a little house and a small family" nearby didn't learn of the massacre until two days after it occurred.[36]

The Aftermath

In the wake of the uprising, the Indians returned to several outlying plantations to drive off their frightened and demoralized inhabitants. When they succeeded, they put the settlers' homesteads to the torch. The governor declared martial law and ordered the colonists to draw in toward Jamestown. Military commanders were appointed for the eight settlements to be held. Refugees flocked to Jamestown Island and the Governor's Land and congregated at other sites considered relatively safe. But concentrating the population created food shortages and fostered the spread of contagious diseases, especially during the warmer months. Although the colonists undertook retaliatory raids, burning the Indians' villages and destroying their food supplies, the Natives continued to fight back by attacking remote settlements and capturing or killing those who ventured out alone. Virginia Company officials, though sympathetic to the colonists' plight, blamed them for settling so far apart they couldn't rush to each other's assistance. Despite the danger, they urged the settlers to return to their plantations and offered some incentives to those who would.

In early April 1623 an emissary from Opechancanough brought word to Martin's Hundred that "blud enough had already been shedd on both sides" and that the Indians were starving as a result of the colonists' raids. They offered to return their English captives and to allow the colonists to plant in peace, if they could do the same. A week later, 19 women (most, if not all, of whom were from Martin's Hundred) were redeemed with glass beads. Mrs. Sarah Boyse, considered "Chiefe of the prisoners," was sent home "appareled like one of their Queens." Jane Dickerson, a widow whose release was secured by Dr. John Pott of Jamestown in exchange for two parcels of beads, later contended that the servitude to which he subjected her as a servant in his home was little different than "her slavery with the Indians." In December word reached England that "ye English despite a treaty with ye Natives for peace and good quarter have poisoned a great many of them," a reference to Captain William Tucker's May 22, 1623, attempt to kill Opechancanough and other Indian leaders by toasting a spurious peace treaty with a cup of poisonous wine.[37]

The Colonists Return to Their Homesteads

During the fall and winter of 1623, as the colonists' fears subsided, they gradually re-occupied the outlying plantations they had abandoned. Many of them were armed with outmoded military equipment Virginia Company officials had obtained from the Tower of London. One colonist said that planters were "working with our Hoe in one hand, and our peece [gun] or sword in the other." Retaliatory raids were undertaken against the Indians from time to time, and one man declared that the colonists "may now by right of warre . . . invade the country and destroy them who sought to destroy us." He added that "now their cleared ground in all their villages (which are situate in the fruitfullest places of the land) shall be inhabited by us." It is doubtful that Captain Jabez Whittaker and the Virginia Company's servants ever returned to the land they once occupied at the mouth of the Chickahominy. The Governor's Land, however, was inhabited continuously. Martin's Hundred's settlers went back to their plantation, although the Indians continued to harass them and destroy their crops. New colonists continued to die in droves, for they arrived meagerly outfitted and found that neither food nor shelter awaited them. It was a low point in the colony's history. By April 1623 Martin's Hundred's inhabitants had built fortifications to shield themselves from the Indians. However, living conditions were miserable. Richard Frethorne, a young indentured servant, wrote his parents that he was starving and clothed in rags and that the Indians kept returning to the plantation to pick off anyone who ventured out alone.[38]

In 1624, March 22 was declared a holy day to be celebrated with prayer and fasting. Some officials called the Indian massacre the judgment of a wrathful God requiring appeasement; however, commemorating the date served to remind the settlers not to let their guard down. They were ordered to fortify their houses against the Indians and were forbidden to trade with them.[39]

The Virginia Company's Downfall

Captain Nathaniel Butler, former governor of Bermuda, visited Virginia during the winter of 1622–1623 and declared that the colony was a death trap. He sent word to England that when new immigrants arrived in winter, they died in such droves that their corpses lay unburied for days. He also said that the colony lacked protection against its enemies. A group of settlers and governing officials attempted to refute Butler's allegations. They admitted that many people met with sudden death in Jamestown, but said that their corpses were not allowed to lie uninterred. As to the charge that the colony had no defenses, they said that Jamestown had heavy ordnance and that in 1622 they had begun building fortifications but shortages of food and labor had stopped their work momentarily. They added that almost all of the houses in the colony were defended by strong palisades.

One Virginia Company officer, who favored a return to martial law, claimed that the wharf at Jamestown was "broken down & demolished; the fort unfortified; the Ordnance unserviceable." Some mariners, who came to Virginia in 1623, agreed. They said that the landing at Jamestown was very bad and that goods put ashore "right against the companies store howses, and the governors howse, Armours, swords, musquets, truncks and such like goods, lye a fortnight together uncared for, everie tide beeing overflowed with water and the trunks ready to be swallowed." They said that "Likewise Iron bars and sowes of Ledd and millstones and Grindstones and Iron furnaces lye right against the same places, sunk and covered with sand, the water dayly overflowing them." They closed by saying that most old-timers wished that the government was still under martial law.[40]

But most of the surviving Ancient Planters swiftly and vehemently disagreed. They insisted that martial law had yielded immense pain and little gain and contended that when Governor Yeardley arrived in 1619, he found no fortifications and only two mounted cannon "fitter to shoot down our houses than to offend an enemy." Moreover, the only houses in Jamestown were those erected by Sir Thomas Gates' men, including "one wherein the governor always dwelt," plus a 20-foot-by-50-foot frame church built during Captain Samuel Argall's brief term as deputy-governor. The colony's burgesses agreed. They said that Yeardley's arrival and the implementation of the Great Charter ushered in an era characterized by substantial, enduring progress. Ultimately, infighting among Virginia Company factions led to the revocation of its third and final charter.

The Transitional Period

By June 1624 Virginia had become a Crown colony. Although there were some attempts to revive the Virginia Company, most colonists were convinced they would fare better under the Crown. Some of the defunct organization's landholdings had come into the hands of its former servants by 1626. Within the corporation of James City, Francis Fowler, Thomas Harvey and John Tyos patented part of the Company Land, as did Bridges Freeman.

During the 1620s, many of the freemen who immigrated to Virginia at their own expense leased land while meeting residency requirements for acreage under the headright system. Established planters brought indentured servants to the colony, placed them upon their property, and generated the income they needed to acquire more servants and land. Many people invested in two or more tracts and circulated among them. A list of patented land, compiled in May 1625, indicates that within what became James City County were 16 parcels of 100 to 300 acres that were claimed by individual planters. Many of those tracts were classified as "planted."[41]

The Corporation of James City's Settlements

By the early-to-mid 1620s, family life had taken root in Virginia. Quite a few households consisted of a married couple and one or more children, plus a small number of indentured servants. Often, families embraced the children of one or more prior marriages. Thus, step-, half-, and full-blooded siblings frequently progressed with a parent or step-parent through a series of marriages almost always ended by death. The accumulation of wealth through serial marriage and the rigors of survival on the frontier likely made widows and widowers eager to remarry. As the colony became better established, more women came to Virginia and the number of marriages and births rose. The orphaned and the infirm received care in the homes of those willing to shelter them.

In February 1624 183 people were living within urban Jamestown, whereas 39 others resided elsewhere on the island. But 89 had died since April 1623. On January 24, 1625, when a new tabulation was made, Jamestown Island's population consisted of 175 people, 122 of whom were men and boys. Nine blacks (three men and six women) lived in Jamestown, which had 21 houses, three storehouses, a church and a large court of guard; elsewhere in the island were ten houses. Jamestown Island's inhabitants generally had more provisions, military equipment, and livestock than those who lived elsewhere. In 1625 75 people lived in The Maine and Pasbehay, two communities located east of Deep Creek, within the Governor's Land. Nearly half of the men there had come to the colony as Virginia Company servants.

The settlers inhabiting Archers Hope lived between College Creek and the corporation of James City's glebe, which abutted east upon Mill Creek and west upon the Neck Lands (Neck O' Land) directly behind Jamestown Island. During the mid-1620s Archers Hope, which had a population of approximately 16 men, women, and children, took on an air of permanency. In February 1625, eleven people were residing in five households in the Neck O' Land behind Jamestown Island. Only Richard Kingsmill was credited with buildings, which raises the possibility that the inhabitants of the Neck O' Land had drawn together for safety and mutual support. As Kingsmill was guardian to the late Rev. Richard Buck's minor children, who inherited acreage in the Neck O'Land, he apparently decided to occupy the Buck patent to preserve the orphans' claim.

In 1625 27 people were living at Martin's Hundred, where there were seven houses and at least one storehouse. In May, brick-maker John Jackson and his 47-year-old indentured servant, Thomas Ward, a potter, informed the Society of Martin's Hundred that their clothing and shoes were completely worn out and that they lacked ammunition to defend themselves. They claimed that the settlement's leader, William Harwood, hoarded food and other supplies, which he used to curry favor with high ranking officials. Robert Adams of Martin's Hundred added that while he and another man were working in their garden, they were attacked by Indians and he received a gunshot wound in the leg. During the melee, Adams' wife fled to Harwood, who reportedly locked himself and his guards in the storehouse and refused to let her in. She was forced to take refuge in the wash house, where she hid until the attack ceased. Several residents of Martin's Hundred (indentured servants whose terms had expired) clamored for permission to seat land of their own within the Society's patent. On the east side of College Creek, in what eventually became known as Kingsmill Neck, were several parcels of land which by May 1625 were patented but unseated.[42] The colonists' hesitancy to invest their time and resources in clearing and developing this area may have stemmed from the fact that the Society of Martin's Hundred had asserted a claim to 80,000 acres that would have encompassed it.

By the mid-1620s the Virginia colony had become well established and few doubted it would survive. The settlers had demonstrated that they could produce their own food supply and officials in England had learned that farmers and skilled artisans were essential to the colony's well-being. The headright system enticed many people to seek their fortunes in Virginia, whereas the opportunity to reap substantial profits from growing tobacco served to fuel the spread of settlement. Despite the objections of the Native population, the Europeans were here to stay.

Notes

1. Captain John Smith, TRAVELS AND WORKS OF CAPTAIN JOHN SMITH, PRESIDENT OF VIRGINIA AND ADMIRAL OF NEW ENGLAND, 1580–1631, Edward Arber, ed. (Edinburgh, 1910), lvii–lxi; K. R. Andrews, "Christopher Newport of Limehouse, Mariner," WILLIAM AND MARY QUARTERLY, 3rd Ser., 11 (January 1954):28–41; Quinn, NORTH AMERICA, 392–393.

2. Wallis, RALEIGH AND ROANOKE, 79–80; Arthur P. Middleton, TOBACCO COAST: A MARITIME HISTORY OF THE CHESAPEAKE BAY IN THE COLONIAL ERA (Newport News, 1953), 34–35.

3. Quinn, NORTH AMERICA, 392–393; Tyler, NARRATIVES, 125–126; McIlwaine, MINUTES, xvi; David H. Flaherty, ed., LAWES DIVINE, MORALL, AND MARTIALL, ETC. (Charlottesville, 1969), x.

4. Tyler, NARRATIVES, 5–23; Smith, TRAVELS, xii–lxiii, xc, 49–51; Quinn, NORTH AMERICA, 202; Conway Sams, THE CONQUEST OF VIRGINIA, THE SECOND ATTEMPT (Norfolk, 1929), 807–810; George Percy, OBSERVATIONS GATHERED OUT OF A DISCOURSE OF THE PLANTATION OF THE SOUTHERN COLONIE IN VIRGINIA BY THE ENGLISH, 1606 (New York, 1965), 16.

5. The settlers' fears were not unfounded, for a short time later a Spanish official informed King Philip III that it would be a service to God to expel the English from Virginia, "hanging them while so little is needed to make it possible" (Tyler, NARRATIVES, 223–224).

6. Tyler, NARRATIVES, 5–23, 35, 123, 127; Captain John Smith, "Virginia Discovered and Discribed [sic]," 1610; Smith, Barber, ed., TRAVELS, I, 206. Unfortunately, it was not until later that the link between environment and good health was appreciated fully. Marine scientists now know that during the summer months, when the James River drops to its lowest level, its salinity increases markedly and contaminants, such as stagnant water, sewage, and sediments, are trapped.

7. Smith's assessment was remarkably similar to Thomas Harriot's, for in 1586 he declared that some of the Roanoke colonists languished for lack of English cities, "faire houses," or "daintie food."

8. Tyler, NARRATIVES, 140–141; Cary Carson et al., "Impermanent Architecture in the Southern American Colonies," WINTERTHUR PORTFOLIO 16:140; Smith, Arber, ed., TRAVELS, 127, 140–141.

9. During this period a small fort was built across the James at the head of Gray's Creek, a retreat if a Spanish invasion appeared imminent.

10. Tyler, NARRATIVES, 140–141; Smith, Arber, ed., TRAVELS, 471, 486–487, 610, 612; Philip A. Bruce, SOCIAL LIFE IN VIRGINIA IN THE SEVENTEENTH CENTURY (Williamtown, 1907), 39–42; Flaherty, LAWES, xi, xiv–xix.

11. Tyler, NARRATIVES, 5–23, 117, 191. The colonists were forced "to devoure those Hogges, Dogges, and horses that were then in the colony, together with rats, mice, snakes or what vermin or carrion soever we could light on . . . that would fill either mouth or belly."

12. Flaherty, LAWES, xi, xiv–xix. Dale was said to have had people hanged, tortured, broken on the wheel and chained to trees until they starved. Joan Wright and Anne Burras Laydon, who was pregnant, were whipped because the shirts they had been making for the Virginia Company's servants became unraveled. Mrs. Laydon had a miscarriage (Tyler, NARRATIVES, 423; McIlwaine, MINUTES, 62).

13. Charles E. Hatch, THE FIRST SEVENTEEN YEARS: VIRGINIA, 1607–1624 (Charlottesville, 1957), 92; John Rolfe, A TRUE RELATION OF THE STATE OF VIRGINIA LEFTE BY SIR THOMAS DALE KNIGHT IN MAY LAST 1616 (Charlottesville, 1957), 8–10; Ralph Hamor, A TRUE DISCOURSE OF THE PRESENT ESTATE OF VIRGINIA AND THE SUCCESSE OF THE AFFAIRES THERE TILL THE 18TH OF JUNE 1614 (Richmond, 1957), 18–19, 23, 32–33.

14. AN ACCOUNT OF THE ANCIENT PLANTERS, [1624], British Public Records Office, Colonial Office 3/21, 72; Tyler, NARRATIVES, 284–286; Lyman Carrier, AGRICULTURE IN VIRGINIA, 1607–1699 (Charlottesville, 1957), 20; Tyler, NARRATIVES, 263, 285.

15. Susan M. Kingsbury, ed., RECORDS OF THE VIRGINIA COMPANY OF LONDON (Washington, D.C., 1906–1935), I, 513.

16. McIlwaine, MINUTES, xvii; Frank Craven, THE VIRGINIA COMPANY OF LONDON, 1606–1624 (Charlottesville, 1957), 45; Warren M. Billings, JAMESTOWN AND THE FOUNDING OF THE NATION (Gettysburg, 1990), 47–48. In 1617 the Virginia Company promised 50 acres per head to those who sent people to the colony.

17. Martin's Hundred had not yet been seated, but many of its would-be settlers already were in the colony.

18. Tyler, NARRATIVES, 247–278; William G. Stanard et al., THE COLONIAL VIRGINIA REGISTER (Baltimore, 1965), 52–53.

19. Thad W. Tate, THE NEGRO IN EIGHTEENTH CENTURY WILLIAMSBURG (Williamsburg, 1965), 1; Kingsbury, RECORDS, III, 243; Smith, Arber, ed., TRAVELS, 541–542. See Chapter 16 for a fuller treatment of the black experience.

20. Craven, VIRGINIA COMPANY, 45; McIlwaine, MINUTES, xvii; W. Stitt Robinson, MOTHER EARTH, LAND GRANTS IN VIRGINIA, 1607–1699 (Charlottesville, 1957), 21–22; Thad Tate et al., THE CHESAPEAKE IN THE SEVENTEENTH CENTURY (Chapel Hill, 1979), 93.

21. Kingsbury, RECORDS, III, 98–109, 245.

22. The subdivisions known as Drummond's Field, Field Crest, First Colony, and the St. George's and Maine farms, and a small portion of Green Spring are located within the Governor's Land tract.

23. Much of the Company Land tract is encompassed by Governor's Land at Two Rivers.

24. Hatch, First Seventeen, 35–38, 92; Gary Parks, Virginia Land Records (Baltimore, 1982), 276; Robinson, Mother Earth, 21–22; Kingsbury, Records, III, 99–101, 310.

25. McIlwaine, Minutes, 14–15, 93, 149–150; Virginia Land Office Patent Book I:3–8, 61; H. R. McIlwaine et al., eds. Journals of the House of Burgesses, 1619–1776 (Richmond, 1905–1915), 1619–1659, 41; Philip A. Bruce, "Viewers of the Tobacco Crop," Virginia Magazine of History and Biography, 5 (October 1897):120; Virginia M. Meyer et al., Adventurers of Purse and Person, 1607–1624/25 (Richmond, 1987), 476; Ambler Manuscript No. 11.

26. He also had land in Archers Hope.

27. Tyler, Narratives, 312; Smith, Arber, ed., Travels, II, 268; Virginia Land Office Patent Book I:9, 15; Kingsbury, Records, IV, 555. William W. Hening, The Statutes At Large: Being a Collection of All the Laws of Virginia (Richmond, 1809–1823), I, 126, 191, 245–246; II, 135. William N. Sainsbury, et al., comp., Calendar of State Papers, Colonial Series, America and the West Indies (Vaduz, 1964), I, 256; Patent Book 1:6; McIlwaine, Minutes, 486–487; Meyer et al., Adventurers, 28–36; Patent Book I:1, 3–8.

28. Virginia Land Office Patent Book I, 10–11, 423; I, Part II, 630; McIlwaine, Minutes, 4, 57, 84, 154; Ambler Manuscript No. 16, 23, 133; McIlwaine, Minutes, 99, 107, 158; John C. Hotten, Original Lists of Persons of Quality, 1600–1700 (Baltimore, 1980), 182; Meyer et al., Adventurers, 42.

29. Kingsbury, Records, III, 99–101, 226–227, 245–246, 310–315, 441–442, 477, 489, 494; Hotten, Original Lists, 180.

30. Tyler, Narratives, 335, 338; Kingsbury, Records, III, 99–101, 154, 175–176, 247, 255; IV, 104–105, 555.

31. Ibid., I, 587; Hatch, First Seventeen, 104–105. The story of the plantation's material culture and layout has been described by noted archaeologist Ivor Noel Hume.

32. Ferrar Papers No. 138, 139, 159; Hotten, Original Lists, 173–176. These are the earliest dated Virginia censuses discovered to date.

33. Contrary to a popular belief that seems to have originated in the late nineteenth century, the 1622 massacre did not occur on Good Friday, for in 1622 (1621 Old Style) Easter was on April 21st.

34. This was Richard Pace of Pace's Paines in what is now Surry County. The Indian was Chanco (Kingsbury, Records, IV, 98).

35. Lyon G. Tyler, ed., "Two Tragical Events: Schepps-togt von Anthony Chester in Virginia, gedaan in het jaar 1620," William and Mary Quarterly, 1st Ser., 9 (July 1900):212.

36. Kingsbury, Records, 570–571; IV, 41, 98–99, 232; Smith, Arber, ed., Travels, 362.

37. Kingsbury, Records, IV, 221–222, 473; Smith, Arber, ed., Travels, 378, 385.

38. Kingsbury, RECORDS, III, 60, 556–557; IV, 41–42, 58, 61, 104–105, 107, 236–237, 239; Martha W. McCartney, "Seventeenth Century Apartheid: The Suppression and Containment of Indians in Tidewater Virginia," JOURNAL OF MIDDLE ATLANTIC ARCHAEOLOGY, Vol. 1 (October 1985), 52–54; Ferrar Manuscript No. 569, No. 572.

39. Hening, STATUTES, I, 123; McIlwaine, MINUTES, 25, 147, 151, 155.

40. Tyler, NARRATIVES, 413–416; McIlwaine et al., HOUSE OF BURGESSES, 1619–1659, 24; Edmund Randolph, HISTORY OF VIRGINIA, Arthur H. Shaffer, ed. (Charlottesville, 1970), 133; Sir Nathaniel Rich, "A Brief declaracon of Th'estate of the Plantacon in Virginia during the first twelve years, April–May 1623"; Kingsbury, RECORDS, IV, 93.

41. McIlwaine et al., HOUSE OF BURGESSES, 1619–1659, 22–23, 35; Hotten, ORIGINAL LISTS, 176–177; Craven, VIRGINIA COMPANY, 57; Nugent, CAVALIERS, I, 19, 33, 36–37, 63, 113, 123–126, 160, 224; Meyer et al., ADVENTURERS, 294–295; Kingsbury, RECORDS, III, 556.

42. Hotten, ORIGINAL LISTS, 173–176, 178, 191–192, 218–221; Meyer et al., ADVENTURERS, 28–37; Kingsbury, RECORDS, IV, 58–61, 555–556; Ferrar Manuscript No. 569, No. 572.

EXTENT OF SETTLEMENT BY 1650

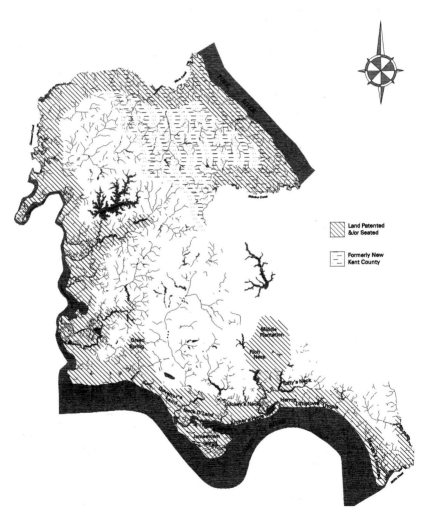

Map by Deborah L. Wilson.

CHAPTER 3

"Our Plantations, Beautifull and Pleasant"
1626–1650

Maintaining Law and Order

As the colony's population increased and settled into loosely defined communities, squabbles among neighbors sometimes required arbitration. Local courts were established in a few places and the inhabitants of privately-sponsored plantations like Martin's Hundred could seek justice from a local leader. But most people were obliged to air their complaints before members of the Council of State (or governor's council) who convened periodically as a General Court. They deliberated over matters that ranged from infractions of church law (such as hunting hogs on Sunday) to murder and treason. Many of the punishments handed down by the General Court today would be termed barbaric. For example, a man's ears might be loped off for committing perjury. But this was a brutal era when corporal punishments such as whipping, hanging, maiming, and dismemberment were sanctioned by law and belief in witchcraft and supernatural phenomena was commonplace.[1]

Slander

Ensign John Uty, who owned land near Grove Creek but lived at Hog Island, sued a neighbor who called him "a common rogue, rascal and thief." Thomas Alnutt of Jamestown was fined for gossiping about the minister of a neighboring parish and Captain Ralph Hamor's wife, Elizabeth, was called to testify about someone's calling Martha Syzemore a "Virginia whore." The General Court typically required slanderers to apologize publicly and post a bond guaranteeing their good behavior. When high ranking officials committed slander, they sometimes took communion together, signifying their willingness to forgive and forget.[2]

Moral and Social Offences

Another type of suit occasionally aired before the General Court was breach of promise. Mrs. Jane Kingsmill of Jamestown overheard Eleanor Sprage (Spradd), a maid servant, pledge to marry Robert Marshall. But before the couple's marriage bans were posted in the parish church, Eleanor became engaged to another. She was chided for her behavior and ordered to publicly apologize to her fellow parishioners. On another occasion, rumor had it that the minister at Hog Island intended to "steal away" the orphaned daughter of Jamestown minister Richard Buck. This sparked a considerable amount of gossip that reached the General Court. Twelve-year-old Mara Buck reportedly was slow-witted, but she was a young heiress at a time when females (especially wealthy ones) were scarce and didn't stay single for long.[3]

Churchwarden Richard Kingsmill was zealous in reporting fellow parishioners who got drunk, swore, or hunted on the Sabbath: offenses against ecclesiastical law. Several residents of Archers Hope and Pasbehay (Thomas Farley, Thomas Jones, Robert Hutchinson, and John Osborne) were censured for being drunk and disorderly late at night. Others were accused of "nightwalking" (venturing abroad late at night) and "nicknaming houses" (making defamatory remarks about their contemporaries, especially those in the upper ranks of society). During the 1620s Archers Hope was an especially raucous community. Mrs. Amy Hall and William Harman exchanged insults and then blows, whereupon he seized her by the hair and threw her to the ground. Hall, whose angry confrontations with her neighbors were well known to the General Court, was placed in Jamestown's ducking stool and dunked in the river three times. Afterward, she was trussed up and towed across the James River and back, behind a ship. The community's most volatile couple was

The course of justice. Courtesy of Dover Publications.
Photo by Carl Aschman.

Joseph and Margaret Johnson, whose violent domestic disputes frequently landed them in court. On one occasion, Joseph attacked local commander Thomas Bransby, who intervened in one of their quarrels. Later he told the court that he was tired of "partinge Newgate birds and Bridewell whores." Pasbehay also had its share of hotheads. Margaret Jones attacked her neighbor, John Butterfield, in his garden, and commenced flailing him with a tobacco stalk. It was not her first infraction of the law, for she already had been punished for committing adultery with Robert Hutchinson, her husband's drinking companion. She, like the irascible Amy Hall, was towed behind a ship to cool her fiery temper.[4]

Couples guilty of fornication or adultery were punished severely, as were whites who had sexual relations with blacks. Usually, men, boys, and black women were whipped and white women and girls were shamed publicly by being made to stand before the congregation of their church, draped in a white sheet and holding a wand. As most of the indentured servants who came to Virginia during the early seventeenth century were young and single, many unauthorized sexual liaisons probably occurred that simply escaped detection.[5] Mrs. Margaret Beard of Pasbehay was found guilty of "behaving scandalously" with servant Thomas Bates. Her husband complained about her "lewd and idle life" but asked the General Court not to impose corporal punishment because she was pregnant. The cuckolded William Beard's revenge came later, for when he made his will, he left Margaret, "the whore," a bed, pillow, and sheets, but bequeathed the rest of his ample estate to others. Perhaps one of the saddest cases ever tried at Jamestown involved two young girls (ages 7 and 10) who had been raped by a young male servant. Both girls were "openly whipped in the fort at James City" and one child's mother was flogged for failing to report the crime more promptly. The rapist was executed and his corpse put on display.[6]

Disputes Over Debts and Property

Many of the cases brought before the General Court involved unpaid debts. Surgeon Thomas Bunn, a tenant who lived upon the Governor's Land, went to court to collect payment from John Proctor, who lived across the James River. Bunn had provided medical treatment to a maid servant who died after Proctor had had her flogged with a line containing fishhooks.[7] John Johnson of Jamestown Island was ordered to fulfill his agreement to repair the dwelling of the late Ensign William Spence, and Johnson's neighbors, John Haule and Thomas Passmoure, went to court to settle a dispute over a debt. Problems sometimes arose over the ownership of cattle, many of which roamed at large, and over swine that destroyed crops. Disagreements between indentured servants and their masters sometimes reached the General Court because one or both parties failed to live up to their obligations. In 1624 when Captain John Harvey's former servant, William Mutch, demanded the corn he was owed, Harvey struck him "over ye pate with his trunchion,"[8] ending the discussion. From time to time, planters disagreed over how to divide a tobacco crop. In February 1626 Dr. Pott's servant, Thomas Leyster (Lister), and Roger Stanley, who lived upon the Governor's Land, drew swords over how much tobacco Stanley owed Pott. In the scuffle that followed, Leyster struck Stanley with a jug, raising the possibility that both men had been drinking. They were brought before the General Court.[9]

Loss of Life

The General Court held inquests when unexplained deaths occurred. In 1625, when little George Pope of Jamestown Island tumbled into an open well and drowned, his caretaker Margaret Osborne, was queried about his death. She testified that she often sent him to fetch water, which he scooped up with a dish and poured into a small barrel. A five-year-old neighbor said that he saw George lean forward to dip up water and fall in. On another occasion, the hanging death of a servant boy was ruled a suicide, as he was known to have been troubled by severe depression.[10]

Theft

In 1623 laborer Daniel Frank (Francke) and gunsmith George Clarke, both of Jamestown Island, were accused of stealing a calf from Governor George Yeardley. Clarke, who testified that Frank had killed the calf, admitted helping butcher it. Calf-stealing was not Frank's first offence, for he already had stolen several items from Provost Marshall Randall Smallwood. Both men were sentenced to death but the gunsmith was reprieved, perhaps because his skills were highly prized. The case of Dr. John Pott, a Jamestown resident and one-time governor found guilty of cattle-rustling, reveals that law-breaking cut through all ranks of society.[11]

Criticizing the Government

Offending government officials brought dire consequences. In March 1624, Captain Richard Quaile of James City, a mariner and author of a "controversial document," had his ears nailed to the pillory in the market-place at Jamestown, was stripped of his command, and fined heavily. In further degradation, he was given an axe and designated a carpenter. Quaile, who pled for clemency, claimed that he was ill, impoverished, and alone in "this mere plantation of sorrows." When Edward Sharples, clerk of the Council of State, was found guilty of sending unauthorized documents to the king, his ears were nailed to the pillory and then cut off. He also was banished from Jamestown

Island unarmed. Somehow, he managed to survive and a year later was back in Jamestown as a servant in the household of Clement Dilke. Richard Barnes, who made derogatory comments about the governor, received the most severe and protracted corporal punishment on record, for his arms were broken, his tongue was bored through with a sharp needle-like instrument, and he was obliged to run a gauntlet of forty men who were to butt him and kick him out of the fort at Jamestown. Peter Martin, who remarked that a man had been wrongfully executed, was "whipped from the fort to the gallows and then back again," after which he was to be "set upon the pillory and there to lose one of his ears." Martin, an indentured servant who had just fulfilled his contract, also was required to serve another seven years.[12]

Acquiring and Disposing of Land

Although most colonists obtained their land through the headright system, people sometimes came into court to record leases, confirm the title to property they had inherited, or ask for acreage that had reverted to the Crown.[13] For example, in 1628 John Uty asked the General Court to assign him the patent of John Jefferson, who relocated to Barbados, abandoning his waterfront acreage in what became Kingsmill Plantation. The surviving records of the General Court also include some early land sales. For example, Percival Wood and his wife, Ann, testified that they had sold a dwelling and 12 acres of land at Jamestown Island's Black Point to Sir George Yeardley.[14]

Settling Estates and Providing for Widows and Orphans

Before county courts were established and authorized to probate estates, executors were obliged to present their accounts to the General Court. Guardians appointed for orphaned children found homes for them and managed their property, making regular reports to the court. For example, when Jamestown minister Richard Buck and his wife died, leaving four youngsters, guardians were appointed to watch over their inheritance. Buck owned 12 acres on Jamestown Island and 750 acres in the Neck O' Land, adjacent to the parish glebe. Richard Kingsmill, one of the Buck children's guardians, moved to their property in the Neck O'Land, just across the Back River from his Jamestown Island home. Usually, executors' responsibilities were much simpler. They inventoried the decedent's estate, settled and collected all debts, and made final distribution of the property. Sometimes they had to see that contractual obligations were fulfilled. For example, Thomas Swinhowe, a casualty of the 1622 Indian uprising, had agreed to construct a palisade around Dr. John Pott's house on the mainland. Therefore, Swinhowe's executor, Randall Smallwood, had to hire someone to fulfill his legally-binding obligation.[15]

Strengthening the Colony

When the Council of State convened as a General Court, decisions sometimes were made that affected the colony as a whole. For example, in 1624 every male head of household, age 20 and over, was required to set out four mulberry trees and 20 vines and to fence his garden. Men were appointed to make sure that every household planted an adequate amount of corn. As the 1620s closed, colonists had to grow two acres of corn "for every head that worketh the land" and could raise no more than 2,000 tobacco plants per person.

Growing uneasiness over the prospect of a French invasion led officials to station a light shallop in Hampton Roads to meet all incoming ships. Vessels entering Virginia waters had to "break bulk" (open their cargoes) at Jamestown before going elsewhere. No one was allowed to relocate from one plantation to another without official permission and all men were ordered to keep their firearms in good condition.

By 1628 Virginia authorities had begun trying to regulate the quality and quantity of the colony's tobacco. They placed restrictions upon planting and harvesting the crop and appointed inspectors to examine it before shipment abroad. Tobacco storage warehouses were built on the banks of navigable waterways, where packed barrels called hogsheads were kept until they were loaded aboard outbound ships. By 1633 there were seven tobacco warehouses in the colony. Virginians' over-dependence upon tobacco as their principal money crop created economic problems, for fluctuations in the market produced dramatic "booms" and "busts." Even so, many Virginians continued to consider tobacco their mainstay.[16]

Relations with the Indians

Memories of the 1622 Indian uprising were kept alive by the Natives' sporadic but persistent attacks. In October 1626 the colonists were given six months to build palisades around their homes and plans were made to undertake marches against the Indians. Consideration was given to colonizing Chiskiack (on the York River) and to running a palisade across the peninsu-

EXTENT OF SETTLEMENT BY 1650

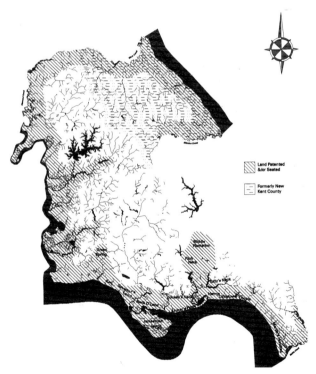

Map by Deborah L. Wilson. See enlarged map, page 60.

la. In April 1627 the governor issued a warning that the Indians were expected to attack at any time. As some of the colony's leaders continued to believe that the Natives' attacks were a punishment from God, all households were commanded to assemble for prayer at least once a day and every plantation had to have a special place for worship services and a fenced-in area as a cemetery. The colonists were forbidden to waste powder by firing weapons during times of celebration, such as weddings and funerals, and to venture out unarmed or alone. Local military leaders had to muster and drill their men on every holiday.

On April 24, 1628, four Indians brought a message to the governor from several men being detained by the Pamunkey. A decision was made to secure their release, seizing the opportunity to learn where the Indians were planting their corn. This evolved into a dishonorable peace treaty that was made in August. According to the minutes of the Council of State, "a pease is to be made till they [the prisoners] are del'd up *and ye English see a fit opportunity to break it.*" By late January 1629 the governor and council found the excuse they had been looking for. Because:

. . . *the people and planters of the colony have grown secure and utterly neglected to eyther stand upon their guard or keep their Arms fitt. . . . The condition of our people being soe wretchedly negligent in this kinde that neither proclamations or other strict orders have remidied the same . . . that all the former treaties of peace be utterly extinct.*

It was thought "a safer course for the colony in general (to prevent a second Massacre) utterly to proclayme and maintayne enmity and warres with all the Indians of these partes." Thus, the peace treaty was not broken on account of the Natives' treachery but because the settlers were negligent in maintaining their own defenses. There was a moratorium on shooting or killing Indians until February 20th, when they officially became "utter Enemies."

A lone Native, who entered the colonized area before his people had been notified of the treaty's dissolution, was sent home with word that the agreement had been annulled because of the Indians' failure to abide by it. Henceforth, official Indian messengers were obliged to come in only "at the appoynted place, at Pasbehay," west of Jamestown Island.[17] An intriguing reference to a "trucking" or trading point at "old Pasbehay," found in a 1637 patent for land near Bush Neck, raises the possibility that Natives entering the territory held by the colonists traveled the so-called Chickahominy Path, which followed portions of what later became Routes 5 and 614.[18]

The Texture of Daily Life

In 1629 Captain John Smith wrote a description of conditions in Virginia, based upon interviews with several colonists who visited England. He spoke of the abundance of livestock, food, and beverages, and Virginians' preoccupation with growing tobacco. Most of the plantations toward the falls of the James reportedly were so well fortified with palisades that their inhabitants didn't worry about the Indians and most male colonists were outfitted with "a peece, a Jacke, a Coat of Maile, a Sword, or Rapier." Indians seldom were seen along the James, although their fires could be observed at a distance and they occasionally killed "some few stragglers." Governor John Pott and two or three councilors then resided at Jamestown, the capital, where "most of the wood [is] destroyed" and "all converted into pasture and gardens." On Jamestown Island "all manner of herbs and roots we have in England" grew in abundance "and as good grasse as can be." This had induced some who lived in outlying areas to pasture their cattle there. Smith said that the Virginia colonists raised domesticated geese, ducks, and turkeys and trained their servants to shoot game and wild fowl. Peaches, apples, apricots, figs, grapes, and other fruit grew well and the colonists found "the Indian corne so much better than ours [English wheat] they beginne to leave [off] sowing it." Smith likened Virginia's plantations to English country villages.[19]

Maintaining an Adequate Defense

In March 1629 commanders were appointed for the colony's loosely defined communities, whose males were organized into military units. John Jackson was responsible for the plantations in the Neck O'Land behind Jamestown Island; John Uty, for those in Martin's Hundred and Archers Hope; and Bridges Freeman, for those in Pasbehay and the Chickahominy

River basin. During the early 1630s the Indians made sporadic attacks and the colonists retaliated from time to time. John Uty, John West, and a few others also established homesteads on the York River at Chiskiack. A summer drought in 1632 led to a shortage of corn, which forced the colonists to initiate trade with the Indians. Fall brought a peace treaty with the Pamunkey and the Chickahominy; however, the settlers were warned not to trust them, for all Indians were considered "Irreconcilable enemies." Meanwhile, the relentless encroachment of land-hungry planters did little to sooth racial tensions. By the mid-1630s land had been patented along the Chickahominy River inland as far as Tyascan (Diascund) Creek.

In February 1633 the assembly revived a proposal to build a palisade across the James-York peninsula, cordoning off an area for the colonists' exclusive use. Fifty acres were offered to each man willing to settle between Queens and Archers Hope (College) Creeks. Construction began on March 1, 1633; the palisade was rebuilt at least once.[20]

Rolling Back the Forest

Virginia planters, when seating new land, usually constructed crude huts they occupied while erecting weatherproof but insubstantial frame houses. Building a simple dwelling or "Virginia house" allowed a patentee to legitimatize his land claim while fulfilling his need for shelter. As prospective planters had to make a substantial investment in workers to cultivate their land, they tended to skimp on housing costs in order to channel their limited resources into the purchase of labor. Some people rented their undeveloped property to tenants, often landless freedmen who agreed to build "a convenient dwelling and other necessary houses and . . . to leave all in good repair."[21]

The Company Land

During the 1630s and '40s people laid claim to portions of the 3,000-acre tract called the Company Land, at the mouth of the Chickahominy River. Bridges Freeman, who moved there around 1629–1630, was commander of the munitions at Jamestown and served several terms in the assembly, at first representing Pasbehay and the Chickahominy River area and finally, James City County. He became the tobacco inspector for Sandy Point and the Chickahominy Parish and in 1647, the region's collector of the revenue. Freeman by 1643 had accumulated 750 acres that extended from the mouth of the Chickahominy to Merryman's (Gordon's) Creek. To the east of his frontage on the James was the patent of Thomas Harvey, who like Freeman's partner, Francis Fowler, and near-neighbor John Tyos, were former indentured servants of the Virginia Company. During the mid-seventeenth century the entrance to the Chickahominy River was known as the Chickahominy Gate and Freeman's land was called Piney or Freeman's Point.[22]

The Governor's Land

In 1627 several inhabitants of the Governor's Land sought permission to leave. They complained about "the barrenness of ye ground . . . the badness of their utterly decayed houses & of their small strength & ability to defend themselves." Almost all of these people had resided there for several years and some were former servants of the Virginia Company. Throughout the seventeenth century a number of Jamestown lot owners leased small parcels in the Governor's Land.[23]

The Neck O'Land and Archers Hope

Richard Kingsmill, who patented 500 acres in Archers Hope sometime prior to May 1625, seated his property by 1626. In time it became known as Kingsmill Neck. As Kingsmill divided his time between his Jamestown Island plantation and the late Richard Buck's acreage in the Neck O' Land, he probably placed indentured servants upon his Archers Hope patent. After Buck's orphans matured, they took possession of his property. Daughter Elizabeth married Jamestown burgess Thomas Crumpe, who patented 750 acres between the James City Parish glebe and Powhatan Creek, directly above the Buck patent. Later he became burgess for the Neck O'Land community and in 1639 was appointed the region's tobacco inspector. Thomas and

Elizabeth Buck Crumpe's son and heir, John, patented 1,500 acres in the Neck O'Land in 1654. Included were 250 acres he acquired on the basis of headrights, his maternal grandfather's 750 acres, and his uncle Peleg Buck's 500 acres. After John Crumpe's death, his widow and heir, Elizabeth, married Matthew Page. It was through their union that the Buck property in the Neck O'Land descended to the Pages who developed Rosewell in Gloucester County.[24]

Nearby in Archers Hope was Jockey's Neck, which name is derived from Joachim (Joakin, Jockey) Andrews of Jamestown Island, who acquired his patent in 1619 but failed to seat it. John Johnson, another island resident, patented some Jockey's Neck land that stayed in his family for several generations. Close by was Ensign William Spence's homestead, which was attacked during the 1622 massacre with the loss of several lives. The guardian of the Spence couple's four-year-old orphan, Sara, leased their land to Thomas Farley. Later, it came into the hands of Roger Webster, a cowkeeper. Thomas Pettus owned land on the west side of College Creek that lay somewhat inland.[25]

Thomas Farley, a gentleman, patented land on the east side of College Creek in Farleys or Farlow's Neck. Nearby was the acreage of John Davis, who owned part of the Great (or Barren) Neck, which abutted south and east upon Halfway Creek. Richard Brewster, Edward Goldbourne, and Thomas Pettus also owned land on the east side of College Creek.

Humphrey Higgenson, who had nearby Tuttey's Neck, acquired the Farley and Kingsmill Necks during the 1640s, combining them with his Harrop plantation. Thus, he unified the western part of what became Kingsmill Plantation. Higginson's property abutted east upon Richard Richards' 350 acres called Littletown, which included parcels that William Claiborne, Jochim Andrews, and William Fairfax (Fierfax, fferFax) had patented earlier on. Further east was John Jefferson's land, which John Uty repatented after it reverted to the Crown. In 1639 tobacco viewers were appointed to serve the territory between College Creek and the Wareham River or Ponds, later known as Grove Creek.[26]

Martin's Hundred

To the east of Grove Creek was Martin's Hundred, which extended along the banks of the James to Skiff's Creek, the boundary line between the corporations of James City and Elizabeth City. Early land records suggest that after the dissolution of the Virginia Company, patentees quickly laid claim to what was considered very desirable acreage. Some of these people formerly may have been associated with the Society of Martin's Hundred as servants or employees. Captain William Whittaker's landholdings abutted Grove Creek's mouth and extended inland for a considerable distance. To his south and east was the land of Thomas Loving. Clement Hardon, David Mansell, John Hayward, William Stafford, and John O'Berry had patents in the eastern part of Martin's Hundred and George Holmes and Samuel Snead owned land that lay inland along what became known as the Green Swamp.[27]

Middle Plantation and Rich Neck

Shortly after a palisade was built across the James-York peninsula between the heads of College and Queens Creeks, a small settlement developed that became known as the Middle Plantation. Near the southerly end of the palisade line, Dr. John Pott of Jamestown built a home. Close to the head of College Creek was a 600-acre tract that Secretary Richard Kemp was allowed to use as a privilege of office. On the west side of the creek was a broad, elevated promontory called the Rich Neck that official merchant George Menefie developed into a 1,200 acre plantation he called Littletown.[28] Dutch trader David DeVies visited Menefie's manor house in March 1633 and described the abundance of roses, fruit trees, and herbs in his host's garden. In 1638 Secretary Kemp, who patented 840 acres known as "the Meadows" adjacent to Littletown, purchased the Menefie property and combined the two tracts into a country estate he called Rich Neck. After Kemp's death in 1656, his widow, Elizabeth, married Sir Thomas Lunsford, a hotheaded Royalist and former captain of the Tower of London. The couple resided at Rich Neck.[29]

Plantations Along the Chickahominy

As settlement slowly spread inland along the Chickahominy, tree after tree yielded to the axe and the forests upon which the Indians relied for hunting and gathering were converted into tobacco fields. Although much of the Chickahominy's shoreline was marsh-rimmed, its channel could accommodate sea-going vessels. Planters showed a preference for headlands, such as Mattahunk and Checkeroes (Bush) Necks, that were covered by rich, alluvial soils. As time went on, patentees tended to reaffirm and enlarge their earlier land claims. In the vicinity of Checkroes or Checkerhouse (Gordon's) Creek were the patents of John Felgate, Edward Oliver, Thomas Wombwell, and Richard Bell. Richard Kingsmill's daughter, Elizabeth, was part-owner of three islands in that area.

By the late 1630s Samuel Trigg and Raphael Joyner had laid claim to 300 acres on Diascund Creek, two miles inland from its mouth. Their patent abutted south upon William Wigg's island, later known as Hicks Island. At the mouth of Diascund Creek was the patent of Edward Coles (Cowles). Despite the fact that settlers began claiming land in this vicinity at a relatively early date, a significant number of patents were left unseated, with the result that they reverted to the Crown for reassignment to others. Wallingford Parish was established in 1642, an indication that a significant amount of population growth had occurred within the Chickahominy River basin. The creation of Wilmington Parish out of the upper part of Wallingford in 1657–1658 indicates that expansion was both rapid and continuous.[30] It is likely that a lingering Native presence somewhat inhibited the seating of patents along the Chickahominy.

The Ware and Skimino Creek Drainage

Paralleling the York River was the Rickahock Path which followed the ridgeback roughly bisecting the James-York peninsula. Patentees began claiming land along that primitive trail during the late 1630s. Acreage within the Ware Creek drainage was settled by the early 1640s. These people, who inhabited a sparsely populated frontier beyond the reach of military protection, would have borne the brunt of any friction with the Indians. Within the territory defined by Skimino and Ware Creeks were the holdings of a Mr. Rosier, whose acreage on the east side of Ware Creek's mouth was reassigned to John Broach in 1642. The Rosier-Broach patent formed the nucleus of what became known as the Mount Folly tract. Others who owned (and perhaps occupied) land along Ware Creek during the mid-seventeenth century were William Hockaday and John Boatwright, whose dwelling was mentioned in a 1652 patent. The patents of John Holding, Charles Edmonds, John Barber, John Cocker, and Thomas Gardner lay somewhat inland. Along the west side of Skimino Creek was John King's patent, which abutted the landholdings of Robert Booth (Bouth) whose 800 acres by 1651 had been were absorbed into the patent of Arthur Price, a wealthy merchant and York County burgess. Price owned the land between Skimino and Taskinask Creeks that was developed into Riverview and Shellfield plantations.[31]

The Establishment of Virginia's First Counties

In 1634, when the colony was subdivided into eight shires or counties, James City County was formed.[32] Each was to have a local court with justices (or commissioners) of the peace, a sheriff, a clerk, and other lesser officials. County justices were authorized to take depositions, settle petty disputes and minor criminal cases, and try civil cases involving less than 10 pounds sterling. The establishment of county courts, which authority increased over time, relieved the General Court of many routine matters and freed it to handle important cases and function as an appellate body. Each county also had a lieutenant, who was responsible for organizing the local militia, which members were to be properly armed and drilled regularly. Burgesses were elected at the county seat, which was at the hub of local life.

James City County's seat of government was at Jamestown until around 1715 to 1721, when it was moved to Williamsburg. During the second half of the seventeenth century, James City County's justices usually convened in the statehouse in the same chamber the General Court used for quarterly meetings.[33] The General Court's clerk traditionally served as James City County's clerk of court, although the two judicial bodies' records were kept separate, and the county sheriff usually functioned as the House of Burgesses' sergeant-at-arms. The General Court shared a jail, pillory, whipping post, and stocks with the county court, which the law required to have a ducking stool. A gallows stood by as a silent but grim reminder to would-be lawbreakers.

County courts came into existence around the time the colony's population entered a period of great expansion. In 1634 James City County had 886 inhabitants, making it the most populous jurisdiction in Virginia. Its territory on the upper side of the James stretched from Skiffs Creek west to a point just above the Chickahominy River's mouth, and on the lower side of the river, from Lawnes Creek to Upper Chippokes Creek, taking in what later became Surry County. James City County extended north until it met the southerly boundary of Charles River or York County, near the Rickahock Path. Between 1634 and 1653 the territory between Ware and Skimino Creeks lay within the bounds of York County; later it became part of New Kent and then James City County.[34] When Virginia's county governments were first formed, Governor John Harvey chose as local justices men with experience in the General Court or in the old, obsolete monthly courts. But as there was a shortage of such men, it was necessary to select some with little or no familiarity with the workings of a court. By the late 1640s it had become traditional for incumbent county justices to recommend prospective appointees. In time, local courts became increasingly competent in handling administrative duties. A significant number of justices were burgesses and the largest landowners in their counties. Such men typically used their political offices to enhance their personal wealth and secure their family's position in society. What we call "conflict of interest" was then the norm among high ranking officials. For example, George Menefie of James City County served simultaneously as a member of the Council of State and as first the corporation's, and then the county's, official merchant. He hosted a May 1636 council meeting when several important decisions were made about trade.[35]

Expanding the Role of Local Government

When the Grand Assembly convened in January 1640, it was agreed that Jamestown would remain "the chief town and residence of the Governor." A number of new laws were passed that affected county government. Local justices had to see that a cemetery was laid out in every parish and church-wardens were responsible for having it fenced in and maintained properly. This may have been when the Jamestown church's burial ground was first enclosed. It became legal to export cattle and sell corn to the New England colonies or other neighboring plantations. For the first time, it became illegal to hunt on other people's land without their permission. Churchwardens were ordered to report infractions of ecclesiastical law to their local court justices. This meant that moral offences, such as bastardy and fornication, could be punished on a local level.

During the 1640s county justices took on the task of maintaining roads, bridges, and ferries. Local sheriffs were empowered to seize colonists' goods to satisfy their debts, and the value of the civil cases county justices were allowed to try was raised substantially. They were given the responsibility of overseeing orphans' inheritances and could try all cases in common law and in equity, which in effect gave them original jurisdiction in most civil cases. Local court justices saw that wills were probated properly, taxes were col-lected, and arms and ammunition were made available to the local militia. They also had a role in setting prices and wages and the fees charged by tavern-keepers and millers. By 1652 county justices exerted control over most local affairs. Later, they gained the right to try capital cases and hold jury trials. Thus, as the colony moved into the second half of the seventeenth century, the county court had the right to undertake a wide variety of criminal, civil, ecclesiastical, admiralty, and administrative functions.[36]

Fostering Economic and Urban Development

The 1630s and '40s brought repeated efforts to strengthen Virginia's economy and improve the capital city. Governor John Harvey sought to stim-ulate interest in the production of marketable commodities and tried to encourage skilled artisans to come to the colony. To improve the reputation of Virginia tobacco, five warehouses were built where it could be inspected and stored before being shipped abroad. At least one inspector per warehouse had to be a local member of the Council of State. William Peirce and Richard Stephens, who resided on New Town lots in Jamestown, were qualified to officiate in the capital city's warehouse, which served the territory from Weyanoke (in Charles City) to Lawnes Creek. By law, all incoming ships had to land first at Jamestown, where all "contracts, bargains and exchanges in tobacco" were to be transacted. The community's merchants and storekeepers were to be involved in virtually all sales of imported commodities. These measures were designed to make Jamestown the center of Virginia's commerce and trade.[37]

Dutch traders found trading with the Virginia colonists advantageous and profitable. David DeVries advised would-be traders to maintain a house in Virginia to receive planters' tobacco as soon as it was ready for shipment. He paused at Jamestown and stayed in the home of Governor Harvey, a titled nobleman. Although Harvey insisted that "there was no other house but his for hospitality," its excessive use for official functions was his own fault. Instead of constructing or renting a building to serve as the colony's statehouse, as he had been told to do, he chose to have the governing bodies meet in his home, which he used for official entertaining. Harvey's caustic personality and political leanings eventually made him so unpopular with members of his own council that they literally thrust him from office.[38]

In February 1636, while the temporarily-deposed Harvey was out of the country, the assembly enacted legislation promoting Jamestown's development. Those willing to build on undeveloped land in the capital city would be awarded the acreage they improved. Several merchants, a mariner, a brickmaker and others responded by patenting Jamestown lots around this time. In 1639 Governor John Harvey, who had succeeded in getting reinstated, told the Privy Council that in response to the legislative incentives promoting Jamestown's development, "twelve houses and stores" had been built and Secretary Richard Kemp had erected a brick house that was "the fairest ever known in this country for substance and uniformity." He added that "others have undertaken to build framed houses to beautify the place" and contributed toward "the building of a brick church." Harvey said that funds were being raised to construct a statehouse and that the storehouses recently built would accommodate "far more goods than have been sent this year." He claimed that there wasn't a foot of land for half-a-mile along Jamestown's waterfront that wasn't improved or scheduled for development. But before Harvey's glowing reports reached England, he was replaced by Sir Francis Wyatt. Ultimately, Harvey succumbed to financial problems and was forced to dispose of his property to satisfy his creditors. One he sold was the residence that had served as the colony's statehouse, which he conveyed to the government. Governor Francis Wyatt was authorized to erect a special building in which the council could meet and to relocate the capital, if his council and the assembly agreed. But by the time he took office, a substantial investment had been made in improving Jamestown and the colony's principal officials, like their predecessors, opted not to change locations.[39]

In 1641 the king instructed newly-appointed Governor William Berkeley to see that a statehouse was built and authorized him to move the seat of government, if the council and assembly agreed. Anyone patenting 100 acres or more was to enclose a quarter-acre as an orchard or garden and patentees of 500 or more acres were ordered to construct at least one 16-by-24-foot brick house with a cellar. No one was "to build slight cottages" to substantiate land claims and people with skills in trades and handicrafts were supposed to practice them in towns. The Grand Assembly responded to the king's directives by enacting legislation designed to encourage Jamestown's development. A flurry of patentees responded by claiming small lots in the western end of the island. A March 1643 law authorized people to keep land upon which they had "built decent houses" even though it had been patented by someone else. In March 1643 the assembly presented the very popular Governor Berkeley with two houses and an orchard, the same structures the government had purchased from the bankrupt John Harvey in 1641. Provisions also were made for Berkeley to be compensated from locally-generated taxes on agricultural commodities. He quickly patented approximately 1,000 acres at Green Spring, directly behind the Governor's Land, and commenced developing it into a manor plantation. In February 1645 Richard Kemp wrote Berkeley, then in England, that construction of his brick house at Green Spring was progressing well, but "that att towne" had progressed "no higher than ye first storye above ye cellar." Kemp was referring to the three-bay brick rowhouse Berkeley erected at Jamestown, to the west of the church.[40] One or more of its bays at times served as the colony's statehouse.

Commerce and Trade

During the mid-1640s Virginia's governing officials decided to build two public flax-houses at Jamestown where two children from each county could be taught to make cloth from raw flax. The flax-houses had to be readied for use by April 1, 1647.[41] Official encouragement was given to other types of businesses and twice during the 1640s the Dutch were invited to trade in Virginia. They apparently welcomed the opportunity, for in 1648 one man reported that at Christmastime there were ten ships from London, two from Bristol, twelve Hollanders, and seven from New England all trading at Jamestown.[42]

In 1649 one writer said that in Virginia prosperity was in evidence everywhere. The colonists had plenty of barley and excellent malt and generally "brew their owne Beere, strong and good" although "they have Six publike Brewhouses." He said that trade was brisk and that "above 30 saile of ships" bearing at least 700-800 mariners came to the colony annually. Virginia offered excellent opportunities to turners, potters, and coopers "to make all kind of earthen and wooden Vessels" and "to sawyers, carpenters, tile-makers, boatwrights, tailors, shoemakers, tanners, fishermen and the like." There also was an abundance of iron ore. Another man reported that earlier, there had been "two or three bru [brew] houses" at Jamestown that went out of business because their customers refused to pay their bills. One was owned by Captain John Moon, who eventually moved to Isle of Wight County.[43]

It is easy to envision the excitement on Jamestown's waterfront when a foreign ship was sighted coming up the river! The prospect of bartering for imported goods, catching up on the latest news, or simply gawking at strangers would have been riveting. In 1644 Adam Bland of Jamestown received a shipment from London merchant John Bland that included everything from vessels for food preparation and consumption to agricultural implements and nails. Runlets of aquavitae and several types of wine came in aboard the SIVILLA MERCHANT, as did containers of thread, fabric, lace, and readymade clothing. Barrels of gunpowder were stored in the ship's hold along with four grindstones, a shallop, a wherry with oars, 3,744 tobacco pipes, and an assortment of knives. At mid-century, when the English government imposed a Navigation Act that outlawed the importation of goods in anything other than English ships or those of the goods' country of origin, the Virginia colonists clung to their right to "free trade as the people of England do enjoy to all places and with all nations."[44]

A 1649 law created an official market-place at Jamestown. It was vast in size and encompassed the entire upper end of the island west of Orchard Run. The market was open from 8 A.M. to 6 P.M. weekly, on Wednesdays and Saturdays. All transactions were recorded by a special clerk and were legally binding. Within Jamestown's ample market zone, merchants could exchange imported goods for tobacco and vendors could haggle with their customers over vegetables, fruit, meat, livestock, and other commodities. In 1655 the concept of trading zones resurfaced when the assembly authorized each of Virginia's counties to establish one or two markets that extended a mile or two along both sides of a navigable waterway. Throughout this period Jamestown was the colony's official port of entry and as such, retained its role as the premier center of trade.[45]

The Workings of Government

The rise of representative government occurred gradually, in part because the Crown didn't interfere in its evolution. In 1643 Virginia's Grand Assembly became bicameral, for the burgesses began meeting apart from the governor and council. The Secretary of the Colony, Clerk of the Council, Clerk of the House of Burgesses, and Clerk of the General Court kept the records of the official bodies to which they belonged. Virginia's legal system was based upon English law. Legislation was enacted from time to time to meet changing needs.

The burgesses and General Court worked closely with local officials in solving whatever problems arose. For example, in October 1640 James City County Under-sheriff Raphael Joyner of Diascund claimed that some people refused to contribute toward his salary. The burgesses responded by lightening his work load: they made local sheriffs responsible for jailing accused criminals until right before trial by the General Court.[46]

The 1640s saw changes in laws that governed the conduct of indentured servants. A 1642 act set four-year terms for servants who arrived in the colony at age 20 or older. Those between 12 and 20 were bound for five years and children under 12 were obliged to serve seven years. Sometimes, servants married secretly or engaged in unsanctioned sexual liaisons, both of which were considered detrimental to their owners' financial interests. People sometimes harbored runaways instead of returning them to their rightful owners. Such offences typically brought fines and a lengthening of the servant's term of service. Anyone absconding more than once was branded upon the cheek with an "R." However, indentured servants gained a few legal rights during the 1640s. They were authorized to file formal complaints against owners that failed to provide them with food and clothing or treated them "in an unchristian manner." Although indentured servants probably were at a considerable disadvantage when filing complaints against their owners, a few such cases did make their way into the colony's legal records.[47]

Dealings with the Natives

Court records reveal that during the late 1630s and early 1640s there was a considerable amount of interaction between the colonists and the Indians. Those who took Indian children into their homes and reared them in the Christian faith were eligible for compensation. Cross-cultural contact also occurred when Natives became servants in planter households or were hired to hunt or fish. Although it was illegal to sell firearms to Indians, restrictions on trading with them eased somewhat. The Powhatan Indians' paramount chief, Opechancanough, leader of the 1622 uprising, came to Jamestown in 1640 to testify before the General Court on behalf of a colonist accused of killing one Native to avenge a crime committed by another. In 1641 Walter Chiles and Joseph Johnson of James City County and two other men secured official permission to explore the territory beyond the head of the Appomattox. They were entitled to 14 years' profits from their discoveries, except for precious metals. The assembly renewed the explorers' license in 1643.[48]

In April 1642 a new Indian treaty was signed. However, steady growth in the colony's population and encroachment upon Native lands inevitably gave rise to conflict. Patents issued during the late 1630s and early 1640s chart the colonists' intrusion into the Chickahominy Indians' heartland. For example, in 1639 Mattahunk Neck and Cuspita were patented, tract names which reflect their association with the Indians. Settlers also ventured into the Pamunkey Indians' territory along the lower side of the Pamunkey River and moved across the York into the Middle Peninsula. In 1641 colonists were authorized to venture into the countryside along the Piankatank River, as long as they seated in groups of a hundred men or more and paid a barrel of corn a year to Opechancanough. Settlers also moved into the territory along the Rappahannock River.[49]

The 1644 Indian Uprising

The Natives responded to the growing pressure by rising up in defiance. This second major uprising occurred on Thursday, April 18, 1644, and claimed 400 to 500 settlers' lives. Again, Opechancanough was credited with leading the massacre. Hardest hit were those who lived along the upper reaches of the York River and on the lower side of the James, near the Nansemond River. The Grand Assembly resolved to "abandon all formes of peace and familiarity" with the Natives and vowed to seek out and destroy those involved in the attack. Again, retaliatory marches were undertaken for the expressed purpose of destroying the Indians. April 18th joined March 22nd as a holy day, an annual reminder that the Indians were enemies. Eighty men were garrisoned at Middle Plantation and "all private trade, commerce, familiarity and entertaynment with the Indians" was prohibited, for governing officials believed that the weapons the Natives had used were procured through trade.[50]

Although official records contain relatively little information on the 1644 massacre, it is certain that retaliatory marches were undertaken against the Pamunkey, Chickahominy, Weyanoke, Waresqueek, and Nansemond Indians, and two tribes that lived far below the James River, in what became North Carolina. Captain William Claiborne, as "General and Chief Commander," led a large and well equipped army against the Pamunkey Indians' stronghold in Pamunkey Neck, destroying their villages and corn fields. But the Indians withdrew into the forest and dropped out of sight. It was around this time that the colony was subdivided into two military districts and local leaders were given greater authority. James City Parish's minister asked the assembly to create a new parish out of the land between College and Grove Creeks because local people were afraid to commute to church at Jamestown or Martin's Hundred during "the dangerous times."[51]

In February 1645, while Sir William Berkeley was in England procuring military supplies, Richard Kemp updated him about the previous summer's expeditions against the Indians. Captain Leonard Calvert took his ship into the Chickahominy River and helped the colonists attack the Chickahominies in their homeland. Besides burning the Indians' towns and destroying their king's dwelling and treasure house, they laid waste to their corn and took numerous prisoners. Kemp said that Captain Ralph Wormeley was extremely valiant and his horsemen brought in many captives. Wormeley "with his own hands" killed two Indians and brought in one "by ye necke to ye great joy of ye Army," which forced him to disclose where his people's towns and corn fields were located. The colonists pressed the offensive until their powder ran out. Kemp added that if the Indians had realized how little ammunition they had, they would have been in great jeopardy. Frontier settlers were in great danger and no one dared to venture out unarmed. Because there was such a desperate need for ammunition, the Council decided to ask the assembly for authorization to purchase some from in-coming ships. But because there wasn't enough tobacco on hand to cover the cost, the burgesses fixed upon the idea of building forts or garrisons in strategic locations along the frontier to provide surveillance over the Indians.[52]

Controlling Access to the Peninsula

In February 1645 the assembly chose three sites they considered critical to the colonists' defense. Carpenters and other workmen were pressed into service as were men to garrison the forts. Fort James, on the Chickahominy River, was located at Moysenac, on the west side of Diascund Creek's mouth, within what was then James City County. The fort, a small frame building, was erected under the supervision of Thomas Rolfe, who was awarded the land upon which it stood in exchange for seeing that it was manned and maintained for three years. The site at Moysenac was selected because it was in the Chickahominy Indians' heartland. In March 1646 the assembly decided to construct a garrison called Fort Henry at the falls of the Appomattox River. A third of the 45 soldiers stationed there were from James City County.[53]

Because the burgesses realized that it was impossible to defeat the Indians conclusively, as they had fled into the woods, a search party (including 13 James City County men) was sent out to capture Opechancanough, dead or alive. Governor Berkeley, upon learning that the chief's people had been seen, rallied a party of horsemen and set out in pursuit. The aged Indian leader was captured and brought back to Jamestown, where he was jailed and allegedly "treated with all the Respect and Tenderness imaginable." However, a soldier, distraught over "the calamities the colony had suffered by this Prince's Means, basely shot him through the Back." The death of the Native emperor, known to the English as "that Bloody Monster," heralded the demise of the Powhatan chiefdom. Afterward Berkeley, who was credited with subduing the Indians, pressed for strengthening the colony's defenses against a foreign enemy. These accomplishments reportedly made him the "darling of the people."[54]

The 1646 Treaty

In October 1646 Necotowance, immediate successor to Opechancanough, concluded a formal peace agreement with the Virginia government, which agreed to protect his people from their enemies. In return, the Indians were to let the governor appoint or confirm their leaders and they promised to pay an annual tribute to the Crown's representatives. They conceded their willingness to withdraw from the James-York peninsula, east of the fall line, and to abandon their land on the lower side of the James, south to the Blackwater River.[55] All Natives entering the ceded territory could be slain lawfully, unless they were garbed in "a coate of striped stuff" that messengers were to wear as a badge of safe conduct. All trade with the Indians was to be conducted through the garrisons on the Appomattox and Pamunkey Rivers, where Indian messengers' striped coats were kept when not in use.[56]

The Natives took their treaty obligations seriously. In March 1648 Necotowance and "five more petty kings attending him" came to Jamestown to deliver a tribute of 20 beaver skins. But they may not have fully comprehended the need to wear a striped coat when entering the ceded territory. An account published in 1649 quoted Necotowance as saying "My countrymen tell me I am a liar when I tell them the English will kill you if you goe into their bounds." The writer hastened to add that the "valiant Captain Freeman made him no liar when lately he killed three Indians without badge incroaching," a reference to James City County's Bridges Freeman. As European settlement continued to advance toward the head of the Chickahominy River, the Chickahominy Indians withdrew into the Pamunkey Indians' territory, where they stayed for several generations. In 1648 one colonist patented the site of the Warrany Old Town, above Diascund Creek.

Arthur Price, who lived between Taskinask and Skimino Creeks, informed York County's justices that "some inhabitants on York River above Skimino due [do] dayly Entertain the Indians in their houses, day and night" contrary to law. He was authorized to arrest lawbreakers and kill any Indians he found associating with them. Ironically, Price himself had an Indian maid servant he had purchased from the estate of a local man.

In October 1649, a 5,000-acre patent was allocated to three Indian leaders whose territory was enveloped by colonized land. Three years later, legislation was passed whereby "all the Indians of the collonye shall hold and keep those seats of land that they now have." The burgesses noted that "many Complaints have been brought to this Assembly touching wrongs done to the Indians in taking away their lands." Thus was born the concept of cordoning off Indian preserves or reservations in Virginia. As racial tensions eased, the colonists and the Indians again began to intermingle.[57]

Class Differences Emerge

As the seventeenth century wore on and the colony's population increased, social and political distinctions between the classes became more apparent. Servants, having fulfilled their terms of indenture, sought to procure land of their own but often lacked the means to do so. This led to a growing number of landless freedmen. Some of these people rented land from larger planters; others simply became transients. The gap widened between those with greater and lesser opportunities for economic advancement, with the result that Virginia became a distinctly stratified society. At the pinnacle were the governor and his councilors, who shared some of their power with members of the assembly. Below the burgesses were county justices of the peace and other local officials. At the bottom were the lesser planters and landless freedmen, who ranked just above ethnic minorities such as blacks and Indians, whose legal rights and opportunities for advancement were very limited. Somewhere between the top and bottom rungs of the socio-economic ladder was a substantial number of Virginians with landholdings of modest size. These were the middling farmers, skilled workers, and others with a limited but adequate amount of disposable income. Despite expansion in the colony's population, the old ruling families and their kin, augmented by new arrivals who came with money and good political connections, clung tightly to their power and dominated Virginia's government.[58]

Stimulating Virginia's Economy

As the half-century mark drew nearer, Governor William Berkeley, who constantly sought new ways to enhance Virginia's economic potential, put its agricultural diversity on display at Green Spring by growing rice and other crops and planting numerous varieties of fruit. He also showcased industries, such as pottery-making, that he felt had good potential. But Berkeley was keenly aware of the need for inland exploration to search for minerals, precious metals, and other natural resources, and to further Indian trade. In 1650 he assembled a small group of men, who set out from the head of the Appomattox River. They probably trekked into the wilderness by following a southwesterly trade path that became established around 1646 when Fort Henry was built. The explorers were led by two Indian guides, an Appomattock and a Nottoway, who took them as far as the Meherrin River.[59] Thanks to Berkeley's keen interest in inland exploration, new trade routes were opened and the groundwork was laid for Virginia's claim to the Ohio River valley. While he was still in office, Thomas Batts and Robert Fallam set out to "discover the mountains."[60]

The Civil War in England

Even before England became embroiled in a bloody Civil War, tensions between the Royalists and the supporters of Parliament (dubbed the Roundheads) spilled over upon the colonies. During the spring of 1645, when Dutch sea captain David DeVries returned to Virginia, he witnessed a hostile encounter between an armed flyboat from Bristol and two London ships. In a sharp engagement that occurred at Newport News Point, all three vessels were damaged and several people were killed. DeVries said that the Bristol men were loyal to the king and the Londoners, to Parliament.

Virginia colonists by and large were sympathetic to the monarchy and after they learned that King Charles I had been beheaded, the burgesses met at Jamestown to proclaim his son's right to the throne. They also declared that anyone expressing doubts about Charles II's right of succession would be considered treasonous. Governor William Berkeley, who was fiercely loyal to the Crown, opened his home to royalists who sought refuge in Virginia. As a result, the colony became a haven for those in exile. One such man was Sir Thomas Lunsford, who married Richard Kemp's widow and took up residence at Rich Neck, in relatively close proximity to Sir William Berkeley's Green Spring plantation. Another was Francis Morrison, whom Berkeley befriended and placed in command of the fort at Jamestown.[61]

The Colony in 1650

By the mid-seventeenth century, settlement was well established throughout eastern Virginia, as far west as the fall line, and on the Eastern Shore. The colony's mortality rate had begun to level off and in 1649 there were an estimated 5,000 people in Virginia. By 1675 that figure had climbed to around 50,000.[62] The colony not only had managed to survive, it was gaining momentum.

Notes

1. Virginia's first accused witch was Goodwife Joan Wright of Elizabeth City, whose "spells" allegedly made one neighbor's chickens die and another's servant woman "dance starke naked" for stealing a piece of lightwood. Mrs. Wright's husband, Robert, was on land in the eastern end of Jamestown Island (McIlwaine, MINUTES, 111–112, 114, 480).

2. Ibid., 18–19, 61–62.

3. Ibid., 15–17. Mara's younger brother, Benomi, was identified as "the first idiot" born in Virginia (Meyer et al., ADVENTURERS, 142).

4. Ibid., 70, 108, 116, 119, 123, 133, 153, 166, 480. Newgate and Bridewell were English prisons.

5. Indentured servants needed their master's permission to marry.

6. Ibid., 142, 149–150, 475, 479–480; British Public Records Office, Principal Probate Registry, 140 Twisse.

7. Proctor and his wife were especially cruel taskmasters. Witnesses testified that she had been whipped on at least six occasions, in one instance receiving as many as 200 blows. They also were credited with beating one man servant to death.

8. A short stick.

9. McIlwaine, MINUTES, 19, 24, 46, 94–95.

10. Ibid., 38, 53–54, 194–195, 480. The court also was called upon to determine the gender of an individual who probably was a hermaphrodite.

11. Ibid., 4, 479.

12. Ibid., 12, 14, 17, 52; Kingsbury, RECORDS, IV, 468. Sentencing wrong-doers to servitude or increased servitude became an increasingly common mode of punishment as the colony's labor shortage worsened. Often, these people were made to serve those who had handed down the sentence.

13. When land lapsed because its owner abandoned it, died without heirs, or was convicted of a capital crime, it "escheated" or reverted to the Crown, whose agents could to reassign it to someone else.

14. McIlwaine, MINUTES, 44–45, 173. Virginia's early surveyors typically laid out patents for riverfront land by running an arbitrary straight line parallel to the river bank and then striking a perpendicular line inland for a distance of one mile. Thus, a two-acre plot would measure 16. 5 feet (one pole) from point to point along a river bank and extend one mile inland.

15. Nugent, CAVALIERS, I, 109; McIlwaine, MINUTES, 85–86, 103, 152; Meyer et al., ADVENTURERS, 142–143. 16. Hening, ed., STATUTES, I, 134–135, 204–206, 488; II, 32, 119, 126, 152, 190–191, 200, 209–210, 221, 224–226, 231–232, 251–252; Kingsbury, RECORDS, III, 473; McIlwaine, MINUTES, 28, 104–105, 129, 143, 483.

17. This exclusionary policy was perpetuated by Indian treaties enacted later in the seventeenth century.

18. McIlwaine, MINUTES, 44, 104, 116, 129, 136, 147, 151, 153, 155, 172, 184, 189–190, 198, 484; Hening, STATUTES, I, 130, 156; Nugent, CAVALIERS, I, 69,

19. Smith, TRAVELS, Barbour, ed., II, 215–218.

20. McIlwaine, MINUTES, 192; Hening, STATUTES, I, 140, 151, 153, 167, 176, 192–193, 208–209, 219; Nugent, CAVALIERS, I, 22, 89, 91, 94, 143, 160–161, 249, 323, 388, 515.

21. Carson et al., IMPERMANENT ARCHITECTURE, 141, 158, 168–170.

22. Nugent, CAVALIERS, I, 19, 33, 36–37, 63, 123–126, 160, 224.

23. McIlwaine, MINUTES, 129.

24. Meyer et al., ADVENTURERS, 223–225; Hening, STATUTES, V, 278; Virginia Land Office Patent Book 1, 287; Nugent, CAVALIERS, I, 83, 125, 394.

25. Kingsbury, RECORDS, III, 570; McIlwaine, MINUTES, 76; Nugent, CAVALIERS, I, 76, 107, 161, 178. Pettus's acreage probably encompassed the Williamsburg Airport and the Birchwood subdivision. Later, part of the Pettus property was repatented by Philip Ludwell and added to his family's vast estate, Rich Neck.

26. Nugent, CAVALIERS, I, 15, 25, 30, 80–81, 124, 159, 162, 166, 174, 178, 486, 495; II, 33, 170, 207, 250. By 1660 the Uty tract had been absorbed into Thomas Pettus's Littletown plantation, consolidating the eastern portion of what became eighteenth century Kingsmill Plantation.

27. Ibid., I, 29–30, 33, 108, 114, 224.

28. This plantation encompassed the Holly Hills subdivision.

29. Nugent, CAVALIERS, I, 24, 54, 104–105, 159–160, 465; David DeVries, VOYAGES FROM HOLLAND TO AMERICA, LED 1632 TO 1644 BY DAVID PETERSON DEVRIES, Henry C. Murphy, trans. (New York, 1853), 49–50; Lyon G. Tyler, "Ludwell Family," WILLIAM AND MARY QUARTERLY, 1st Ser., 1 (January 1893):209–210. Kemp's 840 acres seems to have included the 600 acres assigned to him as secretary of the colony.

30. Warren M. Billings et al., COLONIAL VIRGINIA: A HISTORY (Chapel Hill, 1986), 66–68; Nugent, CAVALIERS, I, 18–19, 26, 43, 47, 74, 89, 98, 107, 116, 124, 212, 240, 323; Cocke, DIOCESE OF VIRGINIA, 33, 62–64.

31. Nugent, CAVALIERS, I, 130, 166–167, 176, 186, 267–268, 496; York County Deeds, Orders, Wills 2:289, 328. 32. The other original counties were Charles City, Henrico, Elizabeth City, York, Accomac, Isle of Wight, and Nansemond.

33. At times when no statehouse existed, it is uncertain where they met.

34. Wesley F. Craven, THE SOUTHERN COLONIES IN THE SEVENTEENTH CENTURY 1607–1689 (Baton Rouge, 1970), 166–170; British Public Records Office, Colonial Office 8/55 f 155; Warren M. Billings, THE OLD DOMINION IN THE SEVENTEENTH CENTURY (Chapel Hill, 1975), 43–44.

35. Warren M. Billings, "The Growth of Political Institutions in Virginia from 1634 to 1676," WILLIAM AND MARY QUARTERLY, 3rd Ser., 31 (April 1974):232–233; Billings, OLD DOMINION, 43–44; Craven, SOUTHERN COLONIES, 166–170; Hening, STATUTES, I, 223–224; McIlwaine, MINUTES, 481, 492.

36. J. A. C. Chandler et al., eds., "Acts of the General Assembly, January 6, 1639/40, "William and Mary Quarterly," 2nd Ser., 4 (January 1986):145–162; Billings, "Growth," 228–231; Hening, STATUTES, I, 287, 290–291, 301–303, 319.

37. McIlwaine, HOUSE, 1619–1659, 124–125; Hening, STATUTES, I, 204–206, 210, 221.

38. Force, TRACTS, II:8:14; DeVries, VOYAGES, 77; Sainsbury, CALENDAR, I, 151; McIlwaine, MINUTES, 497–498; Billings, OLD DOMINION, 237–239.

39. Sainsbury, CALENDAR, I, 268–269, 281, 287–288; B.P.R.O., C.O. 1/9, f 98; Patent Book 1:II:98, 466–467, 587–588, 595, 598–730; 2:105; McIlwaine, HOUSE, 1619–1659, 126; Ibid., MINUTES, 497–498; William G. Stanard, ed., "Instructions to Sir Francis Wyatt, January 1638/39, " VIRGINIA MAGAZINE OF HISTORY AND BIOGRAPHY 11 (July 1903):55–57.

40. B.P.R.O., C.O. 5/1354 f 231; McIlwaine, MINUTES, 500, 514; Patent Book 1:II:944; 2:47; 4:88; Hening, STATUTES, I:226, 252, 267; Nugent, CAVALIERS, I, 160; Richard Kemp, February 27, 1645, letter to Sir William Berkeley and Sir John Berkeley, Clarendon Manuscript No. 24, ff 48–51. The ruins of this rowhouse are situated on the property of the Association for the Preservation of Virginia Antiquities.

41. One man who visited the colony during the 1640s said that many Virginians, whose soil was exhausted by tobacco, had turned to cultivating flax and wheat (DeVries, VOYAGES, 181).

42. Hening, STATUTES, I, 258, 336; William G. Stanard, ed., "Acts, Orders and Resolutions of the General Assembly of Virginia at Sessions of March 1643–1644," VIRGINIA MAGAZINE OF HISTORY AND BIOGRAPHY 23 (January 1915):246–247; Peter Force, comp., TRACTS AND OTHER PAPERS, RELATING TO THE ORIGIN, SETTLEMENT AND PROGRESS OF THE COLONIES IN NORTH AMERICA (Gloucester, Mass., 1963), II:8:14.

43. Force, TRACTS, II:8:3–9; John Stirring, January 26, 1649/50 letter to John Ferrar; Lyon G. Tyler, "The Armistead Family," WILLIAM AND MARY QUARTERLY, 1st Ser., 8 (January 1899):31.

44. Neville Williams, "The Tribulations of John Bland, Merchant," VIRGINIA MAGAZINE OF HISTORY AND BIOGRAPHY 72 (January 1963):30–40.

45. Hening, STATUTES, I, 362–363, 412–414.

46. Force, TRACTS, II:8:8; Jon Kukla, POLITICAL INSTITUTIONS IN VIRGINIA, 1619–1660 (Garland, New York), 289; Hening, STATUTES, I, 264–265; McIlwaine, MINUTES, 470, 479. James City County land owners who served as Speaker of the House during the 1640s, '50s, and '60s were Thomas Stegg, Edward Hill, Ambrose Harmer, Walter Chiles, William Whitby, Francis Moryson, Theodorick Bland, and Henry Soane.

47. Hening, STATUTES, I, 253–255; Edmund S. Morgan, AMERICAN SLAVERY, AMERICAN FREEDOM: THE ORDEAL OF COLONIAL VIRGINIA (New York, 1975), 215–220.

48. Hening, STATUTES, I, 239, 386, 410; McIlwaine, MINUTES, 477–478, 483; William G. Stanard, ed., Virginia Assembly in 1641, VIRGINIA MAGAZINE OF HISTORY AND BIOGRAPHY, 9 (July 1901):51. 76

49. Hening, STATUTES, I, 237; Stanard, "Assembly of 1641," 51; Nugent, CAVALIERS, I, 131–132, 135.

50. Force, TRACTS, II:8:1; Robert Beverley, HISTORY OF THE PRESENT STATE OF VIRGINIA (1705) (Chapel Hill, 1947), 60–61; Hening, STATUTES, I, 239, 290; McIlwaine, MINUTES, 277, 296, 501; William G. Stanard, ed., "Acts, orders and Resolutions of the General Assembly of Virginia at Sessions of March 1643–1644," VIRGINIA MAGAZINE OF HISTORY AND BIOGRAPHY 23 (January 1915):229.

51. Stanard, "Acts, March 1643–1644," 230–231; "Assembly in 1641," 51; Hening, STATUTES, I, 239, 298, 317.

52. Kemp to Berkeley et al., February 27, 1645.

53. Nugent, CAVALIERS, I, 234; Hening, STATUTES, I, 293, 315, 323–329. Thomas Rolfe was the son of Pocahontas and the great–nephew of Opechancanough, leader of the 1622 and 1644 uprisings. In 1974 the College of William and Mary conducted archaeological excavations at Fort James, which is on the National Register of Historic Places. Forts Charles and Royall were built at the falls of the James and on the Pamunkey River near Manquin Creek.

54. Hening, STATUTES, I, 315, 318; Beverley, HISTORY, 60–62; Force, TRACTS, II:7:6; Force, TRACTS, II:8:13; Wilcomb E. Washburn, THE GOVERNOR AND THE REBEL: A HISTORY OF BACON'S REBELLION IN VIRGINIA (New York, 1972), 17.

55. In 1666 these boundary lines were reaffirmed and demarcated.

56. Hening, STATUTES, I, 293–295, 325.

57. Nugent, CAVALIERS, I, 175, 214; Hening, STATUTES, I, 289; II, 34; York County Deeds, Orders, Wills 2:289, 328; Force, TRACTS, II:8:13, 25; Billings, OLD DOMINION, 229–230.

58. Billings et al., COLONIAL VIRGINIA, 66–68; Washburn, REBEL, 153–166; Kukla, POLITICAL INSTITUTIONS, 286–287.

59. At one point in the journey, the Indian guides performed a ritual at a site they deemed significant. The Nottoway made reference to Opechancanough as his people's "late Great Emperour." Thus, his influence apparently extended as far south as the Chowan River and included more Native groups than ethnohistorians generally assume.

60. Force, TRACTS, II:8:14; III:10:49–50; Washburn, REBEL, 17; Salley, NARRATIVES, 5–20; Anonymous, "A Journal from Virginia beyond the Appalachian Mountains in September 1671," WILLIAM AND MARY QUARTERLY, 1st Ser., 15 (July 1906):235.

61. DeVries, VOYAGES, 185; Hening, STATUTES, I, 359–361; Force, TRACTS, III:10:49–50; Nugent, CAVALIERS, I:229, 465.

62. Bruce, SOCIAL LIFE, 18–20.

CHAPTER 4

"The Anger of God Almighty Against Us"
Three Tumultuous Decades 1651–1680

Boundary Changes and the Impact of Settlement

The early 1650s brought changes that had a significant impact upon James City County. During spring 1652 Surry County was formed from James City's territory on the lower side of the James River. This had both political and economic ramifications, for it reduced from six to four the number of delegates James City County sent to the assembly and it decreased the tax base. James City Parish already had experienced the loss, for in 1647 Southwark Parish was created out of its southerly territory.[1]

Settlement continued to fan out in every direction and forest lands were converted to cleared fields used for agriculture. Tidewater Virginia was dotted with small and middling farmsteads that were interspersed with the larger plantations of the well-to-do. Between Ware and Skimino Creeks were the patents of Edward Folliot and James Wilson. Folliot's 1,700 acres were situated on the northwest side of Ware Creek's main branch, near the land of Richard Taylor, whereas Wilson's acreage lay on the east side of the creek's head, abutting Cow (Cowpen) Swamp. References to the Mount Folly (or Holly) path suggest that it was the forerunner of Croaker Road (Route 607). By the early 1650s, Robert Wilde, Phillip Chesley, William Owen and William Morgan had acreage bordering Skimino Creek, near the land of

William Pullam, Martin Baker, Thomas Bigins, Henry Ashwell, Thomas Collins, and Arthur Price. John Handkin, possible forebear of the family that later developed Riverview, also lived in that vicinity.[2]

Land near Diascund Creek changed hands frequently, usually because would-be patentees failed to seat the acreage they claimed. For example, between 1668 and 1682 Thomas Maples and William Hitchman, Thomas and Theophilus Hone, Henry Hartwell, and Edward Chilton patented the same tract in rapid succession. In every instance the acreage reverted to the Crown because it was allowed to languish, unimproved. Among those who patented—and retained—substantial quantities of land within the Diascund Creek drainage were Sir John Ayton, Edward Cowles (Coles, Coale), William Edwards, Robert Sorrell, and the Rev. Thomas Hampton, one-time rector of James City Parish. William Browne in 1681 patented nearly a thousand acres that included Moysenac or Fort James and at the close of the seventeenth century Henry Duke amassed nearly 3,000 acres near the Diascund Bridge.

Distribution of settlement, as depicted on Augustine Herrmann's 1670 map entitled "Virginia and Maryland." Library of Congress.

Plantations were then scattered along the banks of Virginia's navigable waterways.[3] Most of those who lived within the Chickahominy River basin were middling planters and yeoman farmers, not members of the planter elite.

Generally, when settlers moved into new territory, they vied for waterfront property that had good soils for agriculture and access to shipping. Successful planters usually managed to acquire several small tracts and consolidate them into relatively large holdings. By the mid-seventeenth century, Humphrey Higginson had combined Farley's, Kingsmill's, and Tuttey's Necks with his Harrop plantation, amassing acreage that extended for a considerable distance along the James River, just east of College Creek. Meanwhile, Richard Richards patented 350 acres called Littletown that included small tracts once owned by William Claiborne, Joachim Andrews of Jockey's Neck, and John Jefferson. By 1660 Littletown had come into the hands of Colonel Thomas Pettus, who united it with the Utopia property, which included relatively small patents once owned by George Sandys, John Uty (Uti, Utye), and others. Thus, Pettus amassed acreage that extended west along the James from Grove Creek toward Humphrey Higginson's landholdings. Pettus, a member of the Council of State, personifies the highly successful Virginia planter who accumulated wealth and joined the ranks of the elite.[4]

Virginia at Mid-Century

After England's civil war came to an end, a Parliamentary fleet set sail for Virginia to proclaim the supremacy of the Commonwealth government. Oliver Cromwell's agents also wanted to assert their authority over a colony known as a royalist stronghold. In April 1652 when they arrived at Jamestown, Sir William Berkeley was obliged to surrender the colony and relinquish his governorship to Richard Bennett of Isle of Wight County. The articles of surrender Berkeley signed acknowledged that Virginia was under the purview of the Commonwealth's laws, which had not been imposed upon the colonists by force. The burgesses were authorized to conduct business as usual, except for enacting legislation contrary to the laws of the Commonwealth. Virginia's charter was to be confirmed by Parliament and its land patents' legality upheld. The colonists, like all English citizens, were entitled to free trade and no taxes could be imposed upon them without their assembly's consent. All publicly-owned arms and ammunition had to be surrendered. The clergy could continue using the Book of Common Prayer as long as all references to the monarchy were omitted. Anyone refusing to subscribe to the Articles of Surrender had to leave Virginia within a year.[5]

Former Governor Berkeley retired to Green Spring, where he channeled his energies into agricultural experimentation. He enlarged his plantation by purchasing nearly a thousand acres of neighboring property and disposed of his three-bay brick rowhouse at Jamestown, selling one unit to the new governor and another to tavern-keeper Thomas Woodhouse. During Berkeley's decade in office, two of the rowhouse's units were used at times as the colony's statehouse. After Governor Bennett took office, Woodhouse sometimes hosted meetings of the General Court and the assembly occasionally convened in taverns. This may be why a 1659 law allowed the burgesses to fine fellow members who were excessively drunk during assembly meetings.[6]

During the 1650s several of Jamestown's waterfront lots changed hands and patents were issued for land in the extreme eastern and western ends of the island. In 1652 Edward Travis, who married the daughter and heir of John Johnson, patented nearly 200 acres on Jamestown Island near Black Point, consolidating several small farmsteads that had belonged to Ancient Planters a quarter century earlier. Travis quickly expanded his holdings which extended from the north side of Goose Hill Marsh to Black Point. He continued to acquire land and by 1677 he had amassed 550 acres. The Travis plantation then extended from Black Point to Kingsmill Creek and followed Passmore Creek west, almost reaching Orchard Run. By the close of the eighteenth century the Travises owned more than 800 acres in the eastern end of Jamestown Island and one or more town lots. The southeastern end of Jamestown Island extended much further south than it does today and Thomas Woodhouse, William Hooker, and William Sarsen held patents for more than 200 acres there, below Goose Hill. In the extreme western end of the island, near the isthmus that led to the mainland, John Baldwin patented a tract that adjoined the land upon which Governor Berkeley's brick rowhouse stood. A quarter century later, Baldwin's land came into the hands of William

Sherwood, who during the 1680s and 90s amassed much of the land in the western end of Jamestown Island. On the mainland was a 24-acre tract known as the Glass House, where the Italian glassworkers had plied their trade during the 1620s. During the 1650s the Glass House property was owned by Colonel Francis Morrison.[7]

While Virginia was under the sway of the Commonwealth government, the assembly modified the laws that regulated bound servants' contracts. As England's over-supply of workers had been depleted, yet a growing number of people were needed to toil in Virginia's expanding tobacco fields, the burgesses decided to lengthen the terms of newly-arrived servants. Within five years the law was repealed, for the burgesses perceived that their policy was discouraging servant immigration. In 1656 a law was passed doubling the terms of servants who ran away more than once.[8] During Governor Samuel Mathews' administration, three Quakers, considered lawbreakers because of their dissenting religious views, were imprisoned at Jamestown while awaiting deportation. They were deprived of writing materials and communication with others because officials suspected they would promote their doctrine while incarcerated. Later, Quaker George Wilson was jailed at Jamestown where he was "chained to an Indian wch is in prison for murder." Wilson said that they "had our legs on one bolt made fast to a post with an ox chain" and described the prison as a "dirty dungeon." Quaker preachers Josiah Cole and Thomas Thurston also termed Jamestown's jail "a dirty dungeon where we have not the benefit to do what nature requireth, nor so much air to blow in at a window, but close made up with brick and lime."[9]

During the 1650s and '60s, several James City County residents appeared before York County's justices of the peace. Ann Barnhouse of Martin's Hundred asked them to assign her slave woman's son to his father, a black indentured servant in York County, noting that she had had the child baptized. The names of William and Abraham Spencer, Edward Ramsey, Nathaniel Hunt and Robert Shore of James City County appeared in York County's court records, as did that of Miles Chafie, a James City runaway caught in York. Sarah Morris, a maid servant in Joseph Crowshaw's Archers Hope household, blamed Richard Anderson, a fellow servant and runaway, for fathering her bastard child. James City County's justices undoubtedly dealt with similar matters.

Settling with the Indians

During the 1650s relations with the colony's tributary Indian tribes gradually stabilized. The 1652 legislation assigning specific tracts to the Indians
was upheld because officials, through experience, knew that conflict over land
was at the root of most disputes with the settlers. Also, the land the Indians
were assigned lay beyond the fringes of the colony's frontier. However, as
increasing numbers of planters ventured into the Middle Peninsula and
Northern Neck and the territory beyond the fall line, they paid little heed to
whether they were intruding upon the acreage assigned to the Indians. Some
people blatantly established homesteads on the Indians' land. Others tried to
trick them into selling part of it. Meanwhile, the Native population dwindled
and that of the colonists increased. This put pressure upon the Indians, whose
hunting and foraging habitat gradually was reduced. Also, their special tracts
(or preserves) eventually were surrounded by planter homesteads. Despite
official policy, influential people sometimes tried to circumvent the law by
claiming part of the Indians' acreage, perhaps in anticipation of their dying
out or abandoning it. One such individual was Sir Thomas Lunsford of Rich
Neck, who secured a patent for land on the lower side of the Rappahannock
River within territory set aside for the Nanzattico and Portobago Indians.[11]

During the early-to-mid 1650s the tributary Indians began making use of
the colony's legal system and occasionally served as allies of the Virginia government. In March 1656 the Pamunkey and Chickahominy Indians helped the
colonists drive off 600 to 700 Natives "drawne down from the mountaynes
and lately sett down near the falls of the James River." This conflict, the Battle
of Bloody Run, claimed the life of Totopotomoy, the Pamunkey Indians'
leader. Commencing in 1656, Indians had to carry written authorization
whenever they entered fenced plantations to hunt or forage. A 1662 law
required those entering the colonized area to wear silver or copper badges
inscribed with the name of their tribe; any lacking badges were subject to
arrest. Free men were permitted to trade with the Indians in special marts.
Although Governor Berkeley declared that "the Indians around us are
subdued," raids sometimes occurred on the frontier near the fall line. The
people of James City County probably didn't live in fear of an Indian attack,

but they knew that they could be sent to defend the frontier. After the death of Governor Samuel Mathews in January 1659, the burgesses elected Sir William Berkeley as Virginia's chief executive.[12]

Promoting Economic Development

During 1659 the Commonwealth government strengthened the Navigation Acts, intended to restrict Virginia's trade with foreign nations. This prompted Governor Berkeley to remind his superiors that "the privileges granted us by our articles of surrender [are] to have free trade with all nations in amity with the people of England." In 1660, when word reached Virginia that the monarchy had been restored and King Charles II was installed upon the throne, Berkeley issued a proclamation and celebrants marked the occasion with trumpeting, the firing of guns, and drinking. In fact, one man was paid for providing more than 200 gallons of hard cider to the merry-makers at Jamestown.[13]

In March 1661 Berkeley set sail for England to make sure that Virginia's economic interests were given consideration in the policy-making decisions of the newly-formed Restoration government. Throughout the summer he made numerous appearances before high ranking officials, lobbying against the Navigation Acts. He presented a report on the colony's economic status, proffering that Virginia needed the Crown's financial and political support in order to take full advantage of its abundant natural resources. He asserted that England's best hope of economic supremacy lay in making Virginia the keystone of the empire. However, Charles II paid little heed to Berkeley's arguments and sometimes pursued public policy that ran contrary to the colony's interests, such as bestowing Virginia's Northern Neck upon several favorites.[14]

Berkeley, upon returning to Virginia, tried to showcase enterprises that demonstrated the colony's economic potential. At Green Spring he experimented with trials of potash, flax, hemp, silk, and wine, and the production of glass, earthenware, and salt.[15] In April 1663 Berkeley informed an associate in England that he had sent him a ton of potash and enough black walnut lumber to wainscot five or six rooms. He claimed that the wine he had produced was as good as any that "ever came out of Italy." Early eighteenth century historian Robert Beverley, whose late father was a frequent visitor to Green Spring, said that Berkeley planted trees that served as a trellis for his grapevines.[16]

Updating the Colony's Laws

In 1661 Virginia's legal code was revised extensively and summarized. For the first time, each county could send only two burgesses to the assembly. Jamestown, as the capital city, retained its ancient right to representation and any county that set aside a hundred acres upon which resided a hundred tithable citizens was entitled to the same privilege. County courts were to have eight justices each, with the first man appointed to office serving as sheriff. Vestries could have no more than twelve members. Tax rates were established by law and for the first time, county courts could issue marriage licenses. When the Assembly formally adopted English common law in 1662, legislation was enacted to regulate local elections and set public officials' fees. Procedures were established for probating estates, determining land ownership, setting the prices tavern-keepers and millers could charge, and formalizing land transfers. These duties added to the workload of the county court. Other issues the burgesses addressed in 1662 included relations with the Indians, the treatment of indentured servants, controlling the quality of tobacco, and the proper observance of the Sabbath. Only escaped prisoners, accused felons, or those suspected of rioting could be arrested on Sundays, because it was felt that the prospect of being taken into custody would discourage church attendance. Quakers and other non-conformists could be fined for failing to attend or support the Established Church and informants were rewarded for turning them in. Three or four sites were set aside in every parish for public burial grounds, where all the dead were to be interred unless prior arrangements had been made. This law was intended to prevent the concealment of wrongful deaths. Every four years vestrymen had to procession the boundaries of land within their parishes, renewing boundary markers whenever necessary, and seeing that disputed property lines were surveyed. A procedure was established for appointing the surveyors of public highways, whose duties were defined by law.

Every county seat had to have a pillory, stocks, whipping post, and ducking-stool near the courthouse and meeting dates were established for local courts. James City County's monthly court convened on the sixth day of the month, Sundays excepted, and all justices were expected to attend the sessions from beginning to end. Half of each county's eight justices were "of the quorum," i.e., one or more of them had to be in attendance at every court session. All plaintiffs and defendants had to present a written summary of their cases and were guaranteed the right to trial by jury. The General Court continued to serve as an appellate body for the county judiciary. For example, in March 1676 George Marable appealed (and won) a decision James City County's justices had made in Henry Burton's favor. On the other hand, the General Court's justices sometimes sent cases to the county court. When Hubert Farrell of James City County "most wickedly and maliciously scandalized, abused and defamed" Tabitha Bowler at the home of Mr. William White in Jamestown, he was fined, forced to apologize, and ordered to post a bond guaranteeing his good behavior. However, the case was forwarded to the next court session.[17]

In accord with Governor Berkeley's economic initiatives, several of the laws enacted in 1662 were intended to strengthen and diversify Virginia's productivity. County officials were given flax seed to sell to local inhabitants. Those who raised and processed it, spun the fibers into yarn, and wove it into cloth a yard wide were eligible for a bounty. Rewards also were offered to those who planted mulberry trees or built ships. Each county had to erect a tanhouse (where tanners, curriers, and shoemakers could process hides into leather goods) and set up a loom and weaver to produce fabric for the manufacture of clothing. The weaver, a male supplied with thread spun by five women or children, was "with much ease" to produce enough clothing for 30 people. All counties that failed to comply with these legislative mandates were subject to a fine. It is uncertain how James City County officials responded. The masters of all incoming ships, upon arriving at Old Point Comfort, had to present a manifest, pay customs duties, and account for their passengers. Then, they had to go directly to Jamestown to obtain a trading license. This law would have given the capital's residents (many of whom were high ranking officials) first access to newly imported goods. Another important piece of legislation established the requirements for planting or seating new land. Specifically, anyone who built a house, kept livestock upon his property for a year, or cleared an acre of ground and planted crops, could secure his patent.[18]

Converting Jamestown to a Metropolis

In September 1662 Governor Berkeley's superiors in England ordered him to see that towns were built on each of the colony's rivers, commencing with the James. He was to set a good example by building some houses there himself and to tell his councilors that the king would view it very favorably if they followed suit. He was supposed to report who built houses in response to the directive. Three months later, the assembly passed an act intended to foster Jamestown's development. The government was to underwrite the cost of constructing 32 brick houses that measured 20 feet by 40 feet, were roofed with slate or tile, had walls 18 feet high and a roof of a certain pitch. They were to be aligned in a square or other configuration Berkeley deemed appropriate. Workmen's rates were set by law and public levies were earmarked to meet the cost of construction. Each of Virginia's 17 counties was supposed to build a house and private individuals who did so were entitled to a stipend and the privilege of constructing a store. No more frame houses were to be erected at Jamestown, nor older ones repaired, but it was not considered necessary to raze existing buildings.[19]

In September 1663 the burgesses decided to compensate the counties that had built brick houses. They noted that "the next year four houses more [should] be built" and so on, until each county had fulfilled its obligation. The speaker of the House was authorized to make agreements with private citizens interested in building houses "with good sufficient bricks, lime and timber," offering would-be developers the land upon which their structures stood. Berkeley was to see that a statehouse was built. He had the right to determine its size and layout, as long as it would accommodate the General Court, the assembly, and its committees. There is some evidence that Berkeley responded by converting one of his own dwellings into a statehouse, pocketing the funds earmarked for construction. One burgess declared that it was disgraceful that "all our laws [are] being made, and our judgements being given, in alehouses."[20] Prior to the time the new statehouse was readied for use, James City County's justices, like the burgesses, may have conducted business in local taverns.

To underwrite the cost of improving the capital, all of the tobacco grown in James City, Charles City, and Surry Counties was to be handled by Jamestown's storehouses. The processing fees would have funnelled tax revenues into the community. Although it is uncertain how many new houses were built at Jamestown during the early 1660s, archaeologists have identified nearly a dozen likely candidates. At least one new wharf was erected there and two ferry routes were established to points across the James. In April 1665 Thomas Ludwell informed officials in England that they had "begun a town of brick and have already built enough to accommodate both the publique affairs of ye country and to begin a factory [retail building] for merchants." Flax, silk, potash, and English grains were being produced and small vessels constructed for use in trading with neighboring colonies. A contemporary writer estimated that Jamestown then had approximately 20 houses. Robert Beverley, the historian, later said that most of the capital's new buildings "were soon converted into Houses of Entertainment."[21]

In 1668 James City County's justices received permission to convert one of the publicly-funded brick houses into a jail that would accommodate their prisoners and those of the General Court. Written records reveal that a unit in the long brick rowhouse near Pitch and Tar Swamp was chosen. This, perhaps, explains a macabre discovery made by National Park Service archaeologists, who unearthed half of a human pelvis, a leg and a foot from a nearby well. Undoubtedly, when the General Court convened at Jamestown, people flocked to town. In November 1663 a case involving a Dutch ship, the Arms of Amsterdam, was tried before the General Court, litigation that had international implications. Tributary Indian leaders sometimes sought justice from the General Court, and in 1665 English sea captain William Whiting was hauled into court and accused of piracy. In 1664 James City County's sheriff was fined for arresting a member of the General Court and the assembly. That may have prompted the burgesses to enact legislation excluding everyone (except James City County residents) from arrest in Jamestown five days before or after the General Court or assembly convened. In 1682 amnesty was extended to the people of James City County.[22]

The Dutch Threaten Virginia

In early June 1665 Governor Berkeley learned that England was at war with the Dutch. He was ordered to see that the colony's defenses were in a state of readiness and that all trading ships were protected. Local militia companies were pressed into service to construct battery platforms at Jamestown and three other locations. Berkeley had ordnance from Old Point Comfort brought up to Jamestown and he sent an urgent request to England for munitions. However, before the summer's end, Virginia officials adopted a strategy that allowed them to concentrate their firepower in one place. They decided to build a fort at Jamestown. The militia of James City and Surry Counties were to contribute six days per man toward building the fort, which earthen walls were shored up with wood. In late March 1666 Berkeley received orders from the king to build a fort at Old Point Comfort, a site favored by some influential Bristol merchants. He and the council openly questioned the efficacy of the plan, for they knew that Hampton Roads' breadth would allow invading ships to elude onshore cannon. But they complied and the ordnance at Jamestown was returned to Old Point Comfort. In early July, however, a Dutch man-of-war entered Hampton Roads, captured two ships, and threatened some people on shore. That prompted Berkeley to ask the king for a frigate or two to patrol the bay and to order the men at Old Point Comfort to withdraw. Later, he and the council sent word to England that they had "designed a fort at James Town in the center of the country," where 14 great guns had been brought at great expense. Secretary of State Thomas Ludwell added that they had decided to construct only one fort because they couldn't afford to build more and that there were enough men at Jamestown to form a local guard without expense to the government.[23]

The Turbulent 1660s

The late 1660s were a time of trial for Governor Berkeley. While he struggled to understand Charles II's attitude toward the colony and attempted to promote economic development, severe weather wrought massive destruction and the Dutch attacked again. In April 1667 a storm that produced hail "as big as Turkey Eggs" destroyed spring crops, broke "all the glass windowes and beat holes through the tiles of our houses," and "killed many young hogs and cattle." Then, on June 5th, the Dutch sailed into the James and captured or sank 20-some vessels of the tobacco fleet, loaded and awaiting the outbound tide. Mid-summer brought a 40-day rainy spell that drowned the season's crops and on August 27th, a killer hurricane struck that lasted for 24 hours and destroyed an estimated 10,000 houses. Thomas Ludwell said that the storm "began at North East and went round northerly till it came to West and so on till it came to South East where it ceased."[24] The strong winds were accompanied by heavy rain that caused severe flooding and forced many families from their homes. Wave action ripped vessels from their moorings. Fences were blown down and escaped livestock roamed freely, damaging what was left of the year's corn, tobacco and field crops.[25] The disasters of 1667, taken as a whole, must have been demoralizing for the colonists and their aging governor.

In September 1667 the burgesses decided that forts should be built on each of Virginia's major rivers within six months.[26] Special commissioners were to oversee construction of the fort at Jamestown, which cost was to be borne by James City, Surry, Charles City, and Henrico Counties. Its ten-foot-high earthen walls had to be capable of supporting at least eight large cannon, with a riverside wall at least ten feet thick. Five men, including a gunner, were to be on constant guard and incoming ships had to obtain their trading licenses there. Again, conscript labor was used. A map made by James City Parish minister John Clayton in 1688 reveals that the earthen fort on Jamestown Island (which Clayton labeled "ye old fort") stood upon the river bank just west of Orchard Run. He said that the "old fort of earth" was "a sort of Tetragone with something like Bastions at the four corners" and proffered that it was too far from the river's channel to be very effective. Five months after the forts were scheduled for completion, they became obsolete, for peace was restored. When the burgesses convened in 1668, August 27th was declared a day of annual fasting and atonement, for many people felt that the recent hurricane was attributable to "the anger of God Almighty against us."[27]

The burgesses authorized parishes to build workhouses where poor children (not necessarily orphans) could be educated and trained to spin, weave, and perform other useful tasks. For the first time, black female indentured servants were subjected to a poll or capitation tax, even though they were free.[28] To discourage "idleness and debaucheryes" attributable to drunkenness, local justices were ordered to see that county seats had no more than one or two taverns. A limited number was permissible at ports, ferry landings and major roads, where they were necessary "for the accommodation of travellers."[29]

Local Cases Aired Before the General Court

During the late 1660s and early 1670s, the justices of the General Court continued to deal with local issues, both public, and personal. They redefined the boundaries of the James City Parish glebe and saw that Thomas Hunt was paid for repairing the mill dam and bridge across Powhatan Swamp, part of the road to Middle Plantation. They decided to use some abandoned land as a glebe for Middletowne Parish (established in 1658 out of Harrop and Middle Plantation Parishes) and appointed John Summers's widow, Tabitha, as administrator of his estate. They heard Captain White's suit against Edward Thruston of Martin's Hundred, who had married Thomas Loving's widow, and listened to John Phipps' claim against James City County sheriff Francis Kirkman, who also was a local justice, militia captain, and vestryman of James City Parish. The justices gave Richard Holder of Jamestown some wasteland that abutted his acreage on Orchard Run and they ordered William May and Richard Lawrence to investigate a dispute between Robert Sorrell and Thomas Ballard involving some of the late John Newell's property.[30]

In October 1670 the General Court found the Rev. William Nelson (alias Peter Atherton) guilty of lying, blasphemy, forgery, and mutiny. He also appears to have fleeced his flock. He was defrocked, made to stand in the doorway of the courthouse next to a list of his crimes, four hours, two days in a row, and then was jailed until he could be expelled from the colony. John Greenfield, who fled to New Kent County, was jailed until he could answer to a lawsuit initiated by Thomas Ludwell of Rich Neck. Captain Christopher Wormeley, who owned part of Powhatan plantation, sued the churchwardens of James City Parish as a means of recovering funds owed to the late Rev. Justinian Aylemer, whose widow he married. John Hull, an apprentice, successfully sued his master, William Drummond. Executors' squabbles often ended up in court. Thomas Harris's widow and executrix, Alice, brought suit against the late George Woodward's estate and there was a case against David Newell, Mr. Hunt's executor.[31]

Mrs. Sarah Bow of James City County was found guilty of calling her neighbor, Mrs. Deacon, "a whore." Sarah's husband, Jeffrey, had to pay a fine toward construction of "the New Fort at James City" and Mrs. Bow was sentenced to a ride in Jamestown's ducking-stool as soon as her baby was born. Innkeeper Richard Lawrence of Jamestown accused his neighbor, Richard Awborne (Auborne), of causing John Senior's death. So damning was the evidence that Awborne had to post a bond to guarantee his appearance in court. Later, Awborne sued Lawrence for slander. John Knowles' maid servant, Mary Blades, who fatally stabbed fellow servant Philip Lettice (Lettie), was sentenced "to be hanged by the necke till she be Dead." Knowles lived on Jamestown's Back Street, where the crime probably occurred. Several Jamestown residents asked the General Court to make the island's unpatented marsh land a common pasture and William Whittaker of Martin's Hundred received permission to patent some vacant acreage near his plantation. Samuel Weldon of James City County and Elizabeth Wood went to court over the ownership of a horse. Thomas Lane and Mrs. Perry sued William Drummond for defamation of character and Robert Weekes took Thomas Davis to court for slander. These cases demonstrate that despite the county courts' growing authority, the General Court's docket still was cluttered with local matters. James City County sheriff Francis Kirkman sued Robert Brian to recover a black male he allegedly lured away and a runaway slave from Gloucester County received "a good and well laid on whipping" for failing to report another black's escape from jail. By 1674 Kirkman apparently began shirking his duties, for two plaintiffs successfully sued him for failing to make their defendants appear in court. Three of Richard Lawrence's man servants absconded in his shallop. When captured they were made to serve an additional seven years. Robert Sorrell, Andrew Reader, Gabriel Harper, William Drummond, George Proctor, Thomas Hye, John Pittman, Mathew Collins, Ralph Deane, William Fisher, and surveyor James Minge, who were residents of James City County, brought personal disputes to the General Court during the mid-to-late seventeenth century.[32]

Perhaps one of the most unusual suits the justices heard was instigated by Phillip Corven of James City County, a black man and indentured servant of the late Mrs. Anne Beazley. Beazley bequeathed eight years of Corven's service to her cousin, after which time he was to be freed. But the cousin sold Corven's indenture to a Warwick County man who tricked him into signing a paper extending his contract another three years. This prompted Corven to sue for compensation for the extra years of service plus his "freedom dues." He contended that "persons of good creditt" would corroborate his statements. As the seventeenth century wore on, Virginians increasingly sought legal arbitration. Occasionally, the General Court sent cases back to county courts or forwarded them to neighboring jurisdictions.

New Problems with the Dutch

In September 1672 the assembly ordered the construction of brick forts on all of the colony's major rivers, for there was a resumption of hostilities with the Dutch. Local militia companies were placed on alert and William Drummond, Major Theophilus Hone, and Mathew Page of James City County were hired to build a 250-foot-long brick fort at Jamestown. However, Page died and his partners' work was declared "very bad and altogether Insufficient." Even so, in July 1673 when the Dutch invaded Hampton Roads, some ships reached safety "above the fort" at Jamestown. Nineteen others, vessels in the tobacco fleet that were anchored near Old Point Comfort, were destroyed. In April 1674 Drummond and Hone were ordered to repair the brick fort, taking "Downe all such worke as is cracked and insufficient."[33]

In 1688 the Rev. John Clayton told an English friend that Jamestown was defended by "a silly sort of fort, that is, a Brick Wall in the shape of a Half-Moon" situated at the edge of the Pitch and Tar Swamp, where the James River's channel ran close to the shore. He claimed that the brick fort was "little better than a blind Wall to shoot wild Ducks or Geese" because it "stands in a vale" (or low place) where its guns were likely to lodge their shot in the rising embankment. Clayton said that ships approaching Jamestown had to be almost on top of the fort to come under its guns and that one broadside from an enemy ship would create Pandemonium. Clayton's sketch of the brick fort and an early land patent indicate that it was west of the church in a low-lying area.[34]

Governor Berkeley's Decline

In April 1670 Virginia's 64-year-old Governor William Berkeley married Frances Culpeper Stephens, the 36-year-old widow of the one-time governor of Albemarle (Carolina). By 1672 Berkeley had sold three of his rowhouses in Jamestown, and his wife had disposed of a valuable Warwick County plantation that had belonged to her first husband. That infusion of wealth probably gave the Berkeleys the funds they needed to expand the Green Spring house into a large mansion. In autumn 1674 when the assembly confirmed the governor's title to Green Spring plantation, which he had enlarged during the Commonwealth period, the burgesses noted that he "hath expended a great summe of money in building . . . upon the land."[35]

Berkeley's advancing age and lengthy tenure in office appear to have made him somewhat testy, arrogant, and possessive of his privileges. In 1673 he had Benjamin Eggleston of James City County hauled before the General Court for having "presumptuously and impudently intrenched upon the perogative and abused the Authority of the Right Honorable Governor." For that offence, Eggleston received 39 lashes at Jamestown's whipping post and a heavy fine. His father, Richard, had begun patenting land along the east side of Powhatan Creek during the 1640s and '50s and by 1662 had amassed 2,277 acres adjoining Green Spring. Thus, the man the aging governor had flogged was his neighbor's son. In late summer 1674 some indentured servants

Artist Sidney King's portrayal of the rebel Nathaniel Bacon's confrontation with Governor William Berkeley. Courtesy of the National Park Service.

Jamestown in flames, September 19, 1676. Library of Congress.

belonging to Governor Berkeley, George Loyd, and Richard James absconded and were gone for two months. When the men were captured, the county sheriff applied the lash to all but one: a carpenter belonging to Berkeley. The men's terms of indenture were extended and they had to give William White a year and a half of service to compensate for stealing his boat.[36]

The Prelude to Bacon's Rebellion

The mid-1670s brought an administrative crisis for Governor Berkeley, who was nearly 70 and in declining health. During his lengthy period in office, members of the colony's planter elite gradually solidified their position. As a result, those outside the circle of privilege came to perceive government officials as opportunists who reaped a handsome profit from positions considered a public trust. Personality conflicts among the colony's leaders also fueled dissention. Giles Bland insulted Secretary Thomas Ludwell of Rich Neck, who promptly called for his arrest. Bland was so incensed that he called Ludwell "a Sonne of a whore, [a] mechannick fellow, puppy [puppet] and coward" and challenged him to a duel. Jamestown attorney William Sherwood, the county's sub-sheriff, also swore out a warrant against Bland, who owed money to the estate of Richard James, whose widow he'd wed. But it was when Bland dispatched "a mutinous and scandalous letter" to Governor Berkeley, forwarding a copy to England, that he was thrown in jail.[37]

However, the colony's troubles were more deeply rooted than quarrels among its leaders. Virginia planters chafed under the restraints of the Navigation Acts, which prohibited them from selling their tobacco to countries other than England, and few people followed Berkeley's lead in trying to diversify the economy. Meanwhile, Charles II, like his late father, began to bestow grants of Virginia land upon his favorites. This reduced the tax base and cast doubt upon the legality of land titles in the Northern Neck. As taxes soared, there were troubles with the Indians on the fringes of the colony's rapidly expanding frontier. The tributary Indians, to whom the 1646 treaty offered government protection, found themselves trapped between the colonists' plantations and the strong, warlike tribes who lived in the interior of the continent. Fear and rumors spread like wildfire. One writer sent word to England that Indians outfitted with French artillery came into the settlements in broad daylight and killed the colonists at will. To these domestic problems was added a genuine fear of foreign invasion.[38]

It was into this scenario that Nathaniel Bacon Jr. was thrust in 1674. Contemporaries described him as quick-witted, ambitious but arrogant, "impatient of labor," and a troublemaker. His father, a wealthy English gentleman, had withdrawn him from Cambridge in the wake of a scandal, provided him with 1,800 pounds sterling, and packed him off to Virginia. Soon after his arrival, he purchased a plantation near the head of the James River and built a home. In March 1675 Governor Berkeley, young Bacon's cousin-by-marriage, appointed him to the Council of State, where he joined his uncle, Colonel Nathaniel Bacon.[39]

As Virginians learned of Indian troubles in New England and rumors spread of an all-out war, they became increasingly uneasy while they waited—and waited—for their governor to act. Many settlers on the Rappahannock River frontier abandoned their homesteads. In March 1676 the assembly decided to construct garrisons at nine strategically important locations near the heads of the colony's rivers. Fifty-five James City County men were pressed into service and sent to a fort at the falls of the James. Horses, provisions, tools, and matériel were procured through public levies. Soon it became obvious that the forts were ineffective against the Indians, whose strategy was one of surprise attacks. Building the forts was a costly error in judgment that fostered resentment against the Berkeley government.[40]

The Rebellion Gets Underway

Young Nathaniel Bacon, whose Henrico County plantation was attacked by Indians, eagerly agreed to lead a group of vigilantes on a retaliatory march. They set out for the southern part of the colony in April 1676. Although Governor Berkeley sent word to Bacon to cease his military operations and report to Jamestown, he demanded a commission to pursue the Indians and continued on his way. This prompted Berkeley to declare Bacon a rebel and send soldiers to intercept him. But Bacon eluded Berkeley's men and attacked the friendly Occoneechee Indians. Thus began the popular uprising known as

Bacon's Rebellion, which spread throughout Tidewater Virginia and left a bloody imprint upon the history of James City County. Nathaniel Bacon, upon returning from his Occoneechee campaign, set sail for Jamestown with 50 armed men. He arrived on June 6th and slipped ashore to confer with two of his more prominent supporters, Richard Lawrence and William Drummond. However, after he returned to his sloop he was taken into custody and brought before Governor Berkeley. As word spread of Bacon's capture, literally hundreds of his supporters streamed into Jamestown, determined to rescue him unless he was freed. From this position of strength, Bacon apologized to Berkeley, who pardoned him and restored him to his Council seat. Bacon then went home, purportedly to tend to his sick wife. But on June 23rd, he returned to Jamestown at the head of 500 to 600 supporters, with whose backing he demanded a commission to march against the Indians. Although Berkeley at first refused, Bacon's followers reiterated his demands at gunpoint and threatened to kill any councilors and burgesses who refused to cooperate. Under this duress, Berkeley granted Bacon's commission. Bacon also prevailed upon the assembly to enact laws that included some of his ideas. One expanded Jamestown's corporate limits to encompass the entire island and gave the city's voters the right to enact any regulations they saw fit, as long as they didn't impinge upon the rights of James City County or neighboring jurisdictions. Another allowed colonists to patent Indians' land as soon as they abandoned it, even if they had been driven off.[41]

On June 26, 1676, Berkeley withdrew to Green Spring and Bacon and his partisans commenced roving the peninsula, rallying support and gathering weaponry to use in a war against the Indians. This prompted Berkeley to go to Gloucester in an attempt to recruit troops. But he met with little success, for local farmers sympathized with Bacon, who was fighting Natives they considered enemies. It was then that Berkeley became fully aware of his own vulnerability. He and some of his loyalists withdrew to the Eastern Shore and took up residence at Arlington, the Northampton County home of John Custis.[42]

Bacon, meanwhile, headed for Middle Plantation and on July 29th made Captain Ortho Thorpe's house his headquarters. He drafted a treatise he called a "Declaration of the People" that leveled charges against Governor Berkeley and followed it with a "Manifesto" justifying his own actions. Some of his a followers commandeered three ships and set out for the Eastern Shore to confront Berkeley in his hideaway. Bacon, meanwhile, attempted to raise men for a march against the Indians on the colony's frontiers. Upon meeting with little success, he vented his wrath upon the Pamunkey Indians, who recently had signed a peace agreement with the Berkeley government. His men pursued the Pamunkeys into Dragon Swamp, where they killed men, women, and children indiscriminately, took captives, and plundered their goods. While this was going on, Berkeley overcame the rebels' attack, rallied his supporters, and on September 7th returned to Jamestown, where he offered a pardon to the 800 men Bacon left garrisoned there. He had his men erect a palisade across the isthmus that connected the island with the mainland and then settled in to wait for the confrontation he considered inevitable.

As Bacon's Pamunkey expedition drew to a close, he learned that the men he sent to the Eastern Shore had been captured and that Berkeley's men were in possession of Jamestown. At that juncture, Bacon offered freedom to all slaves and servants willing to join his ranks. He then set out upon the lengthy trek to Jamestown, displaying his Pamunkey captives along the way. On September 13, Bacon and his rebel army passed by Green Spring, traversed the Governor's Land, and reached the isthmus that led to Jamestown Island. As he advanced toward the capital on horseback, one of his men sounded a trumpet to herald his arrival. Bacon then fired his carbine. He saw that the palisade Berkeley's men had erected across the far end of the isthmus was so strong that he would have to lure his adversaries out of their defensive lines. Bacon dispatched some of his men to Green Spring to raid the governor's provender, while others built a "French work" near Glass House Point. One eyewitness estimated that the opposing lines were about 500 feet apart.[43]

The next day, when Bacon commenced his siege, he placed the wives of several loyalist leaders (including his own aunt) upon the ramparts of his trench.[44] He also put his Pamunkey captives on display to demonstrate his prowess as an Indian fighter. Although Berkeley's men made a sally against the rebels, they fled so hastily from their opponents' retaliatory gunfire that one wag likened them to "scholars goeing to schoole [who] went out with hevie harts but returned home with light heeles." Next, Bacon began bombarding Jamestown with two cannon, taking (as one man put it) "delight to see stately structures beated downe and Men blowne up into the aire like shuttle cocks."[45] At that point Berkeley's dispirited supporters urged him to abandon the capital city. Reluctantly, the aging governor withdrew to safety on the Eastern Shore. Bacon and his followers then put Jamestown to the torch. Richard Lawrence and William Drummond set fire to their own dwellings, reputedly among the finest in the town. An estimated 16 to 18 buildings were burned on September 19, 1676, including the church. Although the statehouse deliberately was set ablaze, one of the rebels, William Drummond, hurried many of Virginia's official records from the building, sparing them destruction.[46] One eyewitness claimed that as Berkeley's men set sail for the Eastern Shore, they "saw with shame by night the flames of the town which they had so basely forsaken." But destroying the capital city apparently made some of Nathaniel Bacon's followers question his judgment. They also may have begun to wonder what would happen if Berkeley regained the upper hand.[47]

The next day, Bacon went to Green Spring, where he drafted a protest against Berkeley. Meanwhile, some of his men, giddy with confidence and spoiling for a fight, commenced plundering the property of the governor's supporters. When Bacon attempted to bring his partisans under control, he met with little success for they had evolved into an unruly mob that made little distinction between friend and foe. On October 26, 1676, the popular uprising was dealt a mortal blow, for Bacon succumbed to the bloody flux and what was termed "a lousey disease."[48] Joseph Ingram, his successor, lacked Bacon's magnetism and verve. He divided the rebel army into small bands that withdrew into the upper reaches of the York River, where they fortified themselves against assault.[49]

The Rebellion Subsides

Governor Berkeley's men quickly seized the opportunity to quell the uprising and during November and December many of the rebels were hunted down and captured. At Green Spring, where an estimated 100 men and boys were holed up in the governor's house, Captain Drew, their leader, resolved "to keep the place inspite of all opposition" and was quoted as saying that he had made the plantation "the strongest place in the Country what with grate [great] and small Gunns." He swore to retain the plantation until the governor himself dared to claim it.[50]

During the second week of January 1677 four rebel leaders were hauled before the governor and council, given a court martial hearing, and sentenced to hang. On January 16th, Joseph Ingram surrendered at his West Point stronghold and four days later, court martial proceedings were held at James Bray's home in Middle Plantation, where two more rebel leaders were sentenced to death. Berkeley returned to Jamestown on January 22nd. He viewed the ruins of the capital city and then rode to Green Spring, where he found his plantation "much spoilt and plundered."[51]

On January 24, 1677, several of Bacon's followers were brought before a military tribunal held at Green Spring, then the interim seat of the colony's government. All but one were found guilty of treason and sentenced to death. Mrs. Ann Cotton of York County wrote her husband that some were "hanged at Bacon's Trench" at the entrance to Jamestown Island; the remainder were put to death at Green Spring. Berkeley's loyalists confiscated the personal property of convicted or suspected rebels. This prompted William Drummond's widow, Sarah, and several others to dispatch protests to the king.[52]

Meanwhile, Charles II, upon learning that the popular uprising was underway, sent three commissioners to Virginia to investigate its causes. One was Colonel Francis Morrison, who had been Speaker of the House of Burgesses in 1655-1656. The men arrived in late January 1677 with a thousand royal troops and orders for Governor Berkeley's recall. They quickly discovered that Jamestown lay in ashes and that the rebellion had been quelled. Because the governor's residence at Green Spring was "very much ruined by the rebels," they stayed in Surry County at the home of Colonel Thomas Swann, a member of Berkeley's council who sympathized with Bacon.[53]

Berkeley told the commissioners that his houses in Jamestown were burned, Green Spring was almost destroyed, and his personal property, "totally plundered." William Sherwood, Theophilus Hone, Thomas Swann, Colonel Nathaniel Bacon and others also lost dwellings in the fire that consumed Jamestown. One man sacrificed 63 casks of wine, some of which was consumed by fire and the rest by Governor Berkeley's supporters. Thomas Ludwell, who had a house in Jamestown and the plantation called Rich Neck, claimed that his "stock was utterly ruined and taken away by the late Rebells." His brother, Philip, said that Bacon's men had plundered him "of all within their Reach."[54]

As the days wore on, the dialogue between the commissioners and Berkeley became increasingly strained. Ten James City County residents (Thomas Bobby, John Dean, Thomas Glover, Andrew Goedean, William Hoare, Henry Jenkins, John Johnson, James Barrow, John Williams, and Edward Lloyd) filed formal complaints in which they claimed that their goods had been plundered by Berkeley's men or that they were imprisoned without just cause. Lloyd, a mulatto, alleged that the trauma his pregnant wife suffered as a result of the intrusion caused her to lose their baby and then die. On February 13, 1677, the commissioners warned Berkeley that the king would take a dim view of his seizing private property. He, in turn, contended that most of his neighbors had stolen his belongings, which were "still to be seen in their houses" and that if his supporters had retaliated, it was without authorization.[55]

Many of those living between Ware and Skimino Creeks, in what later became James City, were followers of Nathaniel Bacon. James Wilson, whom Berkeley had executed for his role in the popular uprising, lived near Mount Folly, the home of Bryan Smith, one of the governor's most avid supporters. Smith and a band of vigilantes that included Roger Potter, Richard Awborne, William Hartwell, and Samuel Mathews III, seized the personal belongings of Richard Clarke, a Bacon supporter who lived near the mouth of Skimino Creek. In a grievance Clarke filed with the king's commissioners, he claimed that in late December 1676 Smith and his men raided his plantation, where some neighbors had sought refuge, and "carryed away fower English servants, seven Negroes, and all his household goods and other estate" including tobacco notes worth a substantial sum. He said that Smith and Robert Beverley (a staunch Berkeley supporter) still had some of his servants. Clarke's neighbors, Robert Lowder, John Cocker, and Robert Porter, asked the commissioners for protection against Smith, who was trying to force them to pay for some hogs consumed by Bacon's followers. The men claimed that

Smith threatened to send them to prison unless they paid up.[56]

Contemporary narratives reveal that the intensity of the opposing sides' partisanship fueled a cycle of looting and retaliation. After the king's troops arrived in January 1677, a ship was sent out to round up five groups of insurgents that had fled into the countryside. It was shortly before order was restored that Bryan Smith raided the plantation of Richard Clarke; it was afterward that Smith's men extorted a large quantity of tobacco from neighboring planters who had supported Bacon's cause. Smith's heavy-handed treatment of his neighbors demonstrates clearly that both sides' supporters did their share of pillaging. His leadership role in guerrilla activities raises the possibility that he erected the ancient structure known as the Stonehouse, which stood at the rear of his Mount Folly tract and had defensive features. It would have served as a cache for loot and matériel and as a place of retreat if Bacon's rebels gained the upper hand.

The king's commissioners asked each county's freeholders to list their complaints about the government. James City County's residents responded that tax revenues were being misused and that the colony was defenseless against foreign invasion. They recommended that the Indians captured during Bacon's Rebellion be sold for public profit and that local officials' salaries be reduced. They felt that land should be taxed and that all landowners, including public officials, should be subject to taxation. In virtually every instance, the king's commissioners replied that the issues raised by the people of James City County already had been put to rest.[57]

In February 1677 the assembly met at Green Spring and passed 20 new legislative acts, four of which had to do with Bacon's Rebellion. Fines and other penalties became the established punishment for those who had participated in the uprising or insulted public officials. Pardons were issued to all but those found guilty of treason. Plundered goods were to be restored to their rightful owners and those who suffered losses in the rebellion were authorized to sue for compensatory damages. The burgesses nullified the legislation Bacon forced upon them at gunpoint and they designated two official holy days: May 4th, a fast day in repentance for the rebellion, and August 22nd, a day of thanksgiving to commemorate its end.[58]

In March 1677 several of the uprising's ringleaders were tried in civil tribunals conducted by Governor Berkeley at Green Spring. Although some were fined or given relatively mild punishment, nine were sentenced to hang. In late March, commissioner Francis Morrison asked Lady Frances Berkeley to intercede with her husband on behalf of one condemned man. But she replied that she would "rather have worn the canvas the Rebels threatened to make her glad of" than ask for him to be spared. In April, immediately prior to Sir William Berkeley's departure for England, the commissioners experienced what they deemed a major insult: when the governor's coach transported them from Green Spring to Jamestown, the common hangman served as postillion. The outraged commissioners informed Berkeley that the incident was "an insult to the King's Great Seal" and that they were going to report it to Charles II himself. Berkeley responded that he was as "innocent in this as the blessed Angels themselves" and that he had sent his slave "to be racked, tortured or whipt till he confesses how this dire misfortune happened." But the commissioners claimed they had seen Lady Berkeley spying upon them "through a broken quarrel of glass, to see how the show looked" and refused to believe that the affront was unintentional.[59]

Sir William Berkeley's Exodus

After Berkeley set sail for England, some of his most ardent supporters ("the Green Spring Faction") resisted Lt. Governor Herbert Jeffries' more lenient attitude toward convicted rebels, none of whom were sentenced to death. Philip Ludwell I, known for his "rash and firey temper," viewed Jeffries and his policies with disdain. Once, when he had consumed an ample quantity of hard cider he accused the lieutenant governor of perjury and called him "a worse rebel than Bacon." He also declared that "if every pitiful little fellow with a periwig that came in to govern this country had liberty to make laws," no one's real estate or personal property would be safe. In late May Jeffries and his council discussed building or repairing a structure to serve as a statehouse and finding a suitable governor's residence. The destruction at Jamestown was so widespread that several criminals were returned home until time for them to appear before the General Court.[60]

The 1677 Treaty

On May 29, 1677, a formal peace agreement was made with the colony's tributary Indians, what became known as the Treaty of Middle Plantation. Cockcoeske, the Queen of the Pamunkey, her youthful son, "Captain John West" (her child by one-time Governor John West), and several other native leaders came to Middle Plantation, where they knelt before Lt. Governor Jeffries, "kissed the paper of peace" and endorsed it with their signature marks. Afterward, guns were fired to commemorate the occasion. Other Indian tribes, who heard about the treaty, in 1680 became signatories to an expanded version. Special gifts were ordered for some of the Indian kings and queens who signed the treaty. The Queen of the Pamunkey received special recognition because of her steadfast loyalty to the English. The Indians, by endorsing the Treaty of Middle Plantation, acknowledged their allegiance to the Crown and conceded that entitlement to their land was derived from the monarch.

The tributary Indian tribes quarreled among themselves from time to time and asked the colonial government to intercede. This led some officials to declare that the peace agreement had created as many problems as it had solved. Sporadic outbreaks of violence continued to plague the frontier, where Iroquois, Susquehannock, and Seneca Indians swept down upon isolated homesteads. In May 1679 the king dispatched enough military equipment to the colony to outfit 200 horse soldiers and the assembly ordered the construction of forts at the heads of the colony's four major rivers. They served as the armed horsemen's base of operations while they maintained vigilance over the frontier.[61]

The Restoration of Green Spring

Sir William Berkeley died shortly after returning to England. He left his Virginia landholdings to his widow and bequeathed Mrs. Sarah Kirkman, the James City County sheriff's widow, enough money to buy a mourning ring. Lady Frances Berkeley set about repairing the Green Spring mansion, hoping that she could rent it to Virginia's governors and live comfortably in England. But life presented her with another alternative. In October 1680 she married Philip Ludwell I of Rich Neck, deputy-secretary of the colony. It was through their union that the Berkeley and Ludwell fortunes were joined, with the result that literally thousands of acres of James City County land descended through successive generations of the Ludwell and Lee families.[62]

In 1681 when Thomas Lord Culpeper arrived in Virginia and assumed the governorship, he used Green Spring as a personal residence. His successor, Francis Howard, Lord Effingham, followed suit. During their administrations the assembly and General Court occasionally convened at Green Spring.[63] Time eventually healed the rifts caused by Bacon's Rebellion and other issues became more compelling.

Notes

1. McIlwaine, MINUTES, 556, 559; Surry County Deeds No. 1:371; Cocke, SOUTHERN VIRGINIA, 47–48.

2. Nugent, CAVALIERS, I, 335, 339, 360, 364, 393; II, 16, 129, 170; III, 84, 169–170; York County Deeds, Orders, Wills 2:289, 328.

3. Nugent, CAVALIERS, II, 44, 169–170, 200, 212, 240, 323, 354, 387; Thomas J. Wertenbaker, THE PLANTERS OF COLONIAL VIRGINIA (Princeton, 1922), 212; Nugent, CAVALIERS, II, 222; Augustine Herrmann, "Virginia and Maryland, 1670."

4. Billings et al. , COLONIAL VIRGINIA, 66–68; Nugent, CAVALIERS, II, 207; Mary A. Stephenson, CARTER'S GROVE PLANTATION: A HISTORY (Williamsburg, 1964), 52; Mary Goodwin, KINGSMILL PLANTATION (Williamsburg, 1972), 8.

5. Randolph, HISTORY, 150–151.

6. Hening, STATUTES, I, 366–367, 407, 508; II, 204; Nugent, CAVALIERS, I, 173, 415.

7. Virginia Land Office Patent Book I, Part II, 890; II, 11–12; III, 8, 158, 367–368, 391; IV, 88, 150; V, 145; VI, 42; VII, 97, 228–229; James City County Land Tax Lists 1792; Ambler Manuscript No. 53, No. 134.

8. Hening, STATUTES, I, 401, 411, 435, 440, 517–518, 538–539.

9. McIlwaine, MINUTES, 505–506; Hening, STATUTES, I, 446; J. A. C. Chandler et al. , "George Wilson," WILLIAM AND MARY QUARTERLY, 2nd Ser. , 5 (January 1897):266–267; Lyon G. Tyler, ed. , CRADLE OF THE REPUBLIC (Richmond, 1906), 61.

10. York County Wills, Deeds, Orders 1657–1659:18, 35, 54; Records 1665–1672:1, 8, 17, 29, 40–41, 76.

11. McIlwaine, MINUTES, 493, 41, 227, 365, 400, 517. Lunsford patented part of what became Camden, a Caroline County plantation.

12. Hening, STATUTES, I, 5, 393, 402, 530, 547; II, 141–142; Force, TRACTS, I:8:14–15; McIlwaine et al., HOUSE OF BURGESSES, 1659/60–1693, 4, 74, 95.

13. Billings et al., COLONIAL VIRGINIA, 78; Hening, STATUTES, I, 540.

14. Hening, STATUTES, II, 17; William Berkeley, A DISCOURSE AND VIEW OF VIRGINIA (London, 1663), 2, 4; Washburn, THE GOVERNOR, 104–105.

15. Excavations conducted by National Park Service archaeologists at Green Spring in 1928–1929 led to the discovery of a small glass furnace and some old brick kilns on the banks of Powhatan Creek. One furnace brick was inscribed "H. A. L." and the date "August 6, 1666." In 1955 a pottery kiln also was found on the Green Spring property, southeast of the mansion site.

16. William Berkeley, April 18, 1663, letter to Lord ?, Egerton Manuscript 2395 f 365; Beverley, PRESENT STATE, 135.

17. Hening, STATUTES, II, 4, 20–28, 52–53, 59, 70, 86, 101–103, 113, 124; McIlwaine, MINUTES, 368, 390, 447.

18. Hening, STATUTES, I, 123, 135; II, 70, 75, 124, 166–167, 170, 219, 238–254.

19. B.P.R.O., C.O. 5/1354, 273–274; Hening, STATUTES, II, 172–176.

20. McIlwaine et al., HOUSE, 1659–1693, 27–28; Hening, STATUTES, II, 204. 107

21. Hening, STATUTES, II, 173–176; McIlwaine, MINUTES, 508–509; B.P.R.O., C.O. 1/19:75–76; 1/21:344–346; Beverley, HISTORY, 67–68; Warren M. Billings, JAMESTOWN AND THE FOUNDING OF THE NATION (Gettysburg, 1990), 80–81.

22. McIlwaine et al., HOUSE, 1659–1693, 27, 53, 152; McIlwaine, MINUTES, 447, 485, 508, 573; Hening, STATUTES, II, 213, 502.

23. McIlwaine, MINUTES, 484–488; B.P.R.O., C.O. 1/20, 199–201, 218–219.

24. He thought that the hurricane passed around him in a counter–clockwise direction. Actually, its eye had passed overhead.

25. Billings et al., COLONIAL VIRGINIA, 76.

26. They were to be erected at Jamestown, Tindall's (Gloucester) Point, Corotoman, Yeohocomico, and a site on the Nansemond River.

27. Hening, STATUTES, II, 256–258, 264–265; John Clayton, [Untitled map of Jamestown Island], 1688. A 1689 patent for land on the west side of Orchard Run makes reference to an "an old ruin'd turf fort" in that location.

28. That racism figured in legal decisions is evidenced by the dismissal of a case against a white indentured servant named Hannah Warwick, who refused to obey her overseer, a black man (McIlwaine, MINUTES, 513).

29. Hening, STATUTES, II, 267–269.

30. McIlwaine, MINUTES, 205–206, 218, 221, 226, 240, 258, 510, 513–516.

31. McIlwaine, MINUTES, 226, 266, 277, 288, 308, 319, 321.

32. William P. Palmer, CALENDAR OF VIRGINIA STATE PAPERS (New York, 1968), I, 8, 10; McIlwaine, MINUTES, 313, 329, 337, 341, 344, 346–349, 367, 370, 375, 378, 382–383, 394, 402, 407, 420, 436, 441.

33. Hening, STATUTES, II, 293–294; B.P.R.O. , C.O. 1/29, 72–75; 1/30, 169–170; William G. Stanard, ed., "Miscellaneous Colonial Documents," VIRGINIA MAGAZINE OF HISTORY AND BIOGRAPHY 20 (January 1912):26; H. R. McIlwaine, comp., EXECUTIVE JOURNALS OF THE COUNCIL OF COLONIAL VIRGINIA (Richmond, 1925–1945), 533; MINUTES, 334, 342, 367, 371, 512.

34. Force, TRACTS, III:12:23–24; Clayton, [Untitled map], 1688.

35. William G. Stanard, ed., "Notes to Council Journals," VIRGINIA MAGAZINE OF HISTORY AND BIOGRAPHY 33 (July 1925):352; Hening, STATUTES, II, 319–321; McIlwaine, MINUTES, 503, 514.

36. McIlwaine, MINUTES, 348, 382–383; Nugent, CAVALIERS, I, 160, 228, 294, 465.

37. Billings et al., COLONIAL HISTORY, 91; McIlwaine, MINUTES, 390, 418, 423.

38. Morgan, AMERICAN SLAVERY, 250–292; Craven, SOUTHERN COLONIES, 389 note; Washburn, THE GOVERNOR, 1972:153–166.

39. Washburn, THE GOVERNOR, 18–19. The colonel was married to Elizabeth, the daughter and heir of Richard Kingsmill, and owned a farm on Jamestown Island.

40. Hening, STATUTES, II, 326–328; Washburn, THE GOVERNOR, 32–33.

41. Washburn, THE GOVERNOR, 18–19, 46–47, 51–53, 58–59, 65, 68; Billings et al., COLONIAL HISTORY, 77–96; Hening, STATUTES, II, 351.

42. Jane Carson, BACON'S REBELLION 1676–1976 (Jamestown, 1976), 78; Washburn, THE GOVERNOR, 18–19, 69–70); Billings et al. , COLONIAL HISTORY, 77–96.

43. Washburn, THE GOVERNOR, 76, 80–83; Charles Andrews, ed., NARRATIVES OF THE INSURRECTIONS, 1665–1690 (New York, 1967), 130–131; Force, TRACTS, I:11:24; III:8:21.

44. Bacon had dispatched small parties of horsemen to round up the women. Among those used as pawns were Colonel Nathaniel Bacon's wife, Elizabeth; Colonel James Bray's wife, Angelica; Colonel John Page's wife, Elizabeth; and Colonel Thomas Ballard's wife, Anna (Force, TRACTS, I:9:8; Tyler, CRADLE, 156).

45. McIlwaine et al., HOUSE OF BURGESSES, 1659–1693, 69–70; Andrews, INSURRECTIONS, 71. At least five local men lost their lives in the assault: William Senior, William Simkler, John White, Robert Sorrell, and Richard Jones. Their widows later submitted pension claims.

46. He may have carried them to his farm on the Governor's Land. Later, Secretary Thomas Ludwell took the records to his home, Rich Neck (Andrews, Insurrections, 136).

47. Washburn, THE GOVERNOR, 80–83; Neville, BACON'S REBELLION, 309–310; Billings et al., COLONIAL HISTORY, 94; Andrews, INSURRECTIONS, 130–131. According to one official account, when Jamestown was burned, it contained twelve new brick houses, a number of frame dwellings with brick chimneys, the colony's statehouse, and a church.

48. Berkeley proffered that the rebel was felled by the hand of Providence and said that "An honest Minister wrote this Epitaph on him: Bacon is Dead I am sorry at my hart That lice and flux should take the hangmans part" (Washburn, THE GOVERNOR, 85).

49. Washburn, THE GOVERNOR, 84–85; Andrews, INSURRECTIONS, 92; Billings et al., COLONIAL HISTORY, 94–95. One contemporary said of Ingram, "The Lion had no sooner made his exitt but the Ape (by indubitable right) steps upon the stage." Another writer said that "the Titmouse . . . was become an Elliphant."

50. Carson, BERKELEY, 10; Andrews, INSURRECTIONS, 86, 95.

51. Hening, STATUTES, II, 545–547; Carson, BERKELEY, 196:10; Washburn, THE GOVERNOR, 84–91; Neville, BACON'S REBELLION, 313, 323.

52. Hening, STATUTES, II, 547–549; III, 569; Neville, BACON'S REBELLION, 90, 315, 368, 372; Force, TRACTS, I:9:10; 10:4; Washburn, THE GOVERNOR, 84–91.

53. Swann, dubbed "ye Great Toad," allegedly "did sitt in ye council of war for burning the town." His son, Samuel, was married to William Drummond's daughter.

54. Washburn, The Governor, 74, 60, 80–84, 217–218, 255; William G. Stanard, ed., "Vindication of Sir William Berkeley," Virginia Magazine of History and Biography 6 (October 1898):143; Sainsbury, Calendar, X, 167–168; B.P.R.O.: C.O. 5/1371 f 179.

55. Sainsbury et al., Calendar, I:50–53; Washburn, The Governor, 105–106; Neville, Bacon's Rebellion, 254.

56. Chamberlayne, Blisland Parish, xxxix, xli–xliii; William G. Stanard, ed., "Virginia Gleanings in England," Virginia Magazine of History and Biography 12 (July 1904):54–55, 140; Hening, Statutes, II, 375; Nugent, Cavaliers, I, 393; II, 170.

57. Neville, Bacon's Rebellion, 338–340. The Stonehouse Archaeological Site was added to the National Register of Historic Places in 1973.

58. Hening, Statutes, II, 366–406. Men found guilty of promoting rebellion had to stand upon the pillory for two hours and be fined, unless they committed the same offence three times; women guilty of a like offence were to receive 20 lashes for the first offense, 30 lashes for the second, and trial as a traitor for the third.

59. Neville, Bacon's Rebellion, 71, 73, 276; Hening, Statutes, II, 548–558; William G. Stanard, "Virginia in 1677," Virginia Magazine of History and Biography 21 (April 1913):370.

60. William G. Stanard, "The Randolph Manuscript," Virginia Magazine of History and Biography 18 (January 1910):5; Lyon G. Tyler, "Ludwell Family," William and Mary Quarterly 1st Ser. , 19 (January 1911):210; Neville, Bacon's Rebellion, 90; Hening, Statutes, II, 557–558; McIlwaine, Minutes, 516, 519.

61. Herbert Jeffreys, Letter to the Rt. Honorable, June 11, 1677, Coventry Papers Vol. 73, Bath 65, ff 64–65; Thomas Ludwell, Letter to the Rt. Honorable, August 3, 1678, Coventry Papers 73:281; Anonymous, Articles of Peace, [1680], Virginia Records, 1606–1692, Papers of Thomas Jefferson, 8th Ser. 14:226–233; Hening, Statutes, II, 433–434; Nicholas Spencer, Letter to ?, dated 1680, B.P.R.O., C.O. 1/44 f 425.

62. Hening, Statutes, II, 59, 558–560; McIlwaine, Minutes, 494, 519; William G. Stanard, "Proprietors of the Northern Neck," Virginia Magazine of History and Biography 33 (July 1925):352; McIlwaine, Minutes, 523; Lee Papers, 1679–1685.

63. Carson, Berkeley, 6; Philip A. Bruce, "Bacon's Rebellion," Virginia Magazine of History and Biography 1 (July 1893):113, 116; "Culpeper's Report on Virginia in 1683," Virginia Magazine of History and Biography 3 (January 1896):229; William G. Stanard, ed., "Historical Notes and Queries," Virginia Magazine of History and Biography 21 (April 1913):319.

CHAPTER   5

"Great Helps and Advances . . .
Towards the Beginning of a Town"

The Capital Moves to Williamsburg 1681–1699

The Business of Government

At the close of the seventeenth century, three James City County men (Henry Hartwell, the Rev. James Blair, and Edward Chilton) prepared an official report, describing conditions in Virginia. Their narrative, which provides a bird's-eye view of how the colonial government functioned, reveals that the highest ranking officials needed to spend lengthy periods of time at Jamestown. It also offers many insights into the role the government played in the lives of ordinary citizens.

The governor as chief executive had the right to grant land, fill government positions, and issue treasury warrants for public funds. He presided over the Council of State and the General Court. He could summon or dismiss the burgesses, veto the laws they passed, and call for elections, if he so desired. As commander-in-chief of the armed forces, the governor made sure that the colony's defenses were maintained and he commissioned all military officers. His power was restrained by the monarch.[1]

The Council of State advised the governor on matters that ranged from military and trade policies to the State Church. Council members also served as justices of the General Court, the colony's highest ranking judicial body, which sometimes served in an appellate capacity. In 1699 the inhabitants of James City County's lower Wilmington Parish, which straddled the Chickahominy, asked the Council of State to adjust their parish's boundary lines so that they could attend church in Jamestown, which was more convenient. On another occasion, James City Parish churchwardens William Broadribb and Edward Travis asked for funds to repair the parish church's steeple and improve the road to the church. Church-related personnel problems sometimes were aired before the councilors as justices of the General Court. In 1695 the vestry of Wilmington Parish expelled the Rev. John Gourdon from his position because of a salary dispute, but the General Court decided to reinstate him. The justices also overturned a decision made by the James City County court regarding a local man who duped a customer by substituting spoiled barley for good malt. The General Court tried capital cases such as treason and murder. For example, Samuel Bray of James City County, who was accused of murdering his wife, Sarah, was tried, convicted, and executed at Jamestown. When a Grand Jury was needed by the General Court, the sheriff of James City County impaneled those he considered "the most able and discrete men" in Jamestown, a practice which origin lay in tradition. Decisions made by the General Court could be appealed to the monarch. For example, Mrs. Sarah Drummond, the executed rebel's widow, exercised this appellate procedure when seeking compensation for the damages her plantation sustained at the hands of Governor William Berkeley's agents, some of whom were members of the General Court.[2]

Members of the Council of State served as the colony's secretary, escheator, and auditor. The secretary maintained copies of all important public documents, whereas the escheator kept a record of all land that had reverted to the Crown. The auditor accepted from county sheriffs the taxes, quitrents, and government officials' fees paid by local inhabitants. He also received the customs duties collected by naval officers, fellow councilors who inspected all seagoing vessels entering and leaving Virginia. Council members served as military officers: colonels, who were in command of county militia units. If a county were too distant from its colonel's residence, the governor usually appointed a local military leader and gave him the rank of major. The governor, with input from his colonels and majors, commissioned local captains and lieutenants, who headed the military companies and units directly under their charge. Virginia's white adult males, with some exceptions, were obliged to participate in the militia.

Councilors were handsomely compensated for performing their numerous duties. They also were privy to "inside information" they could use to their own advantage. For example, because they had convenient access to the escheator's records, they usually knew when land reverted to the Crown and could patent it before others learned that it was available. Council members as military officers sometimes agreed to outfit the militia or undertake fort construction, which entitled them to compensation from public funds. The heads of James City County's most prominent families typically served as councilors.

At the close of the seventeenth century, the assembly (or House of Burgesses) consisted of two delegates from each county and one from Jamestown. As soon as the governor called the House into session, elections were held at county seats. Free white adult males had the right to vote and hold office in every county in which they owned a certain minimum amount of real estate. Thus, a man could vote in several localities' elections and hold office in a jurisdiction in which he didn't reside. As the more successful owned land in two or more counties, they had a greater opportunity to wield their influence over local and regional affairs. For example, Captain Miles Cary, who resided in Elizabeth City County but owned land in Jamestown, served as the capital city's burgess in 1692-1693. Daniel Parke, who in 1693 was elected a burgess for both James City and York Counties, was allowed to choose which jurisdiction he preferred to represent. Philip Ludwell of James City County was a perfect example of someone who held a number of public offices. In 1695 he was elected a burgess for James City County even though he was a member of the Council of State, Secretary of State, and a militia colonel. Whenever elections were held, men went to the county courthouse to cast their ballots. The sheriff, who officiated at local elections, made sure that only eligible voters participated. He set the date of the election and the time at which the polls would open and close. On election day, he sat with the candidates and their clerks around a table while voters approached, one by one, to announce their choice. Thus, all votes were cast aloud, in public, and in front of the candidates.3

The House of Burgesses chose its own Speaker (or chairman) and formed standing committees. Among the James City County men who served as Speaker during the seventeenth century were Ambrose Harmer, William Whitby, Francis Morrison, and Henry Soane. Legislation enacted by the House and approved by the Council of State was forwarded to the governor for his endorsement. Laws that survived this process became effective but did not become permanently binding until the monarch consented. People who performed duties on behalf of the government presented their burgesses with claims for public funds. Citizens sometimes voiced common concerns by drafting petitions they submitted to the House.

Because Jamestown was the capital of Virginia as well as the seat of James City County, many local men played an official role in both governments. The county sheriff served as sergeant-at-arms to the General Court and the House of Burgesses, and as jailor had custody of county and General Court prisoners. In 1696 when sheriff Edward Ross refused to serve as the General Court's sergeant-at-arms because he felt he was underpaid, another man filled in until the salary dispute was resolved. The Rev. Robert Holderby of James City Parish was paid for offering prayers at assembly meetings and John White of Jamestown was compensated as official bell-ringer. William Drummond, son of the late rebel, was among those paid for delivering official messages and William Edwards of Jamestown, Clerk of the General Court, received extra compensation. Later, Edwards' widow was paid for hosting a meeting of the assembly's Committee for Public Claims. In 1692 James City County sheriff George Marable sought compensation for providing room and board to three pirates and the under-sheriff of Middlesex County. Marable's successor, Michael Sherman, was paid for incarcerating two men. Thus, it appears that the county sheriff was paid for whatever duties he performed.4

During the late seventeenth century Virginians paid several types of taxes in support of their government. White males age 16 and older and slaves were considered "tithable." That is, a poll or capitation tax had to be paid on their behalf. Every June, household heads were obliged to present a list of the tithable people for whom they were responsible. The lists were posted at the courthouse door for all to see. County taxes financed capital improvements such as courthouse and prison construction, the maintenance of bridges and causeways, and the payment of local burgesses' salaries. Every October, Virginians paid parish levies or church dues that supported their local parish of the State Church. With these funds vestries paid ministers' salaries, maintained church property, and provided public welfare. The House of Burgesses, with the approval of the governor and council, assessed the public levy. Such revenues were used to maintain the statehouse or rent other facilities, and to cover the expenses incurred by the assembly, such as buying candles or writing materials and paying messengers and doorkeepers.[5]

The Government Buildings at Jamestown

Because the colony's statehouse was destroyed when Bacon's rebels put Jamestown to the torch, the assembly, the Council of State, and the General Court were forced to seek other accommodations. The justices of James City County, which formerly convened in the General Court's chambers, also had to find another meeting place. The burgesses met at Green Spring on several occasions, but usually held their meetings at Jamestown in taverns or space they rented in private homes. This led to complaints on the part of the citizenry. In 1684, eight years after Jamestown burned, the House of Burgesses hired Colonel Philip Ludwell to repair and remodel the statehouse. But after it was readied for use, the council continued to meet in rented rooms in William Sherwood's home or houses in other parts of Tidewater.[6] On February 7, 1691, James City County's justices of the peace asked the Council of State for permission to hold monthly court in the General Court's chambers. They said that after the statehouse was destroyed, the county built its own courthouse, which eventually had fallen into disrepair. They added that Lt. Governor Francis Nicholson had offered to repair the building and turn it into "a school house for the inhabitants of James City County and others" if the justices would deed the property to him. Although it is doubtful that Nicholson established a school at Jamestown, the local justices were allowed to use the General Court's chambers as long as they kept its windows and plaster in good repair. In November 1693 Thomas Beckett, Thomas Lun, and Mrs. Alice Goolrick, all of James City County, sought compensation for repairing the General Courthouse, which had become "extremely decayed and rotten," and for digging a vault beneath a newly-built powder house. The statehouse was repaired several times during the late 1690s and at least one of the building's offices was enlarged and remodeled.[7]

Relations with the Indians

In December 1682 the assembly voted to abolish the frontier forts established in 1679, for they were too costly to maintain. Instead, horse soldiers (or rangers) garrisoned in the abandoned forts were to use them as a base of operations. In 1684 men from every county were pressed into service; however, within a matter of months they were sent home, for the need for protection had diminished considerably. Trading practices commenced being regulated by law, for unscrupulous dealings often were at the root of troubles with the Indians. Also, Indian servants employed by the settlers had to be registered in the nearest local court. In 1697, when sporadic outbreaks of violence occurred beyond the fall line, "flying armies" that consisted of a lieutenant and twelve mounted rangers were placed on constant guard at the head of the James, York, Rappahannock, and Potomac Rivers to keep watch over the colony's frontiers. James City County, like other localities, had a troop of 48 horse soldiers and a company of 60 foot soldiers, which formed a standing army.[8]

During the late seventeenth century, tributary Indian tribes, whose villages were attacked by stronger, warlike Natives from beyond the colony's frontier, sometimes asked the Virginia government for the protection to which they were entitled under the 1677 treaty. In the mid-1680s food and supplies were provided to certain tribes that had come under siege and some of the weaker Native groups were urged to unite for mutual protection. Sometimes, tributary Indians took up residence on the outskirts of the colonists' plantations. When Natives crossed from one colony into another to commit a crime, the two governments were supposed to cooperate in bringing the perpetrators to justice. In 1696 an Indian from Maryland was jailed at Jamestown until he could be sent north to stand trial.[9]

Urbanization and Change

In June 1680 Governor Thomas Culpeper told the House of Burgesses that the king wanted Virginia to have towns and ports, like his other colonies. The assembly responded by passing an act that was designed to encourage urban development, trade, and manufacturing by establishing port towns in each of Virginia's 20 counties. Jamestown, was the choice for James City County. All exports after January 1, 1681, and all imports (including slaves, English servants, and merchandize) after September 29, 1681, had to be landed and sold in one of the new ports of entry. The 50-acre port towns were to be laid out in half-acre lots and those who purchased lots had a year in which to develop them. The 1680 act encouraged development by offering planters fixed rates at port warehouses and extending to tradesmen, such as carpenters and bricklayers, five years immunity to prosecution for bad debt. Despite these incentives, most Virginians demonstrated little interest in urbanization.[10]

In 1682 the king again ordered Culpeper to see that towns were built in Virginia. As he believed that Jamestown, "the most antient [and] the most convenient place for ye Metropolis of our said Colonie," was still ruinous, he wanted the city rebuilt as soon as possible. This prompted some of the community's property owners to ask the assembly to define the town's legal limits. They pointed out that the recent town act created 50-acre ports and said that Jamestown was much larger, for it encompassed all of the acreage from Sandy Bay to Orchard Run and from the James River to Back Creek. They added that the modest price set for purchasing 50-acre town sites was inapplicable to Jamestown, where every acre was worth far more than the sum being offered for 50 acres of undeveloped land. They sought permission to build storehouses, offering to forfeit their land if they failed to do so, and asked that the city limits be expanded to include the whole island. They also recommended that all vacant marsh land be converted to common ownership so it could be used for pasturing livestock. A new town act, passed in 1691, basically reaffirmed the 1680 legislation. Many of the formerly-designated ports of entry, including Jamestown, were confirmed and a few new town sites were added. In September 1692 the king and queen sent word that since

Jamestown was to be remain the seat of government, they would be pleased if each councilor built a house there. This sparked a flurry of patenting and perhaps development.[11]

Francis Howard, Lord Effingham, arrived in Virginia in 1686 to assume the governorship. As he had been instructed to rent a suitable home until a proper residence could be built, he, like his predecessor, decided to live at Green Spring which he leased from Lady Frances Berkeley and her new husband, Philip Ludwell I. But Howard's tenancy was marred by the summertime deaths of his wife and several household members and in the fall he moved to Rosegill, Ralph Wormeley's plantation in Middlesex County. In late October 1687 the king's "Declaration for Liberty of Conscience" was read in Jamestown. This so-called act of toleration, which gave non-Anglicans the right to assemble for worship, was announced "with the beat of the drum and the firing of two great guns and with all the joyfulness this collony is capable to express."[12] Even so, the State Church's authority remained intact.

Howard was in office in July 1688 when three accused pirates were captured and brought to Jamestown to stand trial before the General Court. The precious metals and other valuables in their possession were seized. Although the three men were acquitted and their belongings were returned, they were obliged to compensate the James City County sheriff for the cost of their imprisonment. Thus, they were forced to pay for their own wrongful confinement! Howard was still governor when several James City County residents' names made their way into the records of nearby York County. John Davis of Jockey's Neck warned the public not to do business with his wife, Ann, who had absconded, and Elizabeth Hambleton publicly declared that Mr. John Childe of James City Parish had fathered her bastard son. Meanwhile, Joseph Firth was paid for the use of his horse, which had been pressed into service at Jamestown, and Isaac Goddin of York County bestowed some James City County land upon his daughter, Sarah. William Chesleyn of upper James City County agreed to accept two cows in satisfaction for a debt and John and Elliner Cooper's orphaned daughter, Mourning, was apprenticed to a York County man until she reached age 21 or married.[13]

Defending James City

When Francis Nicholson, Virginia's interim governor from 1690 to 1692, arrived in the colony, he found that its defenses were in poor condition. In 1690 Colonel John Page was ordered to make an inventory of the military stores in the fort at Jamestown, the curved brick structure the Rev. John Clayton once likened to a duck blind. Colonel William Browne, who owned part of a rowhouse in Jamestown, agreed to shelter the ammunition while a vaulted magazine and store house were built. However, in 1693 when Governor Edmund Andros arrived, he found the fort in disrepair and its guns "lying on the ground." Colonels William Byrd and Edward Hill, who inspected the old fort, concluded that it would be more costly to repair than replace. John Tullitt (Tullett) of Jamestown was hired to demolish it and George Harvey of Pasbehay was authorized to build "a platform for the great guns."[14]

In 1697 the Rev. James Blair, an outspoken critic of Andros, informed officials in England that the governor had

. . . *thrown away a great deal of money in raising [razing] an old fort at Jamestown, & in building a powder house, and in making a platform for 16 great guns there. . . . I never heard one man that pretended to understand anything of Fortification, that upon sight of these works, did not ridicule & condemn them as good for nothing but to spend money.*

He added that:

The Guns at Jamestown, are so placed that they are no defence to the town, which being much lower in the river, might be taken by the Enemies shipping, without receiving any the least assistance from those Guns. The powder House stands all alone without any Garrison to defend it, and is a ready prey for any foreign or domestic enemy.[15]

Blair exaggerated, however, for the powder magazine stood upon a bluff on the riverbank, a relatively short distance above the fort.

The College of William and Mary

On February 8, 1693, King William and Queen Mary granted a charter to the college that bears their names, to establish "a certain place of universal study, or perpetual college, for divinity, philosophy, languages and other good arts and sciences." Public revenues were earmarked for its construction and support. The newly created educational institution was endowed with 20,000 acres of land. On December 20, 1693, Thomas Ballard, who in 1675 bought 330 acres of James City County land from Thomas Ludwell (part of Rich Neck) sold it to the government as the campus of the new college. It was located in the Middle Plantation, where it straddled the forerunner of Jamestown Road and followed the old "road to New Kent," Richmond Road. By 1694 a small grammar school stood close to the site selected for construction of the college's main building. Its first bricks were laid in August 1695. In April 1699 the assembly convened in the college building at Middle Plantation. That meeting foreshadowed Jamestown's demise as the colony's capital and the seat of James City County.[16]

The Impetus for Relocating the Capital

On October 20, 1698, fire broke out next door to the statehouse. It spread quickly, consuming both statehouse and jail. James City County yeoman Arthur Jarvis, a convicted burglar awaiting execution, was blamed for the blaze, but there was insufficient proof of his guilt. The governor sent word to England that many of the public records kept in the statehouse were thrown from its windows before flames completely engulfed the building; however, nearly 200 guns stored there were burned. Later, the documents were collected and sorted and some of the charred weapons were salvaged. At that juncture the General Court began convening in the late William Sherwood's home, where space also was rented for storage of official records. John Tullitt, who occupied a nearby rowhouse, was asked to outfit his dwelling to accommodate the House of Burgesses. In early 1699 Governor Francis Nicholson, who was strongly in favor of moving the capital to Middle Plantation, declared that Jamestown was in such wretched condition that the assembly and the General Court couldn't meet there at the same time. Later in the year, the fort at Jamestown was abandoned and the munitions stored there were removed. Plans also were made to take the government's records to the College of William and Mary for safekeeping. Despite this exodus,

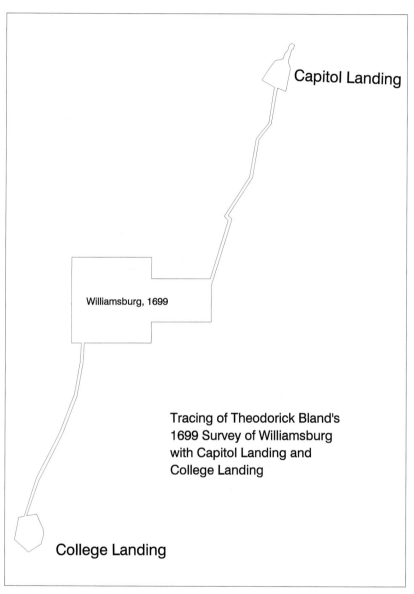

Capitol Landing

Williamsburg, 1699

Tracing of Theodorick Bland's
1699 Survey of Williamsburg
with Capitol Landing and
College Landing

College Landing

Map by Christina A. Kiddle.

Jamestown continued to serve as the seat of the James City County court for another 15 to 20 years.[17]

The Move to Middle Plantation

On May 1, 1699, a group of students from the College of William and Mary made a presentation to the House of Burgesses in which they advocated moving the capital to Middle Plantation. They claimed that "great helps and advances" had been made "towards the beginning of a town," for the fledgling community already had "a Church, an ordinary, several stores, two Mills, a smiths shop, a Grammar School, and above all the Colledge." One scholar pointed out that Middle Plantation's position between two navigable creeks made it well suited to trade and that it was far enough inland to be safe from enemy invasion. With little deliberation, the assembly voted to abandon Jamestown and passed "An Act Directing the Building the Capitoll and the City of Williamsburgh." The 220 acre town site lay in both James City and York Counties and included acreage on College and Queens Creeks intended for development as inland ports: Princess Anne's Port (or College Landing) in James City and Queen Mary's Port (or Capital Landing) in York. Duke of Gloucester Street, which ran along a ridgeback that divided the drainages of the James and York Rivers and roughly separated James City and York Counties, formed the central axis of the town, which was to be laid out regularly into lots. Williamsburg was destined for success, for the spread of settlement inland was accompanied by steady population growth. Construction of the new capitol building was funded by a special tax on liquor, servants and slaves.[18]

Life in James City County at the Close
of the Seventeenth Century

Durand de Dauphine, a French Huguenot who visited Virginia during the late seventeenth century, said that "Jemston" (Jamestown) was the colony's only town and that most people lived on plantations of various sizes. He said that tobacco, not currency, commonly was used to purchase land, livestock, and commodities, such as clothing, hats, shoes, and wooden furniture. Farmers typically left about half of their land wooded and placed the remainder under cultivation. They rotated their crops every four years, converting tilled ground to pasture and vice-versa. According to Durand, Virginia farmers "do not know what it is to plough the land with cattle, but just make holes into which they drop the seeds." Most sowed wheat in late October or early November, planted corn in April, and transplanted tobacco in May. He said that most farmhouses were frame and were roofed over with narrow chestnut planking. The more affluent coated their dwellings' interior walls with mortar. Virginians, "whatever their rank," tended to build "only two rooms with some closets on the ground floor" and two rooms overhead in an attic. Many plantations had a detached kitchen, a tobacco house, and separate houses for servants and black slaves. Durand said that "when you come to the home of a person of some means, you think you are entering a fairly large village." Farmers allowed their cattle to roam in the woods, where wolves were kept

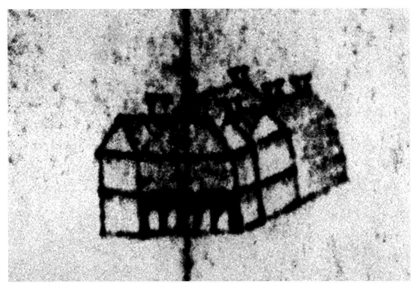

The Green Spring mansion, shown on John Soane's March 20, 1683, map of the Governor's Land, "Plan of Lord Culpeper's Estate on the James River, Virginia." Courtesy of the William Salt Library, Stafford, England, and the Library of Congress.

at bay by faithful dogs, and most livestock was allowed to roam free. Had he made a tour of rural James City County, he would have found large plantations intermingled with small and middling farms and a loosely defined network of roads that enabled local residents to communicate with each other and the outside world.

Durand spoke warmly of Virginia hospitality, for most people freely shared whatever they had with travelers. He described a wedding he attended, where the guests dined sumptuously upon meats of all kinds and quenched their thirst with beer, cider, and punch. The merrymakers smoked, sang, and danced the night away, until overtaken by a combination of drunkenness and fatigue. Another early writer, who attended a funeral feast, indicated that the mourners consumed 25 gallons of beer, 22 of hard cider, 5 of brandy, and 12 pounds of sugar, some of which undoubtedly was used in making punch.[19] The three James City County men, who prepared an official report on conditions in Virginia, said that by the 1690s most of the land east of the fall line had been patented. They claimed that the ancient headright system had been much abused, thanks to the submission of fraudulent documents to county courts, and that dishonest surveyors sometimes produced drawings of property they never visited or included more (or different) acreage than had been patented. Patentees were supposed to build a house upon their land within three years or place an acre or more under cultivation. But because a simple hog-pen met the ambiguous definition of minimum housing and a poorly tended acre of ground fulfilled planting requirements, many Virginians owned large tracts of land they never used. Perhaps for this reason, in 1705 the minimum requirements for seating land were strengthened and made more specific. Although officials in England continued to decry what they called a straggling mode of settlement, Virginia planters, who were hungry for new lands upon which to grow tobacco, kept expanding the colony's frontier.[20]

James City County Landmarks

Near the close of the seventeenth century James City County's official surveyor, John Soane, made plats of several local properties, some of which drawings survive. In 1681 he surveyed William Sherwood's landholdings on

Jamestown Island, one of which plats shows the site of "blockhouse hill," a slightly elevated piece of ground upon which Virginia's first colonists built a watchtower that enabled them to maintain surveillance over the isthmus and Back River. Another Soane plat, prepared in 1684, depicts Christopher Wormeley's 600 acres, part of the vast tract called Powhatan. In 1679 Lady Frances Berkeley hired Soane to survey a tract near Green Spring that she intended to lease to tenants.

The Governor's Land

John Soane's 1683 plat of the Governor's Land delimits the 3,000 acres set aside in 1619 for the support of the colony's incumbent governors. It also defines 16 lesser-sized parcels that in 1683 were in the hands of Governor Culpeper's tenants. Among those lessees were Sarah Drummond (widow of the executed rebel), Edward Challis, Thomas Easter, William Armiger, William Lord, John Tallent, Daniel Workman, John Hobson, Joseph Pettit, William and George Marable, William Wilkinson, William Sherwood, William Olister, James Bayley, and Thomas Rowse. Soane identified the sites upon which certain leaseholders' dwellings stood upon the Governor's Land and he showed the forerunner of Route 614, which extended toward Green Spring.[21]

Jamestown Island

Relocating the colony's capital to Middle Plantation irrevocably changed the course of Jamestown's history, for its importance as an urban community diminished almost immediately. Although some lot owners retained their property, the bulk of the island's acreage was absorbed into two large and important plantations that belonged to William Sherwood's heirs and those of Edward Travis I.

William Sherwood, an attorney with good connections in England, married the widow of Richard James, a well-to-do merchant and owner of nearly 200 acres in the western end of Jamestown Island. As the residence Sherwood shared with his wife and stepson was destroyed during Bacon's

Rebellion, he purchased a lot in the New Town and built a new brick house. During the early-to-mid 1680s, Sherwood continued to acquire land, in time amassing around 430 acres in the south-central and western portions of Jamestown Island. At his death in 1697, his widow married Edward Jaquelin, whose son-in-law eventually consolidated over 900 acres into what became known as the Ambler plantation.

Meanwhile, Edward Travis I, who in 1652 married the daughter and heiress of Ancient Planter John Johnson, patented 196 acres in the eastern end of the island near Black Point, consolidating a number of small tracts that were settled during the first quarter of the seventeen century. Travis continued to acquire land and by 1677 had accumulated more than 550 acres. The Travis plantation extended from Black Point westward to Kingsmill Creek and southward to Passmore Creek. In time, Edward Travis's descendants amassed more than 800 acres in the eastern and north-central part of Jamestown Island.[22]

Green Spring and Rich Neck

Lady Frances Berkeley, who inherited the Green Spring plantation, restored the mansion to habitable condition and rented it to two Virginia governors. In 1680 she married Philip Ludwell I, who around 1678 had inherited Rich Neck from his brother, Thomas. The couple made their home at Rich Neck. As they produced no living heirs, both properties descended to Philip Ludwell II, his son by a prior marriage. It was likely around 1693–1694 that the younger Philip moved from the family home at Rich Neck to Green Spring and made it his manor plantation. In 1697 he married Hannah Harrison, with whom he produced three children, one of whom was son and heir Philip Ludwell III.[23]

Powhatan

In 1684 Christopher Wormeley, who owned 660 acres called Powhatan on the south and east side of the Drinking Swamp (a branch of Powhatan Creek), had part of a nearly 2,300-acre tract that formerly belonged to Richard

Eggleston. In 1690 Wormeley bequeathed Powhatan to his son, William, who in 1695 patented another 700-plus acres on the east side of Powhatan Creek. Meanwhile, Richard Eggleston's son, Benjamin, in 1698 repatented the rest of his father's land on Powhatan Creek and enhanced its size by 300 acres. During the eighteenth century, Richard Taliaferro, who married Elizabeth Eggleston, developed part of the Eggleston property into a family seat called Powhatan.[24]

Kingsmill

Colonel Thomas Pettus, who in 1660 consolidated the Littletown and Utopia tracts into what became the eastern part of Kingsmill Plantation, left his property to his son, whose widow married James Bray II. Bray, like the Pettuses, was wealthy and influential and served as a burgess, county justice, and alderman of the city of Williamsburg.[25] Under his skillful management, the plantation prospered.

The Old Company Land Tract (Piney Grove)

In 1685 John Turner patented land that extended "from Chickahominy Gate [mouth] along Bridges Freeman's land to the ferry path." Turner's property and that of George Harvey abutted "Freeman's alias Chickahominy Path," the forerunner of Route 5. During the 1690s the Barretts patented acreage that lay inland, behind Freeman's landholdings. During the early eighteenth century, the Chickahominy ferry was moved to the Barretts' property and became known as Barretts Ferry.[26]

The Weldon Plantation

Samuel Weldon, a James City County justice and sheriff, who immigrated to Virginia around 1675, married Sarah Efford, heiress to several hundred acres of land approximately four miles west of Middle Plantation. Samuel and Sarah Weldon's son, Benjamin, inherited his maternal grandfather's land and developed it into what by the mid-eighteenth century was a relatively well known local landmark.[27]

Mount Folly and Taskinask

After the close of Bacon's Rebellion, Bryan Smith of Mount Folly and Taskinask became deeply indebted to Daniel Parke. As Smith used his plantations as collateral and was unable to repay his debt, in April 1689 both properties reverted to Parke, whose daughters inherited them. Later, son-in-law William Byrd II of Westover came into possession of Mount Folly and Taskinask by agreeing to accept Parke's assets and debts.[28]

Notes

1.   Henry Hartwell et al., THE PRESENT STATE OF VIRGINIA AND THE COLLEGE [1697] BY HENRY HARTWELL, JAMES BLAIR AND EDWARD CHILTON (Princeton, 1940), 20–23.

2.   McIlwaine, EXECUTIVE JOURNALS, I, 326–328, 409; II, 20, 310; LEGISLATIVE JOURNALS, I, 260, 263, 438, 463; Palmer, CALENDAR, I, 28; Hartwell et al., PRESENT STATE, 46–48; Neville, BACON'S REBELLION, 89.

3.   Hartwell et al., PRESENT STATE, 33–35, 40–44, 50, 52–53, 63–64; McIlwaine, EXECUTIVE JOURNALS, I, 315, 324; LEGISLATIVE JOURNALS, 194, 247; William G. Stanard et al., THE COLONIAL VIRGINIA REGISTER (Baltimore, 1965), 88; Daniel J. Boorstin, THE AMERICANS: THE COLONIAL EXPERIENCE (New York, 1958), 114–116.

4.   Hartwell et al., PRESENT STATE, 40–44; Stanard, REGISTER, 51; McIlwaine, EXECUTIVE JOURNALS, I, 356, 363; LEGISLATIVE JOURNALS, 118, 130, 142, 207; Sainsbury et al., CALENDAR, I, 38, 45.

5.   Hartwell et al., PRESENT STATE, 54–56.

6.   In 1704 the council met in western James City County at Colonel Henry Duke's home.

7.   McIlwaine et al., HOUSE OF BURGESSES, 1659–1693, 78, 245; 1695–1702, 36; McIlwaine, LEGISLATIVE JOURNALS, 93, 206; EXECUTIVE JOURNALS, I, 161–162.

8.   Hening, STATUTES, II, 143, 433–434; McIlwaine, EXECUTIVE JOURNALS, I, 57, 60, 140; LEGISLATIVE JOURNALS, 81, 111–112, 287; Hartwell et al., PRESENT STATE, 63–64.

9.   McCartney, "Apartheid," 73; McIlwaine, EXECUTIVE JOURNALS, I, 342.

10.   John W. Reps, TIDEWATER TOWNS IN COLONIAL VIRGINIA (Princeton, 1972), 66; Hening, STATUTES, II, 473.

11.   Sainsbury et al., CALENDAR, 10:341; 14:471–473; 15:584; Force, TRACTS, III:12:23; Ambler Manuscript No. 23; McIlwaine et al., HOUSE, 1695–1702, 20, 22, 24; McIlwaine, EXECUTIVE JOURNALS, I, 269; Hening, STATUTES, III, 59; Reps, TIDEWATER TOWNS, 86–87, 141.

12.   McIlwaine, EXECUTIVE JOURNALS, I, 517; William G. Stanard, "Genealogy," VIRGINIA MAGAZINE OF HISTORY AND BIOGRAPHY 36 (January 1928):100; York County Deeds, Orders, Wills 1687–1691:70–73.

13.   Sainsbury et al., CALENDAR, 1:21, 45; McIlwaine, EXECUTIVE JOURNALS, I, 520; York County Deeds, Orders, Wills 1687–1691:79, 118, 167, 205, 378; Deeds, Orders, Wills No. 10 (1694–1697):10, 185, 279.

14. McIlwaine, EXECUTIVE JOURNALS, I, 117, 187, 255, 275, 322, 331, 344, 349–350; B.P.R.O., C.O. 5/1308 f 150; Sainsbury et al., CALENDAR, 14:132, 517.

15. Perry, HISTORICAL COLLECTIONS, I, 14.

16. Hugh Jones, THE PRESENT STATE OF VIRGINIA (Chapel Hill, 1956), 5–7; Hartwell et al., PRESENT STATE, 1964:69–71; James D. Kornwolf, GUIDE TO THE BUILDINGS OF SURRY AND THE AMERICAN REVOLUTION (Surry, 1976), 33–37; Beverley, PRESENT STATE, 265.

17. McIlwaine et al., HOUSE OF BURGESSES, 1695–1702, 154, 160, 175, 198, 214; McIlwaine, EXECUTIVE JOURNALS, I, 392–393, 409–410; II, 40, 152–153, 432–433; LEGISLATIVE JOURNALS, 257, 262, 463; Sainsbury et al., CALENDAR, 18:92.

18. Jones, PRESENT STATE, 7, 190; Reps, TIDEWATER TOWNS, 141–142, 147–150; Waverley K. Winfree, THE LAWS OF VIRGINIA BEING A SUPPLEMENT TO HENING'S THE STATUTES AT LARGE, 1700–1750 (Richmond, 1971), 22.

19. Durand de Dauphine, A BRIEF DESCRIPTION OF AMERICA WITH A LONGER ONE OF VIRGINIA AND MARYLAND, Gilbert Chinard, trans. (New York, 1934), 107–111, 117–120, 138; Philip A. Bruce, SOCIAL LIFE IN VIRGINIA IN THE SEVENTEENTH CENTURY (Williamtown, 1907), 255. Durand's punch recipe required three jugs of beer, three jugs of brandy, three pounds of sugar and some nutmeg and cinnamon, all of which were mixed together and allowed to stand for a while.

20. Hartwell et al., PRESENT STATE, xvii–xviii, 16–20; Hening, STATUTES, III, 304–329.

21. John Soane, Survey for Thomas Lord Culpeper, 1683; Plott of 660 acres of land survey'd for Honble. Christopher Wormeley, 1684; Land for William Sherwood, 1681; The plott of 76 acres of land survey'd for Henry Jenkins, 1690.

22. Ambler Manuscript No. 7, 10, 14, 26, 34, 43_92, 142; Virginia Land Office Patent Book 3:8, 158; 7:228–229; James City County Land Tax Lists 1792.

23. Hening, STATUTES, II, 558–560; Lee Papers 1679–1685; Carson, BACON'S REBELLION, 6; Billings et al., COLONIAL VIRGINIA, 58. Thomas Ludwell came into possession of Rich Neck via Elizabeth Kemp Lunsford, who after Sir Thomas's death, married Robert Smith.

24. Soane, Wormeley, 1684; Jenkins 1690; Nugent, CAVALIERS, I, 160, 228, 294, 465; II, 4, 21. The Powhatan mansion was added to the National Register of Historic Places in 1970.

25. William M. Kelso, KINGSMILL PLANTATION (Orlando, 1984), 37, 39.

26. Nugent, CAVALIERS, II, 293, 371; Hening, STATUTES, III, 219, 471; McIlwaine, MINUTES, 619–621; Gary Parks, VIRGINIA LAND RECORDS (Baltimore, 1980), 256.

27. Nugent, CAVALIERS, I, 405; William G. Stanard, "Virginia Gleanings in England," VIRGINIA MAGAZINE OF HISTORY AND BIOGRAPHY 13 (July 1904):195–196. The Efford–Weldon property enveloped the land upon which the Williamsburg Memorial Park is located.

28. William Byrd Title Book, n.d. 128

C H A P T E R   6

"Labour Spread Her Wholesome Store"
1700–1750

Conducting the Business of Government

Despite the 1699 decision to make Middle Plantation the colony's capital, the transition was gradual. In December 1700 burgess William Leigh reported that many of the public records still were at Jamestown, awaiting removal to the College of William and Mary. Space there already had been assigned to the Secretary of the Colony and the Clerk of the House of Burgesses. Although the House and the Council of State began convening at the college, the General Court continued to meet regularly at Jamestown, perhaps in the accommodations used by the James City County Court. However, the General Court moved to Williamsburg as soon as the capitol building was ready for use.[1]

Mrs. Elizabeth Harrison, a James City County widow, asked the governor's council for an increase in the pension she received on behalf of her late husband, Benjamin, former treasurer of the colony. In 1718 Robert Goodrich, requested a patent for some land on Scotland Swamp, at the head of Checkerhouse Creek. The tract, which formerly belonged to John Smith of James City County, had escheated to the Crown. Goodrich was obliged to have the 170-acre parcel laid off by the county's official surveyor, Simon Jeffreys. Alexander Kerr of James City County sought to acquire some acreage on Warrany Creek, which he claimed was escheat land that Thomas

Green of Gloucester had had surveyed but failed to patent; investigation revealed, however, that the property Kerr wanted was "overplus" or excess acreage included in a neighboring patent that belonged to Robert Sorrell. Similarly, Samuel Woodward Sr. attempted to patent some land on the north side of Timber Swamp, acreage that was part of the Duke family's holdings.[2] These persistent attempts to claim land in Virginia's oldest settled area demonstrate that James City County real estate was considered very desirable, despite the seemingly limitless supply of land on the colony's frontier. One reason probably was the local soil's suitability for the production of sweet-scented tobacco, the most valuable and marketable type.

Because the laws of primogeniture were part of Virginia's legal code, property that descended to a primary heir was "entailed" or attached to the decedent's estate and descended from generation to generation. If an heir needed to dispose of entailed land or slaves (for example, to settle debts against the estate), he needed the assembly's consent to do so.[3] For example, in 1712, John and Frances Custis asked the House of Burgesses for permission to sell Mount Folly and Taskinask, plantations that had belonged to her late father, Daniel Parke, whose estate was encumbered by debt. Likewise, in 1732 Thomas Bray's heir requested the burgesses' permission to dispose of some entailed land in order to cover debts incurred by the decedent. On the other hand, heirs sometimes asked for an entail to be transferred from one piece of property to another of comparable or greater value. For instance, Charles Barham of Martin's Hundred sought to sell 50 acres of entailed marsh land between the Martin's Hundred road and Samuel Pond's acreage at the old churchyard, substituting a 400-acre tract he also owned.[4]

Throughout the first half of the eighteenth century Virginia's governing officials were obliged to deal with Native groups' interaction. In May 1700 the greatmen of the Nottoway, Meherrin, Nansemond, Chickahominy, Rappahannock, and Nanzattico Indians, which tribes were tributaries to the Crown, came to Jamestown to confer with the governor and council about a treaty they wanted to make with some Natives that lived outside of Virginia. The tributary leaders agreed to give the governor the wampum peake belts they would receive when the treaty was signed; he agreed to return the belts when they came to Jamestown to pay their next annual tribute. The government's symbolic show of authority served to remind the tributary Indians that they were subservient to the Crown. In September 1700 Thomas Monck was arrested by James City County's sheriff and jailed at Jamestown because he had spent a considerable amount of time with certain Indians above the fall line, who were suspected of committing some murders in Stafford County.[5] Conditions on the colony's lengthy frontier were unstable throughout the first half of the century.

During autumn 1700 approximately 170 French Protestant refugees arrived at Jamestown, having fled religious persecution in their Catholic homeland. They were supposed to proceed to the site of the old Manakin Indian town above the falls of the James River. However, because winter was coming on and the newcomers were impoverished and unfamiliar with "the customs of this country," they were allowed to disperse until the following year. In spring 1701 William Byrd II visited Manakin Town, where the refugees had laid out a small village and subdivided it into small farmsteads.[6]

Messages from on High

In February 1702 a comet spewed across the sky in a brilliant arc that passed from west-southwest to east-southeast, over Williamsburg. Sir Jeffrey Jeffreys reported that he saw "ye Tail . . . of a blazing star" about two hours after dusk on two consecutive nights. The comet, which he called a "hairy star," was "of ye color of ye Milky Way and of ye breadth of a Rainbow." Although Jeffreys had a scientific interest in the comet, many of his contemporaries viewed it as a religious omen, for they clung to the belief that "Blazing stars [were] messengers of God's Wrath." In 1759 a broadside warned sinners to repent and good Christians to stay indoors "when God is in this wise speaking from Heaven." The belief that shooting stars foretold disasters, such as wars and epidemics, was a deeply rooted tradition shared by much of the world's population.[7]

In 1703, four years after a decision was made to relocate the colony's capital and construction of a new statehouse already was underway at Middle Plantation, Queen Anne sent word that she wanted Jamestown rebuilt as the seat of government. The colony's officials, after much deliberation (and probably a certain amount of uneasiness) decided to inform the queen that they already had moved the capital. They covered their position by pointing out that she had failed to disallow the legislation authorizing the change. Another issue that arose was whether Jamestown would continue to send a representative to the colony's assembly, something to which Governor Nicholson was adamantly opposed. Although his viewpoint prevailed, in 1705 when Governor Edward Nott took office, representation was restored.[8]

Land Ownership and Development in James City County

A list of Virginia counties' quitrents, compiled in 1704 and sent back to England, reveals that 114,780 acres of James City County land were held by at least 284 individuals. However, the quitrent roll included the names of both landowners and leaseholders and some people's names (for example, for those who eluded the tax assessor) were missing altogether. Also, James City County in 1704 spanned both sides of the Chickahominy River, taking in some acreage that now lies within Charles City's borders, and it extended west of Diascund Creek but did not include the territory between Skimino and Ware Creeks. Tobacco collected in payment of James City County quitrents was offered for sale at auction, which revenues were used to pay public officials and other governmental expenses.[9]

In 1705 the criteria for seating newly patented land were defined more clearly. According to law:

. . . *the building of one house of wood, after the usuall manner of building in this colony, being at least in length 12 foot and in breadth 12 foot, and clearing, planting and tending at least one acre of ground [within three years] shall be and is hereby declared to be a good and sufficient seating and planting of land.*

In 1713 the legal definition of planting-and-seating was amplified. Those patenting land they deemed unfit for cultivation unless they improved the soil were given three years to build "one good dwelling house after the manner of Virginia building, to contain at least 20 ft. in length and 16 ft. in breadth, and to put thereon three cattle and six sheep or goats." Would-be patentees of arable land could secure its title by draining or clearing three acres of marsh or swamp out of every 50 acres they sought to acquire. Anyone claiming 50 acres of barren land could legitimize the title by maintaining three neat (dairy) cattle or six sheep or goats upon it, to enrich the soil. By 1720, anyone who cleared and fenced three out of 50 acres as pasturage or expended 10 pounds current money on constructing buildings or planting trees and hedges, fulfilled the minimum planting and seating requirements. How conscientiously these laws were obeyed or enforced is uncertain. Roving livestock continued to be a problem and in 1726 some of James City County's inhabitants sought passage of a law that would prohibit those who owned swine from allowing their animals to run at large "within 10 miles of the flowing of the tide."[10]

Throughout the mid-to-late seventeenth century and almost all of the eighteenth, ferries plied the James River from Jamestown Island to Gray's and Crouches Creeks in Surry County and from Archer's Hope to Hog Island. Ferries also crossed the Chickahominy at its mouth and at Cowles Ferry, near Diascund Creek. Further upstream, in the Chickahominy's narrows, were bridges that provided a direct link with Charles City County. In the vicinity of Providence Forge was Soanes (Soans) Bridge and still further west was a span known as the Long Bridge. The ferries that operated at Yorktown, at Skimino and Taskinask Creeks, and at West Point provided important links between the James-York and Middle Peninsulas. In time, inland transportation corridors became more sophisticated, fostering a more widely dispersed pattern of settlement. By the mid-eighteenth century a major thoroughfare ran up the James-York peninsula, following the track of a well-established horsepath. Scattered along the way, especially at crossroads, were taverns or ordinaries whose proprietors catered to the traveling public. Among these establishments were the well known taverns six, twelve, and sixteen miles west of Williamsburg and at ferry-landings on the James River. Mills, churches, stores, blacksmith shops, and other service-related facilities also served as focal points of community life. In western James City County, Captain Cowles' mill on Diascund Creek's tributary, Mill Creek, was one such important local landmark, whereas nearby Cowles Ferry, which landing was on the east side of Diascund Creek's mouth, would have brought travelers into the area. Mills also were situated on Grove, Mill (Jockey's Neck), Powhatan, Ware, and Skimino Creeks.[11]

Virginia's burgesses realized that shifting the capital from Jamestown to the new planned town at Middle Plantation would whet the appetite of real estate speculators. Therefore, the act establishing Williamsburg and its inland ports stipulated that no lots would be sold before October 20, 1700, "to the end that the whole country may have timely notice of this act and equal liberty in the choice of the lots." Anyone purchasing a lot in Williamsburg or one of its ports had to erect a building upon it within two years or forfeit the land. Structures within the town had to conform with certain specifications and setback rules.[12]

The earliest known development of acreage associated with College Landing dates to 1705, when John Holloway patented a small plot of James City County land, low ground upon which he already had erected a wharf. Holloway, who was speaker of the House of Burgesses and Public Treasurer, was described by John Randolph as a cunning, avaricious barrister who practiced law with more guile than erudition and used his influence to further his own means. For example, shortly after the House instituted a tobacco inspection system designed to regulate the quality and uniformity of Virginia tobacco, Speaker Holloway's newly-patented acreage at the College and Capitol Landings was chosen for the construction of official inspection warehouses. In 1750 Leonard Henley and William Browne of James City County were appointed tobacco inspectors for the warehouse at Hog Neck on the Chickahominy and Benjamin Eggleston, Thomas Cobbs, and Henry Tyler served as inspectors in the warehouses at Capitol and College Landings. The warehouse at College Landing was intended to serve James City County planters who lived along the James, from Skiffs Creek to the mouth of the Chickahominy River, but others were free to utilize its facilities. People who brought their hogsheads of tobacco to the College Landing warehouse could do business with the merchants, artisans, tavern-keepers, and others who had establishments there or they could make the short trek into Williamsburg. At College Landing, raw agricultural products were bought and sold and seagoing vessels arrived with merchandize from foreign ports. Charles Taliaferro, a Williamsburg carriage-maker, operated a popular tavern at College Landing and also had a brewhouse there.[13]

James City County Officials and Their Duties

In 1702, when Governor Francis Nicholson sent a detailed report to England, describing each county's attributes, he indicated that James City County encompassed four parishes (Wallingford, Wilmington, James City, and Martin's Hundred) and part of a fifth. James City Parish's rector, the Rev. James Blair, had the greatest number of parishioners. Sheriff Thomas Cowles, Philip Lightfoot, Henry Duke, Benjamin Harrison, Philip Ludwell, Michael Sherman, James Bray, Thomas Mountfort, Hugh Norvell, William Edwards, William Drummond, John Frasier, Dionisius Wright, John Geddis (Gaddis), and Henry Soane served as justices of the James City County Court, with John Lightfoot as county escheator and James Minge as surveyor. The clerk of the county court was Chickeley Corbin Thacker, who also was clerk of the General Court. The justices were drawn from various parts of the county, a tradition that endured. Shortly thereafter, Nicholson appointed Philip Ludwell as colonel of the county militia with John Frayser as lieutenant, Edward Jaquelin as coronet and Sheriff Thomas Mountfort as captain of the cavalry in the lower county. The James City County militia then consisted of 30 horsemen and 40 dragoons, and a minimum number of foot soldiers.[14]

In March 1701 the General Court reviewed and reversed a decision made by James City County's justices. County coroner and justice James Geddis confiscated Mrs. Lucy Doran's ferry-boat because her servant boy and ferryman, Thomas Lunton, overturned it and drowned. But the General Court decided to return Mrs. Doran's boat because she was a poor woman and the ferry was her primary means of support. In other action involving the James City County court, the General Court ordered its clerk to determine whether anyone was seated upon the Governor's Land whose lease hadn't been recorded and to compile a list of all leaseholders and the conditions upon which they held their property. The county sheriff was supposed to see that all such leases were entered into local court records. The clerk of court was to contact the brother and executor of James City County surveyor John Soane to determine whether there was a survey of the Governor's Land among his personal effects. Curiously, the missing survey made its way to England, where it ended up in the Staffordshire Record Office. John Soane's will, recorded in Henrico County in August 1699, reveals that he owned a James City County plantation called Poplar Spring, which he bequeathed to his brother, William. He left his surveying and mathematical instruments and his "books and papers thereto belonging" to his cousin, Henry Soane, a James City County justice.[15]

In 1702 local freeholders asked the House of Burgesses to make the Chickahominy River the dividing line between James City and Charles City Counties, but no decision was made. The issue resurfaced in 1710, but lay dormant for another decade. In 1720 the east side of Wallingford Parish, which straddled the Chickahominy River, was added to James City Parish and three years later, when Wilmington Parish (above Wallingford) was dissolved, its lower portion was appended to James City and its upper portion to Blisland. Typically, adjustments in parish boundary lines came in response to population growth or changes in its distribution. In 1724 when Virginia's clergy were asked to report upon conditions within their parishes, those of James City County said that there were no public schools although reading, writing, and arithmetic were taught in a few little schoolhouses. They also said that young paupers sometimes were made apprentices in crafts or trades.[16]

Public Holidays for Feasting or Fasting

When the House of Burgesses designated public holidays (holy-days), services usually were held in parish churches and the colonists were forbidden to perform "all Servile and bodily labour." In 1700 May 3rd was appointed a day of fasting and prayer "for delivering the colony from the great plague of caterpillars"; after the "plague" subsided, June 5, 1701, was designated a day of thanksgiving. August 13, 1701, and March 11, 1702, were solemnized as fast-days in anticipation of war with France and on April 23, 1702, the colonists marked the restoration of peace with a day of thanksgiving. A few months later, when war was declared, October 7th was designated a day of prayer and fasting. Besides observing special holidays in commemoration of military and political events, the colonists kept fast-days on which prayers were offered for relief from "pestilential and infectious sickness."

Sometimes, holidays also were established to mark significant occasions. For example, Governor Francis Nicholson, despite his intense dislike of Jamestown, apparently acknowledged its historical significance, for in an April 21, 1704, address to the General Assembly, he said he hoped to hold a centennial jubilee there in two years to commemorate the colony's first settlement.[17]

Updating the Colony's Laws

In 1705 Virginia's laws were summarized and updated to address the colony's changing needs. It was then that the so-called Black Code was formalized. This group of laws, which affected all non-whites, conferred upon enslaved blacks the status of personal property and made them chattels for life. It also deprived Indians of the legal rights they formerly had enjoyed. Ironically, this occurred at a time when the tributary Indians were making increased use of the colony's legal system rather than settling disputes on their own. Under the 1705 legal code, Indians and other non-whites were forbidden to testify in court under any circumstances, a prohibition that prevented them from collecting just debts. Likewise, Indian servants no longer could sue for their freedom if their masters detained them after their contract expired. Bans against inter-racial marriage made it illegal for ministers to unite whites and non-whites, thereby discouraging the Natives' assimilation into the white population. Those who married despite the law were fined and subject to six months imprisonment. Non-whites were ineligible to hold any public office (whether civil, ecclesiastical, or military) and if they dared to forcibly oppose a white Christian, they could be flogged. Thus, 1705 brought profound erosion of ethnic minorities' civil rights. A 1711 law required both tributary and non-tributary Indians who ventured into colonized areas to wear badges and three years later, a law was passed prohibiting the use of the titles "king" and "queen" in reference to Indian leaders.[18] These changes suggest that as Virginia's Indians became increasingly acculturated and assumed a more visible, but less forceful, role in society, and as they declined in population and strength, they became legally susceptible to the same types of discrimination to which blacks and other minorities were subjected.

One law the House of Burgesses enacted in 1705 specified that the General Court and county courts were the only judicial bodies that had authority in the colony. This probably was a reaction to Governor Howard's attempt to establish a chancery court. A 1705 act updated the 1691 town-founding legislation. All goods entering the colony were to be sold in one of the officially sanctioned port towns except servants, slaves, and salt. Each town was authorized to hold market days twice a week, have an annual fair, and establish a hustings court at which cases of less than 30 pounds sterling could be tried. Jamestown again was declared an official port. Its market days were Tuesdays and Saturdays and the annual fair was to be held from October 12th through 16th, excluding Sundays. In 1705 Jamestown was the only community that had representation in the House of Burgesses, although Williamsburg gained that privilege a few years later. During the late 1720s it was decided that the burgesses for Jamestown, Williamsburg and the College of William and Mary should be receive the same compensation as those representing counties.[19]

In 1706 the House of Burgesses agreed to allow James City's justices to salvage bricks from the old statehouse that had burned in 1698 so that they could use them to build a new county courthouse at Jamestown. In 1715, however, a few of James City County's justices asked Lt. Governor Alexander Spotswood to make Williamsburg the county seat. But a group of local citizens adamantly opposed the change and asked the House of Burgesses to see that the county court was "continued in the place where it formerly stood, or [was] settled at some Convenient place as near as may be to the Centre of the County." The same day they voiced their obligations, some of the county's justices asked the House to allow them to meet in the newly-built statehouse; however, because the capitol building lay within the bounds of York County, the petition was rejected. George Marable, a James City County burgess and Jamestown property owner, submitted a petition to Spotswood in which he contended that Williamsburg was an inconvenient location for the county seat. The testy Spotswood took umbrage at Marable's tone and declared that he was "as good a Judge as Mr. Marable's Rabble" when it came to selecting a suitable site! Sometime after 1715, but before 1721, a James City County Courthouse was erected in Williamsburg at the corner of Francis and England Streets. The city and county shared the building for more than 20 years "on courtesie." In 1734 James City County's sheriff was authorized to summon juries from all parts of Williamsburg, not merely that portion which lay within the county's bounds.20

Military Defense

In 1700 the governor and council decided that the great guns at Jamestown should be spiked to prevent them from being used by an enemy. Two years later, when England and France were at war, Virginia's governing officials grew uneasy about the prospect of foreign invasion and took steps to shore up the colony's defenses. A shipment of newly arrived military stores was placed in the old magazine at Jamestown, despite the site's vulnerability. Although some arms and ammunition were moved to Williamsburg for safekeeping, a supply of "great Shott" was kept at Jamestown, buried in the ground. When the burgesses learned that the French were establishing a military power-base in the West Indies, they recommended that Jamestown be fortified and "made so strong, considering the natural advantages of its situation, that no naval force of an enemy could pass by it" to plunder the colony's shipping. Spotswood and his council agreed and platforms were built at Jamestown and at Gloucester Point so that guns from the ships seeking protection could be used to form a battery. A vessel was stationed upstream from each battery, to prevent enemy ships from eluding its guns. Spotswood believed that Jamestown's natural setting made it almost impervious to an overland attack. He also felt that because the river's channel ran so near the shore, it would be next to impossible for a ship to avoid the battery's guns.21

Although the French threat subsided for a time, by August 1711 tensions had increased to the point that some new defensive measures were deemed necessary. A sloop was stationed at Capes Henry and Charles to signal the approach of enemy ships and beacons were placed at strategic sites along the major rivers. If the beacons at Jamestown and Yorktown were lit and two cannon shots were heard, all other beacons were to be set ablaze to alert Tidewater's militia units that an invasion had occurred. A line battery for 16 cannon was raised at Jamestown "and a line [was] cast up for covering the same from the James River to Back Creek." Lines also were laid out from

Back Creek to Archers Hope, and from there to Queens Creek, so that palisades could be erected if it became necessary to defend Williamsburg.
William Byrd II of Westover sent down 2,000 palisades for use in protecting
Jamestown and Williamsburg, and a Surry man sought payment for "500 pal-
lisadoes delivered to the fortification at Jamestown." During August and
September 1711 Spotswood made six trips to Jamestown to examine the line
battery there. On October 15, 1711, he informed Lord Dartmouth that he had
had forts armed with cannon built on the colony's major rivers, "not finding
at my arrival such a thing as either Parapet, Pallisade or one single piece of
ordnance mounted throughout the whole Government." But despite
Spotswood's claims, the Rev. John Fontaine, who visited Jamestown in 1716,
found only "a small rampart with embrasures remained . . . which was
deserted and gone to ruin," plus "a church, a Court House, and three or four
brick houses" that were somewhat deteriorated. The courthouse Fontaine
mentioned would have been James City County's.[22]

James City County's New Seat

In 1717 the citizens of Williamsburg asked the assembly for a charter of
incorporation, but action was deferred. Five years later, when the request was
resubmitted, it was approved. Williamsburg, as an incorporated city, was
entitled to a mayor, recorder, six alderman, and a dozen common councilmen.
The first city officials, who were appointed, had the right to choose their successors. The mayor, aldermen, and recorder were to serve as justices, who
convened monthly as a hustings court. Williamsburg could have up to two
weekly market days (Wednesdays and Saturdays) and two fairs a year, on
December 12 and April 23. Taxes on livestock and commodities that were
sold during market days were intended to underwrite the cost of city government, at least in part. Commencing in 1734 the justices of James City and
York Counties were required to levy taxes toward the support of
Williamsburg's sergeant and constable. In 1739 several local residents began
offering bounties and prizes to those who won races and other contests held
during Williamsburg's December fair, a wintertime event with traditionally
poor attendance.[23]

Williamsburg's Hustings Court earned a reputation for rendering swift justice and in 1734 it gained the right to try all cases of minor indebtedness, whether or not the debt was contracted in the city. The three-to-four months turn-around time for such cases made Williamsburg's Hustings Court very popular with litigants from other jurisdictions. The complaints of masters, servants, and apprentices also could be heard and people arraigned on capital offences made a preliminary appearance there before going on to the General Court. In 1745 city officials acquired William Levingston's old playhouse on Palace Green so that they could hold "Common Halls and Courts of Hustings." Strange as it may seem, balls were held in the James City County courthouse from time to time, just as gala affairs were given in the capitol.[24] In 1747 the new capitol building burned. Afterward, the government records stored there, which were "so carelessly kept" that they were "broken, interrupted and deficient . . . and lie in such a confused and jumbled state (at least the most ancient of them) being huddled together in single leaves and sheets in books out of the binding," were gathered up and sorted. A year later, a public records office was built. While the capitol was unusable, the assembly convened in the main building of the college. During the 1747 smallpox epidemic in Williamsburg, James City County's justices held court in Jamestown.[25]

Legislation and Litigation

A law the House of Burgesses enacted in 1705 made it illegal for horse owners to allow their animals to intrude upon ground enclosed by fences, hedges, and ditches of various types. The measure was undertaken to promote the breeding of superior livestock. The burgesses also established a ferry route from College Landing to Hog Island. The ferry-keeper, whose rates were set by law, had the right to operate a tavern at the landing. To the east of College Creek, at Higgenson's (or Burwell's) Landing, was another ferry to Hog Island. Both ferries were still in use at the close of the eighteenth century. By 1718 the public ferry at the mouth of the Chickahominy River had been shifted somewhat inland from Freeman's Point, to the Barretts' property. From Jamestown Island, ferries traversed the James River to Crouches Creek and Swann's Point, both of which routes were in continuous use through the 1760s. A ferryman plying an expanse of open water was required to use "a substantial flat-bottomed boat" at least 15 feet long for the conveyance of horses and a 12- to 13-foot long "foot-boat" for passengers, attended by three men. In 1738 another measure was undertaken to make travel easier. Local surveyors of public roads were required to erect wooden or stone signposts at crossroads to point the way to important communities.[26]

In-fighting among James City County's justices came to the attention of the General Court in 1702 and three years later, Thomas Cowles resigned his position because of the abuse he purportedly received from fellow justice James Bray. Other local matters were aired before the General Court. Colonel Philip Lightfoot requested clemency on behalf his male slave, who was to receive 31 lashes at the county court's whipping post, and in 1707 the General Court made provisions for the orphans of Henry Nicholson, a James City County suicide victim. Twelve local men served as jurors when six Tuscarora Indians were tried for killing a New Kent County man.[27]

In March 1710 some slaves from James City and York Counties were jailed for conspiring to rebel on Easter Sunday. The plot also involved black and Indian slaves in Surry and Isle of Wight Counties. The local slaves who were implicated belonged to the Rev. James Blair (the owner of Jockey's Neck), Philip Ludwell (who had Green Spring, Rich Neck, Indigo Dam, the Hot Water tract and several other properties), and Edward Jaquelin, George Marable, Edward Ross, and John Brodnax, all of Jamestown Island. Ludwell asked the governor to release his men from jail because "of ye danger of catching cold this sickly time." Although most of the accused James City blacks eventually were released into the custody of their owners "to receive correction," Jamy (a Brodnax slave) and Essex (a Ross slave) were detained.[28]

In 1710, when the burgesses updated the colony's legal code, a law was passed that affected several local landowners. All mill owners whose dams served as the bed of a public road had to see that they were at least 10 feet in breadth. This would have applied to mill dams in several parts of James City County, including those spanning Powhatan, Mill, Skimino, Ware, and Diascund Creeks. Other new laws altered somewhat the procedural conduct of local courts. County justices had to take an oath of office in which they promised "to do equal right to the poor and to the rich" and to use their "cunning, wit and power" in accord with the law. For the first time they had to promise not to accept bribes or try cases in which they had a personal interest. Local court justices were empowered to try all cases except capital crimes and outlawry and a solitary justice of the peace could hear civil cases that involved less than 20 shillings. James City County's court convened on the second Monday of every month. The justices had to meet until all business was conducted. Before adjournment could occur, the minutes of the session had to be read and signed by the senior-most justice in the group. In 1710 James City County's justices were scolded by Spotswood and his council for failing to collect the annual levy that paid high ranking public officials' salaries. The lieutenant governor not only got angry, he got even! He exercised his right to dismiss the incumbent justices, appointed new ones, swore them in, and then ordered them to collect the taxes.[29]

In 1714 when Virginia's governing officials updated their superiors in England about conditions in the colony, they reported that James City County had 1,535 tithables and that quitrents were paid on 117,337 acres of land. Four parishes lay wholly or partially within James City County: James City, Wallingford, Wilmington, and Bruton. William Marston was the incumbent county sheriff and Thomas Cowles, John Geddis, and David Bray served as coroners. George Marable and Henry Soane Jr. represented James City County in the House of Burgesses and Edward Jaquelin appeared on behalf of Jamestown. William Robertson served as clerk of the county court and Simon Jeffreys as the official surveyor. James City County had three tobacco warehouses, which principal agent was burgess Henry Soane Jr. In accord with the duties of office, he and tobacco inspector Edward Jaquelin were furnished with scales and weights imported from England.[30]

The Tempo of Daily Life

The Rev. Hugh Jones, who immigrated to Virginia in 1717, was rector of the church at Jamestown, chaplain to the General Assembly, and a professor at the College of William and Mary. Between 1722 and 1724 he wrote a descriptive account of life in the colony. He said that in Williamsburg, near

Bruton Parish Church, was a large octagonal tower that served as the magazine or repository of arms and ammunition. It stood "far from any house except James Town [James City County] Court-House, for the town is half in James Town County and half in York County." Williamsburg was a market town and a rich array of goods was available in local stores. The townspeople were neat and fashionably dressed, there was an abundance of artisans, and "the servants here, as in other parts of the country, are English, Scotch, Irish, or Negroes." Williamsburg had some brick dwellings but most were frame. In the countryside, houses were distributed randomly, sometimes in clusters of two or three, but more often half-a-mile or more apart. Jones observed that gentlemen's houses often were built of brick, although some had handsome frame dwellings. The kitchen usually was separate from the main house because of the summer heat.[31]

Real estate advertisements that appeared in the VIRGINIA GAZETTE during the 1730s and '40s suggest that approximately 90 percent of the dwellings in Tidewater Virginia were of frame construction. The smallest measured only 12 feet by 16 feet and was situated upon a 890-acre plantation, whereas the largest measured 25 feet by 30 feet, had a brick chimney and a bricked cellar, and was on a 600-acre tract. The average house enclosed only 420 square feet. All of the James City County farms offered for sale had domestic complexes that included a main house, outbuildings (such as kitchens, tobacco houses, hen-houses, dairies, smokehouses, and barns) and slave quarters.[32] This pattern of development seems to have been evident throughout Tidewater Virginia.

According to the Rev. Hugh Jones, James City County was "nicely adapted for sweet scented or the finest tobacco" and had an abundance of tidal creeks, near which planters preferred to build their homes. When farmers needed to convert forested land into fields for agriculture, they cut down trees "about a yard from the ground" and then hoed the earth between the stumps, using it for planting. Jones said that soil exhausted by successive crops of tobacco was capable of bearing Indian corn, English wheat, and other crops. Indian corn was the colonists' staple crop, which they used to make bread, cakes, mush, and hominy. It also served as an excellent livestock feed and its blades and tops, when well cured, made good fodder. Hogs usually were allowed to run at large to forage for roots in the marshes and woods. Jones said that the quality of Virginia's beef and veal was excellent and its pork was famous (especially bacon and hams), but lamb and mutton generally were not well liked. There was an abundance of wild geese and ducks, fish (including sheepshead, rock, trout, drum, and sturgeon), and shellfish (oysters and crabs), but venison was less plentiful in Tidewater than it formerly had been. Mulberry and fruit trees reportedly flourished but had a relatively short life cycle.

Many Virginians made their apples into cider, which they drank liberally, but the most commonly consumed beverage was water, which was abundant almost everywhere. Virginia planters sometimes made a beverage from persimmons and produced beer from molasses. According to Jones, some people raised barley and made malt, whereas others imported theirs. The most common imported malt-drink was Bristol beer, which was consumed in large quantities the year around. But wine, arrack, brandy, rum, and punch were the preferred beverages and "the common sort, when they drink in a hurry," consumed drams of rum or brandy. Madeira, Jones said, was Virginia's most popular wine, for it relieved the heat of summer and warmed "the chilled blood in the bitter colds of winter." More affluent Virginians consumed French and other European wine (especially claret and port) and chocolate, coffee, and tea were popular non-alcoholic beverages.

The Reverend Jones said that Virginia planters and native-born blacks were articulate and conversant on many subjects. White servants made up a substantial segment of Virginia's population and fell into one of three categories: those who were indentured, hired workers, and convicts or forced labor. Indentured servants, upon being freed, sometimes rented land, hired on as farm managers, or followed a trade they knew. Virginia farmers, in Jones' opinion, led relatively easy lives, for they relegated the bulk of their labor to servants and slaves. They enjoyed horse-racing, cock-fighting, and socializing. They also liked traveling about on horseback, although most roads ran down ridge-backs and often it was necessary to detour around the head of creeks. Jones considered public ferries dangerous, thanks to "sudden storms, bad boats, or unskillful or willful ferry-men . . . especially if one passes in a boat with horses." He added that his brother died in an accident while using the Chickahominy Ferry.[33]

Pinewoods. Photo by Nan Maxwell.

The observations of the Rev. Devereux Jarratt, a native of eastern New Kent County, provide a somewhat different perspective on life in mid-eighteenth-century Virginia. Jarratt, who was a carpenter's son, said that his family, which was of middling means, "always had plenty of plain food and raiment, wholesome and good, suitable to their humble station." Their food was "altogether the produce of the farm or plantation, except a little sugar, which was rarely used," and their clothing (with the exception of hats and shoes) was homemade. Jarratt said that meat, bread, and milk "was the ordinary food of all my acquaintance" and that his family "made no use of tea or coffee for breakfast or at any other time." His family looked upon "gentle folks" as "beings of a superior social order" who were easily recognized because they usually wore wigs. He said that if he "saw a man riding the road near our house, with a wig on, it would so alarm my fears . . . I would run off, as for my life." Jarratt indicated that his parents' greatest ambition was to teach their children to read, write, and do arithmetic. At the age of eight or nine he was sent to a local school, where he learned to read and "write a sorry scrawl." Jarratt's early religious training came from the Rev. David

Rural life. Courtesy of Dover Publications.

Mossom of St. Peter's Parish, who reportedly was such "a poor preacher" that he aroused his congregation only when he erupted into violent outbursts. Mossom also preached in James City County, for he was one-time rector of Blisland Parish.[34]

Edward Kimber, an English tourist, shared Jarratt's view that only "the very elevated Sort" of Virginians wore wigs. In 1736 he noted that "few [ordinary] Persons wear Perukes, so that you would imagine they were all sick or going to bed. Common People wear Woollen and Yarn Caps, but the better ones wear white Holland or Cotton. . . . It may be cooler, for ought I know, but methinks 'tis very ridiculous." He also said that Virginia planters were great horsemen "and have so much Value for the Saddle, they'd run eight miles to catch their horses rather than ride five miles to church. Churchyards, in his opinion, typically "look'd like the Out-Skirts of a Country Horse Fair." Kimber described Williamsburg as "a most wretched contriv'd Affair for the Capital of a Country" and said that "there is nothing considerable in it but the College, the Governor's House and one or two more." He expressed his preference for Jamestown, Hampton, and some of the other towns he'd seen.[35]

The Powhatan Plantation manor house. Photo by Ralph Maxwell.

Legal Issues Affecting James City County

In December 1720 the freeholders of James City and Charles City Counties again asked the House of Burgesses to make the Chickahominy River the dividing line between the two counties. The burgesses agreed and in 1721 the new boundary became official. It was shortly thereafter that Wilmington Parish was dissolved and its land was assigned to parishes in the neighboring counties. At least twice during the 1720s statistical reports sent to England listed the number of tithables in James City County and the names of local officials. The county was described as producing oronoco or sweet-scented tobacco, the most valuable type.36

The link between church and state remained tightly forged until after the American Revolution. In 1733 the vestry of Blisland Parish ordered William Browne, former churchwarden of the defunct Wilmington Parish, to surrender its communion silver so that it could be used in Blisland Parish's new

A dependency at Kingsmill Plantation. Photo by Ralph Maxwell.

Lower Church, Hickory Neck. Browne refused to do so and the matter eventually ended up in court. Even after the disestablishment of the State Church, Blisland's vestry sought the aid of the county sheriff in collecting church taxes that were in arrears.[37]

In 1734, while burgess Edward Jaquelin controlled much of the western end of Jamestown Island and had a leasehold in the adjoining mainland, some of the old capital's freeholders petitioned the House for funds to pay for stabilizing the river banks at Sandy Bay, where the James and Back Rivers converged. They noted that in recent years there had been "such great breaches between the river and creek at Sandy Bay that it is now so dangerous to pass." Even so, the funding request was denied and erosion continued unchecked. Two years later, the petitioners informed the House that the road crossing the isthmus, providing access to the ferry to Swann's Point, was so badly eroded that the tide regularly inundated it. Again, the petitioners' request for funds was turned down. In 1748 local citizens again complained about the eroding isthmus and ferry road. This time, they asked that Richard

Ambler (who by then owned the Jaquelin plantation and leasehold) be required to repair the causeway or lose his right to operate the ferry. They added that "several responsible freeholders" had offered to do so if the ferry-landing were moved to their lots in Jamestown. Ambler, who was highly influential, protested and the ferry stayed where it was.[38]

In 1748, when the assembly convened, county justices were authorized to appoint inspectors for pork, beef, flour, tar, pitch, and turpentine. A new law made it illegal "to cast corpses in the rivers and creeks," for the masters of slave ships frequently threw the dead overboard "to the annoyance of the adjacent inhabitants." Another law that reeks of cruelty made it legal to dismember slaves "going abroad at night or running away and staying out," unless they already had been disciplined by another authority.[39]

Well Known Local Properties

Green Spring and Rich Neck

By 1716 Philip Ludwell II owned and occupied Green Spring. Lt. Governor Spotswood's animosity toward him was so great that he asserted a legal claim to 500 acres of the plantation, contending that it was part of the Governor's land. Ludwell's attorney in England won the case, for he demonstrated that the James River was steadily eroding the Governor's Land and that if another 500 acres were taken from Green Spring, his client would lose possession of the mansion and other buildings Sir William Berkeley had erected there. Ludwell, like his father and step-mother, Lady Frances Berkeley, leased part of his plantation to tenants, two of whom were Richard Goodrich and Edward Hooker. Ludwell sold 100 acres of Rich Neck to his brother-in-law, the Rev. James Blair, who lived there until his wife's death in 1713.

When Philip Ludwell II died in January 1727, his 11-year-old son, Philip, was his primary heir. Six months before Philip Ludwell III came of age, he hastily wed Frances Grymes of Morratico. They lived at the Green Spring mansion and following in his father's footsteps, treated Rich Neck as a subsidiary farm. Philip Ludwell III served as a burgess and member of the Council of State. He also was an avid horticulturist and was keenly involved in Green Spring's farming operations. He cultivated citrus fruit and exotic plants and exchanged specimens with Thomas Jefferson, Henry Lee of Leesylvania, and other prominent Virginians. After Frances Grymes Ludwell died, Philip and his daughters moved to London and entrusted his landholdings to farm manager Cary Wilkinson. Among the properties under Wilkinson's care were Green Spring, Rich Neck, Indigo Dam, the Hot Water plantation, the Powhatan Mill, and the Mill Quarter.[40]

Powhatan

Sometime after 1701, William Wormeley inherited his father's 660 acres called Powhatan, which he supplemented with another 700-plus acres. Later, 375 acres of his Powhatan property came into the hands of Edward Jaquelin of Jamestown Island. Jaquelin, who died in 1739, conveyed his acreage at Powhatan to his spinster daughter, Martha, who sometime prior to 1766 sold it to her brother-in-law, Richard Ambler. Meanwhile, Benjamin Eggleston, whose forebears had owned the bulk of Powhatan since the mid-seventeenth century, divided it between his sons, Joseph and Benjamin Jr. Although Joseph Eggleston took up residence upon his share of Powhatan, Benjamin Jr.'s acreage descended to his wife and daughter, both of whom were named Elizabeth. During the 1740s, daughter Elizabeth and her husband, Richard Taliaferro, a highly skilled architect, built a brick residence upon the property she inherited, the restored Georgian mansion that still survives.[41]

Kingsmill

James Bray II, having married Thomas Pettus's widow and purchased the legal interests of his heirs, accumulated 3,500 acres of James City County land. In 1725 he bequeathed his plantation called Littletown to his grandson, James Bray III, who assumed control of the property as soon as he matured. A plantation ledger book maintained from 1736 to 1744 reveals that Littletown flourished under James Bray III's skillful management. He grew large quantities of tobacco with slave labor, had a water-powered gristmill, and was involved in a variety of industrial activities, such as tanning, shoemaking, brickmaking, and the manufacture of lumber products. Cider also was produced for sale commercially. James III's widow, Frances, and his sister, Elizabeth Bray Johnson, inherited Littletown at his decease. Mrs. Johnson received the western part of the property, which contained the Bray family home, whereas the widowed Frances Bray was assigned the eastern part of the tract, called Utopia. Later, Frances Bray married her neighbor, Lewis Burwell IV, who resided upstream at Kingsmill. At the close of the eighteenth century, the Burwells reunited Littletown and Utopia, which they consolidated with their landholdings at Kingsmill.

Lewis Burwell IV's great-grandfather, Lewis I, came to the colony during the 1650s and quickly rose to wealth and prominence. His son, Lewis II, purchased the Harrop plantation and Farley's Neck. By 1734 Lewis Burwell III, who had inherited his father's property, was residing in a mansion in Farley's Neck. He was a county justice, burgess, and the Upper James River District's naval officer, positions that would have enabled him to enhance his income. At Burwell's Landing at Kingsmill were a warehouse and tavern and a ferry that ran to Hog Island. Lewis Burwell III's land descended to his son, Lewis IV, as did his public offices. Through Lewis IV's marriage to James Bray III's widow, Frances, he expanded his family's landholdings in the county to nearly 2,800 acres. Like most well-to-do planters, Burwell employed overseers to manage his various properties.[42]

Carter's Grove

Sometime prior to 1723 Robert "King" Carter of Corotoman purchased approximately 1,400 acres of land in the extreme eastern end of James City County, in Martin's (or Merchants) Hundred. Carter was motivated by a desire to provide for his widowed daughter, Elizabeth, and grandson, Carter Burwell. Robert Carter's plantation account books indicate that he took an active role in managing his landholdings but employed overseers to handle routine matters.

In 1738, when Carter Burwell attained his majority and took control of the land he had inherited from his grandfather, he married Lucy Grymes of Brandon, in Middlesex County. During the early 1740s Burwell began construction of the stately brick mansion that today attracts visitors from around the world. His ledger books list the sums expended for building materials and hiring skilled craftsmen, such as bricklayers, carpenters and blacksmiths, and the artisans who finished the mansion's interior. Burwell's ledgers list the quantities of wheat and corn produced on his James City County farms and shed light upon how he provided for his slaves. Burwell sold beef to the governor's wife and supplied wheat, pork, veal, and mutton to the College of William and Mary and some Williamsburg tavern-keepers. After Carter Burwell's death in 1756, his plantation descended to his five-year-old son, Nathaniel, who took possession of the property in 1771.[43]

Mount Folly, Taskinask and Skimino Mill

Perhaps one of James City County's most colorful figures was Daniel Parke, who owned Mount Folly, Taskinask and the Skimino Mill and was wed to Philip Ludwell I's daughter, Jane. Parke, a burgess and councilor, was described by his contemporaries as quick-tempered, arrogant, and adulterous. His will, which named his legitimate and illegitimate offspring as heirs, suggests that he boldly eschewed conventional morality. In 1704 Parke was appointed governor of the Leeward Islands and on December 7, 1710, he was murdered by a group of insurgents during a riot in the streets of St. John, Antigua. At Parke's death, his James City County property descended to his daughters, Frances (the wife of John Custis) and Lucy (who was married to William Byrd II of Westover).

Byrd struck a bargain with the Custis couple, whereby he assumed ownership of the entire Parke estate along with liability for its debts. It was a bargain he lived to regret, for he had underestimated Parke's indebtedness. He was obliged to dispose of many valuable assets, including the Skimino Mill, which he sold to Quaker minister James Bates of York County. William Byrd II entrusted Mount Folly and Taskinask to the care of an overseer and later left the plantations to his daughter Wilhimena. She and her husband, Thomas Chamberlayne, gradually disposed of the entailed land she had inherited and some time prior to 1759, sold Mount Folly to Stephen Bingham, whose son still owned it at the close of the Revolutionary War.[44]

Jamestown Island

Edward Jaquelin immigrated to Virginia at the close of the seventeenth century and married Rachel James Sherwood, a wealthy widow who may have been many years his senior. She had outlived two previous husbands, Richard James and William Sherwood, and held life-rights to their property. The Sherwood dwelling at Jamestown often was used for meetings of the Council of State, the General Court, and the House of Burgesses. In 1704 Jaquelin, a merchant, purchased property on Jamestown Island from Sherwood's reversionary heir. As early as 1700 Jaquelin requested compensation for the council's use of the Sherwood dwelling. He continued to add to his landholdings and purchased 24 acres at Glass House Point and a half-acre waterfront lot in Jamestown. After Rachel James Sherwood Jaquelin died, Edward married Martha Cary of Warwick County with whom he had children. He continued to reside at Jamestown, which he represented in the House of Burgesses, and he served as a justice of the James City County court. When Edward Jaquelin died in November 1739, having outlived his wife and sons, he bequeathed life-rights to his Jamestown Island landholdings and leasehold in the mainland to his son-in-law, Richard Ambler. He also left him outright ownership of a two-acre lot on the west side of Orchard Run's mouth.

Richard Ambler, within a few years, consolidated several Jamestown Island parcels into an aggregate that he developed into a family seat. In January 1745 he purchased nearly 300 acres from Christopher Perkins, and then in April, procured a quit-claim deed to the Jaquelin property from his wife's sisters, Edward Jaquelin's reversionary heirs.[45] Richard Ambler's consolidation of the Perkins and Jaquelin landholdings enabled him to amass slightly more than 698 acres of land that enveloped almost all of Jamestown Island's frontage on the James River. The Travis plantation, meanwhile, encompassed the northeastern part of the island.

The Neck O' Land

In September 1744 Mann Page Jr., the son of Mann Page of Rosewell, asked the House of Burgesses to dock the entail on part of his late father's land so that he could settle the decedent's debts. One of the tracts Page wanted to sell was 1,700 acres in the Neck O' Land near Jamestown Island. In 1752 Robert Carter purchased the Neck O'Land plantation and later, it came into the hands of William Holt, who later sold it to William Allen of Claremont. Allen's heirs retained it until the late nineteenth century.[46]

Notes

1. McIlwaine, EXECUTIVE JOURNALS, II, 46, 62, 118, 517.

2. Sainsbury et al., CALENDAR, I, 194; Simon Jeffreys, Survey for Robert Goodrich, last day of July, 1714; McIlwaine, EXECUTIVE JOURNALS, IV, 100, 129, 191, 204; V, 216.

3. This was known as "docking" an entail.

4. Winfree, LAWS, 60–61, 367–368, 381.

5. Sainsbury, CALENDAR, 18:79; McIlwaine, EXECUTIVE JOURNALS, II, 104.

6. Sainsbury, CALENDAR, 18:620.

7. Sir Jeffrey Jeffreys to Mr. William Blaithwayt, February 25, 1701/02 letter; John L. McKnight, Comets, WILLIAM AND MARY (Williamsburg, summer 1985):32.

8. McIlwaine, EXECUTIVE JOURNALS, I, 323, 330; Sainsbury et al., CALENDAR, 21:285, 310–311, 552, 655, 761; 22:625–626.

9. Wertenbaker, PLANTERS; McIlwaine, EXECUTIVE JOURNALS, II, 408; III, 74.

10. Hening, STATUTES, I, 313; IV, 81; V, 424–425; McIlwaine, LEGISLATIVE JOURNALS, 709.

11. John Henry, "Virginia," 1770; Joshua Fry and Peter Jefferson, "A Map of the Most Inhabited Part of Virginia . . . ," 1755; Nugent, CAVALIERS, III, 192.

12. Hening, STATUTES, III, 423–428.

13. Nugent, CAVALIERS, III, 174; William Maxwell, VIRGINIA HISTORICAL REGISTER, 2:199–122; Hening, STATUTES, IV, 267; McIlwaine, EXECUTIVE JOURNALS, V, 328, 331; Dixon's VIRGINIA GAZETTE, June 3, 1775; November 27, 1779. College Landing was added to the National Register of Historic Places in 1976.

14. Louis des Cognets, comp., ENGLISH DUPLICATES OF LOST VIRGINIA RECORDS (Baltimore, 1981), 2; McIlwaine, EXECUTIVE JOURNALS, II, 132, 135; LEGISLATIVE JOURNALS, 326.

15. Henrico County Deeds and Wills 1654–1737:145; McIlwaine, EXECUTIVE JOURNALS, II, 131, 149–150; Hening, STATUTES, III, 112, 220.

16. Hening, STATUTES, III, 220; McIlwaine, LEGISLATIVE JOURNALS, 354, 496; Winfree, LAWS, 194; McIlwaine, LEGISLATIVE JOURNALS, 691, 700–701; William S. Perry, comp.HISTORICAL COLLECTIONS RELATING TO THE AMERICAN COLONIAL CHURCH (New York, 1969), I, 645.

17. McIlwaine et al., HOUSE OF BURGESSES, 1702–1712, 43–44; George Brydon, VIRGINIA'S MOTHER CHURCH (Richmond, 1947), 239–240. However, Nicholson had left the colony by 1705 and there is no evidence that a celebration was held.

18. Hening, STATUTES, III, 251, 298, 449–459; McIlwaine, EXECUTIVE JOURNALS, II, 286, 365.

19. Hening, STATUTES, III, 236, 267, 302, 415; McIlwaine, LEGISLATIVE JOURNALS, 769.

20. McIlwaine et al., HOUSE OF BURGESSES, 1702–1712, 204; William H. Gaines, "The Courthouses of James City County," VIRGINIA CAVALCADE, vol. 18, no. 4:23, 26–27; Palmer, CALENDAR, I, 169; Robert M. Barrow, WILLIAMSBURG AND NORFOLK, MUNICIPAL GOVERNMENT AND JUSTICE IN COLONIAL VIRGINIA, (Williamsburg, 1967), 61–62.

21. McIlwaine, EXECUTIVE JOURNALS, II, 64, 90, 124, 208; III, 40, 56, 95–99, 102. McIlwaine et al., HOUSE OF BURGESSES, 1702–1712, 200.

22. McIlwaine, EXECUTIVE JOURNALS, III, 283; McIlwaine et al., v, 1702–1712, xli; J. A. C. Chandler et al., "Journal of the Lt. Governor's Travels, Expeditions Undertaken in the Service of Virginia," WILLIAM AND MARY QUARTERLY, 2nd Ser. 3 (January 1923):41; William Byrd, THE SECRET DIARY OF WILLIAM BYRD OF WESTOVER, 1709–1712 (Richmond, 1941), 401; Surry County Orders 1691–1713:377; Alexander Spotswood, THE OFFICIAL LETTERS OF ALEXANDER SPOTSWOOD (New York, 1973), 121; John Fontaine,THE JOURNAL OF JOHN FONTAINE, AN IRISH HUGUENOT SON IN SPAIN AND VIRGINIA, 1710–1719 (Williamsburg, 1972), 90; McIlwaine, EXECUTIVE JOURNALS IV, 91.

23. Barrow, Municipal Court, 11–14, 25, 49; McIlwaine, LEGISLATIVE JOURNALS, 828, 969; Hening, STATUTES, V, 264, 386.

24. Gaines, "Courthouses", 23, 26–27; Palmer, CALENDAR, I, 169; Barrow, Municipal Court, 61–62; Hunter's VIRGINIA GAZETTE, April 11 and October 24, 1751.

25. Gaines, "Courthouses", 26–27; McIlwaine, EXECUTIVE JOURNALS, V, 247. In November 1781, when there was another epidemic, the county justices were authorized to convene "anywhere in the county" (Hening, STATUTES, X, 458). AT

26. Hening, STATUTES, III, 219, 416, 470–471; V, 33; VI, 13; McIlwaine, LEGISLATIVE JOURNALS, 619–621; Winfree, LAWS, 29; Goodwin, KINGSMILL, 89; Surry County Orders 1691–1713:232.

27. McIlwaine, EXECUTIVE JOURNALS, II, 261–262, 435; III, 58, 141, 159.

28. William G. Stanard, ed., "Philip Ludwell to Edward Jennings, 1709, In Regard to A Negro Plot," VIRGINIA MAGAZINE OF HISTORY AND BIOGRAPHY 19 (January 1911):23–24; McIlwaine, EXECUTIVE JOURNALS, III, 234–236.

29. McIlwaine, LEGISLATIVE JOURNALS, 578; Hening, STATUTES, III, 504–516; V, 490; Palmer, CALENDAR, I, 146; Sainsbury et al., CALENDAR, 1:146.

30. Des Cognets, LOST RECORDS 6, 24; McIlwaine, EXECUTIVE JOURNALS, III, 381.

31. Jones, PRESENT STATE, 70–71, 74, 77–79.

32. William Parks, VIRGINIA GAZETTE, 1736–1745, passim.

33. Jones, PRESENT STATE, 55, 72–73, 77–79, 84–87, 92, 221–222.

34. Devereux Jarrett, "The Life of the Rev. Devereux Jarrett," WILLIAM AND MARY QUARTERLY (3rd Series) 3 (January 1946):360–364.

35. Edward Kimber, "Observations in Several Voyages and Travels in America," WILLIAM AND MARY QUARTERLY, 1st Ser. 15 (July 1906):23.

36. Cocke, DIOCESE OF SOUTHERN VIRGINIA, 62–64; DIOCESE OF VIRGINIA, 37–38; Chamberlayne, BLISLAND PARISH, xxx–xxxi; Des Cognets, LOST RECORDS, 34, 47.

37. Chamberlayne, BLISLAND PARISH, 220–228.

38. McIlwaine et al., HOUSE OF BURGESSES, 1727–1740, 216, 276; 1742–1749, 300, 305, 310.

39. Hening, STATUTES, VI, 75, 101, 111.

40. Richard L. Morton, COLONIAL VIRGINIA (Chapel Hill, 1956), 238; Lee Papers 1714, 1735; Susan H. Godson et al., THE COLLEGE OF WILLIAM AND MARY: A HISTORY (Williamsburg, 1993), I, 145; Archibald B. Shepperson, JOHN PARADISE AND LUCY LUDWELL OF LONDON AND VIRGINIA (Richmond, 1942), 8, 18–19, 23–24, 32.

41. Ambler Manuscript No. 123; York County Wills and Inventories 21:278–282; Annie L. Smith, THE QUITRENTS OF VIRGINIA (Gloucester, 1957), 29; Robert Eggleston, personal communication, 1976; Williamsburg–James City County Tax Lists 1768–1769; Willie Graham, personal communication, May 1994.

42. Goodwin, KINGSMILL, 22, 25, 73–75; Kelso, KINGSMILL, 40; James P. McClure, Littletown Plantation, 1700–1745 (Williamsburg, 1977), 19. During the 1760s, Mathew Moody Jr. operated the tavern at Burwell's Landing, served as the ferry–keeper, and managed a storehouse there.

43. Stephenson, CARTER'S GROVE, 2–7, 42–54, 294–296, 312–314.

44. Stanard, "Virginia Gleanings," :372–381.

45. McIlwaine et al., HOUSE OF BURGESSES, 1695–1702, 219; Lyon G. Tyler, "Personal Notices from the VIRGINIA GAZETTE," WILLIAM AND MARY QUARTERLY, 1st Ser., 5 (January 1897):51–53, 243; Joseph Chermaison's Executors, January 12, 1712, deed to Edward Jaquelin; Ambler Manuscript No. 73, No. 101; York County Wills and Inventories 21:278–282; John H. Smith et al., April 4, 1745, deed to Richard Ambler; Ambler Manuscripts No. 53, No. 106, No. 107, No. 123.

46. Goodwin, KINGSMILL, 59; Hening, STATUTES, V, 278. 157

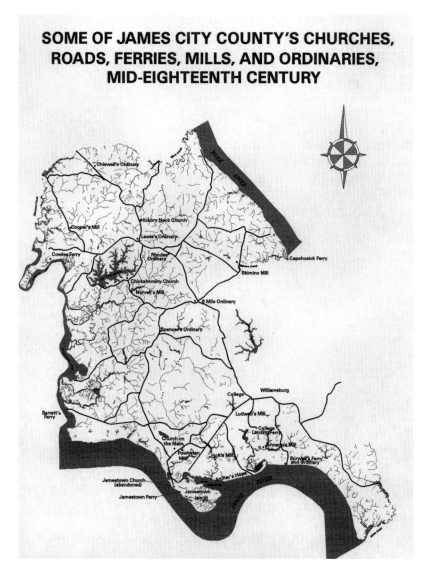

SOME OF JAMES CITY COUNTY'S CHURCHES, ROADS, FERRIES, MILLS, AND ORDINARIES, MID-EIGHTEENTH CENTURY

Map by Deborah L. Wilson.

CHAPTER 7

"How Wide the Limits Stand Between a Splendid and a Happy Land" 1751–1775

Accommodating Change

By the mid-eighteenth century development was widely dispersed throughout James City County. Local residents made regular trips to the county seat to vote and pay taxes, take care of business, attend the monthly court, or procure goods and services unavailable closer to home. Occasionally they asked the legislature for assistance in solving problems that exceeded the authority of the county court. In 1752 some James City County freeholders asked the assembly to adjust the boundary line with New Kent County. The burgesses agreed, but the governor vetoed the law effecting the change. The vestry of Blisland Parish sought permission to sell 200 acres of James City County land that Edward Wade had bequeathed to the churchwardens of Wilmington Parish. As Wilmington was defunct and the 200 acres lay within the expanded bounds of Blisland Parish, the vestry wanted to sell it, using the proceeds toward the purchase of some communion silver. Thomas Chamberlayne asked the assembly to dock the entail on some land he inherited and David Bray's heirs requested a similar accommodation. Because some local farmers thought slaves' dogs were killing their sheep, they asked the burgesses to pass a law prohibiting them from owning dogs. The resulting law forbade slaves from keeping more than two dogs at their quarters and from taking dogs with them when they left home.[1]

James City County as depicted on Joshua Fry and Peter Jefferson's map, published in 1775. Library of Congress.

In 1755 the House of Burgesses exempted certain groups of freeholders from compulsory military service. Excluded were prominent political officials; the president, faculty and students of the College of William and Mary; Williamsburg's mayor; clergy; millers; founders; and overseers (that also were sharecroppers) who were responsible for four or more slaves or servants. Quakers, free blacks, and mulattoes were prohibited from carrying arms, but were authorized to serve as drummers and trumpeters and to perform manual labor. Regular musters were to be held in March and September. During this period, James City County and Williamsburg had separate militia companies. County justices and the city's common council recommended potential military officers, but the governor made the actual appointments.[2]

In 1759 Virginia's governing officials decided to levy a tax upon riding carriages, a policy that was the ancestor of today's personal property tax on motor vehicles. Local tax rolls for 1768 and 1769 indicate that free whites

The courthouse of 1770. Courtesy of the Colonial Williamsburg
Foundation.

Plantation life in eastern Virginia.
Henry Howe's HISTORICAL
COLLECTIONS OF VIRGINIA.

were assessed upon the number of slaves and wheeled vehicles in their possession and the amount of acreage they owned. They also paid a poll tax and
church levies, which were part of the tax structure. Joshua Jones of James
City County ran afoul of the law when he failed to list himself and a slave as
tithables (polls) subject to taxation. In 1762 the qualifications of voters and
voting officials became more explicit. Free white males age 21 or older, who
owned at least 50 acres, or 25 acres with a house at least 12 feet square, were
deemed eligible to vote. Deliberately excluded from franchisement were all
women, underage white males, Catholics, convicts, criminals transported to
Virginia because of crimes in Great Britain or Ireland, and all free and
enslaved blacks, mulattoes, and Indians. For the first time since 1619, when
representative government was introduced, a man was limited to voting in his
county of residence and could not cast ballots in every county in which he
owned real estate.[3]

During the 1760s James City County's boundary lines were altered significantly. Late in 1766 the territory between Ware and Skimino Creeks was
taken from New Kent County and added to James City and that portion of

At Green Spring. Library of Congress.

James City County which lay west of Diascund Creek was made part of New Kent. This land exchange created the westernmost county boundary line we know today. The new boundary line commenced at the mouth of Diascund Creek, which it followed inland to John Blair's millpond and swamp, then continued northward to a tree at Isaac Goddin's spring, crossed the main road that ran up the peninsula, ran along James Hockaday's spring branch to Russell's mill, and then traced Ware Creek to the York River. In 1769 the boundary line separating James City and York Counties within the city of Williamsburg was defined more precisely. The new line extended "from the main road by the north end of the college," ran down the middle of Duke of Gloucester Street "to the east end of the Market Place," followed "the lane separating James Anderson's storehouse from William Lightfoot, then [passed] through the middle lots on the north side of Francis Street, then through the Nelsons' lots," and "crossed Capitol Square to the street to the York road."[4]

During the third quarter of the eighteenth century Williamsburg officials were given permission to hold an unlimited number of market days and to build a market house. The structure stood upon the south side of Duke of Gloucester Street within the market square. In November 1769 the House of Burgesses authorized James City County's justices and Williamsburg's mayor to build a new brick courthouse for both governments' use. Because the most convenient site was on the north side of Duke of Gloucester Street, in York County, the northern half of market square, between Nicholson Street and "the line of Hugh Walker's lot on the west and the pailing where H. Dixon's store is on the east," was annexed to James City County. The county justices were allowed to sell the old courthouse and its lot to the highest bidder at a public auction. The property was purchased by Robert Carter Nicholas, who converted the building into an office. The new courthouse, which was begun in 1770 and completed by 1772, was shared by James City County and Williamsburg until 1930, when the land upon which it stood was purchased by the Rockefellers. A clerk's office near the colonial powder magazine reportedly was razed by Union soldiers during the Civil War.[5]

The Texture of Life in James City County

Sometimes, violent weather captivated everyone's attention. On Sunday, July 9, 1758, around 4 P.M., a small cloud passed overhead. According to Lt. Governor Francis Fauquier, it spewed jagged pieces of ice that were three-quarters of an inch wide and twice as long, with half-inch spikes protruding from one side. He said that the hailstones broke every pane of glass on the north side of his house and destroyed his garden, but he used the ice chunks to chill his wine and "froze cream with some the next day." He also said that the summer had been unseasonably hot, with temperatures in the mid-to-upper 90s. Thomas Jefferson noted that in August 1766 the temperature in Williamsburg reached a record high of 98 degrees and that the winter of 1740–1741 was known as "the cold one." However, the most frigid in his recollection was the winter of 1779–1780, when the temperature in Williamsburg dropped to 6 degrees, the Chesapeake Bay was frozen from its head to the mouth of the Potomac, and people were able to walk across the James and York Rivers. According to the VIRGINIA GAZETTE, once the temperature in Tidewater dipped below freezing, it rose on only three occasions. By mid-January 1780 the rivers had frozen solid and wagons were able to cross the James at Burwell's Landing and the York at Yorktown. While the James River was choked with ice, the privateer brig JEFFERSON sank off Jamestown and two boats went down between the island and Swann's Point.[6]

In mid-September 1769, a hurricane swept into Hampton Roads bringing torrential rain and strong winds that leveled crops of corn, wheat, and tobacco. Reportedly, not a house was left dry in Williamsburg and many older buildings were leveled. Fallen trees blocked the roads and numerous mills were destroyed. So great was the storm's fury that a vessel loaded with coal broke apart in front of Jamestown Island, where Major Edward Travis's schooner was wrenched from its moorings and driven ashore a good distance away. The surging tide undoubtedly hastened the erosion of Jamestown Island's isthmus, for only two months later, James City County's justices and other local freeholders asked the House of Burgesses to relieve them of the burden of maintaining the causeway that provided access to the Jamestown ferry.[7]

Ebenezer Hazard, who had the task of finding postmasters and riders who would serve a route from Philadelphia to Savannah, passed through James City County in 1777. When he rode into Williamsburg on the "very deep and sandy" road from New Kent Courthouse (Richmond Road), he commented that the city's main buildings were "the College, the Mad-House, the Palace & the Capitol, all of brick." He said that there were 40 Cherokee Indians in town with whom he had "smoaked Part of a Pipe" and that they were adorned with paint and feathers. He attended worship services at Bruton Parish Church and on the evening of June 4th went to a ball and musical entertainment at the capitol. Hazard noted that "the water at Williamsburgh is very bad; no Beer or Cyder in Town—Grog or Toddy or Sangaree made with vile Water is the only Drink to be had" and commented that such beverages and the heat were "sufficient to keep a Man in a continual fever."[8]

A French visitor said that when the legislature or court was in session, people spent the day "hurrying back and forwards from the Capitoll to the taverns, and at night, Carousing and Drinking," with a beverage in one hand and a box and dice in the other. He said that there wasn't a tavern in Virginia with tables that weren't "all battered with the boxes" and that "Madeira wine and punch made with Jamaica rum is their Chief Drink." He observed that the plantations of the well-to-do lined the banks of the James and York Rivers, where the best soil could be found for growing sweet-scented tobacco. Wheat also was an important crop in the Tidewater.[9]

John Harrower, an indentured servant who came to Virginia during the 1770s, detailed numerous aspects of everyday life, including the burial of the dead. Mrs. Lawrence Taliaferro, whose husband was interred in the cemetery of Hickory Neck Church in western James City County, was "drest in a Calico Gown and a white apron," wrapped in a sheet, and then carefully laid in a flannel-lined black walnut coffin which lid was screwed down. After the coffin was lowered into the grave, which was five to six feet deep, it was partially back-filled and then overlaid with plank. Afterward, the rest of the earth was piled on. Harrower also set down his observations about agriculture. He said that wheat and corn were sown together so that they could be harvested simultaneously. Corn was planted two stalks per hill in mounds about six feet apart. Wheat was strewn upon the ground and then trod into the earth with the hoofs of horses. When Ebenezer Hazard visited the Ambler plantation at

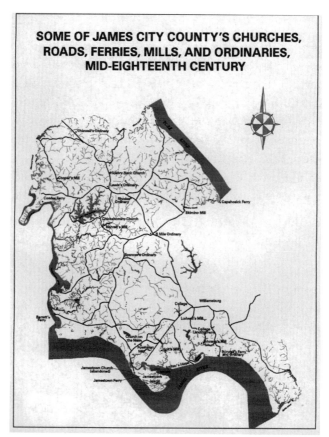

Map by Deborah L. Wilson. See enlarged map, page 176.

Jamestown, he sketched an elaborate machine for threshing wheat; it was powered by horses walking in a circle.[10]

Local Transportation Corridors

Historical maps and other documentary sources reveal that during the late eighteenth century ferries traversed the James River from Jamestown Island (and after 1779, the mainland), College Landing, and Burwell's Ferry (at Kingsmill) to Swann's Point, Crouches Creek, and Hog Island. Ferries also plied the Chickahominy River at two sites between its mouth and the upper limits of James City County. Ferry-keepers, like millers and tavern-keepers, were licensed and their rates were set by law.

By the second half of the eighteenth century a major public thoroughfare (the forerunner of Richmond Road) ran up the James-York peninsula toward the New Kent County courthouse and lesser byways followed the track of old, well-established paths toward the York, James, and Chickahominy Rivers. The forerunners of Route 615 (Ironbound Road), Route 614 (Green Spring Road), Route 613 (Brickbat Road) and Route 612 (Long Hill Road) then connected with a network of other small roads. By using Ironbound Road's forerunner, travelers could cut across the countryside as they headed toward the Jamestown Ferry. They also could follow Long Hill Road to Centerville, turn south, and then head for the river road (forerunner of Route 5) that would take them to Barretts Ferry near the mouth of the Chickahominy. The forerunner of Route 646 (Lightfoot Road) led to Route 604-697 and the Capahosick Ferry. The forerunners of Maxton and Cokes Lanes and Route 607 also extended toward the York River. Routes 610 and 603 (Old Forge and the Diascund Road) were important thoroughfares, as were the Chickahominy Road (Route 631) and Route 632, which went to Centerville. Important highways extended in an easterly direction down the peninsula toward Warwick and Elizabeth City Counties and northeast toward Yorktown.[11]

Commercial Development

Public Warehouses

In March 1761 planters in James City and Charles City Counties asked the House of Burgesses to establish "publick warehouses for the inspection of tobacco . . . at Jamestown on the land of John Ambler, Esq." The petition was rejected, for such warehouses already were in existence at College Landing, on Taskinask Creek, at Capitol Landing, and in neighboring counties. The men who built and operated official inspection warehouses derived income from the tobacco they processed and stored and the inspectors themselves were entitled to fees that were set by law.[12]

Accommodations for Man and Beast

Taverns or ordinaries existed at Jamestown throughout much of the seventeenth century. Some of them were popular gathering-places in which government officials sometimes congregated to do business. Among those who owned taverns in Jamestown during the seventeenth century were Thomas Woodhouse, Thomas Swann, Henry Gawler, George Marable, and Richard Lawrence. One or more taverns were opened in Middle Plantation around the time the college was built and several were in business in Williamsburg during the eighteenth century. Taverns also were kept at the College and Capitol Landings and on the east side of Williamsburg in York County. By the 1720s there was a popular establishment called Forneau's Ordinary on the old road from Williamsburg to New Kent Courthouse, not far from Routes 30 and 601, Old Stage and Firetower Roads. Stephen Forneau's tavern was open for business by at least 1726, when the vestry of Blisland Parish met there. In 1736 Thomas Jones of Caroline County advised his wife and her traveling companions to stay at Forneau's, where they (and their horses) would be well provided for. He said that although Mrs. Holdcroft's establishment was closer to Williamsburg, Forneau's was more comfortable. In 1751 when Stephen Forneau's 500-acre plantation was offered for sale, reference was made to the "well accustomed Ordinary thereon." Forneau's property straddled the northerly portion of the boundary line between New Kent and James City Counties.[13]

By the mid-1750s Forneau's Ordinary and the farm upon which it stood had come into the possession of Colonel John Chiswell. Chiswell's Ordinary was shown prominently on the map published by Joshua Fry and Peter Jefferson, who indicated that it was 16 miles from Williamsburg. On May 12, 1755, when Daniel (George) Fisher stopped at Chiswell's Ordinary around 8 A.M., he found two planters playing cards. He noted that a letter to a Williamsburg man was lying on the table, but no one was willing to take it there. During the late 1750s Chiswell sold his ordinary to John Robinson, whose executors offered it for sale in 1759. By that date Thomas Doncastle was renting it. He retained the ordinary until January 1776, when it was bought by Thomas Cartwright, former proprietor of the tavern at Burwell's

Ferry. Ebenezer Hazard, who in 1777 stopped overnight at Cartwright's, found the tavern agreeable. By 1780 Cartwright's Ordinary had come into the possession of Adam Byrd. During the Revolutionary War, British, French and American troops encamped there and Patrick Henry stopped by. Byrd's Ordinary was popular with travelers throughout the late eighteenth century. By 1812 it had come into the hands of William L. Allen, whose executors sold it to Truman Parker during the 1830s. During the mid-nineteenth century the tavern, which was still known as Allen's Ordinary, was open for business.[14]

The Six Mile Ordinary, was which stood upon the southwest corner of the intersection formed by Richmond and Centerville Roads, six miles west of Williamsburg, was very popular with the traveling public. It was in business throughout the second half of the eighteenth century and probably was the establishment run by John Crawley who in 1745 advertised that he had "for many Years entertained Travellers with Accommodations for themselves and Horses." When the American Revolution first got underway, the Six Mile (or Allen's) Ordinary, which took its name from proprietor Isham Allen, was a rallying point for local patriots. On July 1, 1774, a group of freeholders congregated there and drafted the James City Resolves. Precisely two years later, they gathered there again to declare their support for American independence. In 1787 William Allen was the proprietor of the Six Mile Ordinary which was owned by William Lightfoot. By 1814 it had come into the hands of Nelson W. Hall of York County. Later, it was owned by William B. Taylor and then his widow, Elizabeth. The Six Mile Ordinary was still in business when the Civil War began.[15]

A few miles southwest of the Six Mile Ordinary was Spencer's Ordinary, which saw a considerable amount of military action during the American Revolution. It was situated at the corner of Centerville and Longhill Roads, where the Forest Glen subdivision is located. British and American forces clashed there during June 1781 and it is thanks to that engagement that the ordinary and the plantation upon which it was located were sketched by British and German cartographers.[16]

Rhodes Ordinary, which was located 11 miles from Williamsburg, on the western outskirts of what became Norge, was another small but busy tavern that was in business during the mid-to-late eighteenth century. It was in the vicinity of Cokes Lane's intersection with Route 60, not far from Olive Branch Christian Church. In 1769 John Lewis placed a real estate advertisement in the VIRGINIA GAZETTE, offering to sell Rhodes Ordinary and the 50-acre farm upon which it stood. Five years later, when Lewis again tried to dispose of his tavern, he said that Captain John Lightfoot was then occupying it and that it was surrounded by "mostly cleared, good land for corn and grain." Rhodes Ordinary was still in existence in 1781, when the Marquis de Lafayette's men encamped in that vicinity.[17]

Besides Rhodes Ordinary, John Lewis had another tavern that stood at the intersection of the roads to New Kent Courthouse (Route 60) and Coles Ferry (Old Forge or Route 610). He was residing upon the premises during the 1760s when he offered to take queries about the late Mrs. Mary Holdcroft's Hickory Neck Plantation, which Alexander Walker wanted to sell. John and David Lewis had a store near the ordinary and sold yard goods, sundries, and other items. By the late 1770s John Lewis's Ordinary had become Fox's. In January 1780 the VIRGINIA GAZETTE reported that Fox's Ordinary had burned to the ground and in October 1781, when the French Army's wagon train passed by, Alexander Berthier remarked upon the "two old chimneys" that stood in the fork of the road. Samuel Dewitt, who was George Washington's cartographer, and Christopher Colles, who mapped a route between Annapolis, Maryland, and Williamsburg, identified the site of the "Burnt brick Ord." that stood on the north side of Old Forge Road, opposite the James City-Bruton Fire Station.[18] In time, the cluster of buildings at the crossroads became known as Burnt Ordinary and later, Toano.

Grist and Saw Mills

Throughout James City County's rural countryside were mills, small mercantile establishments, and the shops of artisans who catered to local residents and travelers. The way millers conducted business was regulated by law. Toll mills' proprietors were allowed to charge an eighth of the meal or flour yielded by the corn and grain they processed. On the other hand, merchant millers purchased grain, ground it into flour or meal and then sold it to the public. The weights and measures millers used, which were sealed, were calibrated in accord with standards set by law. Mill dams traversed by public roads had to be kept in good repair and support a 12-foot-wide bridge with sturdy railings. A miller who failed to maintain his dam-road was fined for every day it was unusable.[19]

In November 1776 someone offered to sell a "good grist mill" on Diascund Creek, noting that it had two stones, a good set of bolting cloths, a granary, a storehouse, and coopering and blacksmith shops. This was likely Blair's Mill, which by the time of the Revolutionary War had become Cooper's Mill. The British Army encamped there in 1781. On Ware Creek, which lay head-to-head with Diascund Creek, were Russell's, and Goddin's Mills, which served to define James City County's boundary line.[20]

Near Jamestown was Kennon's Mill, which was situated on Mill Creek upon land that belonged to Colonel Thomas Pettus during the mid-seventeenth century. During the early 1760s the heirs of Colonel Richard Kennon of Charles City County sold the mill to William Holt and the Rev. Charles Jeffrey Smith. The two men built a blacksmithery, storehouse, granary, gristmills, and dwellings at what became known as Providence Forge and converted Kennon's Mill into a bakehouse-milling complex, where ships' biscuits were baked and sold. The biscuits, which resembled hard-tack and were made from flour and a minimal amount of water, were mass-produced; they were a valuable commodity for which mariners paid a good price. By 1775 William Holt was the sole owner of what he called Holt's Mill. He manufactured ships biscuits and sold beef, pork and other commodities at his mill complex.[21]

The Powhatan Mill, on Powhatan Creek, which was owned in succession by the Ludwells and Lees of Green Spring, was another active milling establishment. Near Williamsburg, on a branch of College Creek, was Ludwell's Mill, which was in existence throughout the eighteenth century and later became known as Jones' Mill. Several miles west of Williamsburg, on the boundary line between James City and York Counties, was the Skimino Mill, which had been in business since the early eighteenth century. Further up Skimino Creek was Nathaniel Piggott's Mill, which eventually became Fenton's. Not far from the site of the Chickahominy Church was Norvell's Mill, which was in operation throughout the eighteenth century. It was located where Route 632 crosses Yarmouth Creek, at Cranston Pond. During the mid-nineteenth century it was owned by the Bush family. In the eastern end of James City County, there was a mill at Kingsmill Plantation and Burwell's Mill was located just over the York County line.

Natural Disasters

On February 21, 1774, the residents of James City County were jostled by an earthquake. According to a Williamsburg correspondent to the PENNSYLVANIA GAZETTE, "Last Monday, about 2 o'clock, an Earthquake was felt at Westover. . . . It was likewise felt in this city by a few people." So strong was the quake "further up the country" that some houses reportedly were dislodged from their foundations. Two days later there was a strong after-shock. One Williamsburg resident reported feeling "a violent tremor of the earth."[22]

A little more than a year later, a weather-front passed through Tidewater Virginia, causing extensive damage in Williamsburg and the surrounding countryside. According to the May 26, 1775, edition of the VIRGINIA GAZETTE: *Last Monday between 2 and 3 we had three severe hail storms from the west, which quickly succeeded each other. The first lasted very near 5 minutes and most of the stones were as big as pidgeon's eggs, some much larger. A number of windows were broken, particularly at the Palace, which lost upward of 400 panes. The gardens likewise sustained considerable damage and we hear that the storm was very violent at Greenspring and sundry other places near town.*[23]

It is likely that the hail damaged spring crops, orchards, and livestock.

James City County Properties

The Ludwell Holdings

Throughout the eighteenth century, members of the Ludwell family were in possession of Green Spring, Hot Water, Powhatan Mill, Indigo Dam, Rich Neck, and several other local properties, including acreage in Archers Hope and lots in Williamsburg and Jamestown. An inventory of Philip Ludwell III's estate, compiled shortly after his death in 1767, sheds a great deal of light upon the furnishings of a wealthy planter's home and his subsidiary farms. At Green Spring were large quantities of black walnut and mahogany furniture, mirrors, pictures, and window curtains of various fabrics, items that reflect the family's affluence and cultivated taste. Ludwell may have been hard of hearing, for he owned an ear trumpet. He also had on hand seven old swords, a bayonet, three pistols, four guns, shot and bullet molds, and other military equipment. Playing cards, smoking-pipes, a backgammon table, and a spinet offer clues to some of the leisure activities the Ludwells enjoyed, whereas a set of globes, a reading frame and books, and a compass reflect their interest in the outside world. Specialized vessels for serving food (such as fruit glasses, salts, cruets, tart molds, beer and wine glasses, dessert knives and forks, and chocolate and sweetmeat pots) denote the Ludwells' refinement. Sets of mosquito curtains, tubs and troughs for processing and salting meat, an apple press, pickle bottles, scrub brushes, spinning wheels and cards, looms, and butter churns were a few of the utilitarian items associated with everyday life at Green Spring. Tools for shoemaking, blacksmithery, wheelwrighting, and carpentry were on hand as were substantial quantities of cowhide, tobacco, wheat, and corn.[24]

Among the more unusual items in Philip Ludwell III's inventory were special hoes and knives used in processing indigo and a substantial quantity of the plant itself. Although indigo may have been raised at Green Spring, it probably was grown on the Ludwell tract that eventually became known as the Indigo Dam. At the time of Ludwell's death Green Spring was subdivided into subsidiary farms known as Scotland, Pinewood Meadow, and the Mill Quarter. He also owned several outlying tracts (Rich Neck, the Hot Water tract, Cloverton, the New Quarter and Archers Hope) and rented 825 acres of the Governor's Land. All of these properties were run in synch with Green Spring. The Ludwell family's subsidiary farms, which had herds of livestock, were staffed with gangs of slaves, who had on hand agricultural equipment and rudimentary utensils they used in processing their food.[25]

A plat of the Green Spring property, prepared around 1770 when the estate of Philip Ludwell III was passed on to his daughters, identifies the plantation's subunits and reveals that three prominent roads traversed Green Spring's nearly 4,300 acres: the main road from Barretts Ferry to Jamestown (forerunner of Route 5); the road from Jamestown to Chiswell's Ordinary (now Route 614); and one that ran toward Barretts Ferry and crossed diagonally through Mr. Warburton's land (Route 613). Gordon's Creek and a branch of Deep Creek (Lake Pasbehay) defined portions of Green Spring's boundaries.[26]

Hannah Philippa Ludwell Lee, who was 30 years old when she inherited Green Spring, was married and residing in England at the time of her father's death. Because her sister, Frances, died before their father's estate was settled, ultimately it was divided between Hannah Philippa and her sister, Lucy, who at age 16 married John Paradise of London. Lucy Paradise received Rich Neck and her father's other landholdings on the east side of Powhatan Creek, whereas Hannah Philippa Lee was assigned Green Spring and the property on the west side of the creek. Hannah Philippa's husband, William Lee, eagerly embraced the opportunity to manage his wife's extensive landholdings. Unfortunately, his relationship with Cary Wilkinson, the late Philip Ludwell III's farm manager, was strained. Lee, who tended to be suspicious, fractious, and stingy, dispatched a series of letters to Wilkinson in which he provided him with highly detailed instructions on the management of his wife's property. As Lee had left Virginia at a relatively early age and had had little or no practical experience in farming, and as Wilkinson was accustomed to having a relatively free hand in managing the Ludwell properties, the two men were at odds more often than not. Lee had his own ideas on how crops and livestock should be raised and how slaves should be treated. He also demanded a detailed accounting of all profits and losses and regular inventories of the livestock and slaves. Wilkinson, after a barrage of quarrelsome letters from Lee, finally responded in broken but caustic language to the issues his employer raised. He also pointed out some of Lee's shortcomings and closed by saying "Their is nothing that I can do semes to give Satisfaction and without I can, I will sarve no man."[27] After Wilkinson resigned in a huff, William Lee had a lengthy succession of overseers.

The Ambler Plantation on Jamestown Island

Richard Ambler of Yorktown, having acquired nearly 700 acres of land on Jamestown Island in 1745, continued to enhance the size of his plantation. On October 6, 1753, he purchased a small waterfront lot from Edward Champion Travis. It was located in front of the site upon which he built an imposing brick mansion for his second son, John. Richard Ambler died in February 1766, having survived his wife by nearly a decade. He left John the Jamestown Island plantation, a 310-acre leasehold in the Governor's Land, and fee simple ownership of his acreage at Powhatan. He bequeathed his York County property to sons Edward and Jaquelin. An inventory of the late Richard Ambler's estate reveals that he considered his farm on the mainland and the Powhatan acreage subsidiaries of the Jamestown Island plantation.[28]

John Ambler I, an attorney educated in England, represented Jamestown in the House of Burgesses from 1759 to 1761 and was re-elected in 1765. He died on May 27, 1766, only three months after his father's decease. As he was single and childless, his landholdings descended to his brother, Edward, a Yorktown merchant slightly more than a year his senior. Edward Ambler moved to Jamestown Island, which he made his family seat, and succeeded his brother in the House of Burgesses, serving in the sessions of 1766, 1767, and 1768. But Edward's life, like John's, was cut short and he died on October 30, 1768, "after a tedious illness." Two months later, tragedy struck again, for in late December one of the Amblers' outbuildings at Jamestown burned to the ground and a male slave perished while attempting to save his belongings. An inventory of Edward Ambler's personal estate, compiled in 1769, suggests that he carried on mercantile activities while he was living at Jamestown.[29]

The widowed Mary Cary Ambler, who revered Jamestown for its antiquity, stayed on in the family home with her six-year-old son, John II. In 1779, when combat came to Jamestown Island, she withdrew to Hanover County and leased the plantation to her neighbor's brother. Around that time, a group of James City County freeholders asked the legislature to relocate the Jamestown ferry's landing from the island to the Ambler farm on the mainland. John Ambler II inherited the ancestral plantation on Jamestown

Island, the lease for the Maine farm in the Governor's Land, part of Powhatan, plus land and slaves in several other Virginia counties.[30]

Powhatan Plantation

In 1768 James City County's tax assessor credited Richard Taliaferro with Powhatan, 975 acres that formerly belonged to his father-in-law, Benjamin Eggleston Jr. Eggleston's widow, Elizabeth, retained the residual 450 acres, which were still in her possession in 1768. Meanwhile, Edward Jaquelin's spinster daughter, Martha, who inherited his Powhatan property, sold it to her brother-in-law Richard Ambler, who left it to his son, John. It, like the rest of John's James City County property, descended to elder brother, Edward, whose principal heir was John Ambler II. A detailed inventory of the late Edward Ambler's estate reveals that he used his acreage at Powhatan as a subsidiary farm and had slaves, livestock and farming equipment on the premises.[31]

Piney Grove and the Travis Plantation on Jamestown Island

Edward Champion Travis inherited his forebears' approximately 840 acres in the eastern end of Jamestown Island and resided there. Sometime prior to 1768 he acquired Piney Grove, which extended along the James from Deep Creek to the mouth of the Chickahominy River. Travis was one of James City County's wealthiest citizens and served as a burgess and colonel in the local militia. During the early 1770s, he acquired a plantation on Queens Creek in York County and developed it into a personal estate. He allowed his son, Champion, to occupy the ancestral home on Jamestown Island. The Travis domestic complex at Jamestown sustained considerable damage during the Revolutionary War, as it was shelled by the British and then occupied by Virginia troops.[32]

In December 1778, when Edward Champion Travis made his will, he left son Champion the plantation on Jamestown Island and Piney Grove. An eighteenth-century plat of Piney Grove, based upon a survey commissioned by Champion Travis, reveals that the 1,200-acre tract was subdivided into 27 small parcels, which boundaries conformed to the lay of the land. A number of houses (including a substantial dwelling identified as "the Brick House") were located at Piney Grove. Benjamin Warburton's land lay to the east of Piney Grove and William Barrett's, to the north. Champion Travis, like his father, took an active role in public life. He represented Jamestown in the House of Burgesses, served as a county justice and sheriff, participated in the Conventions of 1774 and 1775, held the rank of colonel in the state regiment, and was appointed a naval commissioner in 1776. Travis retained his James City County landholdings until after the close of the American Revolution.[33]

Kingsmill

Lewis Burwell IV, who inherited his father's acreage at Kingsmill and enlarged his holdings on the James River through his marriage to James Bray III's widow, Frances, employed overseers to help him manage his property. In 1775 he turned his enlarged Kingsmill Plantation over to his son, Lewis Burwell V, whom contemporaries described as indolent, opportunistic, and volatile. Young Lewis lost his appointment as a county justice because he "declined to act" and once, in the heat of anger, he stabbed his brother-in-law, Peyton Randolph, in his side. During the Revolutionary War Burwell sold supplies and shelter to American troops but also provided commodities to the British.[34]

Jockey's Neck

The Rev. William Bland, the son of Richard Bland II of Jordan's Point, was ordained in 1767. He returned to Virginia and married Elizabeth, the daughter of William and Mary College President William Yates, and began serving as interim lecturer at Bruton Parish Church. By the late 1760s, however, he began assisting with services in James City Parish's Church on the Main, a brick structure that was built during the 1750s after the church at Jamestown was destroyed by fire.[35] In 1774 Bland became rector James City Parish, and therefore had use of the glebe. He rented it to William Spratley, whose farm was nearby, and supplemented his income by serving as the

Ordinary of Newgate, chaplain of the local jail. Bland is believed to have acquired Jockey's Neck from the Yates family through a marriage contract. He resided in Williamsburg and placed Jockey's Neck in the hands of an overseer.

Although Bland was an ardent supporter of the American Revolution, some of his outspoken opinions led colleagues to question his patriotism. One of the many issues over which Virginians disagreed with the Crown was the lack of an American bishopric. As there were no Anglican bishops in North America, those desiring ordination had to go to England. Bland's vocal opposition to the establishment of an American bishopric convinced some fellow clergy that he had Loyalist leanings. During 1785 the Rev. William Bland sold Jockey's Neck to Dr. James Carter of Williamsburg, a prominent physician, and moved to Norfolk. After Carter's death in 1794, the farm was credited to his estate. Thomas Coleman of Williamsburg bought it in 1820.[36]

Drinking Spring

By the mid-eighteenth century plantations of middling size were scattered throughout James City County's interior. On the north side of Richmond Road, at the head of Yarmouth Creek and just west of Norge was the Drinking Spring plantation, which was owned by the Burwells during the early eighteenth century. In 1768 Drinking Spring owner Julius Allen offered to rent his 250 acres and five valuable slaves "used to plantation business." The Drinking Spring plantation's domestic complex lay within a triangular land mass delimited by Routes 60, 658 and 602. It was identified by Alexander Berthier, whose map indicates that Rochambeau's Army encamped there from July 1 through July 4, 1781. In 1799 the Drinking Spring plantation came into the hands of Henley Taylor, whose descendants retained the property until 1987.[37]

Morecock's Island

In January 1773 Patrick Coutts, who owned Morecock's (Mocock's) Island, on the Chickahominy River, advertised it for sale in the PENNSYLVANIA

GAZETTE. He indicated that his acreage consisted of three islands, the largest of which had two springs and 150 acres of high ground that contained an overseer's house, slave quarters, and a barn. Coutts said that the Chickahominy was navigable inland for 20 miles and would accommodate vessels capable of transporting a cargo of 4,000 bushels.[38]

The Weldon Plantation and Lilliput

Enveloping what became Williamsburg Memorial Park was Benjamin Weldon's plantation, which he inherited from his mother's family, the Effords. Weldon's farm, which was about four miles from Williamsburg, was a frequently used reference point in real estate advertisements, suggesting that it was a well known local landmark. Nearby was Lilliput, a plantation that by the 1760s belonged to the colony's treasurer, John Robinson of King and Queen County. Benjamin Weldon, a county justice and relatively prosperous middling farmer, succumbed to financial hardships after the Revolutionary War.[39]

Gathering Storm-Clouds:
"In Freedom We're Born and in Freedom We'll Live"

The long, bumpy road to American Independence was paved with debt and taxes, largely attributable to the cost of the French and Indian War. The Virginia government issued treasury notes secured by future taxes and released paper currency with a face value of more than 500,000 pounds sterling. The colonists began to worry about the growing debt and British merchants became increasingly uneasy about being paid in currency that had little real value outside of Virginia.[40]

In May 1763, approximately three months after the war officially ended, Lt. Governor Francis Fauquier lectured the House of Burgesses on the necessity of placing British merchants on a more favorable footing. The burgesses responded with a document that acknowledged Virginians' allegiance to the Crown but asserted their rights as British subjects. Thus, they side-stepped a concept usually taken for granted: that the colonies existed primarily for the benefit of the Mother Country. In April 1764 Parliament addressed British merchants' complaints by passing the Currency Act, which forbade colonial legislatures to issue paper currency after September 1st.

George Grenville, Great Britain's prime minister and chancellor of the exchequer, was confronted by the need to reduce the enormous national debt accumulated during the French and Indian War. Concluding that a stamp tax would make the American colonists shoulder their share of the debt, he introduced a measure that required the purchase of stamps for many types of documents. In February 1765 the Stamp Act became law. When word of its passage reached Virginia, the House of Burgesses, led by Patrick Henry, enacted a series of resolutions in opposition, for they felt that the new tax was being imposed without the colonists' consent. This prompted Lt. Governor Fauquier to dissolve the assembly. Meanwhile, Parliament passed the Quartering Act, which required colonial governments to furnish barracks and supplies to British troops stationed in America. It, like the Stamp Act, was enormously unpopular.

As the date the Stamp Act took effect drew near, some of Virginia's county justices resigned. Others simply declared that the act was unconstitutional and refused to enforce it. Citizens in the Northern Neck pledged to prevent implementation of the Stamp Act, with "no regard to danger or to death." In February 1766 Parliament repealed the Stamp Act but preserved the Quartering Act and the Declaratory Act, which asserted Parliament's right to pass laws that were binding upon the colonies. In May 1766 when word of the Stamp Act's repeal reached Virginia, it was received with broad acclaim. In May 1767 Charles Townshend, then-chancellor of the exchequer, introduced legislation that called for duties on certain types of imported goods and slaves, part of which funds were to go toward the support of colonial governors and judges. Many everyday items (such as paper, paint, glass, lead, and tea) were to be taxed. General search warrants were authorized for use in enforcing the Townshend Revenue Act, but Virginia court justices (and those of several other colonies) flatly refused to issue them. Massachusetts' General Court justices dispatched a petition to the king and prime minister, disputing the new acts' constitutionality, and they circulated a letter among other colonies' legislatures. Virginia's House of Burgesses dispatched a written protest to England and furnished copies to the other colonies' assemblies. The burgesses noted "how necessary we think it is that the Colonies should unite in a firm but decent Opposition to every Measure which may affect the Rights and Liberties of the British Colonies in America." Locally, the VIRGINIA GAZETTE began publishing letters from John Dickinson of Pennsylvania, summarizing the colonies' opposition to the Townshend Acts. Through such communication, the seeds of common opposition were propagated and nurtured throughout Virginia.

It was into this situation that the colony's new governor, Norborne Berkeley, Baron de Botetourt, was thrust when he arrived in Williamsburg in October 1768. He was instructed to win "principal Persons of Influence and Credit" away from the "erroneous and dangerous Principles which they appear to have adopted." Therefore, in May 1769 when he called the House of Burgesses into session, he told its members to "follow exactly the interests of those you have the Honour to represent." The burgesses responded with a resolution in which they declared their exclusive right to levy taxes upon the colony's inhabitants. They also asserted Virginia officials' right to contact their counterparts in other British colonies. The governor, upon learning of the burgesses' actions, promptly adjourned the assembly. But most of the delegates reconvened in the Raleigh Tavern's Apollo Room, where they signed an agreement not to import any goods or manufactures (except paper) that would be taxed in America until the offensive parliamentary acts were repealed. Among the prohibited goods were alcoholic beverages, meat, fish, dairy products, tallow and candles, fruit, sugar, pewter, tools, watches and clocks, furniture, jewelry, fabric, and leather goods. Champion Travis, James Walker, and Lewis Burwell, who represented Jamestown and James City County, subscribed to the 1769 non-importation agreement.

On April 12, 1770, Parliament repealed all of the Townshend duties, except the tax on tea, and allowed the Quartering Act to expire. However, the controversial Declaratory Act was upheld. A new non-importation agreement was signed in June 1770, but many colonists abandoned the boycott after they learned of the Townshend Act's repeal. Meanwhile, the House of Burgesses decided to ask the king to prohibit Parliament from levying taxes upon the colonies. It was around that time that Lord Botetourt died, leaving William Nicholson as acting governor.

In September 1771 John Murray, the fourth Earl of Dunmore, arrived in Williamsburg and took office as governor. When the House of Burgesses convened in February 1772, the possibility of reviving import duties on slaves sparked a spirited debate. It gave rise to the preparation of a resolution that prohibited the importation of African slaves, "long been considered as a Trade of great Inhumanity." The burgesses asked Lord Dunmore to forward their treatise to the king.

On March 4, 1773, Dunmore called the House into session and announced that counterfeiters had been at work and that "all the Emissions of your paper Currency now in Circulation are forged." But the royal governor's plan to have the accused men tried in England resurrected an old and controversial issue: the propriety of sending colonists abroad to stand trial. Again, some of the burgesses adjourned to the Raleigh Tavern, where on Friday, March 12, 1773, they resolved to establish a committee of inter-colonial correspondence. This moved the American colonies one step closer to offering a common resistance to Great Britain.

Parliament's April 1773 passage of a new Tea Act convinced many colonists that officials in England were trying to trick them into acknowledging their tax policy's legality. The new law also gave the East India Company a monopoly on tea and the right to choose their own agents. In Massachusetts, the public outcry culminated in a December 16th riot known as the Boston Tea Party. Officials in England retaliated by closing the port of Boston and restricting Massachusetts' government until reparations were made. Shortly after the VIRGINIA GAZETTE reported upon the events in Massachusetts, some burgesses drafted a resolution designating June 1 as a day of fasting and prayer for divine intervention on behalf of the American colonies. Dunmore responded by dissolving the House of Burgesses. The next day, the burgesses convened at the Raleigh Tavern, formed another non-importation association, and declared that "an attack made on one of our sister colonies, to compel submission to arbitrary taxes, is an attack made on all British America." They also called for "an annual meeting of colonial delegates in a general congress," a very early proposal for a Continental Congress.

On Sunday, May 29th, letters from the Massachusetts Committee of Correspondence reached Peyton Randolph, chairman of Virginia's Committee of Correspondence. He quickly assembled as many burgesses as he could find. Plans were made to hold a general meeting (the Virginia Convention) in August to discuss ceasing all trade with Great Britain. Tensions continued to mount. In June, the Fee Bill expired, which authorized county officials to be paid for the duties they performed. This led to the closing of county courts. Parliament meanwhile passed legislation designed to punish Massachusetts and it threatened anyone disrupting trade with Great Britain with criminal prosecution. Some of Virginia's port towns, upon learning of Massachusetts' plight, immediately enacted bans upon British trade. Meetings were held throughout the colony. James City County freeholders convened on July 1, 1774, at Isham Allen's Six Mile Ordinary and resolved "not import any article whatever from Great Britain" after whatever date the Virginia Convention's delegates set at their August meeting. Local citizens were asked to donate money, corn, wheat, or any other commodities that would provide relief to the people of Boston. The James City Resolves were published in the Virginia Gazette on July 14, 1774. By that time, Governor Dunmore had left on a six-month junket to Virginia's western frontier. During his absence county associations re-affirmed the principle of non-importation and in some places, companies of militia volunteers formed and began to drill.

The delegates to the Virginia Convention met in Williamsburg during the first week of August 1774. They were burgesses from the last session of the House and those elected to serve in its next session. Robert Carter Nicholas and the newly elected William Norvell represented James City County, whereas Champion Travis attended on behalf of Jamestown. Former burgess Lewis Burwell also may have been present. Convention delegates chose six men to attend the First Continental Congress and they agreed to halt British imports after November 1, 1774, and exports after August 10, 1775. The resolutions drafted at the Virginia Convention on August 6, 1774, in essence were a blueprint for those adopted by the First Continental Congress.

When Dunmore returned to Williamsburg in December, he learned what had transpired. When he updated his superiors, he received a stinging rebuke and was told that Virginia's trade might be interdicted as Boston's had been. In February 1775 Dunmore was notified of a ban on exporting gunpowder and arms to the colonies and he was ordered to secure all military stores that were on hand. He also was told to prevent the election of delegates to a second Continental Congress. The VIRGINIA GAZETTE commenced printing accounts that purportedly emanated from Great Britain and publishing private citizens' opinions of what the British government might do. The British, meanwhile, assumed that a relatively small number of American colonists were resisting their policies.[41]

Pedantic William Lee of James City County was the unlikely prophet who accurately forecast the breach that lay ahead. On April 3, 1775, while he was living in London, he wrote an associate in Virginia that the argument between Great Britain and her colonies "must now come to a final decision." He closed by venturing his opinion that "it will end in absolute independence of the colonists."[42]

Notes

1. McIlwaine, LEGISLATIVE JOURNALS, 1091, 111; Hening, STATUTES, VI, 295, 393, 412–414, 488.

2. Hening, STATUTES, VI, 531–533; Barrow, MUNICIPAL GOVERNMENT, 25.

3. McIlwaine, EXECUTIVE JOURNALS, VI, 454; Hening, STATUTES, VII, 262, 518.

4. Hening, STATUTES, VIII, 208, 405; McIlwaine, LEGISLATIVE JOURNALS, 1355.

5. McIlwaine, EXECUTIVE JOURNALS, V, 469; LEGISLATIVE JOURNALS, 1404, 1420; Barrow, MUNICIPAL GOVERNMENT, 46, 49; Hening, STATUTES, VIII, 364–365, 419, 556; IX, 239; Lyon G. Tyler, WILLIAMSBURG: THE OLD COLONIAL CAPITAL (Williamsburg, 1928).

6. Francis Fauquier, July 21, 1758, letter; Thomas Jefferson, NOTES ON VIRGINIA (Chapel Hill, 1972), 78; PENNSYLVANIA GAZETTE, February 8, 1780; Dixon's VIRGINIA GAZETTE, September 15, 1780; John E. Selby, REVOLUTION IN VIRGINIA: 1775–1783 (Charlottesville, 1988), 245.

7. Purdie–Dixon's VIRGINIA GAZETTE, September 14, 1769; McIlwaine et al., HOUSE OF BURGESSES, 1766–1769, 258.

8. Fred Shelley, "The Journal of Ebenezer Hazard in Virginia in 1777," VIRGINIA MAGAZINE OF HISTORY AND BIOGRAPHY 62 (October 1954):400, 410–411.

9. Carson, WE WERE THERE, 15.

10. John Harrower, THE JOURNAL OF JOHN HARROWER, AN INDENTURED SERVANT IN THE COLONY OF VIRGINIA, 1773–1776 (Williamsburg, 1963), 59–60, 87, 107, 112; Shelley, HAZARD, 416.

11. Hening, STATUTES, VI, 494; VII, 263; Fry and Jefferson, Virginia, 1755, 1775; Henry, Virginia, 1770; Alexander Berthier, [untitled map of the peninsula], ca. 1781.

12. McIlwaine et al., HOUSE OF BURGESSES, 1758–1761, 223, 231; 1761–1765, 72, 97.

13. Chamberlayne, BLISLAND PARISH, 26; William G. Stanard, ed., "Thomas Jones to Mrs. Jones, 1736," VIRGINIA MAGAZINE OF HISTORY AND BIOGRAPHY 26 (January 1918):179; VIRGINIA GAZETTE, April 4, 1751.

14. Daniel George Fisher, "Narrative of George Fisher," WILLIAM AND MARY QUARTERLY, 1st Ser., 17 (July 1908):165; Shelley, HAZARD, 405; James City County Land Tax Lists, 1782–1861.

15. VIRGINIA GAZETTE, May 9, 1745; Purdie's VIRGINIA GAZETTE, July 5, 1776; James City County Land Tax Lists 1781–1861; Personal Property Tax Lists 1781–1861.

16. John G. Simcoe, A HISTORY OF THE OPERATIONS OF A PARTISAN CORPS CALLED THE QUEEN'S RANGERS (New York, 1844).

17. Purdie and Dixon's VIRGINIA GAZETTE, June 29, 1769; November 24, 1774.

18. Rind's VIRGINIA GAZETTE, September 29, 1768; Dixon's VIRGINIA GAZETTE, October 25, 1776; January 15, 1780; Chamberlayne, BLISLAND PARISH, 172, 178, 191, 195; Howard C. Rice et al., THE AMERICAN CAMPAIGNS OF ROCHAMBEAU'S ARMY (Princeton, 1972), II, 104–106; Samuel Dewitt, [Untitled map], 1781; Christopher Colles, "From Annapolis to Williamsburg," 1789. Continued on following page 182

19. Samuel Sheppherd, THE STATUTES AT LARGE OF VIRGINIA (New York, 1987), 137–138.

20. Purdie's VIRGINIA GAZETTE, November 22, 1776; Chamberlayne, BLISLAND PARISH, XXX.

21. Parks, LAND RECORDS, 225–226; Lyon G. Tyler, "Providence Forge," WILLIAM AND MARY QUARTERLY, 1st Ser., 5 (July 1896):20–21; York County Deed Book 7:171–173; Judgements, Orders 4:344; Order Book 1765–1768; Purdie's VIRGINIA GAZETTE, September 15, 1775; Public Service Claims 1777–1778.

22. PENNSYLVANIA GAZETTE, February 24, 1774.

23. Purdie's VIRGINIA GAZETTE, May 26, 1775.

24. William G. Stanard, ed., "Appraisal of Estate of Philip Ludwell," VIRGINIA MAGAZINE OF HISTORY AND BIOGRAPHY 21 (October 1913):395–416.

25. Ibid., 245–248.

26. William G. Stanard, "Some Notes on Green Spring," VIRGINIA MAGAZINE OF HISTORY AND BIOGRAPHY 37 (July 1929):289.

27. Shepperson, JOHN PARADISE, 54–57, 455.

28. Ambler Papers, No. 115, No. 116, No. 123; York County Wills and Inventories 21:278–282, 386–391.

29. William G. Stanard, "Notes to Council Journals," VIRGINIA MAGAZINE OF HISTORY AND BIOGRAPHY 33 (January 1925):187; McIlwaine et al., HOUSE OF BURGESSES, 1766–1769, 13; Purdie–Dixon's VIRGINIA GAZETTE, December 29, 1768; Edward Ambler, Appraisal of Edward Ambler's Estate, 1769.

30. Church, LEGISLATIVE PETITIONS, No. 1133; John Jaquelin Ambler, History of the Ambler Family in Virginia, 1826.

31. James City County Tax Lists 1768–1769; York County Wills and Inventories 21:278–282; Inventory of the Estate of Edward Ambler, 1768. 32. Meyer et al., ADVENTURERS, 378; York County Wills 1771–1783:458–459.

33. James Thompson, Property of Champion Travis Esquire, Surveyed and Delineated the 20th of M[–], n.d.; James City County Land Tax Lists 1782–1801; William G. Stanard, "Travis Family," WILLIAM AND MARY QUARTERLY, 1st Series (July 1909) 18:141–145.

34. Kelso, KINGSMILL, 46–47; Goodwin, KINGSMILL, 34.

35. The Church on the Main was located near the Jamestown 1607 townhouse development.

36. James City County Tax Lists 1768–1769; William Meade, OLD CHURCHES, MINISTERS AND FAMILIES OF VIRGINIA (Baltimore, 1966), 113, 168–170, 272–274; James City County Land Tax Lists 1790–1834. After the Rev. Bland moved to Norfolk, he became embroiled in a dispute with another clergyman, which brought his church unwanted notoriety. Mid–nineteenth century Episcopal bishop and church historian William Meade described Bland as a man of intemperate habits.

37. York County Records, Wills, Orders No. XIV (1709–1716):60–64; Rind's VIRGINIA GAZETTE, September 22, 1768; Rice et al., ROCHAMBEAU'S ARMY, I:159; II:174; Plate 109; James City County Land Tax Lists 1781–1861; Deed Book 365:253.

38. PENNSYLVANIA GAZETTE, January 1, 1773. Continued on following page 183

39. James City County Land Tax Lists 1782–1792; Personal Property Tax Lists 1782–1792.

40. John E. Selby, CHRONOLOGY OF VIRGINIA AND THE WAR OF INDEPENDENCE (Charlottesville, 1973), 2.

41. William J. Van Schreeven et al., REVOLUTIONARY VIRGINIA: THE ROAD TO INDEPENDENCE (Charlottesville, 1973–1979), 1:1–2, 9–10, 15, 48–49, 52–54, 69–70, 74–77, 81–87, 90–91, 93–98, 106, 143, 200–221, 230; Selby, CHRONOLOGY, 2, 4–5, 7, 9–11, 13–14, 18; Revolution, 20–21.

42. William C. Ford, ed., LETTERS OF WILLIAM LEE (New York, 1967), 282.

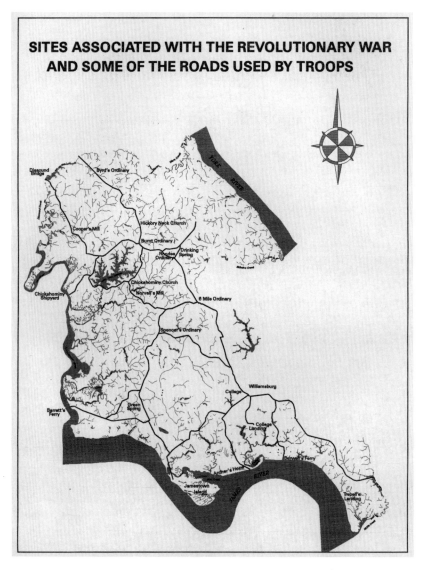

SITES ASSOCIATED WITH THE REVOLUTIONARY WAR
AND SOME OF THE ROADS USED BY TROOPS

Map by Deborah L. Wilson.

C H A P T E R   8

"This Great Good Cause We Will Defend"

The Revolutionary War in James City County 1776–1781

A British Intrusion: The Gunpowder Incident

On March 3, 1775, the VIRGINIA GAZETTE alerted the citizens of James City County to the presence of an armed British ship at the ferry landing at Kingsmill:

A Caution to the Publick. Be it known that his Majesty's armed schooner MAGDALEN, HENRY COLLINS, ESQ. commander, mounting four carriage guns . . . now lies moored opposite to Burwell's ferry, for the purpose of bringing to and searching all vessels going up and down the James river. (Note well, masters and owners, that the King pays no costs or damages in his Admiralty courts, whether your vessels, after seizure and libelling, be condemned or not).[1]

If the embargo's imposition left doubts that the colonies' relationship with Great Britain had deteriorated dramatically, another event made it painfully clear. On April 21, 1775, a detachment of royal sailors and marines slipped into Williamsburg before dawn, seized the gunpowder stored in the city magazine, and loaded it aboard the MAGDALEN. As soon as the theft was discovered, drums sounded an alarm, summoning local citizens to the market square. The crowd quickly evolved into an angry mob set on a confrontation

Courtesy of the Colonial Williamsburg Foundation.

with Lord Dunmore. Peyton Randolph, Robert Carter Nicholas, and Williamsburg's mayor were the prevailing voices of calm, for they convinced the crowd that it was preferable for a delegation to make a "decent and respectful protest." People dispersed but rumors that the royal marines were returning rallied another mob. The next day, the outraged Dunmore threatened to arm the colonists' slaves if calm were not restored. On April 29th, when word of the battles of Lexington and Concord reached Fredericksburg, three horsemen rode to Williamsburg to see whether armed assistance was needed. Again, Peyton Randolph made a plea against violence. Dunmore, uneasy about the safety of his wife and children, moved them to a ship anchored at Yorktown. Later, after violence no longer seemed imminent, they returned to the Governor's Palace.[2]

On April 26, 1775, the Henrico County Committee passed a resolution terming the gunpowder's seizure "an insult to every freeman in this country." The following week, Patrick Henry persuaded members of the Hanover County Committee to send one party of militiamen to Williamsburg and another to King William County, to seize Richard Corbin, the colony's receiver-general.[3] The two groups converged at Doncastle's (Byrd's) Ordinary in western James City County. Afterward, the James City County Committee expressed its gratitude to Henry and his men for their assistance. Lord Dunmore summoned the assembly on June 1st. He aired Lord North's proposal that the colonies wouldn't be taxed if they agreed to tax themselves in accord with quotas set by the Mother Country. The burgesses adjourned without taking action. Two or three days later, several young men, who broke into Williamsburg's powder magazine around midnight, were surprised by a blast from a spring-loaded gun; two were slightly wounded. A mob of angry citizens stormed the magazine, calling Dunmore an assassin of youth. Because the royal marines were expected to return, Williamsburg's volunteer company mobilized and men from James City and New Kent Counties were invited to "assist the citizens in their nightly watches [and] guard against any surprise from our enemies." On June 8th, Dunmore and his family slipped out of Williamsburg before dawn and took refuge aboard the Fowey. Later, Lady Dunmore and her children set sail for England and Lord Dunmore moved to a ship anchored near the mouth of the James River.[4]

Readying The Colony's Defenses

During late July and much of August 1775 the Third Virginia Convention convened at St. John's Church in Richmond, for it was feared that Dunmore's men would attack Williamsburg. Robert Carter Nicholas and William Norvell attended on behalf of James City County and Champion Travis represented Jamestown. County committees and delegates were chosen and an eleven member Committee of Safety was empowered to make and enforce rules that would maintain social order. Plans were made to recruit two regiments and an ordinance was passed to encourage the manufacture of saltpeter, gunpowder, refined sulphur, and arms for the use of Virginia troops. The county committees of James City and York and the city of Williamsburg were warned that the British might attempt to land troops in their neighborhood. If so, they were to be repelled by force. The College of William and Mary's faculty and students joined military units. Patrick Henry established a campground at the college, where Virginia troops assembled and trained.[5]

A small but sinister-sounding item in the August 19, 1775, edition of the VIRGINIA GAZETTE reveals that tensions had tightened to the breaking point: *We are informed by a gentleman of credit that this morning about daybreak, he discovered a man of war's barge in the College Landing creek with eight men on board, one of which was dressed in red and had all the appearances of a certain lord. The oars were all muffled, and the people seemed in the greatest hurry to get away. Beware, my penetrating lord, lest one day or other you pay dear for your curiosity.*[6]

Two more news reports that appeared during August reflect the same militant mood. Anthony Warwick of Isle of Wight County, found guilty of selling goods to the British, was hauled before the county committee which decided that he should be outfitted in:

. . . a fashionable suit of tar and feathers, being the most proper badge of distinction for men of his complexion. They then mounted him on a horse and drove him out of town, through a shower of eggs, the smell of which, our correspondent informs us, seemed to have a material effect upon the delicate constitution of this motleyed gentleman.[7]

A Williamsburg man, who made derogatory remarks about the American cause, narrowly escaped the same fate. He was seized and taken to the volunteer companies' encampment at Carter's Grove, where he was interrogated. After a spirited debate over whether he should be "complimented with a coat of thickset" (tar and feathers), drummed through the city, or simply forced to apologize, the latter course was taken. But a warning to "those who may hereafter sport with the great and glorious cause of America" was published in the VIRGINIA GAZETTE.

On August 21, 1775, the Third Virginia Convention's delegates divided the colony into 16 military districts, each of which was to furnish 500 men and compensate them for their service. Each county's Committee of Safety was to appoint its milita company's officers. Thomas Jefferson later said that every able-bodied freeman from 16 to 50 was enrolled in the militia. Militia members had to outfit themselves with arms that were "usual in the regular service." He added that "This injunction was always indifferently complied with." Each county militia was headed by a lieutenant, who held the rank of a colonel when on the battlefield. General officers were appointed as the need arose; their rank depended upon the seriousness of the situation. Virginia's governor was the commander-in-chief of the state militia. In 1780–1781, 235 out of Virginia's 49,971 militiamen were from James City County and another 120 came from Williamsburg.[8]

James City, Charles City, New Kent, Warwick, York, and Elizabeth City Counties, and Williamsburg comprised the Military District of Elizabeth City. When district leaders met at the Williamsburg-James City County Courthouse in early September 1775, Robert Carter Nicholas, William Norvell, and Nathaniel Burwell represented James City County and Champion Travis served on behalf of Jamestown. Nicholas was chosen chairman of the District's leadership committee, which decided how many companies of minutemen each county should provide and chose each company's officers. James City County was to furnish 50 minutemen, which comprised one company. James Walker was elected captain of the James City Company, with William Johnson as lieutenant and Henry Brown as ensign. By mutual agreement, "the place of general rendezvous" for the District of Elizabeth City's battalion was "in the neighborhood of the city of Williamsburg." The leadership committee advertised for someone to furnish provisions and supplies to the District's companies of minutemen and James Bray Johnson, who owned land in James City and Charles City Counties, was appointed Commissary of Musters. In December, when the Fourth Virginia Convention distributed salt to County Committees of Safety, James City received 36 bushels.[9]

The only surviving excerpts of the James City County Committee of Safety's minutes are those published in the VIRGINIA GAZETTE. A September 17, 1775, account of a recent committee meeting indicates that William Holt, whose mill near Jamestown had a bakehouse for ships' biscuits, was censured for furnishing supplies to some British naval vessels "now in the county." Holt replied that "he hath for several years contracted to furnish the men-of-war with supplies of bread and flour for immediate use" and that after he moved to Norfolk he had secured its Committee of Safety's permission to proceed with the sale. Even so, the James City County Committee ordered him and other "proprietors of mills and bakehouses not to manufacture any larger quantities of bread or Indian corn into flour, meal or bread than may be necessary for the internal consumption of this country." Two years later, Holt was paid for various commodities he sold to the American Army and he seems to have continued producing ships biscuits.[10]

A Formal Declaration of War

By late summer 1775, the breach between Great Britain and her American colonies had become irreparable. The November 10th edition of the VIRGINIA GAZETTE carried King George III's August 23rd declaration that the colonies were in "open and avowed rebellion" and his call for loyal British subjects to aid in suppressing them. Nearly a week before the king's call-to-arms was published locally, two British tenders fired upon Jamestown and some American sentinels stationed there, "driving two or three small balls through the ferry-house." The attack must have frightened the widowed Mary Cary Ambler and her household, whose dwelling was nearby. Lord Dunmore placed the sloop KING FISHER at Burwell's Ferry Landing to search all incoming ships. When its men attempted to board a small vessel, they were driven off by the gunfire of rifle guards posted on shore.[11] The KING FISHER and its tenders commenced a heavy cannonading, during which the storehouse at Burwell's Ferry was stuck by a six-pound cannon ball that went in one side and out the other. A number of shots also hit the ferry house in which Thomas Cartwright and his household lived.[12] Three or four hours later, the KING FISHER fired a few broadsides at the ferry landing, then withdrew and anchored just off shore. Later, it dropped down to Mulberry Island. The VIRGINIA GAZETTE reported that Burwell's Landing was attacked by the same vessels that fired upon Jamestown Island a week earlier. In mid-November, a boat load of British soldiers tried to land at Jamestown, half a mile below the American battery. Although they were repelled, a man-of-war stationed nearby fired upon the Travis plantation at the eastern end of the island, sending a shot through the kitchen chimney.[13]

More than one British vessel ran afoul of the local militia. John Lee of James City County and 15 other men were standing guard at Jamestown on a windy night in November 1775, when a sentinel spied two enemy sloops sailing up the James "on a plundering party." However, when the vessels reversed their course, one ran aground and Lee's men commenced fire. Later, they seized the sloop and its cargo, which included ivory, beef, pork, and military stores. The British sloop was outfitted for use by Virginia's state navy and put under the command of Captain Edward Travis, whose brother's Jamestown Island home recently had been shelled. During this period Dunmore and his men, despite the colonists' resistance, were relatively free to cruise Virginia waters and touch land almost anywhere. The British were in control of Norfolk, Portsmouth, and Gosport and Dunmore had declared martial law. He signed an Emancipation Proclamation that freed all of the rebelling colonists' slaves and indentured servants and invited them to bear arms on behalf of the king. Two black slaves, who offered their services to men aboard what they thought was a British tender, were executed at Jamestown by the Americans they mistakenly approached.[14] However, a significant number of blacks (enslaved and free) served on behalf of the American cause and later, some slaves were freed on account of their meritorious service.

Achieving Independence

Early in 1776 the Virginia Committee of Safety made plans to build salt works and powder mills and to undertake other projects that would provide support to the military. A Board of Naval Commissioners was created for the purpose of establishing a small navy. The commissioners were to oversee the construction and repair of all state navy vessels and supervise all public rope-walks, dockyards, and shipyards. They also were to procure several armed vessels from owners of the merchant fleet and to seek out suitable locations for the construction of state shipyards. In June 1776 master shipbuilder John Herbert was authorized to hire ships-carpenters "to examine and view all such places on James River or its branches as he may think proper and convenient for erecting shipyards." A readily available supply of timber and iron were considered essential. In July the Continental Congress adopted Richard Henry Lee's resolution for independence and on the 4th, the Declaration of Independence was accepted.[15]

On April 24, 1776, a large group of James City County freeholders gathered at the Six Mile (Allen's) Ordinary where they drafted written instructions to Robert Carter Nicholas and William Norvell, the county's delegates to the Fifth Virginia Convention. The document stated that:

Reason, drawn from justice, policy and necessity, are everywhere at hand for a radical separation from Great Britain. From justice, for the blood of those who have fallen in our cause cries aloud, 'It is time to part.' From necessity, because she hath of herself repudiated us by a rapid succession of insult, injury, robbery, murder and a formal declaration of war.

The text went on to say that it was time to dissolve "the connexion between America and Great Britain, totally, finally and irrevocably." The delegates' instructions were published in the VIRGINIA GAZETTE, which editor noted that they had been signed "by a majority of the freeholders living in the county."[16]

In May 1776, when British General Henry Clinton invaded North Carolina and large numbers of Virginia troops went to oppose him, there was concern about Williamsburg's vulnerability to attack. The Fifth Virginia Convention's delegates decided to station "as strong a force as possible" in the city and its dependencies, which were identified as Jamestown, Yorktown, Burwell's Ferry, and Hampton. During the spring and summer months, two militia companies were based at Burwell's Ferry, where they constructed fortifications and worked on the road leading to Williamsburg. Men also were posted at the College of William and Mary and at Jamestown, where three companies (despite ill health) were building a battery. Captain Massie, who was the first commander of the fortifications at Burwell's Landing, was succeeded by Captains Fox and Hobson. At the close of 1776 Philip Johnson resigned as James City County's lieutenant due to his age and infirmities; he was replaced by Nathaniel Burwell.[17]

In June 1776, when George Mason's proposed Declaration of Rights was approved by the Virginia Convention, a new government was established in Virginia. It resembled its colonial antecedent but had some major differences. The General Assembly had much greater power than the House of Burgesses

Site of the Chickahominy Shipyard. Photo by Ralph Maxwell.

had had and it chose the governor, whose role was much weaker than it had been during the colonial period. Thanks to Thomas Jefferson's influence, Virginia's legal codes were revised, special privileges were abolished, and the penal code was made more humane.

Throughout 1776 a considerable amount of military activity took place on Jamestown Island. A ship-load of Scottish Highlanders was captured and brought ashore there and military stores, food, and other commodities were sent to Jamestown where they were loaded aboard outbound ships. Naval vessels were repaired and outfitted there with supplies and equipment from the Warwick rope walk, Portsmouth, and Cabin Point. Captain Edward Travis used Jamestown Island as a staging area for the naval vessels under his command. A British brigantine captured by a privateer was offered for sale at Jamestown, as was a Surry County man's newly outfitted sloop. During the summer of 1776, an alleged counterfeiter was apprehended at Jamestown, tried by the military and then released.[18]

Ebenezer Hazard, who strolled around the western end of Jamestown Island in June 1777, observed that a small battery had been erected "a little above the town" and that a dozen or so men of the Allied army were garrisoned there. It was curvilinear and stood in a swale just west of the church, probably in the same low area in which a curved brick fort was located a century earlier. Hazard visited the ruinous old church and transcribed William Sherwood's epitaph, which described him as "A Great Sinner Waiting For A Joyfull Resurrection." He said that there was a fine, but badly neglected, fruit orchard at Jamestown, near which was a large brick house "with large Rooms, well papered, lofty Ceiling, Marble Hearths and other Indications of Elegance and Taste," which was "decaying fast." He identified the abandoned dwelling as Mrs. Ambler's, adding that after she had fled from the area, her home was used as the ferry house. Hazard described Jamestown as gloomy and melancholy, although it formerly had been a small but thriving county seat. Captain Edward Travis later signed a four-year lease with Mrs. Ambler, entitling him to the use of her plantation. Thus, the Travises briefly controlled almost all of Jamestown Island.[19]

By March 1777 shipbuilder John Herbert had selected a site on the Chickahominy River that he deemed suitable for the construction of the

Virginia navy's shipyard. There, on Phillip, William, and James Bray Johnson's land near the mouth of Yarmouth Creek, W. Pointer and a gang of slaves erected the buildings of the Chickahominy Shipyard.[20] The shipyard had dwellings that housed its superintendent and paymaster, warehouses in which naval stores were kept, and at least two boat slips. Ship construction and repair got underway at the Chickahominy Shipyard by June 1777. Expenditures for rope, sail cloth, saws, and military stores, recorded in navy account books, reflect the scope of the facility's operations. In an attempt to attract skilled workers, the state assembly in 1778 voted to exempt from military service all ships carpenters, blacksmiths, joiners, and clerks associated with the shipbuilding industry.[21]

Captain James Maxwell, at General George Washington's request, served as the superintendent of the Chickahominy Shipyard. He resided there with his family, as did first clerk and paymaster Jonathan Browne and his successor Isaac Smith. John Herbert, the first master shipbuilder, died in 1780; his replacement was William Cole, reputedly an equally capable artisan. Blacks and whites, both male and female, were employed at the Chickahominy Shipyard and probably resided on the premises. The size of the shipyard's payroll suggests that there was a substantial work force. A December 1780 list of winter clothing (jackets, breeches, stockings, and caps or hats) ordered from the Commissary of Stores indicates that there were at least 26 male workers. Those employed at the shipyard also were provided with staple foods, such as flour and corn, and an occasional barrel of rum.[22]

Several ships were built at the Chickahominy Shipyard between 1777 and 1780 and many vessels were repaired and outfitted. By mid-summer 1780, government officials decided to dispose of certain state-owned ships and offered them for sale to the public. Letters exchanged by James Maxwell and Governor Thomas Jefferson indicate that in October 1780 several naval vessels at the Chickahominy Shipyard were ready for mobilization. In January 1781 Jefferson ordered Maxwell to have his men build 20 portable boats of a new design, suitable for use in shallow waters. He also told Maxwell to fabricate several bateaux that could be used in the James River above the fall line.[23]

The British fleet arrived in the James during January 1781 and began sailing upstream. When Benedict Arnold reached Burwell's Ferry and sent a

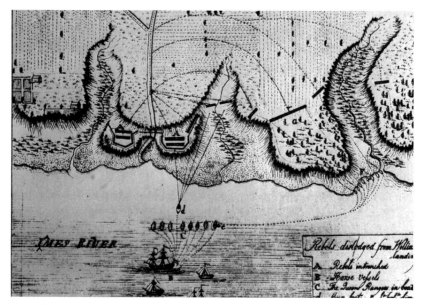

The British invasion at Kingsmill, depicted by Lt. Colonel John G. Simcoe on his map, "Rebels dislodged from Williamsburg landing," 1781. National Archives.

man ashore with a flag of truce, to determine the mood of the people, he was surprised to find that they were armed and ready to fight. When word of the British invasion reached the Chickahominy Shipyard there was a flurry of activity. The galley LEWIS was outfitted and sent downstream and guns were loaded aboard the brig JEFFERSON, which had been stripped for repair. By February the JEFFERSON and TEMPEST were ready to join the French fleet and the TARTAR and SAFE GUARD were ready to sail as soon as crews could be found. The LIBERTY and the NICHOLSON, which had been sunk for conceal- ment in deep holes in the bottom of the Nansemond River, were raised and outfitted as part of the general military build-up. Edgar Joel planned to raise the decrepit DRAGON, sunk near the Chickahominy Shipyard for an extended period of time, in order to outfit it as a fire ship that could be sent into the British convoy. But the plan went awry when a bungling pilot put the DRAGON onto a sand bar and the British learned of his plan.[24]

In mid-March 1781 the Chickahominy Shipyard's superintendent asked his superiors for weapons that could be used for defense and he requested the return of the state sloop. On April 4, he informed the governor that "by the latter end of this week all the publick stores will be removed from this place." He added that he had sent the TEMPEST and the JEFFERSON up the James to join several other armed vessels.[25] Meanwhile, the LEWIS and the boat PATRIOT were stationed between Hampton Roads and Burwell's Ferry. Despite these measures the British moved up the James and ultimately reached the fall line.

Relocating the Capital to Richmond

Although James City County largely escaped the ravages of war until the spring of 1781, a political decision made in 1779 had a profound effect upon the counties of the lower peninsula. On June 12th the General Assembly voted to shift the seat of Virginia's government from Williamsburg to Richmond, which was presumed less vulnerable to enemy attack. On April 7, 1780, the state's executive department ceased transacting business in Williamsburg and on April 24th resumed its duties in Richmond. A week later, the General Assembly held its first session in the new capital city.[26]

After the capital was moved, Williamsburg no longer was at the hub of Virginia's social and commercial life. In 1783 Johann David Schoepf observed that the community was:

. . . a poor place compared with its former splendor. With the removal of the government, merchant, advocates and other considerable residents took their departure as well. . . . The merchants of the country round about were accustomed formerly to assemble here every year, to advise about commercial affairs and matters in the furtherance of trade. This also has come to an end.[27]

Thus, in some respects, Williamsburg's decline mirrored that of Jamestown when the capital was moved in 1699. Although the people of James City County continued to make regular visits to the county seat, the city lost much of its cosmopolitan atmosphere.

In mid-April 1781 when British General William Phillips arrived in Hampton Roads with 2,600 men, he decided to move up the James River and capture Williamsburg. He had Lt. Colonel John Simcoe and the Queen's Rangers land below the city and he sent Lt. Colonel Abercrombie's men ashore further upstream. When Simcoe and his men reached Burwell's Ferry Landing on April 19th, they discovered that the Americans had thrown up entrenchments, which were manned. Employing a diversionary tactic, he opted to land a short distance downstream, on the west side of a small estuary now known as Wareham's Pond, but dispatched a gunboat and some other small vessels toward Burwell's Ferry. According to Baron von Steuben, the

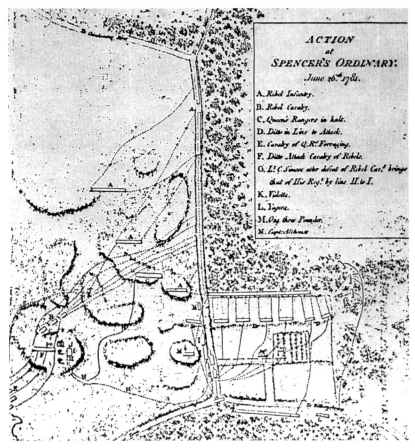

Lt. Colonel John G. Simcoe's portrayal of "Action at Spencer's Ordinary," June 26, 1781. National Archives.

American troops fared as well as they did because of "an accidental occurrence which happened, much to the soldierly credit of old Chancellor Wythe and one or two other old Gentlemen" who "took a pop" at the British while partridge-hunting near the mouth of College Creek. Later, Phillips and the rest of his army went ashore at Burwell's Ferry. He ordered Simcoe to spend the night in Williamsburg before continuing on to Yorktown.[28]

On April 21st, Colonel James Innes sent word to the governor that 500 British infantrymen, 50 horses, and four pieces of artillery had come ashore at Burwell's Ferry and that their unexpected arrival had forced him to withdraw to the Six Mile Ordinary around midnight. He said that 14 British ships were above of Jamestown, and that 16 flat-bottomed boats had ascended the Chickahominy and were within three miles of the shipyard. Meanwhile, General Phillips and a large body of troops marched to Barretts Ferry where they boarded vessels that transported them to the mouth of the Appomattox River. Simcoe and the Queen's Rangers lagged behind, for they "formed the rear guard and lay on shore the whole night in a position which a little labor rendered unassailable." Phillips' army reportedly inflicted extensive damage upon everything in its path.[29]

On April 22nd at 4 P.M. a detachment of British soldiers seized and destroyed the Chickahominy Shipyard. Colonel Innes, who was encamped in the yard of Hickory Neck Church, sent word to Governor Jefferson on April 23rd that the British had set the shipyard ablaze, which flames illuminated the night-sky. The next day, Innes reported that the shipyard's buildings and an unfinished 20-gun ship were destroyed, along with some naval stores that had been stashed at the Diascund Bridge. The destruction of the state shipyard and the loss of more than a dozen vessels at Osbornes marked the demise of the Virginia State Navy.[30]

In late May General Charles Lord Cornwallis and his army of seasoned veterans arrived in Petersburg and joined forces with General Phillips' men, temporarily under the command of Benedict Arnold. This union of forces created a British Army 7,000 strong. Cornwallis left Petersburg, crossed the James and set out in pursuit of Lafayette, who had retreated toward Fredericksburg while awaiting reinforcements. The savvy French general embarked upon a strategy of paralleling the British Army's movements while staying just out of reach. In mid-June Cornwallis moved eastward along the old road that ran through New Kent Courthouse and Burnt Ordinary.[31] Simcoe's men, meanwhile, followed the upper side of the Chickahominy River, then crossed and burned the Diascund Bridge. Simcoe and Cornwallis met up at Cooper's Mills on Diascund Creek.[32] Cornwallis and the vanguard of his army set out for Williamsburg and arrived on June 25th. Meanwhile, Lafayette, who joined forces with Generals Anthony Wayne and von Steuben, amassing an estimated 1,900 Continentals and 3,000 militia, also headed for Williamsburg. On June 26th, part of the Allied Army was encamped at Byrd's Tavern. According to a British intelligence report, Lafayette held forth in the yard of the Chickahominy Church, near Burnt Ordinary, and some of his men were near Rhodes Ordinary and the Drinking Spring. His advance detachments were approaching Spencer's Ordinary and plantation near Centerville, where main roads to Williamsburg and Jamestown converged.[33]

Some of Cornwallis's men were already there, resting while they awaited

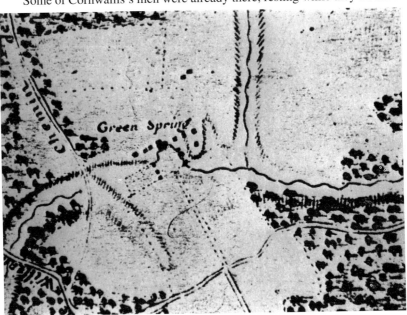

Green Spring as depicted on Nicholas Desandrouin's 1781 map, "Plan de Terrein a la Rive Gauche de La Riviere du James." Library of Congress.

Major Armstrong's ranger battalion and the army's baggage train. Johann Ewald, a Hessian officer with the British Army, arrived at the Spencer plantation on June 26th, around six or seven in the morning. He and his men camped in platoons along the road, had breakfast, and relaxed. Although Edwald hoped to resume his march before "the awful heat" became oppressive, he was tired and decided to take a nap:

I had hardly closed my eyes when several shots were fired . . . I jumped up and asked where the shooting was, whereupon several officers shouted that the farmers had fired on the [Loyalist] refugees . . . driving the cattle. . . . I had scarcely fallen asleep for the second time when I was awakened by a number of shots. I jumped up, mounted my horse, called the men to take up arms, and rode with my orderly and a ranger dragoon into Spencer's orchard, behind which I crouched.

I had hardly ridden fifty paces into the apple orchard, when I discovered a man in a blue uniform a short distance away from me. I was aware of him before he saw me and I sprang upon him. The man was more frightened than I, and after he was in my hands I saw that he was an officer of the Armand Legion and a Frenchman. . . . I handed him over to my orderly, sprang back without saying one word more, and shouted "Up, up, forward march!" Everyone followed. But to my astonishment, when I was barely across the orchard I found a long line deployed behind a fence, two or three hundred paces away, just on the point of moving forward.

During the military engagement that followed, men from both sides were killed or captured. Ewald said that his soldiers found it difficult to move through the thick undergrowth. A map he made to illustrate his account reveals that troop movements and intense fighting encompassed both sides of Centerville Road.[34]

Colonel Simcoe, who was present at Spencer's when combat occurred, saw the day's events from another perspective. He claimed that the British emerged victorious and the Allies fled in confusion, discarding their weapons. Lt. Colonel Banastre Tarleton, who approached Spencer's via Longhill Road, also spoke of the arms the Allies threw away. The Marquis de Chastelleux, who was with the Allied Army, said that Lafayette's vanguard made a surprise attack upon the British, who were stealing cattle from the neighborhood.

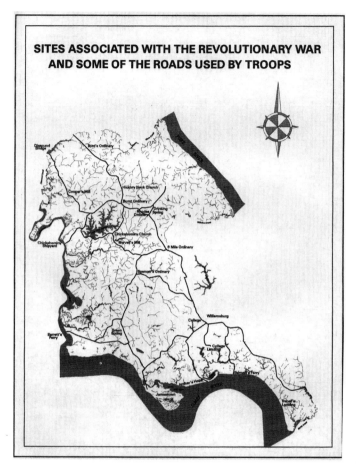

Map by Deborah L. Wilson. See enlarged map, page 206.

Thus, they were caught off-guard and forced to fight. Chastelleux claimed that only when Cornwallis came to his men's rescue were the Allies obliged to retire, by which time nearly 150 men had been killed or wounded.[35] This battle probably gave rise to the name War Hill, a large tract between Centerville and Longhill Roads.

The Battle of Green Spring

While the British were occupying Williamsburg, they destroyed some horseboats they found on Jamestown Island and then moved up the Chickahominy River to Morecock's Island, where they burned more horseboats and some canoes. Lafayette, meanwhile, made the Tyree plantation near the Diascund Bridge his headquarters but maintained a patrol and picket line toward Williamsburg. His army, which was in close range of the British, was constantly on the move. Both armies parried each other's movements, pausing occasionally to rest. On June 30, 1781, Cornwallis decided to withdraw to Jamestown so that his men could cross the James, march to Portsmouth, and set sail for New York, in accord with orders from his commander-in-chief. By July 4th, the British Army's main body was encamped at the Ambler plantation on the mainland west of Jamestown Island, preparing to depart. Meanwhile, on July 5th Lafayette's advanced units were positioned at the Chickahominy Church and Norvell's Mill.[36]

While Lafayette was at Norvell's Mill he received word that the British had left Williamsburg and that the main part of the army had crossed the James. He resolved to draw closer to Jamestown so that his men could attack what few enemy troops remained. He dispatched a detachment of men under the command of General Wayne but held the greater part of his force in abeyance. Little did he know that British Colonel Banastre Tarleton had bribed two local men to tell any Allied troops they met that almost all of the Red Coats had crossed the James. As luck would have it, one of the informants encountered General Wayne, to whom he imparted the misinformation.[37]

Early in the afternoon of July 6, Wayne and the Pennsylvania Line reached William Lee's "large brick house" at Green Spring, where he paused to assess the strength of his enemy. Around 2 P.M., he sent out a small group of American riflemen and a scouting party who advanced across the long, narrow causeway that extended from the front of the Green Spring mansion toward Jamestown. They came face to face with a British cavalry patrol, with whom they briefly exchanged fire. Next, they encountered a group of British pickets, who fired and then fell back. In this halting manner, the Americans were lured into Cornwallis's carefully contrived trap. Lafayette arrived at Green Spring and was told that the British were continuing their withdrawal across the James. But when he moved to a vantage point on the river bank, he saw that the British had not crossed over after all. Realizing that he had been duped, Lafayette hastily returned to Green Spring and found combat already underway. He positioned two battalions of Virginia troops in an open field at the west end of the causeway so that they could cover General Wayne's retreat.

Meanwhile, the American advance guard, still unaware of the ruse, continued on toward Jamestown. When they caught sight of a British field piece slowly being withdrawn, they followed it and came face-to-face with British troops concealed in the woods. The Americans rapidly withdrew toward Green Spring, covered by the firepower of the men Lafayette had stationed to cover their retreat. As darkness fell, both sides retired from the battlefield and Lafayette moved inland, leaving three companies of light infantry at Green Spring. At daybreak on July 7th, Tarleton, with 200 dragoons and 80 mounted infantrymen, crossed the causeway to Green Spring, where they encountered a patrol of mounted riflemen, who retired toward the main army's position. Tarleton also withdrew. The next day, the British left Jamestown and Lafayette took up a position on the Ambler farm, where his enemies had encamped only two days before.[38]

A soldier, who returned to the battlefield after all fighting ceased, reported that both armies' lines could be traced by the trail of empty cartridge boxes on the ground. In September 1781 an American officer informed his superiors that he had "employed a person to collect from the people the arms picked up after the action at Jamestown, which are chiefly State property." Thus, the fought-over ground seemingly was littered with discarded weapons. As late as 1852, evidence of the Battle of Green Spring still was still visible. Historian Benson J. Lossing, a guest at the Ambler farm, said that the dwelling of his host, John Coke, had "many bullet marks, made there during the battle at Jamestown Ford, on the 6th of July, 1781." He added that the French Army had camped at Amblers' when enroute to Yorktown.[39]

The battle's impact upon the neighborhood apparently was considerable. On July 15, 1781, William Lee's brother, Richard Henry Lee, informed him that Richard Taliaferro of Powhatan Plantation and Champion Travis of Jamestown Island had lost all of their slaves when the British came through and that John Paradise of Rich Neck had only one. He said this was typical of areas the British Army occupied and that:

The enemies Generals here appear to carry on the war much more upon views of private plunder and enriching individuals than upon any plan of national advantage. . . . The British General [Cornwallis] has been travers-ing an undefended part of Virginia, with an Army employed in taking off Negroes, plate, &c. and destroying Corn, Cattle and Tobo. . . . So soon as our militia could be collected and joined by a few regular corps from the army, his Lordship rapidly retreated.[40]

He said that the British had taken 60 head of cattle from Green Spring. A French military officer said that "a certain Mr. Egleston, one of the richest inhabitants of these parts" (probably Joseph Eggleston Jr., who then owned part of Powhatan) took refuge in a beaver lodge when he heard that the British were coming to pillage his house. Eggleston, who had shot and killed a British soldier, hid throughout the six weeks there was a price on his head.[41]

An agreement negotiated during spring 1781 made provisions for pris-oners-of-war to be exchanged at Jamestown. "Cartel vessels" bearing American detainees landed periodically between July 1781 and November 1782. The men released there were in dire need of provisions, money, and transportation out of the area. The Chevalier d'Ancteville, who arrived at Jamestown in late summer 1781 right after the British departure, said he found "burned debris, tombs opened, other beautiful monuments broken to pieces, [and] a temple partly knocked down." He claimed that "the houses still existing breathed a cadaverous odor and enclosed cadavers" and said that "all means of devastation had been employed to the city and to the country-side." One army physician commented that the local people were "generally genteel and hospitable, the ladies handsome and witty, and what is still better, they have fortunes." A young French lieutenant said that he had "chatted awhile with a couple of Virginia girls—one of them as big as a horse (almost)."[42]

Prelude to the Yorktown Campaign

In mid-August 1781 General George Washington, upon learning that the Comte de Grasse was sailing toward the Chesapeake Bay, began moving his and the Comte de Rochambeau's armies southward to Virginia. Cornwallis, meanwhile, already had decided to occupy Yorktown and Gloucester Point, for he considered the harbor between them essential to the defense of his shipping. By August 22 the British were busily throwing up earthworks on both sides of the river, with the assistance of an estimated 2,000 black slaves.[43]

By late summer Hickory Neck Church, just west of Burnt Ordinary, had been converted into a hospital for Continental Army soldiers. On August 6th the hospital's general surgeon, Dr. John Lehmann, reported that he had 35 patients from the navy and the militia, who were from North and South Carolina, Maryland, and Virginia. The men suffered from ailments that ranged from dysentery and the ague to gonorrhea. Only one man was wounded. The following week, Dr. Thomas Tud. Tucker, physician-in-charge of the hospital at Hickory Neck, sent word to Cornwallis that when his apothecary's mate and several other hospital employees went to Williamsburg to procure medical supplies, they were seized by British troops and taken to Yorktown. Tucker said that "the sick at Hickory Neck Church are a part of those who came lately from Charleston" and had been removed from Yorktown before there was assurance they would receive treatment from British doctors. He said that the Marquis de Lafayette had indicated his hospital was to remain open and asked that his medical workers and their cart be released.[44]

On August 29, 1781, the French fleet sailed into the mouth of the Chesapeake and anchored near Lynnhaven Inlet. Several ships then moved inland to the mouth of the York River, cutting off Cornwallis' means of communication and preventing him from receiving reinforcements. French troops began streaming into James City County as part of the overall military build-up. A shortage of seagoing vessels forced some of Rochambeau's men to trek overland to Annapolis, where they boarded ships that set sail for Williamsburg. As there were not enough vessels to carry the French Army's horses and wagons, they were sent overland. Victor Collot and Louis-Alexandre Berthier, assistant quartermasters-general, escorted the 1,500 horses, 800 oxen, and 220 wagons from Annapolis to Williamsburg, pausing at suitable sites along the way. Perhaps because Berthier anticipated following the same itinerary when returning north, he made detailed sketches of the campsites his men used along the way and described the neighborhoods in which some of them were located. On October 6, 1781, the French wagon train left New Kent Courthouse, crossed into James City County and camped overnight at Byrd's Ordinary. Berthier noted that "The camp would be well situated [for the army]. The tavern is large. There are several houses in the neighborhood for lodging the headquarters staff." He observed that the road to Williamsburg was good and was bordered by large clearings and wooded areas. He passed a meetinghouse on his left (Hickory Neck Church), emerged from the forest and came to "a fork where there are two old chimneys," the ruins of Fox's Ordinary. He said that "The right-hand road goes to Petersburg via Cole's Ferry over the Chickahominy." Berthier wrote of passing several more roads, clearings, and houses and then "you come to Allen's Tavern," six miles from Williamsburg. In 1789 Christopher Colles retraced the French wagon train's itinerary. He recommended that it be used by the postal service and made a map on which he identified Byrd's Tavern and the site of the "Burnt brick Orny."[45]

The men of Jean-Francois-Louis, the Comte de Clermont-Crevecour, set sail from Annapolis on September 20, 1781, and five days later disembarked near the mouth of College Creek. They set out for Williamsburg as soon as their artillery pieces, baggage, and horses had been brought ashore. They placed a piquet and one or more cannons on the east side of South Henry Street, overlooking College Landing, and a cannon at the mouth of the creek. By September 28th the Allied Armies were on their way to Yorktown. Meanwhile, transport ships arrived at Trebell's Landing (at Kingsmill) with siege artillery. On the 30th the British abandoned their outermost earthworks at Yorktown, for the siege had begun. They holed up in the town, which the Allies commenced to bombard. On October 16th Cornwallis asked the Allies to parley. Leaders from the opposing sides met at the Moore house, east of Yorktown, where they drew up articles of surrender that were signed on October 19, 1781. With the surrender of Cornwallis's 7,247 man army, the American colonies' independence was won. However, another 17 months elapsed before a formal peace treaty was signed.[46]

The Aftermath

Rochambeau and his army wintered-over in Williamsburg and other parts of Hampton Roads and lingered until the following summer. As soon as the French military units received their marching orders, they assembled in Williamsburg and then set out toward Annapolis, retracing the itinerary the wagon trains had used the previous fall. The army's four divisions departed on four successive days. Thus, each of their camp sites was occupied four times in rapid succession. The first division of Rochambeau's army, upon leaving Williamsburg, paused for the night of July 1, 1782, at the Drinking Spring. A sketch map indicates that the spring was located north of Richmond Road, between Cokes and Maxton Lanes. Artillery pieces were parked on both sides of the road to Williamsburg and French troops encamped on the west side of the road. The next night, the men stopped two miles above Byrd's Tavern, at which point they exited James City County.[47]

Although most local people didn't seem to mind playing host to the French, their refusal to return the slaves they'd seized from the British generated a certain amount of ill feeling. One French officer said that the army had "garnered a veritable harvest of domesticks. Those among us who had no servant were happy to find one so cheap." A few citizens eventually filed claims for the French troops' damage to their property. But by and large, Virginians considered their French allies considerate guests whose discipline and behavior were praiseworthy.[48]

On April 23, 1783, Governor Benjamin Harrison asked Williamsburg's mayor to proclaim "a general peace and American independence" in accord with a proclamation from Congress. He responded by scheduling a special event on Thursday, May 1st. At 1 P.M., when a bell was rung, a crowd assembled at the courthouse, where the proclamation was read aloud. People then processioned to the college and the capitol, where the proclamation again was read. Heading the line of marchers were two attendants carrying ribbon-decorated staffs, followed by a herald on a "neatly caparisoned" gelding and two more attendants carrying decorated staffs. Then came the city sergeant with his mace, and the mayor and recorder, carrying the city charter. They were followed by the clerk with a map of the city, the city's aldermen, the Common

Council, and the townspeople. Afterward, everyone adjourned to the Raleigh Tavern to "pass the rest of the day."[49] A new nation had been born.

Notes

1. Purdie's VIRGINIA GAZETTE, March 3, 1775.

2. Purdie's VIRGINIA GAZETTE, April 21, 1775; Dixon and Hunter's VIRGINIA GAZETTE, April 22, 1775; Selby, CHRONOLOGY, 18–19; Kelso, KINGSMILL, 49–51; Van Schreeven et al., REVOLUTIONARY VIRGINIA, 3:63–64.

3. He wasn't home.

4. Van Schreeven et al., REVOLUTIONARY VIRGINIA, 3:62–63, 188–189, 218; Selby, CHRONOLOGY, 19–20.

5. Van Schreeven et al., REVOLUTIONARY VIRGINIA, 3:303, 440; 5:25; Wilford Kale, HARK UPON THE GALE: AN ILLUSTRATED HISTORY OF THE COLLEGE OF WILLIAM AND Mary (Norfolk, 1985), 52, 57–59; Jefferson, NOTES, 150–151, 153.

6. Pinckney's VIRGINIA GAZETTE, August 17, 1775; Mary A. Stevenson, QUEEN MARY'S PORT (CAPITOL LANDING), PRINCESS ANNE'S PORT (COLLEGE LANDING) (Williamsburg, 1951), 22; Palmer, CALENDAR, II, 410; III, 214; VIII, 131. College Landing was strategically important, for it provided easy access to the capital city and it was a major supply point for the Allied Army

7. Van Schreeven et al., REVOLUTIONARY VIRGINIA, 3:485–486.

8. Ibid., 1:72–73; 4:53, 74, 94–95, 100–101; Jefferson, NOTES, 88–89; Anonymous, "Militia A.D. 1780," 1780.

9. Van Schreeven et al., REVOLUTIONARY VIRGINIA, 4:53, 74, 94–95, 100–101; 5:272.

10. Purdie's VIRGINIA GAZETTE, September 17, 1775; Public Service Claims 1776–1778. By 1783 William Holt's son–in–law, William Coleman, was operating his mill and bakehouse, then called Newport Mills (Lee Letter Book V, 2–6).

11. The KING FISHER'S purser later complained that a faithful servant dared "not even shew his Nose, " there were so many "Rebels" on the river bank (Van Schreeven et al., REVOLUTIONARY VIRGINIA, 6:9).

12. In January 1776 he announced his purchase of Thomas Doncastle's ordinary on the road to New Kent (Purdie's VIRGINIA GAZETTE, January 26, 1776).

13. Selby, CHRONOLOGY, 21–22; Purdie's VIRGINIA GAZETTE, November 10 and 17, 1775.

14. Jean P. Hall et al., "Legislative Petitions from Virginia Counties with Significant Record Losses, No. 3," MAGAZINE OF VIRGINIA GENEALOGY 29:149; Virginia Legislative Petitions 1775; Van Schreeven et al., REVOLUTIONARY WAR, 6:10; Selby, Chronology, 23. Dixon's VIRGINIA GAZETTE, April 13 and August 3, 1776.

15. Selby, CHRONOLOGY, 25, 29; H. R. McIlwaine, ed., JOURNAL OF THE COUNCIL OF STATE (Richmond, 1931), II, 513.

16. Van Schreeven et al., REVOLUTIONARY VIRGINIA, 6:458. Unfortunately, the list of names has been lost.

17. Ibid., 6:65–66; Goodwin, KINGSMILL, 83–84; McIlwaine, COUNCIL OF STATE, I, 37, 96, 254.

18. William B. Clark, NAVAL DOCUMENTS OF THE AMERICAN REVOLUTION (Washington, D. C., 1966), 5:386, 686, 688, 720, 1147; 6:132, 174–175, 727; Charles E. Hatch, "Jamestown, The Revolution," WILLIAM AND MARY QUARTERLY, 37–38; McIlwaine, COUNCIL OF STATE, I, 35; Purdie's VIRGINIA GAZETTE, November 8, 1776; July 4, 1777; Dixon's VIRGINIA GAZETTE, August 3, 1776.

19. Shelley, HAZARD, 414–416; Nicholas Desandrouin, "Plan du terein de la Rive Gauch," 1781; Hatch, "Jamestown" 32; Clark, Naval Documents, 5:386, 686, 688, 720, 1147; 6:132, 174–175, 727; Ambler Manuscript No. 129.

20. The river, though somewhat brackish, has a reduced saline level that would have served a natural deterrent to the teredo worm, a destroyer of wooden ships. The Chickahominy Shipyard Archaeological Site was added to the National Register of Historic Places in 1979.

21. Virginia Papers Concerning the State Navy, 1776–1784:I–A, March 22, 1777; Journal of the Navy Board I: Mar, 19, 1777; II April 3, 1777; Virginia Navy Account Book 1776–1781:23, 26.

22. Palmer, CALENDAR, I, 396; II, 9; Virginia Papers Concerning the State Navy 1776–1784:I–B–H, November 8, 1780.

23. Claiborne's VIRGINIA GAZETTE, July 15, 1780; Julian P. Boyd, PAPERS OF THOMAS JEFFERSON (Princeton, n.d.), IV, 380.

24. PENNSYLVANIA GAZETTE, January 31, 1781

25. On April 27, 1781, the British attacked several naval vessels at Osbornes. Nine Virginia Navy ships were lost, several were scuttled, and the remainder were captured. The British also seized 12 private vessels carrying 2,000 pounds of tobacco (Selby, REVOLUTION, 273).

26. As it turned out, the British reached Richmond and on January 5 and 6, 1781, inflicted great damage upon the new capital. Buildings were burned, public records were destroyed, and substantial quantities of gunpowder and tobacco were captured (Selby, CHRONOLOGY, 40; Louis Manerin et al., THE HISTORY OF HENRICO COUNTY [Charlottesville, 1984], 139–140).

27. Reps, TIDEWATER TOWNS, 189.

28. Goodwin, KINGSMILL, 58, 86–87.

29. Simcoe, QUEEN'S RANGERS, 193; Goodwin, KINGSMILL, 86–88; Selby, CHRONOLOGY, 2.

30. Palmer, CALENDAR, II, 9, 65, 69; IV, 106; IX, 400; VIRGINIA GAZETTE AND GENERAL ADVERTISER, January 1, 1794; Robert A. Stewart, HISTORY OF THE VIRGINIA NAVY (Richmond, 1923), 94, 101–102. After the war was over, several cannon and cannon balls were retrieved from the Chickahominy Shipyard and the vicinity of Diascund Bridge. The shipyard property was sold at public auction.

31. That is, they marched along Routes 30 and 60 to Toano.

32. Michael Captaine, Untitled Map, 1781. It belonged to John Cooper, a wealthy James City County planter, who owned nearly 1,300 acres of land in that vicinity. Later, Cooper's real estate came into the hands of William Brown (James City County Land Tax Lists 1782–1823).

33. Selby, CHRONOLOGY, 43–44; Howard C. Rice, trans., TRAVELS IN NORTH AMERICA IN THE YEARS 1780, 1781, AND 1782 BY THE MARQUIS CHASTELLEUX (Chapel Hill, 1963), 963:378; Simcoe, QUEEN'S RANGERS, 226; B.P.R.O., P.R.O. 30/11/5 ff 1–2. The opposing armies used Centerville Road (Route 614), Chickahominy Road (Route 631), and Longhill Road (Route 612) in their progress toward Williamsburg.

34. Joseph P. Tustin, trans., Diary of the American War, a Hessian Journal: Captain Johann Ewald, Field Jager Corps (New Haven and London, 1979), 308–311, 341.

35. Simcoe, Queen's Rangers, 226–237; Rice, Chastellux, 378–379.

36. B.P.R.O, P.R.O. 30/11/5 ff 1–2; Hatch, "Affair," 170–196; William G. Stanard, "Letters of Lafayette," Virginia Magazine of History and Biography 6 (July 1898):59. Lafayette seems to have spent a considerable amount of time in the vicinity of Norvell's Mill, for in early September 1781 he was encamped there when he dispatched a letter to Governor Thomas Nelson, urging him to send provisions to his men.

37. Hatch, Affair, 170–196; William Maxwell, "Lord Cornwallis's Movements and Operations in Virginia in 1781," Virginia Historical Register, VI (October 1853):202–203.

38. Hatch, "Affair," 170–196. At that juncture, commander–in–chief Henry Clinton countermanded his former orders and instructed Cornwallis to fortify Old Point Comfort rather than proceeding to New York (Selby, Chronology, 45).

39. Benson J. Lossing, Pictorial Fieldbook of the American Revolution (New York, 1851–1852), 240–240; Hatch, Affair, 170–196.

40. James C. Ballach, The Letters of Richard Henry Lee (New York, 1911–1914), II, 242–244.

41. Rice et al., American Campaigns, I, 137, 154. Joseph Eggleston Jr. and his mother, Elizabeth, owned property that straddled News Road and a branch of Powhatan Creek. Originally it was part of the plantation called Powhatan.

42. Hatch, "Jamestown," 35; Chevalier de Ancteville, Journal of the Chesapeake Campaign, 1781; Hugh F. Rankin, The American Revolution (New York, 1964), 317–318.

43. Selby, Chronology, 45; Rankin, Revolution, 317–318.

44. John Lehmann, August 6, 1781; B.P.R.O., P.R.O. 30/11/6 ff 359–360.

45. Rice et al., American Campaigns, II, 83–84, 104–106; Colles, "Annapolis to Williamsburg," 1789. A map made by George Washington's cartographer, Samuel Dewitt, also shows these features.

46. Alexander Berthier, "Camp a Williamsburg le Septembre 7 miles de Archers hope," 1781; Palmer, Calendar, IX, 400–401; Rice et al., American Campaigns, I, 55–56, 138; Selby, Chronology, 46; Revolution, 310.

47. Rice et al., American Campaigns, I, 159, 173–174, maps 109 and 110.

48. Selby, Revolution, 312.

49. Lyon G. Tyler, "Historical Notes, " William and Mary Quarterly 1st Ser., 14 (July 1905):278–279. 208

The James City Parish Glebe is identified on J. G. Swift's 1818 map, "Reconnoitering the Chesapeake Bay." Swift also indicated that in 1781 two ferries ran from Jamestwon Island to the lower side of the James. Library of Congress.

CHAPTER 9

"Where Liberty Is, There Is My Home"
1782–1830

Recovering From the War

After the French and British went home, the people of James City County set about rebuilding their lives. But some local families were destitute, for they had lost their main breadwinner. Ellinah, the widow of James Milby, a soldier in Colonel Charles Harrison's artillery regiment, asked the General Assembly for assistance on her own behalf and that of her year-old child. Likewise, Mrs. Anne Hayes asked for a subsistence allowance because her late husband, Daniel, a soldier in Anthony Singleton's Artillery, had left her with six children age 10 or younger. Mrs. Mary Dorton requested a pension for herself and seven small children, for her husband, John, perished while serving with the 5th Virginia Regiment in Williamsburg. Some James City County citizens wanted compensation for services performed on behalf of the military. Walter Hopkins and William Rose asked to be paid for quartermaster duties they performed and Joseph Hay, a surgeon in the Virginia State Hospital, requested a bounty of land. Benjamin Trent sought back pay on behalf of his young son, who died in June 1777 while on duty in Williamsburg. On the other hand, Robert Carter Nicholas's executor requested reimbursement for the 6,000 pounds interest due on the funds the decedent had borrowed to purchase gunpowder for the state.[1]

Some local people asked the General Assembly to reimburse them for losses they sustained during the war. John Pierce presented a claim for money

Lord Dunmore owed him for two years' hire of a slave. Champion Travis asked for compensation because his dwelling and offices on Jamestown Island were ruined by the Virginia troops using them as guardhouses. Lewis Burwell Jr. of Kingsmill requested reimbursement for the destruction of his gardens and ferryhouse and damage to the outbuildings Virginia troops used as guardhouses. Dionysius Lester, Jamestown Island's ferry-keeper, asked to be paid for transporting American troops across the James during November 1775 and Mrs. Anne Cocke requested reimbursement for a slave captured by Lord Dunmore's forces while he was ferrying the 2nd Virginia Regiment from Jamestown to Edward's Landing below Cobham. The citizens of James City and four other Tidewater counties were told to forward their claims against the French to Dudley Digges, who would give them to Count Rochambeau. However, William Lee took a more direct approach. In February 1782 he informed his brother that he had dispatched a complaint to the Marquis de Lafayette about "all [the] damage done to the Estate at Green Spring last Campaign."[2]

For many people, times were hard. Those who leased portions of the Governor's Land near Jamestown refused to pay their annual rent unless they were absolved from paying taxes upon their property. This occurred at a time when the General Assembly was considering whether to sell publicly-owned real estate, such as the Governor's Land; the farm associated with the royal Governor's Palace; and property belonging to parishes of the defunct State Church. In 1784 the assembly decided to bestow all public land (except that of the church) upon the College of William and Mary, along with authorization to sell it. The college nullified the leases of those renting portions of the Governor's Land and threatened to sue them if they didn't vacate the premises. This prompted William Lee, John Ambler, William Wilkinson Jr., John Warburton, and the guardians of John Harris's orphans to file a November 1785 petition with the General Assembly, asserting that their rental agreements were legally binding. Ultimately, the lessees were given the opportunity to buy the acreage they had been renting. Real estate and personal property tax rolls suggest that during the late 1780s and early 1790s the fortunes of Champion Travis and other James City County planters waned, for the quantity of livestock and slaves they owned decreased markedly. They, like many other supporters of the American Revolution, probably found themselves deeply in debt at a time when the new nation's economy was weak.[3]

James City County residents called upon the legislature for assistance with various types of problems. Thomas Smith asked for a land grant under the headright system, for he had brought 52 indentured servants into the colony during 1774 and 1775, when there was a moratorium on the acquisition of western lands. Henry Martin of the island of Tortola, who purchased Kingsmill and planned to make it his home, requested permission to bring 12 slaves to Virginia, his domestic servants. William Holt, who had merchant mills in James City and New Kent Counties, asked the assembly to establish a flour inspection station locally. He claimed that although his mills were capable of processing 75,000 bushels of wheat a year, he was hindered by the lack of a convenient inspectorate. Holt apparently expected business to improve, for he hired Humphrey Harwood to build two new bake-ovens and a storehouse at his mill complex on Mill Creek. Local farmers petitioned the legislature to establish a bounty on crows, which had done extensive damage to their corn crops.[4]

Glimpses of Life in James City County

Journals maintained by French military officers during the early 1780s provide insights into everyday life in James City County. One diarist interviewed Adam Byrd (Bird), proprietor of the well known ordinary on the road to New Kent Courthouse. He recalled vividly the havoc wreaked by the British Army when it passed through in June 1781 and said that Cornwallis's men were "a hurricane, which destroyed everything in its path." In their wake came

. . . a scourge yet more terrible, a numerous rabble under the names of Refugees and Loyalists . . . not to assist in the field but to share the plunder. The furniture and clothing of the inhabitants was in general the only booty left to satisfy their avidity; after they had emptied the houses, they stripped the owners.

Byrd said these intruders "had forcibly taken the very boots from off his feet." But despite his losses and the indignities he suffered, Byrd was able to reopen his popular tavern and in 1786 was playing host to stage passengers.[5]

A French officer, who disembarked at Jamestown shortly before the Battle of Yorktown got underway, claimed that Lt. Colonel Banastre Tarleton's men had committed some heinous crimes. One was a brutal attack upon a local pregnant woman whose husband had gone off to war.[6] Other French soldiers reported that Williamsburg had severe food shortages and that its drinking water was polluted because the departing British had tossed corpses into local wells. St. George Tucker, who arrived on the heels of the British departure, said the army left two legacies: a smallpox epidemic and a plague of flies. He said, "It is impossible to eat, drink, sleep, write, sit still or even walk about in peace on account of their confounded stings."[7]

Some of the accounts penned by the French were relatively lighthearted. One man described the local damsels as "much gayer by nature than the northern women, though not so pretty. They love pleasure and are passionately fond of dancing, in which they indulge both summer and winter." Another wrote that "Virginians live almost exclusively on salt meat, of which they keep an ample store." He observed that in summer, fresh-killed meat had to be consumed within 24 hours. He said that thanks to eating so much salted meat, "the men and women all have poor teeth. A girl of twenty here, even more than in the north, has lost her freshness." He claimed that the men in Tidewater were "exceptionally lazy" and lived like lords whether or not they could afford it. They drank a lot, chewed tobacco, and left to their wives the task of running the household. One French visitor said that Tidewater residents made little effort to cultivate good gardens, although they lived in a beautiful, fertile area. He said that the summer heat was oppressive, especially at night, and that locals drank a mixture of rum and water (grog) to restore their vigor. He concluded that few people enjoyed bathing, which they were convinced brought on diarrhea and fever, and that if anyone had to enter the water, he did so done before dawn or after sundown, and then *very briefly*.[8] One officer in General Rochambeau's army observed that corn, which was grown in substantial quantities, was ground into flour and baked into bread or cakes; it comprised the mainstay of black slaves' and poorer whites' diet. He said Virginia's thoroughbred horses compared favorably with the finest in England and that local men were exceptionally fond of horse racing and fox-hunting, especially in the Williamsburg area, where "several inhabitants keep excellent packs of hounds and hunt on horseback." A doctor who moved to Williamsburg in 1770 noted that horse races were held at an excellent track "adjoining to the town." He said that two, three, or four mile heats were run there and that the size of the wagers was substantial.[9] A French nobleman declared that Virginia men were devotees of boxing-matches and conducted themselves "with a barbity worthy of their savage neighbors." He said that England's ferocious stage-boxing was tame in comparison, for Virginia's boxing-matches included biting, gouging and worse. He had a great deal of compassion for the enslaved black, whom he felt was doomed to misery, but also spoke of the "miserable huts inhabited by whites whose wane looks and ragged garments bespeak poverty." He attributed slaves' plight to their owners' vanity and sloth and ascribed poorer whites' lack of opportunity to the greed of plantation owners, who monopolized many thousands of acres of land. However, wealthy William Lee, who returned to Virginia after the war and took up residence at Green Spring, told a different story. He declared that "This country is nothing like what it was, nor can it ever again be the same" and claimed that local economic conditions were so bad that "a Dutch blanket wrapt round the shoulders and fastened before with a wooden skewer is now a genteel and the most common kind of great Coat."

During this period of adjustment Williamsburg, like James City County, lost much of its vitality even though it continued to function as a county seat. In 1783 Johann David Schoepf said that the city was "a poor place compared with its former splendor." In his opinion, as soon as the capital was moved, "merchants, advocates, and other considerable residents took their departure as well." This cost the city half its population and its trade diminished.[10]

Adjusting to Changes in Government

In June 1776, when the Virginia Convention adopted a constitution for the new Commonwealth of Virginia, the structure of county government stayed intact, as did the link between church and state. As a result, county courts and parish vestries, which were appointive bodies, retained their taxing authority. Many people felt that this was equivalent to taxation without representation. Nathaniel Burwell and Robert Andrews represented James City

County in the State Convention of 1788, which met during June, and they voted in favor of ratifying the Federal Constitution. As time went on, some important changes proved necessary in the upper levels of government. The House of Burgesses readily evolved into the House of Delegates, but a number of new public offices (positions formerly occupied by royal appointees) had to be filled and the judicial system had to be modified. The fledgling state government had to address needs that ranged from civil defence, trade, and the monetary system, to public welfare, a responsibility formerly relegated to the Established Church.[11]

In 1782 locally-appointed tax commissioners commenced compiling assessments on real estate and personal property, which were submitted to the state auditor's office and the county clerk of court. Tax assessments were listed in pounds, not dollars, until around 1820, despite the fact that an American monetary system already had developed. At first, land tax rolls included only a property owner's name and the quantity of acreage in his/her possession. But as time went on, the amount of information tax commissioners recorded became more comprehensive. For example, in 1815 tax assessors began listing each tract's distance and direction from the county courthouse and when and by what means property changed hands. To establish parity in the value of the land being assessed, state officials divided Virginia into four enormous tax districts considered geologically similar. James City County was assigned to a district that included almost all of the counties east of the fall line. The clerk of the county court had to furnish tax commissioners with a list of all land transactions that had occurred within the previous year.[12] Tax commissioners, appointed by the county court, made periodic visits to the properties within their assigned territory, estimating each one's worth. Those who owned real estate or personal property were required by law to respond truthfully when queried by the tax commissioners. People who felt that their assessment was unjust could file an appeal with the county court. Commencing in 1820, tax commissioners began recording the collective worth of all buildings that stood upon a landowner's acreage. When they compiled personal property tax rolls, they listed each household head (regardless of gender) and noted the number of tithable free white males age 16 or older. The property of the deceased was attributed to their estate. Tax criteria changed from time to time, but slaves, livestock, and wheeled passenger vehicles typically were deemed taxable. In 1815 certain types of wooden furniture (such as bedsteads and tables made of walnut or mahogany) were taxed as luxury items, as were gold watches, clocks, gold and silver plate and large musical instruments, such as pianos and harps. The following year, furniture was excluded from taxation.[13]

After the Revolution county justices were appointed by the governor, just as they had been before, and when a vacancy occurred, the surviving justices recommended a replacement. They had the power to levy taxes, try cases, and appoint lesser local officials, all in a single session, and they were supposed to rotate the sheriffry among themselves. In 1796 John Pierce, a justice from upper James City County, wrote the governor that he strongly opposed allowing local courts to appoint sheriffs. He said that justices tended to select someone who had never served before rather than rotating the office as was proscribed by law.[14]

During the post-war period many James City County households found it difficult to keep their taxes from falling into arrears, even though commodities such as wheat, rye, oats, barley, corn, and bacon were an acceptable medium of payment. Sheriff William Barrett, when accused of delinquency in collecting local taxes, "cited the hardships of the people due to shortness of crops during the past year [1784] as a reason for their not being able to pay taxes promptly." In 1785 he asked for a deferment because local citizens "were exceedingly poor and unable to pay taxes." Two years later a group of approximately 120 James City freeholders from virtually every part of the county signed a petition requesting relief from fiscal problems they attributed to the state government's monetary policy.[15] During the late 1780s Charlotte and Mary Dickinsons' slaves, Sall and Samson, were convicted of burglary, a capital crime. But both women filed a petition with higher authorities, which resulted in the slaves' being pardoned.[16] The inference was that the slaves had been stealing on behalf of their impoverished owners.

Local lawbreakers were committed to the public jail in Williamsburg "just as if it were in the county," and John Fenton and his successor, John Power, served as the county jailor. As the old capitol building was dilapidated, city officials were authorized to sell its eastern wing and place the colonial secretary's office in the hands of a tenant, using the proceeds toward repairing the capitol's western (or front) wing. The renovated structure was readied for use by 1807 and the circuit court of James City County began meeting there.[17]

Protecting the Homeland: A Need for Military Defense

After the close of the Revolutionary War, there was some concern that the British would return to attack their break-away colonies. In 1782 Colonel Nathaniel M. Burwell, commander of the James City County militia, informed his superiors that his men would be insufficiently armed, if called to active duty. The state still utilized the military districts that had been established in 1775, and James City County was grouped with Charles City, Elizabeth City, and several other neighboring counties. In September 1782 Lt. William P. Quailes informed Captain William Davies that he was ready to begin recruiting men in James City and New Kent Counties, whereas John Pierce reported that he had received beef and clothing from James City and

Ferrying passengers and horses. Courtesy of Dover Publications.

Charles City Counties but that York, Warwick, New Kent, and Elizabeth City residents were uncooperative. Two months later, 500 men from James City and five other counties were ordered to Yorktown "to level the works . . . for fear that the enemy might take possession if left standing." The James City County militia was part of the 68th Regiment, which consisted of free white males, age 16 or older. The 68th Regiment was 1,491 strong and included field officers and 12 companies, one of which consisted of light infantry. The regiment was part of Brigade 2, Division 4.[18]

County militia units mustered in their home communities and elected their own officers, whose names were submitted to the county court. The justices, in turn, sought confirmation from the governor, who actually commissioned the officers. In essence, this procedure was a holdover from the colonial era. Most counties' high ranking militia officers served as justices or held other important government positions. Thus, even after the Revolution, local political power largely resided in those who were relatively affluent and influential in their communities. Many of these men also headed up individual militia companies. In July 1785 Captain Pinkethman Taylor, Lieutenant John James, and Ensign W. Stanhope Richardson led James City County's First Company of militia, whereas Colonel John Warburton, Lieutenant Thomas Barham and Ensign Thompson Fitzhugh headed the Second Company. Captain John Goddin, Lieutenant Jeremiah Taylor, and Ensign William Lightfoot were in command of the Third Company and Captain William Walker, Lieutenant Jones Allen, and Ensign John Allen led the Fourth Company. Almost all of these men were still serving as company leaders two years later. In 1787 James City County's highest ranking militia officers were Colonel Edward Power, Lt. Colonel Champion Travis, Major John Warburton, Captain John Goddin, and Lieutenants Nathaniel Burwell and William Richardson. In 1797 Captain John Ambler of Jamestown was in command of the local cavalry, which office he still held in 1801.[19]

Occasionally, militia companies and county justices wrangled over whose names should be submitted to the governor as officer candidates. For example, one James City County militia company chose Royal R. Allen as its leader instead of William Lightfoot, whom the justices argued was older and much more experienced. Lightfoot also was a justice; Allen was not. Both sides dispatched petitions to the governor, who selected Allen on the basis of his youthful vigor. Sometimes, local men sought to advance their own military rank or that of their kin. For example, in 1808 James Semple asked for a commission as captain of the county's light infantry, whereas Lieutenant John Ambler approached the governor on behalf of his son, Edward. However, Ambler was lukewarm about his son's advancement and was frank with the governor. He said that although Edward wanted a major's commission in the infantry or a captaincy in the cavalry, he was "a strong, active young man without military experience except what he may have acquired in his present station in as first lieutenant in the Williamsburg Troop."[20]

Laws Affecting Everyday Life

During the 1790s, the laws pertaining to race relations and moral conduct were redefined. It became legally possible to manumit slaves by bequeathing

The Farmer going to Market

Courtesy of Dover Publications.

them their freedom or executing a deed of manumission. On the other hand, slaves who perjured themselves in court could be executed.[21] Other laws made it illegal for anyone to be drunk or profane, and to work or conduct business on Sunday. Those who committed adultery were fined $20 and those guilty of fornication, $10. One new law shielded clergymen from arrest while conducting church services.[22]

Fees were set for the ferries that operated at several sites along the James and Chickahominy Rivers, all of which routes had been in use since the eighteenth century or longer. Ferries still ran from Higginson's Landing (on the east side of College Creek) to Hog Island and from Jamestown Island to Swann's Point and Cobham in Surry. At the mouth of the Chickahominy River was Barretts Ferry, which ran to Dancey's Land and Edloe's in Charles City County. In 1805 John Pierce of James City County and Robert Chandler of Charles City asked the General Assembly to establish a ferry on their property, approximately two miles below Coles Ferry, which was near

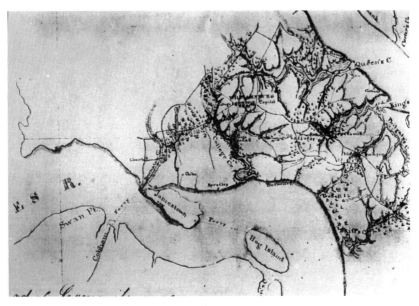

The James City Parish Glebe is identified on J. G. Swift's 1818 map, "Reconnoitering the Chesapeake Bay." Swift also indicated that in 1781 two ferries ran from Jamestwon Island to the lower side of the James. Library of Congress. See enlarged map, page 234.

Diascund Creek.[23] Other local freeholders submitted petitions to the state legislature. In December 1824 a group of upper county men recommended that money derived from the sale of the Blisland Parish glebe be set aside to fund public schools. A year later, local residents asked the General Assembly *not* to pass a law calling for a state constitutional convention.[24]

Tobacco still was an important money crop in James City County and the state maintained an inspection system to regulate its quality. Locally, William James Lewis served as the College Landing warehouse's inspector. But in 1788 Charles Hunt and Mathew Anderson questioned his competency and claimed that upon occasion Lewis refused to inspect tobacco or "committed blunders" because he was "too fond of liquor." Ultimately, Lewis, who was found guilty of misconduct, was replaced by William Wilkinson Sr. and Edward Cowles.[25]

One thorny issue the General Assembly was obliged to address at the close of the Revolution was disestablishment of the former State Church. In 1799 all property belonging to the Established Church "devolved on the good people of this Commonwealth upon the dissolution of the British government here." An 1801 law gave county Overseers of the Poor the right to sell glebe land whenever it was vacated through the death or removal of the incumbent parish clergyman. Once that occurred, the glebe was offered to the highest bidder in an auction held at the courthouse door. Parishes that had leased their glebe lands to tenants prior to 1801 could let the agreement expire before a sale occurred. In 1807, when James City and New Kent Counties' Overseers of the Poor sold the old Blisland Parish glebe, in accord with the law, James City's Overseers were given their share of the proceeds. In 1824 they resolved to apply $1,000 toward funding primary schools in James City County and to use the remainder to convert Hickory Neck Church into a schoolhouse.[26]

The Tempo of Rural Life

A Frenchman, who visited Virginia in 1794, said that scattered throughout the countryside were:

. . . a few mediocre houses; frequently a fence encloses a rather large plot of ground on which is built the most primitive sort of log or weatherboarded

dwelling. Nor is the picture enhanced any by the tree stumps, half consumed and blackened by fire, that have been left in the fields.[27]
Thus, he viewed life in rural Virginia as bleak, especially for those of very limited or middling means. Land and personal property tax rolls suggest that during the early nineteenth century, the ranks of Tidewater Virginia's middle class declined, while the number of small farmers increased and the position of the large landowner became more firmly solidified. Concurrent with this reduction in farm size came growth in personal wealth, as evidenced by increases in the quantity of taxable personal property owned by Virginians.

The everyday lives of rural people, though filled with workaday drudgery, included moments of pleasure and diversion. Household members and visitors entertained one another with conversation that ranged from serious discussions to gossip and light banter. Gatherings at churches, fairs, political rallies, court days, and militia musters also provided levity. Taverns or ordinaries sometimes hosted traveling musicians, magicians, and other performers who offered locals an opportunity to escape from everyday routines. One form of entertainment for the literate was reading newspapers. The press typically offered news of a local, national and international nature, printed advertisements and legal notices, and presented informative articles on everything from medical ills to personal and political complaints.

The War of 1812

In June 1812 the United States declared war on Great Britain. It was the culmination of several years of conflict between the British and the French, the Americans' allies during the Revolutionary War. Virginia Governor James Barbour, who was concerned about a possible British invasion, decided that if a fort were built at Jamestown, where the river channel runs close to the shore, it would be almost impossible for an enemy vessel to elude its guns. However, before action was taken on Barbour's recommendation, the British entered the James River, attacked Craney Island, and blockaded Hampton Roads. Early in February 1813 infantrymen from James City and York Counties (part of the 68th Regiment) were sent to Norfolk and Hampton to repel the British if they came ashore. This made local officials uneasy about

James City and Warwick Counties' vulnerability. Their concern was justified, for on June 25, 1813, 900 British troops landed on the lower peninsula and began advancing west. Meanwhile, armed vessels in the James fired at some people on shore. Shortly thereafter, a regiment from New Kent and Charles City Counties was sent to defend Williamsburg.[28]

During the summer, 14 British barges, an armed brig, and six or seven tenders moved freely up and down the James, plundering homes near the shore and sometimes venturing inland. Colonel John Ambler II was stationed at Camp Bottoms Bridge when the British invaded his home on Jamestown Island. On July 1, 1813, a raiding party reportedly came ashore and carried off whatever they could and laid waste to everything else. Four days later, a British brig, several schooners and eight to ten barges sailed past Jamestown and continued upstream. As soon as William H. Waller's elderly mother learned that the British "had Landed at Kings Mill and were marching towards the old city," she "immediately snached [sic] up her silver spoons, put them into her red trunk with her papers" and sent them to Mr. Semple's house, for she recalled the British Army's looting during the Revolutionary War. Mrs. Semple said "that she went to bed to receive the Brittish," implying that she had concealed valuables in her bed-clothes. In April 1814 a high ranking military officer recommended that a fort and battery be constructed at Jamestown, or further up the James at Hoods, to prevent the British from reaching Richmond.[29]

An American soldier, who encamped on the grounds of Blisland Parish's ruinous upper church in mid-September 1814, described life in what he called Camp Warranigh. His comrades cleared debris from Warrany Church's crumbling interior and used loose bricks to enclose their camp fires. There, just west of James City County's upper boundary line, they constructed crude shelters from brush, erected a small log building, and cleared a vista that opened to the York River. The soldiers mustered three times a day and took nightly turns at sentry duty. Toward late December 1814 a considerable number of Williamsburg people grew concerned that the British might return, especially while so few men were on hand to mount a defense. But on Christmas eve 1814, the Treaty of Ghent was signed, ending the war.

Afterward, the state entered a period of economic stagnation. Conditions continued to deteriorate and America experienced its first great depression, the Panic of 1819. In nearly half of the counties east of the Blue Ridge, the population dwindled, thanks to a general out-migration. In Tidewater, where very little attention had been devoted to replenishing the soil, farmland was devoid of nutrients and relatively unproductive. During this period, many large estates were broken up and redistributed when old, well-established families moved west in search of better land. Members of the lower and middling classes also moved on, for they foresaw opportunities to better themselves. All of these changes occurred amidst agricultural prices that fluctuated wildly and economic conditions that were relatively unstable. As a result of the state's diminishing population, Virginia's influence on the political scene lessened.[30]

James City County's First Tourist Attraction

In May 1807 a jubilee was held on Jamestown Island to commemorate the first colonists' arrival. Although relatively little is known about "that immense assembly which was convened on the plains of Jamestown," a number of distinguished citizens and students from the College of William and Mary gave speeches. One participant reported that "Many yards of the palisades erected by the first settlers are yet to be seen at a low tide standing at least 150 to 200 paces [375 to 500 feet] from the present shore."[31] The posts the writer saw probably were remnants of the approximately 2,000 palisades used to fortify Jamestown Island in 1711 when a French invasion was expected.

John Henry Strobia, a steamboat passenger who visited Jamestown in July 1817, remarked that there were "few traces of its ancient importance." He said that "Two or three old houses, the ruins of an old steeple, a church yard and faint marks of rude fortifications are now the only memorials of its former inhabitants." English diarist Henry Beaumont, who visited Jamestown in 1818, agreed with a fellow traveler who thought that the island was "a fine situation for a Town." The two men weighed the merits of purchasing and developing the island, but ultimately discarded the idea. Between 1818 and 1822 steamboats from Richmond, Petersburg, and the Potomac River made regular stops at Jamestown and passengers were accommodated at the old Ambler house.

In 1822, after David Bullock bought the Ambler property in the western end of Jamestown Island, a celebration was held to commemorate Virginia's first colonists' arrival. Literally thousands of visitors flocked to the island for the event. The celebrants, in their unbridled enthusiasm, "burnt down one of the two large brick houses on the island [the Travis house] and broke the tombstones into fragments and scattered them over the face of the earth so that the whole island exhibited one wide field of desolation." A newspaper man reported that five steamboats, 35 other vessels, and an infinite number of small boats brought even more tourists to Jamestown Island than had been in attendance at the 1807 celebration. He noted, however, that in 1822 there were no formal ceremonies or speeches and that throngs of visitors dispersed to go picnicking. He was present when "the old brick building belonging to Colonel Travis' estate" caught fire and was destroyed.[32]

Local Issues Before the General Assembly

The state legislature at its 1818–1819 session enacted several new laws that affected local citizens. Freeholders who resided in Williamsburg no longer were able to vote in both city and county elections, but the sheriff of James City County retained the right to summon prospective jurors from both jurisdictions. The justices of the James City County court were responsible for seeing that the local jail was equipped with iron bars, bolts and locks and that a pillory, whipping post, and stocks were on hand. Those convicted in the court of James City County were to be incarcerated in Williamsburg's jail. Fifteen Tidewater counties and Suffolk were grouped with James City and Williamsburg in a newly created chancery court district. The circuit court of law and chancery was to convene twice a year in the old capitol building in Williamsburg and its judge was obliged to reside in the city.[33]

In June 1825 a group of York County freeholders asked the General Assembly to annex "that part of York County lying north of Kings Creek and Burwell's Mill Pond" to James City County. Although their petition died in committee, the issue of annexation resurfaced three years later. This time, several York County men announced in the PHOENIX PLOUGH BOY that they intended to approach the legislature about annexing some land in the upper end of the county. They wanted "so much of the county of York as lies north of the road leading from the Six Mile Ordinary [now Lightfoot] to Littleton T. Waller's Mill [Skimino Mill]" to be added to James City County, noting that "in going to our courthouse we are compelled necessarily to pass the courthouse of James City in Williamsburg 6 miles on our way and thence to travel 12 miles further to reach our seat of justice." They contended that "The present county line is a circuitous and indistinct one of marked trees" and that the proposed boundary line was a public road, i.e., the forerunner of Route 646 (Lightfoot Road). No significant action was taken on the proposal in 1829 or when it was revived a decade later.[34]

Promoting Economic Development

As the economy of the new nation took hold, Virginians became increasingly interested in the development of internal improvements, such as canals, railroads, turnpikes, and better public roads. In 1794 a French visitor declared that Tidewater was criss-crossed by roads that were:

. . . *mere tracks large enough for wagons, occasionally bridged, across ditches, streams or mudholes, by small tree trunks placed close together. One meets coaches, wagons, and carts on these roads, the carts sometimes drawn by yoked oxen; and occasionally one passes a horse with a husband in the saddle and his wife riding behind.*[35]

One visitor to Williamsburg during the 1820s said that:

The streets give an idea of the wonderful fertility of this soil, by their being covered with grass and several cows, pigs, horses, mules and goats are to be seen pasturing all undisturbed among them. I thought I was transported to Noah's Ark when I first came to this town, so prodigious was the quantity of animals! [36]

In February 1816 the General Assembly, in response to public demand, established and endowed the Board of Public Works. This created a fund to underwrite the construction of turnpikes, railroads, and canals. Private companies were encouraged to build turnpikes and bridges with the state as a co-investor. The development and improvement of transportation corridors linked rural areas with urban markets, which fueled the expansion of agricultural productivity and specialization. In 1818 the Directors of the Virginia Canal Company proposed building a canal from College Creek to Williamsburg. Its proposed right-of-way, which was surveyed, passed through the Tazewell (formerly Greenhow) farm's meadow.[37]

One mode of transportation readily available to the residents of James City County was the stagecoach, which made regular runs, carrying passengers, mail, and news. It was thanks to stage traffic that the forerunner of Routes 60 and 30 between Williamsburg and New Kent Courthouse became known as the Old Stage Road. During the second decade of the nineteenth century steamboats began plying a route between Hampton Roads and Richmond, making regular stops at towns and private wharfs along the way.

State officials hoped to foster economic development by publishing a map that depicted Virginia's relatively elaborate network of public roads, thoroughfares that would accommodate commerce and trade. In 1819 the General Assembly enacted legislation that required local officials to have maps made of their counties. These county maps were to be used in preparing a composite: a large, detailed map of Virginia. Cartographer John Wood was hired to make a map of each county in the state. On October 25, 1819, he reported to the General Assembly that he had surveyed nine counties, including James City, and he presented the legislators with two copies of each map he'd made.[38] Although some of Wood's maps have survived, many others have not. One or both copies of Wood's map of James City County may have been destroyed in 1865 when Richmond burned, or they may be tucked away somewhere, awaiting discovery.

Some James City County Properties

The Ambler Plantation on Jamestown Island

John Ambler II, Edward Ambler's son, came of age in 1783 and took possession of the property he had inherited. He made his home on Jamestown Island and was one of James City County's wealthiest farmers. Ambler's plantation ledgers reveal that he procured much of his family's clothing, footwear, and household furnishings from London, but relied heavily upon merchants in Richmond, Williamsburg, and Cobham for everyday items. Ambler had Williamsburg goldsmith James Galt repair and clean his watches and mend his incense case. He had his blacksmithing done at Green Spring and hired local craftsmen to repair his saddle, mend farming equipment, and fabricate a wheat machine. He paid local practitioners for dentistry and inoculating some of his household members against smallpox. Wheat and pork produced on Jamestown Island and the Main were sold to local people, usually in large quantities. Ambler's business records indicate that he operated a prosperous and extremely active working plantation, which he ran with the help of large numbers of slaves who worked under the supervision of overseers William Chick, Robert Chancellor, and Henry Taylor.

But John Ambler II's life was not idyllic, for his first and second wives "fell martyrs to their attachment to Jamestown . . . known to be unhealthy during the months of August and September," and when he married for the third time in 1799, he resolved to spend only the winter months there. He had a brick wall built around the Jamestown Church's graveyard and erected a log-and-stone causeway that connected Jamestown Island to the mainland at the mouth of Sandy Bay, where it was subject to tidal flooding.

In October 1798 four of Ambler's friends from Williamsburg, who were on their way to his house, found the causeway inundated by the tide. According to Dr. Philip Barraud, portly Bishop James Madison disembarked from their coach and insisted on crossing the causeway on foot. But before he had gone very far, he toppled into the river and had to be rescued. Later, after a hearty meal at the Ambler house and an ample supply of wine, one of the Bishop's companions waggishly observed that "his Holiness received this correction as a Lesson not to assume so broad a Bottom for the Mother Church" and reminded him that despite his piety, he couldn't walk upon water.

Even though the Ambler plantation enveloped most of Jamestown Island's western end, a few town lots still existed during the late eighteenth century. In 1771 Hannah Philippa Ludwell Lee inherited two Jamestown lots her late father owned, one of which contained improvements. In 1789, when her widower, William Lee, prepared his will, he left the lots and some land in

Williamsburg to their son, William Ludwell Lee. John Parke Custis, who inherited two or more Jamestown lots he considered useless and dwindling in value, in May 1778 sought the advice of his step-father, George Washington, about selling them. Although it's uncertain what became of the Lee and Custis lots, in time they probably were absorbed into the Ambler family's landholdings.[39]

During the early nineteenth century John Ambler II moved to Richmond, but returned to Jamestown and Williamsburg each winter. According to family tradition, he gave his Jamestown Island plantation to his son, Edward II. In 1820 when the tax assessor began estimating the value of buildings that stood upon local property, the 900 acre Ambler plantation on Jamestown Island had structures worth $3,600, making it one of James City County's most elaborately developed pieces of real estate. After Edward Ambler II's departure from James City County around 1821, the plantation was sold three times in rapid succession, finally coming into the hands of David Bullock of Richmond. In 1831 Bullock bought the late Samuel Travis's estate and for the first time since Virginia was colonized, Jamestown Island in its entirety was united under one owner. Bullock retained the farm until 1835.[40]

The Maine

Besides Jamestown Island, John Ambler II inherited his father's leasehold in the Governor's Land known as "the Main" or "Amblers." In 1788 he purchased the property his family had been leasing from officials of the College of William and Mary, to whom the land had devolved after the Revolution. Later, he gave it to his daughter, Mary Cary Ambler, the wife of Williamsburg attorney John Hill Smith. The Smiths eventually sold it when their debts became overwhelming.[41]

The Travis Plantation on Jamestown Island

In 1782, Champion Travis, whose plantation encompassed the northeastern end of Jamestown Island, had a substantial number of slaves and a large livestock herd. He relied upon the assistance of William Steiff and other overseers to manage his property. In May 1793 two of Travis's slaves, Nelly and

Daphney, who were ploughing his fields, struck and killed overseer Joel Gathright when he commenced beating one of them. Both slaves were found guilty of murder and sentenced to death. A contingent of neighboring landowners asked Governor Henry Lee to spare one slave's life, for she was pregnant, but another group (led by the governor's brother) urged him to proceed with the hanging as an example to other slaves. In the end, the woman's execution was postponed long enough for her to deliver the child she was carrying. The circumstances surrounding this highly emotional case are open to conjecture. In 1818, nearly a decade after Champion Travis's death, his Jamestown Island plantation was transferred to his son, Samuel. In 1820 there were no buildings on the Travis property that the county assessor deemed taxable.[42]

Piney Grove

In 1801 Champion Travis sold Piney Grove to Francis M. Whittle of Norfolk, whose son, Conway, moved to the farm and eventually acquired it. During the mid-1830s Piney Grove was owned briefly by Nelson W. Hall of York County. In 1849 the plantation came into the hands of Moses R. Harrell, who erected some new buildings on the tract and moved his family there. Harrell, who was James City County's sheriff, sometimes conducted slave auctions, perhaps as part of his official duties. Like many other successful farmers of his day, he kept abreast of the latest advances in scientific farming and invested a substantial amount of money in agricultural equipment.[43]

The Warburton Property

To the east of Piney Grove was the plantation of Benjamin Warburton, an affluent planter whose ancestors had been living in that vicinity since the early 1660s. Warburton died during the mid-1780s but his 925 acre plantation remained intact until the close of the century. By 1803 part of the Warburton estate had been sold to John D. Wilkinson, the owner of a neighboring farm. Tax records demonstrate that Wilkinson, a man of modest means, slowly but surely improved his financial lot. When he moved to James City County in

1790, he had only one horse to help with his farming operations and no slaves; when he died around 1814, he had several horses, ten adult slaves, and a wheeled vehicle, a taxable luxury item. After Wilkinson's death the farm passed through the hands of William P. Harris and William S. Bacon, both of whom were middling farmers. Later, it was purchased by John S. Miles, who

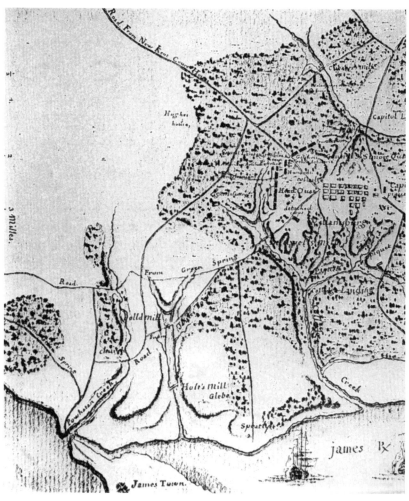

Holt's Mill, where ships' biscuits were manufactured, is shown on an untitled map of the Williamsburg area. National Archives.

called it Deep Bottom. During the mid-nineteenth century, Deep Bottom was owned by Nathaniel Piggott, a wealthy western James City County farmer.[44]

Powhatan

John Ambler II of Jamestown inherited his father's 375-acre quarter at Powhatan, part of the acreage that belonged to the Wormeleys during the seventeenth century. He sold it in 1815, the same year he bestowed his Jamestown Island plantation upon son, Edward II. Peter Desverges, who purchased almost all of Ambler's Powhatan acreage, quickly conveyed it to William Hewlett, who retained it until the early 1840s. In 1820 Hewlett's farm contained only $20 worth of buildings, a reflection of its use as a subsidiary property. In 1829 William Hewlett added a house of modest but middling value and appears to have moved in.

Meanwhile, Richard Taliaferro I, who owned much of the Egglestons' share of the Powhatan tract, died of "gout in the head." He left a widow, the former Elizabeth Eggleston, and a son, Richard Taliaferro II, his ultimate heir. Richard II and his wife, Rebecca Cocke, were residing at Powhatan when he died around 1790. She stayed on, managing the farm very capably, and significantly enhanced its productivity. After Rebecca Cocke Taliaferro's death in 1811, her executors sold Powhatan to Richard T. Hannon of Petersburg. The property passed through the hands of other absentee owners before Thomas Martin bought it. His son, Dr. William Martin, who inherited Powhatan around 1845, still owned it at the time of the Civil War.[45]

Green Spring

By summer 1795 William Lee was dead and Green Spring and its subsidiary farms were in the possession of his son, 22-year-old William Ludwell Lee. Young Lee asked the noted architect Benjamin Latrobe to design a new dwelling for Green Spring, a house suitable for a gentleman. Latrobe, who visited Green Spring in 1796, noted that "Poverty and decay seem indeed to have laid their withering hands upon every building public and private between Hampton and Shockhoe Creek at Richmond." He also found almost unbearable the "swarm of Muskitoes or galinippers" at Green Spring and remarked that in the very room in which the Virginia Assembly held many of its early meetings, he "was plotting the death of muskitoes" in much the same way the burgesses had sought to exterminate the Indians "and for the same tendency and reasons. They were weak and troublesome." Latrobe tried in vain to persuade his young host to preserve the ancient Green Spring mansion, but when he made a return visit in 1797, he found that Lee had razed the old house and replaced it with a new one.

William Ludwell Lee defied tradition in yet another way: he freed all of his slaves. When making his will, he instructed his executors to see that his young slaves were educated in one of the Northern states and he arranged for his adult slaves to be provided with food and shelter on his Hot Water plantation, where comfortable houses were to be built for them at his expense. Thanks to Lee's bequest, a community of free blacks became established at Centerville, on what had been a subsidiary farm of Green Spring.[46]

After William Ludwell Lee's death in 1803, his acreage descended to his sisters, Portia Hodgson and Cornelia Hopkins, who during the 18-teens began selling it off. Finally, in 1824 Portia and her husband, William Hodgson, sold Green Spring to George Mason.[47] The plantation was owned by David I. Anderson and several others before being bought by John and Robert C. A. Ward of New Jersey. They relocated to James City County and commenced farming with slave labor.[48]

Rich Neck

Lucy Ludwell Paradise and her husband, John, spent almost all of their married life in London. In 1805 she returned to Virginia as a widow and took up residence in Williamsburg. Within a couple years she began selling off large portions of Rich Neck, the plantation she inherited from her father, Philip Ludwell III. In time, mental illness took its toll and Mrs. Paradise was committed to the Public Hospital. After her death, her executors leased Rich Neck to Robert Anderson. Mrs. Paradise's grandsons were her intended heirs, but her nieces, Portia Hodgson and Cornelia Hopkins, seized her estate on the basis of a legal technicality: the youths were not Americans and therefore were ineligible to inherit land in this country. Although grandson Philip Barziza Jr. immigrated to Virginia, married a local girl, and became a naturalized American citizen, he was unsuccessful in recovering part of his grandmother's estate. The law suit was aired before the Virginia Supreme Court.[49]

Kingsmill

Shortly before the close of the American Revolution Lewis Burwell V began trying to sell Kingsmill Plantation and an adjoining 1,100-acre tract that was "very good for all kinds of grain." In April 1783 John Carter Byrd of Charles City County bought Kingsmill and quickly sold it to Henry Martin of Tortola. Martin moved to James City County and commenced repairing and remodeling the Kingsmill manor house. During the mid-1780s John Southall, William Milby, and Alexander Terence served as his farm managers. After Martin's untimely death in 1786, attorney Henry Tazewell of Brunswick County bought Kingsmill. He married Benjamin Waller's daughter, moved to Williamsburg, and began taking a prominent role in public life. In 1789 Tazewell was named chief justice of the state's General Court and in 1793 was made a judge in the Court of Appeals. He was elected to the United States Senate and became its president. During Senator Tazewell's frequent absences, he entrusted Kingsmill to his son, Littleton Waller Tazewell, who reportedly detested rural life. In 1801 William Allen of Surry County, who already owned the adjacent Littletown/Utopia tract, bought Kingsmill from the senator's son and consolidated it with the property he already owned. Allen's slaves and livestock were distributed among his Kingsmill, Jamestown, and Neck O'Land plantations, which were entrusted to overseers.[50]

Neck O'Land and Holt's Mill

William Holt, owner of the 2,000-acre Neck O' Land farm, sold it to John Allen of Surry County in 1785. Allen's brother, William, acquired the tract in 1805, along with approximately 900 acres formerly owned by James Southall.

William Allen, who lived at Claremont, was one of Virginia's wealthiest men and owned 700 to 800 slaves and an estimated 30,000 to 40,000 acres of land. In James City County alone, his river frontage on the James extended from Sandy Bay to Grove Creek. The Neck O' Land tract was the focal point of Allen's farming activities on the west side of College Creek.[51]

William Holt's son-in-law and business partner, William Coleman, by 1782 was running the Newport Mills, a grist-and-saw mill complex and bake-house on Mill Creek. At Holt's death, his interest in the property descended to his brothers, who called it the Jockey's Neck Mill. The Holts sued William Coleman in an attempt to gain his share of the property, but he succeeded in becoming its sole proprietor and in time significantly enhanced its value.[52]

The Centerville Area

In western James City County, near the Spencer plantation, was the acreage of Samuel Durfey, a middling farmer who had a few slaves and some livestock. Samuel Durfey Jr. inherited the family farm, which abutted that of Daniel Jones of War Hill. Young Durfey fell upon hard times and in 1828 his creditors sold his land to John Warburton Sr.[53] Today the Durfey property is part of the subdivision known as Fox Hill.

Drinking Spring and Foster's

By 1796 Henley Taylor owned the approximately 300-acre Drinking Spring farm, just west of Norge. In 1828 his son, Richard E. Taylor, who was in possession of slightly more than half of Drinking Spring, built a home there. To the east of the Taylor farm was that of Major W. Mahone, who by the 1790s owned acreage on the northeast side of the Stage Road. The build-ings on the Mahone property were worth only $50. In 1840 then-owner William Spencer Mahone built a new home, the storey-and-a-half dwelling that later became known as Foster's and is now the Bradshaw home.[54]

Roslyn and Breezeland

During the early nineteenth century Allen Marston began accumulating the acreage that eventually became known as Roslyn (Roslin), the modern-day Massie farm west of Lightfoot. Marston built a home there, which he occupied until his death in the early 1830s. One of his heirs, John T. Marston, resided at Roslyn up until the time of the Civil War. Nearby was the home of the Farthings, called Breezeland.[55]

The Diascund Creek Area

By 1782 Henry Browne owned over a thousand acres on the east side of Diascund Creek, land that during the mid-eighteenth century belonged to James Jennings and Henry Duke, Esquire. During the late 1780s, Browne's acreage descended to his son, William, who by 1811 had accumulated more than 1,650 acres in that vicinity. Browne's near-neighbor was James Pride, another large landowner. By the mid-1820s, part of the Brownes' land had come into the possession of Benjamin Hicks (Hix), whose descendants inherited it.[56]

Aspen Grove or Moss Side

Near the Croaker interchange of Interstate 64 was acreage that belonged to the Hankins family. In 1782 Charles Hankins, a middling planter, owned 270 acres there which descended to his heirs, Nathaniel and Alexander H. Hankins. At various times the Hankins farm was known as Aspen Hill (Aspen Grove) and Moss Side. Family members owned it until recently.[57]

Riverview and Shellfield

By the early 1780s William Hankins I was in possession of the York River acreage above Skimino Creek that became Riverview Plantation. A map prepared by a French cartographer at the close of the American Revolution indicates that two buildings within a fenced yard then stood near the site now occupied by the Riverview dwelling. Hankins, a prosperous farmer, left the bulk of his James City County land to his son, William II, plus some York County acreage he developed into the estate called Cherry Hall. In 1828 William Hankins II purchased George B. Lightfoot's 366-acre farm, Shellfield, just east of Riverview. As Lightfoot and his siblings had inherited some real estate from William Norvell, this transaction probably gave rise to the local tradition that Riverview was the home of the Norvells.[58]

Taskinask and Mount Folly

During the late eighteenth century, Taskinask and the acreage directly behind it belonged to John Richardson, whose heir, Allen Richardson, inherited it in 1804. The Richardsons' nearly 1,200 acres encompassed almost all of Taskinask's original 900 acres, with the exception of a small parcel owned by John R. Knewstep. By 1812 Elizabeth Richardson was in possession of Taskinask, which she renamed Cedar Grove. She retained it until her death in the early 1850s.

By the early nineteenth century James Banks owned Mount Folly, having acquired it from former owner Stephen Bingham's heirs. The Banks' retained the farm until the eve of the Civil War. In 1857 then-owner James A. Banks bought part of Taskinask from the Knewsteps and combined it with Mount Folly.[59]

The Burnt Ordinary Community

Near the crossroads known as Burnt Ordinary, formed by the intersection of Richmond and Chickahominy Roads (Routes 60 and 631), was the plantation of James Norvell Walker. During the early nineteenth century Walker sold most of his land to his neighbor, Henley Taylor, who left it to his widow, Mary. Taylor bequeathed the rest of his land to his son, Richard E. Taylor. The landholdings of James Shelburn (Shelbourn) also were close at hand. He was the son of the Rev. James Shelburn, a well-known Baptist minister, James City County native, and avid supporter of the American Revolution.[60]

La Grange

Located on the Old Stage Road between Burnt Ordinary and Barhamsville is the land upon which the La Grange farmhouse was built. During the late eighteenth and early nineteenth centuries it belonged to Edward Power, who in 1826 sold it to Francis Piggott, the owner of plantations called Huic and New Design. Within four years Piggott sold the Power tract to his daughter and son-in-law, Edmund Taylor Jr. The Taylors were living at La Grange in October 1832 when the Marquis de Lafayette paused there to execute a certificate of services, recognizing Ludwell Lee's services as a volunteer aide-de-camp during the battle of Green Spring. According to local lore, the Power farm became known as La Grange (the name of Lafayette's estate in France) because the Marquis quartered his troops there in 1781.[61]

Notes

1. Hall et al., "Legislative Petitions," 144–149, 151.

2. McIlwaine, COUNCIL OF THE STATE, III, 21; Randolph W. Church, VIRGINIA LEGISLATIVE PETITIONS (Richmond, 1984), No. 96, No. 107, No. 161, No. 240, No. 962; William G. Stanard, "Some Notes on Green Spring," VIRGINIA MAGAZINE OF HISTORY AND BIOGRAPHY 37:292; "Some Notes on Green Spring, " Virginia Magazine of History and Biography 38:44.

3. McIlwaine, COUNCIL OF STATE, III, 124; Hening, STATUTES, X, 189; XI, 406; Sheppard, STATUTES, I, 237; VIRGINIA GAZETTE AND GENERAL ADVERTISER, January 1, 1794; James City County Petitions, November 22, 1813.

4. Palmer, CALENDAR, II, 681; Humphrey Harwood Account Book 1785; Hall et al., "LEGISLATIVE PETITIONS," 144–148, 151.

5. Rice, CHASTELLUX, 378–379; Carson, WE WERE THERE, 72.

6. Another writer attributed the gruesome assault to the Hampton area.

7. Rice et al., AMERICAN CAMPAIGNS, I, 137, 154; Hugh F. Rankin, THE AMERICAN REVOLUTION (New York, 1964), 316.

8. Rice et al., AMERICAN CAMPAIGNS, I, 66, 71.

9. A Revolutionary War map indicates that there was a large oval track a few miles west of Williamsburg, on the north side of what is now Route 60 but south of Route 645, just over the York County line.

10. Carson, WE WERE THERE, 20, 66–67, 76–77; Rice, CHASTELLUX, 437–438, 441; William Lee, Letters to Edward Browne, December 31, 1783; January 10, 1784; Reps, TIDEWATER TOWNS, 191.

11. Nan Netherton et al., FAIRFAX COUNTY: A HISTORY (Fairfax, 1992), 118; Davis Bottom, REGISTER OF THE GENERAL ASSEMBLY OF VIRGINIA, 1776–1918 (Richmond, 1917), 243–244; Selby, REVOLUTION, 310, 317–318.

12. Assessors sometimes listed this information in special "alteration" books.

13. Hening, STATUTES, XI, 142–145; Thomas Richie, comp., THE REVISED CODE OF THE LAWS OF VIRGINIA, BEING A COLLECTION OF ALL SUCH ACTS OF THE GENERAL ASSEMBLY, (Richmond, 1819), II, 10–25. Real estate and personal property tax rolls provide a good estimate of individual wealth.

14. Manerin et al., HENRICO COUNTY, 151; Palmer, CALENDAR, VIII, 374.

15. Included were William Bowles, William Farthing, Joshua and John Morris, John Godden, Henley and Isham Taylor, Alexander W. Green, William Wilkinson Jr. and Sr., William Bush, Thomas Pate, John and William Hankins, Joseph and Hubbard Hix, George Hatton, Edmund and Thomas Cowles, Henry Brown, Filmer Green, John Goodall Jr. and Sr., William Spragen, John Cooper, John Drummond, Samuel Durfey, Andrew Banks, William Allen Jr. and Sr., William Lee, John Graves, John and W. Browne, Dudley Williams, William Lightfoot, Richard Gaddy (Geddy), Thomas Wright, Jeremiah and Isham Taylor, Leonard Henley, Isham Christian, Benjamin Bridges, Daniel and John Jones, Wells Dunford, Dudley Richardson Sr., Stanup and Edward Richardson, J. and Edward Linsey, Edward Digges, William Piggott, James Pride, James McDowell, James Jennings, Edward Farthing, Isa Lamden, Jeremiah and James Wade, Richard Brack, James N. Walker, Luke Anderson, John Weathers, Thomas Lyons, William James, Adam Byrd, and John and Stephen Manning.

16. Hening, STATUTES, X, 490; Palmer, CALENDAR, IV, 77; Hall et al., "LEGISLATIVE PETITIONS," 144–148, 151; McIlwaine, COUNCIL OF STATE, IV, 176, 210.

17. Hening, STATUTES, XI, 381; Palmer, CALENDAR, IX:23; Sheppard, STATUTES, I, 273; III, 427–428.

18. Palmer, CALENDAR, III, 203, 324, 329; IV, 394, 430; V, 56; VI, 504; VII, 165; IX, 410; X, 12; McIlwaine, COUNCIL OF STATE, III, 171–172.

19. Executive Papers, July 27, 1785; October 8, 1787.

20. Palmer, CALENDAR, IV, 394, 430; VI, 504; VII, 165; IX, 410; X, 12; Executive Papers, July 27, 1785; October 8, 1787; February 20, 1813.

21. Their owners were compensated for their monetary value.

22. Shepphard, STATUTES, I, 127, 134–135, 192–193.

23. Local signatories to Pierce's and Chandler's petition included William L. Allen, Sandy and William Lindsey (Linsey), John Browne, George Pate, Francis Pierce, Isaac Otey, Samuel Allen, Royal R. Allen, Richard Allen, John Slater, Charles Lindsey, Mann Spencer, Thomas S. Morris, James Baker, John Fisher, Rob L. Ware, Julius and Richard Allen, John Timberlake, Richard Crump, James Young, William Walker, John Walker Jr., Richardson D. Taylor, John Piggott, William Bush, William Brown Sr., W. D. Waddile, Daniel Taylor, B. Crenshaw, Dudley Curle, Nelson Jones and someone named Bullock (Hall et al., LEGISLATIVE PETITIONS, 154).

24. Ibid., I, 154–155.

25. Palmer, CALENDAR, IV, 480, 519; McIlwaine, COUNCIL OF STATE, IV, 304; V, 13.

26. Sheppard, STATUTES, I, 237; II, 314–315; III, 427–429; James City County Petitions, December 15, 1824.

27. Moreau de Saint–Mery, "Norfolk, Portsmouth and Gosport as seen by Moreau de Saint Mery in March, April and May 1794," VIRGINIA MAGAZINE OF HISTORY AND BIOGRAPHY 48 (July

1940):263.

28. Virginia State Library, A HORNBOOK OF VIRGINIA HISTORY (Richmond, 1965), 80–81; George B. Tindall, AMERICA, A NARRATIVE HISTORY (New York, 1984), 338–343; Palmer, CALENDAR, X, 134, 187, 212, 232, 237; Virginius Dabney, VIRGINIA (Richmond, 1971), 206–207.

29. Palmer, CALENDAR, X, 240, 244, 325–327; John Jaquelin Ambler, History of the Ambler Family in Virginia, 1826; Goodwin, KINGSMILL, 89; Tindall, NARRATIVE HISTORY, 350.

30. Charles G. C. Chamberlayne, THE VESTRY BOOK OF ST. PETER'S PARISH (Richmond, 1937), 685–689; Palmer, CALENDAR, X, 406; Virginia State Library, HORNBOOK, 82–83; Tindall, NARRATIVE HISTORY, 365; Colonial Williamsburg Foundation, Resource Protection Process for James City, York County, Williamsburg and Poquoson, Virginia, Draft Report II (Williamsburg, 1985), Section XII.

31. Lyon G. Tyler, "Glimpses of Old College Life," WILLIAM AND MARY QUARTERLY, 1st. Ser. 5 (January 1897):222.

32. John Henry Strobia, July 18, 1817, diary entry; Henry Beaumont, 1818 diary entry; Ambler, History, 1828; RICHMOND DISPATCH, May 25, 1822; Tyler, "Glimpses," 222.

33. Ibid., I, 124, 156, 197, 250–251, 267. Included in the district were Accomac, Charles City, Elizabeth City, Gloucester, Isle of Wight, James City, Mathews, Surry, Warwick, Princess Anne, Middlesex, Nansemond, New Kent, Northampton, and York Counties, plus the cities of Williamsburg and Suffolk.

34. York County Legislative Petitions 1825–1839.

35. Saint–Mery, "Norfolk," 264.

36. Lyon G. Tyler, "Williamsburg Caricature," TYLER'S QUARTERLY OF VIRGINIA HISTORY, 3 (October 1921):164–165.

37. John T. Schlotterbeck, PLANTATION AND FARM: SOCIAL AND ECONOMIC CHANGE IN ORANGE AND GREEN COUNTIES, VIRGINIA, 1716–1860 (Baltimore, 1980); Netherton et al., FAIRFAX COUNTY, 191–192; Palmer, CALENDAR, XI, 475; Thomas M. Ladd, "A Plan of That Part of the Virginia Canal from College Creek to Williamsburg," 1818.

38. Richie, REVISED CODE, II, 207; Palmer, CALENDAR, X, 488–489.

39. Ambler Family 1770–1860; John Ambler Papers; James City County Land Tax Lists 1783; Personal Property Tax Lists 1782–1798; Ambler, History, 1826; History of the Ambler Family in Virginia, 1828; Philip Barraud, October 28, 1798, letter to St. George Tucker; John Parke Custis, May 11, 1778, letter to George Washington; George Washington, THE WRITINGS OF GEORGE WASHINGTON FROM ORIGINAL MANUSCRIPT SOURCES, John C. Fitzpatrick, ed. (Washington, 1936), 13:56–58.

40. Ambler Family 1770–1860; James City County Personal Property Tax Lists 1801–1815; Land Tax Lists 1820–1836.

41. Ambler, History, 1826.

42. James City County Land Tax Lists 1782–1821; Personal Property Tax Lists 1782–1821; Palmer, CALENDAR, VI, 461–465, 521, 532–533, 543.

43. James City County Land Tax Lists 1830–1845; Agricultural Census 1850.

44. James City County Land Tax Lists 1782–1854; Personal Property Tax Lists 1782–1854.

45. James City County Land Tax Lists 1782–1845.

46. James City County Land Tax Lists 1802–1850. In 1804 there were 606 free blacks and mulattoes in York and James City Counties (Palmer, CALENDAR, IX, 443).

47. He should not be confused with the well known American patriot.

48. Martha W. McCartney, THE HISTORY OF GREEN SPRING PLANTATION, JAMES CITY COUNTY, VIRGINIA (Williamsburg, 1992).

49. James City County Land Tax Lists 1782–1838; Shepperson, JOHN PARADISE, 447–448.

50. Goodwin, KINGSMILL, 56, 59; James City County Land Tax Lists 1796–1812.

51. James City County Land Tax Lists 1783–1819; Personal Property Tax Lists 1805; Goodwin, KINGSMILL, 59.

52. Petersburg Hustings Court Will Book 1:223–224; James City County Land Tax Lists 1782–1820.

53. James City County Land Tax Lists 1782–1838; Personal Property Tax Lists 1800.

54. James City County Land Tax Lists 1796–1843.

55. Ibid., 1805–1861.

56. James City County Deed Book 9:423; Land Tax Lists 1782–1865.

57. James City County Land Tax Lists 1782–1861; Deed Book 210:150, 156–257.

58. James City County Land Tax Lists 1782–1813. Virtually all of the Norvells' land in James City County during the late eighteenth and early nineteenth centuries was located on the lower side of Route 60, east of Yarmouth Creek's Mill Creek branch, or on the Chickahominy River.

59. James City County Land Tax Lists 1782–1861.

60. Palmer, CALENDAR, VIII, 100; James City County Land Tax Lists 1782–1860.

61. Marquis de Lafayette, Certificate, October 18, 1832; James City County Land Tax Lists 1783–1835; Rice et al., AMERICAN CAMPAIGNS, passim; La Grange, Historic American Buildings Survey Form 47–31. As William Ludwell Lee would have been 8 years old when the Battle of Green Springs occurred and as he had been dead many years when Lafayette made the presentation, the identity of the man being recognized is uncertain.

CHAPTER 10

"Where Every Rood Of Ground Maintain'd
Its Man" 1831–1860

Maintaining Law And Order

During the early-to-mid the nineteenth century, when James City County's court justices convened on the second Monday of every month, their responsibilities differed little from their colonial counterparts. They heard civil suits, held preliminary hearings in criminal cases to be tried in the circuit court, issued tavern licenses, naturalized new citizens and decided whether freed slaves should be allowed to remain in the county. They also were responsible for seeing that local roads were kept in usable condition. On the days court was in session, people flocked into Williamsburg, often with their families in tow. There, they sold produce, purchased goods and services, and attended auctions of slaves, livestock and real estate. They also gossiped with friends and neighbors, caught up on the news, and socialized. According to one local woman, between the Wren Building and the Bright house on Richmond Road was the so-called "dressing tree," where "poor country people coming to town stopped to put their shoes on."[1]

But court days had a somber side. Eliza Baker, a black woman born in Williamsburg in 1845, recalled that a whipping post stood in the ravine near the corner of Francis and South England Streets. She said, "There was a big cage there which they put you in before they whipped you" and that Allen Lindsey and a Mr. Britain "used to do the whipping." Afterward, free blacks were kept caged until they paid a dollar for their release; slaves were held until their owners paid the fee. Blacks convicted of criminal acts were detained in the old jail near the Garrett house. Slave auctions were held on the courthouse green, where blacks were placed on a block and hawked to the highest bidder. Eliza Baker, who had witnessed slave auctions, said that the auctioneer (often, Sheriff Moses R. Harrell) would describe the skills of the person being sold. A good carpenter might go for $400 and a good cook or seamstress for even more. A healthy woman would bring $175 to $200, whereas little children under the age of 8 would sell for $60 to $80. She also recalled that dark-skinned slaves were the most highly prized. She said that there was a local slave trader named Hansford.[2]

One visitor to Williamsburg during the 1830s said that the Lunatic Hospital housed 60 patients and that its facilities were then being enlarged. Besides the asylum, college, courthouse and jail, the city had Episcopal, Methodist, and Baptist churches, 16 stores, three tanyards, a saddler's shop and four nearby merchant mills. Williamsburg also had two benevolent societies, nine attorneys and five medical doctors. The city's older public buildings reportedly presented "the appearance of decaying grandeur."[3]

When the State Convention of 1829–1830 was held, James City, Charles City, Elizabeth City, Warwick, York and Henrico Counties, and the city of Richmond, were represented by John Tyler, John Marshall, Philip N. Nicholas, and John B. Clopton. Thanks to redistricting, James City County was placed in a new district that included only York County and the city of Williamsburg and sent one delegate in the General Assembly. When a new State Convention was held in 1850–1851, Robert McCandlish and Lemuel J. Bowden attended on behalf of James City, Gloucester, Warwick and Elizabeth City Counties, and Williamsburg. The formula for representation was revised and in 1852–1853 James City County became part of a district that included only New Kent and Charles City.[4]

By the mid-1840s Virginians began complaining about the method by which county justices were chosen and the property requirements for suffrage. Some people contended that allowing county justices to appoint their successors and select sheriffs, deputy-sheriffs, and other county officers was inconsistent with the principals of a republican form of government. This wave of discontent culminated in a state-wide referendum and constitutional convention. The new state constitution, ratified in 1850–1851, brought about numerous changes in the structure of Virginia's government. For the first time, the governor, lieutenant governor and state attorney general were to be elected by popular vote, not chosen by members of the General Assembly. Also, county justices, sheriffs, and other local officials were subject to election. Significant changes were made in suffrage, for voting rights were broadened and linked to local residency requirements. All white males age 21 and over, who had lived in the state for two or more years, were allowed to vote in the county or city in which they resided. In May 1852, when Virginia counties held their first local elections under the new constitution, many former justices were returned to office. Thus, it appears that most people found fault with the old method of choosing local justices, not the office-holders themselves.[5]

In April 1842 voters in the Burnt Ordinary district were asked to decide whether public school funds should be loaned to private individuals at a competitive rate of interest, in order to generate income for education. The money in question included the proceeds from selling the Blisland Parish glebe and the Hot Water plantation near Centerville, which William Ludwell Lee had left as a bequest for a free school. The majority of voters agreed that James City County's Board of School Commissioners should be authorized to lend the funds "to dependable persons that use their real estate as security."[6]

The General Assembly in 1860 enacted several pieces of legislation that affected the citizens of James City County and Williamsburg. The two juris-dictions were to share a jointly-owned jail and the city sergeant was to serve as the county jailor. He was obliged to see that prisoners' cells were kept "clean and decent" and were whitewashed twice a year and that inmates were served wholesome food. Convicts and slaves were to be segregated from other prisoners. The county sheriff was authorized to supoena jurors from any part of Williamsburg to serve in the James City County Court or the Williamsburg Hustings Court and Grand Jury members could be selected from both juris-dictions. The county's Overseers of the Poor were told to "continue the poorhouse and school established under the act of February 3, 1817, for edu-cating and maintaining the poor." As neither maps nor written records have come to light that show where the poorhouse was located, its whereabouts is uncertain. Local officials probably rented a structure they used to accommodate the indigent. When the State Convention of 1861 was held, John Tyler attended on behalf of James City, Charles City, and New Kent Counties.[7]

Public Health

As advances in medical science gave rise to increasingly sophisticated methods of treatment, American doctors began wondering about the quality of health care their peers were providing to patients. In 1847 the fledgling American Medical Association conducted a survey of the country's doctors, inquiring how many of them had attended medical school. The statistics compiled for Virginia reveal that only two-thirds of the state's 972 doctors had had any formal medical training whatsoever and of those, some had attended only one or two courses of lectures. More than a fourth of Virginia's physicians practiced without any formal qualifications whatsoever. In 1847 none of the three physicians practicing in James City County were graduates

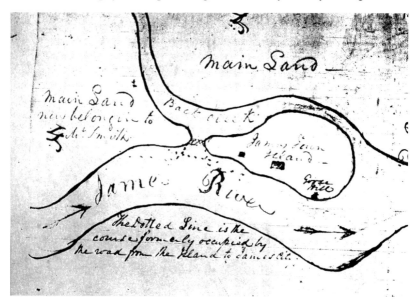

Durfey and Edloe's proposed toll bridge to Jamestown Island. James City County Legislative Petitions, 1832. Library of Virginia.

of a recognized medical school. Williamsburg, meanwhile, had ten doctors whose educational background is uncertain.[8]

A Bridge to Jamestown Island

In 1832 Goodrich Durfey and William Edloe of James City County asked the General Assembly to relocate the landing of the James River ferry from the old Ambler farm on the mainland to Jamestown Island, where steamboats and ferries could dock more conveniently. They also requested the right to erect a toll bridge across the Back River to accommodate traffic to the proposed ferry landing and submitted a sketch showing the site at which they wanted to build a bridge. Williamsburg attorney John Hill Smith, whose wife owned the Ambler farm, strenuously objected. He contended that "the old road on the Jamestown side has been wholly washed away by the river and the place where it ran is now in the river at a distance of 75 or 100 yards from the present shore." He added that "on the opposite side of the creek [where his wife's farm was located] the former road is partly covered by water," having been abandoned for more than 50 years. He also pointed out that the Amblers had built "a stone bridge [causeway] across the creek at a great distance from the old road, which was good as long as it lasted." Despite Smith's protests, the ferry landing was moved to Jamestown Island and the Durfey-Edloe bridge proposal was approved. The new bridge, which was in place by January 1833, reportedly stood at the site formerly occupied by John Ambler II's stone-and-log causeway.[9]

Life in Rural James City County

On Saturday, June 21, 1834, around 5 or 6 P.M., a storm-front that moved into James City County from the northwest spawned a large, powerful tornado. At Jockey's Neck, Thomas Coleman and one of his servants were crushed to death when a building in which they had taken refuge was leveled. Coleman's overseer and a few of his workers received serious injuries and some of his livestock were killed. In Williamsburg, numerous chimneys and frame houses were destroyed and "trees which had stood the utmost fury of the elements for centuries" reportedly were "uprooted or shattered to pieces." The tornado also did extensive damage in York and Gloucester Counties.[10]

However, rural life usually was much more peaceful. Robert Morris, a schoolteacher and farmer, who lived near Croaker, kept a daily diary in which he recorded his observations. He mingled with George Geddy, Richardson Henley, William Lightfoot, Lemuel Bowden, Albert H. Hankins, Nathaniel Piggott, and other relatively prosperous members of the community, although he was of very modest means. Morris, a Baptist, was fond of visiting local churches to hear guest speakers. He owned no slaves and often hired free blacks to help him with his farming operations. He did most of his shopping in the store at Burnt Ordinary and in January 1845 noted that he had bought coffee, paper, whiskey, cashmere, quinine, fencing, thimbles, magazines and newspapers, nails, pork, cotton, ginger, and a shovel there. He also went to Burnt Ordinary to attend militia musters and it was there that he caught the stage to Williamsburg or Richmond. Morris was licensed by James City Baptist Church to give religious instruction to slaves and to conduct their funerals. Occasionally he baptized free and enslaved blacks at local churches.

On March 11, 1846, Morris noted in his diary that 28 grampus whales, 18 feet long and 8 feet wide, had come ashore at Yorktown. The following spring he mentioned that a whale beached at the mouth of the Warwick River measured 62 feet long and was 10 feet high and "12 1/2 feet wide from eye to eye, with a tongue as big as a feather bed." Another unusual event Morris recorded was that he had "helped to tie a lunatic in the road" to Burnt Ordinary. He wrote about local fox-hunting and mentioned the 1845 smallpox epidemic that affected several Tidewater counties. He discussed traveling by steamer from Port Walthall (on the Appomattox River) to the wharf at The Grove and paying a dollar for hack service to Williamsburg. In April 1845 Morris went to Burnt Ordinary to vote in the elections. Emotions ran high and "Waller and Pierce struck each other across the table and Lucius Edloe half-dressed [was] lying in the sand." Toby Henley was "full of talk" and Morris said that men from New Kent and Charles City Counties came to Burnt Ordinary "to vote against Bowden."[11] Toward evening, fights broke out and "D. Jones [was] thrashed well, B. Trebel and N. Piggott and T. Henley [were] fighting." He said that "Philbates and B. Trebel [were] sparring" as were

Howard and Bowden. Morris implied that these men's combativeness was fueled by an ample supply of liquor.[12]

In 1854 Felix Peirce described Burnt Ordinary as "a healthy, prosperous community" with a post office, churches, and stores. When he advertised for a good shoemaker, a tailor, a blacksmith, and a coachmaker or wheelwright, he expected those he hired to live in the community. Burnt Ordinary had a debating society, which met regularly in the local post office, and the VIRGINIA GAZETTE provided local residents with some intellectual stimulation. The GAZETTE was published from August 1853 to October 1854 by Thomas Martin of Powhatan Plantation and afterward, by Peyton and A. A. Neel. After A. A. Neel soloed briefly as publisher, J. Harvey Ewing took over and served until E. H. Lively became the paper's owner. The GAZETTE carried the usual advertisements and notices of deaths and marriages, but it also contained national and international news, poetry, and serial short stories. One regular feature many James City County farmers read avidly was the agricultural market report. The newspaper also published lists of people for whom letters had arrived at the local post office.[13]

The Status of Blacks at Mid-Century

In 1854 a runaway slave named John, who belonged to Francis M. Jones of James City County, was captured and jailed in Middlesex County. He earned a considerable amount of notoriety by setting the county prison ablaze. One eyewitness saw flames coming from an upper room. He surmised that John had set the door of his cell on fire in order to free its hinges and had concealed his actions by hanging a quilt across one window and a straw mattress across the other. Although John managed to escape, he was recaptured, tried, and sentenced to banishment from the United States. In accord with the law, John's owner was compensated for what Middlesex County's justices thought he was worth: $250. Later in the year, a group of James City and York County citizens submitted a petition to the General Assembly, asking that John's owner be paid his true value: $600. They argued that Middlesex County's justices had undervalued John because of the seriousness of his offence and that he "did not burn the jail from malice nor from any other motive than to escape confinement . . . to which he had been subjected as a runaway."[14]

In 1857 a group of laws passed by the General Assembly placed new restrictions upon the rights of free blacks. They were prohibited from owning slaves other than their own children. This would have prevented a free black from purchasing a spouse who was enslaved. Free blacks couldn't purchase wine or liquor without the consent of three local justices of the peace and the beverages had to be bought from a licensed tavern. No blacks (enslaved or free) in James City, New Kent, Essex, or King and Queen Counties were allowed to own or keep dogs, or pass through those counties accompanied by a dog, without written permission. Black lawbreakers could be whipped and slave owners who failed to enforce the dog law could be fined. Another new piece of legislation allowed free black inmates of the state penitentiary to be used in public works projects. A map depicting the distribution of slaves throughout Virginia in 1860 reveals that counties in the lower Tidewater

Detail from Herman Boye's "Map of the State of Virginia," 1826. Library of Virginia.

region (with the exception of Warwick) had fewer slaves than those in the upper Tidewater or Piedmont. Further west, the percentage of enslaved blacks dropped off dramatically and few or none lived in numerous counties west of the Blue Ridge. In 1860, 54.4 percent of James City County's population was comprised of enslaved blacks.[15]

James City County and the Agricultural Revolution

The financial Panic of 1837 was followed by a long agricultural depression. Tidewater farmers found themselves in dire straits, for their land's value was reduced by its lack of productivity. In nearby New Kent County the tax assessor noted in his record book (line after line) that the farms he visited had "old worn out soil." However, economic conditions began to improve once it was discovered that lime and marl could be used to restore the fertility of soil acidified by the long-term production of tobacco. In 1842 Edmund Ruffin reported that Tidewater land values had risen significantly and that farm income had increased by hundreds of thousands of dollars. He said that advances in agricultural technology (such as improved equipment to till the soil) also had enhanced productivity substantially. According to Ruffin, prior to 1817, an estimated 99 out of every 100 acres under cultivation were tilled by primitive one-horse ploughs, half of which were trowel-hoe or fluke-hoe ploughs, which rarely penetrated deeper than three inches, if that. Wheat usually was trodden out by horses or oxen and threshing machines were rare. By the mid-nineteenth century, however, progressive farmers eagerly embraced improvements as they came along.[16]

In 1831 the mowing machine replaced the labor-intensive process of hand-cutting hay with scythes. Then, during the 1840s the grain-reaper came on the market. The 1850s brought the grain drill and in 1860 the steam thresher was perfected. All of these modernizing inventions enhanced the farmer's efficiency and productivity. In March 1839 Congress authorized funds for the collection of agricultural statistics. By 1850 the state of Virginia had begun compiling agricultural censuses. These records, which were collected every decade from 1850 through 1880, list how many acres per farm

The Ancient Stone house as it appeared in ca. 1845. HENRY HOWE'S
HISTORICAL COLLECTION OF VIRGINIA.

were under the plow and how much land was fallow or forested. They also
include the value of a farmer's agricultural equipment and livestock and the
number of acres planted in various types of crops. As time went on, the data
collection process became more comprehensive and encompassed dairying,
egg production, and the value of fruit and crops produced for market.[17]

One way Virginia farmers stayed abreast of the latest developments in
agronomy was by joining agricultural societies and farmers clubs that published journals, held fairs, and promoted progress and reform. As scientific
farming gained acceptance and was put to use, land values rose. By the time
of the Civil War a mixed crop system of agriculture predominated throughout Virginia, with wheat and corn followed in importance by potatoes. Animal
husbandry also became popular.[18] Although the advent of scientific farming
strengthened Tidewater's economic position, the region did not reach its
zenith until much later in the century, when the railroad and commercial
shipping made urban markets readily accessible.

Agricultural census records for 1850 reveal that in James City County, the fair market value of the average farm was approximately $4,300. Most local farmers cultivated a third of their land and allowed the rest of it to lay fallow or in woodland. Animal husbandry was important and the average farmer's livestock herd was worth a twelfth the value of his real estate. The overwhelming majority of James City County farmers owned cattle and horses or mules, but only 40 percent raised sheep. Almost everyone grew corn, wheat, hay and Irish and sweet potatoes and some farmers raised fruit and vegetables for sale at market. Between 1850 and 1860 local real estate values rose but land use management patterns changed little.[19] Most local agronomists farmed with slave labor.

On May 18, 1854, an advertisement in the VIRGINIA GAZETTE invited "all farmers interested in having an agricultural society in this part of the state" to meet at the city/county courthouse on Election Day. This was the origin of the Middle Plantation Agricultural Society, which on November 15, 1860, held an exhibit on Williamsburg's fairgrounds. Farm families from James City, York, and Warwick Counties and Williamsburg were invited to display their livestock, agricultural produce (such as fruits, vegetables, honey, and butter) and handicrafts (including needlework, quilts, and knitting). Prizes were offered for the best entries in each category. In 1860 James W. Custis was president of the Middle Plantation Agricultural Society and E. H. Lively (publisher of the VIRGINIA GAZETTE) was secretary.[20]

Local Historic Attractions

The Stonehouse

During the 1830s and '40s several antiquarians voiced their interest in a local historic site that has intrigued successive generations of Virginians: the ancient stone structure that once stood high upon a hilltop overlooking Ware Creek. In September 1838 John Galt Williamson, a guest at nearby Cedar Grove (Taskinask), visited the site, which was then enveloped by a thick forest of old oaks. He said that according to local lore, it was a lair of Blackbeard the pirate. Williamson, however, believed that the old building was erected as a place of defence, basing his opinion upon the strength of its walls, the size of its doors and windows, and the presence of loopholes that would accommodate guns.[21]

A few years later, Edmund Ruffin, the agronomist, described his visit to the Stonehouse. He said that the structure, which stood on a high, narrow promontory, was nearly inaccessible by land or water. He added that it:

. . . is now in ruins, more or less of each wall having tumbled down, no trace of either the roof or floor being left. It was a rectangular building 18 1/2 by 15 feet. The four corners stand nearly at their original height, being 6 feet above the level of the floor. The chimney rises in a good state of preservation 5 feet higher, but there is sufficient evidence that it was originally still more elevated. . . . Its elevation was only one story, with a basement room half below and half above the surface of the earth. It stands nearly north and south. At the south end is the chimney, which projects outside of the wall, but has no fireplace in the basement, but a well finished semi-circular fireplace in the room above, 3 1/2 feet wide and 2 feet deep, with only one flue 12 by 12 inches. On the west end is the doorway giving entrance into the upper and also into the basement room; this doorway is 6 feet wide.

On the north there is a door 3 feet wide into the basement and on each side of the door a hole through the wall (which is 2 feet thick) resembling a small port-hole, measuring on the inside 20 by 10 inches and on the outside 20 by 4 inches. Each hole is exactly the same size, and constructed with care. If these holes were merely intended for purposes of ventilation, why were they made wider within than without, and why were they both put on the same side with the door? On the east side is one jamb of a window or port hole, and from its position, not being in the middle, there is every reason to believe there must have been a second opening corresponding thereto in the same side. A half-burned door lintel, which has recently fallen from the door of the basement room, is the only remnant of wood left; it is of white oak and was evidently sawed with a whipsaw. The walls of the house, which are 2 feet thick in the basement, and 18 inches above, are constructed of ferruginous sand stone, of which an abundance is found in the hill on which the building stands. The stones, which are not large, have generally flat beds and are hammered to a true face, and all the openings are finished with great care. The cement used is lime mortar and must have been very good. The measurements are all very exact, and the work bears ample testimony of great care and nicety in its structure.

Edmund Ruffin was convinced that the Stonehouse "was no doubt erected by someone as a permanent place of secret retreat and probably of defense." Because he thought the building's doorway would accommodate a piece of small artillery, he speculated that it might be associated with some of Virginia's earliest settlers or perhaps with Bacon's Rebellion.[22] Ruffin's second theory has considerable validity, for the old Stonehouse was close to the back line of Mount Folly plantation, which was owned by Bryan Smith, one of Governor William Berkeley's avid supporters, who turned vigilante in the aftermath of the popular uprising.

A few years after Edmund Ruffin wrote about the Stonehouse, Henry Howe quoted an author whose speculations were even more melodramatic. He raised the possibility that it was the site of a fort constructed in 1609 by Captain John Smith, intended "for a retreat neare a convenient river, upon a high commanding hill, very hard to be assaulted and easy to be defended." Howe's informant apparently never had seen a copy of Smith's well known map, which shows his "new fort" at a site near the head of Grays Creek in Surry County.[23] Today the remains of the mysterious stone building have disappeared from view, thanks to desecration of the site by looters. In 1972 the Stonehouse Archaeological Site was added to the National Register of Historic Places. It is located within the Stonehouse Magisterial District.

Jamestown

In 1837 when historian Charles Campbell visited Jamestown Island, he commented that "The fragment of a wall of the old church, standing solitary in a ploughed field, is all that remains." He added that "The water hereabouts is gaining on the land and the time may not be far off when the ground on which it stood shall be submerged." Richard Randolph, who also stopped by in 1837, spoke of seeing the church ruins, "some of the remains of the walls and mounds of the ancient fortress of Jamestown" and "a small brick building that tradition says was a powder magazine."[24] He added that:

. . . at a little distance from this house are the remains . . . of a very large building. This was apparently the Governor's or State House.[25] *There are similar remains in other places lying on the surface of the ground in regular order in a long, narrow line, which probably indicates the direction and location of the principal streets of the town.*

He noted that "In digging the foundation of a house in the Island some time since the workmen discovered several human skeletons. Indeed, these may be found in many places near the site of the town." Randolph said that:

The part of the Island not embraced within the limits of a town appears to have been apportioned into numerous lots of small size, each one of which was surrounded by a dyke. Many of these ditches are still visible and plainly indicate the extent of the lots they enclosed. On some of these lots are to be found remains of buildings. On one there is an old well, the brick walls of which are quite perfect and sound.[26]

When Benson J. Lossing visited Jamestown Island in 1848, he stayed with its owner, John Coke, who then had "all the soil that is left unsubmerged on which the English built their first town in America." Lossing paused on the western bank of Sandy Bay and made a sketch of Jamestown Island, noting that "what was once a marsh" had become "a deep bay, 400 yards wide." He depicted "the remains of a bridge, destroyed by a gale and high tide a few years ago," and said that his host was living upon Jamestown Island when the floodwaters came and that "for three days himself and family were prisoners." Lossing said that John Coke's father-in-law "well remembered when a marsh, so narrow and firm that a person might cross it upon a fence rail, was where the deep water at the ruined bridge now is." Lossing predicted that within a few years Jamestown Island would "have a navigable channel around it, so great was the encroachment of the waters of the river." He said that "already a large portion of it, whereon the ancient town was erected, has been washed away" and that "a cypress-tree, now many yards from the shore, stood at the end of a carriage-way to the wharf, 60 yards from the water's edge, only 16 years ago." Lossing urged Virginians to build a wall of masonry to check the river's encroachment and closed by saying that "Some remains of the old fort may be seen at low water several yards from the shore."[27] Historian Henry Howe also described Jamestown's appearance during the mid-nineteenth century. He said that the first fort had been on "a point of land projecting into the James" and that "the water is gaining on the shore, and the time will arrive when the waves will roll over it." He quoted from the Rev. Hugh Jones, who in 1747 stated that Jamestown consisted "at present of nothing but abundance of brick rubbish and three or four good inhabited houses."[28]

When Richard Randolph returned to Jamestown at mid-century, he concluded that:

. . . the great body of the town, which however was never very large, was certainly west of the Old Steeple [church tower] still visible, and is now entirely or very nearly submerged in the river. This is clearly proved by the old deeds for lots in the town, recorded in the office of James City County court, which call for bounds that are now under water; and more palpably, by vast numbers of broken bricks, and other relics of buildings that may still be seen in the Western bank at low tide.[29]

Artist Robert Sully spoke eloquently of an 1854 sojourn on Jamestown Island and made pencil sketches and watercolor renderings of the church tower, Travis house ruins, and a cypress tree he estimated stood 60 yards off-shore. He also drew a picture of what he believed was "the site of the old fort," which was "two hundred yards above the church, on an elevated point." He indicated that a magazine, the foundation of which was "still in good preservation" and "of the same kind of bricks as the church," stood 40 yards to the rear and noted that its 10-foot-square powder pit extended to a depth of "about 5 feet." William Allen's overseer gave Sully an old musket barrel he recovered from the vicinity of the fort and Sully himself admitted collecting "some blue beads, Indian arrow heads, a stone hatchet, Indian pipe bowls, &c." He stated that "the encroachment of the water on the land has been long going on, but of late years, particularly at the point where the Church stands, it has been fearfully rapid." He said that "A little below the Fort Point, there is some distance from the beach a Cypress Tree, under water to its lower branches" and that "in the recollection of the living, Carriages once drove around this tree." Moreover, "A considerable distance from the Beach, at low water, there is distinctly seen the Inclosure of a well Brick'd round in a circle." Sully proffered that "at a former period, the little tongue of land on which the Church stands projected much further out—a gentle slope. It is now washed away to an abrupt half circle."[30] Although Robert Sully assumed that the magazine and fort site were associated with the colony's first settlers, his rendition of the vaulted building's ruins and a sketch made later in the century raise the possibility that he was seeing the brick magazine erected by Governor Edmund Andros during the mid-1690s.

The Jamestown Jubilee

In 1854 the Jamestown Society of Washington began making plans for an 1857 celebration to commemorate the 250th anniversary of the first settlers' arrival. They joined forces with the Virginia Historical Society and with the cooperation of Jamestown Island's owner, William Allen, began erecting cabins to accommodate visitors. They also built a 175-foot-long refreshment saloon, a dining hall that seated 500, and a speakers platform. As the big day drew near, would-be celebrants from Washington, Baltimore, Norfolk, and Richmond boarded steamboats that would take them to the Jamestown Jubilee. On the morning of May 13th, "a large fleet of bright winged craft of all sizes and characters, jubilant with gay streamers, booming guns and sonorous music" was afloat off Jamestown Island. By noon, 13 steamers, several schooners, and a yacht were on hand and several bands were playing. One visitor remarked that "All that remains at Jamestown is a portion of the tower and walls of the old church and a brick magazine, now used as a barn." Another man observed that souvenir-hunters "cracked off a suitable chunk from one of the old slabs" in the graveyard, while others "contented themselves with a brickbat apiece" from the old church tower. According to one report, "a beautiful grove and wild thicket of underbrush" then sur-rounded the church ruins. "Beyond the grove, on all sides, the land is cleared and under high cultivation; about two hundred acres nearest the church are in wheat." The Jamestown Jubilee included patriotic rhetoric, an elaborate military review, dancing, and free-flowing champagne. Judge John B. Clopton's son, William, told a friend that May 13th was very hot and that his father was exhausted by "hard walking through corn fields." He said that the elderly judge kept saying "Take me to the stand, take me to the stand," which his son assumed was the speaker's stand. But when they reached it, the judge said "I don't *want* to hear John Tyler now. Take me to the stand where the *mint julep* is!"[31]

Three illustrations published in an 1857 HARPER'S WEEKLY article on the Jamestown Jubilee depict the church ruins, military encampment, the waterfront, and a prone celebrant imbibing from a jug. Artist-reporter David H. Strother ("Porte Crayon") wrote that:

Drums were beating, colors flying, pots boiling and glasses rattling; gallant-looking officers on horseback were galloping about the field; companies of soldiers were marching and maneuvering, while the great unorganized mass just swarmed about the pavilions, without doing anything in particular that we could perceive.

He added that "The field was alive with tents; among them a huge one, in which every variety of gambling was in full blast," but as soon as the commanding officer found out, "he 'closed the bank.'" The 1857 celebration ended with "Everybody pleased, everybody tired, and almost everybody sober." Although many of the celebrants departed from Jamestown Island, those who remained overnight were treated to fireworks and a grand ball.[32] Taking excursions to Jamestown Island, especially for picnics, was a popular pastime with local residents during the mid-nineteenth century and a special celebration was held there on May 13th, nearly every year.

Some Local Properties

Jamestown Island and "Amblers" on the Maine

David Bullock of Richmond, who bought the Ambler family's Jamestown Island plantation in 1822, purchased Samuel Travis's estate in 1831. This gave him possession of the island in its entirety. Four years later Bullock sold the island to Goodrich Durfey, a local real estate speculator who at various times owned Jockey's Neck, Indigo Dam, Kingsmill, Piney Grove, and Newport Mills and in 1832 undertook construction of a toll bridge to Jamestown Island. Durfey, like Bullock, maintained the Ambler plantation's buildings, which retained their assessed value of $3,600. In 1844, less than a decade after purchasing Jamestown Island, Durfey offered it for sale. In a newspaper advertisement he claimed that it consisted of nearly 2,000 acres, approximately half of which were arable and "in a high state of improvement and cultivation." He indicated that the farm had "the best wheat soil in the state, one of the fields having produced last year, by actual measurement, over 30 bushels to the acre, mostly on a heavy clover fallow." Moreover, it was "one of the best stock farms in Eastern Virginia," with ample pasturage for 300 head of cattle. Durfey stated that there was "a substantial three story brick house, 40 by 60, with 4 rooms on a floor, in good repair" and "a kitchen, a laundry, an overseer's house, a dairy, a smokehouse, barns and stables, together with negro houses, all of which are new and in good order." He added that the farm had "a young apple and peach orchard of the best improved fruit from Baltimore and Richmond nurseries," a ferry that produced $300 a year in revenues, and a steam boat wharf that rented for $300 a year.[33]

During 1845 Goodrich Durfey deeded Jamestown Island to John Coke, who already owned the old Ambler farm on the mainland. He took up resi-

View of the Jamestown Jubilee, 1857. David H. Strother in HARPER'S WEEKLY, June 27, 1857. Library of Congress.

dence on the island and bought a stagecoach to use as a hack to convey passengers from the ferry-landing to Williamsburg. Martha Orgaine purchased Jamestown Island in 1847 on behalf of her young son, the great-nephew and principal heir of William Allen of Claremont. When William Orgaine came of age and changed his surname to Allen (a prerequisite to receiving his inheritance), he assumed control of more than 3,000 acres on the west side of College Creek in the Neck O'Land, plus Jamestown Island, and the Kingsmill and Littletown plantations. Thus, Orgaine-alias-Allen's river frontage extended from Grove Creek to Sandy Bay. He, like his benefactor, resided at Claremont and entrusted his outlying properties to the care of farm managers, who were supervised by a principal overseer. The ferry-landing was moved back across Sandy Bay to "Amblers," which John Coke still owned. Coke leased the Kingsmill Wharf from Allen and ran hack services from there and "Amblers" to Williamsburg.[34]

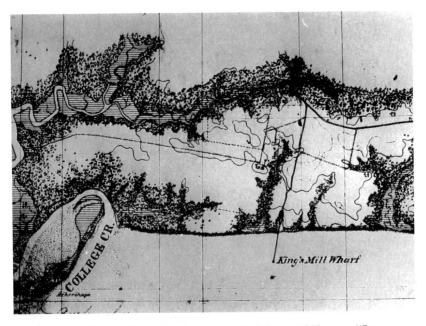

The wharf at Kingsmill as shown on John W. Donn's 1873 map, "James River, Virginia, from Burwell's Bay to College Creek." National Archives.

Ewell Hall, now surrounded by the Williamsburg Memorial Park.
Photo by Ralph Maxwell.

Foster's, now the Bradshaw home. Photo by Nan Maxwell.

Green Spring

In 1843 the nearly 3,000-acre Green Spring plantation was purchased by Robert C. A. and John Ward of New Jersey, who despite being Northerners, owned slaves whom they entrusted to the care of farm manager George C. Richardson. Green Spring was an active and prosperous working farm up until the time of the Civil War.[35]

Egglestons

A few miles above Williamsburg and next door to the Martins' Powhatan Plantation, was a 450-acre tract that Elizabeth Eggleston inherited prior to 1768 from her husband, Benjamin Eggleston Jr. "Egglestons," which originally was part of Powhatan, lay along the north side of News Road (Route 613). By 1844 it had passed to Green Spring overseer George C. Richardson, who was living on his own land at the time of the Civil War. Nearby was Benjamin Green's farm. During the 1860s News Road was a minor thoroughfare that had a "bad crossing" at Powhatan Creek.[36]

The Indigo Dam Farm

Not far from "Egglestons" was the Indigo Dam plantation that Lucy Ludwell Paradise inherited from her father, Philip Ludwell III. His estate inventory included indigo knives and hoes. An archaeological feature tentatively identified as an indigo-processing site has been excavated there by Colonial Williamsburg Foundation archaeologists, working under the direction of Dr. Marley R. Brown III. The Indigo Dam plantation was a subsidiary of Green Spring. In 1839 nearly 560 acres of Mrs. Paradise's estate came into the hands of John N. Maupin, who also owned the Mill Quarter, a subsidiary farm associated with Powhatan Mill. After the Civil War, the Indigo Dam tract was owned in succession by David S. and William T. Cowles, Goodrich Durfey, R. B. Gilliam and Moses R. Harrell.[37]

Rich Neck

The litigation that pitted the late Lucy Ludwell Paradise's nieces against her grandsons (the children of her daughter and an Italian nobleman) was settled during the 1830s. Afterward William B. Morecock and William Edloe purchased 600 acres of Rich Neck, that portion which contained the old Ludwell family seat. Morecock relinquished his interest in the property to Lucius Edloe, whose kin sold their land to Robert F. Cole of Williamsburg in 1848. Cole immediately constructed new buildings upon the tract.[38]

Jockey's Neck and the James City Parish Glebe

Thomas Coleman of Williamsburg, who in 1820 purchased the Jockey's Neck farm from Dr. James Carter's executors, perished in the 1834 tornado. In 1846 Coleman's executors sold his farm to Benjamin E. Bucktrout of Williamsburg, who also bought the old James City Parish glebe from the Rev. John Bracken. The minister had purchased the glebe in 1814 when real estate belonging to Virginia's defunct State Church was sold off. Bracken was rector of Bruton Parish Church from 1773 to 1818, served briefly as president of the College of William and Mary, and was one of the Williamsburg area's wealthiest citizens.

In 1848 Benjamin E. Bucktrout's executors sold Jockey's Neck to Goodrich Durfey, who in 1856 joined with John Coke in purchasing the seat of Holt's (Newport) Mill from Francis C. Coleman, one of the late William Coleman's heirs. Immediately prior to the Civil War, Durfey became sole owner of the Newport Mills, a grist and saw mill complex.[39]

Carter's Grove

In 1839 Carter's Grove plantation came into the hands of Thomas Wynne, an affluent local farmer who immediately capitalized upon his property's commercial potential. He built a public steamboat wharf and began operating a hack service to Williamsburg and Yorktown. Vessels that regularly plied the James bought both passengers and freight to the Grove Wharf, which teemed with activity. During the late 1840s Wynne added carriages and stagecoaches to his fleet of livery vehicles. In 1846 he was hired by the government to provide mail delivery to Williamsburg six times a week; he also had a postal route to Yorktown. In 1848, when Wynne asked the General Assembly for permission to repair and enlarge his wharf, he said it extended into the river more than a hundred yards. Failing health eventually forced Wynne to sell his farm.

In 1856 Lewis Ellison purchased Carter's Grove. He moved his family there and used slaves and hired labor to work the land. Wheat, corn, hay, oats, and potatoes were among the crops raised at Carter's Grove and Ellison also had substantial herds of cattle, sheep, and horses. Much of the Ellison family's garden produce was sold in urban markets. Lewis Ellison's investment in farming equipment, which included a threshing machine and two reapers, was five-and-a-half times that of other James City County agronomists. On the eve of the Civil War, Carter's Grove was one of James City County's most productive farms. Ellison supplemented his household's income by transporting mail from Grove Landing to Williamsburg. Despite his resourcefulness, he was forced to sell off three small parcels of land immediately prior to the Civil War.[40]

The Ewell Farm

During the early 1790s Benjamin Browne of Surry County came into possession of the farm that eventually became known as Ewell Hall. At his death, the acreage descended to his son, Benjamin Jr., who sold half of it to William L. Bacon. In 1840 William Smith and his wife, who owned the remainder, conveyed it to George W. Cardwell. Cardwell fell on hard times and in 1858 his creditors conveyed his property to Benjamin S. Ewell, president of the College of William and Mary. He immediately constructed a large frame dwelling there, which he made his family home. In 1863, when Confederate cartographers mapped part of James City County, they attributed the house to "Col. Ewell." Today the Ewell Hall mansion forms the centerpiece of the Williamsburg Memorial Park.[41]

Lombardy, near Toano. Photo by Ralph Maxwell.

Riverview, overlooking the York. Photo by Ralph Maxwell.

Foster's

In the heart of what eventually became the village of Norge was the farm Frances Foster bought from William Spencer Mahone in 1841. Although Foster died within a year, her name had a lingering association with the property. In 1845 Nathaniel Piggott, a wealthy James City County farmer and owner of nearby Farmville, purchased the Foster estate and significantly enhanced the value its improvements, perhaps elaborating upon the brick-encased dwelling that still exists. Piggott, an active member of Olive Branch Christian Church, owned land on both sides of Route 60's forerunner, had riverfront land above Jamestown Island, and a mill on Skimino Creek. The ruins of his mill (later Fenton's) are still standing.[42]

Surprise Plains

Just east of Burnt Ordinary was the eighteenth-century Walker farm, which by the early nineteenth century belonged to James City County School Commissioner Henley Taylor. During the 1850s it was in the possession of E. Beverley Slater, whose dwelling stood close to the intersection of Chickahominy Road and the road to Richmond (Route 60). While Slater owned the farm it was known as Surprise Plains. The recently built Toano Middle School stands upon the tract.[43]

The Six Mile Ordinary Farm

Mrs. Elizabeth D. Taylor, a York County widow, inherited life-rights to the 150-acre Six Mile Ordinary farm that her late husband, William, bought in 1827, a year before his death. Mrs. Taylor's popular tavern, which was on a well traveled stage road six miles west of Williamsburg, would have provided her with a steady source of income. In 1842 she purchased a neigh-boring farm from John C. Davis and built a home there. It was on Mrs. Taylor's land that the James City (or Smyrna) Baptist Church was built.[44]

Lombardy

A letter written by William Barton Rogers in April 1859 provides an intimate look at life in western James City County on the eve of the Civil War. Rogers, who was heading for Williamsburg, boarded a little steamboat in Richmond and intended to disembark at the mouth of the Chickahominy River. As a bad storm prevented the steamer's landing there, Rogers persuaded the captain to take him up the Chickahominy to a site near the road to Burnt Ordinary. From there, he made his way to Lombardy, the home of his old friend, Littleton Waller. Rogers said that Mrs. Waller welcomed him cordially and took him upstairs to her husband, who was "basking in the warmth of a luxurious wood fire, the very picture of philosophic and benevolent cheerfulness." Rogers said that Waller, "after visiting all quarters of the globe and sharing in the dangers of the Mexican War as a purser in the navy," had retired to his country home, "where he has made himself the model farmer of the neighborhood and spends his time in doing good to his neighbors." The next morning, Rogers visited Waller's marl bank and collected some specimens. After dinner, he "was driven in a buggy to dear old Williamsburg." Rogers said that he observed along the road "proofs of prosperous and improved agriculture" and that at the old crossroads known as Burnt Ordinary, where there once had been a "ruinous charred inn," was "a hamlet of neat white houses, and on all sides . . . evidences of neatness and thrift."[45]

Warrenton

John Walker, who owned a substantial amount of land in western James City County at the close of the eighteenth century, left his acreage on Old Forge Road to Robert Walker, who lived upon the property with his wife, Elizabeth. During the mid-1820s the Walker heirs sold the family farm to Dr. Michael S. Warren, who moved there and called the farm "Warrenton." Dr. Warren constructed a new building upon his property and in 1840 erected a second one of comparable value. In 1845 he commenced paying taxes upon a mill and during the early 1850s the value of the buildings on his farm rose dramatically. It may have been then that he built the large frame dwelling now known as Warrenton. By that date, Dr. Warren was in possession of the Chickahominy Shipyard tract and two other farms in the neighborhood. At his death in the early 1850s, his widow (the former Elizabeth B. Allen) inherited life-rights to Warrenton, which she farmed with slave labor. After her death in the late 1880s, her son and daughter became embroiled in a legal dispute that made its way to the state supreme court.[46]

Windsor Castle

Windsor Castle, a frame dwelling that architectural historians date to the third quarter of the eighteenth century, in 1810 was part the estate of William Browne, whose landholdings were concentrated on the east side of Diascund Creek. By 1832 John R. Pierce had acquired the acreage that contains Windsor Castle. Within two years, the farm came into the possession of Mathew Pierce. William Bush purchased the Pierce property in 1840 and in time, significantly enhanced the value of its improvements. Colonel Bush and his wife, the former Matilda Elizabeth Finch, were living in Windsor Castle at the time of the Civil War.[47] The structure is on the National Register of Historic Places.

Ashland

Near Cowles Mill and Diascund Creek was the Ashland farmhouse, built upon some vacant land that William B. Gregory bought from Thomas Mann Randolph's executors in 1838. As Gregory died shortly after making his purchase, his executors in 1839 built a domestic complex to enhance the property's value. William B. Morecock purchased the Gregory farm, which he called Ashland, and moved his family there. Confederate map-makers mislabeled the Morecock dwelling as "Bowcock."[48]

La Grange

La Grange, the home of Edmund and Ann B. Taylor, was next door to George Geddy's farm, White Hall, and Eliza Piggott's property, Temple Hall. In 1856 the Taylors' heirs sold La Grange to Warner Enos. He purchased an adjoining parcel from William Pumphrey's executors and built a new house, leaving La Grange to the occupancy of Dr. A. J. E. Jennings. Both the Enos and Jennings dwellings were identified by Confederate cartographers in 1863–1864. Dr. Jennings, upon moving to La Grange, began practicing medicine out of a dispensary he built onto the back of his home. The physician's household included his wife, Virginia H., 8-year-old son John Melville Jennings, and farm manager R. G. Wood.[49]

Riverview Plantation

Albert W. Hankins, the son of Cherry Hall owner William Hankins II, was living in James City County by 1830, most likely upon his father's farm called Riverview. In 1835 he inherited the tract and a legal interest in nearby Shellfield. Between 1839 and 1840, the value of Riverview's buildings increased somewhat. It was around that time that Hankins married Zelica Whitaker of York County. During the next decade the couple nearly doubled the value of the buildings on their property. It was likely then that Riverview's old frame dwelling was enlarged substantially. During the late 1850s several members of Albert W. Hankins' household succumbed to contagious diseases. One was his wife, Zelica, who died of consumption (tuberculosis).

Albert W. Hankins exemplifies the prosperous James City County farmer, who by wisely husbanding his resources, maintained a high standard of living. He employed 23-year-old Richard Hix to oversee his 18 adult slaves and manage his farming operations, which included a large and valuable livestock herd and the production of wheat, corn, oats, peas, beans, and potatoes. The Hankins' owned gold and silver flatware, expensive household furnishings, two pleasure carriages, and bank certificates, all of which are evidence of their wealth. A highly detailed topographic map prepared during the late 1850s depicts Riverview's layout. The Hankins' farm included four houses in which their slaves resided.[50]

Cloverdale

To the southeast of Ware Creek, near the crossroads known as Croaker, was a large farm called Cloverdale. During the 1840s it was owned by Henry B. M. and Eliza H. Richardson, who by 1848 had a mill upon their property. The Cloverdale mill is shown on maps made by Confederate cartographers during the 1860s.[51]

Ware Creek's Free Black Community

Tax rolls and census records for the first half of the nineteenth century reveal that a substantial number of free blacks, who owned the land they occupied, were living along the east side of Ware Creek. The community included farmers of various economic means and people with specialized skills, such as millers, blacksmiths, bricklayers, tailors, painters, carpenters, mechanics, teachers, watermen, sailors, and midwives. Otway (Ottoway) Hodson (Hudson, Hotson), a 45-year-old farmer, shared his home with his wife Alley, Pryor Ashlock (a young oysterman), William Taylor (a young laborer), and two children (Isaiah Ashlock, age 13, and James A. Taylor, age 7). Hodson owned five cattle and household furnishings worth only $5. Nearby was David (or Davy) Taylor, a farmer who owned 150 acres of land and a building worth $15. As the tax assessor indicated that his farm formerly was part of La Grange, David or his forebears may have been slaves of the late Edmund Taylor Jr. and his wife, who originally owned the land. In 1860 David Taylor and his wife, Elizabeth, had eight children between the ages of 4 and 22. They owned a substantial herd of livestock, $25 worth of household furnishings and a clock, then considered a taxable luxury item. Near the Taylor farm was the household of George Nelson, another free black. His 50 acres had structural improvements with an estimated value of $50, a sum that exceeded many of his white neighbors' assessments for buildings. Nelson's household included his wife, Marie, and five other people who seemingly were unrelated. Tax records credit George Nelson with a horse, three cattle, 12 hogs, a clock, a pleasure carriage, and $70 worth of furniture. He was one of the most prosperous men in his neighborhood, irrespective of race.[52] Even so, most of the free blacks living in the Ware Creek community seem to have eeked out a marginal existence. Little did they know what lay ahead: the end of slavery, which brought freedom to all.

Notes

1.   Albert O. Porter, COUNTY GOVERNMENT IN VIRGINIA: A LEGISLATIVE HISTORY, 1607–1904 (New York, 1947), 109, 163; Victoria and Petricolas Lee, Typescript of Interview (Williamsburg, 1939). The Bright dwelling is now William and Mary's Alumni House.

2.   Eliza Baker, Memoirs of Williamsburg, Virginia (Williamsburg, 1933), 3, 5.

3.   Carson, WE WERE THERE, 99.

4.   Davis Bottom, comp., REGISTER OF THE GENERAL ASSEMBLY OF VIRGINIA, 1776– 1918 (Richmond, 1917), 245, 249.

5.   William J. Van Schreeven, THE CONVENTIONS AND CONSTITUTIONS OF VIRGINIA, 1776–1966 (Richmond, 1967), 7.

6.   James City County Legislative Petitions 1777–1858. The Blisland Parish glebe was sold in 1807 and the bulk of James City County's share of the proceeds went toward converting Hickory Neck Church into a school. Lee bequeathed his Hot Water plantation to the College of William and Mary so that a public school would be built in the center of James City County (see Chapter 17).

7.   William F. Ritchie et al., THE CODE OF VIRGINIA, 1860 (Richmond, 1860), 289, 296, 689, 693; Bottom, GENERAL ASSEMBLY, 247.

8.   American Medical Association, "Report on the Number of Practitioners of Medicine in Virginia," TRANSACTIONS OF THE AMERICAN MEDICAL ASSOCIATION 1 (1847):359–365.

9.   James City County Legislative Petitions 1832–1833.

10.   AMERICAN BEACON, June 23, 1834; NORFOLK AND PORTSMOUTH DAILY ADVERTISER, June 26, 1834.

11.   This was likely Lemuel Bowden of Williamsburg, whose views set him apart from many of his neighbors.

12.   Robert Morris, Diary, March 3, 1845, to February 22. 1857.

13.   VIRGINIA GAZETTE, September 15, 1853; April 27, 1854; January 4, 1855.

14.   York County Legislative Petitions 1777–1858.

15.   William F. Ritchie, comp., ACTS AND JOINT RESOLUTIONS PASSED BY THE GENERAL ASSEMBLY, 1857–1858 (Richmond, 1859), 39, 46, 51–51, 152; Anonymous, "Map of Virginia Showing the Distribution of the Slave Population from the Census of 1860," [1860].

16.   Kathleen Bruce, "Virginia Agricultural Decline to 1860: A Fallacy," AGRICULTURAL HISTORY 6:12.

17.   Anonymous, One Hundred Years of Agriculture, n.d.; U.S.D.A., ABRIDGED LIST OF FEDERAL LAWS APPLICABLE TO AGRICULTURE, 1949; James City County Agricultural Census, 1850–1880.

18.   Charles W. Turner, "Virginia Agricultural Reform, 1815–1860," AGRICULTURAL HISTORY 26:80–81; Bruce, Agricultural Decline, 12.

19.   James City County Agricultural Census 1850, 1860; Lou Powers, Owners of 'the Grove' from 1839 to 1906 . . . A Preliminary Report (Williamsburg, 1984).

20.   VIRGINIA GAZETTE, May 18, 1854; November 4, 1860.

21.   John Galt Williamson, Letter to Alexander D. Galt, September 4, 1838.

22.   Edmund Ruffin, THE FARMER'S REGISTER 9:710–711.

23. Henry Howe, HISTORICAL RECOLLECTIONS OF VIRGINIA (Charleston, 1845), 390–393; Smith, "Virginia Discovered and Discribed [sic]," 1610.

24. Lyon G.Tyler, "Jamestown," WILLIAM AND MARY QUARTERLY, 1st Ser., 21 (October 1912):133–138. During the mid–nineteenth century Bishop William Meade noticed the powder magazine. He indicated that "the old brick magazine and a small frame room near it" both "must soon tumble into the James River" unless preventive measures were taken against erosion (Meade, OLD CHURCHES, I, 114).

25. Randolph saw the brick rowhouse known as the Ludwell–Statehouse Group, which is on the property of the Association for the Preservation of Virginia Antiquities.

26. Tyler, "Jamestown," 58–59.

27. These were likely the same off–shore palisades that were visible in 1807, remains of the line battery built in 1711.

28. Lossing, AMERICAN REVOLUTION, II, 240–241; Henry Howe, HISTORICAL RECOLLECTIONS OF VIRGINIA (Charleston, 1845), 319, 321; William Maxwell, ed., "Jamestown," VIRGINIA HISTORICAL REGISTER 4 (1851):172.

29. William Maxwell, ed., "Old Letters," VIRGINIA HISTORICAL REGISTER 2 (1849):138–139.

30. Robert Sully, October 1854 letter to Lyman Draper.

31. William M. E. Raschal, ed., "The Jamestown Celebration of 1857," VIRGINIA MAGAZINE OF HISTORY AND BIOGRAPHY 66 (July 1958):259–271; William G. Stanard, ed., "History of the Virginia Historical Society," VIRGINIA MAGAZINE OF HISTORY AND BIOGRAPHY 39 (July 1931):308.

32. Raschal, Celebration, 259–271.

33. James City County Land Tax Lists 1821–1846; Goodrich Durfey, Old Jamestown For Sale, [1844].

34. James City County Land Tax Lists 1831–1861; Personal Property Tax Lists 1844–1848; Deed Book 1:170, 172; VIRGINIA GAZETTE, October 6, 1853.

35. McCartney, GREEN SPRING

36. James City County Land Tax Lists 1830–1860; Deed Book 1:283; 5:518; Gilmer, "Vicinity," 1864.

37. James City County Land Tax Lists 1782–1861; Deed Book 2:458; 3:437; 4:691, 767; 8:13–14.

38. James City County Land Tax Lists 1838–1861.

39. James City County Land Tax Lists 1820–1874; Deed Book 4:790–791; H. W. Flournoy, ed., "Note on the Rev. William Bracken of Williamsburg," VIRGINIA MAGAZINE OF HISTORY AND BIOGRAPHY 29 (July 1921):268; Palmer CALENDAR, IX, 153.

40. Lou Powers, "Owners of 'the Grove' from 1839 to 1906 . . . A Report" (Williamsburg, 1987), 2–14.

41. James City County Land Tax Lists 1790–1861; Gilmer, "Vicinity," 1864.

42. James City County Land Tax Lists 1841–1861; York County Land Tax Lists 1850–1861.

43. Gilmer, "Vicinity," 1864; A. A. Humphereys, "Yorktown to Williamsburg," 1862; James City County Deed Book 4:732–734.

44. James City County Land Tax Lists 1830–1861.

45. Carson, WE WERE THERE, 108–109.

46. James City County Land Tax Lists 1782–1888; Channing M. Hall, An Abstract of Title for Mr. Charles N. Dozier, 1944.

47. Gilmer, "Vicinity," 1864; Virginia Department of Historic Resources, Windsor Castle National Register Nomination, 1987.

48. James City County Land Tax Lists 1837–1850; Personal Property Tax Lists 1838–1850; Gilmer, "Vicinity," 1864.

49. James City County Land Tax Lists 1830 1861; Personal Property Tax Lists 1861; Census Records 1860; Gilmer,"Vicinity," 1864. John M. Jennings enjoyed a distinguished career as director of the Virginia Historical Society.

50. James City County Land Tax Lists 1830–1860; Death Records 1849–1896; Census 1850; Slave Schedules 1850; Agricultural Census 1850, 1860; Personal Property Tax Lists 1850; York County Wills and Administrations 1831–1858 No. 3–A:71–73; A. D. Bache, "York River, Virginia, from Clay Bank to Mount Folly," 1857–1858.

51. James City County Land Tax Lists 1840–1861; Gilmer, "Vicinity," 1864.

52. James City County Land Tax Lists 1850–1861; Census 1860; Personal Property Tax Lists 1850–1861.

CHAPTER 11

"O, Darkly Now the Tempest Rolls"
The Civil War in James City County
1861–1865

The Specter of War

The first shots fired at Fort Sumter, South Carolina, on April 12, 1861, signaled the beginning of the Civil War. Politicians, North and South, had been heatedly debating secession for several years, but neither side seemingly realized that the issues under dispute might culminate in a long, bloody war. When President Abraham Lincoln issued a call to arms, the response was enthusiastic. Several states in the upper South reacted by quickly aligning themselves with the Confederacy. Virginia seceded on April 17, 1861, and the state's voters ratified a secession ordinance on May 23rd. The Confederate States of America's seat of government was shifted from Montgomery, Alabama, home of its president, Jefferson Davis, to Richmond, Virginia. From then on, the focus of the war in the east was the territory separating Richmond from Washington, D. C., the federal capital. As a result, much of eastern Virginia's landscape was devastated by war and the state was bereft of a large portion of its male population.[1]

In June 1861 Virginia's Trans-Alleghany counties, which opposed secession, set up the so-called Restored Government, with Wheeling as capital. Thus, Virginia had two state governments: a Confederate one in Richmond and another in Wheeling that was part of the Union. Within two months the Restored Government's legislature voted to form the state of West Virginia out of the western eounties that had opposed secession. At that juncture, Governor F. H. Pierpont, head of the Restored Government, shifted its seat to Alexandria, Virginia, where it was shielded by the Union Army until 1865 and the fall of the Confederacy.[2]

Early Development of Richmond's Defenses

In April 1861, when Virginia decided to secede, federal troops left Fort Monroe and marched into Hampton in a show of force. Although local residents were told they wouldn't be disturbed unless they acted with hostility, shortly thereafter, a Union gunboat fired upon the Confederate battery at Sewell's Point. Later, when it became clear that occupation of Hampton was inevitable, Confederate Colonel John B. Magruder ordered his men to put the town to the torch. In late summer, Virginia's Confederate forces were concentrated in the northern part of the state. This left the peninsula especially vulnerable to a Union Army advance from the direction of Fort Monroe.[3]

General Robert E. Lee, as military advisor to President Davis, was responsible for seeing that Richmond was defended. His ability to protect the Confederate capital proved far more important than anyone could have guessed, for seven military campaigns were launched against Richmond prior to surrender. Initially, approaches to the city were defended by small bodies of strategically-placed troops. Lee had earthworks built on Jamestown Island and two upstream locations, and had water-batteries erected at Mulberry Island and Day's Point. The fortifications were intended to prevent Union naval vessels from moving up the James, circumventing the land-based defenses the Confederates intended to build. But the work of erecting earthworks around Richmond progressed so slowly that Lee began to perceive the delay as a defense crisis. The General Assembly responded by passing a law that required all free black males between 18 and 50 to participate in public works projects, such as building fortifications. They had to furnish their names and addresses to the court of the city or county in which they lived and could be summoned to serve up to 180 days at a time. The conscripted workers were to receive food, lodging, and medical care in exchange for their labor, plus pay commensurate with the jobs they performed. Some of James

City County's free black males joined slaves and Confederate troops in constructing earthworks in front of Williamsburg and on Jamestown Island.[4]

James City County Prepares for War

A journal kept by Thomas George Wynne of Greenmount, a schoolteacher and nephew of the Wynnes who owned Carter's Grove earlier on, sheds a considerable amount of light upon how James City County residents felt about secession and the prospect of war. On April 21, 1861, only four days after Virginia left the Union, he noted that:

Much excitement has been caused to-day in our neighborhood by noisy rumor of the reinforcement of old Point [Comfort] with one thousand troops, of the burning of Norfolk City and various other groundless reports. Two companies of soldiers from Gloucester passed by on their way to the Grove Wharf where they expected the West Point Steamer to take them down to Norfolk, but up to six o'clock this evening she had not arrived. . . . We have to send down breakfast to the troops in the morning. Great uneasiness amongst the ladies. May the Lord avert civil war.

The following day, Wynne noted that the Gloucester men had gone home and that he and his neighbors had transported them to Yorktown. He said that "A dispatch came from the Governor this morning, stating that an attack would be made on York River in 48 hours, and ordering out all the companies in this neighborhood. . . . There is still much excitement." On May 2nd, Wynne added that the GLEN COVE, a steamer enroute to Norfolk, had been turned back by a Union ship sealing off Hampton Roads. He said that the steamer had paused briefly at the Grove Wharf before returning to Richmond.

On the morning of June 12th, several hundred French-speaking Louisiana Zouaves, enroute to Yorktown, disembarked at the Grove Wharf. Their brilliantly colored Turkish-style uniforms with bright red jackets and baggy pantaloons, inspired great admiration. Wynne described them as "a brave, desperate looking set of men" and said that "the sight of them will frighten the Yankees." On June 17th approximately 250 men of the 10th Virginia Regiment pitched camp at the Grove Wharf, which they intended to fortify. But two days later Colonel Magruder countermanded their orders and told them to burn the wharf instead. On the afternoon of July 1, 1861, Wynne heard cannon fire that seemed to emanate from Yorktown and Newport News Point. Three days later he wrote in his journal that "a large fire is seen to night in the direction of Hampton." He also said that on July 2, the night-sky was illuminated by "a beautiful comet moving in a northwesterly direction, with its hairy tail streaming behind some considerable distance across the heavens."

During mid-July the Confederate troops stationed at the Grove Wharf, with the assistance of local residents, began throwing up entrenchments. The 2nd Louisiana Regiment pitched camp at Grices Landing and the 5th Louisiana Regiment went to the site where Grove Wharf had stood. On the night of August 25th, Thomas G. Wynne noted that Mr. Charlton of the 5th Louisiana had joined him for dinner.[5] A week later, the women of the Wynne household heard the 5th Louisiana Regiment's chaplain preach a sermon. On November 1, 1861, Thomas G. Wynne estimated that there were between 35,000 and 40,000 Confederate troops on the lower peninsula. He said that men from the 1st and 10th Louisiana Regiments were encamped at the Spratley farm, on the west side of College Creek's mouth.[6]

Jamestown Island's Strategic Importance

Even before the Confederates took steps to fortify Jamestown Island as part of Richmond's defenses, owner William Allen had begun constructing a battery there and ordered eight 32-pound cannon from Norfolk. Allen's battery was almost complete by early May 1861, when Lieutenant Catesby ap Roger Jones, a Confederate naval officer, informed his superiors that Jamestown Island was suitable for an 18-gun battery. On May 3, 1861, Jones reported that Allen had promised him 250 hands to aid in its construction and that wheelbarrows were needed to transport guns. He said that the battery was to be extensive, "owing to the course of the [river's] channel," and that it would have five faces and 16 guns. Three companies totaling 214 men were then stationed on the island. Work on the battery progressed swiftly and on May 10th, Lieutenant Jones reported that eight guns had been mounted.[7]

The Confederate engineer who oversaw construction of Jamestown

Island's earthworks later recalled that in 1861 there was no bridge across the Back River and that he had had to build one for the army's use. He remembered seeing a mansion that was "not in very good repair, but entirely habitable, and the ruins of the old church." The island "was in a very good state of cultivation" and he recollected General Lee's "bemoaning the sacrifice of a promising wheat field to a square redoubt." He added that "the battery, which was built just above the old tower, was not far from the brink of the river bank, which I understand . . . has been heavily encroached upon by the river." A Confederate veteran's widow recalled her husband's saying that "at low tide about 75 yards east of the old church" were "the brick walls of an old house, and from these walls his men obtained bricks for the fireplaces and chimneys of the tents."[8]

On May 4, 1861, Major Benjamin S. Ewell dispatched the 86 men and boys of Williamsburg's Junior Guard to Jamestown Island to protect the battery there.[9] Later in the month, when Colonel Magruder assumed command of the forces between Jamestown Island and the York River, he decided to erect a five-gun battery on the island. The steam tender, TEASER, was sent there to ferry troops to the mainland, as landing in the lower part of the James had become very risky. Magruder ordered Lieutenant Jones to "keep a bright lookout" and if necessary, to spike the guns and abandon the island. In July all cannon not bearing directly upon the main channel were shifted to the Spratley farm on the mainland and an eight-inch Columbiad was placed where it would protect the bridge, platform and equipment on the island. The 68th Regiment, which included James City County's troops, then had two active volunteer companies on Jamestown Island, under the command of Colonel Leonard Henley. Lieutenant Jones made occasional trips to Williamsburg to teach an army detachment how to use a 42-pound carronade. In September 1861 he was advised to abandon Jamestown Island unless he had a bombproof shelter to shield his men from an enemy advance that was expected.[10]

On October 12, 1861, Lieutenant Jones conducted ordnance experiments on Jamestown Island on behalf of the Confederate Navy, which was preparing to outfit its first ironclad vessel, the VIRGINIA. He aimed an eight-inch Columbiad at twelve-foot square wooden targets that were more than 300 feet away and shielded with various types of iron. Ultimately, the Confederates built five forts on Jamestown Island: near the old church tower, behind it, midway down the island, at Black Point, and at Goose Hill. They also erected earthworks on the nearby mainland and placed chains across the Back River near Black Point.[11]

Overture to the Peninsular Campaign

Major-General Benjamin F. Butler of the Union Army arrived in Hampton Roads in late May 1861. His decision not to return runaway slaves, whom he considered Confederate property or "contraband," gave thousands of enslaved blacks an incentive to flee to Fort Monroe. Butler's pronouncement preceded the Emancipation Proclamation by more than 18 months. It created massive problems for the Union Army, which was obliged to provide food and shelter to vast numbers of black refugees, who arrived with only the clothes upon their backs. It is uncertain how many James City County slaves fled behind Union lines.

Early in 1862, Fort Monroe became the Union Army's base of operations in the drive to capture the Confederate capital and bring the war to a timely end. Richmonders grew increasingly uneasy about the military build-up in the lower peninsula and the fact that their city was considered a prime target. A huge public outcry spurred Confederate officials into action and construction of concentric rings of defensive earthworks around Richmond earnestly got underway.[12]

On March 19, 1862, General Magruder declared martial law, in anticipation of a Union Army advance. The region encompassed by his order included James City, York, Elizabeth City, Warwick, Gloucester, and Mathews Counties, and the city of Williamsburg. On the eve of the Peninsular Campaign, there were 184 Confederate officers and men stationed on Jamestown Island along with 15 pieces of heavy artillery and four pieces of field artillery. The batteries at Jamestown were considered an integral part of the defences of Richmond.[13]

Major-General George B. McClellan, who was cautious by nature, headed the Union forces that participated in the Peninsular Campaign. When he arrived at Fort Monroe, he found only a third of the 155,000 troops he had requested, thanks to major revisions in military policy. Faced with what he considered a serious shortage of men and the need to commence his campaign, he decided to split his army into two columns, sending one toward the Halfway House (midway between Yorktown and Williamsburg) and the other to Yorktown. He hoped his strategy would prevent the Confederates on the lower peninsula from receiving reinforcements. On April 4, 1862, McClellan and his men left Fort Monroe and began advancing up the peninsula. Many people gathered up their personal belongings and fled from the approaching army. McClellan was hindered by woefully inaccurate maps and by over-estimating the strength of his enemy. He quickly discovered that the Confederates had taken elaborate steps to cover their withdrawal. He learned too late that he might have prevailed, had he pressed his offensive.

It was the considerable tactical skill of General Magruder that enabled the Confederate Army to slip away to the outskirts of Richmond. He had his men erect three parallel lines of earthworks across the peninsula, taking maximum advantage of the terrain's numerous creeks and ridges. By March 1, 1862, all three defensive lines were partially built and a line of canal boats had been sunk across the Warwick River. Magruder's first line extended between the heads of the Poquoson and Warwick Rivers, where the intervening land was narrow and flanked by swamps and marshy ground. His second line ran from Yorktown to Mulberry Island, and his third, which was situated just east of Williamsburg, included a string of earthworks that stretched out between College and Queens Creeks. A large redoubt known as Fort Magruder formed the third line's centerpiece.[14]

Benjamin S. Ewell, a West Point graduate, was architect of the Williamsburg line. He was made a lieutenant colonel, placed in temporary command of the peninsula's land forces, and in May 1861 was ordered to recruit at least ten companies of men from James City, York, Warwick, and Elizabeth City Counties, Williamsburg and Hampton. Ultimately he assembled twelve companies, which drilled and trained at Camp Page, a field outside of Williamsburg, on Capitol Landing Road. General Lee ordered Ewell to lay out a line of fortifications at Williamsburg. He commenced construction during the last week of May 1861 but was severely hindered by shortages of men and equipment. Because local citizens, though favoring the war, were reluctant to part with their slaves, even temporarily, Ewell was forced to impress all able-bodied blacks, free and enslaved. He also asked the Secretary of War for 1,500 slaves from the counties west and south of Richmond. In early March 1862 Magruder informed his superiors that, in accord with his orders, he had sent some of his men to Suffolk via the Kingsmill Wharf. He added that numerous blacks were then building defensive works across the peninsula. Although the right (southeastern) and central portions of the Williamsburg line were completed in less than a year, the left (or northwestern) end was not.[15]

After William and Mary's faculty voted to close the college, its buildings were rented to the Confederate government, which used the Wren Building as barracks and later, as a hospital and storage facility. While Confederate troops were concentrated in Williamsburg, they used as fuel many of the wooden fences that enclosed the college's grounds. The first regiment to pitch its tents on the College of William and Mary's campus was the 15th Virginia Infantry.[16]

The Confederate Decision to Retreat

On April 17, 1862, General Joseph E. Johnston arrived on the lower peninsula to assume the Confederate command. He appointed General James Longstreet chief commander of the field, thereby superseding General Magruder. Under Johnston were the divisions of Longstreet, Magruder, G. W. Smith, and Daniel H. Hill. The brigades of Generals Cadmus M. Wilcox, A. P. Hill, Jubal A. Early, and J. E. B. Stuart also were involved. Johnston, upon assessing the situation, ordered a retreat to the outskirts of Richmond, for he was wary of sending his 53,000 men (3,000 of whom were sick) against 133,000 Union soldiers.[17] Consequently, the Confederates abandoned the Warwick line (their middle position) and then fell back toward Williamsburg to their third (and final) line of defense. Then, they slowly withdrew up the stage road toward Richmond, so that they could protect the Confederate capital.[18]

While Confederate troops passed through Williamsburg on their way up the peninsula, Longstreet was in command. He was supported by Daniel H.

Hill's division and the brigades of Wilcox, A. P. Hill, Early, and Stuart. Victoria and Petricola Lee of Williamsburg, who witnessed the Confederate Army's exodus, handed biscuits and fried meat to the men passing by. While they were standing in front of their home dispensing food, General Johnston rode by and gesturing in their direction, shouted to his troops "That's what we're fighting for, boys." While Johnston was in Williamsburg, he occupied the abandoned dwelling of William W. Vest, a wealthy merchant and treasurer of the Eastern Lunatic Asylum, whose large brick house stood at the east end of Duke of Gloucester Street. One departing Confederate officer handed his sword to Victoria Lee and asked her to keep it until he returned. He never did.[19]

Eliza Baker, a black woman who was 17 when the war came to Williamsburg, recalled that some local residents abandoned their homes as soon as they learned that Union troops were approaching. Later, "the Yankees came and carried out all the furniture and things they wanted [and] then the plain [poorer] people helped themselves to what was left." They reportedly "took the carpets off the floors and they took the bureaus and everything else they wanted."[20]

Sometime prior to May 5, 1862, when the Battle of Williamsburg was fought and the area fell under the control of the Union Army, the court records of James City County and Williamsburg were removed from the courthouse and taken to Richmond for safekeeping. Although precisely when and by whom the official documents were moved remains a mystery, one early twentieth-century historian claimed that they were transported by wagon to Richmond at the orders of former Governor-then-General Henry A. Wise. Upon reaching the capital city, the records were stored in the General Court Building on the southeast corner of Capitol Square, along with those of several other Tidewater counties. A Williamsburg deed book dating to the 1850s reportedly fell off the wagon near the Chickahominy River. Later it was recovered and rebound as Deed Book 1. It was likely through the same quirk of fate that James City County Deed Book 1 (which also dates to the 1850s) survived.[21]

The Battle of Williamsburg

On May 4, 1862, Union Army General Hooker's brigade moved along the Yorktown Road and attacked the Stuart cavalry's position east of King's Creek. Confederate General Johnston, whose men had withdrawn from Yorktown the night before, parried the move by ordering two of Magruder's brigades to occupy Fort Magruder, which they reached by nightfall amid cold, drenching rain.[22] At daybreak on May 5th, the Confederates held the redoubts that flanked Fort Magruder and controlled the road to Yorktown above its junction with the highway to Hampton. Woods and thickets, too dense for the effective use of artillery, lined the roads, which the rain had converted into seas of mud. The clearings were pock-marked with rifle pits from which emanated a deadly fire. General Hooker sent out a call for reinforcements or diversionary assistance from Generals S. P. Heintzelman and Sumner, who were occupied in another part of the field.[23]

When Heintzelman's troops attacked the Confederate center and right, Longstreet reenforced his position with four brigades, a holding action that temporarily thwarted the Union advance. By early afternoon, however, W. S. Hancock's brigade occupied two vacant redoubts on the northeast side of the Yorktown Road, threatening the left end of the Confederate line. When Early's men attempted to drive them off, they were met with heavy musketry and a devastating charge. The entire Confederate line was obliged to fall back. Hancock moved forward with the brigades of Philip Kearney, David B. Birney, and Hiram G. Berry, and as the day wore on, Darius N. Couch's and John J. Peck's brigades joined in the fray. But despite the relentless pressure, the Confederates held their line and ultimately Hancock withdrew, convinced that he was outnumbered. The Confederates' staunch resistance at Fort Magruder enabled the army to make good its retreat, but the Battle of Williamsburg was very costly to both sides in terms of human suffering. Toward nightfall, as General McClellan approached Williamsburg, the Confederates withdrew. The next day, Union troops swarmed into town.[24]

Alfred Bellard, a Union soldier who took part in the Battle of Williamsburg, said that Fort Magruder stood in an open field and was flanked by supportive works. Rifle pits dotted the terrain and trees, felled for a

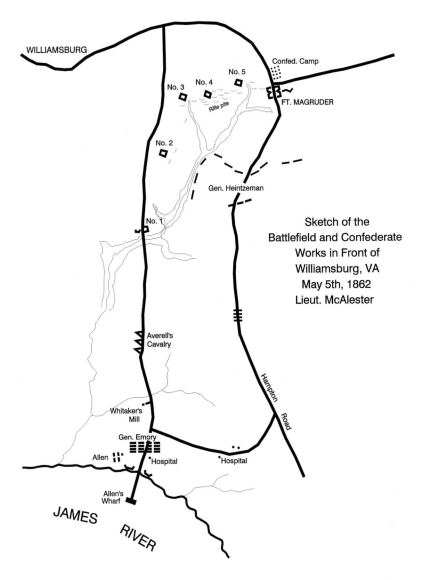

WILLIAMSBURG

Confed. Camp

No. 5

No. 4

No. 3

FT. MAGRUDER

Rifle pits

No. 2

Gen. Heintzeman

No. 1

Sketch of the
Battlefield and Confederate
Works in Front of
Williamsburg, VA
May 5th, 1862
Lieut. McAlester

Averell's
Cavalry

Hampton Road

Whitaker's
Mill

Gen. Emory

Allen

Hospital

Hospital

Allen's
Wharf

JAMES

RIVER

Map by Christina A. Kiddle. Kiddle and McCartney, Williamsburg Cultural
Resources Map Project, City of Williamsburg. Colonial Williamsburg
Foundation Department of Archaeological Research.

hundred yards on both sides of the road, formed a primitive abatis, in some places eight to ten feet high. Bellard recalled that at one point, when the Union Army was losing ground, the regimental bands were ordered to consolidate and play. He said that as soon as they struck up "Three Cheers for the Red, White and Blue," two guns were moved to the road and the Union infantry, which only moments before had been on the run, regrouped and pressed forward with renewed vigor. According to Bellard, as soon as darkness fell, the battlefield grew quiet, the wounded were withdrawn, and the dead were interred in mass graves. In the May 5, 1862, Battle of Williamsburg, the Union Army lost 2,228 men and the Confederates, approximately 1,500.[25]

The Confederate Withdrawal

Major General Daniel H. Hill's division, which served as the retreating Confederate Army's rear guard, reported that on the night of May 5th, literally thousands of soldiers took refuge in barns and outbuildings that shielded them from the drenching rain. He described the demoralized men as "cold, tired, hungry and jaded" and said that "many seemed indifferent alike to life or capture." The next morning, the Confederate withdrawal continued. Hill said that the roads were "in a truly horrible condition" and that "the straggling was enormous." Meanwhile, the Union cavalry, like scavengers, followed close behind the retreating column, ready to pick up those who lagged behind. Hill indicated that when his men were about six miles from Williamsburg, they encountered a formidable swamp in which were mired numerous wagons and ambulances abandoned by Confederate units at the head of the column, but destroyed so that they would be useless to the enemy. Four days after Hill's men left Williamsburg, they reached Long Bridge, on the Chickahominy. They suffered greatly from hunger, for they lacked provisions and were obliged to subsist upon parched corn and whatever they could find along the way.[26]

Captain John Pelham of the Stuart Horse Artillery, which preceded Hill's division, also recounted the Confederate Army's withdrawal from Williamsburg. His men left town on May 6th, early in the morning, and by evening reached a brick schoolhouse (Hickory Neck Academy) about half a

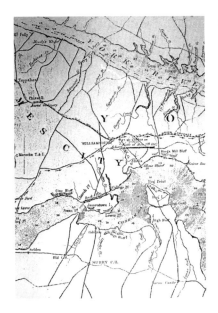

I. Knowles Hare's 1862 "Map of the Vicinity of Richmond and the Peninsula Campaign," showing troop movements. National Archives.

mile above Burnt Ordinary. At 10 A.M. the next day, Pelham was ordered to send a rifle gun and howitzer toward the rear of the retreating column. Later, he reported that he left the howitzer "at the Methodist Church to the east of Burnt Ordinary" (the James City Chapel) and placed the rifle gun at a location a mile closer to town.[27]

The testimony of Union sympathizer Lemuel Bowden, a Williamsburg resident, who during July 1862 participated in a federal inquiry into General McClellan's conduct during the Battle of Williamsburg, also sheds some light upon the Confederate retreat. Bowden said that he was on the porch of his sister's house, about nine miles west of town, when Confederate soldiers began straggling by.[28] Some crowded into the dwelling, asking for food and according to Bowden, his sister "had to keep five or six cooks constantly employed" to feed them. He said that "About 1 o'clock in the day, an officer rode up . . . and supposing I was the proprietor of the house," inquired whether Generals Longstreet and Johnston could use the dwelling as their headquarters, adding that they'd likely arrive around 1 A.M. Bowden, whose Unionist views made him a pariah in his home community, was uneasy about being in the midst of so many Confederates, lest he be recognized. He advised his sister to entertain the generals but to request a guard to control the common soldiers' access to her home. According to Bowden, "In a short time, a Mr. Washington, a son of Mr. Hampton, and some others, came to the house and at one o'clock at night General Johnston and General Longstreet and their staffs [arrived], some 25 or 30 in all." Bowden stayed in his room to avoid

being seen. Johnston informed Bowden's son that there had been "a pretty severe skirmish at Williamsburg" and that he had lost around 500 men. According to local lore, Johnston and his men paused the next night in the yard of Hickory Neck Church, resuming their journey the following day.[29]

The Union Army Occupies Williamsburg

A. A. Humphreys' map, "Map No. 2, Williamsburg to White House," September 1862. National Archives.

On the morning of May 6th the Union cavalry under George Stoneman entered Williamsburg. It was then General McClellan learned that the Confederates had abandoned the city. He received word that Magruder's division had reached Diascund Bridge the night before and that G. W. Smith was at Barhamsville. McClellan then realized that the battle fought at Williamsburg had given the Confederates 24 hours in which to make good their escape. He ordered his troops not to disturb local citizens or property. Then, he sent a telegram to his wife, informing her that "The battle of Williamsburg has proved a brilliant victory" and that "This is a beautiful little town and quite old and picturesque." Later, McClellan learned that Hill's and Longstreet's divisions, which brought up the rear of the retreating Confederate column, didn't reach Burnt Ordinary until nightfall on May 6th. Thus, they had narrowly slipped his grasp. This tactical error prompted federal officials to launch an inquiry into McClellan's conduct during the battle. McClellan, upon arriving in Williamsburg, informed his superiors that he had captured 300 uninjured Confederate soldiers and taken custody of more than 1,000 wounded the retreating army had left behind. But the Union casualty list also was quite large. Within the next few days, an estimated 800

Confederate dead were buried by the Union troops.[30]

The Union Army, upon taking possession of Williamsburg, established its lines just west of the College of William and Mary and placed a large reserve force in tents pitched on the campus. One Union Army officer commented that many of Williamsburg's inhabitants had "fled precipitately, leaving much valuable portable property." He cited as an example "a family of wealth [that] left costly plates on the dining table which they hastily deserted in the midst of dinner." Miss Harriette Cary of Williamsburg, who maintained a diary during May, June, and July 1862, noted that on May 6th at 9 A.M. McClellan's men took possession of the city. They were "splendidly equipped," healthy-looking, and well uniformed. An officer and two men made a room-by-room search of local houses and McClellan moved into the Vest mansion which had been occupied by Confederate General Johnston the day before. Sentinels or "safe-guards" were placed at the doors of some local dwellings to prevent thievery. The Methodist, Baptist, and Episcopal churches and the college were converted into hospitals for the Confederate wounded, who were attended by Union Army surgeons. Miss Cary said that at first an incessant stream of Union troops, wagons, and ambulances passed through the city. Later, Vest's store was converted into a hospital for injured men brought in from the direction of Richmond. Many of the Confederate wounded were evacuated to Fort Monroe and the dead were buried in the graveyard of Bruton Parish Church and what became Cedar Grove Cemetery. Color-coded maps prepared by Union Army cartographers reveal that the Confederates built earthworks overlooking William Allen's wharf at Kingsmill and that McClellan's soldiers encamped along the road to the wharf. Military hospitals also were located at Kingsmill, where General Heintzelman's men were headquartered.[31]

While Williamsburg was under the control of the Union Army, the 5th Pennsylvania Cavalry occupied the town. The college's main building served as a hospital and commissary, just as it had when the Confederates were there, and the Brafferton was converted into an office and temporary living quarters for the military officer in charge of the town. John S. Charles, who was 11 years old when the Battle of Williamsburg was fought, recalled that almost every house in town was filled with refugees from Hampton and the lower peninsula. He said that the Confederate wounded sometimes were placed in private homes because the town's make-shift hospitals were full. On Boundary Street was the home of a black preacher and his family, who fled behind Union lines as soon as McClellan's men moved on. According to Charles, most of Williamsburg's unoccupied frame houses were dismantled and converted to kindling.[32]

Miss Harriette Cary said that one of the ways local women demonstrated their disdain for the occupying army was their intentional "indifference to dress." She called Williamsburg's mayor "Bowden the Traitor" because he had sided with the enemy. She and her friends swapped stories about local families who had been "secretly and openly" deprived of their horses, mules, sheep, bacon, grain, and slaves, taken as booty by "marauding parties." Another woman indicated that several of Williamsburg's leading citizens, who refused to take the oath of allegiance, were driven to the Kingsmill Wharf with a certain promise of imprisonment in Norfolk. But the men were detained briefly and then released. According to Captain David E. Cronin of the 1st New York Mounted Rifles, who was stationed in Williamsburg throughout the Union occupation, it was only General Henry M. Naglee's countermanding Colonel David Campbell's orders that spared the local men extradition to Norfolk. In Cronin's opinion, Campbell's heavy-handed treatment of the respected townsmen led Confederate General Henry A. Wise to make a bold and rash counter-move a short time later.[33]

Victoria Lee said that the Union Army established a commissary in a large frame building on the main street and suspended a sizable flag over the sidewalk. As local women deliberately avoided walking beneath the flag, Union troops, not to be outdone, procured a very long flag that stretched across the street. One Union officer said that "The condition of the 'housed-up' inhabitants . . . was trying in the extreme" and that "the expression on the faces of the people . . . was one of undisguised hatred and contempt." After the first year, the occupying army relaxed a little, as did the city's inhabitants. Victoria Lee spoke of tending Confederate wounded in the Baptist Church's make-shift hospital. She said that "one of the most terrible sights I have ever seen" was "a pile of human arms and legs" amputated from the numerous men who had been shot through their extremities. Lee said that the courthouse accommodated two druggists' apothecary shops, run for the benefit of Confederate sick and wounded. Eliza Baker, on the other hand, spoke of the carnage that preceded the Battle of Williamsburg, bloodshed attributable to the intense combat on the lower peninsula. She said that "a week before they [the Union Army] took Fort Magruder the rainwater in the road and street was all bloody" and that numerous men were buried around the powder magazine, which earlier had served as a market house and Baptist church. One writer said that in the wake of the Battle of Williamsburg, the opposing sides hired the Bucktrout funeral establishment to re-bury the dead hastily interred when the firing first stopped.[34]

When Williamsburg fell into the Union Army's hands, it was placed under martial law. The 5th Pennsylvania Cavalry seized the VIRGINIA GAZETTE's printing presses and began publishing a military newspaper called THE CAVALIER. It contained war news, propaganda aimed at the local populace, public announcements, short stories, and poetry. In one of the little newspaper's early issues, it was announced that daily mail service was available between Williamsburg and Fort Monroe. Only eight issues of THE CAVALIER were published before the GAZETTE's printing presses were moved to Yorktown. But publication quickly resumed and THE CAVALIER continued to provide news of happenings in Williamsburg, which the Union Army classified as a picket post of Yorktown.[35]

A June 1862 letter written by Judge John M. Gregory, who once represented James City County in the General Assembly, sheds some light upon conditions in the rural countryside. He said that most farmers had lost their slaves and that it was difficult to hire free blacks willing to work as field hands. Sandy Point, at the mouth of the Chickahominy, was in the hands of the Union Army and blacks had congregated there in large numbers, many of whom were runaway slaves. Gregory said that Union gunboats had gone up the Chickahominy River as far as Windsor Shades and that there were so many enemy vessels on the James that there was little reliable communication with Richmond. He added that "Very few have any salt now" and that before long, people's only food would be what they produced themselves.[36] On May 20, 1862, Miss Harriette Cary noted in her diary that "Two Yankee gun boats [were] very much disabled by our batteries on the narrows of James

River—Many killed—15 buried at James Town who had died of their wounds on their return." By May 22nd, some of the Union soldiers garrisoned in Williamsburg had begun acknowledging that their army had met with strong resistance toward Richmond.[37] While Williamsburg was occupied, Miss Cary and her friends worshiped in secret, praying for Confederate victories and the Union Army's departure. When Dr. John Galt died, a Union officer replaced him as director of the Eastern Lunatic Asylum. Federal authorities, upon inspecting the asylum in August 1862, found its inmates "in a very destitute condition, [with] nothing at all in the way of clothing or supplies being left except one piece of bacon . . . hung so high in the meat house that it could not well be reached." Ultimately, Mayor Lemuel Bowden (ex-president of the hospital's Board of Directors) and some of his fellow officials were accused of absconding with the asylum's supplies, leaving almost nothing behind for the patients.[38]

While the Union Army was in control of Williamsburg, there was a telegraph station on Jamestown Island. McClellan's men reportedly robbed bricks from the wings of the Ambler house and used them to construct chimneys for the cabins they built in various parts of the island. In June 1862, the crew of the U.S. gunboat AROOSTOOK burned almost all of the buildings, magazines, and carriages associated with the Confederate gun batteries on Jamestown Island, sparing only a barracks in the rear of the large battery on the western end of the island, then occupied by "contrabands" or runaway slaves. They also spiked all of the guns the Confederates hadn't disabled. One naval officer recommended posting a sentinel on Jamestown Island to prevent the Confederates from slipping across the James to infiltrate Union-held territory on the peninsula.[39]

Afterward, a company of dismounted cavalrymen was posted at Jamestown Island, with a mounted reserve on the mainland to maintain contact with the Union Army's headquarters in Williamsburg. Sometimes, the men on duty at Jamestown climbed to the top of the church tower ruins to gain a more commanding view of the river. However, one observer said that the tower was little higher than the nearby Confederate fortifications. Union Army sentries were especially vigilant at night, for spies and smugglers were expected to cross the river under the cover of darkness. Each evening, a few boards were removed from the plank bridge that linked the island with the mainland, to keep the pickets from being surprised from the rear. The mounted reserves also stood watch. Jamestown Island was considered a good duty station, for there was an abundance of fish, shell-fish, and game, along with fruits and nuts. There was plenty of time for reading and according to Captain Cronin, the encampments near Williamsburg "did not lack for books of an entertaining kind, either light or serious, taken from the fine libraries found in the abandoned town mansions."[40]

However, serving on Jamestown Island was not without risks. In 1864 an inexperienced company of black horse soldiers from the 20th New York Cavalry, mounted upon steeds unaccustomed to gunfire, was sent to Jamestown Island to relieve another unit. According to Captain Cronin, the cavalrymen were ambushed near the foot of the bridge to the island by Confederate Lieutenant F. Charles Hume and his band of sharpshooters. The men of the 20th New York were driven back toward Williamsburg, where their ranks were strengthened. Cronin said that they regrouped, returned to the bridge, and reportedly held Jamestown Island for several weeks. Military records, however, provide a somewhat different view. On September 3, 1864, a Union Army ambulance, sent to Jamestown Island to retrieve three sick men, was escorted there by black cavalrymen of Troop H of the 20th New York Cavalry. Within a mile of the island, they were ambushed by 15 Confederate guerillas, concealed in the woods. The next day, 21 Union cavalrymen set out on a retaliatory mission. Its leader concluded that the "guerilla party in question was composed of citizens of the neighborhood" in which the attack occurred.[41]

On September 9, 1862, men from General Henry A. Wise's legion under the command of Colonel W. P. Shingler, staged a highly successful but short-lived raid on Williamsburg. Wise, then commander of the Confederate forces on the peninsula, was intimately familiar with the city, for as a practicing attorney he had tried many cases in the local courts. His men drove the 5th Pennsylvania back to Fort Magruder, captured 33 reserves asleep on the college lawn, and then swept down Duke of Gloucester Street to the Vest mansion, where they seized Colonel David Campbell, the Union provost marshal, and spirited him away. One Union officer claimed that the 5th

Pennsylvania was "disgracefully beaten" by men they greatly outnumbered. Afterward, General H. W. Halleck, the regional commander, was prompted to ask his superiors, "What is the object of holding Williamsburg?"[42]

The Union Army regained control of the city the same day they lost it and some of the 5th Pennsylvania Cavalry's men, who, celebrating their victory with ample quantities of liquor, set fire to the Wren Building. One eyewitness said that they "were smarting under defeat by Col. Shingler's cavalry and also fired by a liberal supply of 'The Rosy.'" J. L. Slater, who also saw the college ablaze, said that on his way home, he encountered a man from the 5th Pennsylvania who called out "I burned the damned College and I intend to burn this damned town."[43]

Afterward, Union troops erected a line of defensive works across the college yard, incorporating the walls of the Wren Building and the kitchens of the President's House and the Brafferton. They also bricked up the doorways and windows of the structures' north and west sides, to make loopholes for small arms. Their strong line of palisades across Jamestown and Richmond Roads, was defended by chevaux-de-fris and a trip-wire. Deep ditches were dug across both roads at the periphery of the college's grounds. John S. Charles said that "In these ditches were placed vertically big logs 10 ft. long and 3 ft. in the ground" that were fitted up with port-holes so that they could be defended against approaching enemy cavalry. He indicated that "Some distance in the rear of the college and extending in a curved line far beyond the mill [Jamestown] and stage [Richmond] roads was constructed an abatis consisting of big oak and beech trees with sharpened limbs set in the ground, standing westward and all entangled with wire."[44]

Union Army Captain David E. Cronin, who eventually became Williamsburg's provost marshal, took a more neutral view of Shingler's raid, for he said attacks and counter-attacks by opposing forces were typical of all warfare. He felt that the arrests made by Colonel Campbell inspired General Wise's foray and that the 5th Pennsylvania retaliated barbarously by burning the college. He added that "the closing of Bruton Church" also was followed by a raid. He surmised that placing a regiment of black cavalry "in the hallowed precincts of the college" was what led the "ruthless ambuscade" of the 20th New York's men enroute to Jamestown Island.[45]

A tragic event that occurred during autumn 1862 suggests strongly that while the Union Army held Williamsburg, little effort was made to maintain peace in the surrounding countryside. In October, an estimated 100 slaves from William Allen's Neck O'Land and Jamestown Island plantations shot and killed his main overseer and some other visitors to the island. They also destroyed the buildings on both farms and at Kingsmill. A lone survivor of the incident (a free black employee of Allen's, wounded and left for dead) made his way to Surry County, where he informed the authorities. It appears that little (if any) action was taken by the occupying army. It is possible that the "contrabands" hiding out on Jamestown Island in the early summer were Allen slaves, who threw off the yoke as soon as the Union Army began advancing up the peninsula.[46]

On October 24, 1862, the Eastern Lunatic Asylum's attorney, Talbot Sweeney, secretly dispatched a letter to Governor John Letcher, requesting food and clothing for the inmates. He said that the Union provost marshal had invited the hospital's former steward and matron to return, but failed to furnish them with supplies. The patients were suffering from a lack of medical treatment and some had died. It was rumored that the Union Army planned to transfer them to institutions in the north. In Sweeney's opinion, if that occurred, the hospital would be torched.[47]

Besides an update on conditions at the asylum, Sweeney provided the governor with some important intelligence data. He said that no enemy pickets were stationed on the stage road west of Casey's, two miles from the college, and that on the College Mill (Jamestown) road they were a mile from the campus.[48] He indicated that Williamsburg still was held by the 5th Pennsylvania Cavalry, which scouting parties of approximately 75 men sometimes ventured out the stage road six or so miles west of the city. Scouting rarely (if ever) was done on the Jamestown road. The 5th Pennsylvania was camped on the road to Yorktown, about four and a half miles from Williamsburg, and a cavalry company equipped with eight pieces of mounted artillery was stationed at Fort Magruder, a mile and a half below the city. Sweeney said that McClellan had fortified Yorktown against an attack from the direction of Williamsburg and that the Union Army had control of the York River and Gloucester Point. He said that a fourth of the estimated 8,000 Union troops were sick and unfit for duty and speculated that the only reason McClellan held onto Williamsburg was that he could do so easily. Sweeney closed by saying that the Confederates could re-take the city any time but lacked the strength to hold it. He asked the governor to communicate with him through William L. Spencer on Centerville road, who would see that he got messages. Throughout this period, the Union troops occupying Williamsburg were subjected to constant harassment by a wily band of Confederate sharpshooters, who made surprise attacks and then sped away, eluding capture. This guerilla-style warfare was carried out by Lieutenant F. Charles Hume and his men, who were highly skilled marksmen, good riders, and seasoned woodsmen.[49]

Union cavalrymen occasionally undertook lengthy reconnaissance missions outside of Williamsburg. On December 17, 1862, three months after Shingler's raid, they made a tour of Burnt Ordinary and reached Diascund Bridge (Lanexa). In early January another party of horse soldiers was sent out to spy upon Confederate troops, who had been sighted at both locales. Major William G. McCandless of the 5th Pennsylvania Cavalry reported that on January 10, 1863, he dispatched two scouting parties on a sweep through the countryside. One moved west, skimming the lower side of the York River, and then turned south to join the main column at the Six Mile Ordinary (Lightfoot). The other rode out Jamestown Road, turned toward the Chickahominy River, and then headed for Centerville and Six Mile Ordinary to meet up with their comrades. No Confederates were sighted there, but McCandless' men encountered three mounted men at the lane to Mrs. Piggott's house, Farmville. Half a mile further west, "at the brick church" (Olive Branch Christian Church), the advance guard confronted 16 Confederate cavalrymen, whom they pursued as far as Burnt Ordinary. There, the men of the 5th Pennsylvania came face to face with superior numbers of Confederates, who had reached Burnt Ordinary by means of the Chickahominy Road (Route 631). With what McCandless called "a sudden swoop," the Confederate cavalry captured four Union horsemen and then drew up in a line of battle. The Union advance guard drew their sabers and charged. According to McCandless, "The flashing of our sabers in the air and the shouts of the men as they charged upon the foe" caused the Confederates

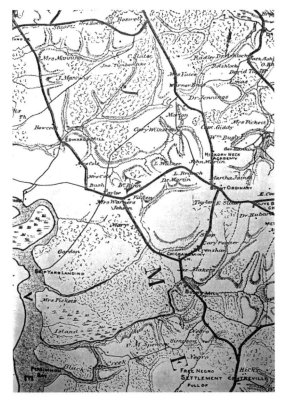

Confederate cartographers mis-identified Dr. Marston as Dr. Martin. His home was west of Burnt Ordinary (Toano). J. F. Gilmer, "Vicinity of Richmond and Part of the Peninsula," 1864. National Archives.

to flee down the Chickahominy Road toward Centerville and make a dash toward the Diascund Bridge. The 5th Pennsylvania set out in pursuit and rescued three of their four men, took four prisoners, and wounded a fifth man who escaped into the woods. But McCandless, upon hearing that 500 Confederate cavalrymen and a regiment of infantry were stationed at Diascund Bridge, ordered his men to withdraw toward Centerville. Confederate Colonel W. B. Tabb, who reported upon the same incident, said that his men were victorious and that seven or eight Union cavalrymen had been captured, 20 to 30 had been wounded, and that 35 prisoners were taken.[50]

Across the Opposing Lines

Because Williamsburg, as a Union Army outpost, was relatively close to Richmond, the city was frequented by spies from both sides. Telegraph lines linked Fort Magruder to Yorktown and Jamestown and tree-tops on the outskirts of Williamsburg served as observation posts. Mail was left at the lines, an acknowledged point of exchange, and letters could be sent to Fort Monroe for distribution within Union-held territory. Captain Cronin said that after the burning of the college, skirmishes occurred almost daily and random shots were heard from time to time on Richmond and Jamestown Roads. On March 29, 1863, General Wise's legion advanced toward the city by means of Richmond Road, intent upon surprising and recapturing Fort Magruder. Colonel Tabb and his men reached the Pettit farm, not far from Colonel Ewell's home, and then turned north, heading toward the Capitol Landing bridge. But the Confederates' plan was foiled when they were spotted by Union pickets stationed near the foot of the bridge.[51]

The Union Army commander of the territory around Williamsburg was incensed by Wise's boldness. On March 30th he revoked "all privileges to all storekeepers in the city of Williamsburg and vicinity to purchase and sell goods." Moreover, "All willing to take the oath of allegiance to us [are] to do so before April 1, 1863. All others (except servants and employees of the Lunatic Asylum) will prepare to be placed beyond the lines now occupied by the government." But the same day the order was released, it was rescinded by General John A. Dix, who said that Williamsburg was not to be destroyed unless it was retaken by the Confederates. Dix, however, imposed his own set of restrictions upon those who lived in and around the city. No one could enter Williamsburg from any point below Fort Magruder without first taking the oath of allegiance and city residents could venture no further toward Yorktown than the fort. Likewise, only those who took the oath of allegiance could trade in Williamsburg. These restrictions were designed to eliminate opportunities for spying, which reportedly was undertaken by both blacks and whites. Dix's order stated that "No further supplies will be . . . taken to Williamsburg for the use of the inhabitants except the produce of neighboring farms, until further notice." Those caught aiding the enemy were to have their houses burned.[52]

The April 14, 1863, edition of THE CAVALIER described the Confederates' recent attempt to retake Williamsburg. The abortive strike upon Fort Magruder reportedly had involved 3,000 infantrymen, a cavalry regiment and a six gun battery. In mid-May THE CAVALIER published an open letter from General Dix to General Wise. Dix insisted that the asylum's inmates be moved to Richmond so that the Union Army no longer would be responsible for them. He said that his men would raze virtually all Williamsburg houses from which anyone fired upon his men and that anyone belonging to a group organized for the purpose of attacking them would be executed.[53] Dix's statements imply that the 5th Pennsylvania was plagued by sniper-fire. The organized band of partisans he mentioned probably was Lt. Hume's.

Although General Wise's March 29, 1863, attempt to retake Williamsburg was his last, conditions remained unstable. In April four Union naval vessels made a reconnaissance visit to Jamestown Island, to make sure that the Confederates weren't receiving reinforcements from the lower side of the James River. The 5th Pennsylvania's scouting parties continued to

The Geddy house, White Hall. Photo by Ralph Maxwell.

make excursions into the countryside and they skirmished with the Confederates at Diascund Bridge on June 10 and 20, 1863. Gradually, however, the Confederates drew in toward Richmond.[54]

An article in the September 21, 1863, edition of THE CAVALIER reveals that Mondays and Thursdays served as Williamsburg's official market days. People who lived outside of the city were allowed to approach the Union lines to swap produce for commodities available to those residing within the occupied territory. Generally, these exchanges were held once a week, but in summer they were scheduled more often.[55]

According to one Union officer:

Many of the townspeople owned plantations on the peninsula, still sparsely cultivated by old slaves willingly adhering to their masters' fortunes; and in secluded sections near the rivers, there were many well cultivated fields yielding corn, fruit and vegetables. Poultry, eggs, butter and sweet potatoes were quite abundant. On Market Day, so called "Line Day," people living outside were permitted to meet the townspeople at fixed boundaries on the Jamestown and Richmond Roads and trade within view of watchful guards ordered to prohibit the exchange of letters and articles contraband. At these market days our greenback currency never was refused.

The people outside [the lines] consisted almost wholly of white women and half-grown children. A few aged blacks of both sides sometimes attended them. They came in creaking carts drawn by infirm horses or mules of an age too great to tempt the confiscating propensities of the soldiers. . . . The market women hid their features at "the sight end" of a long telescopic sun bonnet. . . . Most of these market women were in fact ladies. Some of them owned plantations of hundreds of acres, naturally fertile.

The practice of holding "Line Day" eventually was discontinued by the local U.S. Army provost marshal.[56]

Tales of the Civil War

According to Captain David E. Cronin, a wedding ceremony was held where the Union Army line crossed Richmond Road.[57] Although he failed to record the names of the local couple being wed, he said that the bride was

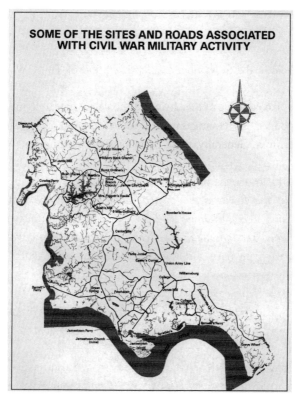

SOME OF THE SITES AND ROADS ASSOCIATED WITH CIVIL WAR MILITARY ACTIVITY

Map by Deborah L. Wilson. See enlarged map, page 332.

between 18 and 20 and the groom was in his 50s. The New Kent County clergyman who performed the service was escorted to the outskirts of Williamsburg by the notorious Confederate Lieutenant Hume, and a Union Army officer brought the bride to the ceremony in a gig borrowed especially for the occasion. Members of the wedding party were decked out in their finest and despite the watchful presence of Union troops, the occasion was filled with merriment. Cronin said he heard later that the couple lived together happily for many years.

During 1864, while Cronin was provost marshal, he tried to keep abreast of what was going on outside of Williamsburg. One of the most interesting episodes he recounted was his attempt to capture the elusive Lieutenant Hume. In June Cronin learned that the guerilla leader often spent the night at

the Marston plantation near Burnt Ordinary, so he took 15 dismounted cavalrymen, hoping to surprise him at dawn. Cronin and his men made a
thorough search of the Marston dwelling and then began checking the slave
cabins. He said,

*In passing the door of one, an aged "auntie" was sitting in the doorway.
I peered within at a bed which I saw, by the heaped-up covering, was
occupied. I asked her who was in the bed. She replied "Dat's only my ole
man, Sah. He's dreadful sick wid de chills, but I've kivered him up warm and
if he gets a sweat he'll be all right." I hesitated a moment about going in.
She pushed her chair back and turned aside so I could pass, saying, "Why
go right in and see, Sah, if you don't believe me." This perfectly natural assurance was enough, so I didn't go in.*

Cronin said that later he heard from a Confederate acquaintance that Hume
often joked about the "sweat" he was in when a Union officer, carbine in
hand, appeared at the door of the slave cabin in which he was hiding. He also
spoke of how quickly he recovered from his "dreadful chill," retrieved his
gun from under the bed, and departed. Hume said that he hadn't had time to
tell the Marstons' elderly slave what to say and that her subterfuge was spon-
taneous.[58]

The following month, Cronin made another attempt to capture Hume. This
time, he expected to overtake him "at the picturesque planter's residence of
Mrs. Cowles, not far from Cowles Ferry on the Chickahominy." He likened
"the peaceful old dwelling which stood on a little eminence" to "the English
farmhouses in the landscapes of Gainsborough." Again, Cronin and 15 dismounted cavalrymen attempted to slip up on Hume and his men at dawn. But
at the sound of a shot, four Confederate scouts, who were upstairs playing
cards, leaped from the windows and darted away. Hume was nowhere in sight.
Cronin later recalled capturing six or eight young soldiers from that neighborhood, who were at home on furlough. One of them was Mrs. Cowles' son.[59]

Cronin spoke highly of Dr. Marston, whose house was a stone's throw
from Burnt Ordinary.[60] On one occasion he loaned Cronin a horse and lumber
wagon to use as an ambulance for his footsore cavalrymen, to whom he also
provided a soothing salve. The provost marshal repaid the physician's
kindness by providing him with some hard-to-get commodities. During the

summer of 1864 a party of Union cavalrymen paused at the Bush plantation, between Burnt Ordinary and Green Spring, to seek information on Lieutenant Hume's whereabouts.[61] When they threatened to set the house afire if its occupants refused to tell what they knew, one woman said if they burned it, they would be guilty of destroying a hospital, for a wounded man was upstairs. Cronin went up and saw Lieutenant E. M. Ware, who had been seriously injured at Cold Harbor. He said that the Confederate officer was one of the most severely wounded men he had ever seen, for one bullet had passed though his jaw, another through his shoulders, and a third through his arm. When Cronin reached Williamsburg, he found a doctor to treat Ware and some local women to provide nursing care. Then he arranged to have him brought to town. Lieutenant E. M. Ware survived his war injuries and eventually became a James City County justice of the peace.[62]

According to local lore, someone in Albert W. Hankins' household posted a smallpox sign on the door of the main dwelling at Riverview, to discourage Union soldiers from stopping in. Another anecdote alleges that the chimney of the house was struck by a shell from a Union naval vessel and a third claims that the house was used as a military hospital. However, there is no written evidence that lends credence to any of these tales.

Dr. Alvan J. E. Jennings, who resided at La Grange, told his son that Hickory Neck Church fared very badly during the war because both armies camped there. He said that the pulpit was dismantled, the flooring was used for firewood, and that one of the building's walls was damaged. An elderly female member of the Hankins family, whose home was near Hickory Neck, reportedly hid a young Confederate soldier in a little closet beneath the stairs while Union troops searched her dwelling. The woman indicated that while the Confederates were holed up in Hickory Neck, they placed a trip-wire across the road to detect the approach of the enemy. One Union soldier, who received medical treatment from the Confederates at the church, later was shot and killed by a man from the lower peninsula, bitter about the ill treatment his family had received from General McClellan's men.[63]

A Toano man, born in 1905, whose grandmother lived at Sunnyside, said that Union soldiers going down Forge Road snatched some of her white Peking ducks. She hurried out, confronted the officer-in-charge, and insisted that the ducks be released, but she also invited him and his men to breakfast. The soldiers reportedly returned the ducks but declined her offer of a meal. Another local man recalled his grandmother's saying that Union troops camped around her home on Diascund Creek, just across the New Kent County line. Although the family successfully concealed some flour and salted fish in a cellar hole beneath their house, the soldiers passing through slaughtered and ate their sheep and cattle. The Confederates, when withdrawing toward Richmond, reportedly burned the wooden bridge across Diascund Creek. Later, Union troops took floor boards from Liberty Baptist Church (in New Kent) to fabricate a replacement.[64]

During the Civil War the Olive Branch Christian Church reportedly was occupied by Union Army cavalrymen, who slept in the gallery and stabled their horses in the sanctuary. The church's windows were broken, its communion silver was carried off, and its flooring and pews were torn apart for firewood. The interior walls were blackened by fires used to heat the building. In 1917 the congregation of Olive Branch received a $500 check from the United States Congress in compensation for wartime damage the church had sustained.[65]

Provost marshal David Cronin said that once, when he and his men were on patrol near Burnt Ordinary, he paused at a large frame house near an intersection about eight miles above Olive Branch Christian Church. He indicated that the dwelling, which served as a central distribution point for gossip and military intelligence, stood on a slight rise with its veranda overlooking the crossroads.[66] Confederate pickets and reserves often were stationed nearby and numerous skirmishes had occurred in that vicinity. Cronin said that there were three ladies in the house, an elderly matron and two young ones, and that according to the older woman, the family had been robbed of its cooking utensils the year before when Union troops passed through. There were a few slaves on the premises, who were very young or very old, as the middle-aged ones had gone off to become "contrabands."[67]

In Cronin's opinion, the war essentially was over on the lower peninsula by the summer of 1864. When his men made "various excursions into the enemy's country, whether mounted or dismounted, there was scarce any skirmishing or firing except at New Kent and at Cowles farm in the last attempt to capture Lieutenant Hume." He said that the countryside that stretched out toward Richmond was dotted with abandoned encampments and "the lone chimneys of ruined dwellings stood out grimly." He added that everywhere there was a conspicuous absence of fences, for they had been used as firewood.[68]

According to a letter written by L. W. Lane, a Williamsburg resident and the owner of Lilliput, "When McClellan left Harrison's Landing [Berkeley Plantation] a portion of his troops crossed to Barretts Ferry and on their march applied the Torch to that grand old House" Green Spring, then owned by the Ward brothers of Hackinsac, New Jersey.[69] Lane said that the Wards, "strange to say, had their slaves and overseer on the farm," and that later, "the federal governor gave them over $6,000" in compensation for the damage that was done. Lane indicated that Union troops also burned the old "Powhatan House" (Dr. Thomas Martin's home), and "Dunbar," Parke Jones' dwelling. Real estate tax rolls document the wartime destruction of buildings at Kingsmill, Jamestown, Neck O'Land, Powhatan, Green Spring and Dunbar. An artist's sketch of William Ludwell Lee's "modest gentleman's house" at Green Spring, drawn in 1890, reveals that it was still in ruins despite the Ward brothers' reputed reimbursement.[70]

After the war, David E. Cronin learned from Williamsburg friends, who had been loyal to the Confederacy, that slaves often assisted their owners by eavesdropping on Union military personnel, who tended to forget that they were present. Slaves also helped by smuggling letters and intelligence data out of Union-held territory. As Lieutenant Hume and his men sometimes slipped into Williamsburg, townspeople signaled the whereabouts of Union troops by beating on pans as if they were calling chickens, or by hanging cloth in certain upstairs windows. Cronin spoke appreciatively, but discretely, of "Mrs. Twelve-Trees," a woman who lived outside of town and furnished information to the Union Army. Although he took pains to veil her identity, one likely candidate is Lemuel Bowden's sister, who lived near the Six Mile Ordinary.

The Destruction of James City County's Antebellum Records

On April 3 and 4, 1865, when it was certain that Richmond would fall, Confederate General Richard S. Ewell was ordered to set the city ablaze. The roaring inferno in the heart of Richmond ignited the General Court's wood-shingled roof, which burst into flames, along with the building and its contents. The records of several Tidewater counties were lost, along with those of Virginia's higher courts, from the seventeenth century on. It was then that almost all of James City County's antebellum records were destroyed.[71]

The James City Cavalry

In 1896 James H. Allen of Peach Park in upper James City County, a school teacher and former officer in the James City Cavalry, recounted some of his wartime experiences in an article that appeared in the RICHMOND DISPATCH. He said that the men of Company H of the Fifth Regiment were mustered into service in Williamsburg by Colonel Mumford on May 22, 1861. Although there was a shortage of recruits at first, Allen said the James City Cavalry earned such a good reputation that eventually "it was more difficult to keep out recruits than it was to gain them." Allen quoted Major B. B. Douglas as saying that Company H "illustrates the fact that educated gentlemen always made good soldiers." The men of the James City Cavalry were involved in the Battle of Malvern Hill and then headed north toward Hanover Courthouse. Later, they moved toward the head of the Rappahannock River and acted as the Fifth Regiment's advance guard.

According to Allen's account, when the James City Cavalry arrived at the town of Warrenton, J. E. B. Stuart's men already were there. They crossed Cedar Creek and eventually came to a colonial brick church. Some Union soldiers, who were enjoying "a bountiful supper" there, quickly were disarmed and sent to the rear as captives. As the men of the James City Cavalry continued on their way, they sighted Union General John Pope's wagon train, which had stopped for the night at Bristoe Station. Hearing sounds of revelry amid the pouring rain, E. M. Ware and C. W. Hubbard crept up to the window of a house from which came "the music of the violin and the tread of dancers." Peering in, they discovered that the dwelling was full of Union officers and women, enjoying themselves. But the men of the James City Cavalry, who were badly outnumbered, made no attempt to attack until reinforcements arrived. On another occasion, they tore up the railroad tracks ahead of an approaching train and according to Allen, soon "Yells, cheers, groans, reports of pistols and carbines, and the clashing of sabres were heard" as the James City Cavalry "did its duty dashingly, heroically, and efficiently." The unit also rode with General Jubal A. Early in the Valley Campaign. Allen provided a roster of the James City Cavalry and noted that of its 97 members, 45 survived the war. Of the casualties, eight were killed, ten were wounded, eight were taken prisoner, and the remainder died from other causes.[72]

The Surrender at Appomattox

From mid-June 1864 until early April 1865 Union General U. S. Grant's Army of the Potomac besieged Confederate General Robert E. Lee's Army of Northern Virginia at Petersburg and Richmond. Grant then pursued Lee's men into southside Virginia, where the hungry and exhausted troops were obliged to forage for whatever sustenance they could find. At Farmville, Grant contacted Lee and proposed that he surrender. But the Confederates pressed on in a valiant but vain attempt to obtain reinforcements and supplies. Finally, when Lee was faced with what he perceived as insuperable odds, he decided to confer with Grant to negotiate the terms of a surrender. The two leaders met in the McLean house in Appomattox, where they drafted a document that was signed on April 12, 1865, at 4 P.M. Lee's surrender heralded the end of the war, for the Army of Tennessee capitulated on April 26th and the isolated forces in the Trans-Mississippi West surrendered in May.[73] The war clouds dissipated, but one form of suffering yielded to another.

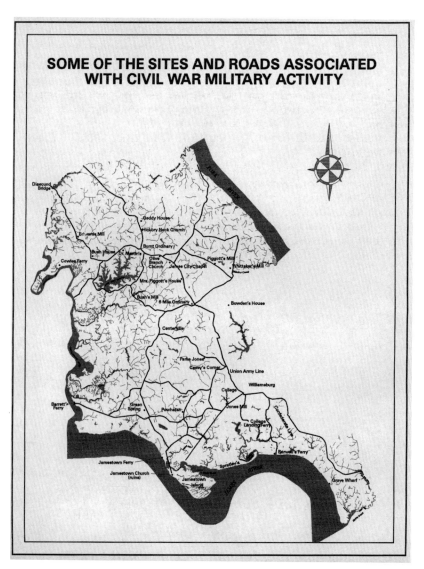

Map by Deborah L. Wilson.

Notes

1. Bruce Catton, THE AMERICAN HERITAGE PICTURE HISTORY OF THE CIVIL WAR (New York, 1960), 59, 62, 75; Bell I. Wiley, EMBATTLED CONFEDERATES, AN ILLUSTRATED HISTORY OF SOUTHERNERS AT WAR (New York, 1964), 12–14, 26, 59, 62.

2. Richard L. Morton, THE NEGRO IN VIRGINIA POLITICS, 1865–1902 (Charlottesville, 1919), 15–17.

3. George B. West, WHEN THE YANKEES CAME: CIVIL WAR AND RECONSTRUCTION ON THE VIRGINIA PENINSULA (Richmond, 1977), 39–41; Emma–Jo Davis, MULBERRY ISLAND AND THE CIVIL WAR, APRIL 1861– MAY 1862 (Newport News, 1967), 30.

4. Francis I. Miller, ed., THE PHOTOGRAPHIC HISTORY OF THE CIVIL WAR (New York, 1911), X:305–306; National Park Service, CONSERVING RICHMOND'S BATTLEFIELDS (Denver, 1990), 5; U.S.W.D., THE WAR OF THE REBELLION: A COMPILATION OF THE OFFICIAL RECORDS OF THE UNION AND CONFEDERATE ARMIES (Washington, 1891), Ser. 1, Vol. 2, Part 3:387; Vol. 9:13–14; E. B. Long, THE CIVIL WAR DAY BY DAY:AN ALMANAC, 1861–1865 (New York, 1971), 163; William F. R. Ritchie, comp., ACTS AND JOINT RESOLUTIONS PASSED BY THE GENERAL ASSEMBLY OF THE STATE OF VIRGINIA PASSED DURING THE SESSION OF 1861–1862 (Richmond, 1862), 61.

5. Later, one of Wynne's sisters married Charlton (Fred Boelt, personal communication, February 24, 1995).

6. Powers, "the Grove," 10–13; Thomas George Wynne, "Farmer's Journal, 1861" (Williamsburg, 1861). U.S.W.D., OFFICIAL RECORDS, Ser. 1, Vol. 4:669.

7. Catesby ap Roger Jones, May 3, 1861 letter to Captain H. N. Cocke; May 16, 1861 letter to Captain S. Barron; E. K. Rawson et al., comp., OFFICIAL RECORDS OF THE UNION AND CONFEDERATE NAVIES IN THE WAR OF THE REBELLION (Washington, 1898), Ser. 1, Vol. 6:699–702,722.

8. Lyon G. Tyler, ed., "Jamestown Island in 1861," WILLIAM AND MARY QUARTERLY, 1st Ser., 10 (July 1901):38–39; "Historical and Genealogical Notes," WILLIAM AND MARY QUARTERLY, 1st. Ser., 10 (July 1901):142.

9. According to an article in the June 24, 1899, edition of the VIRGINIA GAZETTE, Williamsburg's Junior Guard was part of the 32nd Regiment and served in the battles of Yellow Tavern and Gettysburg.

10. Rawson et al., NAVIES, Ser. 1, Vol. 6:698,704,706,712,722,737; Palmer, CALENDAR, XI:185.

11. Catesby ap Roger Jones, Report of Ordnance Experiments at Jamestown, October 12, 1861; VIRGINIA GAZETTE, January 9, 1931; A. A. Humphreys, "Yorktown to Williamsburg," 1862; John W. Donn, "James River from College Creek to the Chickahominy River," 1873–1874; Cotter, "Notes."

12. Bureau of Refugees, Freedmen and Abandoned lands, 1865–1867; Ralph W. Donnelly, "The Confederate Marines at Drewry's Bluff," VIRGINIA CAVALCADE 26:42–47.

13. U.S.W.D., OFFICIAL RECORDS, Ser. 1, Vol. 2, Part 3:386; Vol. 9, 49, 61; Vol. 11, Part 3:369.

14. Alexander S. Webb, THE PENINSULA: MCCLELLAN'S CAMPAIGN OF 1862 (New York, 1881), 37–49, 55–56, 60–62, 71. After the war, Magruder said that he considered Jamestown Island his army's right flank and that the defenses at Fort Magruder and Tuttey's (or Tutter's) Neck were of the utmost importance (U.S.W.D., OFFICIAL RECORDS, Ser. 1, Vol. 9:38–39, 43).

15. Anne W. Chapman, BENJAMIN STODDERT EWELL: A BIOGRAPHY (Williamsburg, 1984), 125, 127–132; United Daughters of the Confederacy, "The Battle of Williamsburg" (Williamsburg, 1991), 1; U.S.W.D., OFFICIAL RECORDS, Ser. 1, Vol. 9:13–14, 38–39; Rawson et al., Navies, Ser. 1, Vol. 7:742.

16. E. G. Swem, "Some Notes on the Four Forms of the Oldest Buildings of William and Mary College," (Williamsburg, 1928), 218, 292; John S. Charles, "Recollections," (Williamsburg, 1928), 2.

17. David E. Cronin, an officer in the 1st New York Mounted Rifles and illustrator for HARPER'S WEEKLY, later wrote that Magruder had 10,000 men on the peninsula, to whom Jubal A. Early added 8,000. When Generals Jones and Hill arrived, the total number was 33,000 (David E. Cronin, "The Vest Mansion, Its Historical and Romantic Associations as Confederate and Union Headquarters in the American Civil War" [Williamsburg, 1862–1865], 8).

18. R. U. Johnson et al., BATTLES AND LEADERS OF THE CIVIL WAR (New York, 1956), II:160–199.

19. Webb, PENINSULA, 69–70; McClellan, PAPERS, 258; Victoria and Petricola Lee, "Williamsburg in 1861" (Williamsburg, 1939).

20. Baker, "Memoirs."

21. Parke Rouse, "James City County's Records and Their Burning in 1865," WHERE AMERICA BEGAN: JAMES CITY COUNTY, 1634–1984 (Williamsburg, 1984); VIRGINIA GAZETTE, June 13, 1930.

22. One local group involved in the defense of Fort Magruder was the Williamsburg Cavalry.

23. U.D.C., "Williamsburg in the Civil War" (Williamsburg, n.d.), 2–3; Webb, PENINSULA, 78–81; U.S.W.D., OFFICIAL RECORDS, Ser. 1, Vol. 11 Part 1:581.

24. U.D.C., "Williamsburg," 2–3; Webb, PENINSULA, 78–81; U.S.W.D., OFFICIAL RECORDS, Ser. 1, Vol. 11 Part 1:581.

25. David H. Donald, ed., GONE FOR A SOLDIER: THE CIVIL WAR MEMOIRS OF PRIVATE ALFRED BELLARD (Boston, 1975), 67–69; U.S.W.D., OFFICIAL RECORDS, Ser. 1, Vol. 11 Part 1:581.

26. U.S.W.D., OFFICIAL RECORDS, Ser. 1, Vol. 11, Part 1:605. Although the main Confederate column withdrew from Williamsburg via the Stage Road (Route 60), some units (especially those involved in the action at Fort Magruder) probably crossed the Capitol Landing bridge and the swamp at the head of Carters Creek, then headed west to Six Mile Ordinary and the Stage Road. Other units may have followed Long Hill Road across the head of Powhatan Creek to Centerville and then turned north toward the Stage Road.

27. Ibid., Ser. 1, Vol. 11, Part 1:575.

28. Bowden's sister, Mollie, the wife of Charles H. Porter, lived just across the York County line, at a site Confederate cartographers' maps identify with the name "Bowden" (Gilmer, "Vicinity," 1864; York County Deed Book 18:424–425,536). The site of the Bowden/Porter residence, which lay between Route 60 and Interstate 64, on the east side of Route 646, may have been obliterated by the extension of the western leg of Route 199.

29. Carol A. Kettenburg, "The Battle of Williamsburg" (Williamsburg, 1980), 84; U.S. Congress, THE REPORT OF THE JOINT COMMITTEE ON THE CONDUCT OF THE WAR (Washington, D. C., 1863), I, 582–586; Martha W. McCartney, HICKORY NECK CHURCH IN BLISLAND PARISH (Williamsburg, 1993), 36.

30. George B. McClellan, THE CIVIL WAR PAPERS OF GEORGE B. MCCLELLAN, Stephen W. Sears, ed. (New York, 1989), 265; P. S. Michie, GENERAL MCCLELLAN (New York, 1915), 256, 275; U.D.C., "Williamsburg," 4; U.S.W.D., Official Records, Ser. 1, Vol. 11, Part 1:449–450,461.

31. Cronin, "Vest Mansion," 15; U.S.W.D., OFFICIAL RECORDS, Ser. 1, Vol. 11 Part 1:453, 462; Lyon G. Tyler, ed., "Diary of Miss Harriette Cary, Kept by Her from May 6, 1862 to July 24, 1862," TYLER'S HISTORICAL QUARTERLY 9 (October 1928):104–116.

32. Swem, "Oldest Buildings," 218, 292; Kale, HARK, 87; Charles, "Recollections," 2, 6–11; WILLIAMSBURG 1944 AND BEFORE REUNION (Williamsburg, 1984), n.p.

33. Tyler, "Harriette Cary," 104–116; Lee, "Typescript;" Cronin, "Vest Mansion," 22.

34. Lee, "Transcript," 1939; VIRGINIA GAZETTE, July 3, 1931; April 9, 1965; "Memoirs"; Charles, "Recollections," 40.

35. THE CAVALIER, June 25, 1862. E. H. Lively, the GAZETTE'S owner and publisher, was away in the Confederate Army when Williamsburg fell into Union hands.

36. Lyon G. Tyler, "Green Spring," TYLER'S HISTORICAL QUARTERLY 10 (October 1928):187–190.

37. There was combat at Drewry's Bluff and Gaines Crossroads on May 15th and Gaines Mill on May 19th.

38. Ibid., 104–116; Palmer, CALENDAR, XI:475.

39. Rawson et al., NAVIES, Ser. 1, Vol. 7:473, 566.

40. Cronin, "Vest Mansion," 172–173.

41. Ibid., 249–250; U.S.W.D., OFFICIAL RECORDS, Ser. 1, Vol.

42. Part 2:696–697. This citation was provided by David Riggs of the National Park Service.

42. Swem, "Oldest Buildings," 292; U.S.W.D., OFFICIAL RECORDS, Ser. I, Vol. 18:11. One report credits Wise with an attack force of 1,800 men, whereas a Union account states that 300 Confederates were involved, units from Georgia, South Carolina, and Virginia.

43. Charles, "Recollections," 2; VIRGINIA GAZETTE, January 4, 1935.

44. Swem, "Oldest Buildings," 292; Cronin, "Vest Mansion," 212; VIRGINIA GAZETTE, January 4, 1935.

45. Cronin, "Vest Mansion," 250.

46. Palmer, Calendar, VI, 233–236. This incident is described more fully in Chapter 16.

47. Ibid., XI, 228–231. On November 27, 1862, General Wise dispatched a letter to General E. D. Keyes, expressing inmates' families' concerns and asking permission for two of his officers to inspect the asylum. He added that no formal protest had been filed when the college was burned. On December 3rd, Keyes replied that there were no plans to move the patients, who were receiving full rations and had been assigned a surgeon. He said "The college buildings were burnt in the confusion of a raid made by your troops within our lines. I know not who burned them" (Henry A. Wise, letter to E. D. Keyes, November 27, 1862; E. D. Keyes, letter to Henry A. Wise, December 3, 1862).

48. The corner of the Casey farm was at Long Hill and Ironbound Roads, where the James Blair Middle School is located. The site where Jamestown Road crosses Lake Matoaka is about a mile from College Corner.

49. Ibid., XI, 231–233; Cronin, "Vest Mansion," 28, 35.

50. Long, AN ALMANAC, 298; U.S.W.D., OFFICIAL RECORDS, Ser. 1, Vol. 18:130–131; Cronin, "Vest Mansion," 28, 55.

51. Cronin, VEST MANSION, 20, 22, 40.

52. Ibid., 37–38, 52, 296–297.

53. THE CAVALIER, April 14, May 12, 1863.

54. Rawson et al., NAVIES, Ser. 1, Vol. 8:709–710; Long, CIVIL WAR, 298, 312, 364, 369; I. Knowles Hare, "Hare's Map of the Vicinity of Richmond and the Peninsula Campaign," 1862.

55. THE CAVALIER, September 21, 1863; Cronin, "Vest Mansion," 57.

56. Cronin, "Vest Mansion," 37–38, 57.

57. The churches in town were closed at that time.

58. Ibid., 206.

59. Ibid., 243.

60. This was likely Dr. Thomas Marston, who during the 1860s resided at "Variety Grove" on Old Forge Road.

61. This was likely "Windsor Castle", owned by Colonel William Bush and his wife, Matilda, during the 1860s.

62. Ibid., 235, 241, 269. Cronin incorrectly reported that Ware became James City County's clerk of court (James City County Deed Books 3 and 4, passim).

63. John M. Jennings, "Address presented at Hickory Neck Church on October 28, 1934" (Toano, 1934); Nancy S. Bradshaw, ed., TALES FROM JAMES CITY COUNTY, VIRGINIA, ORAL HISTORIES (Williamsburg, 1993), 40–41.

64. Bradshaw, TALES, 5, 94–95.

65. VIRGINIA GAZETTE, September 30, 1960.

66. The dwelling's location and description correspond with White Hall, the old Geddy home.

67. Cronin, "Vest Mansion," 261.

68. Ibid., 57, 269.

69. Lane confused William Ludwell Lee's early nineteenth-century dwelling with the ancient Green Spring mansion, razed when the new house was built.

70. Lyon G. Tyler, "The Burning of Green Spring," TYLER'S QUARTERLY 10:176–177; James City County Land Tax Lists 1861–1867; Gaines, "Courthouses," 37.

71. Gaines, "Courthouses," 30.

72. James H. Allen, "Our Confederate Column, the James City Cavalry," RICHMOND TIMES–DISPATCH, June 1, 1896. The unit's roster and that of the Williamsburg Junior Guard appear in Appendix I.

73. Theodore F. Rodenbaugh, THE PHOTOGRAPHIC HISTORY OF THE CIVIL WAR (Secaucus, N.J., 1987), 304–36; Long, CIVIL WAR, 668–669. Johnson et al., BATTLES AND LEADERS, IV, 729–747; James I. Robertson, CIVIL WAR VIRGINIA: BATTLEGROUND FOR A NATION (Charlottesville and London, 1991), 31.

From Swords to Plowshares: Reconstruction and Growth 1866–1880

The Aftermath of War

By April 1865 there had been more than 200 military engagements in Virginia and over half-a-million men had become casualties of one sort or another. Thus, the state had withstood the full fury of the Civil War. Towns and cities were in shambles or had deteriorated. Throughout the rural countryside, fields were ruined, crops and livestock were gone, bridges and railroads were destroyed. Countless homes and businesses were irreparably damaged. An estimated 20,000 to 30,000 Virginia soldiers lost their lives and many thousands of others were permanently disabled as a result of war wounds and disease. Blacks and whites struggled to survive and to redefine their roles in society. The state's economic system was destroyed, for Confederate money and bonds were worthless, inflation was at an all time high, and legal tender was almost nonexistent.

For the first six months after the surrender at Appomattox, at least 25,000 white Virginians subsisted on army rations and many of the state's 360,000 freed blacks lacked food, clothing, shelter, and a means of making a living. Real estate values plummeted and land worth $50 an acre before the war, afterward sold for only $2. So massive was the damage to Virginia's industrial establishment that it was the only state that failed to reach prewar production levels by 1870. In sum, the war, followed by military occupation and Reconstruction, exacted so great a toll that Virginia was reduced to poverty and despair.[1]

Undoubtedly, many returning soldiers were completely demoralized by the conditions they found at home, for they were confronted with what must have seemed like an insurmountable array of problems. In time, many veterans were able to rebuild their lives. However, the more fragile never overcame their sense of hopelessness and some succumbed to depression or alcoholism. In October 1865 the RICHMOND SENTINEL claimed that "thousands of our most gifted and promising young men are fast becoming confirmed sots" or (as another source put it) "whiskey-drinking loafers." But the majority of ex-Confederates, despite their disabilities and economic hardships, persevered. In essence, they did the best they could with what they had, and eventually made a strong recovery.[2] Thus, they exhibited immense courage, stamina, and relentless determination: the same characteristics that had enabled them to give their all to the cause they supported.

After the close of the war, the people of James City County attempted to pick up the pieces of their lives. According to Chesapeake and Ohio Railroad land agent Carl Bergh, the county's

. . . farms lay idle, the slaves had their freedom and the white people had. . . died in battle and many had moved never to return. The few whites who were left had lost all. Their former wealth and standing was at once blown away. Their cattle, sheep, hogs, and chickens were eaten by the soldiers, their horses and mules were stolen, their hoard of Confederate money was not worth the paper it was printed on. . . . Several years went on until the land was sown again and in the meantime, it had grown up in weeds and brush and young pine trees. The people were not used to do[ing] the necessary work . . . which the Negroes had formerly done, so it was difficult for them. Taxes were unpaid and everything was destroyed.

Enormous tasks confronted farmers, for the neglected land had to be cleared of dense vegetation and small trees before plowing could begin. One local man recalled his grandfather's saying that most people could use only part of their land and had to let the remainder grow up in weeds and bushes.[3] Game animals (including predators) multiplied in the underbrush and created problems for those fortunate enough to own poultry and livestock.

Although the social and cultural changes wrought by the war were irrevocable, the economic ones were not. But recovery took time, money, a lot of ingenuity, and a tremendous amount of hard work. Problems created by the loss of slave labor, upon which an estimated half of local farmers depended, were compounded by a substantial reduction in rural families' work force, thanks to the fact that a substantial proportion of Virginia's white males were killed or seriously injured in the war. Because much of the work of farming fell to women, children, and elderly or disabled men, rural families throughout Tidewater shifted to less labor-intensive forms of agriculture, such as animal husbandry or raising fruits and vegetables for sale in urban markets. The amount of acreage put to the plow declined sharply and agricultural productivity dropped by more than half. Most Southern farmers' equipment was worn out or obsolete and they lacked the disposable income they needed to replace it, if indeed new implements were available. Women, who during wartime had learned to shift for themselves, grew crops, tried to make their homes livable, and attempted to give their children a rudimentary education.[4]

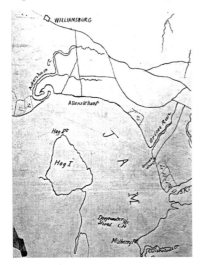

Tracts at Carter's Grove, Kingsmill and other sites, leased to freed blacks for subsistence farming. "Map Showing Position of Government Farms, Freedmen's Bureau," 1866. National Archives.

Census records reveal that a considerable number of households consisted of unrelated individuals who seemingly banded together for mutual support. Many farms were operated by white or black sharecroppers or leaseholders. Some blacks stayed on near the farms upon which they'd been slaves before the war. Throughout eastern Virginia, rural landowners were forced to subdivide their farms and some had to relinquish them altogether. In James City County the actual number of farms increased threefold.[5] Northern speculators with spare capital sometimes seized the opportunity to purchase cheap land, often by paying back taxes. Court records reveal that they often invested in large farms which they quickly resold or subdivided, in an attempt to turn a speedy profit. There were exceptions, however, for some Northern buyers settled upon the land they'd purchased.

Black Refugees

During the mid-1860s the James-York peninsula had a substantial population of homeless blacks, many of whom had fled behind Union lines after General Butler declared runaway slaves contraband of war. These people, who had no means of supporting themselves, posed serious health and welfare problems for federal authorities, before and after the surrender at Appomattox. On March 3, 1865, the United States Congress established the Bureau of Refugees, Freedmen and Abandoned Lands, a little-known branch of government based in the War Department. It was intended to provide food, shelter, clothing, and fuel to "suffering refugees and freedmen and their wives and children." It also had the authority to assign them private property that had been abandoned by its owners or confiscated for back taxes.[6] Bureau agents were entrusted with negotiating labor contracts on behalf of ex-slaves and seeing that they were provided with medical care and schooling, often in cooperation with the American Missionary Association and other private agencies. Because whites left in droves when the Union Army swept through the lower peninsula, a substantial amount of vacant land was available. The Bureau typically subdivided abandoned farm land into small parcels and leased them to refugees who paid rent in crop-shares. Sometimes, Union Army officers simply confiscated private property and issued it to the refugees. It is likely that the buildings on abandoned or confiscated farms sustained a considerable amount of damage from refugees scavenging for boards, nails, and the other building materials they needed to construct simple shanties.[7]

A map of the lower peninsula's so-called Government Farms reveals that several James City County properties were subdivided and placed in the hands of black refugees. Among these farms were Kingsmill, Carter's Grove (called the Martin's Hundred Farm), Spratley's, Neck O'Land, and the Blow farm.

At Kingsmill, freedmen rented William Allen's mill for a third of its toll and 187 acres were assigned to black sharecroppers. Records of the Freedmen's Bureau indicate that the land the refugees used lay just west of Grove Creek and contained houses and cabins.[8] At Carter's Grove four plots, totaling 300 acres, were laid out along the river bank on the west side of Skiffs Creek's mouth; Palen Jones and Jacob Smith were two of the freedmen renting plots there. A notation in the Bureau of Refugees' records states that the acreage at Carter's Grove was seized in accord with orders from General Butler, personally. Confederate Colonel George Blow's farm had 236 acres that were placed in the hands of freedmen. The confiscated properties was restored to their legal owners in 1867.[9]

Two Quaker teachers, sponsored by the Friends Association of Philadelphia, taught local freedmen how to read and write. William and Mary President Benjamin S. Ewell promoted the establishment of schools where illiterate blacks could be educated and he encouraged his maid (who could read) to offer instruction to other blacks. He also urged the passage of the 14th Amendment, which endowed blacks with civil rights. Although it is generally assumed that there was relatively little Ku Klux Klan activity in Virginia at the close of the Civil War, a disabled missionary from New England, who worked in the vicinity of Williamsburg and Yorktown, in 1868 claimed to have been assaulted by Klansmen. He said that he had been dragged from his bed during the middle of the night, taken into the woods, and beaten because he had been teaching blacks.[10] No evidence has come to light to support or refute his story.

Government During Reconstruction

President Abraham Lincoln, who had the foresight to formulate a plan of reconstruction, on December 8, 1863, issued a Proclamation of Amnesty and Reconstruction. It authorized secessionist states to rejoin the Union if they met certain criteria. Lincoln, on the evening of his assassination, declared that he wanted "no persecution, no bloody work." Vice-President and successor Andrew Johnson followed in his footsteps and on May 25, 1865, as president, issued his own Proclamation of Amnesty. Although Johnson, an advocate of the yeomanry, was opposed to the privileges of the gentry, he believed that the Union was indestructible and that reconstruction, per se, was unnecessary. Congress took a sterner, more punitive view.[11]

In May 1865, President Andrew Johnson gave his support to Virginia's Restored Government, which throughout the war had been seated in Alexandria under the protection of the Union Army. With Johnson's encouragement the Restored Government moved to Richmond and incumbent Governor F. H. Pierpont took office. The problems he faced were staggering. He tried to implement the reconstruction policies Presidents Lincoln and Johnson had formulated and he attempted to reestablish local government by appointing commissioners and election officials. County justices were elected, but ordered not to appoint anyone to office who had held a position in the state's Confederate government. As no significant changes were made in the procedures followed by county courts, business was conducted much as it had been before the war. For a time, however, the Bureau of Refugees had special courts that processed cases involving blacks. These judicial units, which were discontinued in May 1866, had the right to impose a maximum fine of $100 or three months in jail. Actions taken on the state level in June 1865 authorized the assessment of taxes and increased the legally allowable interest rate. The marriages of former slaves also were legalized, a measure intended to improve blacks' acceptance in white society and promote economic recovery. Elections were held in October 1865 to fill Virginia's congressional seats and to choose delegates and senators to the General Assembly, which was to convene on December 4, 1865.

Besides dealing with the mechanics of government, Governor Pierpont was obliged to cope with vexing problems such as poverty, lawlessness, and vagrancy that were rampant right after the war. Delegates to the General Assembly's 1866–1867 session rejected the U.S. Constitution's 14th amendment, which granted freed blacks full citizenship. The Southern states' failure to endorse blacks' civil and political equality precipitated a strong backlash and in March 1867, the United States Congress passed the Reconstruction Acts, making Virginia Military District Number 1. Lieutenant-General John M. Schofield was placed in command of the state's military government. He made temporary appointments to vacant public offices and established voter registration procedures that provided for the enfranchisement of the state's blacks. Anyone who had held a state office before the war, but had supported the Confederacy, was deemed ineligible to vote and was disqualified from holding all public positions. This included offices on the local level such as clerks of court, county justices, mayors, aldermen, jailors, and agricultural inspectors. Under the Reconstruction Acts, an estimated 70,000 white males, who formerly had served as government officials, were disfranchised and deprived of the right to hold office. During the Reconstruction period, more than 62.5 percent of James City County's registered voters were black. Delegate F. S. Norton represented James City County and Williamsburg in the General Assembly.

In December 1867 a constitutional convention convened in Richmond in response to General Schofield's orders. Its delegates were both white and black and included native Virginians (some of whom were Confederate veterans), men from out of state, foreign nationals, and Union Army veterans. Daniel M. Norton represented James City and York Counties in the Convention of 1867–1868, which was chaired by John C. Underwood, a New Yorker and judge in Richmond's U.S. Circuit Court. The chairman was so influential that the document the delegates drafted became known as the Underwood Constitution. On the last day of the constitutional convention, General Schofield urged delegates to modify the article that established the criteria for voting and officeholding. He said that he had "been able to find in some counties only one, in others two, and others three, persons of either race able to read and write who could take the test oath." For that reason Schofield believed that "it will be practically impossible to administer the government under your constitution with that provision." He was right. The next time elections were held, more than half of the state's 5,446 offices were left vacant and a substantial number of those elected were disqualified on account of having served the Confederacy.[12]

The New State Constitution

In 1869, when the Underwood Constitution was put to a referendum, its disenfranchisement and test-oath clauses were defeated; the rest of the text was approved. When the General Assembly convened in October 1869, it ratified the 14th and 15th amendments to the U.S. Constitution. In January 1870, when Military District No. 1 ceased to exist and Virginia was re-admitted to the Union, Gilbert C. Walker of New York became governor. The newly ratified constitution effected some major changes in local government. One of the most significant was the establishment of county Boards of Supervisors, which were to assume many of the decision-making duties formerly relegated to county justices. Another was the creation of a state-wide public school system. Although the Underwood Constitution called for Virginia's counties to be subdivided into townships, with one elected super-visor apiece, in 1874 the magisterial district was reinstated as the basic unit of local government.

The Underwood Constitution called for the establishment of a new local court system. Each county court was to have a judge elected by the General Assembly and the courts themselves were placed within a judicial circuit that had a district court. James City County, like other Virginia localities, was required by law to have a Board of Supervisors with elected representatives from each of its districts. It is uncertain, however, when a local Board actually came into existence, for its earliest extant minutes date to September 10, 1887. Thus, if James City had a Board of Supervisors prior to that time, its records have been destroyed or misplaced.

In 1870 the General Assembly placed the entire city of Williamsburg within the bounds of James City County, bringing to an end its division between two neighboring jurisdictions. The 1770 courthouse, which was refurbished after the Civil War, continued to serve both city and county. In March 1872 the James City County and Williamsburg circuit courts were con-solidated into a single judicial body and all cases on both courts' dockets were transferred to the new court.[13]

Bolstering the Economy

During the early 1870s Virginia's financial situation grew increasingly dismal. This made many voters eager for a change. At issue was the state debt and whether Virginia would honor its pre-war obligations, which by 1870 had risen to $45,000,000. The other alternative was to declare bankruptcy and cancel part of the debt. The advocates of full payment (dubbed "Funders") included the wealthier class of Virginians, whereas the "Readjusters" (largely, less conservative whites and newly enfranchised blacks) favored repaying the debt slowly, on a cost-adjusted basis that took into account devastation caused by the war. A number of the state's former political leaders, who had held office before the war, emerged from retirement to run in the elections. This pitted those prominent during Reconstruction (and therefore dependent upon the black vote) against those who had led the state before the war. The standard bearer for the "Readjuster" movement was William Mahone, a former Confederate general-turned-railroad magnate, who reportedly "weighed about 100 pounds, had a squeaky voice, and was so fastidious that his tailor said he would rather make dresses for eight women than one [garment] for the general." During the 1870s "Funder" governors James L. Kemper and Frederick W. M. Holliday made a practice of impounding con-stitutionally-appropriated school funds to pay the state's debts. This ultimately created a backlash that propelled the "Readjusters" into office. In 1879 they won the majority of seats in houses of the General Assembly and in 1881 William Mahone's protégé, William E. Cameron, became governor when Mahone was elected to the United States Senate. Following Governor Cameron's victory, bonds were issued and the state debt was reduced to around $21,000,000. West Virginia assumed responsibility for the remaining third of its antecedent's debt. This freed up funds that could be used to operate the government and run public schools.[14]

Illiteracy had been a major social problem even before the Civil War. During wartime, it became worse, for the state's Literary Fund was channeled into the Confederate military budget and public education, as it was then defined, ground to a halt. As a consequence, Virginia's illiteracy rate soared alarmingly. By 1865 nearly 22 percent of the state's whites were unable to read and write and Virginia had 210,000 illiterate blacks. It was not until the ratification of the Underwood Constitution in 1869 that public education in Virginia really came into its own. It was then that free public schools were established to serve both blacks and whites and school attendance became mandatory. The law provided for a Superintendent of Public Instruction and a State Board of Education, which was to provide suitable textbooks and school equipment. Free schools had to be operational in all Virginia counties by 1876 at the latest, a mandate that closed the legal loopholes that made public education a local option. Many blacks, who previously had had no opportunity to receive an education, responded eagerly to the chance to attend school. But some whites believed that educating children was a responsibility of the home, not the government. Even so, the racially segregated public schools that were established in James City County attracted a relatively large enrollment.

In 1862 Congress passed the first Morrill Land Grant College Act, which awarded 30,000 acres of public land to each state, or the equivalent in land script that could be used to raise money toward building at least one agricultural and mechanical college. Congress also enacted legislation establishing a Department of Agriculture, which purpose was to collect and disseminate information on agriculture and to procure, propagate and distribute improved seeds and plants to farmers.[15]

In 1870 when officials of the United States Department of Agriculture evaluated the status of Virginia's farm economy, they concluded that:

. . . the conditions on which agricultural prosperity rests have been so unsettled by intervening events [the war], and the tenure of lands to a great extent rendered uncertain, that few farmers have been influenced by a spirit of improvement. The great object has been to make a livelihood. The efforts both of farmers and planters have been vigorous . . . but rather with a view to speedy returns than ultimate improvement. No systematic rotation has been practiced. . . . They are still wedded to old habits, from which no change of circumstances has sufficed to divorce them.

Although the grain drill and steam thresher were available and the check-row corn planter had come on the market, few Southern farmers had the disposable income to purchase them or other pieces of new and modern agricultural equipment.[16]

The Asylum Farm

In 1869 the Eastern State Lunatic Asylum's Board of Directors asked the General Assembly for funds to purchase a 170-acre farm adjacent to the hospital grounds. They proffered that the W. F. B. Milliken farm, which was reasonably priced, would soon pay for itself by producing the hospital patients' food supply, then being purchased from outside sources. They also felt that the farm would provide patients with gainful employment and promote their health and recovery. The legislature agreed and within a short time, the asylum farm was yielding sizable quantities of fruit, vegetables, fodder, pork, and beef.

However, on October 24, 1880, at about 5 A.M., fire broke out at the asylum farm, "destroying the brick stable, slaughter house, one ambulance horse" and substantial quantities of hay and fresh produce stored on the premises. Although the hospital's directors asked for funds to rebuild the structures that had been burned, two years later they still were "absolutely without stables, barns or other necessary farm houses" and said that "our team and stock are huddled together in half-rotten sheds and shanties . . . which were made for temporary use several years ago." They received the funds they needed and the refurbished asylum farm became a money-making concern, with excess produce that was offered for sale in the local community.[17]

Williamsburg and the College

After the Battle of Williamsburg and three years of Union Army occupation, what General Philip Kearney called the "lovely sweet College town of charming villas & old mansions" was scarred and dilapidated. So was the college. William and Mary's main building and the Brafferton, were gutted, hollow shells, grim reminders of the war. In June 1865, when President Benjamin S. Ewell assessed the damage, he concluded that the structures could be made usable. Therefore, he set about trying to garner the support he needed to reopen the college. Although he succeeded in gaining the backing of the Board of Visitors, he woefully underestimated the cost of rebuilding. He commenced lobbying the state legislature for funds and tried to obtain a share of the Morrill Land Grant money. He also asked some English gentlemen and a few wealthy Northerners to contribute toward the project. He succeeded in tapping the Mattey Fund and donated some money of his own. When the college reopened on a limited basis in October 1869, enrollment was disappointingly low. At that point, Ewell and the Board of Visitors decided to seek reparations from the United States government. Board member and ex-Confederate general Henry A. Wise sent his old adversary, Massachusetts Congressman and ex-Union general Benjamin F. Butler, a detailed account of the damages the college sustained during the war and asked his advice on how to submit a relief bill to Congress. Butler suggested that college officials emphasize William and Mary's importance as the alma mater of numerous patriots, stressing the accidental nature of the fire that destroyed its buildings. However, he counseled against all other references to the war. Despite repeated attempts to obtain passage of the relief bill, it languished for a decade.[18]

The Pain of Recovery

James City County deed books bear mute testimony to the hardships local people endured during the postwar years. Some, thanks to the loss of farm income and their investment in slaves, were unable to pay off debts they had incurred before the war. Many others, who were obliged to buy merchandize, agricultural equipment and supplies on credit, became hopelessly indebted to storekeepers and other business establishments. Merchants, in turn, went bankrupt because they couldn't collect from their debtors. Labor shortages, worn-out equipment, and land so overgrown with vegetation that it defied the plow were among the numerous problems confronting local farmers. They also lacked the money they needed to buy seed and fertilizer and to replenish their livestock. As a result, many people fell deeply into debt due to circumstances simply beyond their control. A considerable number ended up declaring bankruptcy. The destruction of almost all of James City County's court records in 1865 undoubtedly made it difficult for those buying and selling land to substantiate their titles and boundary lines.

Moss Side

Alexander H. Hankins, like many other James City County farmers, was overwhelmed by debt during the mid-to-late 1860s. He had inherited a farm known variously as Moss Side or Aspen Grove and during the 1840s and '50s managed to make slow but steady economic progress. He added to his land-holdings, purchased additional slaves and livestock, and constructed buildings upon some of his new acreage, perhaps intending to lease it to tenants. But the close of the Civil War found Hankins deeply in debt. He borrowed money from his neighbor, Henley Taylor, and bought merchandize, fertilizer, and household goods on credit. Ultimately, Hankins was obliged to mortgage vir-tually all of his real estate, including his home farm. When he deeded his land to a trustee, he stipulated that if the General Assembly enacted a homestead bill or some other form of exemption for "the relief to the debtor class by reason of great loss sustained in slave property," he would be eligible for benefits. But no such law was passed and in 1870 Hankins was declared bankrupt. A year later, Moss Side was bought by one of his creditors, George Hankins, a kinsman.[19]

Green Spring

The Ward brothers, who purchased Green Spring prior to the Civil War, in 1871 sold it to Leslie E. Sunderland, who used the property as collateral when borrowing his purchase money. Sunderland, a local farmer, already owned a nearby tract. But the economic hardships that characterized the postwar period overwhelmed Sunderland, who fell more and more deeply into debt. He was obliged to mortgage the steam-powered sawmill and lumbering equipment at Green Spring, plus his teams of oxen, carts, and log-carrying sleighs, and his other real estate. Finally, he mortgaged his life insurance and a sixth of all the money he hoped to earn from harvesting the timber at Green Spring. Despite these efforts to secure his debt, Sunderland was forced to default on his mortgage and Green Spring reverted to the ownership of the Wards.

During the mid-1880s Robert C. A. Ward and his brother's heirs sold Green Spring to Leiper M. Robinson of King and Queen County. He subdi-vided the farm, as did his successors, most of whom were from New Jersey. Shortly after the turn of the twentieth century, what remained of the Green Spring tract became the property of the Oriana Stave and Lumber Company of Madison, Wisconsin. Later, it was sold to the Pine Dell Development Company, which also owned Piney Grove.[20] Both companies were in the lumber business.

Piney Grove, Deep Bottom, the Fishery and Kingsmill

Moses R. Harrell, a real estate speculator who bought Piney Grove in 1849 and took up residence on the property, had serious financial problems during the postwar period. In November 1866 he was obliged to mortgage his home farm. Four years later, when Harrell and his wife were unable to repay their creditors, Piney Grove was put on the auction block and sold to the highest bidder. However, the farm's new owners defaulted on their debt and again, Piney Grove was sold at auction. This time, L. W. Lane and Moses R. Harrell were the high bidders. In 1873, when topographic engineers mapped the shoreline of the James River, they indicated that a number of structures were scattered throughout the Piney Grove tract, which consisted of woodland interspersed with marsh and cleared fields.[21]

James S. Morris and his wife, Frances, who owned Deep Bottom and the Fishery, two modest-sized farms just east of Piney Grove, also foundered in debt. As a result, their property was sold at auction. In time, their finances deteriorated to the point that Mrs. Morris had to sell some of her household furniture and personal effects.[22]

In 1876 Moses R. Harrell, having overcome some of the financial problems he experienced right after the war, bought Kingsmill, which he used as collateral when securing his purchase money. Later, he was obliged to sell the bulk of the tract to a partner. As co-investors, they had little success in turning a profit on their property.[23]

Newport Mills and Jockey's Neck

Goodrich Durfey, owner of the Newport Mills, had serious financial problems right after the war. He mortgaged his 100-acre mill farm and mill complex to John W. Lee (Lea), then defaulted on his debt. In 1881 Lea sold the property to William L. Jones, whose grist and saw mills are shown on an 1887 plat of the neighboring Neck O'Land farm. Jones, like Goodrich Durfey, fell on hard times and sold the Newport Mills and mill farm to Galba Vaiden, who quickly conveyed his real estate to the Peninsula Water Company. During the 1920s the property came into the possession of Floyd Powell, whose surname the millpond and dam still bear.

Goodrich Durfey, despite his financial hardships, retained Jockey's Neck, which he owned at the time of his death. His heirs partitioned the property and then sold it to L. Tyler Davis of Williamsburg, who retained it until the early 1890s. Jockey's Neck then came into the hands of a couple from Pennsylvania, who sold the farm to Lewis Layer of James City County. Layer eventually conveyed it to Isaac Johnson, whose successor was Charles E. Dean.[24]

Carter's Grove

After Virginia seceded from the Union, Lewis Ellison of Carter's Grove asked the Inspection Department of the Confederacy to compensate him for delivering mail to Williamsburg, a service he had provided before the war. After the war ended he, like many of his less prosperous neighbors, was overcome by debt. As a result, Carter's Grove reverted to the trustees and estate of former owner Thomas Wynne. In April 1869 Thomas G. Stratton of New York bought Carter's Grove and quickly sold it to Fanny Choles, another New Yorker. Mrs. Choles and her husband, Young, who were English immigrants, moved to Carter's Grove with their six children and set up housekeeping. They seemingly leased their farmland to tenants. Eventually, the Choles,' like Lewis Ellison, fell on hard times and were obliged to default on their mortgage. Again, the farm reverted to the trustees of the late Thomas Wynne. By 1876 another New York couple, Stephen and Mary Roberts, had bought Carter's Grove.[25]

The Drinking Spring Farm and Slater's Store

Richard E. Taylor, who owned the Drinking Spring farm near Olive Branch Christian Church, went bankrupt right after the Civil War. Fortunately, his son was able to purchase the family farm when it was placed upon the auction block. James S. Slater, the proprietor of Slater's Store, which was nearby, also had serious financial problems. He was obliged to mortgage his mercantile establishment, inventory of dry-goods, and food stuffs in order to obtain funds to support himself. Many of his problems were attributable to the fact that his debtors (mostly neighbors) were unable to pay their bills. When Slater finally was overwhelmed by debt, his creditors sold his store and its contents.[26] His situation, as a merchant, was not unique.

Olive Branch Christian Church. Photo by Ralph Maxwell.

The Six Mile Ordinary Farm

At the close of the Civil War, the widowed Elizabeth D. Taylor, owner of the Six Mile Ordinary, was severely encumbered by debt. She owned large sums of money to two mercantile firms and three local people. Many of her financial problems were attributable to her inability to collect from her debtors. Ultimately, she was obliged to deed her real estate to her son, Henley L. Taylor.[27]

Ewell Hall

Another local landowner who suffered financial ruin in the aftermath of the Civil War was William and Mary President Benjamin S. Ewell. In 1858 he bought a farm west of Williamsburg and within a year built the large frame mansion known as Ewell Hall. After the war, Ewell channeled his energies and personal resources into seeing that the college was reopened, seemingly neglecting his farm. As his financial plight worsened, he was forced to borrow substantial sums of money, and used his home farm as collateral. His wife was overcome by mental illness. Ewell was unable to repay his debts and as a result, the family farm was sold at a public auction. It was purchased by his daughter, Mrs. Elizabeth S. E. Scott, and her husband, Beverley, who also owned acreage at Kelton (Lightfoot).[28]

Jamestown Island

William Allen, who owned Jamestown Island, fared better than most James City County landowners, thanks to his immense wealth prior to the war. But thanks to his investment in slaves, he, too, suffered financial vicissitudes. He placed much of his land in the hands of tenants and sold some of his holdings. In May 1865, Allen leased Jamestown Island and the Neck O'Land tract to three men from New York, who were authorized to repair the farms' buildings and erect new ones. In December 1868, two years before the men's lease expired, Allen sold Jamestown Island to one of them, Israel Williams, who moved to James City County and began farming his land. By 1871, indebtedness forced Williams and his business partner to dispose of their property.

In 1874 Frederick Rollin of Brooklyn, New York, bought Jamestown Island. On May 15, 1877, his wife, Mamie, wrote a friend that there had been "quite a jubilee on the island yesterday." She said that excursion boats from Richmond and Norfolk arrived daily and would do so all summer. Despite the Rollins' fledgling tourist business, they defaulted on their mortgage and Jamestown Island was sold at auction in 1879.[29]

The Context of Everyday Life

Because the VIRGINIA GAZETTE went out of business right after the Civil War, local citizens were unable to express their political opinions in print in their home community. Newspapers in nearby Richmond reflected the views of the Conservative majority, which had little confidence in blacks' ability to adjust to their new circumstances and were not especially concerned about their failure. Sometimes written diatribes fanned the flames of bigotry. In 1873 one newspaper in West Virginia reported that "There have been more negroes hung for rape and murder during the last eight years of freedom, than altogether during the 240 years of their bondage in the United States. This is civilization with a vengeance!" Journalists, when reporting upon a crime, always mentioned the race of the accused, if the person was black.[30] This practice became almost universal throughout the South, including the local area, and endured for nearly a century.

But life also had levity. Students at the College of William and Mary sometimes got caught up in tomfoolery that ranged from stealing the college bell's clapper to playing elaborate jokes upon townspeople. One man recalled helping fellow students place carts and buggies on the roofs of buildings, move outbuildings into the streets, and pull other pranks known as "putting the town to rights." One April Fool's Day students lit a large bonfire behind the college's main building, just before midnight. Then they sounded an alarm. People, rudely awakened from their sleep, rushed to the campus only to discover the hoax. But social interaction between the students and local residents usually was much more sedate, for they attended parties, dances, shows, plays, musicals and other social events staged for their mutual enjoyment. There were two literary societies at the college and a few reading clubs. Spirited debates sometimes were held on campus and during the mid-1870s the Ugly Club was established for the purpose of choosing the ugliest, prettiest, wittiest, and laziest man. Students and local people sometimes gathered in the ballroom of the Eastern Lunatic Asylum, where dances were held. It is unclear how freely patients and visitors intermingled during such events. On June 15, 1870, classical music and a series of skits were provided by the 15th Amendment Troop, which performed at the asylum.

Despite the healing that had begun to occur, the wounds of war were still fresh and the women of Williamsburg and the surrounding area made regular pilgrimages to the town cemetery at Cedar Grove to decorate the graves of Confederate war dead. The Wise Light Infantry, a volunteer militia company, was organized during the summer of 1871. It paraded at the state fair and helped to unveil a Confederate monument in Richmond.[31]

The burial records of Olive Branch Christian Church in Norge reveal that many of the men interred in the church cemetery during the late nineteenth and early twentieth centuries were Confederate veterans and at least two had been in the Union Army. The Confederate dead included Richard C. Whitaker, D. R. Ratcliffe, C. W. Hubbard, James F. Hubbard, George W. Tyree, Peter T. Cowles, J. W. Hubbard, John Minor, R. E. Taylor, S. S. Hankins, George E. Richardson, G. W. Otey, George E. Richardson, R. P. James, R. M. (Dick) Garrett, W. B. Vaiden, G. W. Farthing, F. W. Hammond, Tom Wynne, Richard H. Whitaker Jr. and Sr., G. H. Piggott, Benjamin H. Ratcliffe, George E. Geddy, George W. Geddy, Pink Garrett, Dick Higgs, and E. Rogers. Two Union Army veterans, who made James City County their home, were John L. Waterman and Michael Connaughton.[32]

Some Local Place Names

Real estate tax rolls reveal that by the mid-nineteenth century many rural properties in James City County bore colorful, distinctive names. Some were historical in origin. Others were purely whimsical, had a geographic association, or were based upon the surname of a bygone owner. Kingsmill, Neck

O'Land, Jockey's Neck, the Grove (that is, Carter's Grove), Green Spring, Hot Water, Scotland, Pinewoods, Amblers, Mount Folly, Taskinask, Spratley's, Powhatan, and Rich Neck were among the seventeenth- and eighteenth-century names still in use. On the other hand, there were farms named Utopia Island, Lilliput, Alabama, Pudding Bottom, Hobby, and New Design that were a product of their owners' creativity. The names Marlbank, Aspen Grove, Cedar Grove, Riverview, Hickory Neck, Wheatland, Strawberry Fields, Meadowfield, Cloverdale, Peach Park, Hill Pleasant, Piney Meadow, Indigo Dam, Locust Grove, Greenhill, Piney Grove, Hot Water, Deep Bottom, Drinking Spring, and Camp Holly seem to describe their setting, whereas Short, Hog, Bush, Turner's, Mill, Pates Necks and Black Stump have a more strictly topographic association. The tracts called Barretts Ferry, Burnt Ordinary, Old Stonehouse, Fishhouse, Yarmouth, the Shipyard, and Allen's Ordinary made reference to sites or structures that were local landmarks. Perhaps somewhat less well known were the farms called Russell's, Hazelwood's, Warrenton, Ratcliffe's, Bushnel's, Tilledges, Tarpley's, Barnes', Watkins' and Blair's Thicket, which names were attributable to their association with a particular owner or family. Some of James City County's historical place names have been used by twentieth-century developers in designating the names of streets or subdivisions.[33] This continuity between past and present conveys a sense of pride in the county's heritage.

Notes
1. Robertson, CIVIL WAR, 174–176.
2. Netherton et al., FAIRFAX COUNTY, 371–372.
3. Nancy S. Bradshaw et al., VELKOMMEN TIL NORGE (Williamsburg, 1989), 20–21; Bradshaw, TALES, 96.
4. Penelope K. Majeske, Your Obedient Servant: The United States Army in Virginia During Reconstruction (Detroit, 1980), 29, 56.
5. C.W.F., RESOURCE PROTECTION, Section XII.
6. There are indications that some people's property was seized punitively.
7. Tindall, NARRATIVE HISTORY, 672–673; Bureau of Refugees, List of Confiscated Lands, 1862–1866.
8. Allen's land was seized on October 5, 1865.
9. Freedmen's Bureau, "Map Showing Position of Government Farms [for Freedmen in Southeastern Virginia]," 1866.

10. Chapman, Ewell, 175; Godson et al., WILLIAM AND MARY, 345; Suzanne Lebsock, A SHARE OF HONOUR: VIRGINIA WOMEN 1600–1945 (Charlottesville, 1985), 153; Virginius Dabney, VIRGINIA (Charlottesville, 1971), 369.

11. Tindall, NARRATIVE HISTORY, 674–677.

12. Morton, THE NEGRO, 15–17; VIRGINIA POLITICS, 27, 30, 50, 57, 59–60; Manerin et al., HENRICO COUNTY, 310–311, 314; Bottom, GENERAL ASSEMBLY, 249.

13. Manerin et al., HENRICO COUNTY, 317–320; Gaines, "Courthouses," 30; Robert F. Walker, comp., ACTS AND JOINT RESOLUTIONS PASSED BY THE GENERAL ASSEMBLY OF THE STATE OF VIRGINIA PASSED DURING THE SESSION OF 1871–1872 (Richmond, 1872), 217, 331.

14. Manerin et al., HENRICO, 329–330; Netherton et al., FAIRFAX COUNTY, 399–400.

15. U.S.D.A., Abridged List of Federal Laws Applicable to Agriculture (Washington, D. C., 1949).

16. U.S.D.A., Status of Virginia Agriculture in 1870, REPORT OF THE COMMISSIONER OF AGRICULTURE, 1870 (Washington, 1870), 269–270; Anonymous, One Hundred Years of Agriculture (n.p., n.d.).

17. Director's Report 1869:29–30; 1872:10; 1873:8–9; Director's Minutes 1875–1887:18; 1883:23; 1900:28–29.

18. Godson et al., WILLIAM AND MARY, 333–337, 343–344, 348–349, 360–361; James City County Deed Book 5:253; 8:401.

19. James City County Deed Book 2:54–56, 344–345.

20. James City County Deed Book 2:424, 498; 3:302, 328–329; McCartney, GREEN SPRING.

21. James City County Land Tax Lists 1866–1876; C. P. Patterson, "James River, Virginia, College Creek to Chickahominy River," 1873–1874.

22. James City County Deed Book 5:472–473, 557.

23. James City County Deed Book 4:338–339, 388.

24. James City County Deed Book 2:33, 126–127, 150, 153; 4:473, 507; 5:488, 513; 6:89–90, 436–437; 7:326–327, 443; 8:308; 9:220, 590; Land Tax Lists 1885–1900.

25. James City County Agricultural Census 1860; Powers, "the Grove," 15–17; Stephenson, CARTER'S GROVE, 96–109.

26. James City County Deed Book 4:162, 167.

27. James City County Deed Book 2:449, 510; 3:89; 4:58; 5:27.

28. James City County Deed Book 5:253; 8:401.

29. James City County Deed Book 2:198, 204, 281, 394, 426–427; 3:48–51, 503–505; Mamie Rollin, May 15, 1877 letter.

30. Netherton et al., FAIRFAX COUNTY, 44.

31. Godson et al., WILLIAM AND MARY, 397–398; VIRGINIA GAZETTE, May 27, 1869; June 8, 1870.

32. Olive Branch Church Cemetery Record Notebooks I and II.

33. James City County Land Tax Lists 1862.

CHAPTER 13

"Brighter Times A-Coming"
1881–1917

The Struggle for Control

In 1883 Governor William Mahone and his "Readjusters," who fell into disfavor with Virginia voters, were swept from office. They were replaced by members of the Conservative party, who won control of the General Assembly. James City County was then in an electoral district that included Elizabeth City, Warwick, and York Counties. By 1893 James City had been placed in a somewhat larger district that included New Kent, Charles City, York, and Warwick Counties plus the city of Williamsburg. During the 1893 county elections Edward Taylor of James City County was arrested and fined for "intimidating voters."[1]

Two laws were enacted at the 1887 session of the General Assembly in response to James City County citizens' petitions. L. M. Robinson of Green Spring and D. S. Jones, whose property was just above Skiff's Creek's mouth, received permission to erect wharves at their landings on the James River so that they could ship wood products to market. In 1887 Virginia's Boards of Supervisors were authorized to subdivide their counties into precincts so that land could be processioned in an orderly manner. This procedure, a throw-back to the colonial period when parish vestries walked property boundaries with neighboring landowners, was adopted by officials in some of the counties whose court records were destroyed during the Civil War. It was an adjunct means of creating a legal basis for land ownership and boundary line configurations. James City County processioners records reveal that property owners, under oath, described their boundaries in the presence of neighbors and local officials. Sometimes, they also recounted how they had come into possession of their acreage.[2]

As Virginia moved into the 1890s, Conservative party members began devising strategies intended to restrict the voting rights of blacks. In 1894 the General Assembly passed the Walton Law, which gave voters only two-and-a-half minutes to mark their ballots and stipulated that an election judge had to be present when voting occurred. This measure decreased the number of black voters and paved the way for more aggressive changes. In 1901 the majority of delegates to the state constitutional convention decided that no one could register to vote unless he could spontaneously read and explain any section of the state constitution. Moreover, payment of three years' poll tax, six months before general elections, became a prerequisite to voting. M. H. Barnes represented James City and four other counties, plus the cities of Williamsburg and Newport News, in the 1901-1902 state constitutional convention. Virginia's new constitution and voting restrictions became law on May 29, 1902. As a result, the number of qualified black voters in the state dropped from 147,000 to only 21,000, fewer than half of whom had met the poll tax requirement. Although blacks brought the issue of voting rights to the attention of the United States Supreme Court, its justices decided not to intervene in what they considered a state perogative. Disfranchising large numbers of blacks left much of the state's population without a voice in political affairs.[3]

During the late nineteenth and early twentieth centuries laws were passed that legalized racial segregation. These so-called "Jim Crow laws" required the segregation of public facilities such as hotels, theaters, restaurants, and auditoriums; transportation systems such as railroad coaches, streetcars, steamboats, and busses; privately-owned business establishments; and housing.[4] Most predominantly white churches denied access to blacks or discouraged their attendance. Although an 1870 law made it a felony for "any person to conspire with another to incite the white population to make insurrection against the colored population," between 1882 and 1928, 88 Virginia blacks were executed vigilante-style. This led to passage of an anti-lynch law.

In 1912 the General Assembly legalized neighborhood segregation, but during the late 1920s Virginia's law, like Louisiana's, was struck down by the United States Supreme Court. In James City County, blacks outnumbered whites until 1910 by which time there was full scale segregation of public services and housing. During the 19-teens, however, the number of blacks began to decline as they moved elsewhere in search of jobs and greater opportunities. After Booker T. Washington's death in 1915, an organization called the National Association for the Advancement of Colored People (NAACP) assumed a position of leadership among blacks.[5]

The Coming of the Railroad

During the late nineteenth century James City County was considered progressive and many of its citizens were optimistic about the future. Steamboats transported mail, passengers, and freight to and from the county and a network of public roads provided overland access to the outside world. In 1881 when the Chesapeake and Ohio Railroad (C&O) built a rail line connecting Richmond to Newport News, a flag-stop called Vaiden's Siding (later,

The Diascund Train Station. Photo by Nan Maxwell.

Norge) came into existence approximately two miles east of Burnt Ordinary (renamed Toano) and depots were built at Grove and Ewell. Regular freight and passenger service was established by June 1882. The coming of the railroad stimulated the local economy, for it gave farmers convenient access to urban markets and regular mail service became available. But not everyone was pleased with the C&O. In May 1894 the editor of the VIRGINIA GAZETTE claimed that "The C & O has made itself obnoxious to our citizens in many ways" and said that an alternative rail system would be welcome.[6]

The availability of telegraph service accompanied the arrival of the railroad. It, too, stimulated business interests. In 1896 the Western Union Telegraph Company opened a "commercial reporting office" at the C&O's Grove depot. Toano, which contained a train depot, freight station, a hotel, stores, and a bank, was a focal point of commercial activity. Its prominence as an agricultural center was linked to the numerous advances made in farming technology, which heightened productivity. One of James City County's most important crops was potatoes, which were packed in wooden barrels and shipped to Richmond and beyond. Toano had a barrel factory and, when potato production was at its peak, was the largest revenue-producing freight-stop on the C&O route between Newport News and Richmond. Near the intersection of what became Old Forge Road and Route 60 was Toano's public well.[7]

In 1896 C&O land agent Carl Bergh purchased a farm near Vaiden's Siding, midway between Lightfoot and Toano, and began promoting the development of a planned community. As a Norwegian immigrant, he quickly perceived that the area's cheap land, temperate climate, and good soil would appeal to Scandinavians and other Europeans who had settled in the Midwest but suffered greatly from the harsh winters. Bergh prepared multi-lingual promotional pamphlets, encouraging Norwegian, Danish, Swedish, and German immigrants to move to Virginia. Between 1898 and 1902, 61 families moved from the Midwest to James City County and established the community known as Norge.[8]

At a canning factory in Toano, close to the train depot, local farmers' green beans, peas, and tomatoes were processed and their cucumbers were made into pickles. Neighborhood merchants sold oysters in the shell, which they kept cool with damp burlap bags, and Walter Martin's general store in Toano carried everything from custom-made suits and shoes to groceries and baked goods. After the automobile became popular, Toano's livery stable was replaced by a couple of Model-T Fords that were used as taxis or jitneys. R. K. Taylor, who repaired farming equipment, began working on motor vehicles and opened an automobile repair shop that developed into a thriving business. Toano also had a barber shop equipped with billiard tables. Among the businesses in Norge were Hans Kinde's general store, a blacksmith shop, and a gristmill that stood next to the Norge Hall. The Rustads, who were carpenters and cabinetmakers, manufactured everything from kitchen cabinets to custom-made furniture, using lumber they processed in their own sawmill and dressing mill.[9]

THE PENINSULA NEWS

At the turn of the twentieth century western James City County had its own newspaper, THE PENINSULA NEWS, which was produced in Toano by editor-publisher W. Walker Ware and business manager D. Warren Marston. The newspaper appeared on the first and third Saturdays of each month. Local people were encouraged to subscribe to the PENINSULA NEWS, which cost 50 cents a year, to bolster their community's development. Surviving issues of the newspaper reveal that it contained a hodge-podge of local news, book reviews, advertisements, horticultural advice, obituaries, jokes, and occasional editorials. On September 7, 1901, the PENINSULA NEWS reported that C. T. Cowles and his daughter, Ellen, were thrown from their buggy when one of its wheels was struck by those of "some reckless person . . . going at full speed in the opposite direction." Two weeks later, the death of Cornelius H. Richardson of Cloverdale was reported, as was President William McKinley's assassination. The editor of the PENINSULA NEWS heaped "the bitterest condemnation" upon the assassin although he admitted that he didn't share the late president's political views. Business manager D. Warren Marston invited people to leave their dirty clothes at his general store in Toano for shipment to a steam laundry in Richmond and Mrs. W. H. Braithwaite, a Williamsburg undertaker and store-keeper, advertised that her firm accepted telephone orders and that her hearses (black for men, white for women) would be "sent anywhere." The Toano Livery's proprietor, B. H. Ratcliffe, offered to furnish teams on short notice and M. G. Davis, "The Practical House Painter," claimed that carriage work was a specialty. R. E. Richardson and George W. Jones operated general stores in Toano, where they swapped goods for country produce. Jones also did blacksmithing. In the September 7, 1901, issue of the PENINSULA NEWS, the editor asked local farmers to consider holding an agricultural fair the following fall and to decide whether neighboring counties should be invited to participate. It was announced that on October 18, 1901, work would begin on an electric railroad between Toano and West Point.[10]

THE VIRGINIA GAZETTE

During the early 1890s, the VIRGINIA GAZETTE resumed publication. It included the latest local, national, and international news, lavishly embellished with the publisher's opinions. The back pages of the GAZETTE were sprinkled with florid advertisements that hawked everything from patent medicines to professional services and real estate. In October 1893 the GAZETTE reported that "another mad dog" had passed through Toano, causing "a great deal of excitement," and a big fire destroyed the Branch and Company Store and a nearby house. Another calamity involved a runaway horse that dashed down Duke of Gloucester Street, wagon in tow. After careening wildly from side to side, it overturned, injuring several people. In March 1894, Jones Mill was destroyed by fire. Owner D. S. Jones said he planned to rebuild and suspected the blaze was "the work of a fire dink."[11]

The VIRGINIA GAZETTE had society columns that carried news of local families' comings-and-goings. The Eastern State Lunatic Asylum's employees, like the residents of Lightfoot, Toano, and Poquoson, also had a society column. The activities of Sam Harris, owner of "the Cheap Store," were reported in the GAZETTE. As he was the only black (other than lawbreakers) who received news coverage, his inclusion may have been attributable to his sponsorship of large, costly advertisements. One of the most poignant items that appeared in the VIRGINIA GAZETTE during the 1890s was an advertisement placed by a former slave who sought to locate her children, sold away from her before the Civil War. In June 1894, members of the Ewell-Magruder Camp of Confederate Veterans took the train to Richmond, where they attended the unveiling of a monument to General Robert E. Lee. Some men shipped their horses to the state capital so that they could ride in a parade that accompanied the ceremony. Later in the summer, local Confederate veterans organized a youth group known as the Sons of Veterans of the Ewell-Magruder Camp. Veterans, both North and South, were honored annually on Decoration Day, May 31st, forerunner of our modern Memorial Day. The VIRGINIA GAZETTE carried news of the Williamsburgers, a local baseball team that played opponents from Providence Forge, Norge, and other small communities.[12]

The VIRGINIA GAZETTE's editorials reflect the boosterism that characterized the 1890s. The editor publicized the fact that the peninsula welcomed Northern capital. The Williamsburg Land Company, which had farmland for sale in James City, York, Elizabeth City, and Warwick Counties along with Williamsburg and Newport News, began placing large advertisements intended to reach prospective land buyers throughout the United States. On October 28, 1899, a notice in the VIRGINIA GAZETTE stated that men from Williamsburg, James City, and York Counties were going to meet to form a Businessmen's Association. Their organization was the forerunner of what became the Chamber of Commerce.[13]

Modern Communication

One modernizing change that occurred just before the turn of the twentieth century was local telephone service. Around 1890 the area's first telephone was installed in a Williamsburg residence, at a time when the city's population was 1,831. In October 1900 James City County's Board of Supervisors authorized the Chesapeake Telephone and Telegraph Company to install telephone poles and lines along the county's public roads. Apparently, little or no effort was made to control where utility lines were placed, for in 1904 the C.T.&T.'s successor, the Long Distance Telephone Company of Virginia, was ordered "to remove all poles obstructing the public road." In

1908 the Jamestown Farmers Telephone Company was given permission to extend service into rural areas adjacent to public roads. By 1917 there were 126 telephones in service in James City County and Williamsburg.[14]

Agriculture, Backbone of the County's Economy

In 1880 Congress passed an appropriation act to underwrite the purchase and distribution of hybrid seeds, bulbs, and other plant materials to American farmers. Four years later the Bureau of Animal Industry was established for the purpose of preventing the spread of contagious livestock diseases. It became illegal to import and export diseased livestock and to ship infected herds within the United States. The centrifugal cream separator, the combine, and the disk harrow came on the market and by 1890 the gang plow was in general use. Corn husking and shredding machines were developed during the early 1890s and the two-row cultivator became available. Farmers learned that by maximizing the use of horse-power, 20 to 40 animals could work 70 to 80 acres in a day. Around 1906 the first gasoline-powered engines were put to use on farms. A few years later the kerosene tractor became available. All of these advances in agricultural technology greatly enhanced the American farmer's efficiency and productivity. For example in 1830 it took a farmer 61 hours to harvest 20 bushels of grain; in 1900 the same task took less than three hours. The operator of a corn sheller replaced 50 field-hands. Potato planters, manure spreaders, and hay driers all contributed to the considerable progress made in American farming.[15]

Agricultural census records for James City County, compiled in 1880, shed a considerable amount of light upon farming practices. Most local farmers placed approximately a fifth of their land under cultivation and left another two-fifths in pastures, meadows, or orchards; the remaining acreage typically consisted of woodlands. Almost half of James City County's farmers relied upon hired labor, whose assistance was required for nearly half the year. Nearly 80 percent of local farmers kept dairy cattle and 90 percent had swine and barnyard fowl. Almost everyone grew corn, with a lesser number producing wheat and oats. Approximately 70 percent of local farms were involved in timber production.[16]

In 1887 Congress authorized the establishment of agricultural experiment stations under the direction of state land grant colleges. Later, funding was made available for research. The close of the decade saw the creation of forest reserves (now known as National Forests) from public lands and the establishment of the Weather Bureau. The twentieth century brought federal legislation that regulated the quality of milk, butter, butter oil, and meat. Other laws required fungicides, pesticides, and herbicides to be labeled properly. A 1912 plant quarantine act was intended to curb the spread of plant diseases and insect pests within the United States. The Agricultural Extension (or Smith-Lever) Act authorized land grant colleges to offer public instruction in agriculture and home economics and to distribute information useful to rural households. This legislation gave rise to the Cooperative Extension Service, whose agents traditionally have served James City County under the auspices of Virginia Tech. In 1928 funding became available to bring the 4-H program to rural youngsters.[17]

James City County's Board of Supervisors and Their Duties

The first recorded meeting of the James City County Board of Supervisors was held on September 10, 1887, in the city-county courthouse. Board members attended on behalf of the Jamestown, Powhatan, and Stonehouse Districts. The minutes of subsequent meetings suggest that prior to 1891 Board members convened on an as-needed basis, with little heed to a regular schedule. In 1904 Board members decided to begin meeting on the fourth Monday of every month except January, when according to law, they were obliged to convene on the first Monday. Early Board minutes indicate that much of the three Supervisors' time was devoted to making decisions about road maintenance, which also consumed the bulk of their funds.[18] Each of the county's three districts had a paid superintendent (overseer or surveyor) of roads, whose responsibility it was to see that public thoroughfares were kept in good repair. Conflict of interest apparently wasn't an issue, for the local circuit court judge appointed the entire Board of Supervisors as road superintendents, which entitled them to a salary. Each superintendent was supposed to hire a local "low bidder" to drag (smooth) the surface of the public roads in his district and to grade them with gravel and fill potholes. Local citizens also were employed to shore up, resurface, or construct the county's wooden bridges. For example, in January 1887, W. T. Cowles was paid $25 for building a bridge over a dirt dam in the Jamestown District and in 1891 John M. Jennings and R. P. Wright were compensated for repairing the wooden bridges across Diascund Creek. Meanwhile, Robert Hornsby was credited with repairing the Drinking Spring Road; William Apperson received funds for working on Piggott's Mill Road, and Robert Wright made repairs to the Cranston Mill Road. In August 1892 the Supervisors were informed that rising waters sometimes made the stream at Blows Mill dangerous to ford. In accord with the law, they asked the circuit court judge to appoint a special commission to determine whether a bridge was needed and if so, to see that it was built. Board minutes for December 1893 reveal that the special commissioners acted illegally, for they had the bridge built without seeking a low bid. This created a flap among the supervisors.[19]

In 1890 the superintendent of public roads in each of Virginia's magisterial districts gained the right to require all males between the ages of 18 and 60 to do road work two days a year. Those who refused were fined, which funds were applied toward road repairs. The road repair act, which was highly unpopular, was repealed in 1894. Four years later the responsibility of repairing and maintaining public roads and bridges was relegated to the state's Boards of Supervisors, rather than specially-appointed overseers.[20] This procedure already was in place in James City County.

In 1897 James City County's Board of Supervisors received complaints that Green Spring's owner had erected gates across the public road that passed through his property. When asked to remove them, he resisted, for he said that the public road ran through his pasture and that open gates would allow his livestock to escape. In February 1898 Virginia's Boards of Supervisors were authorized to hire contractors or day labor to perform road repairs. They also had the right to purchase teams of draft animals, road machinery, tools, and other implements for use in repairing local thoroughfares. In 1911 a private group called the Peninsula Good Road Association asked the Board of Supervisors for funds to improve the eastern end of Route 60's forerunner, which extended through the lower peninsula. When the road was realigned,

Board members insisted that it pass through Grove rather than Halstead's Point. The General Assembly gave Boards of Supervisors taxing authority so that they could raise the funds that were needed to maintain public roads. A 1916 law permitted them to contract with any person or company willing to maintain public highways, as long as local voters approved.[21]

Another responsibility that fell to county Board of Supervisors was maintaining the public water supply. During the 19-teens James City County's Board disbursed funds to several people for repairing or cleaning public wells at Croaker, Lightfoot, Toano, and Diascund. The supervisors also worked with state officials in preventing the spread of livestock diseases and on several occasions ordered diseased animals' owners to bury or cremate their carcasses. Licensing fees went into the county Dog Fund, which reimbursed local citizens whose livestock was killed by dogs. During World War I the James City County Board of Supervisors allocated funds to the Boys Corn Club and the Girls Canning Club, which like their successors, the 4-H Clubs, promoted an interest in farm life and agriculture.[22]

During the late 1880s and throughout the 1890s the local economy was depressed and in 1894 John M. Dawson, joint treasurer of James City County and Williamsburg, received the General Assembly's permission to delay the collection of taxes. In 1900 treasurer Thomas G. Wynne sought—and received—extra time to collect the taxes that had come due in 1895, 1896, and 1897. In 1894 the local circuit court judge was authorized to appoint a county surveyor and a superintendent of the poor, taking into account the Board of Supervisors' recommendations. The Board, instead of building or renting a poorhouse like some localities did, decided to compensate those who provided for the needy, a system akin to the colonial State Church's approach to public welfare. A page loosely inserted into one Board of Supervisors minute book reveals that in 1915 Drs. E. T. Gatewood, D. J. King, H. U. Stephenson, George A. Hankins, and Albert Snead received funds for providing medical assistance to the poor and Mrs. W. H. Braithwaite was paid for a coffin her funeral establishment had built.[23]

During the 1890s the General Assembly placed restrictions on hunting certain types of game. It became illegal to kill ducks, geese, turkeys, muskrat, and sora rails in James City County after dark. In 1902 partridges, quail, hares, rabbits, and deer were off-limits to local hunters between February 15th and November 15th each year and in 1916 squirrels were added to the list. Bounties were paid to those who brought in crow and hawk bills as proof they had destroyed what were considered pest birds.[24]

At the close of the nineteenth century state officials began taking an active role in promoting public health. In March 1899 the James City County Board of Supervisors passed a resolution requiring smallpox vaccinations. Simultaneously, the Board designated a certain dwelling on Robert P. Wright's farm as a "pest house," where smallpox patients could be quarantined. The building formerly was occupied by a black man named Madison Lightfoot. A year later a yellow fever scare swept the peninsula.[25]

The 1897 Earthquake

Another type of potential disaster literally sent ripples of fear throughout the peninsula during the 1890s. On May 31, 1897, around 2 P.M., an earthquake jarred eastern Virginia and portions of ten other states. In Richmond, buildings swayed violently and a deep rumbling noise was heard, followed by sharp cracking. The ground's upheaval reportedly made some people seasick. In Newport News, "several large buildings tottered and bricks fell from the chimneys" and in Norfolk and Portsmouth, people reportedly "rushed into the streets panic stricken." According to the June 5, 1897, edition of the VIRGINIA GAZETTE, around 2 o'clock in the afternoon, "the people of Williamsburg were startled by a rumbling sound and the rattle of window-glass and furniture in their houses." The earthquake lasted for approximately five minutes and involved movement that traveled from south to north.[26]

The County at the Close of the Century

In late 1898 or early 1899 the VIRGINIA GAZETTE published a Williamsburg and James City County business directory intended to promote the area's development. It provides a wealth of general information on the local community. The Honorable Sydney Smith was judge of the county court whereas J. W. G. Blackstone was the Circuit Court judge and Thomas H.

Geddy served as clerk of the city and county courts. Cyrus A. Branch was commonwealth attorney and Moses R. Harrell was James City County's sheriff with W. Walker Ware as deputy.[27] In 1898 Thomas G. Wynne served as county treasurer and S. S. Hankins as commissioner of revenue, with Peter T. Cowles as the superintendent of schools and Andrew J. Barnes as the superintendent of the poor. The three member county Board of Supervisors was chaired by W. B. Vaiden.

There were post offices in Toano, Lightfoot, Diascund, Ewell, Bacon, Hotwater, Jamestown, Pyrite, Croaker, Grove, and Williamsburg, where local people received their mail, and the business directory listed who got mail at each. Among those who placed advertisements in the directory were W. L. Spencer, a local auctioneer, and Mrs. W. H. Braithwaite, who boasted that her undertaking establishment had been in business since 1823 and that she provided a complete line of caskets and burial robes "with hearse and wagon free." L. T. Hankins, proprietor of a general store in Lightfoot, offered to exchange goods for "country produce such as corn, peanuts, and cordwood," whereas merchant W. Walker Ware of Toano advertised that he sold cordwood and railroad ties. Norvell L. Henley had a law office in Williamsburg and a branch office in Toano's Hotel Felix, where he received clients every Thursday, and commonwealth attorney Cyrus A. Branch had an office in Toano. An advertisement for the steamer POCAHONTAS noted that it made regular stops at Jamestown, a popular tourist attraction.

The editors of the GAZETTE's business directory noted that James City County then had 19 schools, 11 of which served whites, and Episcopal, Methodist, Baptist, and "Christian" churches. They said that "Trucking and general farming are the principal occupations of the people" and added that thousands of cords of pine, oak, and ash and great quantities of lumber were shipped from the county annually. Toano was described as "a great trucking center" from which many boxcar loads of melons, sweet and Irish potatoes, peas, and other vegetables were sent to northern and western markets. Corn was listed as a staple product although wheat, oats, and other cereal crops were raised in abundance. The local soil was described as excellent for growing peanuts and fruit, such as apples, peaches, pears, plums, grapes, cherries, strawberries, and raspberries. Approximately half of James City County's acreage was forested and pine, oak, ash, walnut, chestnut, and hickory grew in abundance. Fishing was an important local industry, for Diascund Creek was noted for its herring, the Chickahominy River for its shad and perch, the James River for shad, rock and sturgeon, and the York River for its oysters, trout and other fish species. Game reportedly was plentiful in the county's forests and marshes.[28]

C&O Service During the Early Twentieth Century

In 1906 the Board of Supervisors called a special meeting to discuss the C&O's proposal to relocate its tracks between Norge and Lanexa and to build overhead bridges across the highway in Toano and Norge. A year later, the Supervisors agreed to allow the C&O to construct a bridge across the tracks at Lightfoot. A Toano man, born in 1895, recalled when the railroad ran through the center of town, close to the town well, and he remembered the tracks' being moved to their present location and a new depot's being built. He said that one morning he and some friends were having breakfast in the Hotel Felix when they heard a loud noise from the direction of the new depot. Hurrying to the site, they discovered that a locomotive from the "fast freight known as 'the 95'" had had a head-on collision with an engine from a work train. No one reportedly was injured. Passengers on the "through train" sometimes disembarked for a hurried meal at the Hotel Felix.[29]

Quite a few men and women from James City County commuted by train to Williamsburg, where they had jobs. People from various parts of the county worked in the Williamsburg Knitting Mill, a manufacturer of men's underwear, which plant was located near the city train depot. One local woman recalled that the tracks of the C&O originally ran down the center of Duke of Gloucester Street, which was illuminated by gaslights. She said that young women from the Female Institute, accompanied by chaperones, sometimes attended movies at the theater run by Mrs. Wolfe. Ice skating on Lake Matoaka and sledding on the snowy slopes by Eastern State Hospital also provided entertainment.[30]

The College of William and Mary

Although the college reopened in 1869, in 1881 it was forced to close due to a lack of funds. In 1888 it became viable again, thanks to Lyon G. Tyler, who modernized and expanded the curriculum and established a state-funded normal school or teacher-training program. Later, the Matthew Whaley Model and Practice School was established, which trained teachers and fulfilled a local need. The college's education curriculum attracted growing numbers of prospective teachers and a summer program of continuing education brought a seasonal influx of "school marms." These changes put William and Mary at the forefront of Virginia education and significantly strengthened its financial position. In 1893, the bicentennial of the college's royal charter, a special celebration was held. During the late nineteenth and early twentieth centuries William and Mary's facilities were enhanced through the addition of several new buildings. The college's landholdings, largely in James City County, then included the main campus, a small plot on the north side of Jamestown Road, and some property on the Palace Green that contained the Mattey School. In 1915, when Williamsburg annexed some James City County land, the college's original campus and some land peripheral to the oldest part of the city were encompassed.[31]

The Williamsburg-James City County Courthouse

In November 1901 the James City County Board of Supervisors voted to build a fireproof office for the clerk of court, a detached structure situated on the green to the west of the courthouse. This was a fortunate decision, for in April 1911 the courthouse James City County and Williamsburg had shared since the 1770s was gutted by fire. County and city officials agreed to remodel the old building, whose walls were still standing, instead of constructing a new one. It was then that Doric columns were added to the front portico of the colonial courthouse, reportedly to give it "a distinctly Federal look." The rebuilt courthouse was in use for two more decades.[32]

The County Seat at the Turn of the Century

On January 1st each year, Williamsburg blacks held an annual celebration for Emancipation and Proclamation Day, the anniversary of President Lincoln's freeing the slaves. Marchers, horses with ribbon-braided manes and tails, buggies and carriages decked out with crepe paper streamers, and sometimes a band from Richmond or Newport News, followed a parade route that extended from the Odd Fellows Hall to the college and back. The event always attracted a large turnout.

The community as a whole made immense progress during the 1880s and '90s. In 1887 the Peninsula Bank and Trust Company was established; its first Board of Directors included a number of men from James City County. The late 1890s saw the construction of an ice plant, a steam laundry, and the Williamsburg Canning Company. The Williamsburg Knitting Mill, which employed approximately 200 people, opened its doors in 1900 but went bankrupt within a decade. An advertisement in the VIRGINIA GAZETTE promised a free site at Kingsmill to anyone who would build a stave factory there. Modern improvements, such as sewer and water lines, were installed in Williamsburg just before World War I, at which time the old community well by the courthouse was back-filled.[33]

Cabell B. H. Phillips, a Williamsburg native, described the city's appearance during the early twentieth century. He said that there were a few new store fronts along Duke of Gloucester Street and that the old knitting mill had been converted into a smoke-belching power plant. Fred Kelley, a former livery stable operator, began selling Ford automobiles. Phillips spoke of the town's "shabby, somnolent and yet proudly aristocratic pre-restoration days" when residents pridefully recalled their kinship with their Revolutionary forebears. At Bruton Parish Church an annual service was held on May 13th to commemorate the arrival of the first Jamestown colonists. Phillips said that a few local landmarks, such as the college's main building and the Blair house, were prized for their antiquity and grace, but most of the town's older buildings were still occupied and "It was considered preferable to let them slowly crumble away rather than to deface them with new roofs or joists or plumbing." He said that many of the town's residences had "incongruous porches or lean-to additions that had accumulated on them like barnacles."

The churchyard and wharf at Jamestown Island. Virginia Navigation Company, AFLOAT ON THE JAMES, 1903.

Duke of Gloucester Street, which had neither pavement nor gutters, was "a mile long, a hundred feet wide and two feet deep" and lined with buildings that ranged from very old to very new. Private residences were intermingled with businesses and some buildings served more than one purpose. Bruton Parish's elderly sexton sometimes took visitors on tours of the church grave-yard and according to Cabell B. H. Phillips, could "find an ancestor for almost anybody among the faded and indecipherable inscriptions." Although the palace green still consisted of open space, a Confederate monument had been erected at one end and "a fiery red brick school had been set virtually on the foundations of the Governor's Palace, at the other." Upon the site once occupied by Chowning's Tavern was the Colonial Inn, Williamsburg's main hotel, and opposite the city-county courthouse were buildings that housed the post office, the bank, and offices of the six or so lawyers who handled most local cases. Near the colonial powder magazine (known to locals as the Powder Horn) were some unpainted shanties occupied by blacks. Phillips said that upon the site originally occupied by the Raleigh Tavern was the store of the Lane brothers, former officers in the Confederate Army. At the end of Duke of Gloucester Street was a plaque that marked the foundations of the colonial capitol. At that point, Duke of Gloucester Street flared into a V, with side streets that led to Francis Street and Capitol Landing Road.

On court days, farmers came into town to trade and often sat under the trees near the courthouse, where they exchanged the latest news. Williamsburg's main business, other than serving as the seat of the city and county court and the district court, revolved around the College of William and Mary and the state-run asylum, which in 1894 became known as Eastern State Hospital. Cabell B. H. Phillips quoted one inmate as quipping that in Williamsburg, "one thousand lazy live off five hundred crazy."

The pace of life was so notoriously slow that a May 14, 1913, editorial in the RICHMOND TIMES-DISPATCH claimed that Williamsburg's residents not only forgot to hold an election, they also failed to budget the $50 it cost to

The steamship POCAHONTAS. Courtesy of Margaret N. Weston.

re-wind the town clock. According to the newspaper's tongue-in-cheek editorial, the residents of "Lotusburg" decided not to have the clock in Bruton
Parish Church's tower wound because they hoped to stop time. He claimed
they "tried abolishing the calendar, but time kept up. Now they will kill time
by stopping the clock." He added that "The native Williamsburger never stirs.
He never lets his anger be aroused for fear it should arouse the rest of him.
He regards a fever as a breach of decorum."[34]

In December 1908 a group of local women, who learned that the state
had traveling libraries for loan to localities, decided to order one which was
placed in Mrs. George Coleman's home. In March 1910 the same ladies
opened the community's first real library in a store on Duke of Gloucester
Street. Its eclectic assortment of books included those on loan from the state
and others donated by friends of the library. This small but important source
of culture was available to the public two half-days a week. Later in the year
when Carter's Grove's owner died, the local library purchased 250 volumes
from his executors for only $20. The decedent's sisters, who knew of his

**The West Virginia house, built for the Jamestown Exposition. Photo by
Nan Maxwell.**

interest in Williamsburg's having a public library, also collected and donated numerous books as a memorial to their brother. In 1925 the Williamsburg City Council allocated $250 toward the salary of a paid staff member for the local library. This was the genesis of public support for what became the Williamsburg Regional Library.[35]

Jamestown, the Area's Premier Historic Attraction

The approach of Jamestown's 300th anniversary generated a considerable amount of excitement, for the celebrations of 1807, 1827, and 1857 demonstrated that there was a great deal of public interest in commemorating the first colonists' landing. By the early 1890s preparations had gotten underway for the May 13, 1907, celebration. On March 1, 1892, several months before Edward E. and Louise Barney of Dayton, Ohio, purchased Jamestown Island, the General Assembly conveyed the state's legal interest in the church ruins and graveyard to the Association for the Preservation of

Some of Toano's old buildings. Photo by Ralph Maxwell.

Virginia Antiquities. The A.P.V.A also had the right to acquire a right-of-way to the property via condemnation and to erect a bridge. The state's interest in the church property stemmed from its reversionary right to land once owned by colonial Virginia's Established Church. In May 1893 the Barneys formally deeded 22 1/2 acres to the A.P.V.A., including the property the state already had bestowed upon the organization. The Barneys and the A.P.V.A. agreed to share the cost of constructing "a wall or some other permanent means of preventing the further washing and caving of the bank" at the western end of Jamestown Island.[36]

One local resident, who witnessed the concrete seawall's construction, said that the laborers who built it earned $1.25 or $1.50 a day. The majority were blacks from the Five Forks area, who reported for work at 7 each morning and typically put in a 10-hour day shoveling cement.[37] Colonel Samuel H. Yonge of the United States Corps of Engineers, who oversaw the construction of the seawall, not only was a skillful engineer but also a diligent scholar whose antiquarian interests led him to explore the island's history and its archaeological features. His publication of THE SITE OF OLD JAMES TOWNE in 1904 provided many insights into the ancient settlement's history.

The Norge Baseball Team. Courtesy of Frances H. Hamilton and Nancy S. Bradshaw.

Articles that appeared in the VIRGINIA GAZETTE in 1893 reveal that Jamestown Island's owner, Edward E. Barney, who was a millionaire and president of the Virginia Navigation Company, planned to turn it into a tourist mecca. He proposed building a large, modern hotel that would "bring to that famous spot myriads of tourists and pleasure seekers." He also hoped to construct an electric railway between Jamestown and Williamsburg that would promote visitation. However, Barney's spokesman told the press that he sought local investors for his projects and would wait for "a ground-swell of interest" before he'd undertake construction. Meanwhile he built a wharf that had a large warehouse, storeroom and pavilion and he planned to erect a bridge from Jamestown Island to the mainland. Between June 1893 and June 1894 an estimated 5,000 tourists flocked to Jamestown Island, despite the poor roads connecting the historic site with Williamsburg. During May 1894, the VIRGINIA GAZETTE reported that the Barneys' employees were busily clearing underbrush, reclaiming marsh land, and developing Jamestown Island into a truck farm and place of scenic beauty. But in February 1895 ice that encrusted the James River ripped away part of the Barneys' wharf and in late March, a fire destroyed their brick mansion, leaving its charred walls to tower over the landscape. While the Barneys owned Jamestown Island, the palace steamer POCAHONTAS made regular stops there. The POCAHONTAS reportedly was 205 feet long, 57 feet wide, had a 2,100 horsepower engine and every imaginable luxury, including an "electric orchestrion giving full musical effects of a full band." Guests were invited to partake of water from Jamestown's artesian wells and fresh produce grown on the island.[38]

On May 13, 1895, the College of William and Mary and the A.P.V.A. jointly hosted a Jamestown Day celebration that was attended by an estimated 2,000 people. The following year Edward E. Barney deeded his interest in Jamestown Island to his wife, Louise, who in August 1906 gave the Williamsburg and Jamestown Turnpike Company access to her wharf and to the A.P.V.A a 100-foot right-of-way. The opening of access to the A.P.V.A. property was in preparation for the 1907 tercentennial celebration. Some A.P.V.A members undertook some exploratory excavations in the old churchyard at Jamestown and within the historic church ruins.[39]

In February 1900 Thomas J. Stubbs, Harry N. Phillips, Norville L.

Henley, Thomas H. Geddy, Robert L. Spencer, Hugh Bird, Arthur Denmeade, L. W. Lane Jr., J. B. C. Spencer and Edmund W. Warburton were incorporated as the board of the Jamestown, Williamsburg and Yorktown Railroad Company, a firm chartered by the General Assembly. They were authorized to issue stock and could acquire the right-of-way for a railroad between Jamestown and Yorktown via the most practical route. They also could extend a spur from the main line to the Kingsmill Wharf. The 1900 legislation that created the JW&Y stipulated that construction had to commence within two years and be complete within five. In April 1902 the JW&Y was consolidated with the Jamestown, Poquoson and Hampton Railroad to form the Jamestown and Old Point Comfort Railroad Company. It received the James City County Board of Supervisors' permission to cross public roads with its equipment.[40]

In 1901 the Order of Jamestown 1607 was incorporated by the General Assembly for the expressed purpose of awakening interest in the origins of the Episcopal Church in America. Members intended to erect a monument to the Rev. Robert Hunt of Jamestown and to restore Bruton Parish Church, which had inherited the Jamestown Church's baptismal font and communion silver. In 1903 the Jamestown Exposition Company received a $200,000 state appropriation to develop a site in Norfolk at Sewell's Point for the 1907 celebration. By 1906 plans also were underway to erect an approximately 100-foot granite marker, patterned after the Washington Monument, on a tiny parcel of land near Jamestown's old church tower. Meanwhile, the Daughters of the American Revolution undertook construction of a colonial-style building at Jamestown and the descendants of Pocahontas and the A.P.V.A. commissioned sculptors to produce bronze statues of Pocahontas and Captain John Smith. The Colonial Dames of America hired experts to reconstruct the Jamestown Church while carefully preserving its foundation walls, and the Virginia Historical Society began assembling an exhibit of important documents for display during the Jamestown Exposition.[41]

As preparations for the Jamestown Exposition got underway, the General Assembly appropriated funds for the construction of buildings, displays, and water lines to the exposition site at Sewell's Point. The legislature also authorized local Boards of Supervisors to compile historical and physical descriptions of their counties that could be published and distributed during the exposition. Each county was to set up an exhibit featuring its industrial, agricultural, mineral, and commercial resources. The Tercentennial was a huge success. Later, the old exposition grounds were sold to the federal government, which established the Norfolk Naval Base.[42] Some of the buildings constructed for the 1907 celebration are still standing.

Powhatan Durham, a local youngster, was "mascot" of the Jamestown Exposition. The five-year-old son of the A.P.V.A.'s first custodian at Jamestown attended the exposition in Indian garb and sold souvenirs embellished with his picture. Young Durham reportedly was born "in the old Confederate Fort . . . while his parents lived in a house that once stood within those ruined embankments." Visiting Jamestown was a long-standing recreational pursuit among locals and during the 19-teens there was regular jitney service to Jamestown Island on Sundays.[43]

Social and Cultural Life in James City County

At the turn of the twentieth century Toano had two hotels and nearly 20 business establishments. But during the mid-to-late 19-teens, the community experienced three disastrous fires. After the Toano High School opened in 1908, it became the center of western James City County's social activities. Chautauquas were held there during the summer months and plays were given at other times of the year. Dancing, fox-hunting, and other forms of recreation were available in Toano, Five Forks, Norge, and other rural communities, some of which also fielded baseball teams. At the Wayside Hotel and the Green Shingle Inn in Toano, people gathered to dance and socialize. During the 1890s the Toano German Club held dances at the Hotel Felix. Occasionally, circuses and medicine shows came to town and the Powhatan Literary Society offered intellectual stimulation.[44]

Around 1904 a group of western James City County men established a Masonic Blue Lodge, Chickahominy 286, whose first meeting was held in Lanexa. The Lodge later relocated to Toano, which was considered more centralized, and eventually had 60 to 70 members. Many of the Masons (and their sons) later became Ruritans and members of the local volunteer fire department. In 1914 a group of local women organized the Norge Club, which met for the first time in the home of Mrs. J. C. Cutler. Seven years later club members purchased the Viking Hall (Norge Community Hall) which they used as their headquarters and meeting place.[45]

In 1916 a large 4th of July celebration was held in Norge that included a baseball game, formal ball, and jousting tournament. Ten costumed "knights" on horseback galloped at full speed toward rings they attempted to spear. The size diminished with each round of the contest. E. S. Cowles, Burtram Cowles, Carter Cowles Jr., and H. B. Warren won prizes for capturing the largest number of rings. R. L. Spencer, C. G. Reeve and E. S. Meanley were judges and Captain L. W. Lane Jr. was the event's chief marshal. Afterward, the merrymakers moved to the Viking Hall, where Mrs. Carter Cowles was crowned queen of the carnival. Teams from Toano and Norge played baseball and in the evening, Kinde's band provided music for a grand ball. At least 2,000 people reportedly attended the day's festivities. Later in the summer local people attended a major musical concert held first in Williamsburg and then in Toano. Vocal ensembles, soloists and instrumentalists performed in the concerts, which were for the benefit of the A.P.V.A. John Robinson's circus came to town and also provided entertainment. In autumn 1916 a teachers' institute was held at the Toano School, where 200 educators from James City, Charles City and New Kent Counties gathered for supplementary instruction.

During the 19-teens VIRGINIA GAZETTE subscribers could learn about the latest trends in ladies' clothing by reading Julia Bottomley's column, "Fancies and Fads of Fashion," or they could entertain themselves with weekly installments of the latest fiction. The more serious-minded could scan the obituaries or read the latest news on the local, national, and international scene. Regular features included columns on agriculture, health, home economics, and cooking. Columns from Williamsburg, Toano, Norge, Five Forks, Grove, and other communities recounted local residents' travels, ailments, and social events. News reports detailed accidents and cases tried in the local courts. In July 1916 the C&O depot in Norge was burglarized. The VIRGINIA GAZETTE's editor reported that hobos were the prime suspects, for they had been seen there from time to time. On another occasion the GAZETTE reported that a gang of 16 crap-shooters had been apprehended in Williamsburg. In 1916 B. F. Garrett, who lived near Yarborough's Mill, was assaulted by four youths while driving home in his wagon. The robbery attempt failed.

W. C. Johnson, long-time publisher of the VIRGINIA GAZETTE, sometimes wrote provocative editorials. On one occasion he claimed that Virginia's highways reputedly were the worst in the nation. He felt that it was useless to spend money on clay-sand roads unsuitable for automobile traffic. In a 1919 editorial he railed against the practice of allowing children to drive automobiles and urged legislators to set a minimum age limit for drivers. Johnson said that there always was "an element of risk when a child drives a car on a street where traffic is heavy" and added that "One frequently sees small boys and girls operating automobiles." The editorial was inspired by a recent motoring mishap in Williamsburg.[46]

Early Attempts at Suburban Development

The Roper-Tilledge Subdivision

In 1912 a large tract on the north side of Ironbound Road, west of modern James Blair Middle School, was subdivided into the streets and lots of the Roper-Tilledge Subdivision. The prospective residential community once was part of the Roper and Tilledge farms, which eventually were absorbed into the Casey property. Nearby was Parke Jones' farm, Dunbar, upon which modern Eastern State Hospital was built. The Roper-Tilledge Subdivision failed to materialize and in 1919 the project was abandoned.[47]

Kingsmill

In 1893 Moses R. Harrell sold 2,400 acres of his land at Kingsmill to Isaac Ketler of Grove City, Pennsylvania. Together they subdivided the central portion of the tract into lots and blocks that were defined by streets. Despite a vigorous advertising campaign, the two men's plans to develop Kingsmill into a planned town met with little success. In 1897 they sold the subdivided portion of the property to several investors whose purchases ranged from nine to forty acres. Repeated efforts to attract industrial development to Kingsmill failed. In 1900 Isaac Ketler sold the balance of his acreage to J. N. Pew, whose heirs conveyed most of it to a lumber company.[48]

Riverview

In western James City County, Riverview Plantation, which was owned by the Hankins family for several generations, was sold in 1895 to a Michigan couple, Oscar and Mary House. During the late 1890s, the widowed Mrs. House subdivided Riverview and the adjacent Shellfield tract and sold lots to a number of Scandinavians living in the Midwest. When many of these people came east, they settled in the community called Norge. In 1906 Christopher C. Moller, who in 1897 purchased the Riverview house tract, sold it to Samuel Swenson of Mount Vernon, New York. In 1913 Riverview, which subdivided parcels were reunited, came into the hands of Louis C. Phillips, a Newport News attorney and brother-in-law of John Garland Pollard, Virginia's governor from 1930 to 1934. Pollard was a frequent houseguest at Riverview.[49]

World War I

In 1914 the outbreak of hostilities between the Allies and Central Powers took many Americans by surprise. Although the country generally supported President Woodrow Wilson's policy of neutrality, in March 1917, when German submarines sank five American merchant vessels, the Wilson cabinet unanimously endorsed a declaration of war. Both houses of Congress supported the resolution and on April 6, 1917, when President Wilson signed the document, the United States officially was at war with Germany. In Williamsburg, the Surgical Dressing Committee worked diligently and on July 7, 1916, the VIRGINIA GAZETTE reported that members had sent off a shipment of nearly 1,600 bandages. B. E. Geddy indicated that a good crop of Irish potatoes was expected in the Toano area, even though local farmers had very little potash to use as fertilizer, thanks to the war.[50]

Before war broke out, the DuPont Company purchased more than 4,000 acres of land overlooking the York River and constructed a dynamite plant. But as soon as war was declared, the federal government took over the facilities and modified them into a powder factory and shell-loading plant. Although DuPont had built homes for its employees, an influx of new workers, many of whom sought accommodations in Williamsburg, brought unexpected prosperity to the area. Land prices soared and business boomed. In time, the facilities at Penniman employed 10,000 people and the community bordering the plant had a population of 10,000 to 20,000. In the Williamsburg area, people circulated a petition asking the C&O to run a daily train to Penniman.[51]

Because of the local population boom, real estate speculators began buying up land for the creation of subdivisions. Fort Magruder Terrace, Lakeside Park, the Williamsburg Business Annex, Kenton Park, and Powhatan Park were surveyed into streets and lots at this time. Fort Magruder Terrace (now part of James Terrace) involved a plan of development that was innovative for its day. An area of green-space was set aside as Fort Magruder Park, which enveloped—and therefore preserved—the ruins of Civil War Fort Magruder. Rumors spread that the federal government intended to convert Mulberry Island into a training facility and in August 1918 newspapers reported that the government was expected to take nearly 11,000 acres of land between Yorktown and Penniman. Purchases by the United States Navy eventually engulfed more than 12,500 acres. The acreage became the Naval Mine Depot and later, the Naval Weapons Station.[52]

Local families whose loved ones went off to war were affected on a deeply personal level. Mobilization also necessitated immense cooperation on the home front. Wartime agencies were established for the purpose of controlling supplies of food, fuel, and raw materials, and Americans were urged to support "Wheatless Mondays," "Meatless Tuesdays," and "Porkless Thursdays" and to plant Victory Gardens and use leftovers. The Fuel Administration introduced the country to "Heatless Mondays" and Daylight Saving Time. Other federal agencies regulated railroads, the highway system, and shipping.[53]

Men from the peninsula's military bases sometimes spent the weekends in Williamsburg. If they didn't have friends or kin to stay with, they pitched their pup tents on the college campus or stayed in the servicemen's club next door to Bell Hospital. The women of the Williamsburg Civic League attended first aid classes and made bandages for the military. Many local citizens became involved in the American Red Cross and other service organizations that supported those in uniform. Youngsters joined the Junior Red Cross, the Junior Farm Bureau, and the U.S. Boys Working Reserve, and through the public schools, learned about health, hygiene, and food preservation. Farmers were encouraged to use modern techniques to raise productivity and agents of the agricultural extension service helped by disseminating the latest information. In 1916 county agent E. M. Slauson reported that the James City County Alfalfa Club, which had 143 members, was the largest on the peninsula and that the Boys Corn Club was small but productive.[54]

Dr. H. U. Stephenson of Toano, the local food commissioner, worked under the direction of state officials. He urged area residents to report storekeepers that violated wartime regulations by overcharging for staple foods, such as flour and sugar. Property owners also were warned about overcharging for the accommodations they rented to war-workers. Everyone was encouraged to buy War Savings Stamps. Those who owned gasoline-powered vehicles, such as automobiles and motor boats, were asked not to use them on Sundays.

Throughout this period, the College of William and Mary had a military battalion that drilled for two hours a day. Academic credit was given to students who enlisted or otherwise helped in the war effort. Many young men left the college to enlist in the armed forces and William and Mary's enrollment dwindled at an alarming rate. Finally, on November 11, 1918, at 5 A.M. an armistice was signed. Six hours later the guns along the front lines fell silent. The following spring, a memorial service was held in Williamsburg in honor of those who had given their lives for their country.[55]

Notes

1.   Manerin et al., HENRICO COUNTY, 329–330; Bottom, GENERAL ASSEMBLY; VIRGINIA GAZETTE, December 15, 1893.

2.   A. R. Micou, comp., ACTS AND JOINT RESOLUTIONS PASSED BY THE GENERAL ASSEMBLY OF THE STATE OF VIRGINIA DURING ITS EXTRA SESSION OF 1887 (Richmond, 1887), 338,341,485).

3.   Bottom, GENERAL ASSEMBLY, 250–251; William L. Katz, THE NEGRO IN VIRGINIA (New York, 1968), 236–238, 241, 244, Philip D. Morgan, THE ETHNIC HERITAGE OF JAMES CITY COUNTY (Williamsburg, 1984); BLACK EDUCATION IN JAMES CITY COUNTY, 1619 1985 (Williamsburg, 1985), 56; Morton, THE NEGRO, 87, 96–97, 155–157; VIRGINIA GAZETTE, March 2, 1934.

4.   The term "Jim Crow" is derived from the name of a song Thomas Rice sang in minstrel shows.

5.   Morgan, ETHNIC HERITAGE; Katz, The Negro, 236–238; Tindall, NARRATIVE HISTORY, 1003. Chapter 16 provides a more thorough treatment of racial discrimination.

6.   VIRGINIA GAZETTE, May 12, 1894.

7.   Bradshaw et al., NORGE, 8–9, 22; Bradshaw, TALES, 6,36–37,80; James City County Plat Book 2:8; VIRGINIA GAZETTE, December 16, 1960.

8.   Bradshaw et al., NORGE, 8–9,22.

9.   Bradshaw, TALES, 46–47,56–57,62–63.

10.   PENINSULA NEWS, September 7 and 21, 1901.

11.   VIRGINIA GAZETTE, October 6 and 20, November 3, 1893; March 17, 1894; June 5, 1897.

12.   Ibid., December 15, 1893; June 1, July 20, August 24, September 28, 1894; June 5, 1897.

13.   Ibid., May 12, 1894; October 28, 1899.

14.   James City County Board of Supervisors Minutes 1895–1908:72, 145, 282; VIRGINIA GAZETTE, July 1949; March 3, 1950.

15.   U.S.D.A., Abridged List; American Petroleum Institute, "Power Farming—A Way of Life," n.d.

16.   James City County Agricultural Census 1880; Powers, "The Grove."

17.   U.S.D.A., "Abridged List."

18.   No James City County Board minutes have come to light that predate September 10, 1887. Earlier records may have been destroyed when the courthouse burned in 1911 or they may have remained in the hands of Board members who lost or misplaced them. In 1912 the VIRGINIA GAZETTE, which already printed ballots, began publishing the supervisors' minutes in the newspaper (James City County Board of Supervisors 1905–1925:116).

19.   James City County Board of Supervisors Minutes 1887–1908:1, 41, 53, 67, 104, 137.

20.   J. A. O'Bannon, comp., ACTS AND JOINT RESOLUTIONS PASSED BY THE GENERAL ASSEMBLY OF THE STATE OF VIRGINIA PASSED DURING THE SESSION OF 1889–1890 (Richmond, 1890), 695.

21. O'Bannon, SESSION OF 1889–1890, 695; ACTS AND JOINT RESOLUTIONS PASSED BY THE GENERAL ASSEMBLY OF THE STATE OF VIRGINIA DURING THE SESSION OF 1893–1894 (Richmond, 1894), 492; ACTS AND JOINT RESOLUTIONS PASSED BY THE GENERAL ASSEMBLY OF THE STATE OF VIRGINIA DURING THE SESSION OF 1897–1898 (Richmond, 1898), 504; Davis Bottom, comp., ACTS AND JOINT RESOLUTIONS PASSED BY THE GENERAL ASSEMBLY OF THE STATE OF VIRGINIA DURING THE SESSION OF 1916 (Richmond, 1916), 459; James City County Board of Supervisors 1895–1908:5; 1908–1925:50, 332.

22. James City County Board of Supervisors 1908–1925:106–107, 111, 113, 146, 181; VIRGINIA GAZETTE, November 9, 1956.

23. O'Bannon, SESSION OF 1894, 140, 794–795; SESSION OF 1897–1898, 764; ACTS AND JOINT RESOLUTIONS PASSED BY THE GENERAL ASSEMBLY OF THE STATE OF VIRGINIA PASSED DURING THE SESSION OF 1899–1900 (Richmond 1900), 293, 572, 975; ACTS AND JOINT RESOLUTIONS PASSED BY THE GENERAL ASSEMBLY OF THE STATE OF VIRGINIA PASSED DURING THE SESSION OF 1901–1902 (Richmond, 1902), 421; Bottom, SESSION OF 1916, 215; James City County Board of Supervisors 1887–1908:78–79 insert).

24. O'Bannon, SESSION OF 1894, 140, 794–795; SESSION OF 1897–1898, 764; SESSION OF 1900, 293, 572, 975; SESSION OF 1902, 421; Bottom, SESSION OF 1916, 215.

25. James City County Board of Supervisors Minutes 1895–1909:41; VIRGINIA GAZETTE, August 5, 1899.

26. VIRGINIA GAZETTE, June 5, 1897.

27. Between 1904 and 1916 Ware served as James City County's sheriff. He was a graduate of William and Mary's law school and lived at Windsor Castle on Old Forge Road. He also was the editor/publisher of the PENINSULA NEWS (Barbra M. Cook, "Sheriffs of James Citty Countie" [Williamsburg, 1994]).

28. VIRGINIA GAZETTE DIRECTORY [1898–1899].

29. James City County Board of Supervisors Minutes 1887–1908:184, 219; Bradshaw, TALES, 13–14, 37.

30. WILLIAMSBURG REUNION, 1942 AND BEFORE (Williamsburg, 1982).

31. Swem, "Oldest Building," 218; Godson et al., WILLIAM AND MARY, 447–450, 458–463, 542; James City County Plat Book 3:23; 5:21.

32. James City County Board of Supervisors Minutes 1887–1908:90; Gaines, "Courthouses," 30.

33. WILLIAMSBURG REUNION, 1944 AND BEFORE (Williamsburg, 1984); WILLIAMSBURG REUNION, 1942 AND BEFORE, (Williamsburg, 1982); VIRGINIA GAZETTE, January 10, 1930.

34. REUNION, 1942.

35. VIRGINIA GAZETTE, March 22, 1940.

36. James City County Deed Book 3:475–477; 5:503–505.

37. Mildred Matica, TALL TALES AND TRUE OF JAMES CITY COUNTY (Williamsburg, 1976), 30.

38. VIRGINIA GAZETTE, May 27, July 23, 1893; May 6, July 13, 1894; February 15, April 5, 1895; E. A. Barker Jr., MAP OF JAMES RIVER AND VICINITY (Richmond, 1899).

39. Lyon G. Tyler, "Historical and Genealogical Notes," WILLIAM AND MARY QUARTERLY, 1st Ser., 4 (July 1895):66; James City County Deed Book 5:536–542; 6:112; 10:371–372, 508–511; John L. Cotter, ARCHAEOLOGICAL EXCAVATIONS AT JAMESTOWN VIRGINIA (Washington, 1958), 219–225; VIRGINIA GAZETTE, June 27, 1930.

40. J. A. O'Bannon, comp., ACTS AND JOINT RESOLUTIONS PASSED BY THE GENERAL ASSEMBLY OF THE STATE OF VIRGINIA PASSED DURING THE SESSION OF 1899–1900 (Richmond, 1900), 398; SESSION OF 1901–1902, 736; James City County Supervisors Minutes 1895–1908:99.

41. J. A. O'Bannon, comp., ACTS AND JOINT RESOLUTIONS PASSED BY THE GENERAL ASSEMBLY OF THE STATE OF VIRGINIA PASSED DURING ITS EXTRA SESSION OF 1901 (Richmond, 1901), 285; SESSION OF 1901–1902, 21; ACTS AND JOINT RESOLUTIONS PASSED BY THE GENERAL ASSEMBLY OF THE STATE OF VIRGINIA PASSED DURING THE SESSION OF 1902–1903–1904 (Richmond, 1904), 264; VIRGINIA GAZETTE, June 27, 1930; James City County Plat Book 2:6; 10:508–511; William G. Stanard, "Proceedings of the Virginia Historical Society," VIRGINIA MAGAZINE OF HISTORY AND BIOGRAPHY 14 (July 1906):xvii–xxii.

42. Davis Bottom, comp., ACTS AND JOINT RESOLUTIONS PASSED BY THE GENERAL ASSEMBLY OF THE STATE OF VIRGINIA PASSED DURING THE SESSION OF 1906 (Richmond, 1906), 196, 209, 293–294, 386, 549; ACTS AND JOINT RESOLUTIONS PASSED BY THE GENERAL ASSEMBLY OF THE STATE OF VIRGINIA PASSED DURING THE SESSION OF 1908 (Richmond, 1908), 242, 565.

43. VIRGINIA GAZETTE July 6, 1917; June 6, 1930.

44. Ibid., February 8, 1895; February 12, 1898; January 1, 1971; Bradshaw, TALES, 6–7, 33.

45. David Waltrip, personal communication, July 7, 1994; VIRGINIA GAZETTE, April 9, 1965.

46. VIRGINIA GAZETTE, November 12, 1898; July 6 and 13, August 10 and 24, October 12 and 24, 1916; March 21, 1918; April 3, 1919.

47. James City County Plat Book 2:22; 19:24; Deed Book 84:257–261.

48. James City County Deed Book 6:236, 260, 270, 309–310, 357, 359, 361, 366–367; 8:340; 43:288, 306–307; VIRGINIA GAZETTE, March 27, 1897; March 18, 1899.

49. James City County Deed Book 6:334–345, 354–355, 412–413; Charles Phillips Pollard, personal communication to G. Alan Morledge, May 31, 1982.

50. Tindall, NARRATIVE HISTORY, 956–959; VIRGINIA GAZETTE, July 6, 13 and 20, August 24, 1916.

51. VIRGINIA GAZETTE, May 18, 1918.

52. H. M. Stryker, THANKS FOR THE MEMORY (Williamsburg, n.d.); James City County Plat Book 2:27, 32, 36, 39, 44–45; Matica, TALL TALES, 17–18; Reunion, 1942; VIRGINIA GAZETTE, July 6, 1916; March 28, May 30, August 29, 1918; Susan Clingan, THE HISTORY OF THE NAVAL WEAPONS STATION, YORKTOWN, VIRGINIA (Yorktown, 1961).

53. Tindall, NARRATIVE HISTORY, 961–963.

54. VIRGINIA GAZETTE, October 12, 1916; January 22, 1932.

55. Ibid., March 21, August 29, 1918; March 20, 1919; Godson et al., WILLIAM AND MARY, 504–505.

CHAPTER 14

"When Johnnie Comes Marching Home Again"
1918–1945

Revitalization And Change

The Transition from War to Peace

After World War I ended, Americans embarked upon making the transition from war to peace. An unforeseen postwar boom eased the process along, but by 1920 there was a general slump in business and farm prices began to drop. The summer of 1919 brought race riots in both North and South and a growing suspicion of those ethnically or culturally "different." With the "Roaring Twenties" came flappers, bootleggers, rumble seats, bathtub gin, and a dance called the "Charleston" and in 1926 the VIRGINIA GAZETTE reported that from time to time local girls could be seen sporting garter flasks. By 1930 the thrill of rebelling against Victorian codes of conduct had begun to subside. However, some of the 1920s' liberating changes became permanent.[1]

Shortly after the armistice was signed, the Williamsburg chapter of the American Red Cross began collecting clothes for Allied countries' refugees. Soon, the VIRGINIA GAZETTE published ads announcing the arrival of the newest automobiles and promoting the latest trends in home improvements. But some local businesses that experienced a wartime boom, thanks to the military build-up on the peninsula, later languished for lack of support. Many farmers found a marketing niche that enabled them to prosper, but some experienced serious economic problems. Early in 1921 approximately one hundred farmers from James City and York Counties met in Norge's Viking Hall to organize a local chapter of the American Farm Bureau Federation. The VIRGINIA GAZETTE's editor observed that a state-wide depression had suppressed the local lumber industry and other businesses.

As economic conditions deteriorated, the crime rate rose and an increasing number of automobile thefts occurred, especially in urban areas. Locally, two boys swiped a Williamsburg man's car and went on a joy-ride to Toano, where they literally ditched the vehicle. When they were brought to trial, the oldest, a 13-year-old, was sentenced to eight years in the Richmond reformatory. But life in James City County usually was relatively placid. There were many sources of entertainment in town and country. Also, social and civic organizations (such as the Masons, the Eastern Star, church circles, and the Toano Hunting and Fishing Club) convened regularly for fellowship. Perhaps the area's most unique social group was the Williamsburg Automobile Fox Hunting Club, which by spring 1919 was on the move, vehicles, hounds and all, to rid the area of the foxes that were "such a bother to farmers."[2]

The Women's Suffrage Movement

Many women, who during World War I found jobs outside the home or became involved in emergency war work, felt a new sense of confidence in their capabilities. Before the war, those of middling means traditionally stayed home to tend children and take care of household duties. Only the relatively affluent escaped the drudgery involved in cooking, cleaning, making clothes and soap, and preserving food. Rural women also tended livestock and sometimes worked in the fields alongside male family members. But as labor-saving devices (such as sewing and washing machines, gas and electric ranges, and packaged and canned food) became available, women gradually began to accumulate leisure time. Those who took wartime jobs tending switchboards, working in factories, stores and offices, and performing administrative duties, began to question the restrictions society traditionally placed on them. One was denial of the right to vote. Although Virginia's General Assembly didn't ratify the 19th Amendment to the constitution until 1952, fortunately the majority of states did. Passage, which took place in August 1920, opened suffrage to women. During the 1920s increasing numbers of women entered the work force. Most were employed in traditional occupations such as secretarial work, teaching, nursing, sewing, and domestic work.[3]

Prohibition

Prohibition, a symptom of some Americans' zealous pursuit of moral rectitude and conformity, was rooted in the temperance movement, a mid-nineteenth century phenomenon. The Anti-Saloon League and Women's Christian Temperance Union spearheaded the drive toward state-wide prohibition, which the General Assembly made law on October 31, 1916. It outlawed the sale and consumption of alcoholic beverages throughout the state. Prohibition in Virginia came three years ahead of the 18th Amendment's passage, which extended the ban nationwide. Many prohibitionists ardently believed that if alcoholic beverages weren't available, there would be fewer people in jails, asylums, and poorhouses and that Americans' health generally would be improved. Around this time Virginia's Sunday "blue laws" were made more stringent, another manifestation of public morality.[4]

Although many Virginians supported the 18th Amendment, others steadfastly resisted it. That backlash gained momentum as jails throughout Virginia began to overflow with Prohibition violators and law enforcement officers were constantly seizing stills and illegal caches of liquor. The VIRGINIA GAZETTE reported numerous arrests for moonshining, alcohol sales and possession, and drunk-driving. For example, in 1930 two men motoring through Five Forks were pursued because they were seen sipping a beverage from a canning jar. In another instance, two Portsmouth men whose small plane made an emergency landing on Jamestown Island were arrested as soon as someone noticed that they were transporting liquor. According to one James City County woman, during Prohibition, "there were two kinds of people . . . as far as the men were concerned: the people who drank and the people who didn't." She said that none of the drinkers went thirsty and that "If you had any means at all, you had three kegs somewhere on your property," one for raw corn whiskey, one for aging, and one that "had been charcoaled and was four or five years old." People commonly justified their "moonshining" by saying that their liquor was "for medicinal purposes." In October 1933

Virginia voters repealed Prohibition through a popular referendum; their action followed in the wake of the federal repeal. As one wag put it, this ended "the era of the amphibious statesman—that notorious species which voted 'dry' and drank 'wet.'" Williamsburg was the first city in Virginia to repeal the prohibition laws. A newly enacted liquor control bill limited the sale of alcoholic beverages to state-run liquor stores. Williamsburg's first Alcoholic Beverage Control store opened in late October 1934.[5]

The College of William and Mary

The 1918 session of the General Assembly brought a significant victory for women interested in attending the College of William and Mary, for "properly prepared" females became eligible for admission and could receive "the same degrees as men." This marked the first time in the college's lengthy history that women could enroll in anything other than the summertime continuing education program for teachers. In July 1919 Julian A. C. Chandler became president of William and Mary. Under his dynamic leadership, the college's enrollment increased significantly. Chandler, who strongly supported expansion and modernization, acquired the 284-acre Bright Farm, to the west of Cary Field Park, and some small lots and houses near the campus. It is thanks to his foresight that the college acquired Lake Matoaka (in 1925), the Mill Neck Farm (in 1928), the Strawberry Plains Road tract (in 1929) and the city of Williamsburg's municipal airport (in 1933–1934).[6] Almost all of these properties were in James City County.

Public Health

Eastern State Hospital, like the College of William and Mary, was an important local employer during the early twentieth century and during Dr. George W. Brown's administration, the size of the hospital's staff increased significantly. Five new buildings were erected on the hospital grounds adjoining Francis Street and nine were erected on the old Parke Jones farm, Dunbar, where the entire hospital eventually was moved. It was then that Eastern State Hospital forged cooperative agreements with the Medical College of Virginia and other nurses training schools in eastern Virginia. Around 1925 Drs. Baxter I. Bell Sr. and Ernest Alderman opened a private hospital in the old Williamsburg Hotel. In 1930 Dr. Bell purchased land on Cary Street, where he constructed Bell Hospital. The twenty-bed facility served the residents of Williamsburg and surrounding counties until late 1966.[7]

During the 1920s the James City County Board of Supervisors appointed C. D. Hart as county health officer and passed a regulation requiring all rental housing to have sanitary privies. In 1932 a state-mandated diphtheria prevention program was implemented by the county. Between March 15 and April 15, the doctors of Williamsburg and Toano were obliged to provide "the complete treatment" for diphtheria for a dollar per patient. Because the county's poor sometimes sought emergency medical care on the lower peninsula, three doctors from Riverside Hospital asked the Board of Supervisors to pay their bills. The Board referred them to A. J. Hall, the county's Overseer of the Poor.

Every summer polio, a highly contagious disease, threatened the lives of local youngsters. During the summer of 1935, when there was a polio outbreak in nearby York County, health department officials prohibited all local children under 16 from attending public gatherings of any kind. The March of Dimes led an annual fund-raising drive for polio treatment and research. Tuberculosis, another major public health concern, received private support. The James City County-Williamsburg Tuberculosis Association was active in the local community and a chest x-ray clinic held during the spring of 1945 attracted nearly 3,000 people.[8]

Law Enforcement

In 1916 Louis P. Trice was elected sheriff of James City County, He was returned to office for 28 years. Although he never carried a gun, he reportedly kept crime to a minimum. Sheriff Trice used his own vehicle on the job and according to one tale, moonshiners once set his car ablaze. Trice, an active and much respected member of the local community, died at age 58. He was succeeded by Vester Wayne Lovelace, who held office for 17 years.

The Chickahominy River Bridge, Route 5. Photo by Ralph Maxwell.

The Ewell Train Station, now a private residence. Photo by Nan Maxwell.

James City County's sheriff was assisted by deputies and sometimes by special policemen who enforced the law in outlying communities. For example, in 1926 a police officer was stationed in Toano to maintain law and order and to assist whenever Commonwealth Attorney C. C. Branch held hearings in his law office. Later, a policeman was headquartered at Five Forks. In December 1931 the Board of Supervisors made it mandatory for the city-county jailor, or a deputy, to stay at the jail every night from 10 P.M. to 6 A.M. and to keep the jail's outside door locked at all times. In 1933 the Board endorsed George A. Marston's appointment as a U. S. Deputy Marshal for the Eastern District of Virginia.[9]

Changes in Political Boundaries

During the first two decades of the twentieth century, James City County was in a state electoral district that included New Kent, Charles City, York, and Warwick Counties, plus the city of Williamsburg. But as the lower peninsula's population grew, especially in the vicinity of Newport News, Warwick County was placed in another district. This revised scheme, which took effect in 1924, was in force until 1966. During 1924 Ashton Dovell replaced Delegate Norvell L. Henley, who died in office. Another change that occurred during the mid-1920s was Williamsburg's annexation of some land in James City and York Counties. The 1923 boundary extension took in some land along South Henry Street and Richmond and Jamestown Roads, enveloping part of the acreage between William and Mary's old campus and the Rich Neck mill dam.[10]

Modernizing Influences in James City County

Transportation

The establishment of the Virginia State Highway Commission somewhat relieved local officials' burdensome task of maintaining public roads. In April 1919 the James City County Board of Supervisors accepted the State Highway Commission's cost estimates for improving portions of Centerville,

Richmond, Jamestown, Grove, Forge, and Longhill Roads. That fall, the Board agreed to see that a new bridge was built across Paper Mill Creek because the old one from College Landing to "Delks" had been washed out. Passage of a Federal Highway Act in 1921 led to the construction of new, improved public thoroughfares throughout the nation. As motor vehicles grew more common, the construction and maintenance of public roads became more costly. By early 1933 there was discussion of building a bypass around Williamsburg.

During the 1920s the railroad was a favorite mode of transportation among peninsula residents. A local train plied the route between Newport News and Richmond, making stops near the old mill at Diascund and at Toano, Norge, Lightfoot, Ewell, Williamsburg, and Grove. People in western James City County often boarded the morning train to Williamsburg and returned home on the evening run. A bus route eventually linked Newport News with Richmond and points in between. Although the road to Richmond was paved with concrete in 1923–1924, the rest of the county's roads were dirt-surfaced. Centerville and Longhill Roads were notoriously bad and one local resident recalled its taking half-a-day to get from Lightfoot to Centerville if the road was muddy. Another person said that there were so few automobiles on the paved road from Lightfoot to Toano that youngsters used roller skates to go from one place to another.

In 1932 the State Highway Commission began hard-surfacing Route 41 (now designated Route 5) from Jamestown Road to Barretts Ferry. There, motorists could board the ferry across the Chickahominy to Charles City County and "many old James River estates." The Board of Supervisors was enthusiastic about the scenic highway, for they expected it to bring tourists to James City County. Route 41, termed one of the best roads on the peninsula, was paved by September 1938. A bridge, built in 1939 to replace Barretts Ferry, was struck and seriously damaged by a barge before being opened to traffic.[11]

Communication

When a telephone directory was published in 1935, there were 595 houses and places of business in the Williamsburg area that had phone service.

The Norge Train Station. Photo by Ralph Maxwell.

Many telephone subscribers lacked mailing addresses because there were so few street numbers. Often, small telephone companies provided service to rural subscribers, sometimes with outmoded equipment. In April 1945 H. G. McCartney of James City County purchased the Toano Telephone Company from R. L. Moody and R. M. Hazelwood Jr. and Sr., because he wanted to improve the quality of local telephone service. Later, his company was replaced by a more modern one.[12]

Electricity and Sanitation

Toano was on the cutting edge of modernity when it came to electricity. R. Kemper Taylor Sr., owner of an automobile repair shop, set up an electrical generating plant and began providing electric current to local customers daily, from 6 A.M. to midnight. In 1927 he sold his equipment to the Virginia Electric and Power Company (V.E.P.C.O.), which had begun extending its power lines up the peninsula. By January 1932 electric lines had reached Toano. In 1936 the Rural Electrification Act made funds available to bring electric power to outlying areas. It was then that vigorous efforts were made to extend power lines into the countryside. Public health concerns gave rise to measures intended to curb the spread of contagious diseases. In 1924 a law was passed to ensure the proper disposal of sewage. It set the stage for counties to begin issuing permits for private wells and waste disposal.[13]

Improving the Farm Economy

In 1921 a group of Warwick County farmers formed a cooperative creamery that evolved into the Peninsula Dairy Association. The Williamsburg area's cooperative creamery, an affiliate, fostered growth in the local dairy industry. Laws passed during the 1930s and '40s regulated the marketing of agricultural commodities, made crop insurance available and generated loans for tenant farmers trying to buy land. Extension agents disseminated up-to-date information on farming techniques and encouraged young people to take an active interest in agriculture. Each year James City County's extension agent and his female counterpart, the home demonstration agent, requested funds from the Board of Supervisors to support local programs. In 1926 funds were allocated to the state forester for fire prevention and in 1933 a 120-foot-tall fire tower was erected at a site on H. P. Hazelwood Sr.'s farm, the highest point in the county.[14]

In 1928 C. J. Jehne, a C&O Railroad agricultural agent, purchased 5 1/2 acres at Glasshouse Point, just west of Jamestown Island. Jesse Dimmick, then-owner of the Main Farm or Amblers-On-The-James, discovered portions of four ancient furnaces in which glass had been manufactured during the early seventeenth century. Jehne donated his land to James City County's 4-H program, whose club members used it until the 1940s, when it was acquired by the National Park Service. In 1949 the Jamestown 4-H Camp's permanent facilities were built at a river front site a little further upstream.[15]

Much emphasis was placed upon enhancing quality and productivity through scientific farming. During August 1930, when eastern Virginia's "leading farm men and women" were invited to an agricultural conference held at the 4-H Camp, families from James City County were urged to attend.

The conference, which was popular and well attended, became an annual event. A State Experiment Station was established in James City County, four miles west of Williamsburg, where small plots treated with various types of fertilizer and pesticides were put on display. In 1931 E. M. Slauson, an Iowa native, received recognition as a "Master Farmer" and his farm, Powhatan, was declared "one of the best" in Tidewater Virginia. The Girls 4-H Club of Norge held a carnival in June 1930 and six months later the Toano Poultry Association held a big show. On October 30, 1931, when a county fair was held in Toano, livestock, agricultural products, canned and baked goods, sewing and other handicrafts were featured. Floral displays, school exhibits, and athletic contests also were part of the day's events.[16]

Frances Bass, a home economics teacher at Toano High School, helped organize the 1932 county fair. Its theme was "the utilization of waste material," what we call recycling. Grace and Rosabelle West of Grove demonstrated how to make hooked rugs from discarded clothing, whereas Dorothy Cooley, Lorraine Benson, Adah Davis, and Margery Anderson "made old clothes into new." Somewhat more difficult to envision is how Thelma Vaiden and Emily Waltrip fashioned vases and bowls from old phonograph records and Frances Cook and Margaret Garrett created serving trays from pine needles. 4-H Club members played an active role in the county fair.[17]

While fairs and contests gave farm families an opportunity to showcase their achievements, Home Demonstration Clubs and 4-H provided women and children with a chance to learn while socializing. Mabel Massey and her successor Miriam Puster served as James City County's home extension agents for several decades and provided leadership to numerous local Home Demonstration Clubs. The women of the Norge area formed a group called the Norgettes, which met regularly during the 1930s, '40s and '50s. Some of the women in western James City County joined the Barhamsville Home Demonstration Club in New Kent. During the early 1950s there were six Home Demonstration Clubs and eight 4-H clubs in James City County. In 1931 Eloise Bangs of Norge won a trip to Washington, D.C., in recognition of being "one of the best 4-H Club members in Virginia."[18]

Local Industry

Although James City County's economy traditionally was dependent upon agriculture, after World War I a number of local people discovered that they could earn a good living by producing saleable goods or performing marketable services.

Pine Dell: Brick and Pottery

In 1926 Clarence B. Sturges purchased the Pine Dell Development Corporation's holdings, which included Piney Grove and portions of Deep Bottom, Green Spring, and several other properties west of Jamestown Island. He challenged Pine Dell employee Paul M. Griesenauer Sr. to produce something useful from the abundance of clay at Piney Grove. Griesenauer, who had a working knowledge of pottery-making, began experimenting with the clays on Sturges' property. He manufactured what became known as Jamestowne Pottery, which became popular and was exported to several foreign countries. Eventually, those involved in restoring Williamsburg to its colonial appearance asked Griesenauer to manufacture brick that could be used in reconstructing and repairing its old buildings. By October 1929 he had begun producing what he dubbed the "James Towne Collony Brick," which was used in the restoration of the Wren Building and in the construction of St. Bede's Church and the Colonial Parkway's bridges.[19]

The Williamsburg Pottery

In 1938 James E. Maloney and his wife, Gloria, purchased a half-acre of land at Lightfoot between Richmond Road and the railroad tracks. They constructed a kiln and a small workshop with a room that served as living quarters. Maloney, who learned his trade from master-potter Paul M. Griesenauer Sr., set up a potter's wheel and began manufacturing ceramic wares, which his wife decorated. He mixed the clays he obtained from two sites on the Chickahominy (the old Hog Neck Brickyard and Barretts Ferry) and then strained them through hardware cloth, using a horse-powered pug mill. Some of the wares the Maloneys produced had a salt-glaze reminiscent of colonial pottery. They sold their vessels to passing motorists and through retail establishments. Eventually, they set up sales counters, which attracted the attention of tourists and other prospective buyers. After World War II the Maloneys began selling "factory seconds" or imperfectly-made dinnerware and glassware they purchased in wholesale lots. As the Williamsburg Pottery's reputation spread, its facilities were expanded. In time, it became a multi-million-dollar business.[20]

Ice Cream and Barrel-Making in Norge

In 1918 Arthur and Rachel Smith bought a piece of land in Norge on the north side of Richmond Road. The Smiths and his parents, the Ward Smiths, began making and selling ice cream. Their lunch room and ice cream parlor attracted customers from Richmond and Newport News. For a while the enclosed front porch of Smiths Ice Cream Parlor served as the Norge post office. In 1921 the Smiths sold some of their land to the Peninsula Barrel Corporation which went bankrupt in 1937.[21]

Other Commercial Ventures

During the 1920s W. E. Topping, a local oil distributor, opened a tourist camp on Richmond Road, outside the city limits. He also had a gas station and a small store. Among the other early entrepreneurs who catered to tourists were Angelo and Nick Costas, Greek immigrants who in 1916 opened the Norfolk Cafe and later, the Norfolk Restaurant. Their business interests eventually included a bowling alley, a poolroom, a barber shop, and the Imperial Theater. In 1932 Angelo Costas and his wife Dora joined Tom and Helen Baltas in opening the Capitol Restaurant on Duke of Gloucester Street. The Costas' later opened a motel on Richmond Road. But James City County's first motel was built by Edward and Cora Olson in upper James City County. Olson's Motel, which was located on Richmond Road in Lightfoot, was built during the 1940s.

On May 30, 1930, the publisher of the VIRGINIA GAZETTE warned local readers about "the menace of the chain-store octopus," which he felt posed a threat to local retailers. But in 1933 Rose's Dime Store opened in Williamsburg and business went on as usual. Every June, July, and August, local merchants closed their stores on Wednesday afternoon to give their employees a holiday. Advertisements that appeared in the VIRGINIA GAZETTE during the 1930s reveal that bread then cost 5 cents a loaf and a three-door ice box with a golden oak finish and equipped with tongs, chipper, and drip pan could be bought for $16.88. An electric refrigerator sold for $169.50 and a new Ford automobile for $430. A telephone call from Williamsburg to Toano or Lee Hall cost a dime and a call to Hampton cost 30 cents.[22]

Jamestown Island, an Emerging Tourist Attraction

In 1918 the General Assembly began planning for the 300th anniversary of America's first legislative assembly. Because the bridge and causeway connecting Jamestown Island with the mainland had become unusable and the A.P.V.A. lacked funds to rebuild them, money was appropriated to cover the cost of construction. Three years later a bill introduced in the United States Senate recommended that the federal government purchase Jamestown Island.[23]

In 1929 the state and federal governments joined forces to build a wharf and pier at Jamestown Island and the A.P.V.A. made plans for excursion boats to land there. During early 1931 students from the Riordon Boys School of Highland, New York, attended classes aboard the steamship SOUTHLAND, which was anchored at Jamestown's "government dock." The school's founder and the president of William and Mary agreed that Riordon students could use laboratory space on campus if one of Riordon's instructors would give flying lessons to four college students. Alexander G. Harwood, then-owner of St. George's Hundred, offered to let the would-be aviators land in one of his fields. Excerpts from the Riordon Boys School's newspaper, THE LUMBERJACK, were published in the VIRGINIA GAZETTE while school was in session at Jamestown. Riordon students also planted a thousand trees that had been sent to Virginia by the New York Conservation Commission.

During 1931 an estimated 36,000 tourists visited Jamestown Island. Ferry Captain A. F. Jester offered a picture of Captain John Smith to the driver of every passenger vehicle that used his boat on Sunday, February 28. Steamships from as far away as Baltimore continued to dock regularly at Jamestown, and commemorative events were held every spring.[24]

Restoration of the Colonial Capital

In 1923 Dr. William A. R. Goodwin, former rector of Bruton Parish Church, returned to Williamsburg after a lengthy absence. He found that many of the city's older buildings were even more dilapidated than when he left and that a hodge-podge of modern structures obscured the rest. Down the center of Duke of Gloucester Street, which had been paved during World War I, was an irregular line of telephone poles strung with wires. Restaurants, laundries, pool rooms, and gas stations were intermingled with aging, sagging eighteenth- and nineteenth-century houses and their gardens. Goodwin, a faculty member and director of an endowment fund at the College of William and Mary, met John D. Rockefeller Jr. in 1924 and tried to interest him in restoring Williamsburg to its colonial appearance. Two years later Goodwin and some local citizens took him on a tour of the city. Although Rockefeller left town after agreeing to provide a few thousand dollars to the college, Goodwin had opened an important line of communication. Later he telegraphed Rockefeller that the Ludwell-Paradise house could be bought for $8,000, quietly and discretely, with no commitment to proceed further. The wealthy philanthropist agreed and had Goodwin purchase the property in his own name. By the end of the year, Rockefeller had become enamored with the idea of restoring Williamsburg. Within the next two years Goodwin quietly acquired one property after another, using checks drafted on his personal bank account whose balance occasionally was swelled by enormous cashier's checks. When Miss Emma Lou Barlow refused to relinquish her old mansion on Duke of Gloucester Street, Goodwin offered to repair and modernize the house with electric lights and plumbing in exchange for life tenancy. Similar agreements were reached with several other local people. In time, Dr. Goodwin held 37 properties, for which he had paid more than $2,000,000.[25] As the time approached for the city's buildings to be restored, Goodwin, in consultation with Rockefeller and his advisors, decided to announce what was going on and who was making it possible. Afterward, a corporation was formed to handle business details and teams of scholars and specialists were hired to work on the buildings and gather information on colonial life. Shops catering to tourists were built in what became known as Merchants Square and the city's streets were paved. In October 1934 the restored colonial capital officially opened as a tourist attraction. At that time, the Raleigh Tavern, the capitol, the palace and a few other buildings on Duke of Gloucester Street were the main attractions.[26]

One of the colonial buildings Rockefeller's agents acquired was the city-county courthouse built in 1770–1772. But restoration of the eighteenth-century courthouse, which was still in use, necessitated the construction of a new one. Officials from James City County and Williamsburg collaborated on erecting the replacement, which stood at the corner of Francis and South England Streets, not far from where a courthouse was built in 1715. On March 27, 1931, a time capsule (a metal box donated by the Riordon Boys School) was inserted into a cornerstone of the new structure. It contained the signatures of local officials and a copy of the Williamsburg Holding Corporation's agreement to restore the colonial capital. By December 1932 the new city-county courthouse was ready for use.[27]

According to one local resident, when Restoration workers uprooted the United Daughters of the Confederacy's monument on palace green and moved it to a side street, the ladies emitted "a shrill cry of anguish." The very next day, a black-draped wooden cross, inscribed "crucified on a cross of treachery," was placed where the monument formerly stood. One woman who mightily resented the intrusion of Rockefeller's restoration project replaced her dwelling's wood-shingled roof with one of shiny tin. Another's determination extended beyond the grave, for her will specified that none of her property was to be sold to the Williamsburg Restoration, ever![28]

A man many people described as a town character wrote a poem about Williamsburg's restoration. In "A Sad Lament," he declared:

> My gawd, they've sold the town,
> They've sold the whole damn town.
> And it is said the news has spread
> For many miles around.

They've sold the courthouse green, I dare say, all the people,
They'll sell the church, the vestry too
And even sell the steeple.
They've sold the Powder Horn,
The School House and the lawn.
It is the tale they've sold the jail
And the streets we walk upon.[29]

Despite occasional protests about the changes that had occurred, the restoration of Williamsburg was a great stimulus to the local economy. It provided jobs to numerous citizens living in James City County and it opened new opportunities to those who provided goods and services. The restoration's impact upon William and Mary also was enormous, for it heightened college officials' interest in preserving its older buildings. Even though some people felt that the restoration of Williamsburg had disrupted a cherished way of life, many others viewed it in a positive light.[30]

Because Williamsburg was expected to become a major tourist attraction, city officials and the college decided to build a municipal airport northwest

The Colonial Parkway as it appears today. Photo by Nan Maxwell.

of town on 70 acres that belonged to Charles Scott. By August 1931 the construction of Scott Field's runways, hangars, and other facilities was underway and college officials were in the process of establishing a flying school. On September 4, 1931, the first college airplane landed at Scott Field. The new airport became a flag-stop on the Ludington Lines route between Washington and Norfolk and other airlines began providing service to Williamsburg. In February 1932 the College of William and Mary exercised its legal option to take over the airport.

As early as 1938 the City Council tried to preserve restored Williamsburg's ambience by enacting zoning restrictions. It was then that special ordinances were passed that prohibited junk yards. In 1941 the city initiated an annexation suit in which it tried to acquire approximately 874 acres of James City County land and a somewhat lesser amount of York County acreage. The proposed annexation would have nearly trebled the size of Williamsburg. But during the summer of 1941, when the suit came to trial, the city was allowed a more modest amount of land. Even so, its territory was doubled. Under the terms of the 1941 court agreement, James City County was paid $7,566 for the land it lost. The issue of annexation lay dormant until 1954, when the city tried to acquire the rest of the acreage it had sought annex in 1941.[31]

The Colonial National Monument

In January 1930 Congressman Louis C. Crampton introduced a bill into the House of Representatives that gave the Secretary of the Interior the authority to designate historic sites in Jamestown, Yorktown, and part of Williamsburg as the Colonial National Monument. Crampton also proposed that all three areas be linked by a scenic boulevard. The Crampton Bill was hotly debated by local citizens, many of whom viewed it as an unwelcome intrusion of "big government." In early February the James City County Board of Supervisors made their opposition to the bill part of the public record. Afterward, Crampton contacted local officials to say that his bill was intended to foster cooperation, not intrude. In June 1930 Secretary of the

Interior Ray Lyman Wilbur made a personal visit to Yorktown, Jamestown, and Williamsburg to promote the proposed designation. The following month Congress passed a modified version of the Crampton Bill, which provided for land in Jamestown and Yorktown to be included in the Colonial National Monument. Plans were made to build a breakwater around Jamestown Island, drain some of its marshes, and plant shrubs and trees to retard erosion. Consideration also was given to restoring the island's historic buildings. During the late summer, an army dirigible from Langley Field began taking aerial photographs of Williamsburg and Jamestown on behalf of the Colonial National Monument Commission. In August the idea of building a bridge from Jamestown Island to Scotland Wharf was revived and the state authorized the Eastern Virginia Bridge Company (a private group of investors) to raise funds for the project. But the would-be builders' permit specified that construction had to get underway by June 18, 1931, and be completed within two years. Ultimately, the project languished for lack of public support, for most people agreed that there wasn't enough traffic to pay for the existing ferry's upkeep, much less that of a bridge.[32]

In 1932 an Act of Congress and a Presidential Proclamation heralded creation of the Colonial National Monument and the acquisition of all of Jamestown Island except what was owned by the A.P.V.A. As Mrs. Louise J. Barney refused to part with her land, it was acquired by condemnation, after a bitterly contested law suit. Surveyors laid out a boulevard that linked Yorktown and Jamestown and passed through Williamsburg via a tunnel. Ironbound Road also was paved to provide additional access to Jamestown. The United States Department of Interior, upon acquiring the bulk of Jamestown Island, placed it under the control of the National Park Service. In 1936 it became a component of the Colonial National Historical Park. Since 1940, the National Park Service and A.P.V.A. have had joint administration of Jamestown Island and its historic sites.[33]

Carter's Grove

In 1928 Carter's Grove Plantation came into the hands of Archibald and Mary Corling McCrea, who intended to restore the old Burwell mansion to its former grandeur. When dark stain was removed from some of the dwelling's elegant interior paneling, traces of red, white, and blue paint came into view, expressions of an earlier owner's aesthetic taste. During the 1930s the McCreas entertained many distinguished visitors at Carter's Grove, including President and Mrs. Roosevelt, direct descendants of the Marquis de Lafayette, the Marquis de Grasse, the Count de Rochambeau, and President Ulysses S. Grant. Frank Lloyd Wright, who took a dim view of architectural restoration, in October 1938 made a speech in which he called restored colonial homes like Carter's Grove nothing better than "a box with air holes." His statements brought a sharp retort from Mrs. McCrea who contended that Wright had "reached a peak of absurdity" when he eschewed colonial architecture in favor of the modern.[34]

The Yorktown Sesquicentennial

In October 1931, the people of James City County and Williamsburg joined York County in sponsoring a celebration of the sesquicentennial of the

The Norge Community Hall. Photo by Ralph Maxwell.

British surrender at Yorktown. "Old Ironsides" was supposed to make a trip to Jamestown Island; however, the visit was cancelled because the water there was too shallow. The VIRGINIA GAZETTE published a commemorative Yorktown Sesquicentennial edition in honor of the occasion. The celebration included patriotic speeches, music and special events. Afterward, state officials claimed that it was the most successful and best attended commemorative event ever held in Virginia.[35]

The James City County Bible and Agricultural Training School

In 1936 evangelist Elder Lightfoot Solomon Michaux and his followers purchased a 1,000-acre farm near Jamestown Island. They made plans to establish a school for delinquent children and a museum commemorating the arrival of Virginia's first blacks. But a lack of funding prevented both projects from coming to fruition. Even so, the faithful gathered at the Gospel Spreading Farm for special prayer services on religious holidays, Memorial Day, Labor Day, and other occasions. The National Memorial Park, a wayside area that contained mechanical rides and a small museum honoring Elder Michaux, were situated on the river bank. Many decades later, the National Memorial Park property was incorporated into the Colonial Parkway's right-of-way.[36]

Local Diversions

During the 1920s and '30s tent shows known as Chautauquas provided afternoon and evening entertainment during the summer months. According to one devotee, a large tent usually was erected in Williamsburg on the courthouse green and in Toano, where special week-long programs were held. People flocked to attend lectures, plays, musicals, and performances by fiddlers, dancers, and yodelers, who paraded upon a platform usually draped with an American flag. Dr. Bennett's Medicine Shows, which visited every year, attracted large crowds and were another favorite diversion. Performances were interspersed with commercial messages promoting the doctor's cure-all elixirs and home remedies.[37]

Sometimes traveling circuses, such as John Robinson's, visited Williamsburg and Toano. They included what some people termed "shameful sideshows" that featured dancing girls and freaks of nature. Occasionally, traveling circuses erected a big top in a field off Capitol Landing Road, where fairs and harness-races sometimes were held, and clowns, a band, prancing horses and exotic animals paraded down Duke of Gloucester Street. In April 1919 a lion escaped from a carnival being held in Market Square. It nimbly darted down the palace green and paused briefly on the porch of the Brush-Everard house. Fortunately, when carnival workers arrived on the scene, the lion went quietly into his cage. Later, Mary Haldane Coleman satirized his nocturnal adventures in a poem she wrote.[38]

The advent of Spring usually brought May Day celebrations, for which a queen and her court were chosen. Dancers circled around a May Pole bedecked with flowers and colorful streamers that were woven together during the ritual. In Toano, an annual May Day celebration was held on the grounds of the high school and in Williamsburg, on the campus of the College of William and Mary. Summer outings frequently included trips to Smiths Ice Cream Parlor in Norge and jaunts to Jamestown Island, where motorists could park and enjoy the scenery. One favorite pastime on warm summer nights was riding the ferryboat to Surry and back. In Williamsburg, the Imperial Theater offered both silent movies and "talkies." On Richmond Road about a mile west of the city limits, the Auto-Torium, the area's first drive-in theater, opened in May 1941. Later it was renamed the Stockade. Dave's Park, located east of town, across from the entrance to Carter's Grove, offered square-dancing every Friday night with live music. The proprietor advertised that he had good food and safe water.[39]

Motorized caravans of Gypsies usually rolled through Grove, Williamsburg, Norge, and Toano twice a year, heading north or south, depending on the season. Some local residents stared with curiosity at their large black cars, piled high with mattresses, cook-pots, and other possessions, which typically traveled over Route 60's forerunner. Sometimes the Gypsies camped in Williamsburg on a York Street lot. Their presence likely added a little zest to everyday living.[40]

Western James City County offered a wide variety of social opportunities. Every Friday afternoon members of the Toano Women's Club served refreshments at Trice's Tea Room in exchange for a silver offering. On the other hand, the James City County Grange met bi-monthly in the Norge Community Hall. The Williamsburg Rotary Club, an all-male group with members from James City County and nearby localities, occasionally convened at the Toano School. The Women's Club of Jamestown also met regularly. All of these civic and social organizations gathered for fellowship, but they also rallied to meet special needs within the community. For example, in June 1930 the Ladies Circle of Olive Branch Christian Church in Norge gave a shower for Miss Kitty Taylor, whose home had been destroyed by fire. In October 1939, 42 men convened in the Norge Hall and established the James City Ruritan Club, the area's first group of its kind. R. L. Moody of Toano served as temporary chairman. Membership was open to farmers and businessmen from James City County and the surrounding area. Later, Ruritan Clubs were established at Five Forks and in Chickahominy.[41]

For youngsters interested in testing their intellectual prowess, there was the annual spelling bee sponsored by the Tri-County School Division with students from James City, Charles City and New Kent. In 1933 the event was held at Toano High School, with $2.50 and $5.00 gold pieces as top prizes. Students from Toano reportedly swept the field. In 1937 a Boy Scout troop was organized at the Toano School, where temporary leaders were appointed for the Wildcat and Beaver Patrols.[42]

One form of entertainment that was extremely popular in the western end of the county was fox-hunting. In February 1931, the Tidewater Fox Hunters Association met in Toano. A large turnout was expected with at least 40 horses and 75 hounds. The 1940s brought the establishment of the James City County Athletic Club, a group of baseball enthusiasts who gathered regularly in Toano.[43]

The C.C.C. in James City County and Williamsburg

In 1929 the country slipped into an economic crisis that became known as the Great Depression. An unparalleled stock market crash plunged numerous businesses into bankruptcy and the unemployment rate soared. One of the offshoots of President Roosevelt's government assistance program, the New Deal, was the Emergency Conservation Work Program or Civilian Conservation Corps (C.C.C.), which undertook public works projects. It was designed for single males, 18 to 25, from families receiving welfare, and unemployed World War I veterans of any age. Each 200-man C.C.C. company was under the command of military personnel. The C.C.C. was racially segregated and black companies were assigned to work in federal or state forests and parks.

In July 1933 William and Mary administrators asked state and federal officials for C.C.C. workers to develop part of the college's woods into a park. By early fall the tents of Camp Matoaka (or Camp SP-9) had been pitched on campus, west of the freshman athletic field. The all-black C.C.C. unit, Company No. 2303 (Camp EM-5), was under the overall command of Major Joseph Mills Hanson. Sixteen local white men were hired as field foremen and clerks. By Thanksgiving the C.C.C. had erected barracks, a mess hall, a recreation building, an infirmary and several administrative buildings. Much of the C.C.C.'s work in the Williamsburg area was done in James City County. One of the C.C.C. workers' first tasks was repairing some of the damage done by the 1932 hurricane. They also constructed roads, trails and picnic areas in the college woods, creating Lake Matoaka State Park, and built a large outdoor amphitheater known as Players Dell. Next, C.C.C. workers began cleaning up Jamestown Island and taking measures to curtail erosion. During the C.C.C.'s four years at Jamestown, workers were trucked-in daily from the William and Mary campus and on nights and weekends they served as watchmen. C.C.C. units assigned to Colonel J. P. Barney, whose parents once owned Jamestown Island, conducted archaeological excavations there. They also performed tasks associated with maintenance and conservation. Among the C.C.C.'s most important contributions at Jamestown Island was the construction of rip-rap from the eastern end of the seawall to a point just east of Orchard Run.

In 1937 when heavy rains caused Lake Matoaka's spillway to collapse, C.C.C. workers brought in rocks and fill dirt to repair the damage. From time to time they assisted in fighting forest fires and they were involved in early phases of construction at the college airport. During 1940 and 1941 the C.C.C. planted trees and grass along the Colonial Parkway between Yorktown and

Williamsburg and placed fill dirt over the newly completed tunnel beneath under the Historic Area. On April 15, 1942, the local C.C.C. camp was closed and its workers were sent elsewhere.[44]

Local News Coverage

On January 10, 1930, publication of the VIRGINIA GAZETTE was revived amid much fanfare. It is thanks to the renascence of Virginia's first newspaper that a considerable amount of local information has survived. For example, the GAZETTE reported that James Fletcher astonished local biologists by snaring an arctic seal in a fishnet near his home at Kingsmill. Inclement weather also made the news. On December 17, 1930, a foot of snow blanketed the area. It was the largest accumulation since February 11, 1899, when it reached a depth of three feet and the temperature fell to zero. In July 1938 a hurricane passed through the area and floodwaters swept away the Lake Powell dam and Route 617.

Sometimes, colorful court cases captivated newspaper reporters' attention. One such incident involved a local contractor who became so enraged at a business acquaintance that he tossed a stick of dynamite at his home. Although the contractor was charged with murder and brought to trial, the judge dismissed the case because the two men had reconciled their differences and no one was hurt. In another incident, burglars broke into the county courthouse and tampered with the records. Sometimes, the police used bloodhounds to track those who fled from crime scenes. On the night of April 12, 1934, the Toano branch of the Peninsula Bank and Trust Company was robbed and thieves stole cash and nearly $2,000 worth of valuables from the safe. All of these incidents, good and bad, gave texture to community life.[45]

Overland Transportation Networks

The residents of James City County and Williamsburg could choose from several modes of transportation if they wanted to go to Richmond or points on the lower peninsula. The C&O operated a daily train that made round trips between Newport News and Richmond and the Peninsula Transit Company offered bus service between Norfolk and Richmond, with stops at Grove Station, Williamsburg, Norge, Toano, Diascund Bridge, Walkers, and other rural post offices. There also was hourly ferry service between Jamestown Island and Scotland Wharf in Surry County.

A network of public highways connected James City County to the outside world, but relatively few roads were paved. Those fortunate enough to own automobiles found travel slow, bumpy, tedious, and sometimes precarious. The editor of the VIRGINIA GAZETTE reported that some people drove while intoxicated or traveled down the middle of the road, to the peril of those heading in the opposite direction. He published an open letter to the State Highway Commission, in which he recommended painting a line down the center of paved roads. He also chided motorists who drove too slowly, too quickly, or too recklessly. In July 1919 the James City County Board of Supervisors made 20 miles per hour the maximum speed limit for automobiles, where there was good visibility. On the other hand, motorists were not exceed to 10 M.P.H. when passing through a village or around a bend, unless there was at least 300 feet of visibility.

As automobile travel grew in popularity, the state assumed a more active role in licensing vehicles. Prior to July 1, 1930, garages, gasoline stations, and other businesses were allowed to sell automobile license plates; afterward, only clerks of court had that perogative. In 1931 when the legal speed limit was raised to 45 miles per hour, the VIRGINIA GAZETTE's editor declared, tongue-in-cheek, that billboards had lost much of their value because "Cars go by them so quickly that occupants are unable to read the messages."

Dr. E. C. Branchi of the College of William and Mary announced in the VIRGINIA GAZETTE that on the morning of January 29, 1930, he and some companions planned to set out on an automobile expedition to South America. Their motoring odyssey was intended to open a highway to Chile and Argentina. The automobiles the men planned to drive were put on display in the windows of Person's Garage, along with their tents and other paraphernalia. Both vehicles were equipped with rubber pontoons and special propeller wheels intended to make them amphibious. The outcome of the men's motoring adventures is uncertain.[46]

World War II

In 1937 Japan joined Germany and Italy in forming what became known as the Rome-Berlin-Tokyo "Axis." As Hitler's tyranny in Europe became increasingly apparent, Americans experienced a growing sense of uneasiness. After the Blitzkrieg and Churchill's announcement that Great Britain would fight to the end, the United States government began strengthening its own defenses. The local Selective Service Board began sending out draft notices and on March 14, 1941, the VIRGINIA GAZETTE announced that two James City County men, Gustavus A. Goddin Jr. and Richard Jones, would report for duty on March 19th. When the Japanese attacked Pearl Harbor on December 7, 1941, the United States abandoned its policy of neutrality and declared war on Japan. Within days, Germany and Italy retaliated by declaring war on the United States.

Industrial conversion was necessary as the country mobilized for war. Automobile and home appliance manufacturers began producing tanks and munitions and clothing manufacturers switched to the production of tents, military uniforms, bedrolls, and mosquito netting. As shortages developed and inflation threatened, price controls and rationing were implemented. Wartime spending caused the national debt to soar and income tax was levied to cover part of the expense. War bond drives were held to encourage the public to invest in America's defense.

Early in 1942 James City County purchased $20,000 worth of Defense Bonds and during the summer months, several men from the county (Elbert T. Elder, Randolph McKown, Shirley Robertson, Howard M. Shockley, and Herbert Epperson) were called into the army. George E. Waltrip enlisted in the navy and Mr. and Mrs. C. M. Bailey's three sons joined the Army Air Corps. Locally, farm wages jumped to their highest level in ten years. Draft deferments were granted to those involved in agriculture, for the military needed food. The James City County extension agent did his part by urging everyone to plant Victory Gardens. Congress passed a law creating Daylight Saving Time, as setting clocks forward one hour was intended to lengthen the work day. As the national debt grew, the James City County Ruritans, the American Legion, and the Chickahominy Lodge A.F. & A.M. jointly held an auction at the Toano School and sold nearly $97,000 worth of War Bonds.[47]

The war effort changed the status of American women forever, for the draft created severe labor shortages. By 1944 over 6 million women had entered the work force, an overall increase of 50 percent, and "Rosie the Riveter" became a well known symbol of patriotism. Nearly 200,000 women entered the armed forces and for the first time, more married women than single were employed outside the home. Although government policy officially opposed racial discrimination, the armed forces were segregated and it took steady pressure to broaden black participation in the defense industries. The prospect of job opportunities revived black migration from the South, which had lagged during the Depression, and blacks began heading for the West Coast and the North.[48]

During the latter part of World War II, the Colonial Parkway tunnel, which was built beneath the courthouse and market square greens between 1940 and 1942, was designated an air raid shelter for the city of Williamsburg. But it was not until 1949, when the tunnel was equipped with paving, lights, and ventilation, that it was opened to traffic. The Yorktown segment of the Colonial Parkway was completed in 1938 but the Jamestown portion wasn't finished until 1957. For the first time, all three historical attractions were connected by a scenic boulevard.[49]

Thanks to Williamsburg's proximity to several military facilities and the Hampton Roads Port of Embarkation in Newport News, members of the armed services flocked to the area in search of rental housing for their families. In February 1944, when rent control was imposed by the Office of Price Administration, the owners of rental property were required to disclose how much they were charging. The building boom on the lower peninsula, a result of the military build-up, produced an acute water shortage that Newport News officials sought to relieve by tapping the Chickahominy River. During the spring of 1942 an agreement was signed, authorizing the construction of a pipeline from the Chickahominy to the city of Newport News. The United States government made plans to build a dam across the river near Walkers, in New Kent County. By March 1943 the new pipeline extended from the reservoir to Lee Hall and was nearly complete.

During World War II local women volunteered in the U.S.O., whose canteen was located over a store on Duke of Gloucester Street. During the summer, dances were held in the VIRGINIA GAZETTE's parking lot, but the most universally popular form of entertainment was attending movies. The college contributed to the war effort by offering classes in camouflage, home nursing, internal combustion engine repair, introductory map reading, military chemistry, telegraphy, and the interpretation of aerial photographs. A combination work-study program was introduced in mid-1942, which allowed students to combine employment with class attendance.[50]

Local Military Facilities

Although James City County had only one military installation, Camp Wallace which was very small, those built in nearby York and Warwick Counties and on the lower peninsula were large. They stimulated the local economy and provided an abundance of employment opportunities.

Penniman (Cheatham Annex)

Many local people worked at Penniman, the powder factory and shell-loading plant that in 1943 was commissioned the Cheatham Annex. One woman who commuted to work at Cheatham during the war recalled making around $85 a month. The facility had warehouses for the storage of food, medical supplies, and other commodities, plus underground storage tanks for fuel.[51]

The Naval Mine Depot or Naval Weapons Station

The Naval Mine Depot, established by the United States Navy in 1918 for the purpose of storing and testing mines, was home to one of America's first torpedo shops. Mines tested at the Naval Mine Depot were stored until shipment to the North Sea. The facility played an important role in World War II, for torpedoes, bombs, and other high explosives were kept there and munitions research and development was carried out on the base. In 1943 an explosion at the Naval Mine Depot claimed seven lives.[52]

Camp Abraham Eustis (Fort Eustis) and Camp Wallace

In March 1918, shortly before the end of World War I, the government purchased nearly 5,700 acres of land on Mulberry Island in Warwick County. The purpose was to establish a training center for the U.S. Coast Artillery, Camp Abraham Eustis. Late in 1918, the government bought 115 acres of James City County land for development into a firing range for artillery and named it Camp Wallace. By August 1918 barracks for 19,000 troops were completed at Camp Abraham Eustis, which had schools for artillery, motor transport, trench mortar, and air balloon training. In 1923 Camp Abraham Eustis was renamed Fort Eustis. In 1931 it was rumored that Fort Eustis would become a prison farm for the detention of convicts from several federal penal facilities. Local opposition was strong, for some people believed that it would deal tourism a death blow. Even so, Fort Eustis served briefly as a federal prison for prohibition offenders.

During the Great Depression, officials from the Federal Emergency Relief Administration (F.E.R.A.) decided to use the abandoned prison camp's facilities as a regional training center for unemployed men from three states. A canning factory was opened to which truck farmers were invited to bring their produce; a bakery and paint shop also served the local community. Facilities were on hand for blacksmithing, clothing manufacture, shoe repair, and other marketable services. By the mid-1930s there was an education center at Fort Eustis jointly operated by federal officials and the State Board of Education.

Shortly after the outbreak of World War II, Fort Eustis reopened as a Coast Artillery and Anti-aircraft training center, where 15,000 men were stationed. In 1944, however, the military base was declared surplus and converted into a detention camp for enemy prisoners-of-war. At the close of the war, plans were made to make Fort Eustis the Army Transportation Corps' training center. Camp Wallace was deactivated and eventually became part of Anheuser-Busch's holdings at Kingsmill. During the early 1950s a proposal to expand Fort Eustis by 4,000 acres met with strong resistance from officials in James City County and the city of Warwick.[53]

Camp Peary

During autumn 1942 local citizens learned that a naval base called Camp Peary was to be built in York County at Magruder, approximately three miles outside of Williamsburg. Many of the black households living there were relocated temporarily to a C.C.C. camp and then to Grove. At Camp Peary, the United States Navy established a Seabee training facility, which was expected to serve 26,000 men. The Seabees used the base until 1944, when it became the Naval Training and Distribution Center. It was then that the Waller Mill Reservoir was constructed on part of the Camp Peary property to supply water to the city of Williamsburg. In November 1945 the Newport News City Council proposed that Camp Peary be the headquarters of the United Nations. Some consideration also was given to making it the site of a United States Air Force Academy. In 1951 Camp Peary became the Armed Forces Experimental Training Activity Area, a facility used by the Central Intelligence Agency.[54]

World War II Draws to a Close

In November 1944, when national elections were held, James City County came out strongly for Franklin Delano Roosevelt, who was elected to his fourth term in office. A substantial number of absentee ballots were cast by men and women of the armed services and there was a higher than usual turnout in the number of women voters.

1945 brought a plethora of changes that had far-reaching effects. In April, President Franklin D. Roosevelt died in his sleep and Harry S. Truman was sworn in as president. By May Hitler was reported dead and Italy's Fascist commander had "unconditionally surrendered." On May 8, 1945, at 6:01 P.M. the war with Germany officially came to an end. In early August, President Truman announced that a new weapon, the atomic bomb, had been dropped on the Japanese city of Hiroshima. A week later, the Japanese surrendered.[55]

Notes

1. Tindall, NARRATIVE HISTORY, 979, 998; VIRGINIA GAZETTE, February 19, 1926.

2. VIRGINIA GAZETTE, March 20, 1919; December 20, 1920; January 13, 1921.

3. Lebsock, SHARE OF HONOUR, 155; Tindall, NARRATIVE HISTORY, 1001.

4. Netherton et al., FAIRFAX COUNTY, 502, 504, 554; Tindall, NARRATIVE HISTORY, 992.

5. VIRGINIA GAZETTE, March 20, 1920; February 14, September 5, 1930; December 18, 1931; July 21, September 1, 1933; February 2, November 2, 1934, Matica, TALL TALES, 9; Netherton et al., FAIRFAX COUNTY, 554.

6. Davis Bottom, comp., ACTS AND JOINT RESOLUTIONS PASSED BY THE GENERAL ASSEMBLY OF THE STATE OF VIRGINIA PASSED DURING THE SESSION OF 1916 (Richmond, 1918), 424; Kale, HARK, Godson et al. WILLIAM AND MARY, 541, 546–547,553; VIRGINIA GAZETTE, January 10, 1930.

7. WILLIAMSBURG REUNION, 1950 AND BEFORE (Williamsburg 1990); VIRGINIA GAZETTE, September 13, 1963; April 2, 1971.

8. James City County Board of Supervisors Minutes 1908–1925: 361; 1926–1930:46; VIRGINIA GAZETTE, March 10, August 5, 1932; July 26, 1935; February 26, 1943; January 19 and 26, April 27, 1945.

9. Cook, "Sheriffs"; James City County Board of Supervisors Minutes 1908–1925:361; 1926–1930:47, 120, 126, 147, 196; VIRGINIA GAZETTE, December 7, 1931; May 5, 1933; August 16, 1935; January 1, 1937.

10. Cynthia M. Leonard, comp., THE GENERAL ASSEMBLY OF VIRGINIA, JULY 30, 1619— JANUARY 11, 1978, A BICENTENNIAL REGISTER OF MEMBERS (Richmond, 1978), 742; James City County Plat Book 3:23; 5:21.

11. Supervisors Minutes 1908–1925, 286, 299; VIRGINIA GAZETTE, August 12, 1932; January 20, 1933; May 18, 1934; July 22, September 16, 1938; August 25, September 29, October 13, 1939; Bradshaw, ed., TALES, 76–77,81.

12. VIRGINIA GAZETTE, December 28, 1934; April 27, 1945.

13. U.S.D.A., Abridged List of Federal Laws Applicable to Agriculture (Washington, D. C., 1949); VIRGINIA GAZETTE, June 12, 1964.

14. E. M. Slauson, "History of the Peninsula Dairy Association" (Williamsburg, n.d.); U.S.D.A., FEDERAL LAWS; James City County Supervisors Minutes 1908–1925, 318; 1926–1930:47, 147; VIRGINIA GAZETTE, October 6, 1933.

15. VIRGINIA GAZETTE, July 7 and 16, 1971; July 7, 1972. The N.P.S. conducted archaeological excavations at Glasshouse Point during the 1940s and 50s.

16. VIRGINIA GAZETTE, August 1 and 29, September 26, December 12, 1930; January 6 and 30, March 6, August 14, September 4, November 6, 1931. Powhatan Plantation was added to the National Register of Historic Places in 1970.

17. Ibid., October 14 and 21, 1932.

18. James City County Historical Commission File "Home Demonstration" (Toano); Bradshaw, TALES, 33; VIRGINIA GAZETTE, June 19, 1931.

19. James City County Deed Book 34:92–95; 114:291, 292, 295; 189:31; Paul M. Griesenauer, THE REMINISCENCES OF PAUL M. GRIESENAUER (Williamsburg, 1956), 14–15, 27–29, 32–33, 35–36; VIRGINIA GAZETTE, August 28, 1931.

20. VIRGINIA GAZETTE, September 4, 1970; Tina C. Jeffrey, THE BIZARRE BAZAAR: THE STORY OF THE WILLIAMSBURG POTTERY (Jeffrey Publishing Company, 1982), 3–8; Griesenauer, REMINISCENCES, 48–53.

21. James City County Deed Book 18:585; 20:269–271; 27:103–104; 29:493; VIRGINIA GAZETTE, September 4, 1970; Bradshaw et al, NORGE, 47.

22. VIRGINIA GAZETTE, May 30, 1930; February 27, April 10 and 17, 1931; May 31, 1935; Bradshaw et al., NORGE, 62, 65.

23. Davis Bottom, comp., ACTS AND JOINT RESOLUTIONS PASSED BY THE GENERAL ASSEMBLY OF THE STATE OF VIRGINIA PASSED DURING THE SESSION OF 1918 (Richmond, 1918), 429; VIRGINIA GAZETTE, May 26, 1921.

24. REUNION, 1944; N.P.S. Land Records File 8–126; VIRGINIA GAZETTE, May 16, June 20 and 27, August 15, September 12 and 19, October 24, November 7 and 14, 1930; May 15, June 19, 1931; January 1, February 5 and 26, 1932.

25. George H. Yetter, WILLIAMSBURG BEFORE AND AFTER (Williamsburg, 1988), 49–52; REUNION, 1942.

26. REUNION, 1942; VIRGINIA GAZETTE, January 10, July 25, August 1, 1930; October 19, 1934.

27. Gaines, "Courthouses," 30; Rouse, WHERE AMERICA BEGAN; James City County Board of Supervisors Minutes 1926–1930, 147; VIRGINIA GAZETTE, March 27, November 20, December 25, 1931. The 1932 courthouse was replaced by a more modern building in 1968.

28. REUNION, 1942; REMEMBER ME? WILLIAMSBURG REUNION (Williamsburg 1978).

29. H. M. Stryker, THANKS FOR THE MEMORY (Williamsburg, n.d.).

30. VIRGINIA GAZETTE, December 11, 1931. In December 1931 Oscar Rustad of Norge was appointed chairman of the America Legion committee formed to plan a tricentennial celebration of Middle Plantation.

31. REUNION, 1942; VIRGINIA GAZETTE, March 6, May 22, June 19, August 28, September 4, November 20, 1931; February 5, October 14, 1932; October 6, 1933; July 2, 1938; March 14 and 21, April 18, July 10, September 12, 1941; March 19, 1954; October 29, 1965.

32. Ibid., January 17, February 14, June 6 and 20, July 11 and 18, August 25, 1930; September 23, 1932; February 21, 1936.

33. James City County Deed Book 27:576–583; VIRGINIA GAZETTE, September 26, 1930; January 2, 1931; May 6, 1932; March 9, 1934.

34. Stephenson, Carter's Grove, 128–129, 157–166, 172–173, 190. A. Burnley Bibb, a noted architect who visited Carter's Grove in 1896–1897, decried its "shrieking tones of red, white, blue, and—mirabile dictu—green! He hastened to add that his hosts, the Booths, "were guiltless of the crime."

35. James City County Board of Supervisors Minutes 1926–1930:201; VIRGINIA GAZETTE, June 19, August 6, October 23, 1931.

36. VIRGINIA GAZETTE, July 30, 1965.

37. REUNION, 1942; REUNION, 1944.

38. REUNION, 1942; THANKS FOR THE MEMORY.

39. REUNION, 1942; REUNION, 1944; VIRGINIA GAZETTE, January 10, May 16, June 20 and 27, 1930; April 11, 1941; November 17, 1944.

40. REUNION, 1942.

41. VIRGINIA GAZETTE, January 24, January 31, February 7 and 13, March 28, June 27, 1930; October 16, 1936; November 3, 1939; David Waltrip, personal communication, July 7, 1994.

42. VIRGINIA GAZETTE, March 10, 1933; January 16, 1937; February 2, 1940.

43. Their first slate of officers included R. M. Hazelwood (president); Roscoe Wilkinson (vice–president), Charles W. Richardson (secretary), H. E. Hailey (treasurer), R. L. Moody (business manager), Oscar Wheeler (coach), R. H. Farthing (assistant coach), Earl Sweeney (umpire), and John H. Jenson (scorekeeper).

44. Charles M. Hunter, "Civilian Conservation Corps (C.C.C.) in Williamsburg, 1933–1942," Williamsburg Area Historical Society Historical Monograph No. 1 (Williamsburg 1990), 1–8; VIRGINIA GAZETTE, November 13, 1931; November 17, 1933; October 29, 1965; James Haskett, personal communication, March 28 and April 4, 1991; Godson et al., WILLIAM AND MARY, 667–669; John L. Cotter, "Notes on Nineteenth and Early Twentieth Century Jamestown as Reported by Mrs. H. L. Munger and Col. J. P. Barney" (Jamestown, 1956).

45. VIRGINIA GAZETTE, January 10, June 6, December 12 and 19, 1930; January 8, 1932; April 13, July 6, 1934; RICHMOND TIMES–DISPATCH, September 26, 1965; James City County Board of Supervisors Minutes 1908–1925:304.

46. VIRGINIA GAZETTE, January 10 and 24, February 7, June 6 and 20, July 4, August 8 and 18, September 5, October 10, December 5, 1930; June 26, 1931; January 2, September 9, 1932; James City County Board of Supervisors Minutes 1908–1925:295; Manerin, HENRICO COUNTY, 420.

47. VIRGINIA GAZETTE, March 10, 1933; February 2, 1934; November 11, 1938; March 14, May 23, 1941; January 9, 16, and 23, June 5, July 10, August 14, November 13, 1942; June 9 and 23, September 1 and 22, 1944; Tindall, NARRATIVE HISTORY, 1009–1111, 1118–1119, 1126–1131, 1138–1139.

48. Tindall, NARRATIVE HISTORY, 1142–1143.

49. THE WILLIAMSBURG REUNION, 1950 AND BEFORE (Williamsburg, 1990); VIRGINIA GAZETTE, July 10, 1942.

50. REUNION, 1944; VIRGINIA GAZETTE, February 27, April 3, December 25, 1942; March 12, 1943; February 4, 1944; Godson et al., WILLIAM AND MARY, 697–698.

51. Matica, TALL TALES, 17–18; REUNION, 1942; VIRGINIA GAZETTE, October 5, 1962.

52. Clingan, NAVAL WEAPONS STATION, 1, 13, 23, 25. In August 1958 the Naval Mine Depot was renamed the Naval Weapons Station.

53. Fort Eustis Historical and Archaeological Association, THE HISTORY OF MULBERRY ISLAND (Newport News, n.d.); VIRGINIA GAZETTE, October 10, 1930; November 20, 1931; June 16, 1933; July 15, 1938.

54. VIRGINIA GAZETTE, September 25, November 20, 1942; June 2, 1944; February 2, November 9, 1945; June 7, July 5, 1946; August 22, 1947; January 13, 1950; January 12, 1957; C.W.F., Resource Protection, Sections IV and V.

55. James City County Deed Book 42:249; REUNION, 1944; VIRGINIA GAZETTE, September 22, November 10, 1944; February 9, April 13, May 4 and 11, August 10, 17 and 31, 1945.

CHAPTER 15

A Place to Live, A Place to Grow
1946–1990

Postwar James City County

After the war ended, the American public eagerly awaited a return to peacetime conditions. The Williamsburg U.S.O. Club closed in August 1946, after serving over three and a half million service men and women. Many veterans, like Toano High School teacher A. A. Williams, returned to enter the work force. Some, however, made the ultimate sacrifice. According to armed forces statistics, twenty James City County men lost their lives during World War II: Clifford D. Anderson; Ellsworth P. Ayers Jr.; John L. Blacknall; Murray E. Borish; Paul Chambers; Phillip P. Chess, Jr; Arthur S. Cosgrove; Charles E. Cox; William A. Goodwin; Alexander G. Harwood; Walter C. Martin Jr.; William W. McGee; James G. Needham; Francis B. Rang; Dewey C. Renick, Jr.; Lawrence M. Rhodes; John N. Richardson Jr.; Herbert C. Roberts Jr; and Ira B. Short.[1] Their passing was felt deeply by the community.

But life went on. The James City Ruritan Club met regularly and youngsters from the county's 4-H clubs continued to descend upon the camp at Jamestown, just as they had before the war. A newly formed post of the Veterans of Foreign Wars chose W. Hooker Harber as post commander. The organization provided local veterans with a chance to socialize and meet for mutual support. Because fuel shortages persisted, the Victory Pulpwood Committee (a holdover from the recent war) advised local citizens to continue using woodlots. In 1946 the Board of Supervisors adopted a $120,000 budget, then a record-breaking sum. Meanwhile, the state highway department undertook construction of a four-lane highway from Toano to Bottoms Bridge, utilizing Route 60's right-of-way. In Norge, the Farm Bureau leased a parcel from the C&O and built a warehouse. Closer to Williamsburg, G. Maxwell Lanier opened a big store on Richmond Road, opposite the Stockade Theater. One local entrepreneur decided to build a frozen food locker plant on Richmond Road and another opened a nearby skating-rink. Although times were tight in some parts of the country, as 1946 ended the local economy was relatively vibrant. The H. L. Smith Motor Company's announcement that new automobiles were on display in its showroom attracted window-shoppers and buyers. There was an upswing in housing starts and during March 1947 the James City County Board of Supervisors adopted an ordinance requiring building permits for structures costing more than $300.[2]

Mable Massey, James City County's Home Demonstration Agent for more than 25 years, resigned in early 1947. She was replaced by Miriam Puster who served for an even longer period. In 1948 Barton A. Jenson, the treasurer of Williamsburg and James City County, died after 20 years in office. His position was offered to Edmond W. Cowles, the county's commissioner of revenue since 1919. In July 1947 Sheriff V. Wayne Lovelace took to the air in a Piper Cub to search for moonshiners. The VIRGINIA GAZETTE reported that his innovative approach led to the unprecedented discovery of three stills in a single weekend. B. L. Marks, a special police officer, was assigned to Toano on Friday and Saturday nights to maintain law and order. In September 1948 the Chickahominy Electric Company, with headquarters in Toano, began supplying power to James City, York, Charles City, New Kent, Henrico and Hanover Counties.

Interest rates were relatively low throughout 1948 and the Peninsula Bank and Trust Company offered to pay one percent on savings deposits of $1,000 or more. But to put a 1948 dollar's purchasing power into perspective, a new Pontiac four-door sedan sold for $1,728 and $124.95 would buy a laundry ensemble that included a new washing machine, an electric iron, an ironing board and twenty boxes of soap powder. At a local grocery store, a pound of vegetable shortening cost 37 cents and soft drinks sold for a nickle.

In 1949 Williamsburg celebrated its 250th anniversary. Meanwhile, the Toano Baseball Club, a member of the Tri-County Semi-professional Baseball League, began holding practice sessions with coaches Oscar Wheeler and A. A. Williams. The league included teams from several peninsula communities plus the C&O. The Board of Supervisors allocated $1,000 toward the development of an athletic field at the Toano School and the James City County Athletic Association sponsored a fund-raising drive to underwrite the cost of building a county stadium there. A new Jamestown 4-H Camp opened at a site a mile and a half west of the old facility established in 1928. There, campers could hike, swim and enjoy educational programs.[3]

Mainstays of the Community

The James City-Bruton Volunteer Fire Department

In March 1947 a group of local citizens interested in establishing a volunteer fire department met in the Norge Community Hall. Out of that meeting came companies of fire-fighters that were based in Toano, Ewell, Grove, Five Forks, and Norge. Each company had a contact person to receive fire reports. The newly formed fire department decided to keep its Model A chemical truck at E. C. ("Pop") Summers' garage in Ewell and to store a truck equipped with a tank, pumps, and hoses in Toano. In January 1948 the fire-fighters appointed G. E. Farthing, Z. O. Smith, and A. R. Lipton as special police to restrain onlookers at the scene of fires. The officers of the James City County Fire Department in 1950 were G. Maxwell Lanier, R. Kemper Taylor, and D. C. Renick. "Pop" Summers served as chief and Robert Piggott as assistant chief, with Willie Jacobson as captain.

During the 1950s, the Five Forks, Grove and Ewell fire companies constructed a station across from James Blair High School. Later, all three companies merged with the Williamsburg Fire Department and moved their equipment to the city station. The fire company located in Toano used as its fire house a two-storey building next door to R. Kemper Taylor's garage. Garland Wooddy was elected fire chief and served ably for many years. In 1957 a new communications network allowed volunteer firemen to have home radio receivers to summon them to fires.

In time, it became a tradition for the Board of Supervisors to purchase fire engines for the James City-Bruton Volunteer Fire Department. In 1965–1966, when the Toano School was razed, a modern fire station was built on the site. When it opened in 1967, the Board of Supervisors agreed to fund a paid fire-fighter who would summon the volunteers and assemble the preliminary equipment. Later, a paramedic and a second paid fire-fighter were hired so that someone always would be on hand. During the early 1960s a Ladies Auxiliary was formed to assist with fund raising, help maintain the fire station, and provide food and coffee to fire-fighters on the job. One money-making activity for which the Auxiliary is famous is its Fish Frys.[4]

The Rescue Squad

The all-volunteer Rescue Squad was established in 1957. At first, members used converted station-wagons to transport the injured. Although the organization traditionally has shared the fire department's facilities, it is a separate entity and purchases its own ambulances and emergency equipment. The Rescue Squad receives public funding for gasoline and the maintenance of life-saving equipment.[5]

Williamsburg Community Hospital and The Pines

In 1955 the Chamber of Commerce first advocated the construction of a public hospital to serve the local community. Three years later a site was chosen and citizens mounted a fund-raising campaign in Williamsburg and six nearby counties. Philanthropist John D. Rockefeller, Jr., offered $500,000, half of the new facility's projected cost. Hospital construction got underway in April 1959 and Robert Shields became the first administrator. The Williamsburg Community Hospital opened its doors on March 12, 1961, and James Overstreet, the first patient, was admitted on April 3rd. The following day, Mr. and Mrs. John A. Cox became parents of the first baby born there. One important addition to the hospital's program was the establishment of a poison control center in autumn 1962. In December 1966 Bell Hospital closed after serving the community for nearly forty years. In 1970 The Pines, a nursing home and convalescent center, was built. The project was undertaken by a group of local doctors and members of the business community.[6]

The National Guard and American Legion

In January 1948 a local unit of the National Guard, an anti-aircraft battalion, was formed with Orlin Rogers as commanding officer. It was on active duty from August 1950 to April 1952 and served as part of the 710th Anti-Aircraft Artillery. Members of the National Guard attended meetings and participated in week-long drills. Another group many local veterans belonged to was the American Legion. In 1950 Douglas Johnson became post commander, succeeding Alfred L. Lipton.[7]

The Korean War

In June 1950, when President Truman, with the support of the United Nations Security Council, sent military units to South Korea, patriotic feelings ran high. The James City Ruritans, like civic organizations throughout America, promoted the sale of Savings Bonds to underwrite the cost of military spending. In early September 1950 the Selective Service was asked to provide 70,000 recruits by November, who could be deployed for the Korean War. On Sunday, July 26, 1953, when the United Nations command and Communist delegates signed a truce, local citizens were ecstatic. In celebration of the armistice Bruton Parish Church's bell was rung and the cannons at the Powder Magazine were fired.[8]

Life on the Local Scene

In 1950 the new Tri-County Baseball League's teams from Toano and Williamsburg took to the field. The local black softball league generated strong support and lights for night softball were installed at Bruton Heights School. Racially segregated women's softball leagues were organized as part of a local summer recreation program. Charles W. Richards, James City

County's agricultural extension agent, tried to start a Grange in Toano. Meanwhile, local Jaycees squared off against Peninsula Post 39 of the American Legion in a Donkey Softball game. In March 1950 the Chesapeake and Potomac Telephone Company (the C&P) installed Williamsburg's 3,000th telephone and four years later took over service to the Peninsula Telephone Corporation's subscribers in the Toano area. In early 1957 telephones on the west side of Williamsburg were converted to a dial system and assigned to an exchange designated "Locust 4"; Williamsburg subscribers already were using a "Capital 9" prefix. Other modernizing developments included the May 1952 opening of the George P. Coleman Bridge across the York River at Yorktown, which replaced a ferry route more than three centuries old.[9]

Moonshining was an ongoing law enforcement problem and Sheriff Lovelace continued to conduct airborne searches for violators. In April 1951 he located and destroyed a 550-gallon still, reputedly the largest discovered since World War II. He also arrested three people involved in a numbers racket and confiscated $12.88. The Board of Supervisors asked the local Circuit Court judge to designate ex-deputy-sheriff Archie Brenegan a special policeman, as he had been fired by Sheriff Lovelace for opposing him in the 1951 election. When Walter C. Martin disclosed that he would not seek another term on the Board of Supervisors, R. L. Moody, Wesley E. Sheldon, and Thomas L. Hockaday announced that they would enter the race.[10]

In September 1951 the James City County School Board replaced the traditional eleven-year educational curriculum with a twelve-year format they inaugurated at the Toano High School.[11] As 1952 drew to a close, a local study commission began weighing the merits of consolidating James City County's school system with Williamsburg's, a change both areas' school boards had recommended three years earlier. Williamsburg schools were badly overcrowded, for virtually all of James City County's black students attended the city's Bruton Heights School and white students from the county's populous Jamestown Magisterial District went to the city's Matthew Whaley School. So controversial was the idea of consolidation that the voters of Stonehouse District asked their School Board representative to resign because his views were out of synch with theirs.[12]

As the Civil Rights movement began to spread across the nation, local blacks gained enough confidence to participate in local politics. In March 1950 M. L. Whiting, a prominent civic and business leader, sought election to the Williamsburg City Council. The following fall, the Urban League announced that it would conduct a survey to assess the business and educational opportunities available to local blacks. In late 1952 James City County blacks filed a petition with the county school board in which they asked for educational facilities equal to those furnished whites. They noted that the upcoming bond issue did not include funds for a much-needed black high school. Commonwealth Attorney Bathurst D. Peachy Jr. urged local officials to replace the Chickahominy Elementary School because it was in deplorable condition. He also pointed out that the United States Supreme Court was then questioning the legality of racial segregation. The Rev. Junius H. Moody, principal of Chickahominy Elementary, said that his school was dark, dingy, in poor repair, and lacked indoor plumbing. Seven grades were crammed into six classrooms, one of which was across the street in a local Masonic Lodge.

1952 brought the death of Judge Frank Armistead only two weeks before his scheduled retirement, and in November, Dwight D. Eisenhower won a sweeping victory over presidential opponent Adlai Stevenson, taking all but one of James City County's electoral districts. In late April 1953 Bathurst D. Peachy Jr., Commonwealth Attorney for 25 years, died suddenly. A month later, Robert T. Armistead was appointed to fill his position. In 1956 when Armistead became Associate Judge of the 14th Circuit Court, J. B. Cowles of Toano was made Commonwealth Attorney.[13]

In December 1952 some local citizens rallied to the support of a terminally ill Henrico County boy, who expressed a strong desire for watermelon. When Ellsworth Owen heard about the boy's request, he contacted the Williamsburg Lodge's purchasing agent. He, in turn, recalled that Stewart U. Taylor stored watermelons in his basement every winter. Some of Taylor's melons were delivered to the youngster, who ate his fill a few hours before he died.[14]

During the spring of 1953, the Welcome Wagon began providing Greater Williamsburg area newcomers with information on local businesses and public services. In the summer James City County voters approved school consolidation by an almost 2 to 1 margin and passed a bond issue to fund construction of a new high school and improve existing facilities. Through the referendum came plans to abandon the all-white Toano School and the Chickahominy School for blacks. A new high school for whites was to be built at Casey's Corner (James Blair High School) and Matthew Whaley was to be enlarged to accommodate all of the city's and county's white elementary school students. Two new wings were to be added to the Bruton Heights School so that black students, grades 1 through 12, could receive instruction there. Members of the James City Negro League protested what they termed the school consolidation plan's inequality. Even so, all of these changes were implemented over a three year period. In early June 1956 James Blair's first senior class received diplomas and 36 seniors graduated from the Bruton Heights School. The Board of Supervisors began requiring motor vehicles to have county license tags, a measure undertaken to generate revenue. A 15 cent fire protection levy was imposed upon the populous Jamestown District and five years later the same policy was applied to the Powhatan and Stonehouse Districts. In other civic matters, Gerald J. Otey of Lanexa was appointed game warden for James City County and Williamsburg, the first person to serve both areas. Meanwhile, Russell M. Carneal was elected to the House of Delegates, defeating the incumbent, a Yorktown man.[15]

As the summer of 1953 drew to a close, "stewmaster" Wise Skillman, applied his culinary talents to the cook-pot in preparation for the Ruritan Club's annual Brunswick Stew feast at the Jamestown 4-H Center. The VIRGINIA GAZETTE reported the end of the year's plague of 17-year locusts, which were expected to reappear in May 1970. Another news story indicated that when Mrs. Rivers Washington's empty house burned to the ground, a 500-gallon still was found amid the glowing embers. November 1953 brought Ike Smith's dramatic rescue from the bottom of his narrow-shafted, 40-foot-deep well. Credited with saving his life was neighbor Francis R. ("Buddy") Jones, who entered the well twice in an attempt to extricate him. State trooper L. F. Craft and Williamsburg Doctor Hugh Stokes also descended the well shaft during rescue operations. Another mishap during the year had a fatal outcome, for an automobile occupied by Comer Jackson, Edwin Gilley, and Homer Cox plunged into the Chickahominy River from the open span of the Route 5 drawbridge. Highway department officials attributed the accident to a combination of human error and equipment failure. An auto theft ring began operating in the area and in early 1954 newly-elected Delegate Carneal sought state funds for a full time police officer for James City County. Mother Nature dealt Tidewater Virginia a reeling blow in 1955 when Hurricane Hazel hit with full force, felling trees, knocking down power lines, and causing widespread destruction. At Carter's Grove 40 trees lay on the ground and some of the mansion's slate roofing was damaged.[16]

But life on the local scene usually hummed along smoothly. In April 1954 the VIRGINIA GAZETTE reported that H. Y. Young's dairy farm in James City County had a modern milking parlour that significantly increased his cows' productivity and the James City Ruritan Club held a fund-raiser to help the Toano Women's Club purchase the Community Building from the School Board. Plans got underway to construct a National Guard armory for James City County and Williamsburg. Also, President Eisenhower announced that he had asked Congress for an appropriation that would allow the Colonial National Parkway to be extended from Williamsburg to Jamestown.[17]

Celebrating Jamestown's 350th Birthday

The early 1950s brought a resurgence of interest in Jamestown, whose 350th anniversary was approaching. In 1957 a relatively elaborate celebration called the Jamestown Festival was held to commemorate the landing of Virginia's first colonists. Large crowds of visitors attended, including Queen Elizabeth II and Vice-President Richard M. Nixon. Extensive archaeological excavations were undertaken by the National Park Service on Jamestown Island and state and federally sponsored visitors centers were opened to the public. Archaeological work also was carried out at Green Spring Plantation. The Colonial Parkway was extended, linking Williamsburg to Jamestown, and a causeway was built that connected the island to the mainland at Glass House Point. In celebration of the arrival of the first Africans at Jamestown, a special ceremony was held at the Jamestown Festival Park, where black military officers were honored and a salute was fired in recognition of World War II naval hero Dorie Miller. In 1960 Native Americans from several states began holding an annual Fall Festival at Jamestown. In 1973, when the state of

Virginia sent its first float to an inaugural parade in 24 years, it featured a conjectural rendition of the first settlers' fort.[18]

Entering the Maelstrom: The 1960s

As the 1950s drew to a close and stereotypical American housewives "waltzed through washday" in their aprons and high-heeled shoes, some members of the younger generation were beginning to question the morality of what John Kenneth Galbraith labeled "the affluent society." As the Cold War grew colder and a nuclear attack was considered possible, official interest turned to civil defense projects. Some people constructed bomb shelters and stored food to sustain them in case of an atomic attack. In James City County, Frank Anderson, as the director of Civil Defense, organized educational programs dealing with radiation hazards and protection from fallout.

Emergencies of a more immediate nature occurred in James City County during 1960. In January an Army helicopter made a fatal crash landing near Norge and in March two heavy snowstorms occurred. Then, on September 12, 1960, Hurricane Donna roared through the area between 5 and 7 A.M. Its 50 to 60 miles per hour winds felled trees and tore down electrical and telephone lines. Extensive damage occurred at Jamestown Island, where trees were uprooted, and at the Jamestown Festival Park, where jetties were damaged. 1960 brought the closing of the Toano's C&O freight office and railway express station and the retirement of D. L. Armstrong, station operator for 28 years.[19]

Demographic Change and Growing Pains

During the 1950s the number of people living in Virginia grew slowly but steadily. In James City County the population rose from 3,879 in 1930 to 4,907 in 1940, to 6,317 in 1950; nearby Williamsburg had 6,726 inhabitants, excluding college students. In 1950 the number of James City County residents involved in agriculture began to decline, a trend that accelerated as time went on and was replicated throughout the state. The median income of Virginia families in 1950 was $2,602, with just over 37 percent making less than $2,000 a year.[20]

By 1960 the nation's population had increased by almost 40 million, thanks to the "baby boom" generation born after World War II. This population explosion created an unprecedented demand for family housing and spurred the proliferation of suburbs. Residential development produced urban sprawl and an increased need for essential public services such as a safe and adequate supply of drinking water, sewage, and refuse disposal, and additional roads and schools. But growth also stimulated business and commercial interests, which provided jobs and enhanced tax revenues. By the early 1960s 20 percent of Americans were living between Boston, Massachusetts, and Norfolk, Virginia, in an expansive corridor that enveloped James City County. This demographic shift was a powerful catalyst for change.[21]

By 1960 there were 11,539 people living in James City County, nearly twice the population in 1950 and three times the 1930 level. Nearby Williamsburg's population almost had doubled as had that of neighboring York County. Between 1910 and 1960 a remarkable 754.4 percent of James City County's growth occurred in Jamestown Magisterial District, where the population increased from 975 to 8,330. Meanwhile, that of Powhatan Magisterial District grew from 1,613 in 1910 to 2,198 in 1960, reflecting a modest 36.3 percent increase. Concurrently, the population of the Stonehouse Magisterial District (1,036 in 1910 and 1,011 in 1960) decreased by 25 people during that 50-year period. Thus, in 1960 72.2 percent of James City County's population resided in the Jamestown Magisterial District. This demographic change had not occurred overnight. In 1930 the Jamestown District had 35 percent of the population, whereas Powhatan had 42 percent and Stonehouse, 23 percent. By 1940 the Jamestown District had 49.4 percent of the total population, whereas Powhatan had 33.6 percent and Stonehouse had 17 percent. In 1953 when the residents of the Jamestown District asked the circuit court judge to subdivide their district, they asserted that 60 percent of the county's population resided there.[22]

Census records reveal that between 1940 and 1960 the number of James City County citizens involved in farming fell by approximately 15 percent and the number of non-farm rural residents rose proportionately. During 1959 alone, nine of James City County's 155 farms were made into subdivisions and another nine were placed in conservation reserve.[23] In 1960 the Board of

Supervisors debated whether to begin requiring developers to build roads in accord with state specifications so that they could be taken into the highway system. By 1960 almost all James City County housing units had some form of heating equipment, such as furnaces, wood or oil stoves or electric heaters; however, only 68 percent had an indoor water supply, flush toilets, and a bath tub or shower. In late 1960 James City and York Counties agreed to collaborate on the construction of a sanitary sewage system for the neighborhoods along Penniman Road, where urban growth had proliferated.[24]

As James City County's population grew, the Board of Supervisors' agenda became increasingly lengthy and in December 1959 they commenced meeting twice a month. The districts the supervisors represented began to take on more distinctive personalities, largely in keeping with how much urbanization had occurred. One controversial issue was zoning. In 1953 the Board appointed a Planning Commission. Among its proposals was recommending a change to the county manager form of government. But the majority of voters soundly rejected the idea when it came to a referendum. In 1956 the county Planning Commission produced a preliminary zoning ordinance and map, which the Board of Supervisors revised and then tabled indefinitely. Charles W. Richards of Powhatan Magisterial District was adamantly opposed to the concept of zoning and announced that he'd try to have his district excluded from any ordinances that were passed. In 1960 the Planning Commission was reactivated and constituents of the Jamestown Magisterial District asked the Board to formulate zoning ordinances exclusively for their area. The draft ordinance and map was shuttled back and forth between the Board and Commission until 1962, when a concensus finally was reached. Ultimately, draft zoning ordinances and a masterplan were developed.[25]

Another weighty issue the Board of Supervisors was obliged to address in 1962 was Williamsburg's attempt to annex nearly three square miles of county land. Ultimately, the matter ended up in court. The operation of the consolidated school system also proved problematic. Although there was general agreement that local schools were badly overcrowded, the county refused to fund its share of new construction until the annexation suit was settled.[26] Later, when the state annexation court reached a verdict the Board

The Williamsburg-James City County Courthouse. Photo by Carl Aschman.

Carter's Grove Plantation. Photo by Ralph Maxwell.

felt favored the city, they filed an appeal. As a result of the 1962 annexation court decision, Williamsburg's limits were expanded to include land along Route 60 West to Skipwith Farms; between Lake Matoaka and Route 5; and between York and Second Streets. It was then that Highland Park was taken from York County and given to Williamsburg in the interest of maintaining a reasonable racial balance. Later, a study commission was appointed to weigh the merits of a merger with Williamsburg. The Williamsburg-James City County Consolidation Study Commission, which first met on January 21, 1963, included elected and appointed officials from both jurisdictions. In August the Commission announced that a merger between the two jurisdictions was feasible. While James City County's Board of Supervisors was pondering whether to put the issue to a referendum, they received word that the Williamsburg City Council opposed consolidation.[27]

As it became increasingly difficult to cover the rising cost of government, the Board of Supervisors sought new ways to curb expenditures. For example, in 1960 the Board decided to make monthly odometer inspections of the personal vehicles driven by law enforcement officers to make sure that they were not being reimbursed for excess mileage. In a fund-raising move, the Board decided to pass local ordinances against certain types of misdemeanors so that the guilty could be fined by the county instead of the state. The Board also decided to raise the cost of local licence tags and to require all vehicles used and kept in the county to be licensed there. In 1962 it became necessary to improve the public sewage facilities in Toano, a septic tank system constructed during the 1930s, because the State Water Control Board determined that it was polluting Ware Creek.[28]

Due to population growth, public landfills were needed for refuse disposal. As rising costs seemed imminent, the Board of Supervisors debated whether to reduce funding for public welfare. They also considered public health issues, such as whether they should require barbers, beauticians, food handlers, and others to be tested annually for tuberculosis. When Board members decided to convert an old road right-of-way on the Gospel Spreading Farm into a public boat landing, they posted signs and and began making improvements. But the Church of God, which owned part of the farmland through which the abandoned right-of-way passed, protested and then threatened to sue. Plans to build a landing on Halfway Creek also came to a halt, for the National Park Service refused to allow access through its property. Because managing the affairs of the county was becoming increasingly time-consuming, in March 1962 the Board of Supervisors decided to hire an Executive Secretary, a position first filled by Lee D. Robbins, a retired Army officer.[29] 1962 brought an offer from Colonial Williamsburg to build a new, more modern city-county courthouse, if officials would agree to relinquish their old lot and facilities. Throughout 1963 and 1964 officials debated whether to construct a county office building in Toano with funds that could be matched with federal monies if the structure were outfitted as an Emergency Operations Center. In June 1965 plans got underway to erect the E.O.C. building in Toano.[30]

The November 1963 elections resulted in the ouster of two long-time members of the Board of Supervisors. In the Jamestown Magisterial District, Dr. Murray Loring replaced James E. Vaiden; in Stonehouse William F. Pettengill won over Frank B. Anderson in a write-in vote. One controversial issue the new Board faced was whether to seek $2.4 million in school bonds that would enable James City County to establish its own school system, or $1.25 million in funds needed for the joint school system. When a public referendum was held, the costlier bond issue was approved by a very narrow margin. However, no action was taken on abandoning the school contract with Williamsburg. In January 1964 when the new Board met for the first time, ultra-conservative Charles W. Richards was elected chairman and A. B. Smith, the County Attorney, was asked to resign. Executive Secretary Lee D. Robbins submitted his resignation in July but offered to stay on if he received unanimous backing from the Board. As Supervisor Richards favored abolishing the position altogether, Robbins departed and Garland Wooddy was hired as the county's new Executive Secretary. The Board also made plans to draft an "escape clause" that would enable the county to withdraw from the 1954 joint-school contract. Meanwhile, a burgeoning number of school-age children necessitated the use of portable classrooms and forced students to attend classes in shifts. Thus, there was an immediate need to build more schools and hire more personnel. In late 1964 the Board of Supervisors discussed the feasibility of a local sales tax and licensing fees for businesses and professionals, both of which measures met with objections.[31]

Shortly after the 1964 presidential election, Circuit Court Judge Robert T. Armistead created a new magisterial district within James City County and made a slight adjustment in the boundary lines of Stonehouse and Powhatan Districts. The newly established Berkeley Magisterial District, which was bound on the east by Jamestown Road, was named after Governor William Berkeley whose Green Spring plantation lay within its territory. Judge Armistead appointed Fred Flanary to serve as Berkeley District's supervisor until elections could be held. Because the addition of Berkeley gave James City County an even number of districts, Judge Armistead designated James E. Maloney to serve as official tie-breaker whenever the four Supervisors were deadlocked on a decision. With the creation of Berkeley District, the county was subdivided in political units that were nearly equal in size, none of which encompassed less than 30 square miles. By 1966 the population of James City and York Counties and the city of Williamsburg had increased so much that when a State Convention was held, the area was allowed to send a delegate to the General Assembly.[32]

Leaping into the Future

In February 1962, when astronaut John Glenn roared into space and orbited the earth three times, local citizens of all ages watched his televised launch and schoolchildren charted the path of the Mercury's orbits. The local Chamber of Commerce declared its support for liquor by the drink, a policy favored by the tourist industry and many others. March 1962 brought what was declared to be the worst snowstorm in twenty years. Later in the year, the Williamsburg City Council approved Colonial Williamsburg's request to close Duke of Gloucester Street's first block to motor traffic during certain hours. It also was during 1962 that Williamsburg got its first traffic signal light. 1963 brought a lengthy drought that was devastating to local crops. Many Williamsburg area residents also faced a water shortage, for the Waller Mill dam broke, releasing the city's supply of drinking water.[33]

In 1964, the year the Chesapeake Bay-Bridge Tunnel opened to use, the General Assembly appropriated the funds needed to transfer all of Eastern

State Hospital's facilities to Dunbar Farm. Dr. William H. Keeler, outgoing director of the Colonial Health District, recommended to the Board of Supervisors that James City County employ two new public health nurses. He noted that the county had not increased the size of the health department's staff in 20 years, despite enormous growth in the county's population.[34]

Celebrating Local History

As the 100th anniversary of the Civil War drew near, local citizens planned commemorative events. The VIRGINIA GAZETTE started publishing "The Civil War, Week by Week," a regular feature recounting war news of the 1860s, and William Geiger, a Civil War buff, asked James City and York Counties and Williamsburg to preserve Fort Magruder by raising and re-seeding its redoubts. Although the Board of Supervisors decided not to contribute toward the fort restoration project, Brantley Henderson, head of the James City County Centennial Committee, met with greater success when he proposed publication of a booklet on the Peninsular Campaign, preparation of a relief map, and re-dedication of the Confederate monument. York County and Williamsburg, meanwhile, agreed to clean up the site of Fort Magruder, reinforce its redoubts, erect a marker and provide parking near the fort. In February 1962 the William and Mary Theater produced "John Brown's Body," the first Civil War centennial event held locally.[35]

Carter's Grove Becomes a Tourist Attraction

In 1963, after Mrs. Mary Corling McCrea's death, Sealantic Fund President David Rockefeller purchased Carter's Grove. The philanthropic organization he headed pledged to preserve and protect the colonial mansion and its grounds for the enjoyment and education of future generations. Shortly thereafter, the plantation was opened to tourists on a limited basis. In January 1970 the board of the Sealantic Fund gave Carter's Grove to the Colonial Williamsburg Foundation. Between 1976 and 1981 Foundation archaeologists under the direction of Ivor Noël-Hume conducted excavations at Carter's Grove where several early seventeenth-century sites associated with Martin's Hundred were

were explored. The remains of a fortified compound likened to an Irish bawn village were discovered and turned into a public interpretative program.[36]

On the Cusp of the Future

Between 1960 and 1969 the population of James City County grew by more than 60.6 percent. New subdivisions, single and multiple family dwellings, and mobile homes proliferated throughout the countryside and convenience stores and shopping centers were built to accommodate their occupants. In 1962 the James City County Chamber of Commerce asked the State Highway Department to make Route 60 four lanes wide from Lightfoot to Anderson's Corner, a corridor they declared was "the lifeline of the county's commerce." They also urged state officials to build a bridge from Jamestown to Surry, noting that a Jamestown Bridge Association already had been formed. Chamber members asked the highway department to place directional signs at Anderson's Corner that would send tourists to Williamsburg by way of Route 60 and they recommended that interchanges of Interstate 64 be placed at Anderson's Corner, Lightfoot, Norge, and Camp Peary. Colonial Williamsburg President Carlisle Hummelsine, meanwhile, urged local business leaders and governing officials to seek clean industry and long-term investors rather than allowing the area to succumb to what he called the "honky-tonk atmosphere" in evidence at Gettysburg, Natural Bridge, and the Great Smokies. A month after Hummelsine's address, the James City County Board of Supervisors revived the issue of zoning, which had been tabled in 1956. A masterplan produced by the Planning Commission included provisions for commercial, residential, agricultural, and light and heavy industrial zoning. County and state planning officials also began working together to formulate feasible ordinances. At the close of 1964, the Board of Supervisors was obliged to approve the construction of a wax museum on Richmond Road despite widespread community opposition, simply because there were no zoning ordinances on the books that would allow them to prohibit it.[37]

In 1965 the James City County Board of Supervisors approved the county's first land use map, a masterplan intended to chart the course of development and yield orderly growth. At the close of 1969, the Roberts

Magisterial District was created, giving the county a total of five districts. In 1971 the boundary lines of James City County's magisterial districts were adjusted to reflect demographic changes that had occurred; in accord with the law, the approval of the United States Department of Justice was sought. As James City County became more populous and tourism increased, the Board of Supervisors passed ordinances that restricted the use of firearms within densely inhabited areas and commenced devoting some attention to maintaining aesthetic values, such as limiting the size and proliferation of billboards, and screening automobile graveyards from view.

During the 1960s the number of housing starts and new businesses proliferated. In 1965 the Williamsburg National Bank (forerunner of Jefferson National) opened for business, making temporary use of a trailer parked at the corner of South Henry and Ireland Streets. Under the leadership of Dr. Davis Paschall, more than a dozen buildings were erected on the William and Mary campus, including the Earl Greg Swem Library, which opened its doors in 1966. The largest structure erected during the Paschall administration was the William and Mary Hall, which was dedicated on February 13, 1971.[38]

Social and Cultural Events

During the early 1960s the Norge Saddle Club's horse shows enjoyed widespread community support. The Williamsburg-James City County League of Women Voters was formed to promote citizen participation in government and the Williamsburg Rotarians and James City County Ruritans held a "city-county night" intended to foster regional rapport. Meanwhile the local Lions Club began staging annual minstrel shows that included an all-male ballet corps clad in tights and tutus. The Cheshire Cats, a folk and jazz group from James Blair High School, commenced performing and the Wedgewood Dinner Theater in Toano staged its first production. In 1964 the Capital Branch of the Association for the Preservation of Virginia Antiquities celebrated its diamond anniversary and three years later the James City County chapter of the American Red Cross marked its golden anniversary.

In 1964 James City County formally honored 94-year-old R. Kemper Taylor Sr., "pioneer of Toano," in a testimonial dinner. He was lauded for his role in bringing electricity and a water system to Toano, being one of Toano High School's original sponsors, and being a charter member of the fire department. Another local man with a devoted following was farmer-huckster Henry Madison Hazelwood of Toano, the "Corn King of James City County," whose produce stand near the Williamsburg Shopping Center attracted hordes of shoppers. Seven-year-old Ashton Hertzler also earned a place in local agricultural history by growing a pumpkin that weighed 101 pounds!

The Chambers of Commerce of Williamsburg and James City County sponsored a joint springtime "Clean-up, Paint-up, Fix-up Week" in 1965 to encourage local citizens to spruce up their neighborhoods. It became an annual event. Meanwhile, the first annual Colonial Cup Regatta was held on the Chickahominy River at Chickahominy Haven, an event in which 80 boaters participated. In 1968 Williamsburg held its first Occasion for the Arts, which attracted large crowds. A highlight of the 1969 Occasion was a visit from the well known children's television personality, Captain Kangaroo. A considerably less welcome visitor also arrived: Hurricane Camille, which dumped several inches of rain upon the peninsula.[39]

Child Development Resources. Photo by Nan Maxwell.

The Civil Rights Struggle

With the May 17, 1954, decision of Brown versus the Topeka Board of Education, school desegregation became mandatory throughout the United States. In September Governor Thomas Stanley responded by appointing a 32-member, bi-partisan legislative commission to formulate a policy for Virginia's public schools. He promised to "use every legal means . . . to continue segregated schools in Virginia." A month later, the James City Ruritan Club went on record as favoring school segregation. In August 1956 when the General Assembly held a special session to devise a school operating plan, the governor recommended that funds be withheld from any locality that allowed integration. Delegate Russell M. Carneal, who represented James City County, supported the majority decision.[40]

In September 1957 President Eisenhower signed into law the first civil rights legislation since Reconstruction. It empowered the U.S. Attorney General to seek court injunctions in order to protect blacks' voting rights in federal elections. Eisenhower also ordered federal troops to enforce the inte-

The Anheuser-Busch Brewery. Photo by Nan Maxwell.

gration of an all-white high school in Little Rock, Arkansas. Although some Virginians (especially in the Southside) mounted what they called the Massive Resistance campaign, the Virginia Supreme Court of Appeals decided that the state had to keep its public schools open. State legislators responded by rescinding Virginia's mandatory school attendance law, making enrollment a local option. In October 1958 the James City County Board of Supervisors passed a resolution endorsing Virginia's school segregation policies. Although 21 black children entered formerly all-white schools in Norfolk and Arlington in February 1959, it was not until 1964–1965 that local schools were desegregated.[41]

In March 1963 the James City County Board of Supervisors began considering the construction of a new black high school on the grounds of the Bruton Heights School. However, local black leaders generally opposed the plan for they favored building a new facility nearer the center of the black population. A fund-raising drive got underway to underwrite construction of a recreation center for James City County, Williamsburg, and upper York County blacks, a facility that became known as Quarterpath Park. The perpetuation of racial segregation in public facilities, despite new federal laws, reflected many local whites' reluctance to accept integration.

In October 1963 the Bruton Heights Parent-Teacher Association formally asked the Board of Supervisors to restore compulsory school attendance, for the drop-out rate among blacks had increased, resulting in higher rates of unemployment and juvenile delinquency. The city and county School Boards also asked for the reinstatement of compulsory attendance, citing the fact that approximately 80 school-age children had dropped out of school and another 55 were chronic absentees. It was not until May 1965 that the Board held a public hearing on the issue, by which time token integration had occurred. A month later, a local ordinance was passed requiring those between 6 and 16 to attend school.[42]

In November 1963, the VIRGINIA GAZETTE published a letter by a writer using the pseudonym "Frederick Douglass,"[43] who urged fellow whites to consider the plight of local blacks. He said that although they had not staged demonstrations or protest marches, they were being harmed irreparably by segregation. He pointed out that no blacks then served on the School Board, the Planning Commission, or other public committees, even though other Virginia communities had included them. He added that only unskilled blacks could find employment, for those with marketable skills couldn't find jobs as fire-fighters, policemen, clerical workers, telephone operators or linemen, repairmen, sales clerks, typists, receptionists, or building trades apprentices. He said that it was understandably difficult for black parents to keep their youngsters in school when there were few prospects of future advancement and that few had the funds to send their children to college. He closed by saying that local blacks in general were orderly, law-abiding citizens who deserved better treatment. Ironically, the letter written by "Frederick Douglass" was published on November 22, 1963, the same day President John F. Kennedy was assassinated.

In 1964 the 24th Amendment to the U.S. Constitution was passed, eliminating the poll tax. A year later, Mrs. Lester N. Opheim was appointed James City County's central Registrar of Voters. In early September 1965 the Southern Christian Leadership Conference assigned to the Greater Williamsburg area two young people who had participated in the Civil Rights movement in the Deep South. Their goal was to persuade local blacks to become registered voters. A registration drive led by both blacks and whites produced 621 new voters. In 1959 the Williamsburg Area Inter-racial Study Group began holding meetings to address multi-cultural issues. The Williamsburg-York-James City County chapter of the National Association for the Advancement of Colored People (NAACP) focused its attention upon seeing that minorities received equal opportunities for jobs and housing. On October 22, 1967, the NAACP held its state convention in the Lake Matoaka Amphitheater with Roy Wilkins as keynote speaker.

When fall classes opened at the College of William and Mary in 1964, Oscar Blayton of Grove entered as a member of the freshman class. Blayton, who had attended Bruton Heights School and was a graduate of North Carolina's Palmer Memorial Academy, was the college's first black undergraduate student, preceded only by two who participated in graduate programs.[44]

During the summer of 1964, three black pupils sought admission to the Matthew Whaley Elementary School and two applied to the James Blair High

Agriculture in modern James City County. James City County file photo.

School. In accord with the law, school superintendent Rawles Byrd forwarded their applications to the State Pupil Placement Board. Later, a new pupil assignment plan was adopted as a means of achieving a more equitable racial balance. So intense were the views of Williamsburg-James City County School Board chairman John E. Wray that he resigned because he was "opposed to voluntarily submitting to integration," a belief he said other Board members didn't share. He also voiced his support for private schools and shortly thereafter became one of the founders of Jamestown Academy. Local public schools first were integrated on September 10, 1964. A week later, the James City County Board of Supervisors voted two to one to provide tuition grants to school-age youngsters enrolled in private school. The following spring, after a new joint-school contract was signed, James City County and Williamsburg, like many other Virginia localities, withdrew from the State Pupil Placement Board. That decision made the local school system eligible for federal funds. Shortly thereafter, students were given freedom of choice with regard to school selection. In July 1965, when children began reg-

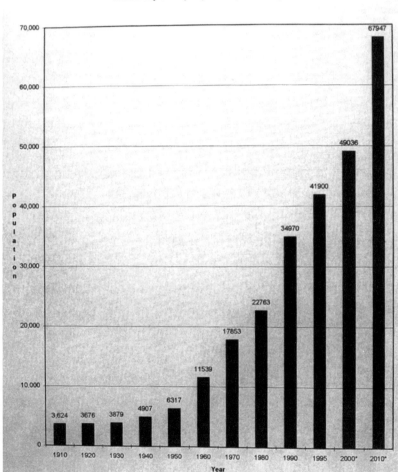

James City County Population (1910-2010)

Courtesy of the James City County Planning Department.

istering for the fall term, 235 black pupils signed up to attend the Williamsburg-James City County system's three predominantly white schools. Of these students, 66 registered for James Blair and 143 for Matthew Whaley, schools in which there had been only two or three blacks the previous year. The local school board's desegregation plan received federal approval.

The Williamsburg-Jamestown Airport. Photo by Nan Maxwell.

1966 brought the establishment of public kindergartens as part of the local school curriculum and Project Head Start got underway at the Matthew Whaley and Bruton Heights Schools.[45]

The Vietnam War

In August 1964, when two American destroyers were attacked in the Gulf of Tonkin, Congress sanctioned American military involvement in what became known as the Vietnam War. There were 184,000 American troops in Vietnam at the close of 1965 and 542,000 in 1969. Americans' opinions about the war were as sharply polarized as they had been during the Civil War. Protesters staged marches in Williamsburg from time to time and in February 1973 a prayer march was held to commemorate the end of American involvement.[46]

During the Vietnam War, local males were drafted into the military, for the Selective Service Act was still in effect. However, few statistics have been compiled on how many James City County citizens actually participated. One such individual was Mark S. Rogers of Norge, who in October 1970 was awarded the Bronze Star. During the early 1970s W. L. Person, the Rev. Junius H. Moody, and R. Kemper Taylor Jr. served on the local Selective Service Board. High school students at James Blair and Walsingham Academy offered their support to those serving in Vietnam by writing them letters and sending hundreds of gift packages as part of "Operation Shoebox." Churches offered Christmas dinners to area servicemen and local residents donated 500 pints of blood in memory of Williamsburg's Lt. Glenn Mann, who was killed in action.[47]

The Kennedy and Johnson Years

During President John F. Kennedy's administration, new social programs were developed as part of the War on Poverty, an official effort to stimulate the nation's economy and reduce unemployment. Kennedy's successor, President Lyndon B. Johnson, sought to accelerate the War on Poverty by proposing federal aid to education. He advocated a medical care program for the elderly (Medicare) supported by the Social Security system, and strongly supported conservation projects. Sixteen-year-old Hurley L. Piggott of Carriage Road was the first local participant in the Job Corps, one of the Johnson Administration's social programs. In September 1964 the James City County Board of Supervisors voiced its opposition to the proposed establishment of a Job Corps camp in York County, which enrollees were to work on the Colonial Parkway. Ultimately, federal officials opted for another location.[48]

The Civil Rights struggle and the Vietnam War forced many Americans to take a long, hard look at the country's foreign and domestic policies. The so-called "generation gap" between the "baby boomers" and their parents widened, as some young people set out to rectify what they considered social ills. Others turned to drugs or mysticism. So sharply polarized were many Americans' views that violence never was far beneath the surface. In 1968 the Ku Klux Klan, which was strongly opposed by Governor Mills Godwin, surfaced in Southside Virginia. In James City County the KKK made the news in 1969 when members staged a rally in a field off Jamestown Road. The VIRGINIA GAZETTE reported that when members of a Newport News motor-cycle gang known as the Soul Wheels learned that the KKK was planning to hold a cross-burning ceremony near a local commune, they armed themselves and stood watch until the rally was over. The turbulent 1960s didn't go quietly, for on December 11, 1968, an earthquake centered on Richmond sent out shock waves that rattled local windowpanes.

On July 4, 1969, Williamsburg and James City County officials moved into the new brick courthouse on the corner of South Henry and Courthouse Way. As the late 1960s faded into the '70s, groups of war protesters continued to march in Williamsburg and the mini-skirt and the Mod Look were popular.[49]

The Williamsburg Preschool for Special Children

In 1966 the Williamsburg Preschool for Special Children was established by a group of citizen volunteers. Its purpose was to assist youngsters with special needs or delayed development by working through a family-centered program. By 1975 the preschool had earned national recognition for its service to the community. During the late 1970s, when public education became available to disabled children age two or older, the preschool turned its attention to infants and toddlers and began receiving federal grant monies for training professionals in the field of early child development and early intervention. In 1978 the Williamsburg Preschool for Special Children was renamed Child Development Resources, a more apt reflection of its mission. Since then, C.D.R. programs have won national recognition and its First Steps program has been heralded as one of five model child care and development programs in Virginia.[50]

Kingsmill and Anheuser-Busch

In September 1969 Anheuser-Busch announced its decision to build a forty million dollar plant on the 2,600-plus acre Kingsmill tract, which it purchased from the Williamsburg Restoration, Inc. The Anheuser-Busch project, which constituted the largest initial investment an out-of-state industry ever made in Virginia, was to consist of a brewery and industrial park, a planned community, golf course, conference center, shopping center, marina, and gardens. In time, it became known that entertainment and amusements would be featured in Busch Gardens.[51] The brewery alone was expected to hire 300 permanent employees and provide temporary jobs to another 1,000. James City County officials were convinced that the new industry would bring in money for public schools and other community services. The Board of Supervisors established a water and sewer authority and an industrial development authority and designated two sanitary districts. In another unprecedented move, Board members passed the county's first zoning ordinance as a planning tool to ensure orderly development. County residents, in turn, approved a $1.6 million bond referendum to underwrite the cost of building a waterline from the Newport News City Reservoir to the Anheuser-Busch brewery. Voters also passed a referendum authorizing the sale of liquor by-the-drink. Ground-breaking ceremonies were held at the brewery site in May 1970. In 1971 plans got underway for the construction of the Ball Metal Company's 10 million dollar beer can manufacturing plant, a supplier to the Anheuser-Busch brewery. A treatment plant to accommodate waste from the brewery was to be built between Carter's Grove and Camp Wallace.[52]

In May 1971 Anheuser-Busch acquired Camp Wallace from the United States government and added it to Kingsmill. On December 22, 1971, the company's brewery processed its first batch of beer, in preparation for shipment the following year. In 1972 Anheuser-Busch agreed to fund a five year archaeological study at Kingsmill in order to preserve and protect the cultural resources on the property. Excavations at Kingsmill were undertaken by Dr. William M. Kelso and his staff in accord with Anheuser-Busch's plans to develop the property. Dr. Kelso's findings, presented in his KINGSMILL PLANTATIONS, 1619–1800, attest to the significance of the archaeological resources on the Kingsmill tract and the peninsula as a whole. In March 1973 ground-breaking ceremonies were held for the establishment of Reynolds Aluminum's recycling center near the Anheuser-Busch brewery. As a regional facility it was to process aluminum from Virginia, the District of Columbia, and parts of Maryland and northern North Carolina.[53]

The Governor's Land Excavations

In 1972 the state undertook an archaeological survey of the eastern part of the Governor's Land, just west of Jamestown Island. The discovery of intact archaeological features within the acreage set aside in 1619 for the support of Virginia's incumbent governor led to the property's inclusion in the National Register of Historic Places and the Virginia Landmarks Register. When townhouse construction led to the discovery of a ca. 1690 trash pit, salvage excavations were carried out by Virginia Historic Landmarks Commission staff members. Two years later, a more intensive field survey was undertaken and in the late 1970s and early '80s, full scale excavations were conducted on acreage scheduled for development. This work was carried out with funding from the National Endowment for the Humanities. In 1990 Alain C. Outlaw's report of excavations at the Governor's Land was published by the V.H.L.C.'s successor, the Virginia Department of Historic Resources.[54]

The 1970s

Between 1968 and 1978 the population of James City County grew by approximately 40 percent, with the result that the area became much more urbanized. Besides residential development, there was considerable growth in the commercial and industrial sectors and in tourist-related enterprises. The amount of land used for agriculture decreased significantly. Between 1959 and 1973 the number of farms in James City County declined by nearly 50 percent, with the result that agricultural land comprised only 20 percent of the county's total acreage. Even so, an impressive amount of farm income was generated from that limited acreage; those earnings were important to the county's economy. Field crops (especially corn, soybeans, and small grains) were the leading sources of farm income in James City County and comprised nearly 50 percent of the market. This was followed by livestock production, which was responsible for approximately 28 percent of the county's farm income. During 1970s dairying and truck farming continued the decline that had gotten underway in the 1960s. In 1971 James City County had a population of just

The James City County Government Center. Photo by Nan Maxwell.

The Grove Fire Station. Photo by Nan Maxwell.

**James City County Transit.
Photo by Nan Maxwell.**

over 19,000. That number was expected to reach 51,000 by 2,000.[55]

As James City County became what some termed a bedroom community, the Board of Supervisors was obliged to provide facilities for increasing numbers of school-children and to fulfill new, unprecedented demands for sewage disposal and drinking water. Some Board members were concerned about the proliferation of new trailers, which occupants' real estate and personal property taxes wouldn't cover the cost of their public services. It was agreed, however, that mobile homes relieved a shortage of low and middle income housing. Applications for large mobile home parks became more numerous, especially in the direction of Route 60 East. It was during the late 1960s and early 1970s that the Board of Supervisors began to consider limiting the number of new trailers moving into the county.

During the early 1970s a food stamp program was adopted. Federal revenue-sharing programs were tapped for funds to assist in building roads and providing child welfare, job training, urban renewal, education, medical care, and other forms of public assistance. One study demonstrated that in 1970 James City County residents received $1.00 in matching funds for every $1.05 they contributed to the new programs. In 1972 alone James City County received $3,369,000 in revenue-sharing funds. Sometimes, the money needed to construct public service facilities became ensnared in government red tape. In October 1971 the Board of Supervisors asked Governor Linwood Holton for assistance in procuring funds earmarked for sewer line construction in Sanitary District 2, where a large number of low income blacks were using substandard septic tanks. The following year a bond referendum was passed to fund public sewerage services for the people of Sanitary District 3, the area between College Creek, the James River and Ironbound Road. Construction of the new sewer lines was expected to produce a building boom in the lower part of James City County.

Environmental concerns were especially popular during the 1970s and local citizens voiced their support of recycling, preserving green space and historic sites, and other issues linked to the quality of life. One topic that sparked a considerable amount of discussion was construction of the Surry Nuclear Plant, which got underway during the summer of 1971. Another was the safety of using pesticides, especially for mosquito control. The Williamsburg-James City Community Action Agency encouraged rural residents to organize and work toward improving their living environment. Two such groups were the Lightfoot Protection and Improvement Organization and the Grove Community Organization. In June 1970 Grove residents celebrated Earth Day by undertaking a major clean-up campaign. Volunteers from the Naval Weapons Station assisted by using heavy equipment to clear away unsightly debris. Mooretown residents, then predominantly black, petitioned county officials for a new bridge across the railroad tracks that would provide fire trucks with ready access to their community. The proliferation of tourist-related facilities and a dramatic increase in the number of visitors to the area brought the need for road improvements and additional law enforcement and fire protection personnel. In May 1970 funds became available to make Route 60 a four lane highway and to commence construction of the Route 199 bypass's eastern loop around Williamsburg. Both projects got underway late in 1972 just as the segment of Interstate 64 between Anderson's Corner and Bottom's Bridge opened to use.

In 1970 the Board of Supervisors decided to adopt building codes that required the inspection of structures whenever electrical, plumbing, gas, and general contracting work was done. The following year, the county's second masterplan was approved and the Board adopted the use of county stickers (decals) instead of metal license tags. Signs with international pictorial symbols were installed along public roadways to steer foreign visitors to accommodations and tourist attractions. Two proposals local residents soundly rejected were the elimination of the Williamsburg postmark and the Norge post office.

Throughout the Greater Williamsburg area, business boomed, tourism flourished, and new mobile home parks and planned communities popped up in record numbers. In 1968 state officials announced the creation of the York River State Park, enveloping approximately 3,000 acres of river front land east of Taskinask Creek. 1970 brought the opening of the Williamsburg-James City County Airport at a site off Lake Powell Road and plans were made to build a new, modern public library. In 1972 recreational facilities were constructed at nearby Waller Mill Reservoir. As the community's population increased, plans were made to add a second storey to the south wing of Williamsburg Community Hospital. Several motels and tourist campgrounds were built and in 1972 alone, 36 new commercial buildings were erected. The Board of Supervisors voted to institute a business tax and as the population grew, the C&P Telephone Company added a new exchange, the 220 series. As business establishments proliferated along the roads entering Williamsburg, James City County officials became increasingly concerned

The James City County-Williamsburg Recreation Center. James City County file photo.

that the city might try to annex what was an important component in the tax base. Therefore, some consideration was given to obtaining city status for James City County, to block future annexations by Williamsburg. In 1972 the General Assembly enacted a state-wide moratorium on annexation that was effective until January 1, 1976. As James City County continued to develop at an unprecedented rate, the Board of Supervisors decided to hire a full-time planner and zoning administrator to manage growth.[56]

Modernizing County Government

As James City County's population density increased, the need for basic public services grew proportionately. By 1970 the county government's work load had become so burdensome that the Board of Supervisors recommended adoption of the county manager form of government, a managerial method first authorized by the General Assembly in 1932. Under that system, a county administrator hired by the Board would draft proposed budgets, establish centralized purchasing and accounting procedures, conduct audits, and oversee long range planning, welfare, and utility services management. The county administrator also would standardize procedures in the offices of the sheriff, commonwealth's attorney, and commissioner of revenue, and see that the buildings, roads, and bridges for which James City County was responsible were maintained properly by county employees. Board members acknowledged that the proposed managerial change was likely to prove somewhat more costly, but it was expected to be an efficient, effective way to address the demands attributable to dramatic growth. A December 15, 1970, referendum led to the adoption of the county manager form of government. Shortly after the change occurred, former Executive Secretary Garland Wooddy was hired as county administrator. A year later, he resigned to head the county's fire protection program. In February 1973 Thomas R. McCann was hired to fill the county administrator's position. Within the next three years, the county staff was expanded to include specialists in such areas as planning, public works and economic development.[57]

From Richmond to Williamsburg in Record Time

During the summer of 1972 an incident occurred that made an indelible impression upon all who witnessed it. A Richmond trucker, involved in a minor accident in Henrico County, panicked and fled down Route 5 at break-neck speed. With the Henrico and Charles City County police in hot pursuit, the driver's tractor-trailer careened from side to side as it headed toward Williamsburg at speeds of 60 to 70 miles per hour. It crashed through a wooden barricade that local law enforcement officers had erected near Walsingham Academy. Then it rounded the corner onto Jamestown Road and hurled toward College Corner at upwards of 60 miles per hour. Thanks to the timely intervention of local police, Merchants Square was cleared moments before the truck roared through. When it entered the grounds of the Williamsburg Inn and sped across the bowling green, startled tourists were sent scurrying! After a few more erratic maneuvers, the truck took off across the 18th fairway of the Golden Horseshoe Golf Course and then came to rest in a grove of trees. By that time it had struck three cars and a bus and caused several hundred thousand dollars' worth of property damage. Miraculously, no lives were lost.[58]

Televising Board of Supervisors' meetings. Photo by Nan Maxwell.

Meeting the Challenge of Growth

Early in 1973, James City County's Board of Supervisors published an open letter in which they asked local citizens' advice on how to direct the county's unprecedented growth and address the problems it generated. They chose this grass-roots approach because there were major philosophical differences among members of the Board. In April 1973 warrants were issued to Colonial Williamsburg, the Williamsburg Pottery, and the Imp Pedlar for violating a new Sunday-closing law enacted by the General Assembly earlier in the year. James City County and Williamsburg were among the numerous communities that challenged the state's new "Blue Law." Williamsburg's first purposefully-built library opened for use in September and in time, became a regional facility. Dow Badische commenced construction of a five million dollar plant and plans were made to establish a national courts center in Williamsburg. Because of the energy crisis, Governor Linwood Holton lowered the maximum speed limit on highways to 55 miles per hour and in November, Colonial Williamsburg announced that electric candles wouldn't be used to illuminate the Historic Area during Christmas.

In marked contrast to the 1973 building boom, 1974 saw fewer construction starts. Although new subdivisions, restaurants and shopping centers were proposed, some local citizens began voicing their opposition to what they perceived as unruly, burgeoning growth. Meanwhile, landowners in both ends

The James City County Human Services Center. Photo by Nan Maxwell.

of the county were unhappy about zoning issues. 1975 brought the adoption of James City County's first comprehensive land use plan. Despite the downturn in heavy construction, the Anheuser-Busch brewery was expected to double its capacity by the end of 1976 and a new wing was added to Williamsburg Community Hospital. County officials also began making plans to construct a government center at Kingsmill during the 1976–1977 fiscal year.[59]

1976, The Bicentennial of American Independence

In 1973 James City County and Williamsburg formed a joint committee to prepare for the nation's bicentennial celebration. A myriad of special programs and social activities were scheduled throughout 1976 and bicentennial garden plots were laid out. A committee was formed to compile local folk lore and a festival was held at Grove in the Community Center. There was a Norwegian worship service at Our Saviour's Evangelical Lutheran Church in Norge and the James City County Planning Department prepared and published "Heritage and Historic Sites," a description of 75 structures and historic sites that had been identified within the county. Classes in eighteenth-century dancing were taught in preparation for a bicentennial ball, which participants were encouraged to wear colonial garb. Colonial Williamsburg celebrated its 50th Anniversary and scheduled a forum on historic site interpretation. There were oratorical contests and British ambassador, Sir Peter Ramsbotham, spoke at a ceremony commemorating the founding of Phi Beta Kappa. The Rev. Billy Graham scheduled a Bicentennial Crusade at the William and Mary Hall and the Trans-American Bike Trail was opened at Jamestown Festival Park. July 4, 1976, was marked by an elaborate local fireworks display sponsored by the Williamsburg Jaycees and the Williamsburg-James City County Bicentennial Committee. Virtually all of these activities and special events were intended to foster interest in America's heritage and cultural traditions.[60]

Addressing the County's Changing Needs

By 1976 James City County officials were faced with deciding how to raise the funds they needed to meet the mounting cost of providing basic services, such as schools, extending sewer and water lines, and paving dirt roads. Concerted efforts were made to attract industry and there was considerable interest in levying a local amusement tax. In 1977 the C&P Telephone Company commenced construction of a $3.2 million communication center at Lightfoot, Anheuser-Busch announced a $200 million expansion of the brewery, and owners of the Toledo Bottling Plant discussed developing a site in Toano. But tourism fell short of the year's expectations and a prolonged drought devastated local crops and threatened the region's water supply. During 1977 the James City County Transit System literally got rolling and Fire Station No. 1 opened in at Grove. A second fire station was built near the intersection of Routes 5 and 199. Construction of the new county government complex also got underway. The South Henry Street extension to Route 199 was completed and the Board of Supervisors approved an expansion of the city-county jail.[61]

In 1978 the Board of Supervisors decided to charge waste disposal companies a dumping fee for using the county landfill and they appropriated funds for the Regional Solid Waste Authority, which served six peninsula counties. The Board debated how to cope with the traffic produced by the Anheuser-Busch and Ball Metal facilities in the eastern end of the county and considered asking the highway department to make Route 60 East a four-lane highway. Board members had to deal with proposed zoning changes, the improvement of dirt roads, and numerous funding requests. The city of Newport News applied for a conditional use permit that would authorize the construction of the Little Creek Reservoir. County planners, foreseeing an opportunity to create a recreation area, advised the Board of Supervisors to require Newport News to make provisions for a boat-launching ramp, public access roads, and facilities for canoeing and fishing. Newport News also was to control mosquitoes and erosion, both of which were identified as potential problems.[62]

As the county's population increased, the need arose for a comprehensive water plan. During 1979 the Toano Sewer Project led to the extension of public sewer services from Williamsburg to Ewell Hall and a new fire station was opened on Olde Towne Road. Another important advance made during the year was the consolidation of emergency dispatch operations so that one emergency number (911) could be used county-wide for fire and medical assistance. Meanwhile, the sheriff's department strengthened its programs in areas of investigation, crime prevention, and narcotics detection.[63]

A spate of new issues came before the Board of Supervisors during 1980, most of which involved the expenditure of tax dollars. As local population growth was accompanied by a rise in the crime rate, more law enforcement officers were needed. With the support of incumbent Sheriff A. M. (Archie) Brenegan, the Board decided to establish a county police department. Its creation made James City County eligible for government funds that could be used to fill 12 new law enforcement positions. Brenegan agreed to serve as both sheriff and police chief during a transitional period in which the two departments' duties would be defined and new staff members hired. In early 1982 it was agreed that the sheriff's office would handle all court and civil process duties and courtroom security, whereas the police department would be responsible for law enforcement duties.

Citizens from Grove came before the Board of Supervisors to voice their objections to a foul odor emanating from the Williamsburg Hampton Roads Sanitation District treatment plant and residents of the Sand Hill development in Toano approached the Board with their public water supply problems. New issues that surfaced during 1980 included the Rescue Squad's need of an additional medical assistance position, providing funds to the S.P.C.A. and the Peninsula Airport Commission, and the feasibility of building a Senior Citizens facility. The Board resolved to establish the Greater James City County Transit Authority so that the local bus service would meet federal guidelines. They also began discussing the construction of the Ware Creek Reservoir. Many of the issues the Board of Supervisors considered during 1980 were still on the table a year later. A public hearing was held on extending cable television service to James City County and the Peninsula Airport Commission proposed that Patrick Henry Airport be renamed the Newport News-Williamsburg Regional Airport. It was agreed that public water mains should be extended along Route 60 West to connect with water systems at Longhill Road, the Williamsburg Pottery, and Toano. Fire chief Garland Wooddy requested funds for the purchase of an aerial ladder truck to serve the county's first high-rise building and four fire-fighters to operate it. County officials recommended to the Board that James City County join the Williamsburg Area Arts Commission and noted that asbestos had to be removed from the county courthouse and E.O.C. building. The Board declared February 19, 1981, "Lawrence Taylor Day" in recognition of his being named First Team Concensus All-American Linebacker at the University of North Carolina. In an attempt to raise revenues to cover the rising cost of public services, a meal and beverage tax proposal was readied for submission to the General Assembly.

One of the most important issues facing James City County officials in 1982 was Williamsburg's desire to annex a considerable amount of land in order to enhance its tax base. The agreement hammered out in a series of work sessions stipulated that nearly four square miles of county land was to be transferred to the city, including some property that belonged to the College of William and Mary and the Colonial Williamsburg Foundation. But in exchange, the Richardson-Meadows tract and certain city waterlines were transferred to the county, with the provision that Williamsburg had the right to sell water to county customers for another 15 years. It was agreed that there would be a 15-year moratorium on annexation and that the joint school contract would be protected.

The local Community Action Agency asked the Board of Supervisors' permission to apply for funds to winterize homes in Forest Glen and Grove. Plans also were made for James City County to join the Pamunkey River Study Committee, which was exploring new sources of potable water; to adopt a new Law Enforcement Radio Communications System; and to develop a street light policy. In 1983 a referendum was held on the sale of revenue bonds to fund construction of a jointly-sponsored city-county recreation center. Near the end of the year, the Board decided to purchase the Twin Oaks Campground for use as an Upper County Park. Board members also considered erecting a Human Services building, and seeking a litter control grant from the Land and Water Conservation Fund. The Board and New Kent

County officials reached an agreement about the proposed Ware Creek Reservoir and the rights and involvement each jurisdiction would have. When Supervisor Abram Frink, county Treasurer Frances Waltrip, and Sheriff Archie Brenegan announced their retirements, all three were formally recognized for their many years of dedicated service.

In 1984 funds were authorized for use in commemorating James City County's 350th anniversary. An official county seal was adopted, a 350th Anniversary Committee was formed, and Robinette Fitzsimmons was named Anniversary Committee coordinator. The Board instructed the 350th Anniversary Committee to plan activities that would have a memorable impact upon local citizens and recommended that oral histories be compiled. Later, a special trust fund was established to receive donations for the celebration and plans were made to hold a special day-long event at the Jamestown Festival Park. The following year the Board of Supervisors decided to create a county historical commission to serve in an advisory capacity on historical matters involving the county.

At the onset of 1984, the James City County Board of Supervisors agreed to commence meeting on the second and fourth Mondays of each month and members concluded that it was necessary to raise the cost of building inspections, which were not being covered by permit fees. The Board also declared January 28, 1984, Leneva Jackson Day to draw attention to her family's need for funds to cover the cost of her liver transplant. Because the number of voters had grown, the Board was obliged to purchase three additional voting machines and funds were appropriated for the Norge Water System. Plans were made to introduce a computerized data processing system to streamline records management. Community block grants were sought for housing rehabilitation and part of the Department of Social Services' budget was earmarked for emergency fuel needs. The county's Industrial Development Authority asked the Board to hold a referendum on revenue bonds to assist investors in constructing motels and restaurants on Richmond Road, just outside of the city. Early in the year the Board asked the highway department to take several new streets into the state system. Water improvements were planned for the eastern end of the county in Tarleton Bivouac and James Terrace, where there had been problems, and the Grove Redevelopment Plan was implemented, which called for upgrading substandard housing and making other improvements.

Among the parade of funding requests the Board of Supervisors reviewed were those submitted by the Task Force for Battered Women; the James City-Bruton Fire Department; and the Williamsburg Regional Library, which requested funds for a cultural wing and bookmobile service. During 1984 plans got underway to construct the community recreation center, with the city of Williamsburg's underwriting a fourth of the cost. Later, Anheuser-Busch offered to donate $250,000 toward the establishment of an outdoor sports complex at the center. The Board was asked to lend its support to keeping the Norge post office open.

One difficult issue the Board of Supervisors was obliged to address was how to regulate mobile home construction in the county. A study revealed that 16.5 percent of James City County's housing consisted of mobile homes, a figure five times larger than the regional average and three times greater than the state average. Board members noted that the number of mobile home permit applications was growing steadily as was the number of unauthorized trailers being used. They decided to declare a six-month moratorium on mobile home construction in order to establish a workable permitting policy.[64]

Housing Partnerships, Inc.

In 1985 a group of private citizens banded together to form a non-profit, volunteer agency called Housing Partnerships to assist people lacking the resources to maintain safe and weatherproof homes. Emphasis was placed upon those ineligible for public assistance. Utilizing private contributions and volunteer labor, Housing Partnerships began undertaking projects at the recommendation of social service agencies, churches, and private citizens. Within the first eight years of its existence, Housing Partnerships was involved in nearly 400 projects.[65]

Closing Out the Decade

James City County's Board of Supervisors continued to face new and unprecedented challenges as the county's population increased and suburbs proliferated. In 1985 when the Board listed state highway projects they considered of the highest priority, they noted their expectation of road improvements when approving the construction of the Williamsburg Landing retirement community, the Mid-County Park, the Powhatan Plantation Resort, the Human Services Building, three new fire stations, the Chisel Run development, the County-City Recreation Center, six new motels plus expansions of existing facilities at Kingsmill, the Outlet Mall, the Williamsburg Pottery, the Busch Corporate Center, and Carter's Grove.

In an unprecedented move, the Board decided to allow its meetings to be televised on a local cable channel. Other issues the Board addressed during 1985 included finding new accommodations for the Crossroads Youth Home, providing funding to the 4-H Educational Center and allowing the county police department to participate in a regional fingerprint program. They also deliberated over whether to renovate or dispose of the Bruton Heights School. One project Board members strongly supported was construction of the Ware Creek Reservoir. Discussions also were held on whether to expand the Williamsburg-Jamestown Airport, to levy a tax to pay for 911 service, and to approve the Burnt Ordinary affordable housing project. A decision was made to urge the Virginia Association of Counties to sponsor legislation that would eliminate involuntary annexation in Virginia. The following year brought construction of the county's first cellular telephone tower and the Croaker Road Water Transmission Main, plus sponsorship of the state-funded Chickahominy Road Community Development Block Grant Program. Preparation of the Ware Creek Reservoir Environmental Impact Statement also got underway. The Board of Supervisors decided to ask the Virginia State Police to assign more officers to the area, noting that there hadn't been a staff increase in 17 years.

In 1987 the 20th of March was designated Lawrence Taylor Day in recognition of his being named the National Football League's Most Valuable Player. Other proud moments for James City County came when Curtis

Strange of Kingsmill won the U.S. Open Golf Championship and Bruce Hornsby received a Grammy award. The Rev. Junius H. Moody was singled out for his 60 years of service as a community leader, educator, and humanitarian and James E. Maloney was publicly recognized as founder of the Williamsburg Pottery, the state's largest shopping and tourist attraction. New school sites were selected at Ford's Colony and Five Forks and the Board of Supervisors decided to build a James City Farmers Market where local produce could be sold. During 1988 the Jamestown-Yorktown Foundation commenced construction of three new exhibition galleries, the Jamestown Settlement museum. The new state facility opened to the public early in 1990. As the 1980s closed, the Board of Supervisors passed a resolution in support of Route 199's completion and agreed to ask the General Assembly for funds to improve the Jamestown Ferry's service. Numerous water mains were built to accommodate new subdivisions and the Board officially declared April 22, 1990, as Earth Day in recognition of its concern for the environment. The 1990s also saw initiation of two major archaeological projects at Jamestown: the Jamestown Archaeological Assessment, sponsored by the National Park Service, and the Jamestown Rediscovery project, sponsored by the Association for the Preservation of Virginia Antiquities. The Jamestown Archaeological Assessment, a multi-disciplinary study involving teams of scholars from the Colonial Williamsburg Foundation and the College of William and Mary, includes an archaeological reconnaissance survey of Jamestown Island and the reevaluation of previous excavations and interpretations. The Jamestown Rediscovery project's purpose is searching for the 1607 fort. Both studies, which still are underway, are geared toward the celebration of Jamestown's 400th anniversary in 2007.[66]

Toward the Twenty-First Century

Census data for 1990 reveal that 47.5 percent of James City County residents then lived in urban settings, whereas the remaining 52.5 percent inhabited rural areas. It was noted, however, that only 167 of the 18,317 people who lived in a rural setting actually were involved in farming. Thus, between 1960 and 1990 the character of the county had changed dramatically.[67] As the peninsula's growth accelerates, this urbanizing trend is expected to present an array of new challenges. But with a proud past as its prologue, James City County is prepared to enter the new millennium.

Notes

1.   Virginia Gazette, January 4 and 11, April 26, June 28, August 9, 1946.

2.   Ibid., January 11, February 15 and 22, March 1 and 22, July 26, August 23, November 22 and 29, December 6 and 27, 1946; January 3 and 24, March 4, May 30, 1947; May 21, 1948.

3.   Ibid., January 10, February 7, March 7, July 11 and 18, September 26, 1947; January 9, April 9, May 21, June 18 and 25, July 16, 23, and 30, August 6, September 3 and 10, 1948; January 28, February 4, April 1 and 15, December 20, 1949.

4.   Warren Smith, personal communication, July 8, 1994; Virginia Gazette, January 30, March 12, August 6, 1948; March 17, 1950; March 20, 1953; January 18, 1957; October 13, December 29, 1967.

5.   Warren Smith, personal communication, July 8, 1994.

6.   Virginia Gazette, November 18, 1955; January 17 and 31, February 14 and 28, March 14 and 21, 1958; January 9, 1959; May 17, 1963; May 13, August 31, 1970; April 2, 1971.

7.   Ibid., January 23, March 19, 1948; May 26, December 29, 1950; April 11, 1952.

8.   Ibid., July 29, 1949; April 28, May 12 and 26, September 8, 1950; July 31, 1953.

9.   Ibid., April 28, May 12 and 26, June 16, July 7, March 3, November 24, 1950; January 19, October 26, 1951; May 9, July 4, 1952; August 20, December 3, 1954; February 1, 1957.

10.   Ibid., December 5, 1947; August 11, 1950; February 23, March 9, April 6, 1951; May 11 and 18, June 22, 1951; December 24, 1954; June 8, 1956; May 22, August 7 and 28, September 4, 1959.

11.   Williamsburg had made the change some years earlier (Virginia Gazette, June 4, 1948).

12.   Ibid., March 20, 1953.

13.   Ibid., September 8, 1950; June 8, September 28, 1951; June 6, July 18, September 5, October 10, November 7 and 28, 1952; March 27, May 1 and 12, 1953; March 9, 1956.

14.   Ibid., December 5, 1952.

15.   Ibid., April 10 and 17, May 8 and 15, June 26, July 3 and 17, 1953; April 1, 1955; June 8, 1956.

16.   Ibid., August 14 and 21, October 23 and 30, November 6, 20 and 27, December 16, 1953; January 8 and 22, February 5, December 3, 1954; Stephenson, Carters Grove, 192.

17.   Virginia Gazette, April 2, 9 and 30, June 11, October 22, 1954; October 25, 1957.

18.   Billings, Jamestown, 110–111; Virginia Gazette, August 23, 1957; October 28, November 4, 1960.

19.   Tindall, Narrative History, 1239; Virginia Gazette, February 5, July 22, September 16, October 14, December 16, 1960.

20.   Commonwealth of Virginia Statistics 1930–1960; U. S. Census of Population

1910–1960; Virginia Gazette, June 16, 1950.

21. Tindall, Narrative History, 1260–1262; Virginia Gazette, July 22, 1960. In June 1957 the James City County Board of Supervisors joined other governing bodies on the peninsula, in asking the State Water Control Board to keep the Chickahominy River free of contamination. A number of sewage plants in Henrico County were cited by New Kent County officials as a source of river pollution (Virginia Gazette, June 7, 1957).

22. Virginia Gazette, June 12, 1953; August 21, 1964.

23. In 1959 the average size of a James City County farm was 196.9 acres. Of the county's farm operators, 100 owned their farms, 44 owned part of the land they farmed and rented additional acreage, and 8 were tenant farmers. The median age of the county's farmers was rising and the average farmer was 55 years old. Nearly a third were age 65 or over (Virginia Gazette, November 25, 1960).

24. U. S. Census of Population 1910–1960; Virginia Gazette, January 15, August 12, November 18, 1960.

25. Virginia Gazette, August 20, October 8, 1954; June 3, 1960; January 5, March 9 and 23, 1962; July 24, 1964; July 9, 1965.

26. Citizens in the upper part of the county formed a committee to protest what they felt was the city's domination of the school system (Virginia Gazette, May 3, 1963).

27. Virginia Gazette, March 18, June 3, August 5, 1960; January 5, August 17, October 12, 1962; January 4 and 25, August 9, December 6 and 20, 1963; February 14, 1964; February 2, 1973.

28. The waste disposal system was installed by the W.P.A. in the early 1930s and given to the county, which had used it ever since. In 1960 the State Water Control Board said that it was the county's responsibility to correct problems in the system and that its users couldn't be charged because Toano wasn't an incorporated town. The county was given three years to complete the necessary improvements (Virginia Gazette, August 5, November 18, 1960).

29. In 1965 James City County was one of only 15 Virginia counties that had an Executive Secretary. It was a management strategy officials in many other counties considered outmoded (Richmond Times–Dispatch, September 26, 1965).

30. Virginia Gazette, February 5, August 5 and 12, November 4, 1960; January 5, March 9, July 13, December 7, 1962; January 4, March 8, April 5 and 12, 1963; September 4, 1964; June 18, 1965.

31. Ibid., January 3, 17, and 31, February 14, March 13, July 3 and 10, August 7 and 21, December 18, 1964; March 12, 1965.

32. Ibid., November 13, 1964; Leonard, General Assembly, 742. James City County and Williamsburg formerly had been in a district with Charles City and New Kent Counties.

33. Virginia Gazette, June 16, 1961; January 5, February 23, March 9, July 27, October 19, 1962; November 22, December 6, 1963.

34. Ibid., February 28, March 13; April 3, 1964.

35. Ibid., April 8, September 30, 1960; February 17, 1961; February 23, 1962.

36. Stephenson, Carter's Grove, 193–194; Virginia Gazette, December 30, 1966;

January 9, 1970; Colonial Williamsburg Foundation, "Wolstenholme Towne in Martin's Hundred at Carter's Grove" (Williamsburg, n.d.).

37.   U. S. Census of Population 1910–1960; VIRGINIA GAZETTE, January 11 and 25, February 8, March 29, 1963; September 11, December 11, 1964; June 25, 1965. 431

38.   VIRGINIA GAZETTE, July 27, 1962; February 7, 1964; September 24, December 30, 1966; December 29, 1967; January 3, 1968; January 2 and 9, October 2, 1970; April 2, July 9, September 17, December 31, 1971.

39.   Ibid.,February 8, March 8 and 22, 1963; June 12, August 5, 1964; April 2 and 9, May 14, July 30, October 29, November 5, 1965; January 2, 1970; December 30, 1977.

40.   Ibid., September 3, October 22, 1954; August 31, September 21, 1956.

41.   Dabney, VIRGINIA, 528,542; Lebsock, SHARE OF HONOR, 155; VIRGINIA GAZETTE, September 13 and 27, 1957; March 7, October 3, 1958; October 25, 1963.

42.   VIRGINIA GAZETTE, March 22 and 29, October 25, 1963; March 12, May 14, June 18, 1965.

43.   The original Frederick Douglass was a nineteenth-century black who escaped enslavement and began lobbying for abolition (Linda Rowe, personal communication, September 8, 1994).

44.   Lebsock, SHARE OF HONOUR, 156; VIRGINIA GAZETTE, July 29, 1960; November 22, 1963. August 5, 1964; June 4, September 17, 1965; December 29, 1967; July 14, 1972; July 10, 1974.

45.   Ibid., June 26, September 18, 1964; May 7, 14 and 21, July 9, August 27, 1965; December 30, 1966; January 3, 1968; August 10, 1994.

46.   Tindall, NARRATIVE HISTORY, 1233–1238, 1275–1276, 1288–1289; VIRGINIA GAZETTE, February 2, 1973.

47.   VIRGINIA GAZETTE, December 10, 1965; December 29, 1967; October 9, 1970; January 7, 1972.

48.   Ibid., September 4 and 18, November 20, 1964; January 8, March 19, May 21, June 18, August 6, 1965.

49.   Dabney, VIRGINIA, 568; VIRGINIA GAZETTE, January 9, April 10, May 8, 1970; August 20, 1971; May 26, June 9, 1972.

50.   Child Development Resources, "Facts About Child Development Resources," n.d.

51.   When Anheuser–Busch purchased Kingsmill, the Williamsburg Restoration Inc. (Colonial Williamsburg) stipulated that the property could not be developed into a tourist attraction of an historical nature associated with American cities, villages, or plantations (VIRGINIA GAZETTE, January 23, 1970).

52.   VIRGINIA GAZETTE, January 2, May 1, 1970; July 9, August 20, 1971; DAILY PRESS, January 9, 1972; June 1, 1973.

53.   Goodwin, KINGSMILL, 60–63; James City County Will Book 2:586; Deed Book 43:288, 306–307; 48:349; 50:447; 124:650; 131:295; VIRGINIA GAZETTE June 11, December 31, 1971; July 28, 1972; March 23, 1973. The Kingsmill Plantation Archaeological District was added to the National Register of Historic Places in 1972.

54. Alain C.Outlaw, Governor's Land: Archaeology of Early Seventeenth Century Virginia Settlements (Charlottesville, 1990).

55. U. S. Census of Population 1910–1960; Virginia Gazette, September 15, 1972.

56. Virginia Gazette, January 3, 1969; May 13 and 29, June 5 and 19, September 25, October 9 and 30, November 13, 1970; January 15, April 2, August 6, 13, 20, and 27, September 24, October 15 and 22, December 3, 1971; January 7 and 14, April 7 and 21, March 17, May 26, June 2 and 9, July 28, August 11, September 22, November 3, December 15 and 29, 1972; January 5 and 26, 1973.

57. Richmond Times–Dispatch, September 26, 1965; Virginia Gazette, September 11 and 18, December 18, 1970; September 29, 1972; January 26, 1973; Beverly Yanich, "Changing Land Use Practices, 1634–1984," Where America Began.

58. Virginia Gazette, August 25, 1972.

59. Ibid., January 3, 1969; March 30, April 6, July 20 and 27, August 10, September 21 and 28, November 11 and 23, 1973; January 2, 1975; January 2, 1976.

60. Williamsburg–James City County Bicentennial Committee, "The Bicentennial in Williamsburg, James City County, Virginia" (Williamsburg, 1976).

61. Virginia Gazette, December 31, 1976; December 30, 1977.

62. James City County Board of Supervisors Minutes, January 9, February 13 and 27, April 11, May 15, 1978; March 9, 1981.

63. James City County Board of Supervisors Report 1978–1979.

64. James City County Supervisors Minutes, January 14, April 15 and 28, July 14, August 25, September 22, October 13, November 24, 1980; January 12 and 26, February 19 and 23, March 9, April 9, June 22, November 16 and 30, 1981; January 15, April 8, June 14, November 15, 1982; March 14 and 28, May 23, October 17 and 23, November 16; December 19, 1983; January 9 and 23, February 13 and 28, March 12 and 26, April 9, June 11, July 13, September 1, October 29, December 17, 1984; April 22, June 12, July 8, 1985. 1984;

65. Housing Partnerships, Inc., "Neighbors Helping Neighbors" (Williamsburg, n.d.).

66. Supervisors Minutes, January 14, February 11 and 25, March 11, April 4 and 22, June 11, July 8, October 7 and 21, December 2, 1985; January 20, April 21, May 19, July 7, August 4, 1986; January 5 and 13, March 16, November 2, 1987; March 21, June 20, July 11, 1988; January 9 and 23, 1989; April 16, 1990.

67. 1990 Census of Population and Housing, James City County Planning Department (Williamsburg, 1994).

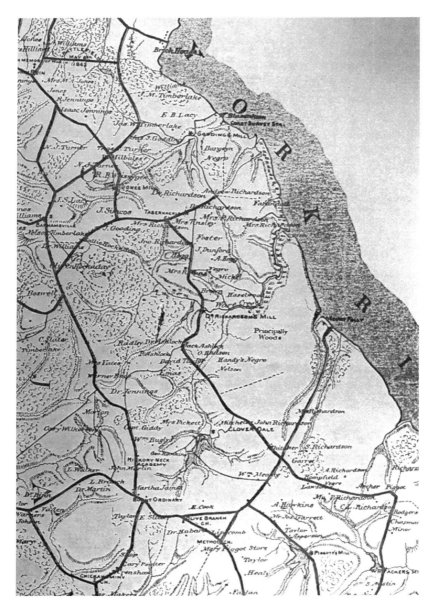

Free black community near Ware Creek, shown on J. F. Gilmer's 1864
map, "Vicinity of Richmond and Part of the Peninsula." National
Archives.

"Go Sound The Jubilee"
James City County's Black Heritage

The First Black Colonists in Virginia

In late August 1619 a Dutch frigate, fresh from a plundering expedition in the West Indies, sailed into Hampton Roads with 20-some Africans aboard, men and women who could not have known the significant place they would occupy in American history. At Old Point Comfort, the ship's captain struck a bargain with Governor George Yeardley and cape-merchant Abraham Peirsey and exchanged his captives for some provisions he needed. Later, the blacks were brought up to Jamestown, where they embarked upon a life of servitude. The Dutch ship's itinerary suggests that these men and women were brought to Virginia from Spanish-held territory in the Caribbean, probably Barbados. Three or four days after the Dutch vessel's departure, a ship called the TREASURER, returning from the West Indies, left another African in Virginia.[1]

Indentured Servitude

By March 1620 there were 32 Africans in the colony (15 men and 17 women) but precisely where they were residing is uncertain. Only 14 black people were included in the February 1624 census, suggesting that some had died or perhaps fled into the wilderness. Two women lived in Sir George

Yeardley's household at Jamestown and a third, Angelo, who came to Virginia in 1623, was part of Captain William Peirce's household. Within the Neck O'Land behind Jamestown Island was Edward, a black man servant under the supervision of Richard Kingsmill, legal guardian to the late Rev. Richard Buck's orphans. In 1625 a more detailed household-by-household muster listed 23 blacks, who resided upon plantations that extended from Hampton Roads to Flowerdew Hundred. Virtually all of them were described as servants, although only a few were listed by name. While some may have shared a dwelling with their white employers, servants typically were housed in separate quarters. Within the corporation of James City were ten Africans, nine of whom (three men and six women) lived on Jamestown Island. Eight of the nine were in Sir George Yeardley's household, whereas Angelo still resided with Captain William Peirce. Edward, meanwhile, was on the Neck O'Land with Richard Kingsmill.

From 1635 on, ships bearing blacks arrived at Jamestown, the colony's port of entry. Some of these men and women were treated as indentured servants whereas others may have been relegated to what amounted to de facto slavery, even though the legal system then made no provision for such an institution. It was during this period that the Virginia colonists' need for increasing numbers of servants to cultivate tobacco, their money crop, created a severe labor shortage. Shiploads of white indentured servants from Europe and blacks from Africa or the Caribbean sailed into the James River and docked at Jamestown, where the services of their human cargo were "hawked" to potential buyers. In time, the immigration of indentured servants from England and the Continent slowed, which led Virginia colonists to rely increasingly upon blacks.[2]

A Heritage of Suffering

The pain, anguish, humiliation, and brutality that Africans endured when they were captured, branded, and transported to an unknown land is hard to imagine. According to surviving accounts, some of the African kings who lived in the interior of the continent had their agents ensnare other blacks, whom they sold to slavers; some were captives of war. These men and women, who were tied together by the neck with leather thongs, were marched overland to the coast in "coffles" or trains. There, they were sold to traders and then imprisoned and branded with the mark of the slaver who bought them. Next, they were loaded aboard ships that were bound for the New World. During the "middle passage" from West Africa to the Caribbean, shipboard conditions were cramped and unsanitary, resulting an alarming death rate. That there were blacks who attempted suicide or mutiny before and during the trans-Atlantic crossing says much about the cruel misery of the voyage. It has been estimated that only half of the Africans sold to slavers lived to reach the New World.[3]

Toward Lifelong Enslavement

There is general agreement that between 1640 and 1660 the status of African-Americans in Virginia society began to erode, with the result that black and white servants were not treated similarly. When white indentured servants became unhappy with lengthy and sometimes ill-defined terms of service, they occasionally took legal action against their masters. But blacks brought to the colony involuntarily had a limited opportunity to become fluent in the English language and even less of a chance to gain an understanding of the law. Thus, they were at a considerable disadvantage when trying to bargain for better treatment or their freedom. An exception, however, was Phillip Corven of James City County, a black indentured servant who sued a white employer that tricked him into signing a paper extending his term of service three years. Although the length of white servants' terms of indenture was established by law in 1643, blacks in servitude gradually came to be regarded as "servants for life," a custom that eventually attained legal status. By that time, other differences had emerged. Commencing in January 1640 there was a prohibition against issuing firearms or ammunition to blacks. Three years later, black and white male servants and black female servants were designated taxable personal property; significantly, white female servants were not.[4]

By 1649 there were approximately 300 blacks in Virginia, two percent of the colony's total population of 15,000. Although many of the Africans transported to the Chesapeake region were from the west coast of Africa, it is generally believed that a substantial number of them had spent some time in the Spanish, Dutch, and British colonies in the Caribbean as laborers on sugar, indigo, rice, and tobacco plantations. Many of the blacks brought to the mainland colonies also were from Barbados.[5]

Although some of the laws passed during the mid-to-late seventeenth century suggest that the status of the black population deteriorated steadily, there is some evidence that the process was piecemeal. In 1655 Ann Barnhouse of Martin's Hundred, a white woman, went to court to convey William, her slave woman Prossa's child, to his father, Mihill Gowen (Gower) of York County, a black indentured servant. Mrs. Barnhouse indicated that she had had young William baptized and she posted a bond, vowing "never to trouble Mihill Gowen or his son, William, or to demand service."[6]

In 1650 James City County blacks numbered approximately 100, or one out of every 12 residents. By 1675 that figure had risen to 300, or one out of every six people in the county. During the 1650s and '60s, when the flow of indentured servants from Europe slowed to a trickle and increasing numbers of laborers were needed to work in the colony's tobacco fields, the legal status of blacks eroded alarmingly. During this period the black population of Virginia grew rapidly through both importation and natural increase. This fueled the development of the plantation system, in turn creating a need for even more labor. It is not surprising that the large landowners who served as Virginia's lawmakers passed legislation that catered to their own interests. One means of meeting the labor shortage was to prolong the service of blacks. For instance, in 1667 the General Assembly eliminated baptism as a possible avenue to freedom. This was a departure from the previous consensus that non-Christians' conversion entitled them to their release. By 1670 service for life was the norm for most blacks entering the colony, for Virginia's lawmakers assumed that few would have been converted to Christianity.[7]

Racial prejudice did indeed play a major role in the status of blacks. This is evident in the 1668 petition of a white female indentured servant who filed a complaint with the General Court because she was forced to work under the supervision of a black overseer. Laws restricting non-whites became even more rigorous by 1682, for legislation stipulated that all servants from non-Christian countries (except Turks and Moors) were considered enslaved.[8]

Occasionally, blacks (like Indians) boldly chose to avail themselves of the colony's legal system. Some met with success. Others didn't. In April 1667 Emannell (Emanuel) Cambew obtained a patent for 50 acres of James City County land, acreage Will Davis had claimed but allowed to revert to the Crown. A decade later, a local African-American named Edward Lloyd was among those who filed a petition requesting compensation for the personal damages he had sustained during Bacon's Rebellion. He claimed that Governor Berkeley's men had plundered his home and frightened his pregnant wife so badly that she had lost their baby and then died. In 1694 Robin Santy, a black indentured servant of Philip Ludwell's, filed an appeal in the General Court. He sought to overturn a decision by James City County's justices who had sided with Ludwell in denying Santy his freedom. The General Court ruled in Ludwell's favor "because Santy was not heard from."[9] Ludwell, a General Court judge, made no apparent attempt to abstain from participating in the decision.

During the early 1690s a special court procedure was established for trying enslaved blacks accused of wrong-doing. Those charged with capital crimes were to be imprisoned immediately and could be indicted on the basis of a confession or two witnesses' oaths. They were tried by courts of oyer and terminer at the county level without the benefit of a jury. In contrast, others (including free blacks) charged with capital crimes went before the General Court, the highest judicial body in Virginia. Because those who had slaves and indentured servants were ever mindful that they might rebel, county constables were authorized to apprehend all runaways. In 1657 constables were empowered to search for blacks thought to have fled to Indian villages. From 1670 on, they were required to whip the runaways they arrested before returning them to their masters. For example, in 1673, Will, a runaway slave from Gloucester, was caught in James City County, where he was soundly whipped by sheriff Francis Kirkman before being sent home. The General Court ordered Will's owner to pay Kirkman for providing "a good, well laid on whipping" in accord with the law. A 1669 law had even more punitive strength. It held that a master who killed a black while inflicting discipline was not guilty of a felony.[10]

A 1680 law forbade slaves to assemble "under the pretense of feasts and burials," to leave their masters' plantations without a certificate or pass, or to possess weapons. These laws may have been a belated response to Bacon's

Rebellion, for a substantial number of armed blacks reportedly were part of his army. In 1682 it became illegal for slaves to leave their owner's property for more than four hours at a time. These efforts to curb blacks' freedom of movement and ability to resist the will of whites preceded a series of legislative acts designed to control and restrict their behavior. Sometimes local officials attempted to impose a more subtle type of subjugation. In 1672 the justices of Surry County decided that blacks shouldn't be allowed to wear white linen, which heightened "foolish pride" and promoted stealing. Instead, they were to wear blue shorts and shifts or other clothing made of lockerham or canvas.[11]

In 1670 it became illegal for free blacks and Indians to own white servants and 20 years later, banishment (or deportation from the colony) was imposed upon any white marrying a black or a person of mixed blood. Legally sanctioned corporal punishments also became more cruel. In 1687 Sam, a black slave from Virginia's Northern Neck, who was accused of inciting others to rebel, was tried and convicted at Jamestown. He was sentenced to be "whipt att a cart tayle from the prison round about the town and then to the Gallows, and from thence to the prison againe." He had to wear a strong, iron collar around his neck for life and was confined permanently to his master's plantation. Blacks' last legal means of escaping a lifetime of enslavement was limited severely in 1691 when owners were forbidden to free them unless they left the colony within six months. In 1723 the General Assembly decided that slaves could be freed only by the governor and council for meritorious service.[12]

The "Black Code" Becomes Law

The colony's slave laws, passed piecemeal in the seventeenth century, were summarized and codified in 1705. Additional legislation stipulated that "all negro, mulatto and Indian slaves, in all courts of judicature and other places, within this dominion, shall be held, taken and adjudged to be real estate."[13] The effect was to relegate blacks and enslaved Indians to the status of personal property. By this time Virginia's black population had increased markedly, slavery had gained widespread acceptance, and large numbers of

Africans were being imported specifically as slaves. Slave trade statistics, 1698 to 1703, reveal that ships registered in Jamestown (still James City County's seat of government) transported blacks from Barbados to the upper James River. During 1725 and 1726 ships licensed in Williamsburg and owned by Jeffrey Flowers, Dudley Digges, John Hutchings, and John Phripp brought blacks from Barbados, Jamaica, Anguilla, and the Windward Coast of Africa to the port of entry at Yorktown and the Lower James River's Naval Office, for which Lewis Burwell of Kingsmill was responsible. During the 1730s, Andrew Mead, John Holt, David Mead, Samuel Riddick, John Tucker, John Saunders, Samuel Barron, Samuel Skinner, Alexander Campbell, Edward Pugh, Cornelius Calvert and other local men imported slaves, most of whom were brought in from the Caribbean, especially Barbados. Edward Champion Travis's sloop, the James Town, carried small numbers of blacks from Barbados to Virginia during the 1750s.

It is estimated that Virginia's black population went from 16,390 in 1700 to 30,000 by 1730; by 1756 that number had climbed to an estimated 120,156. In 1748 it became legal to dismember slaves "going abroad at night or running away and staying out" if they had not already been disciplined by someone else. To regulate the movement of blacks and safeguard against possible insurrection, another new law required owners to issue a certificate of authorization to slaves leaving their home plantations. Whites who caught runaway slaves were empowered to kill them if they resisted arrest.[14]

The Blending of Cultures

Toward the end of the seventeenth century, when large numbers of African slaves were brought to the colonies, especially from the Guinea Coast, a substantial number came to James City County. It is likely that they were from a number of tribes, spoke different languages, and had a diversity of cultural backgrounds. Newly-arrived Africans or "new negroes" generally were considered unruly and disruptive. They were not valued as highly as slaves who understood English and knew how to work in the fields, as house servants, or as skilled artisans. The unique Afro-American cultural tradition (with its rich diversity of music, dance, folklore, religion, crafts, and artistry)

**Reconstructed slave quarters at Carter's Grove Plantation.
Photo by Ralph Maxwell.**

developed gradually. This occurred as newly arrived Africans came into contact with the European heritage of whites and increasing numbers of American-born slaves and whites whose parents had been in the colonies for one or more generations. By 1700 a majority of James City County's work force was black. Within 30 years blacks comprised the majority of the county's total population. This trend accelerated and between ca. 1776 and the eve of the Civil War, approximately two-thirds of James City County's population was black.[15]

Everyday Life

In 1700 there were more than 16,000 blacks in Virginia, the majority of whom worked in the agricultural fields of the Tidewater region. By this time enslaved blacks for the most part had replaced white indentured servants as field hands and slavery was considered an indispensable component of what

was still a tobacco-based economy. Slaves also cleared new land of foresta-
tion, assisted in the construction and repair of buildings, and tended livestock.
Although relatively little is known about the life of a typical field hand, one
English observer noted that a slave's workday began at dawn and ended at
dusk, with time for a brief breakfast and a dinner break. Household slaves led
somewhat different lives. They had more material advantages, but less
privacy. Those fortunate enough to be trained artisans had a greater opportunity to refine their manual and social skills and intellectual prowess.[16]

Virginia planters with a substantial number of slaves typically housed
them in separate quarters a relatively short distance from the main house or
in crude shelters on subsidiary farms. Those with only a few slaves often
provided them with space in a loft, kitchen, barn, or other outbuilding. As
slave families became an integral part of plantation life, separate housing
(usually small huts, log buildings or sometimes, small frame dwellings) were
provided to groups of people related by de facto "marriage"[17] or other kinship
ties. Single adults often lived alone, whereas house servants and other domestics typically resided within their master's home or outbuildings.

In the slave quarters, blacks usually could congregate for food and fellowship after their work was done. There, beyond the pale of white
supervision, they could relax, converse with friends and kin, and enjoy folk
traditions distinctly their own. Slaves often had a small garden plot in which
they could raise food crops for their own consumption or to barter for goods
they lacked. Planters with large amounts of land under their control sometimes subdivided it into quarters or subsidiary farms that had a gang of slaves
who labored under the supervision of an overseer, typically a relatively young
white male. For example, Philip Ludwell III, who owned several plantations
in James City County, had slaves and livestock on each of them, who were
supervised by a central overseer. Ludwell's estate inventory, compiled in the
1760s, reveals that his slaves were furnished with the bare necessities they
needed for farming and food preparation. The Burwells at Carter's Grove and
Kingsmill did likewise.[18]

A Sense of Pride Versus Control

In March 1710 "a great number" of enslaved blacks "and others"[19] in James City, Isle of Wight, and Surry Counties, planned to make a break for freedom on Easter Sunday, vowing to overcome all who opposed them. But one of the slaves, a black male named Will, revealed the plot and the uprising was quelled. Among the James City County slaves jailed for complicity in the plot were blacks belonging to the Rev. James Blair, Philip Ludwell, Sheriff Edward Jaquelin, George Marable, Edward Ross, and John Brodnax, all of whom owned lots in Jamestown. Although most of the slaves were interrogated and then released into their owners' custody "to receive correction," Jamy (a Brodnax slave) and Essex (a Ross slave) were implicated in the plot and therefore were detained. Warrants also were issued for three York County slaves, two of whose names (Bumbara Peter and Mingo) suggest that they

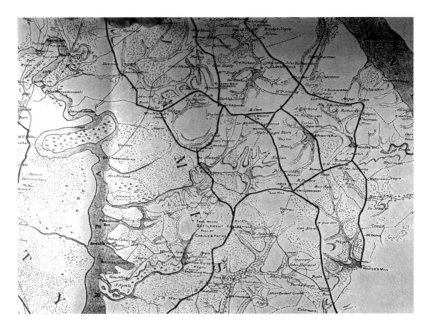

Free black settlement near Centerville, shown on J. F. Gilmer's 1864 map, "Vicinity of Richmond and Part of the Peninsula." National Archives.

were "new Africans." Virginia's governor later reported that two slaves were executed so that "their fate will strike such a terror" that others would not attempt an uprising. During the 1770s unrest among slaves in James City and York Counties led to the establishment of a night watch to patrol the streets of Williamsburg.[20]

A state-wide patrol system, intended to control the movement of slaves, was authorized in 1738. Each county had an officer and four men with the authority to visit "places suspected of entertaining unlawful assemblies of slaves, servants or disorderly persons" and arrest any slave found away from home without a pass. A 1748 law automatically invoked the death penalty whenever five or more blacks were convicted of conspiring to rebel or commit murder. A 1755 law authorized the drafting of blacks and mulattoes into the military to serve as drummers, trumpeters or "pioneers" who performed manual labor. When voting qualifications were established by law in 1762, free blacks, mulattoes, Indians, and women were excluded from enfranchisement, along with all convicts and deported aliens.[21]

Honing Specialized Skills

Although many James City County slaves were involved in agriculture or were domestic servants, advertisements for runaways reveal that quite a few were skilled artisans. A 26-year-old black man who absconded from a plantation near Williamsburg was described as "an extraordinary sawer, a tolerable good carpenter and currier, pretends to make shoes, and is a very good sailor." He also was said to be literate. Other James City County runaways that possessed special abilities included "a very good sawyer and clapboard carpenter," a miller, a baker, a waiter, and a foreman described as "a sensible fellow" who "has no striking fault but an impudent tongue." A considerable number of the enslaved blacks who lived in Williamsburg worked as barbers, blacksmiths, butchers, cabinetmakers, harness-makers, and tailors. Sometimes, slaves escaped to urban areas where they could use their specialized skills to find employment and pass as free.[22]

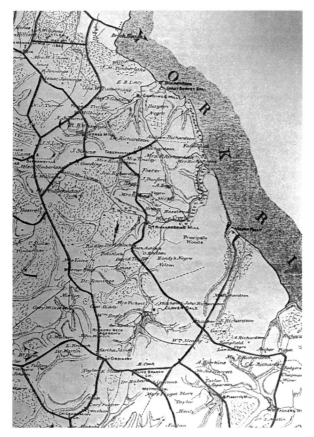

**Free black community near Ware Creek, shown on
J. F. Gilmer's 1864 map, "Vicinity of Richmond and
Part of the Peninsula." See enlarged map, page 474.
National Archives.**

Forging Family Ties

Undoubtedly one of a slave's greatest fears was the prospect of permanent separation from close kin. Slaves sometimes were sold when their
owners fell on hard times or simply were unable to support all of the household members for whom they were responsible. Census records and personal
property tax rolls reveal that middling planters' households during the eigh-

teenth and nineteenth centuries sometimes included 30 or more members (both black and white) who required food, clothing, shelter, and medical care, whether or not they were able to work. This responsibility, which sometimes proved overwhelming, might force an owner to sell one or more of his slaves. Another set of circumstances that led to the disruption of black families was the settling of estates, which often required the sale or redistribution of the decedent's slaves among several heirs. In Williamsburg, slaves were auctioned off from time to time in front of the Raleigh Tavern or occasionally at the James City County courthouse. Such sales typically involved one or two individuals. Slaves also were sold by means of newspaper advertisements.[23]

As slave marriages were not recognized by law, all too few eighteenth-century owners made a conscientious effort to keep families together. Even so, the slaves took their own weddings very seriously, whether they were married in a special ceremony or simply moved in together.[24] Anthony Johnson, Virginia's first demonstrably free black, married his wife, Mary, in a Christian ceremony in ca. 1622 and other free blacks were united in matrimony. However, after black servants were relegated to the status of personal property and slavery became an established institution, such weddings probably were relatively rare. Although there were no laws sanctioning or defining slave marriage, there also were none forbidding it. According to oral tradition, owners usually insisted that their slaves obtain their consent before marrying. Once approval was received, the bride and groom participated in a ceremony generally known as "jumping the broomstick," i. e., with friends and family looking on, they solemnly stepped across a broomstick that was placed on the floor. Sometimes, this rite of passage included a scriptural reading. Occasionally, owners saw to it that their slaves were united in a conventional religious ceremony. When slaves from neighboring plantations married, the husband usually obtained a pass from his master to visit his wife on Saturday nights.[25]

Slave parents often named a child after themselves or other blood relatives as a means of drawing attention to kinship ties, which all too often were ignored by white masters. Slaves sometimes fled to the homes of their loved ones. For instance, 14-year-old Judy, a runaway, was thought to be harbored by her "Mother at Mr. Hornsby's Plantation in James City" and Sam was believed to have fled to "Mr. Benjamin Warburton's Quarter, near Morton's Mill in James City, where he has a wife." The pain and emotional trauma slave families experienced when loved ones were sold is evident in the statement of one Virginia ex-slave, who said that "When your child dies you know where it is, but when it is sold away, you never know what may happen to him."[26]

Fleeting Glimpses of Justice and Freedom

Court cases tried in James City County during the late 1780s reflect the somewhat more lenient attitude toward enslaved blacks that prevailed at the close of the Revolutionary War, when times were hard, economically. In 1787 Charlotte Dickinson's slave, Sall, was spared the death penalty although she was found guilty of burglary, normally a capital offense. A year later the death sentence of Mary Dickinson's slave, Samson, also a convicted burglar, was commuted. Cole Diggs' slave, Harry, who lived in James City County, was found guilty of murder in 1788, but before he could be executed, new evidence surfaced and the county justices granted him a reprieve. Harry was convicted of manslaughter and then pardoned.[27]

In 1782 Virginia's General Assembly broke new ground when it passed a law enabling slave-owners to manumit (or free) their slaves. The result was that an estimated 20,000 Virginia slaves were set free, including more than 250 in James City County. But by 1806 that window of opportunity had slammed shut, for political pressure led to a major revision of the law and newly freed slaves had to be transported out of Virginia. Even so, a significant number of owners already had seized the chance to free them. Some neighboring states responded by forbidding Virginia's free blacks from taking up residence within their territory. In 1816 Virginia officials began to promote the overseas colonization of free blacks.[28]

Crime and Punishment

That the balance of power between slave and owner was delicate is evident in whites' fears that the blacks, who outnumbered them by a substantial two-to-one margin, would rise up in defiance. And sometimes they did. On May 31, 1793, two James City County slaves, Daphne and Nelly, allegedly attacked and killed their overseer, Joel Gathright. The women were ploughing the fields of Champion Travis's plantation on Jamestown Island when Gathright commenced berating them for allowing sheep to get into a corn field. When Nelly hotly denied it, the overseer began flailing her with a small cane. Despite her pregnancy, she fled from his blows. However, she stumbled and fell, whereupon he struck her repeatedly. When Nelly regained her footing, she began to fight back, at which point Daphne joined the fray. The two women then knocked Gathright to the ground and began beating him with sticks and branches. Two young slaves heard Gathright's cries and ran for help, but by the time someone came to his aid, he was almost dead. According to the James City County coroner, the left side of Gathright's skull had been crushed with a large stone. The slave women, who were tried by James City County's court justices without legal representation, were allowed to question those testifying against them. Ultimately, they were found guilty of murder and sentenced to hang. Daphne was led to the gallows on July 19th but Nelly's execution was delayed.

The circumstances surrounding the case apparently aroused some public sympathy, for in September 1793 a group of neighborhood men asked Governor Henry Lee to commute Nelly's sentence. But simultaneously, another group of citizens filed a counter-petition, recommending that clemency be denied. William Lee of Green Spring, who favored execution, contended that "the alarming commotions in this neighborhood and the dangerous example of such a murder" might inspire other slaves to rise up against their owners. The governor agreed and postponed Nelly's hanging only long enough for her baby to be born. Her death sentence was carried out on October 4th. As was customary in a capital crime, the slaves' owner was compensated for their value as personal property.[29]

The Free Black Community at Centerville

Despite William Lee's harsh stance against Nelly and Daphne, his son, William Ludwell Lee, demonstrated that some James City County slave owners refused to deny blacks their basic human rights. Young Lee, who at age 22 inherited nearly 8,700 acres of land that had descended to him from Philip Ludwell III, his maternal grandfather, had few qualms about breaking with tradition. Not only did he raze the ancient Green Spring mansion—in his day considered a historic monument—he also freed his slaves and made provisions for them to start a new life. Lee, who had been reared in Europe and moved to Virginia at age 8, may have found slavery repugnant. But the possibility also exists that he was caught up in the winds of change that swept through America at the close of the Revolutionary War. Some prominent Virginians declared that freedom was the natural condition of all men and that slavery was as unnatural as subservience to a monarch.

In 1802 William Ludwell Lee, who was relatively young, single, and in failing health, made a will in which he bequeathed all of his slaves their freedom on January 1st of the year following his death. But he didn't turn them out into the world to fend for themselves. He instructed his executors to take his slaves, age 18 or less, to a state north of the Potomac where they could be educated at his expense to "acquire an honest and comfortable support." He also made provisions for his adult slaves. They were allowed to settle upon his Hot Water plantation where his executors were to see that "comfortable houses" were built for them. Lee also stipulated that the newly freed slaves were to be given a year's supply of corn (a staple of the black diet) and allowed to reside upon the Hot Water tract for ten years, rent-free. It was thanks to William Ludwell Lee's bequest that a full 60 years before President Abraham Lincoln ever issued his Emancipation Proclamation, a community of free blacks became established at Centerville.

William Ludwell Lee died in January 1803 at age 31 and his executor and brother-in-law, William Hodgson, commenced implementing the terms of his will.[30] Personal property tax rolls suggest more than half of Lee's slaves were freed within twelve months and the remainder the following year. However, fifteen years later, Lee's ex-slaves' homesteads were placed in jeopardy thanks to the wording of his will. Lee, as a proponent of public education, bequeathed an annual stipend of 500 bushels of corn toward the support of a free school he wanted the College of William and Mary to build in the center of James City County. He also pledged a thousand acres of the Hot Water tract toward fulfilling that obligation. In 1818, the college brought

suit against Lee's executor because he had failed to produce the annual allot-
ments of corn to which William and Mary was entitled. William Hodgson, in
turn, contended that in accord with the decedent's will, he had laid off 1,000
acres of the Hot Water tract for the college's use, which officials had declined
to accept.

Ultimately, the case went before Virginia's Supreme Court of Appeals,
which decided that the college's annual allowance of corn was linked to a
thousand acres of the Hot Water plantation, not to Lee's estate per se.
Otherwise, the justices said, the decedent's bequest to the college would
thwart his "benevolent and humanitarian interest" in freeing his slaves. This
was true because the law allowed blacks liberated under the terms of their
owner's wills to be re-enslaved and then sold as a means of raising money to
settle the debts against the decedent's estate. Although it is doubtful that the
college ever attempted to build a free school in the middle of James City
County, from the time of William Ludwell Lee's death in 1803 until 1843, the
local tax assessor attributed the Hot Water tract to his estate and noted
annually that the bounds of the "school lands" were uncertain. Between 1844
and the late 1860s the Hot Water plantation was in the hands of absentee
owners who seemingly did nothing to improve the land. It is likely that any
blacks who resided there were left to their own devices.[31]

Personal property tax rolls for the 1830s reveal that thirteen free black
families then occupied the Hot Water plantation or "free school lands." They
were the Cumbo, Cannaday, Tyler, Browne, Wallis, Johnson, Taylor,
Lightfoot, Harwood, Moore, Armstrong, Cox, Roberts, Mason, and Crawley
households. In 1837 ten of those thirteen households consisted of nuclear
families; i.e., a husband, wife, and children. One included only a father and
son and there were two female household heads with children. All but one of
the households on the Hot Water tract were involved in farming, the exception being Juba Lightfoot, a bricklayer and plasterer. Almost all of these
people were there throughout the 1830s.

Approximately 13 percent of James City County's 119 free black households lived upon the Hot Water tract, whereas 17 percent of the remainder
occupied acreage they owned outright. But 70 percent of free black households resided upon white-owned property or that which belonged to deceased

whites' estates. During the 1830s James City County's free blacks included three carpenters, two shoemakers, a wheelwright, a bricklayer-plasterer, and a midwife. Five of these individuals occupied their own land, which suggests that their marketable skills enabled them to accumulate disposable income.[32] In the wake of the Nat Turner slave revolt in Southampton County the General Assembly strengthened the authority of local "patrollers" to regulate the comings and goings of all blacks. Free blacks were obliged to show their manumission papers upon demand and slaves had to produce a pass from their owners. Those unable to account for themselves properly could be taken into custody. Blacks away from home after the evening curfew (normally 9 P.M.) could be jailed and whipped. Substantial rewards usually were offered for the capture of runaway slaves.[33]

On December 27, 1831, four months after the Nat Turner revolt, approximately one hundred James City County whites signed a petition complaining about the existence of a large free black community in their midst. They claimed that it was a burden upon the county and that free blacks were "degraded, profligate, vicious, turbulent and discontented." During the 1930s, Archie Booker, an ex-slave in his eighties, recalled hearing of a large free black settlement where there were blacksmiths, a wheelwright, and other skilled workers, who made an honest living. That free blacks (some of whom probably were descendants of William Ludwell Lee's former slaves) made the Hot Water tract their permanent home is evidenced by Confederate maps dating to 1863–1864, which identify it as a "Free Negro Settlement Full of Cabins and Paths."[34] Today, dense woods cloak much of the land that once was home to the free black community at Centerville. Much of the area is to be made into a county park.

The Ware Creek Free Black Community

At the head of Ware Creek, near Richardson's Mill, was another small community of free blacks, many of whom were related. Here lived John Ashlock and his kin and the Bervines, the Hodsons, the Nelsons, and the Taylors, who seem to have circulated back and forth across the line between James City and New Kent Counties. Ashlock, who bought land near Ware

Creek in 1817, purchased it from a white woman. The names of free blacks such as Davy Taylor, Ottoway Hodson, George Nelson and John, Peter and Pryor Ashlock were listed in census records and in personal property tax rolls, which identify them as watermen, millers, carpenters, and farm laborers. Most of these male heads of household lived with their wives and children, but some shared their homes with members of their extended family, orphaned children, and others who may not have been related. These free black families' homes (and those of their neighbors) were depicted on maps made by Confederate cartographers, who rarely identified them by race. Real estate tax rolls indicate that the majority occupied very inexpensive dwellings. A house-of-worship and cemetery known as the Six Mile Zion Church, which had a cemetery, served the religious needs of blacks who later lived in this vicinity.[35]

Free Blacks in Nineteenth Century James City County

Census records disclose that in 1800 there were 168 free blacks in James City County who comprised 6.6 percent of the local black population. By 1860, however, 28.8 percent (or more than 1,000 individuals) were free. Some of these people owned real estate and taxable personal property and at least five owned slaves, perhaps spouses or other family members legally unable to obtain their own freedom. In 1833 Abby Hodson, Sylvia Collier, William Cardwell, and Ned Dixon (all of whom were local free blacks) owned one slave apiece and Polly Davis possessed three.[36] In 1817 John Ashlock of James City County, who was identified as "col'd," was credited with 33 1/3 acres of land. During the early 1820s he was able to increase his landhold-ings by purchasing 60 acres from John Dunston, who was white. Ashlock's land was located near Francis Piggott's farm, Temple Hall. Between 1830 and the eve of the Civil War, the amount of acreage owned by James City County's free blacks increased markedly. In 1860 five free blacks were in pos-session of 100 acres or more apiece and Edward R. Crawley, the owner of 232 acres, controlled the largest amount of land. George Nelson, who lived near the head of Ware Creek on a tract he acquired during the 1850s, pos-sessed taxable personal property that exceeded in value that of several white neighbors. He also owned a gig, then a taxable luxury item.[37]

Census records and personal property tax rolls reveal that James City County's free blacks grew crops for their own consumption and perhaps for sale to others, but they also supplemented their income by working as millers, watermen, tailors, sailors, mechanics, midwives, shoemakers, blacksmiths, painters, bricklayers, teamsters, carpenters, and farm laborers. James City County's free blacks included members of the Taylor, Dunston, Jamerson, Wallis, Mason, Mercer, Christopher, Farthing, Cumbo, Ashby, Randolph, Allen, Spratley, Scott, Bartlett, Jones, Ashlock, Hodson, Gary, Harris, Norris, Jackson, Gaines, Moore, Pointer, Tyler, Browne, Copeland, Crawley, Goddin, Dixon, Cannady, Nelson, Johnson, Harwood, Cowles, Lightfoot, Bervine, Simpson, Shepperd, and Carter families. Approximately one-third of James City County's free black heads of household were described as "mulattoes," i.e., they were racially mixed.[38]

Among James City County's most interesting early court documents are the deeds of emancipation that in 1854 were issued to several members of the Mercer family. It was then that the late John Hockaday's administrator presented his will to the county court. He assented "to the desire of freedom . . . as set forth in the said will" thereby freeing William Henry Mercer, John Hockaday Mercer, Israel Henderson Mercer, Benjamin Fleming Mercer, and Matilda Mercer "from all service forever."[39]

Religion as a Galvanizing Force

During the second half of the seventeenth century and the first half of the eighteenth, there appears to have been relatively little interest in offering religious instruction to blacks. Clergy were then in short supply and many slaveholders seemingly were indifferent to their blacks' spiritual well-being. Also, some may have felt that the Christian message would instill pride and make their blacks less governable. By the mid-eighteenth century many whites had decided that it was appropriate to provide their slaves with religious instruction, a belief local Quakers already had acted upon. The register of Bruton Parish Church reveals that approximately 1,000 slaves, whose owners lived in James City and York Counties and the city of Williamsburg, were baptized there.

Before the Civil War white preachers, typically exhorted enslaved blacks to "Be obedient unto them that according to the flesh, are your masters." But to many, the words of the Bible offered a promise of better things to come. During the late eighteenth century many local slaves turned to the Baptist faith. They combined the principals of Christianity with African traditions and produced worship services that included hand-clapping, rhythmic body movements, speaking in tongues, and belief in the presence of the Holy Spirit. This led William Lee of Green Spring to declare that the county's blacks were "crazy with the New Light and their new Jerusalem." Around the time of the Revolutionary War two free black preachers, Gowan Pamphlet and Moses, held Baptist meetings near Williamsburg. Sometimes blacks held religious services in specially constructed brush arbors, one of which was at Green Spring and another at Raccoon Chase, near Ludwell's Mill Pond (Lake Matoaka). At the turn of the nineteenth century, Williamsburg had a black

The Gospel Spreading Farm. Photo by Ralph Maxwell.

Baptist congregation of approximately 500 persons. By 1818 this group, which became known as the African Church, was meeting in a converted carriage house on Nassau Street, midway between the Duke of Gloucester and Francis Streets. Its members included both free and enslaved blacks. The predominantly white congregation of Zion Church (ancestor of the Williamsburg Baptist Church), which came into existence prior to 1828, had some black members, as did many other Baptist churches of the period. Between October 1831 and October 1832, when the memory of the Nat Turner revolt was fresh, a law was passed that prohibited all blacks from preaching and enslaved blacks were forbidden to hold religious meetings unless a white person was present. It is likely, however, that blacks continued to meet for worship in clandestine gatherings. Robert Morris of James City County, a white school teacher who during the late 1840s lived in the Croaker area, noted in his diary the several occasions upon which he baptized blacks in services he conducted in white Baptist churches.

After the Civil War, newly freed blacks flocked to their churches to celebrate a just God's delivery of a long-suffering people and some preachers proclaimed "Hath not one God created us?" The congregations at Shiloh, Chickahominy, New Zion, Gilead, Mount Ararat, and Union built new churches during this period and the Williamsburg Baptist Church became known as the First Baptist Church. The vitality of chanted sermons, the exuberance, and the full-voiced singing that still characterizes many black Baptist worship services offered inspiration. Census records for 1880 reveal that James City County then had eight black Baptist churches with a membership of nearly 3,000 people.[40]

The Civil War's Immediate Effects upon Local Blacks

In late May 1861, when Union General Benjamin F. Butler announced that he wouldn't return runaway slaves, whom he considered "contraband" or Confederate property, thousands of blacks fled to Fort Monroe. Although it is uncertain how many James City County slaves elected to do so, some undoubtedly did. In April 1862 when General George B. McClellan's men set out toward Richmond, many lower peninsula residents abandoned their homes. One local man who witnessed McClellan's arrival in Williamsburg on May 6, 1862, recalled being greeted by crowds of cheering blacks, some of whom tagged along behind the army.[41] The heady prospect of freedom undoubtedly raised local slaves' emotions to a fever pitch.

In October 1862, a few months after Williamsburg came under the control of the Union Army, an event occurred in James City County that outraged white Virginians and sent a ripple of fear through the countryside. On Monday, October 20th, two white men and a young boy, a slave named Littleton, and a free black named Gilbert Wooten[42] set out from Four Mile Tree, in Surry County, and headed for William Allen's Neck O'Land farm. Shortly after they landed their boat at the western end of Jamestown Island, they were seized by five of Allen's slaves, who were armed. Together, they were marched across the Back River bridge to the Neck O'Land plantation's main house, where an estimated 100 black men, women, and children had congregated. A slave named Windsor, who seemed to be in charge, deliberated briefly and then ordered the armed men to return their prisoners to the bridge. Along the way, Allen's overseer antagonized his captors by demanding to know why they hadn't threshed the wheat and he commented that burning the houses on Jamestown Island was needless. As soon the group reached Back Creek, the armed blacks ordered Littleton to step aside and despite the whites' pleas for mercy, shot them and Gilbert Wooten. Then they removed the victims' coats, rifled their pockets for money and threw their bodies into the creek. Wooten, who had been shot in the abdomen, collapsed at the edge of the marsh, where he kept still and pretended to be dead. One of the whites, upon being thrown into the creek, tried to swim away but his attackers bludgeoned him with an oar. After dark, Wooten crept into the marsh and made his way up Powhatan Creek to the home of John Cassidy, a free black at Green Spring. Cassidy helped Wooten cross the river to Surry, where he reported the incident to local officials.[43] Neither Union nor Confederate authorities seem to have taken any action in response to this incident, although newspapers in Petersburg, Richmond, and Lynchburg demanded justice for what were termed cold-blooded, "fiendish murders."[44] Although the records are silent on what caused William Allen's slaves to rebel, they may have been responding to ill treatment or the influence of some "contrabands" who in June 1862 took refuge on Jamestown Island. It is also possible that they were caught up in the anarchy that prevailed on the lower peninsula after the Union Army passed through.

The Freedmen's Bureau in James City County

Shortly after General Butler announced that he wouldn't return runaway slaves, blacks flocked to the lower peninsula. By January 1866 an estimated 70,000 blacks had congregated near Fort Monroe. The monumental task of providing for these former slaves was assigned to the Bureau of Refugees, Freedmen and Abandoned Lands, commonly called the Freedmen's Bureau, which initially distributed food and clothing. Bureau officials sometimes assigned refugees private property that had been abandoned or confiscated. This farm land typically was subdivided into small plots that were leased to refugees in exchange for crop-shares. A map of the lower peninsula's Government Farms reveals that at least five properties in James City County were subdivided into parcels that were placed in the hands of black refugees: Kingsmill, Carter's Grove, the Blow farm, Spratley's, and the Neck O'Land farm. At Kingsmill, freedmen rented William Allen's mill for a third of its earnings. The confiscated property was restored to its owners in 1867.

The Bureau of Refugees' work continued for seven years. It assisted numerous former slaves in adapting to a new way of life and started schools and health care facilities. Philanthropic groups in the North provided support for educational programs, which taught freed blacks how to read and write and imparted knowledge about agriculture and business. But the hardships some ex-slaves (and poor whites) faced right after the Civil War proved insuperable and they succumbed to malnutrition and disease.[45]

Toward a New Way of Life

Many rural ex-slaves, upon being emancipated, gravitated toward cities, where they hoped to find jobs. They quickly discovered that urban areas already had a substantial population of blacks, many of whom lived in ramshackle huts near the docks and marketplaces. Census records demonstrate that by 1870 one out of every six blacks in Virginia lived in urban settings. This trend accelerated until by 1930 one out of every three resided in towns or cities. It is likely that a significant number of James City County blacks went to Richmond seeking work in tobacco factories or gravitated toward the lower peninsula.[46]

In 1869, when Virginia adopted a new constitution, free public schools were established for all and attendance became mandatory. James City County's free schools, which were racially segregated, generated great excitement among blacks, who were eager to learn. In 1872 there were five schools for blacks in the county and one in Williamsburg, all of which were located in private homes. By the mid-1870s public education in Virginia had become universal. In 1885, when James City County's school superintendent compiled statistics for a special exhibition on education, he indicated that schools for whites outnumbered those for blacks by a slim margin and that more blacks than whites attended school.[47]

During the late nineteenth century there were a number of black-owned businesses in Williamsburg, including the "Cheap Store" run by real estate investor Samuel J. Harris, Theodore Harris' theater, the Crump Restaurant, the Crutchfield barber shop and teahouse, Hitchens Store, a blacksmith shop, Skinner's Tavern, and a butcher shop. Later, Robert H. Braxton, a much respected carpenter and builder, developed a subdivision known as Braxton Court. Local blacks also found employment in the knitting mill and in the construction of the C&O railroad line down the peninsula.

At the close of the nineteenth century there were black communities in Williamsburg on York Street and on Francis Street, near the site later occupied by the Williamsburg Inn. The Williamsburg-James City County directory, published by the VIRGINIA GAZETTE in ca. 1898, reveals that blacks and whites often lived side by side in the same neighborhoods until Williamsburg was restored. Some of these people moved to Armistead Avenue's West End and to Franklin Street. By 1916 a subdivision called Highland Park had been laid out. It developed into a predominantly black community.[48]

Grove, Lackey and Magruder

At Grove, a few miles east of Williamsburg, was a small settlement mostly comprised of farmers and fishermen who moved there during the late nineteenth century. During World War I the community grew substantially when development of the Naval Mine Depot (Yorktown Naval Weapons Station) displaced numerous black landowners. Some of these people found employment with the federal government. Many of them formerly lived in Lackey, a small York County settlement northeast of the modern village of Lackey.[49] John Pack Roberts, who was born in ca. 1860, was highly instrumental in the establishment of Grove. A farmer and self-made man who educated himself in the law, he assisted some of the blacks displaced by the government in 1918–1919 in obtaining proper compensation for their land. Grove's population increased markedly during World War II when blacks from Magruder were obliged to vacate their land because a Seabee base (Camp Peary) was to be built. According to Elva G. K. Orr, a local resident, Magruder had a post office, church, lodge, and cemetery. Substantial numbers of blacks also lived in the small settlements that developed near the Chickahominy Church, Mooretown, Centerville, Croaker, and Lightfoot.[50]

Earning a Living

Many rural blacks elected to stay on in their old neighborhoods after the Civil War. A substantial number of them were obliged to seek employment as hired workers, sharecroppers, or tenants simply because a shortage of capital kept them from purchasing land of their own. However, as time went on, a remarkable number of blacks were able to fulfill their dream of owning land. By 1910 there were nearly 180 black-owned farms in James City County, 35 fewer than the number owned by whites. It should be noted, however, that the size of the average black-owned farm was 25 acres whereas the average for whites was 191 acres.[51]

When motorized farm equipment became available, those who could afford to buy it were able to increase their productivity dramatically and use fewer field hands. Thus, mechanization cost some of James City County's black farm workers their jobs. Also, a significant number of small farmers (mostly blacks) were put out of business, for they couldn't compete with their better equipped neighbors. This dampening effect upon the local economy is measured by the fact that during the 1920s the number of black-owned farms in James City County declined by approximately a third. Many of those who lost their means of support were obliged to acquire new, marketable skills. Some found jobs in the barrel-making factory at Toano, which had 70 to 80 workers. Others became laborers in the truck-farming operations that followed the coming of the railroad. Local blacks also worked in timbering and lumbering operations and at the turn of the twentieth century helped to build the seawall at Jamestown. Although the prospects of skilled black workers brightened somewhat during the early twentieth century, their wages typically lagged behind those of whites with comparable expertise and there were many positions for which blacks were not considered at all. Between 1890 and 1920 a substantial number of James City County blacks moved north, seeking work and a greater opportunity to succeed.[52]

Voting Restrictions and the Jim Crow Laws

Reconstruction was followed by two decades in which blacks and whites struggled to re-define their roles in society. During the 1890s the Conservative Party gained control of the General Assembly. Some of its policies, which evolved into the Jim Crow laws, paved the way for more sweeping changes. A new state constitution that took effect in May 1902 required voters to pass a difficult literacy test and pay poll taxes. It was effective in disenfranchising large numbers of blacks and impacted at least one or two generations. As late as 1950 only 17 percent of James City County blacks met the poll tax require-ments for voting. During the late nineteenth and early twentieth centuries racial segregation became legal and was applied to public facilities and pri-vately-owned business establishments. Samuel T. Jones recalled that during the 1920s, when he commuted from Toano to Williamsburg, he sat in the back of the bus. He also said that he and other blacks occupied a special coach when traveling to Richmond by train.

In 1870 it became a felony for large numbers of whites "to make insurrection against the colored population," but lynching still occurred in Virginia. In 1935 Massachusetts authorities refused to permit a black's extradition to Virginia because "with an all-white jury, the man could not expect justice." In 1912 the General Assembly legalized neighborhood segregation. Although the law was struck down by the Supreme Court during the late 1920s, de facto segregation was the norm in urban areas.

Until 1910, blacks outnumbered whites in James City County. By that date, there was full scale segregation of public services and in housing. In 1920 there were fewer local blacks than there had been in the late eighteenth century. During the Great Depression an estimated 24 percent of James City County's black workers were unemployed, statistics that do not include another 24 percent of men and 61 percent of women who needed or wanted work.[53]

Progress and New Opportunities

The unemployment rate declined during the 1940s, '50s, and '60s, when the service sector of the local economy gradually replaced agriculture as the principal form of employment. Central to this improvement were the employment opportunities provided by the Colonial Williamsburg Foundation, the College of William and Mary, and Eastern State Hospital. A local chapter of the National Association for the Advancement of Colored People was organized at the Mount Gilead Baptist Church in 1942 and other social and civic services clubs began working toward the advancement of blacks. Passage of the 1964 Civil Rights Act further improved blacks' opportunities. It was the same year that school integration became a reality.

Statistics suggest that James City County's black and white households differ somewhat in composition, even today. Many black households are multi-generational or include members of the extended family or non-relatives. Also, households headed by women are far more common. The average income of James City County's black families has lagged somewhat behind that of whites and far more blacks have an income below the poverty level. Even so, between 1940 and 1970 the number of James City County blacks employed in professional, managerial, and clerical positions grew significantly and the volume of those employed as laborers and domestics declined.[54]

An especially proud moment for James City County, as a whole, was Abram Frink's election to the Board of Supervisors as representative of the Roberts District, created in 1969. Mr. Frink served on the Board for 13 years, including four one-year terms as chairman. When he retired, he was acclaimed as a consensus builder whose leadership skills were invaluable during a critical period in the county's development.[55] His achievements and those of the Rev. Junius Moody and others are a source of pride to the entire community.

Abram Frink, member of the James City County Board of Supervisors, 1970–1983. James City County file photo.

Notes

1. Tate, The Negro, 1; Kingsbury, Records, III, 243; John Smith, Travels, 541–542. John Rolfe's account of the first blacks' arrival suggests that the Dutch vessel first touched land at Old Point Comfort.

2. Anonymous, "Number of People in Virginia, March 1619 [1620];" Hotten, Original Lists, 173–176, 191–192, 217–218, 224, 229, 241, 244; Tate, The Negro, 3, 5–6; C.W.F., Resource Protection, 1, V, 13.

3. Gary B. Nash, Red, White and Black: The People of Early America (Englewood Cliffs, N. J., 1974), 186–187.

4. Palmer, Calendar, I, 10; Tate, The Negro, 3, 5–6.

5. W. F., Resource Protection, 1, V, 9–10, 12; Tate, The Negro, 12.

6. York County Wills, Deeds, Orders 1657–1659, 18.

7. Hening, Statutes, II, 26, 260. In 1661 a law was passed obliquely recognizing that life servitude for blacks was a possibility.

8. McIlwaine, Minutes, 513; Tate, The Negro, 7–8, 93; C. W. F., Resource Protection, 1, V, 23–26, 34.

9. Nugent, Cavaliers, II, 11; Sainsbury et al., Calendar, V, 52; McIlwaine, Executive Journals, I, 310.

10. Tate, The Negro, 10; Hening, Statutes, III, 333; McIlwaine, Minutes, 347.

11. Tate, The Negro, 91; William G. Stanard, ed., "Notes and Queries: Management of Slaves in 1672, From the Records of Surry County," Virginia Magazine of History and Biography 7 (January 1900):314–335. However, legal restrictions on blacks' clothing were uncommon.

12. Katz, The Negro, 140–141, 174; Tate, The Negro, 9–11.

13. Earlier on, Indians were not considered slaves under the law, for as indigenous inhabitants they were accorded the right to free trade.

14. Walter Minchinton et al., Virginia Slave Trade Statistics, 1698–1775 (Richmond, 1984), 57, 59, 67, 73, 77, 79, 81, 83; Hening, Statutes, III, 447–462; VI, 106–107, 109–111; Katz, The Negro, 140–141, 174; Tate, The Negro, 13.

15. Morgan, Black Education, 1–2, 56; Tate, The Negro, 7–8, 93; C.W.F., Resource Protection, 1, V, 23–26, 34.

16. Ibid., 1, V, 24–25, 34–36; Tate, The Negro, 19–20.

17. A slave couple's mutual commitment was not deemed a legal marriage.

18. C.W.F., Resource Protection, 1, V, 24–25, 34–36.

19. Some of the "others" were Indian slaves, but bound servants also may have participated.

20. Morgan, Black Education, 6; Katz, The Negro, 140–141, 174; Tate, The Negro, 12–13, 111, 113; Stanard, ed., "Negro Plot," : 250–254; McIlwaine, Executive Journals, III, 234–236.

21. Katz, The Negro, 140–141; Hening, Statutes, VI, 31–33; VII, 518.

22. Morgan, Black Education, 19–20.

23. Tate, The Negro, 47.

24. In Africa, marriage was a religious rite often accompanied by weeks of celebration.

25. Robert M. Watson Jr., October 12, 1994, personal communication; T. H. Breen and Stephen Innes, MYNE OWNE GROUND (New York, 1980), 10; Katz, THE NEGRO, 79–81.

26. Morgan, BLACK EDUCATION, 26–30; Tate, THE NEGRO, 46).

27. McIlwaine, COUNCIL OF STATE, IV, 176, 210, 278, 281, 283.

28. Russell, FREE NEGRO, 72–73; Katz, THE NEGRO, 140–141; Morgan, BLACK EDUCATION, 59. Statistics show that in 1783 approximately 38 percent of James City County landowners had 21 or more slaves (C. W. F., Resource Protection, 1, V, 35).

29. Palmer, CALENDAR, VI, 461–465, 521, 532–533, 543.

30. Lee's other executor refused to serve. Hodgson was in an awkward position, for his wife (who appears to have inherited her father's mercenary streak) would have received half of her brother's slaves, had he not freed them.

31. Mumford, SUPREME COURT, VI, 163–164; James City County Land Tax Lists 1803–1869.

32. James City County Personal Property Tax Lists 1834–1839.

33. Katz, THE NEGRO, 140–141.

34. Morgan, "Ethnic Heritage"; Gilmer, "Vicinity."

35. Gilmer, "Vicinity;" James City County Census 1850–1860; Land Tax Lists 1820–1860; Personal Property Tax Lists 1850–1860; U.S.G.S., "Williamsburg," 1906; Simon Ashlock, personal communication, 1988.

36. All of these slaves were age 16 or older.

37. Morgan, BLACK EDUCATION, 11, 22; James City County Land Tax Lists 1817–1850; Personal Property Tax Lists 1817–1850.

38. James City County Personal Property Tax Lists 1837–1850.

39. James City County Deed Book 1, 16–18.

40. Morgan, BLACK EDUCATION, 34–36, 39–40; C. W. F., RESOURCE PROTECTION, 1, V, 44, 59; Robert Morris, "Diary," 1845–1857; Katz, THE NEGRO, 247.

41. Webb, PENINSULAR CAMPAIGN, 39–41; Charles, "Recollections," 3. The Emancipation Proclamation was issued on January 1, 1863.

42. The whites were J. M. Shriver (a British citizen), James A. Graves (William Allen's principal overseer and a former Commonwealth Attorney for Surry County) and Graves' nephew, George. Littleton was Shriver's slave and Wooten was employed by William Allen in Surry.

43. Wooten described Windsor as a slave from the neighborhood; however, a newspaper account described him as a runaway from William Allen's home, Claremont, in Surry County. Some of the blacks in the crowd called him "the Judge." Others Wooten recalled seeing at the Neck O'Land were George Thomas, Norborne Baker, William Parsons, Henry Moore, Jesse, Alick, Mike, Joe Parsons, Jim Diggs (the elder and the younger), Robert Cole, Little Henry, Peter, and Jeffrey, all of whom belonged to Allen.

44. Palmer, CALENDAR, XI, 233–236; RICHMOND WHIG, October 24, 1862; DAILY RICHMOND EXAMINER, October 24, 1862; LYNCHBURG DAILY VIRGINIAN, October 27, 1862.

45. Bureau of Refugees, Freedmen and Abandoned lands, 1865–1867; Freedmen's Bureau, "Map of Government Farms," 1866; Bradley M. McDonald et al., "CAST DOWN YOUR BUCKET WHERE YOU ARE" (Norfolk, 1992), 12.

46. Katz, THE NEGRO, 335–336. By the late 1880s the Newport News Shipyard offered employment to blacks and others.

47. Virginia School Report (Richmond, 1885), 13, 94. See Chapter 17.

48. Morgan, Black Education, 24; C.W.F., Resource Protection, 1, V, 68, 74; James City County Plat Book 2, 33.

49. During the mid–to–late 1860s "old" Lackey was part of the acreage that the Bureau of Refugees assigned to former slaves.

50. C.W.F., Resource Protection, 1, V, 68; Morgan, "Ethnic Heritage;" Clingan, "Naval Weapons Station, 1, 13, 23.

51. Morgan, Black Education, 23–24.

52. C. W. F., Resource Protection, 1, V, 69–70, 74.

53. Katz, The Negro, 237–242, 244; Morgan, "Ethnic Heritage;" Black Education, 26, 56.

54. Morgan, "Ethnic Heritage;" Black Education, 26, 31–32, 67, 74; C.W.F., Resource Protection, 1, VI, 70, 87.

55. James City County Historical Commission Files.

CHAPTER 17

"Only the Educated Are Free"
The History of Education in James City County

The Tradition in Virginia

"I thank God there are no free schools or printing presses and I hope we shall not have them these hundred years," Governor William Berkeley declared in 1671. Though all Virginians didn't share his dour view, disinterest and even outright prejudice against public education persisted until after the Civil War. In 1619 attempts were made to establish a college and university in the corporation of Henrico, where it was hoped that Virginia's Indians could be taught religion and "civilized." Two years later, some private investors agreed to sponsor the East India School in Charles City, where the sons of Virginia planters could receive an education. However, the 1622 Indian uprising put an end to both projects. Settlers who could read and write sometimes shared their knowledge with others. For example, early seventeenth-century records reveal that some of the Jamestown colonists taught children to read so that they could study the Bible. Benjamin Syms of Elizabeth City (now the city of Hampton) in 1634 endowed what became America's first free public school and in 1659 Dr. Thomas Eaton followed Syms' example. Across the James River in Nansemond County (the city of Suffolk), philanthropist John Yeates made a similar bequest in 1731. But these schools were not truly "public," for they were privately sponsored and catered specifically to the needs of poor white children.

Because Virginia planters sought large tracts of land upon which they could cultivate tobacco, their homesteads were broadly dispersed throughout the countryside. Thus, unlike New England, where settlers tended to congregate in small towns and build community schools, they tended to live in relatively isolated settings. As a consequence, Virginians' interest in establishing towns and building public schools never really gained momentum until a much later period. Also, the plantation system (a mainstay of Virginia society) accentuated class distinction. As elected officials (typically, members of the upper class) saw neither the merit nor the necessity of educating those of lesser social rank, there was little incentive to underwrite the cost of public schools. In 1671 Governor William Berkeley told British officials that in Virginia, as in rural England, "every man according to his ability" offered instruction to his children. From this philosophy, which originated in the Mother Country, arose the tradition that individual families were responsible for educating their own youngsters.

Throughout the colonial period, a minimal amount of attention was given to educating poor and orphaned children at public expense. Thanks to that precedent, people came to associate free education with pauperism and charity, a stigma that both haunted and inhibited the development of public schooling until the 1870s. In 1672 county justices were authorized to bind out, as servants, all children whose parents were unable to train them in a marketable skill. Such youngsters' terms of indenture extended to adulthood. A 1705 law compelled orphans' guardians to teach them to read and write and a 1727 legislative mandate specified that the children of poor or neglectful parents be bound out as apprentices.[1]

The College of William and Mary

In 1693 King William and Queen Mary granted a charter to the College of William and Mary, established an endowment, and set aside tax revenues toward its support. The campus of the college lay in James City County, just west of what in 1699 became Williamsburg. By 1694 a grammar school was opened for children age eight and older and in 1695 the first bricks were laid for the college's main building. In 1699 when the colony's capital was shifted from Jamestown to Williamsburg, the college became the Virginia govern-ment's temporary headquarters. Shortly thereafter, an Indian School was established, which in 1723 moved into the new Brafferton Building. By 1710 a small school established by Matthew Whaley's mother had come into exis-tence. At Mrs. Mary Page Whaley's death in 1742 the school land and its buildings became the property of Bruton Parish, which used it to educate poor children. In 1779 the College of William and Mary's grammar and divinity schools were discontinued and professorships were added in a number of liberal arts subjects, including law.[2]

Local School Houses

In 1724 the Anglican clergy of James City County and Williamsburg informed the Bishop of London that there were no public schools in their parishes, although reading, writing, and arithmetic were taught in a few little schoolhouses. These were plantation schools, where one or more families hired a tutor who shared his knowledge with neighborhood children, usually in exchange for room and board.[3] Often, an outbuilding or dependency was outfitted as a classroom or a special building was erected in a less productive field. Classes typically began early in the morning and lasted for about two hours. After a recess for breakfast, instruction continued until around noon. Classes resumed in the mid-afternoon, after the heat had subsided, and con-tinued until early evening. The typical school year ran from April through September, when daylight hours were lengthier. During the eighteenth century Williamsburg had three privately-run schools for boys and plans were made to open a girls' school, where reading, writing, dancing, needlework, and music could be taught.[4]

Blacks' Opportunities for Education

For Virginia's enslaved blacks, the prospects of becoming literate were especially dismal. During the mid-to-late seventeenth century only a few free blacks and black apprentices received religious instruction and were taught to read. By the 1740s there was interest in establishing a school for blacks within the city of Williamsburg. In 1760 a group of English philanthropists, dedicated to promoting education among for blacks and Indians, decided to sponsor a school in Williamsburg and appointed its trustees. By November they had hired Mrs. Anne Wager and rented a dwelling in which she was to live and offer instruction. The school's 24 to 30 students, who were between three and ten years old, were taught how to read the Bible, write, and recite the catechism. Irregular attendance seems to have been a persistent problem, perhaps because slave owners generally were unwilling to part with their blacks for an extended period of time. Mrs. Wager's school closed at her death in 1774.

During the late eighteenth and early nineteenth centuries Methodists, members of the Society of Friends (Quakers), and a few other whites demonstrated an interest in teaching blacks to read, write, and count. But in 1805, a few years after the Gabriel insurrection, Virginia legislators imposed strict penalties upon anyone who tried to educate them. After the 1831 Nat Turner revolt all forms of slave education were prohibited by law. Many whites believed that educated slaves were potentially dangerous and that allowing blacks to congregate in groups (even for worship) was risky. Free blacks sometimes managed to send their children out of the state to be educated, but in 1838 those who left weren't allowed to return. In 1842 it became illegal for blacks to assemble "for the purpose of instruction in reading and writing or in the night time for any purpose." Although some whites believed that slaves should receive basic religious instruction and be taught to read, many feared that literacy would promote rebellion.

Numerous blacks, thanks to their own inventiveness, acquired a rudimentary education. Through stories and songs cultural values and folk lore were transmitted from generation to generation within the slave community. Slaveholders sometimes taught their blacks crafts in order to enhance their usefulness, occasionally conveying other forms of knowledge (such as reading and writing) unwittingly. Probate records and advertisements for runaways reveal that slaves became highly skilled in a variety of trades and often knew how to read and write a little.[5] If they escaped to an urban area, sometimes they could pass for free.

The Genesis of Public Education

Thomas Jefferson, unlike many of his contemporaries, was a strong proponent of public education, for he was convinced that an enlightened electorate was the best protection for free men's rights. In 1779 he proposed building public grammar schools in each of Virginia's counties, where children could be educated gratis for a three year period. However, his ideas were rejected soundly by the state legislature. In 1796 a law was passed that authorized (but did not require) Virginia counties to establish public schools. This was the true beginning of publicly-sponsored education in Virginia. Locally-elected officials could hire, fire, and evaluate teachers, build and maintain schoolhouses, and assess both teachers' and students' proficiency. All free white children of both sexes were entitled to three years of schooling, tuition-free, if their parents or guardians approved. They could attend even longer if tuition were paid. But because the basic cost of public schools was to be borne by local taxpayers, many communities chose not to open schools.

William Ludwell Lee, who inherited Green Spring and several other local properties, bequeathed a thousand acres of his Hot Water tract (near Centerville) to the College of William and Mary, stipulating that the president and faculty would build and operate a free (or common) school in the center of James City County. But when he died in 1803, the college declined to accept the responsibility that went with the endowment. As a result, in 1818 the Hot Water tract became the object of litigation involving the college and Lee family heirs. More than 25 years later James City County's school commissioners (who were entitled to the college's interest in the Hotwater land) succeeded in having the property partitioned. They sold it and invested the proceeds toward the support of local public education.

At the turn of the nineteenth century the schooling of Virginia women began to receive serious consideration. The Williamsburg Female Academy was operational by 1805; classes were held until the mid-nineteenth century. The academy, which was comprised of several buildings, was located on the colonial capital's grounds in Williamsburg. During the 1850s males were admitted but taught separately. Some James City County families sent their children to school at the academy.[6]

The Literary Fund

In 1810 the General Assembly established the Literary Fund, which earnings (if supplemented by local revenues) could be used to pay teachers, build schools, and purchase books. Its principal was derived from fines, forfeitures, confiscations, escheats, and war debts associated with the American Revolution. Money from the Literary Fund was loaned to the federal government during the War of 1812, but later was repaid. In 1816 the General Assembly voted to distribute the Literary Fund's earnings among Virginia's counties, once it achieved an annual income of $45,000 or more a year. Literary Fund revenues were intended to underwrite the cost of providing instruction to poor white children. Under the law, five school commissioners, appointed by local court justices, were authorized to disburse their county's share of the Literary Fund to teachers who presented attendance records on behalf of the poor children they taught. Teachers were paid a penny a week for each pupil. In 1820 the law was amended to allow up to 10 percent of a county's Literary Fund allotment to be used for schoolhouse construction, as long as the locality paid three-fifths of the cost. An additional five percent could be used toward the purchase of books and each county could spend $100 on teachers' salaries as long as local citizens supplied matching funds. Although only the poor were eligible for public school tuition, others could attend classes by paying whatever fees teachers and parents agreed upon. Many families who couldn't afford to send their youngsters to school refused to take advantage of the Literary Fund's tuition subsidy because accepting it meant publicly acknowledging that they (and their children) were paupers.[7]

Old Field Schools

During the first half of the nineteenth century the Old Field School (an updated version of the plantation school) was especially popular in rural communities and some had so-called "Sunday Schools," where religious and secular education were intermixed. A teacher who had attended an Old Field School, said that they typically were constructed of boards or logs and stood in old, abandoned agricultural fields. He recalled that sloping shelves attached to the school room's interior walls served as desks and that pupils sat upon hard, backless benches. Another described his teachers as "a class of stiff, formal pedagogues" that inspired students "to guffaw over their weary platitudes and formal manners." Some who taught in old field schools reportedly "were invalids, some were slaves to drunkenness, some too lazy to work, most of them entirely ignorant of the art of teaching and a terror to their pupils." Students typically learned by rote and had to recite their lessons in front of the teacher and fellow classmates. Punishment (usually inflicted with a ruler, horsewhip, or leather strap) was administered for misbehavior and for failure to learn. Needless to say, recess was a welcome interruption to the rigors of the classroom. One nineteenth-century educator observed that "most young ones go to the school when they must; escape when they can and finally leave it with stubborn resolution to have as little to do with books as possible." The sequel to the Old Field School was the academy, which provided secondary education. There, pupils could learn Latin, Greek, modern languages, higher mathematics and sciences such as physics, chemistry, and botany. Most Virginia counties had one or two academies. The state's only official connection with academies was issuing their charters.[8]

The Hickory Neck School

In 1807 the Overseers of the Poor for New Kent County received permission to dispose of the glebe of the defunct Blisland Parish, which territory lay in both James City and New Kent Counties. James City's Overseers of the Poor, who received $572 out of the $1,000 proceeds, were authorized to use the funds however they saw fit, as long as local householders concurred. The money sat until December 1824 when a group of James City County voters asked the General Assembly's permission to spend it on converting Hickory Neck Church into a school. The General Assembly approved the proposal and incorporated the trustees of the Hickory Neck School Society for the expressed purpose of "repairing a part of the building formerly called Hickory Neck Church" in order to convert it into a primary school for local inhabitants. Six James City County men were named trustees of the Hickory Neck School Society: Archer Hankins, Michael S. Warren, Richardson

Henley, John E. Brown Jr., Thurston James, and Robert Morris. They were authorized to buy, lease or sell land on behalf of the school and had the right to appoint a president, secretary, tutors, librarian, treasurer, and other school officials. However, they could spend no more than $300 of the proceeds of the glebe "for the building and repairs of the said school house." The remainder ($272) was set aside to earn interest that could be used for tuition or any other worthy purpose. It was around 1825 that the oldest part of Hickory Neck Church (constructed in 1734) was demolished and the southern end of the north transept (built in 1774) was extended, bricked up, and converted into a schoolhouse. By the 1840s the Hickory Neck School had become an academy.[9]

James City County's Early Public Schools

In 1823 there were nine so-called common (or public primary) schools in James City County, each of which provided instruction to 25 students, approximately half of whom were from poor families. During the 1820s, '30s, and '40s a growing number of poor children were educated at public expense and spent more time in school. However, school commissioners' returns reveal that the number of young paupers in the population also was on the rise. Henley Taylor and Michael S. Warren, James City County school commissioners during the 1820s, compiled the county's statistical reports, whereas Richardson Henley, Nathaniel Piggott, and diarist Robert Morris served in that capacity during the 1830s, '40s, and '50s. Between 1823 and 1860 James City County had between eight and ten common schools.

An 1829 law made Virginia localities eligible for matching public funds that could be used to build schools and hire teachers, as long as the schoolhouses were in a central location and the land upon which they stood was deeded to the state. Each of these public primary schools was to offer reading, writing, arithmetic, grammar, and geography and if possible, history, and physical science. The poor could attend tuition-free, whereas others had to pay whatever fee teachers and parents agreed upon. In 1837 James City County received only $71 from the Literary Fund, the second lowest sum allocated to a Virginia county school system. The General Assembly in 1845 authorized counties to establish free public schools for poor white children between 6 and 21 and to levy taxes toward their support. However, James City County was not among the localities that opted to do so. Even so, the 1840 school census for James City County indicates that locally there were 140 grammar school students and 93 students in primary schools. By 1850, 150 James City County students were enrolled in private schools, academies and colleges and 165 pupils attended free public schools. Thirty-six percent of whites between the ages of 5 and 20 were enrolled in schools of some sort. During the early-to-mid nineteenth century Virginia's illiteracy rate significantly exceeded that of its more northerly industrialized neighbors. However, as time went on, interest in public education slowly but surely gained momentum. The 1845 act that authorized the establishment of free public schools allowed voters to elect local school commissioners to oversee the management of schools and serve as a school board. School commissioners were obliged to make monthly visits to the public schools within their districts, to examine attendance records, make sure that the schoolhouse was in good repair, and evaluate teaching methods and discipline. They also were authorized to suspend any pupil deemed incorrigible or guilty of gross misconduct.

School commissioners' reports, compiled between 1823 and 1860, list only the number of poor children enrolled, but they demonstrate that more and more youngsters from low income families were being educated at public expense. In 1823 Henley Taylor (upon whose farm the Toano Middle School was built in 1991) was one of James City County's early school commissioners. Robert Morris of Croaker, who taught school during the mid-1840s, also served in that capacity. He noted in his daily diary how many pupils attended his school and how often he held classes. On September 13, 1845, he indicated that he had "heard letters read from applicants for Hickory Neck Academy," apparently one of his duties as a trustee. A short time later Morris was offered a teaching job in Williamsburg, where he held classes in the President's House at the College of William and Mary.

Local census records reveal that in 1860, there were seven school teachers living in James City County, half of whom were women. All but one of these teachers were in their early-to-mid twenties and lived with households that resided near the schools in which they taught. The exception was Thomas G. Wynne, who combined teaching with farming. Lou A. Martin, E. F. Sale, Charles W. Hubbard, Jr., Francis W. Hamilton, Perdia W. Meanley, and James H. Allen were among those who in 1860 taught school in James City County. Nearby Williamsburg had its own contingent of teachers, including Miss Martha James, a James City County native.[10]

The Civil War's Impact Upon Education

By 1860 white Virginians' literacy rate had risen somewhat but illiteracy was still a major social problem. During the Civil War the Literary Fund's revenues were diverted into the Confederate military budget and public education was virtually abandoned. During the 1860s the illiteracy rate soared and at the end of the war nearly 22 percent of the state's whites and an estimated 208,000 blacks were unable to read and write. The College of William and Mary sustained much damage during the Civil War. Afterward, the college reopened, thanks to the Herculean efforts of President Benjamin S. Ewell.[11]

Public Education Becomes Available to All

It was not until 1869, when the controversial Underwood Constitution was ratified, that public education in Virginia really came into its own. By 1876 racially segregated free public schools were established in all Virginia counties to serve blacks and whites. School attendance was mandatory for those between the ages of 5 and 21, regardless of socio-economic status. The educational system established after the Civil War in some respects resembled the one proposed by Thomas Jefferson in 1796. Pupils, who were required to attend school, had to be clean, free of contagious diseases, and vaccinated. Teachers had to keep daily attendance records and provide instruction in reading, spelling, writing, arithmetic, grammar, and geography. A report card from the James City County public school in which Thomas G. Wynne taught indicates that students not only were rated on their academic progress but also their demeanor and attentiveness. A shortage of teachers, who typically had little education beyond high school, was a major obstacle in improving Virginia's public education system. The Peabody Fund, set up by George Peabody to promote education in the Southern states, provided funds that could be used to establish teacher-training schools.

Williamsburg's School Board held its first recorded meeting in December 1870, a year after the Underwood Constitution took effect. Classes, held from February 1st to July 1st in rented rooms, were attended by students from James City and York Counties and Williamsburg. Two teachers were hired for whites and one for blacks. The School Board decided that "white males and females [should] be taught in separate schools" and that the same policy would apply to blacks as soon as they had more than one teacher. As the Williamsburg School Board received a very small sum from the state, they asked the City Council for money to cover the cost of rent, furniture, books, paper, fuel, and other items. In 1873 the School Board leased the Matthew Whaley School (or Mattey Schoolhouse) and its furnishings from the College of William and Mary which held what originally had been Bruton Parish's legal interest in the property. The school was located on the Palace Green, near the site of the colonial Governor's Palace. As the number of pupils increased, the Williamsburg School Board rented rooms throughout the town. During the mid-1880s a schoolhouse for black children was built on Francis Street.

Many blacks, who previously had had little or no opportunity to receive schooling, yearned for an education. In 1871 one James City County writer said that "The free schools are in full blast . . . and great excitement prevails. . . . Young and old, little and big, seem eager to obtain knowledge." A year later there were five black schools in James City County and one in Williamsburg. Virtually all of the county's black schools were in private homes. Some blacks reportedly viewed the chance to receive an education as a second Emancipation Proclamation, which freed them from the bonds of illiteracy. During the 1870s and '80s many whites considered common free schools a drain on tax revenues at a time when the state staggered under massive debt. Some believed that it wasn't the government's responsibility to educate all children, especially blacks, and that educating the young was a function of the home. Many blacks wanted racially integrated free schools, an idea most whites rejected.

During the 1880s Virginia's fledgling educational system became firmly established and began earning the respect of the general public. In 1885, when James City County School Superintendent C. W. Taylor prepared a report for a special exhibition sponsored by the State Superintendent of Public Instruction, he indicated that sentiment and support for public education had waxed and waned, but that by the early 1880s common schools had gained relatively broad acceptance. Taylor prepared a chart in which he summarized how many public schools were in operation in James City County between 1871 and 1883, along with the proportion that were for whites and blacks. He

Report card form used by Thomas G. Wynne, who taught school in Grove. Courtesy of Fred Boelt.

also indicated how many months the schools were in session and the number of teachers and students involved per year. Taylor's statistics reveal that schools for whites outnumbered those for blacks by a slim margin, but that a greater number of blacks attended public school. Between 1871 and 1883 the length of school sessions grew from three to more than six months. Male teachers predominated, especially among blacks, but as time went on, that trend gradually changed. Taylor's statistics reveal that black teachers labored under an especially high student-teacher ratio and that absenteeism among both races was high. C. W. Taylor's report on the history of James City County's schools, which was on display in the chamber of the state senate, earned him an award for preparing "the best comprehensive history of public schools." Between 1871 and 1883 the number of school houses for James City County whites grew from seven to eleven and the number for blacks, from four to nine. During the early twentieth century, when women teachers began to predominate, the gap between black and white teachers' salaries began to widen. By 1890 40 percent of James City County's school-age blacks were

Old schoolhouse in Grove, now used by the Long Horn Hunt Club. Photo by Ralph Maxwell.

The Toano School. Courtesy of Frances H. Hamilton and Nancy S. Bradshaw.

enrolled in school, in contrast to 53 percent of whites. During the 1880s one-room schools for whites were built on one-fourth- to one-half-acre lots on the public roads near Jolly Pond, Yarmouth, Turners Neck, Peach Park, the Diascund Bridge, Lightfoot, Norge, and Croaker.

In 1888 teacher-training became part of the College of William and Mary's curriculum. Simultaneously, the college's property was transferred to the Commonwealth of Virginia in order to provide it with state support. During the late nineteenth and early twentieth centuries the college ran "model schools" where public school teachers were trained. The Nicholson School opened in Williamsburg and according to the 1898 city-county directory, had approximately 100 students who came from Williamsburg, James City and York Counties. The city's black primary school (Public School No. 2) had 75 pupils. In James City County there were eleven schools for whites and eight for blacks, who then comprised two-thirds of the county's school age population.[12]

What School Was Like

Youngsters, regardless of race, typically received all of their instruction from one teacher, who taught several grades in one room. Although the public school curriculum's subject matter was varied, it was oriented toward reading, writing, and arithmetic. One woman who attended a public school during the late nineteenth century described its interior. She said that the teacher's chair and desk, which had a hinged cover secured by a padlock, sat upon a raised platform at the front of the room, which "was furnished with backless benches of unpainted pine." Tall stools were aligned in a row in front of a sloping wall-mounted shelf that served as a desk. Schoolhouses built in accord with state officials' guidelines had walls that allowed blackboards to extend seven feet from the floor. Teachers were encouraged to acquire wall maps, charts, and other graphics to provide students with visual and intellectual stimulation. A bucket and ladle for drinking water and brooms and brushes for cleaning were part of a schoolhouse's equipment.

Mrs. Lucy James, who attended the Hickory Neck School from 1893 to 1896 and later returned as principal, described what it was like, according to old-timers, and later when she was a pupil. When the school first opened after the Civil War, students sat upon backless wooden benches that were arranged in a semi-circle around an open fireplace. During the mid-1890s, when Mrs. James was learning the Three R's, Hickory Neck was heated by a stove set into the old fireplace at the rear of the room. A small frame building near the old building served as a classroom for younger children. Pupils placed their lunch containers (which ranged from tin buckets, shoeboxes, baskets and paper bags to newspaper bundles) on a long shelf in the back of the school room. In one corner was a small shelf with a wooden water bucket and tin dipper, both of which were scoured with white sand from the road and then rinsed clean. Some children walked to school whereas others rode an old work horse. On Friday afternoons, students took part in cultural activities, such as singing and reciting poetry. During recess they played tag, leap-frog, and other games. Mrs. James said that the big boys teased the little ones, who feared being placed "under the big flat tombstones that were then showing in the yard." Across the road and down the hill was a spring that bubbled from a moss-and-fern-covered embankment. It was there that the school's water bucket was filled by the bigger boys. In good weather, the teacher sometimes took all of her students to the spring at lunch time. Classes were held at the Hickory Neck School until September 1908 when the Toano School opened.[13]

Local Educational Facilities

Primary Schools

At the turn of the twentieth century schools for white children were constructed at Ewell, Grove, Diascund, and Blackstump and a black school was erected in the vicinity of the Strawberry Plains. In 1904 a school opened in Norge, on the Flatten farm, where instruction was offered in both English and Norwegian. Although the Jim Crow laws served to further stratify Virginia's public school system, Northern and Midwestern philanthropists established trusts (such as the Slater Fund, the Jeanes Foundation, and the Rosenwald Fund) that provided financial support to black schools. The Chickahominy School Improvement League and the St. John's School League furnished funding to local black schools, including those at Mount Pleasant, Oak Grove, Chickahominy, Centerville, and Croaker. The latter three elementary schools were constructed in 1920, the same year the State Department of Education began furnishing standardized architectural plans to communities building new schools. From then until 1946 Virginia's schools became increasingly standardized as basic specifications were used for construction. The Division of School Buildings, established in 1920, was intended to assist localities in managing school properties.

According to Samuel T. Jones, who attended the St. John's and Chickahominy Schools, finishing the seventh grade made students eligible to seek a higher education. In 1924 the James City County Training School, a public high school for Williamsburg and James City County blacks, was built on the corner of Botetourt and Nicholson Streets. Although it emphasized technical training, one former student recalled that reading, writing and arithmetic comprised its core curriculum. Blacks in the Grove area who wanted their children to attend the James City County Training School purchased a bus and paid $1.35 a month for their children's commute. Eventually, however, the county school board agreed to provide them with transportation. The illiteracy rate among James City County blacks was especially high during the early twentieth century and in 1910 approximately 40 percent were unable to read and write at a time when only 4 percent of whites were illiterate.[14]

The Toano School

Early in 1906 Virginia's General Assembly established a state system of public high schools and appropriated $50,000 from the Literary Fund for school construction loans. According to Dr. H. U. Stephenson, a local school trustee, the citizens of western James City County were convinced that their children were unable to receive an adequate public education because of the high rate of attrition among teachers. He blamed low salaries for the local school system's inability to attract and retain good teachers and said that "Generally speaking, every school had a new teacher every year and every teacher changed the course of study as he or she saw fit." Stephenson also indicated that "There was no

The Five Forks School. Photo by Ralph Maxwell.

James Blair Middle School. Photo by Nan Maxwell.

thought of grading the work. If a child liked mathematics and disliked English, he was allowed to spend his time on the mathematics." Another drawback was that local schools didn't offer an advanced course for older students. Local subscribers pledged $4,500 toward the construction of a high school but little progress was made until 1907–1908 when the Toano High School Fund was established. Into it were deposited monies from the Hickory Neck Academy Fund, the dog tax, school district funds, and $3,000 borrowed from the Literary Fund. A total of $7,000 was raised.[15]

In 1907 James City County's school trustees bought a 1 1/2 acre lot at the intersection of Forge and Stage Roads from Richard H. Slater. They intended to build a regional high school that would serve students from James City, New Kent, and Charles City Counties, which comprised a single school division. According to a report Dr. Stephenson filed with the State School Superintendent, a member of the local school board drew up plans for the new school and a local contractor undertook its construction. A total of $5,500 was spent on the Toano School's buildings and grounds. Two large school wagons were purchased for $100 apiece. The new school opened on September 21, 1908, with a dedication ceremony and address by J. D. Eggleston, the state School Superintendent. Although an initial enrollment of 50 to 60 was expected, the new school, which accommodated students from grades one through eleven, had 95 pupils on the first day.

Toano pupils received instruction from five faculty members, one of whom was a music teacher. The new school's upper level courses, which were graded, conformed to the state's standard for high schools. Each of the Toano School's specially-built school wagons was 12 feet long and held 25 to 30 students. They were pulled by two large horses rented from a local man. One of the school wagons was driven by a high school boy who reported was "steady, sober and industrious." So enthusiastic was the local response to the Toano School that James City County's school trustees believed they might have to add on two new classrooms within a year and purchase two new school wagons. Photographs that appeared in the VIRGINIA JOURNAL OF EDUCATION in 1908 showed the brand new Toano School, its library and school wagons. Also depicted were its five teachers, four of whom were women. The Toano School was at the hub of upper James City County's social and cultural life for nearly a half-century.[16]

Evolution and Change

In the city, Williamsburg High School was erected at a site near the colonial Governor's Palace with money from the Literary Fund and local revenue bonds. In July 1922 James City County school trustees conveyed properties at Five Forks, Strawberry Plains, Toano, Blackstump, Diascund, and Chickahominy to the county School Board. Two years later members of the St. John's School League, which school for blacks was located between Forge and Stage Roads, followed suit.

In 1928 the Williamsburg Restoration purchased the land upon which stood Williamsburg High School and the old Mattey School, the college's model and practice school. Two years later the present Matthew Whaley School was built. During the 1930s the Matthew Whaley School accepted students from Williamsburg, Jamestown District of James City County, and

Bruton District of York County. In 1940 Bruton Heights School, a fully accredited high school for blacks, was built with funds provided by the federal government and John D. Rockefeller Jr. It was the first Virginia high school for blacks which curriculum included elective subjects. Unlike its forerunner, the James City County Training School, Bruton Heights offered an academic program along with technical training. It had 17 classrooms, an auditorium, a gymnasium, and a library and separate buildings that contained teaching space for home economics and industrial arts. Approximately three-quarters of the students enrolled at Bruton Heights were from James City County, which paid tuition on their behalf.

During World War II it was difficult for the school board to attract well qualified teachers, especially males. Between 1940 and 1950 Williamsburg's school population grew to the point that city students comprised a third of enrollees; the remainder were from James City and York Counties. All of the white students from James City County's populous Jamestown Majesterial District, which in 1960 included 72.2 percent of the county's total population, and all but 200 of the county's black students, attended Williamsburg schools, which were rapidly becoming overcrowded. By 1950 there were only two public schools in James City County: the Toano School for whites, where the enrollment was 225, and the Chickahominy Elementary School for blacks, which had approximately 200 students. These two schools served children in the Powhatan and Stonehouse Magisterial Districts. During the late 1940s and early 1950s, when James City County's Toano and Chickahominy Schools were showing signs of age and the city's schools were badly overcrowded, the issue of consolidation arose. City and county officials and citizens groups began weighing the merits of several school consolidation plans.

In 1953 James City County, which formerly was included in a school district with New Kent and Charles City Counties, was paired with Williamsburg. A school contract was signed on January 14, 1954, and full consolidation took effect on July 1, 1955. It was agreed that James City County would construct a new high school for city and county whites (James Blair) and build additions onto Matthew Whaley and Bruton Heights. Both jurisdictions' white elementary school students were to attend Matthew Whaley, whereas all black students (grades 1 through 12) were to be enrolled in Bruton Heights. The Toano and Chickahominy schools were to be closed. Williamsburg agreed not to increase the tuition charge for county children attending city schools. James Blair High School opened its doors to grades 7 through 12 during the 1955–1956 school year.

By the mid-1960s James Blair, Matthew Whaley, and Bruton Heights were overcrowded and the joint school system was obliged to use space in two area church buildings as supplementary classrooms. Plans were made to construct a new elementary school for whites in Birchwood and a new high school for blacks at the intersection of Strawberry Plains and Ironbound Roads. The segregated schools were built despite the landmark Supreme Court decision of BROWN VERSUS THE TOPEKA BOARD OF EDUCATION, which made school integration mandatory throughout the United States.[17]

Desegregation of the Williamsburg-James City County schools began in 1964; however it was on a voluntary basis and relatively few pupils elected to participate. The local School Board mandated integration in 1965, at which time the various school districts in the county and city were reorganized into what comprised the James Blair, Berkeley, Bruton Heights, Norge, Matthew Whaley, and Rawls Byrd districts. Meanwhile, in autumn 1964 Jamestown Academy, a private school, was established in the Smith Memorial Baptist Church in Lightfoot. Instruction initially was offered to students in grades 1 through 4. In 1966, when a school building was erected in Skipwith Farms, the curriculum was expanded to include grades 5, 6, and 7. Jamestown Academy closed its doors during the 1980s.[18]

In 1947 the Rev. Thomas J. Walsh of St. Bede's Catholic Church sought a community of Sisters with teaching experience to establish a parochial school. This led to the founding of Walsingham Academy by Mother Mary Bernard of the Sisters of Mercy. When the school first opened in September 1947, 57 students in grades kindergarten through 12 attended classes in the building that now serves as St. Bede's rectory. Later, a 30-acre parcel on Jamestown Road was acquired for construction of a permanent school facility, which modern campus welcomed its first students in February 1952.[19]

James City County's Schools Today

In 1967 the Norge Elementary School was built to serve youngsters in the western part of James City County. Four years later, plans got underway to construct a new high school, Lafayette, which is located on Longhill Road. When Lafayette High School opened, James Blair was converted to use as a Middle School.[20]

Today, the schools operated by Williamsburg and James City County include the Clara Byrd Baker Elementary School, the Berkeley Middle School, the James Blair Middle School, the Lafayette High School, the Matthew Whaley School, the D. J. Montague Elementary School, the Norge Elementary School, the Rawls Byrd Elementary School, and the Toano Middle School. The Norge NEED Center, Bright Beginnings, and the Turning Point Program also were developed to meet special educational needs. Local private schools include the Walsingham Academy, the Williamsburg Christian Academy and several pre-schools and kindergartens.

Norge Elementary School. Photo by Nan Maxwell.

Clara Byrd Baker Elementary School. Photo by Nan Maxwell.

Berkeley Middle School. Photo by Nan Maxwell.

Lafayette High School. Photo by Nan Maxwell.

Notes

1.   J. L. Buck, THE DEVELOPMENT OF PUBLIC SCHOOLS IN VIRGINIA, 1607–1952 (Richmond, 1952), 3, 5, 12–13, 16, 21, 65; Kingsbury, RECORDS, III, 101–102, 537–540; McIlwaine, MINUTES, 15–16, 109.

2.   C.W.F., RESOURCE PROTECTION, II, 6–29.

3.   Benjamin Bates, a York County Quaker who lived near what became Lightfoot, operated a small school that probably catered to members of his faith.

4.   Fithian, JOURNAL, 25, 243; Manerin et al., HENRICO, 96; Cornelius J. Heatwole, A HISTORY OF EDUCATION IN VIRGINIA (New York, 1916), 56–57; Thomas K. Bullock, "Schools and Schooling in Eighteenth Century Virginia" (n.p., 1961), 115–117.

5.   Russell, FREE NEGRO, 137–144; Tate, THE NEGRO, 77–83; Bullock, "Schools," 53–61; Morgan, BLACK EDUCATION, 4, 8–11; Breeden, ADVICE, 11–12, 226, 231–323.

6.   A. J. Morrison, THE BEGINNING OF PUBLIC EDUCATION IN VIRGINIA, 1776–1815 (Richmond, 1917), 17, 22; James City County Legislative Petitions 1777–1861, 152; Land Tax Lists 1844–1845; Mumford, SUPREME COURT, 163–164; Virginia School Report, THE ANNUAL REPORT OF THE SUPERINTENDENT OF PUBLIC INSTRUCTION FOR THE YEAR ENDING JULY 31, 1885 (Richmond, 1885), 93; C.W.F., Resource Protection, II, 6–30; Reunion, 1944.

7.   Morrison, PUBLIC EDUCATION, 25; VIRGINIA SCHOOL REPORT 1885, 93; Manerin et al., HENRICO, 199.

8. Weaver, "Nineteenth Century Education," 38–47; Ruffner, ORIGIN, 33; Morrison, PUBLIC EDUCATION, 40; Heatwole, HISTORY, 109; Maddox, FREE SCHOOL, 110, 114; James, "Address."

9. Shepperd, STATUTES, III, 427–429; Hall et al., "Legislative Petitions," 154; Virginia General Assembly, ACTS OF THE GENERAL ASSEMBLY, 1825 (Richmond, 1825), 78–80; James City County Legislative Petitions 1777–1861; McCartney, HICKORY NECK, 34–35.

10. James City County School Commissioners Returns 1823–1860; Morrison, PUBLIC EDUCATION, 53, 68; Virginia School Report 1885, 93; C.W.F., RESOURCE PROTECTION, II:6–30,6–31; Maddox, FREE SCHOOL, 132; Ritchie, GENERAL ASSEMBLY, 1855–1856, 47; Morris, "Diary;" James City County Census 1860.

11. Heatwole, HISTORY, 210, 223; Maddox, FREE SCHOOLS, 166; C.W.F., RESOURCE PROTECTION, II:6–26.

12. Buck, DEVELOPMENT, 65, 70, 85; Rawls Byrd, HISTORY OF PUBLIC SCHOOLS IN WILLIAMSBURG (Williamsburg, 1968), 2–3, 6; C.W.F., RESOURCE PROTECTION, II:6–26, 6–31, 6–32; Morgan, BLACK EDUCATION, 13, 15, 62; Virginia School Report 1885:13, 94; Heatwole, HISTORY, 223, 246; James City County Deed Book 4:369–370, 372, 557, 559, 814.

13. Weaver, "Nineteenth Century Education," 38–47; Ruffner, ORIGIN, 33; Morrison, PUBLIC EDUCATION, 40; Heatwole, HISTORY, 109; Maddox, FREE SCHOOL, 110, 114; James, "Address."

14. James City County Deed Book 7:176; 10:393; 11:93–94, 265; 13:341; 16:363; 18:214; 20:339; Bradshaw et al., VELKOMMEN, 30; Katz, THE NEGRO, 273, 338; Byrd, PUBLIC SCHOOLS, 55–58; Morgan, BLACK EDUCATION, 16–17.

15. In March 1908 the James City County School Board reportedly had $1,928.84 in the "Hickory Neck Academy Fund," which had been collecting interest for a number of years.

16. Virginia School Report 1908:24; Virginia Education Association (V.E.A.), "School History of James City County," THE VIRGINIA JOURNAL OF EDUCATION II, 33–35; James City County Deed Book 11:93–94,265; 13:341; Bottom, SESSION OF 1908, 293; SESSION OF 1914, 188. In March 1914 the General Assembly authorized the local school board to issue revenue bonds to pay off debt associated with the construction of Toano High School.

17. C.W.F., RESOURCE PROTECTION, II, 6–36; James City County Deed Book 20:339, 567–568; 21:351, 423; Byrd, PUBLIC SCHOOLS, 18, 55–58, 68, 74–77; VIRGINIA GAZETTE, March 22 and 29, 1963.

18. C.W.F., RESOURCE PROTECTION, II, 6–37; Morgan, BLACK EDUCATION, 18; VIRGINIA GAZETTE, August 14, 1964; January 15, 1971.

19. Walsingham Academy, "Walsingham Academy, the Upper School, Experience for a Lifetime" (Williamsburg, n.d.); VIRGINIA GAZETTE, February 8, 1952.

20. VIRGINIA GAZETTE, January 29, 1971.

CHAPTER 18

"Light to Show Us Where to Go"
Religion and Churches in James City County

The Anglican Church in Colonial Virginia

In the Beginning

In May 1607 when the first English colonists landed in Virginia, they paused at Cape Henry to express their thankfulness to God for a safe voyage to the New World. Shortly after they arrived at Jamestown Island, they suspended an old sail from some neighboring trees and fashioned a make-shift church. Later, they felled timber and built a rough, barn-like structure, covering its walls with sedge and earth. There, according to Captain John Smith, the Rev. Robert Hunt conducted worship services twice a day, every day, and provided a sermon on Sundays.

Four years later, when the faltering colony was put under martial law, a code of justice was imposed that included numerous moral and religious rules. Settlers were required to attend worship services twice a day and catechism on Sunday. Failure to attend church cost first offenders a week's provisions; second offenders were whipped; and third offenders were executed. The death penalty also was invoked for those who committed murder, theft, and certain types of moral offenses, such as drunkenness. No one was permitted to question or deride the Articles of Faith, the Bible, the Trinity or the clergy. Ministers, besides conducting worship services, were required to record all marriages, deaths, and baptisms. They had the right to select four righteous men from the community to report infractions of religious laws, keep the church in good repair, and see that the clergy were paid. The Virginia Company of London's Great Charter, enacted in 1618, instructed the colony's leaders to see that each plantation had "a sufficient Minister and Preacher of the word of God." Those residing upon the Governor's Land, west of Jamestown Island, were to have a clergyman, as were the Virginia Company servants, who lived upon the Company Land at the mouth of the Chickahominy River, and the Society of Martin's Hundred settlers. In time, Martin's Hundred evolved into a parish and the territory between College Creek and the Chickahominy River became part of James City Parish, which church was on Jamestown Island. By 1632 Chickahominy Parish was established. Its territory extended inland from the mouth of the Chickahominy River for an indefinite distance and spanned both sides of the river.[1]

The Role of the Church in Daily Life

When the New World's first legislative assembly convened in the church at Jamestown in the summer of 1619, 12 of the 34 laws the burgesses enacted dealt with religion, morality, or other forms of personal discipline. Each of the colony's four corporations was to have "a godly and learned minister," who was provided with a 100-acre glebe (home farm) and six servants to work his land. Two men, chosen by the clergyman as churchwardens, were to maintain the church, report wrongdoers, and collect church taxes or dues. Those who persisted in "skandulous offences" could be excommunicated, which brought certain arrest and confiscation of all personal property. Plans were made to establish a college and university in Henrico where young Indians could be converted to Christianity, but the March 1622 Indian uprising quelled the colonists' missionary zeal. As some viewed the massacre as "the heavie hand of Almightie God [exacting] punishment of our transgressions," March 22nd was designated an annual day of fasting and atonement. During the early seventeenth century, writers often used Biblical metaphors (particularly those of the Old Testament) to describe their sufferings and days in the church calendar were used to identify secular dates upon which rent and taxes were due and public events occurred. Thus, the State Church and religious law permeated daily life.

Court records for the years 1622 to 1632 reveal that local churchwardens routinely reported those who got drunk, swore, and committed other acts deemed immoral or socially unacceptable. Churchwarden Richard Kingsmill was especially diligent in reporting his neighbors' drunkenness, rowdy behavior, and disorderly conduct. Governing officials in turn meted out what was considered appropriate punishment. For example, a female guilty of fornication might be made to stand at the front of her parish church during services, draped in a white sheet and holding a white wand, a mode of public humiliation. A male who committed a similar offense was likely to be whipped. Sometimes, slanderers were obliged to kneel and offer a public apology. Women who gossiped or fought with their neighbors usually were dunked in the river. On the other hand, a gossip on the Eastern Shore was obliged to stand at the church door during services with a gag in her mouth. In 1634, when the colony was divided into eight shires and county courts were established, some of the church's responsibilities for maintaining public morality were transferred to the local judiciary, to whom the churchwardens reported directly. By 1635 vestries (like those in early seventeenth-century England) had been established in Virginia's parishes. In 1643 Chickahominy Parish's name was changed to Wallingford. Its westerly boundary line extended west to David Jones (Kennon's) Creek, then the westernmost limits of James City County.

During the seventeenth century the clergy's conduct was closely regulated by law. They were obliged to adhere to the canons of the Church of England and live exemplary lives. They weren't not allowed to drink excessively or spend time playing cards, gaming or rolling dice. They had to preach one sermon every Sunday, serve Holy Communion three times a year, and instruct all children and non-believers in the church's teachings. They could charge fees for performing funerals and marriages and for "churching" women, a rite sometimes held after childbirth. As many of Virginia's colonial parishes were large and had two or more churches, a minister was expected to circulate among them.[2]

The Link Between Church and State

Several new laws enacted in 1645 regulated the practice of religion. The last Wednesday of every month was set aside as a day of prayer, fasting, and worship. April 18th was designated an annual day of thanksgiving, for the colony had survived an Indian uprising in 1644. All ministers were obliged to reside within their parishes so that they could visit the sick, baptize weak infants, and conduct religious rites. Vestries, elected by a plurality of free-holders, chose their own churchwardens. Harrop Parish was formed from the territory between Martin's Hundred and College Creek. The Rev. Thomas Hampton of James City Parish favored the new parish's creation because of "the dangerous times and inconveniences for the inhabitants" to commute to church at Jamestown. But Harrop Parish became extinct in 1658 when its inhabitants and those of the Middle Plantation Parish were united into Middletowne Parish. By that time the countryside along the Chickahominy River had become so populous that the upper part of Wallingford Parish was split off and Wilmington Parish was formed. It, like Wallingford, encom-passed both sides of the Chickahominy River and included land in James City and Charles City Counties.

Some time prior to 1653 Blisland Parish was created. Its territory extended in a westerly direction from Skimino Creek, up the York River. It encompassed virtually all of New Kent County, which was then vast in size. Although the location of Blisland Parish's first church is uncertain, it probably was situated in the eastern (or earliest settled) part of the parish. When Wilmington Parish was dissolved in 1725, its territory on the east side of the Chickahominy in James City County was added to Blisland. In 1767 when the boundaries between New Kent and James City Counties were adjusted, that portion of Blisland Parish between Skimino and Ware Creeks was added to James City County. Blisland is one of the few Tidewater Virginia parishes which colonial vestry records *and* church survive.

In an era when books were relatively rare and literacy was highly prized, the church provided intellectual stimulation. Weddings and funerals often were a community's principal social events. Because church attendance was required by law, convenience of access was of primary importance. During the early-to-mid seventeenth century parish churches typically were located on the banks of a navigable waterway that served as a conduit of transportation. As overland routes developed and became more sophisticated, churches were erected further inland, usually along main roads. Parishioners usually spent several hours at church and often traveled considerable distances to get there. Many churches were built near a spring or other source of potable water.

Between 1649 and 1660, when Virginia was under the sway of the Commonwealth government, ecclesiastical law was suspended. Use of the Prayer Book was allowed as long as all references to the monarchy were omitted, and vestries were given more authority in managing parish business. As the colony's population increased, large parishes often were subdivided into two or more smaller ones, usually at the request of petitioners. Sometimes, little houses-of-worship (known as chapels-of-ease) were built in outlying areas for the convenience of parishioners. Whenever a new parish was formed, its inhabitants had to contribute toward building a church and procuring a glebe for the minister.

After the monarchy was restored in 1660, the Church of England again enjoyed full support under the law, which had been modified somewhat. Anglican clergy, upon immigrating to Virginia, presented their credentials to the governor, the colony's highest ranking official on this side of the Atlantic. They were required to administer communion twice a year and to preach every Sunday in one of their parish's churches or chapels-of-ease. Vestries, by law, consisted of twelve "of the most able men of the parish," who upon being elected, could choose their own successors. The vestry was responsible for hiring clergy and for levying the church taxes that were used to meet parish obligations. If a pulpit were vacant, a clerk (usually the vestry secretary) would conduct services although he could not perform rites such as marriage, baptism, and communion. A clerk could conduct a funeral if a minister could not "possibly be had before the corpse would corrupt in hot weather." Parish clerks sometimes assisted the clergy with Sunday services.

During the seventeenth and early eighteenth centuries, there was a shortage of qualified clergy. As a result, non-English ministers, whose accents seemingly were difficult to understand, sometimes were sent to the colony. The vestry of one nearby parish nailed the church's doors shut to keep out the rector, whose heavy Scottish burr made his speech unintelligible! Each parish had to provide its minister with a salary, an adequate glebe and some livestock. However, parish vestries' definition of "adequate" varied greatly. Also, because all clergy received a set sum as their annual salary and that salary was paid in tobacco, parishes whose soil produced the best (and therefore most valuable) varieties tended to attract and retain the most capable clergymen. Some ministers were wary of preaching "against the Vices that any great Man of the Vestry was guilty of" for fear of jeopardizing their own livelihood.

The county sheriff was empowered to collect church taxes and seize the personal property of anyone whose parish levy was delinquent. Even after the passage of the Act of Toleration, which gave non-Anglicans (except Roman Catholics) the legal right to conduct worship services, parish levies were collected forcibly from dissenters (like Quakers) if they failed to support the parishes in which they lived. On at least one occasion, the vestry of James City County's Blisland Parish hired an attorney and brought suit against a man whose church dues were in arrears.

Churchwardens were obliged to appear in the county court every April and December to report parishioners' infractions of religious and moral law. Vestrymen also processioned (walked) the bounds of public and private properties to make sure that neighboring landowners agreed upon their respective boundary lines. Vestries were involved in laying out public roads and seeing that they were maintained. They also were obliged to see that care was provided to the indigent, the elderly, the orphaned, and the infirm. Although vestries commonly bound out the able-bodied men as servants, those unable to work usually received room, board, clothing, and medical care from local householders who were reimbursed from parish levies. As time went on, the cost of providing social welfare became extremely burdensome to most Virginia parishes.

Despite the fact that attending and supporting the church was compulsory, many Virginians were devout Anglicans. Sometimes they displayed their faith through bequests to their parish or clergyman. For example, two men in Elizabeth City County and one in Nansemond bequeathed their land and slaves to their parishes, stipulating that all revenues derived from the rental of their property be used toward the support of schools for the poor. One local man left his farm to his parish. Thus, religious faith played an important role in the lives of many colonial Virginians.[3]

The Church as a Social Center

Church attendance provided Virginians with an opportunity to socialize with friends and kin, transact business, and read the public notices often posted there. Durand de Dauphine, who traveled through Tidewater Virginia in the mid-1680s, said that when people arrived at church they smoked their pipes before going in and afterward, before heading home. He observed that "everybody smokes, men, women, girls & boys from the age of seven years." There were four parishes in James City County in 1680 (Martin's Hundred, James City, Wallingford, and Wilmington) and part of a fifth (Bruton Parish, which was formed in 1674 and included territory in James City and York Counties and Williamsburg). By 1697 Virginia had been subdivided into 50 parishes, many of which were large and had two or three churches and/or chapels-of-ease. Although most Virginians were Anglicans, the colony had some religious dissenters, including several congregations of Quakers and at least one of Presbyterians.

The Rev. Hugh Jones, rector of James City Parish during the 1720s, described the church's role in everyday life. Because many parishes were of vast size and parishioners lived a considerable distance from church, the dead often were buried "in gardens or orchards, where whole families lye interred together, in a spot generally handsomely enclosed, planted with evergreens." Ministers usually preached funeral sermons in the house of the decedent, where most baptisms and weddings also occurred. Jones said that if he insisted upon conducting such rites in church, many parishioners would do without them. Jones felt that it was appropriate to baptize Indians and slaves except "wild Indians" and "new Negroes," who had neither the knowledge nor the inclination "to know our religion, language and customs" and would "obstinately persist in their own barbarous ways." By the 1720s many Virginia churches were made of brick rather than wood and were "very strong and handsome, and neatly adorned." Whenever a church was abandoned or replaced, the old building and its yard were marked with a ditch, perhaps as a means of identifying what had been a burial ground.

In 1720 Charles City's inhabitants asked the House of Burgesses to add the westernmost portion of James City County, which lay west of the

Chickahominy River, to their territory. The burgesses agreed and in December 1720 the Chickahominy River became the dividing line between James City and Charles City Counties. Simultaneously, the eastern portion of Wallingford Parish was added onto James City Parish because it was deemed "too small to continue . . . of itself." This would have been helpful to those living in Wallingford's eastern half who as early as 1699 had complained that their parish had neither a church nor chapel-of-ease on their side of the Chickahominy.[4]

James City County Parishes in 1724

In 1724 the Bishop of London queried Virginia clergy about their parishes. The Rev. William LeNeve reported that James City Parish was approximately 20 miles long and 12 miles wide, had 78 families and neither a school nor a library. Approximately 130 people attended the services he conducted at Jamestown. He also led services in Mulberry Island Parish one Sunday a month and lectured in Williamsburg on Sunday afternoons. Because the James City Parish glebe lacked a dwelling, the vestry paid LeNeve a housing allowance. He worked with Virginia-born black slaves, whom he tried to convert to Christianity, but he felt that newly arrived slaves, "imported daily," had "so little Docility in them that they scarce ever become capable of Instruction."

The Rev. John Brunskil, whose parish straddled both sides of the Chickahominy River and ran inland to the upper limits of James City County, in 1724 reported that Wilmington Parish was 30 miles long and 9 miles wide and included land that lay in both James City and Charles City Counties. It had 180 families and three churches. Brunskil said that the whites in his parish made little effort to provide their slaves with religious instruction, with the result that "the poor creatures generally live and die without it." He spoke disparagingly of vestries' discretionary power and said that his glebe, "a cottage containing one Ground room and a Garret above," was in such poor condition that it was rented to a pauper. Although Wilmington Parish had neither public schools nor libraries, Brunskil said that there were several private schools and "care is generally taken by parents that their children be taught to read."

In March 1725, Wilmington Parish was dissolved by the assembly and its James City County acreage was divided between James City and Blisland Parishes. That portion of Wilmington which lay between Edwards Swamp/Mill Creek and Diascund Creek was assigned to Blisland Parish, whereas its territory to the southeast was added onto James City Parish. It was likely during the late 1720s that James City Parish's vestry constructed what became known as the Chickahominy Church to accommodate parishioners living near its upper limits. They may have used the site of Wilmington Parish's old Lower Church. Some of Wilmington's members formally protested the dissolution of their old parish, perhaps because they were uneasy about dealing with an unfamiliar vestry. William Browne, who lived near Diascund Creek and had been a Wilmington Parish churchwarden, refused to part with its communion silver, in part because he was owed funds when his old parish became extinct.

In 1724 the Rev. Daniel Taylor of Blisland Parish indicated that there were two churches in his parish, which had 136 families. Like other James City County parishes, Blisland lacked schools and libraries. Bruton Parish, which encompassed approximately 10 square miles in Williamsburg, James City and York Counties, had 110 families. In 1724 the Rev. James Blair, commissary to the Bishop of London, was rector. He reported that he had served James City Parish from 1694 to 1710 and then moved to Bruton. Blair indicated that his parish had four little schools where reading, writing, and arithmetic were taught. Although there were neither parish schools nor libraries in Bruton, the college had a public grammar school and an Indian school with an endowment.

In 1727 the House of Burgesses began requiring vestries to provide clergy with good, convenient glebes of at least 200 acres, with adequate housing and outbuildings. Two decades later, the law defined an adequate glebe as one that had a dwelling, kitchen, barn, stable, dairy, smokehouse, cornhouse, and fenced-in garden, all of which were in good condition. If a vestry wanted to dispose of its old glebe and acquire a new one, the burgesses' consent was needed. Blisland Parish's vestry sought such approval on at least one occasion.[5]

The Church's Role in Social Welfare

By the mid-eighteenth century, the poor were so numerous that parish vestries groaned under the burden of caring for them. The problem was especially acute in Bruton Parish, for people flocked to Williamsburg during Public Times and sometimes stayed on even though they lacked a means of support. In 1755 Bruton's vestry asked the assembly for permission to operate an almshouse where the poor could be made to work. The burgesses agreed and authorized virtually all Virginia vestries to operate poorhouses and purchase raw materials and tools that could be used by their inmates. Churchwardens were allowed to have the sheriff seize beggars and take them to the poorhouse. There, they would labor under the watchful eye of an Overseer authorized to inflict corporal punishment upon anyone refusing to work. Poorhouse inmates had to wear a colorful cloth badge upon the right sleeve, identifying them as parish wards, and they could be flogged for failing to do so. Although Blisland Parish's vestry considered building a poorhouse, the project never got underway. Neighboring Bruton, however, erected a poorhouse at a site overlooking Queens Creek. It is uncertain to what extent the poorhouse solved the parish's welfare problems.[6]

The Great Awakening and the Growth of Religious Diversity

By the mid-eighteenth century, the religious revival known as the Great Awakening had permeated rural Virginia. Evangelists or New Light preachers called upon their followers to renounce dancing, horseracing, and card-playing (which they deemed sinful) in favor of prayer and repentance. At emotionally-charged revival meetings, they threatened the unrepentant with hellfire and eternal damnation.[7] During the 1760s, '70s, and '80s the Baptists, Methodists, and Presbyterians attracted a large and loyal following in Virginia. These religious stirrings brought about a revolution in Southern religious life that coincided with growing resentment against the Mother Country and erosion of interest in the Anglican Church.

In 1739 George Whitefield (Whitfield), a Methodist missionary, visited the Williamsburg area and preached to a large crowd at Bruton Parish Church.

The governor received him cordially, probably because Methodism was an offshoot of the Anglican Church. Although Whitefield made several return visits, a Methodist Society was not established in the Williamsburg area until 1772, when Robert Williams, a circuit-riding lay preacher, began carrying his message to scattered groups of Methodists between Richmond and Old Point Comfort. After the American Revolution, Methodism distanced itself from the Church of England, which symbolized the Mother Country. Williamsburg area Methodists at first met in a barn near the James City County Courthouse. Later, they held services in a frame building on Francis Street.

Joshua Morris, who lived in James City Parish, ran afoul of the law in January 1745 when he permitted the Rev. John Roan, a Presbyterian minister, to preach in his home. Roan railed against the State Church and accused its clergy of immorality and negligence. His scathing, imprudent remarks quickly came to the attention of the governor who saw that he was presented to a Grand Jury. Roan was charged with proselytizing and blasphemy, which were illegal, and only his hasty departure for Pennsylvania spared him from standing trial. Shortly thereafter, an order was published that forbade meetings of "Moravians, Muggletonians and New Lights," all of which were considered evangelical sects. By 1765 a congregation of Presbyterians had begun meeting in the city. A century later they organized as the Williamsburg and York River Presbyterian Church, which built a meetinghouse upon a lot on the Palace Green.

During 1773 the Rev. Jeremiah Walker, a Baptist minister and gifted orator, came to James City County and probably conducted worship services. Elder Elijah Baker, another Baptist evangelist, was on the James-York peninsula from 1773 to 1775. He and Elder Joseph Anthony have been credited with founding the James City Baptist Church near Six Mile Ordinary. Joshua Morris, nephew of the man who entertained the outspoken Rev. John Roan in 1745, served as the pastor of the James City Baptist Church until 1776. John Goodall became the congregation's clerk and then pastor.

One little known local group of religious dissenters were the Skimino Quakers, whose meetinghouse, built in 1767, lay within the bounds of Blisland Parish.[8] Converts made by Quaker missionary Thomas Story, who visited the area in 1699, formed the nucleus of the Skimino Meeting. The congregation grew immediately prior to the American Revolution, but dwindled to extinction after hostilities ceased. Quaker congregations were established at Martin's Hundred and Green Spring, perhaps the "little meeting above Jamestown" that Quaker missionary George Fox wrote of in 1699. Robert Perkins of Martin's Hundred and Ann Acres, who lived near Williamsburg, were James City County Quakers, as was William Ratcliffe Heathen, who donated the small York County lot upon which the Skimino Quakers built their meetinghouse. Records maintained by the regional group with which the Skimino Quakers were affiliated reveal that the congregation included a substantial number of James City County citizens. The Quakers' refusal to support the Established Church and to attend militia musters put them at odds with the law, whereas their desire to free their slaves, refusal to be baptized or take Communion, and insistence upon conducting their own weddings also set them apart from their neighbors. Sometimes, Quakers' refusal to support the State Church led to their personal property's being confiscated. As Quaker ministers served without compensation, they objected to being required to support what they termed "hireling priests."[9]

Mount Vernon Methodist Church. Photo by Nan Maxwell.

After the Revolutionary War

In 1786 the General Assembly passed the Statute of Religious Freedom, which disestablished the State Church, denied it the right of general taxation, and allowed abandoned parish-owned real estate to revert to the Commonwealth of Virginia. Churches that were in continuous use were not threatened. Under the new law, vestries were entitled to retain their parishes' glebe until the incumbent clergyman died or left. Money yielded by the sale of parish-owned real estate was set aside for the education of local children or was given to county Overseers of the Poor, who were responsible for public welfare. During this period, many Anglican churches came into the hands of other denominations or simply fell into disrepair. Portions of two colonial churches survive in James City County: the tower of the church at Jamestown and the north transept of Hickory Neck Church in Toano.[10] The archaeological remains of the Martin's Hundred Parish Church, the Chickahominy Church, and the Church on the Main (in existence from ca. 1750 to ca. 1850) also exist. Much of the fabric of Bruton Parish Church has weathered the test of time.

After the Revolutionary War ended, a number of religious denominations took on new life. In James City County and Williamsburg congregations of Methodists, Baptists, and Christians (Disciples of Christ) began establishing churches. In 1797 itinerant Methodist preacher Francis Anbury noted in his journal that "two very good meeting houses" had been erected since his 1790 visit to the Williamsburg area: one in James City County (the James City Chapel) and one in New Kent (the Tabernacle Church, near Holly Forks).

During the 1820s some of Williamsburg's women Baptists asked the Dover Association to send a missionary to establish a local church. During the winter of 1823 and 1824 the Rev. Daniel Witt made numerous visits to Williamsburg, preaching and teaching. By 1828 a group of worshipers was convening regularly. They formed the nucleus of what in 1832 became the congregation of the Zion Baptist Church. At first, the Rev. Scervant Jones led Zion's members in worship services held in the colonial powder magazine. As the foundation of the congregation's first church, built in 1853, included bricks salvaged from the wall surrounding the powder magazine, William and Mary

Our Saviour's Evangelical Lutheran Church. Photo by Ralph Maxwell.

student pundits declared that the Baptists should have "employed a balloon and lifted the whole of the 'powder horn' up" for use as the church's steeple! During the Civil War, Zion Baptist Church was used as a military hospital. Later, it housed a school for blacks established by the Freedmen's Bureau.

By 1842 Williamsburg Methodists had erected a brick church near the powder magazine. During the Civil War it (like Zion Baptist Church and Bruton Parish) was used as a hospital. Sometime prior to the war, a large Baptist revival, led by the Rev. Littleberry Allen, was held at Hickory Neck Church in Toano. He reportedly "delivered a powerful exhortation and was particularly stern toward 'backsliders.'"[11]

James City County's Churches Today

Modern James City County is home to an abundance of religious denominations. Some have shown pride in their heritage by producing written histories, which are summarized below.

Mount Vernon Methodist Church

One of the "very good meeting houses" Methodist minister Francis Anbury said were built between 1790 and 1797 was the James City Chapel, which overlooked the Stage Road, east of the Olive Branch Christian Church. Although little is known about the James City Chapel, in 1844 school teacher Robert Morris attended services there and in July 1845 returned to hear a sermon by a Dr. Penn. In 1884 the leaders of its dwindling congregation decided to purchase land in Burnt Ordinary (then considered an up-and-coming community) and move the old chapel there. They partially dismantled the building and transported it by rail to the foot of what became known as Church Street. From there, oxen pulled it up the hill to the new location. By 1887 the chapel, which had been enlarged, was ready for use. Because it was long and narrow, some people likened it to "a shoe box perched on top of the hill." At first, the Mount Vernon Methodist Church was part of the New Kent Circuit, which minister served five congregations. By 1914 the congregation of Mount Vernon had grown so much that the church had to be enlarged. It was then that a bell tower and an addition were constructed, making the church T-shaped. The old cemetery at the James City Chapel is still used as a burial ground for Mount Vernon members.[12]

Wellspring United Methodist Church

In 1978 several families decided to form a new Methodist church to serve the growing suburbs outside of Williamsburg. By 1981 the congregation of the Wellspring United Methodist had gained enough momentum to break ground for the construction of a church. It stands upon a large wooded lot abutting Longhill Road.[13]

Our Saviour's Evangelical Lutheran Church

The Zion Scandinavian Evangelical Lutheran Church was organized in 1898 by a group of Lutherans of Norwegian and Danish descent, who immigrated to Virginia from the Midwest. At first they met for worship in private homes, such as Riverview. They barely missed being the first organized Lutheran congregation on the peninsula. In 1904 Zion's congregation began holding services in its church on Richmond Road, with the Rev. O. J. Marken as pastor and C. Peterson, Benjamin Rustad, and Nils Kjostelson as officers. In 1908 the Zion Scandinavian Evangelical Lutheran Church, as originally constituted, was dissolved. One part of the congregation retained the Zion name and the other reorganized as Bethany Church.

In 1910 the members of Bethany Church constructed a house-of-worship near Norge, on the road that led to Mount Folly and Sycamore Landing. Among the congregation's founding families were the Madsens, Fennes, Trosvigs, Twetens, Andersons, Levorsons, Endenloffs, Dunhams, Eltons, Jubergs, Hauges, Christophersons, and the Broughtons, who donated the land upon which the church was built. Bethany Church's pulpit, pews, chairs, choir loft and stained glass windows were donated by the First Baptist Church in Norfolk.

In 1917, when the Bethany and Zion Scandinavian Evangelical Lutheran Churches became part of the same synod, the two congregations agreed to

Hickory Neck Episcopal Church. Photo by Ralph Maxwell.

Chickahominy Baptist Church, site of a colonial Anglican church.
Photo by Nan Maxwell.

share a pastor, who preached on alternate Sundays and was fluent in both English and Norwegian. In 1932 they merged to form Our Saviour's Evangelical Lutheran Church, at which time it was agreed that Zion's building would be used for worship services and Bethany's would serve as a parish house. A proud moment came on June 27, 1939, when Crown Prince Olav and Crown Princess Martha of Norway presented the congregation of Our Saviour's with a Norwegian Bible.[14]

Hickory Neck Episcopal Church

In 1734 the vestry of Blisland parish decided to build a new Lower Church on the land of Mrs. Mary Holdcroft of Hickory Neck Plantation. The elaborately-built brick church known as Hickory Neck was oriented east and west, in accord with Anglican tradition, and was served by the same clergymen who provided spiritual leadership to the congregation of the Warrany (or Upper) Church of Blisland Parish in eastern New Kent County. In 1774 a north transept was added onto Hickory Neck.

After the disestablishment of the Anglican Church, Hickory Neck, which had been used as a military hospital, stood vacant and gradually deteriorated. In 1825 the General Assembly authorized the trustees of the Hickory Neck School Society to convert the old church into a schoolhouse. It was then that the 1734 component of the church was razed, the 1774 transept was extended, its windows were enlarged, and its south end was bricked-up. Classes were held at the Hickory Neck Academy until the time of the Civil War and "Union" or inter-denominational worship services sometimes were held there on Sundays. After the war the building was repaired and restored to use as a school that served all grades.

In 1912, after the Toano School was built, the James City County School Board, with the consent of the General Assembly, deeded Hickory Neck's one-acre lot and building to the trustees of the Hickory Neck Protestant Episcopal Church. After the old building was repaired, church services were held there regularly. In 1972 Hickory Neck Church was declared a Virginia Historic Landmark and a year later it was added to the National Register of Historic Places.[15]

St. Martin's Episcopal Church

In September 1963 a group of Episcopalians interested in promoting racial harmony, solving community problems and worshiping simply convened in the restored church on Jamestown Island. Within a year a steel building (the first St. Martin's Episcopal Church) was erected upon a Jamestown Road lot that was donated by Bruton Parish Church. St. Martin's present sanctuary was dedicated in 1972. The congregation takes pride in having initiated community service programs such as the NEED Center and the Pre-School for Special Children, now known as the Child Development Resources Center. The church also provided the impetus for establishing the Cross Roads Halfway House for teenagers.[16]

Chickahominy Baptist Church

The Chickahominy Baptist Church is located upon land that by the 1720s or '30s was occupied by an Anglican church that served the upper part of James City Parish. The site may have been used even earlier by the defunct Wilmington Parish. During the American Revolution the Marquis de Lafayette and his men encamped upon the grounds of the Chickahominy Church, then a well known local landmark. After the disestablishment of the State Church, the structure may have been abandoned; however, the presence of Susanna Willcox's February 1837 tombstone suggests that people continued to use its old burying ground. Robert Morris, a licensed Baptist preacher, gave a sermon in the Chickahominy Church in 1845. According to local tradition, the building was used occasionally by Episcopalians until it burned during the 1860s. A Confederate map indicates that the church was still standing in 1864. A year later the structure now known as the Chickahominy Baptist Church was erected by blacks upon the land formerly occupied by the eighteenth century Anglican church. Chickahominy Baptist Church's large congregation, which has an active ministry, has had seven pastors since the church was established in the 1860s.[17]

St. John Baptist Church

In 1871 some members of the Chickahominy Baptist Church decided to build a new house-of-worship closer to their own homes. They procured a small parcel from Mr. E. T. Martin, owner of Lombardy (Lumberdy), and erected a small log church some people dubbed "Sandy Bottom" or the "Little Indian Trap by the Road." Among St. John's founding fathers were Brothers Washington Page, James Allen, Sam Jones, and D. E. Walker. The Rev. John Smith of Hampton, Virginia, a former slave, was the first pastor of the Sandy Bottom Baptist Church, which had 29 members. By 1883 the 100-member congregation had outgrown its original log building. It was then that the decision was made to erect a new church. The men cut and hewed the wood from which they built the new house-of-worship and the women provided food to those involved in construction. During spring 1884 the first sermon was preached in the new church which was improved as time went on. In 1913 the Sandy Bottom Baptist Church was renamed St. John Baptist Church. Although the 1883–1884 church was enlarged during the 1940s, in 1966 the congregation erected the brick building it now uses.[18]

Shiloh Baptist Church

The Shiloh Baptist Church in Croaker was established in 1866, at which time the small congregation held worship services in a little log cabin near the present building. The Rev. L. T. Whiting of Gloucester served as pastor of Shiloh for over 40 years. It may have been during his ministry that former members of the disbanded Six Mile Zion Church joined the congregation. During the 1920s, when the Rev. C. D. Ellis was pastor, the church was renovated extensively. The Rev. Richard Dias' pastorate saw the addition of some modern improvements. As the congregation grew, the church was enlarged and its exterior was bricked.[19]

New Zion Baptist Church

In 1870 a group of black Baptists decided to build a neighborhood church upon part of the War Hill tract. Brown's Baptist Church (a simple log cabin) was named after Richardson Brown who secured the land upon which the house-of-worship stood. In February 1880 Richard L. Henley formally deeded the church lot to Brown, Henry Ruffin, Benjamin Taylor, Moses Harrard, and John W. Cannaday Sr., the congregation's trustees. In 1900 the original church was remodeled and given the name New Zion Baptist Church. During the early years heat and light were provided by a wood stove and kerosene lanterns; later, modern conveniences were added. In 1982–1983 the new brick church was constructed in which worship services are held today.[20]

Mount Pleasant Baptist Church

The Mount Pleasant Baptist Church on Ironbound Road traces its history to 1891, when the congregation's 58 members had the Rev. J. B. Whiting as pastor. During the Rev. C. S. Boston's ministry at Mount Pleasant (1913–1924) a cornerstone was laid for the congregation's original house-of-worship, which over time has been remodeled and enlarged. In 1975 ground was broken for the construction of a new building.[21]

The James City Baptist Church

The James City (or Smyrna) Baptist Church, established around 1773 at Six Mile Ordinary, was one of the peninsula's first Baptist churches. It is termed the Mother Church of at least four local congregations: the James River Baptist Church, the Smith Memorial Baptist Church, the Grace Baptist Church, and the York River Baptist Church. The congregation of the James City Baptist Church adopted its first written constitution in 1817. Worship services were then held in a frame building that stood upon a lot near the intersection of Centerville and Richmond Roads, later the site of Smith Memorial Baptist Church. The James City Baptist Church's congregation grew quickly despite the lack of a regular preacher. During the early 1830s the teachings of a religious reformer polarized many Baptist congregations, including those of the James City Baptist Church and the Zion Baptist Church in Williamsburg. Among those actively involved in James City Baptist were

school teacher and diarist Robert Morris, William M. Jones, and John
Ratcliffe. During the 1840s William T. Lindsey, Philip J. Barziza (grandson
of Lucy Ludwell Paradise), and Dr. William Martin (a physician-turned-
farmer-and-preacher who lived near Burnt Ordinary) were the congregation's
licensed preachers.

Robert Morris's diary reveals that during 1845 several men preached to
the congregation of the James City Baptist Church. He also frequently visited
other local churches to hear guest speakers. Morris noted that C. Goodall, Dr.
Martin, and Brother Lindsey spoke at his home church, whereas Mr. Henshall
of Olive Branch Christian Church gave a sermon at Hickory Neck. He heard
Mr. Garlic (a Methodist minister) preach and he walked to "the [James City]
Chapel" where he heard Dr. Penn speak. He also traveled to Williamsburg to
attend a service conducted by the Rev. Scervant Jones. Robert Morris and
other members of the James City Baptist Church sometimes delivered
sermons to other local congregations. During 1845 he spoke at the
Chickahominy Church and his brother, Joshua, preached at the "new church,"

Morning Star Baptist Church. Photo by Nan Maxwell

the recently built James River Methodist Church, which eventually became James River Baptist Church. Morris's diary reveals that he and other James City Baptist Church leaders carried their ministry to local blacks. During 1845 he baptized at least eight blacks, one of whom he described as a "free girl" named Wallis. On July 21, 1845, Morris noted that he and Dr. Martin had been licensed "to give instruction to slaves and to attend their funerals." He also made arrangements for his congregation's meetinghouse to be enlarged. In 1857 the James City Baptist Church and Williamsburg (Zion) Baptist Church ceased sharing a pastor and James City's congregation hired their own. During the 1860s Dr. William Martin was the James City Baptist Church's preacher. He also conducted services at the Eastern State Hospital.

In 1880 the Rev. James Henry Barnes became pastor of the James City Baptist Church but he also conducted services at the Williamsburg Baptist Church. He was a graduate of the Hickory Neck Academy and the College of William and Mary and lived on the War Hill farm in James City County. Under the Rev. Barnes' influence church membership grew significantly. Eventually, however, the congregation dwindled and church leaders began allowing Lutherans to use the building. In 1914 James City Baptist Church was dropped from the rolls of the Association to which it belonged. The building became dilapidated and the cemetery and grounds were abandoned. However, the defunct James City Baptist Church eventually gave rise to four other Baptist congregations.[22]

The James River Baptist Church

Around 1836 the James River Methodist Church was erected on Centerville Road on land donated by William S. Spencer. By the late 1880s, however, the congregation was so small that it was dropped from the Methodist Conference. The Williamsburg Baptist Church's pastor conducted a successful revival meeting at James River Methodist and made many conversions. Later, local Methodists and Baptists worked together in what was called a "union" church, with the Baptists supplying the pastors and the Methodists the building. In 1903 the James River Baptist Church became established in the Methodist house-of-worship and a minister was called.

Many former members of the James City Baptist Church joined the James River congregation.

In 1947 the congregation of the James River Baptist Church decided to construct a cinder block tabernacle upon the lot in Lightfoot formerly occupied by the James City Baptist Church. The new building (in which revivals were to be held) was named the Smith Memorial Tabernacle in recognition of member A. T. Smith's unflagging devotion to his church. By 1948 the congregation of the James River Baptist Church had outgrown its old building and undertook the construction of a new one, which was ready for use by October 1949.[23]

Smith Memorial Baptist Church

The number of Baptists living in the Lightfoot area continued to grow and in 1953 the congregation of the James River Baptist Church decided to begin holding Sunday services in its new tabernacle, which they renamed the Smith Memorial Baptist Mission. The Rev. Jesse E. Bowman led both congregations' services. By 1956 the mission had grown to the point that it was reconstituted as the Smith Memorial Baptist Church. Shortly thereafter, Smith Memorial's congregation decided to remodel and enlarge the tabernacle. Later, they built a new church.[24]

Grace Baptist Church

In 1952 Baptists living at Cheatham Annex in York County, who had been commuting to the James River Baptist Church, obtained the Rev. Bowman's permission to conduct worship services at Cheatham. A year later, when they moved off-base, they continued to meet regularly. With the sponsorship of the James River Baptist Church and the Peninsula Baptist Association, land was purchased in James Terrace, where the Grace Baptist Chapel was built. By 1956 the congregation had grown so large that a full time pastor was called. In July 1956 the Grace Baptist Chapel, a mission, was reconstituted as Grace Baptist Church. In 1972 the congregation began construction of its present house-of-worship.[25]

York River Baptist Church

In 1980 the James River Baptist Church, in conjunction with the Peninsula Baptist Association, established a mission at the Croaker interchange of Interstate 64. By June 1981 the Croaker Mission's congregation began holding services in its newly built house-of-worship. Two years later, when the mission became a full-fledged church, its name was changed to the York River Baptist Church. Thanks to the congregation's dynamic growth, a new sanctuary and educational space were built, which in November 1989 were readied for use.[26]

Mount Gilead Baptist Church

The Mount Gilead Baptist Church of Grove, organized in 1876 in the Magruder area of York County, had among its communicants 18 former members of the Bethel Baptist Church. The Rev. J. W. Booth of Bethel Baptist was highly instrumental in establishing Mount Gilead, of which the Rev. William F. Cooke served as first pastor. In 1942 when Magruder's land became part of Camp Peary, its residents (most of whom were members of Mount Gilead) relocated to Grove, where they established new homes. In 1944 the congregation of the Mount Gilead Baptist Church, led by the Rev. S. L. Massie, moved into its new house-of-worship in Grove. Since that time the size of the congregation has expanded considerably. As a result, the church built in the 1940s has been remodeled and enlarged to meet Mount Gilead's changing needs.[27]

Morning Star Baptist Church

The Morning Star Baptist Church, located in Grove, was established in 1888, at which time the congregation acquired the title to the land upon which its house-of-worship was built. Deacons Jackson, Parker and Wynn and Charles Diggs signed the deed to the church property and the Rev. Mazunth was the first pastor. Although Morning Star's congregation traditionally has remained small, the church has been remodeled and expanded over the years.[28]

Little Zion Baptist Church

Another church that serves the people of Grove is the Little Zion Baptist Church, established in 1890 as an offshoot of the St. John Baptist Church. Deacon Isaac Reid, founder and lay-reader, commenced holding outdoor meetings. Later, a church was built. After the U.S. government took over the land upon which the New Zion Baptist Church stood, the congregation obtained other acreage and built a new house-of-worship. As Little Zion's congregation grew and the scope of its ministry increased, the building erected during the 1940s was improved and enlarged.[29]

Walnut Hills Baptist Church

In 1963 two lower peninsula churches sponsored a mission that led to the establishment of the Walnut Hills Baptist Church. At first, services were held in a schoolhouse on Strawberry Plains Road in James City County. During the mid-1980s the congregation built a church in Williamsburg.[30]

Faith Baptist Church

Late in 1989 a group of local people decided to organize an independent, fundamental church in the Greater Williamsburg area. In October 1990, when the Faith Baptist Church officially was organized, the Rev. Michael R. Privett of Norge became its first pastor. The congregation of Faith Baptist has grown steadily.[31]

Williamsburg Community Chapel

The Williamsburg Community Chapel, which held its first services in October 1976, constructed a church on Route 5, where regular worship services are held. The Williamsburg Community Chapel is an inter-denominational faith.[32]

Greensprings Chapel

The Greensprings Chapel was organized in 1965 by a small group of local citizens. As their ranks increased they purchased a lot on Palace Lane in York County where they constructed a sanctuary. In 1988 the congregation erected a new building on Ironbound Road in James City County.[33]

Williamsburg Mennonite Church

The community of faith that became the Williamsburg Mennonite Church stemmed from a Bible study group that began meeting in 1976. Ten Mennonite families that had been commuting to church in Newport News decided that a house-of-worship was needed in the Williamsburg area. With Ken Brunk installed as pastor, the congregation rented the Bethany Church in Norge. In 1978 they purchased the building and enlarged it to accommodate their growing membership.[34]

Olive Branch Christian Church

In 1833 the 20 men and women who founded Olive Branch Christian Church (Disciples of Christ) met for worship at Hill Pleasant farm in James City County. By 1835 the congregation had built a brick church upon a wooded lot donated by Dr. Charles M. Hubbard and his wife, the former Mary Henley. Mrs. Eliza Tribble Piggott of Temple Hall is credited with naming the church. As the congregation lacked a regular minister, services were conducted by elders, visiting preachers, and evangelists. Alexander Campbell, a leader in the Christian denomination, spent a winter at Hill Pleasant farm and conducted worship services at Olive Branch. One convert, Mrs. Araminta D. Morris, the wife of diarist Robert Morris, was baptized at College Landing before being received into Olive Branch's congregation. Others were baptized in the pond of Fenton (or Piggott's) Mill on Skimino Creek.

During the Civil War, Olive Branch Christian Church was occupied by Union soldiers, who reportedly slept in the gallery and used the sanctuary to stable their horses. During their occupancy the church's windows were broken, its flooring and pews were used as firewood, and the communion silver was carried off. The congregation held worship services in the Farthing home until 1866 when the church was restored to usable condition. In 1874 Frederick D. Power of York County became Olive Branch's first paid pastor. Around 1917, when the congregation received $500 from the U.S. government in compensation for damage the church sustained during the Civil War, electric lights and a furnace were installed. In 1924 an annex was added to the church, thanks to a bequest from Miss Nannie Wynne.

Besides Olive Branch Christian Church's finely maintained house-of-worship, its historical treasures include early record books that list the names of founding members. The church cemetery contains a number of early tombstones, including those of both Union and Confederate veterans, and the church's register of burials and its membership rosters contain invaluable genealogical data. Members of the Geddy, Richardson, Piggott, Meanley, Wynne, Marston, Ratcliff, Hankins, Whittaker, and Farthing families were among Olive Branch's most active members.[35]

Williamsburg Christian Church

In 1964 a group of local residents, who had been worshiping at the Lebanon Church of Christ in Lee Hall, received approval to establish a congregation in the Williamsburg area. They purchased land that contained a building they remodeled into a make-shift church. Later, they bought acreage on Route 5 and built a church that was dedicated in December 1968.[36]

Jamestown Presbyterian Church

In 1894 E. J. Campbell of Pennsylvania traded a clydesdale horse for 100 acres of land, two of which he donated toward the establishment of a church. Construction began during the winter of 1895–1896, with local men furnishing the labor and the materials from which the building was fabricated. The Rev. Connelly, a Methodist minister, made weekly visits to the fledgling congregation to conduct worship services. In May 1896 the Powhatan Temple was dedicated as an independent Methodist church.

By 1901 attendance had begun to decline and formal worship services eventually ceased. In 1905 several new families that moved into the area established a non-denominational congregation in the Powhatan Temple, which they renamed the Five Forks Church. Baptist and Methodist clergymen served as supply preachers during this period. During the 19-teens Dr. W. W. Powell, pastor of the Williamsburg Presbyterian Church, began holding services at Five Forks every other Sunday and in 1920 the congregation reorganized as the Five Forks Presbyterian Church. As attendance grew and additional space was needed, the building was improved. Eventually the congregation adopted the name Jamestown Presbyterian Church.[37]

Other Local Churches and Denominations

Many James City County residents commute to worship services in Williamsburg or other nearby communities. These include Quakers, who meet in private homes, Roman Catholics who attend St. Bede's Church in Williamsburg, the Mormons (or Church of Latterday Saints), and members of the Jewish faith who attend Temple Beth El. Local Christian Scientists, meanwhile, worship in Williamsburg at the First Church of Christ Scientist. A new Roman Catholic congregation, recently established in the Norge area, has led to the founding of St. Olaf's Catholic Church.[38] James City County residents and others in the area are members of the Kingdom Hall of the Jehovah's Witnesses on Richmond Road. The diversity of denominations and communities of faith in James City County sustain local religious life.

Notes
1. Smith, TRAVELS, II, 957; Strachey, HISTORIE, 3–5; Cocke, DIOCESE OF SOUTHERN VIRGINIA, 54–55. In 1712 the Martin's Hundred and Yorkhampton Parishes were consolidated.
2. Kingsbury, RECORDS, III, 101–102, 541; Brydon, MOTHER CHURCH, 83; Tyler, NARRATIVES, 249–278; McIlwaine, MINUTES, 33, 57, 136, 142; Edward L. Goodwin, THE COLONIAL CHURCH IN VIRGINIA (Milwaukee, 1927), 76; Hening, STATUTES, II, 157.
3. Hening, STATUTES, I, 290–291, 298, 317, 399–400, 498; II, 44; Cocke, DIOCESE OF SOUTHERN VIRGINIA, 62–64; McCartney, HICKORY NECK, 12–16; Goodwin, COLONIAL CHURCH, 78, 83, 88; Hartwell et al., PRESENT STATE, 65–67; Jones, PRESENT STATE, 98–99; McIlwaine, EXECUTIVE JOURNALS, I, 325–328; Chamberlayne, BLISLAND PARISH, 111.
4. Dauphine, HUGUENOT EXILE, 118; Hartwell et al., PRESENT STATE, 65–67; Jones, PRESENT STATE, 97–99; Cocke, DIOCESE OF SOUTHERN VIRGINIA, 62.

5.   Perry, Historical Collections, 264–266, 298–300, 372–373; George C. Mason, Colonial Churches of Tidewater Virginia (Richmond, 1945), 22; McIlwaine, Legislative Journals, 691, 700; Chamberlayne, Blisland Parish, 20, 53, 58, 92; Brydon, Mother Church, 378–379; Hening, Statutes, IV, 202–207; VI, 89–90.

6.   Martha W. McCartney, "Virginia's Workhouses for the Poor: Care for 'Divers Idle and Disorderly Persons,'" North American Archaeologist VIII (1987), 292. Documentary records suggest that the Bruton Parish Poorhouse later became the Williamsburg Manufactory, where cloth was produced from raw materials.

7.   In 1809 the renowned architect Benjamin Latrobe attended a Methodist camp meeting at which a blacksmith–turned–preacher cautioned his listeners about "the burning billows of hell" that would "wash up against the Soul of the glutton and the miser." He cried out "When hell gapes and the fire roars, Oh poor sinful damned souls . . . all of ye, will ye be damned? Will ye? Will ye?" Latrobe reported that "a general groaning and shrieking was now heard from all quarters" (Latrobe, Journals, 111).

8.   The Skimino Quakers' meetinghouse was located on Route 646 in the northwest corner of the Lightfoot interchange of Interstate 64. The congregation's burial ground (according to the late Garfield Barlow, a local man in his 90s) was located within the York County subdivision Banbury Cross.

9.   Isaacs, Worlds, 37–38; George Whitefield, George Whitefield's Journals (London 1960), 371–372; Mary Norton, comp., "A Brief History of Williamsburg United Methodist Church" (n.p., 1991); Lewis V. Little, Imprisoned Preachers and Religious Liberty in Virginia (Lynchburg 1938), 23; Williamsburg Presbyterian Church, "History" (n.p. 1992); Jesse E. Bowman, History, James City and James River Baptist Churches (Williamsburg, [1953]), 11–12,17–18, 21, 23, 25–26; Martha W. McCartney and Margaret N. Weston, "The Friends of Skimino Meeting" (n.p., 1973). Thomas Story wrote about one Anglican priest in Southside Virginia, whose relationship with his congregation (which included Quakers) had reached an impasse. The clergyman refused to preach unless he was paid, whereas the Quakers in his parish refused to pay him unless he preached. Story wryly observed that "As among some sort of Hirelings and their Employers it is No Penny, no Pater–Noster; here, on the other Hand, it is No Pater–Noster, no Penny" (Thomas Story, Journal of the Life of Thomas Story [London 1747], 155–156).

10.   The Jamestown Church has been rebuilt and is maintained as a historic shrine.

11.   Shepperd, Statutes, I, 311; Mason, Colonial Churches, 15; Norton, Brief History; Susie Dorsey, A History of the Williamsburg Baptist Church, 1828–1978 (Williamsburg, 1978), 1–5, 10–11, 14–15; L. G. Tyler, ed., "Historical and Genealogical Notes," William and Mary Quarterly 1st Ser., 25 (January 1945):72.

12.   Morris, "Diary;" Mount Vernon Methodist Church, Mount Vernon, 1887–1981, A Brief History (Toano, 1981).

13.   Wellspring United Methodist Church, "Wellspring United Methodist Church: A History and a Future," (n.p., 1992).

14.   Our Savior's Lutheran Church, Our Savior's Evangelical Lutheran Church, (Williamsburg, 1973).

15.   McCartney, Hickory Neck.

16. Edith Edwards, "Short History of St. Martin's Church, Williamsburg, Virginia" (n.p., 1989).

17. Gilmer, "Vicinity;" Chickahominy Baptist Church, "History of the Chickahominy Baptist Church," (n.p., n.d.); Meade, OLD CHURCHES, I, 200–201.

18. Saint John Baptist Church, "Saint John Baptist Church: 105th Anniversary," (n.p., 1983).

19. Shiloh Baptist Church, "Shiloh Baptist Church History: 1866–1989" (n.p., 1989).

20. New Zion Baptist Church, "New Zion Baptist Church History" (n.p., 1985).

21. Mount Pleasant Baptist Church, "Mt. Pleasant Baptist Church: 92nd Anniversary" (n.p., 1983).

22. Bowman, HISTORY, 37,40, 47–48, 51–52, 54, 56; Morris, "Diary; Dorsey, A HISTORY, 16–18.

23. Bowman, HISTORY, 58–59, 85–87.

24. Smith Memorial Baptist Church, A DECADE OF DEDICATION (Lightfoot 1966), 1–2, 5, 8–9.

25. Grace Baptist Church, "The History of Grace Baptist Church, 1952–1986" (n.p., 1986).

26. York River Baptist Church, "History of York River Baptist Church" (n.p., 1992).

27. Madeline Gee, GROVE FESTIVAL: A BICENTENNIAL EVENT, JULY 31, 1976 (Grove, 1976).

28. Ibid.

29. Ibid.

30. Walnut Hills Baptist Church, "Sanctuary Dedication, Walnut Hills Baptist Church, Williamsburg" (n.p., 1987).

31. Faith Baptist Church, "History of Faith Baptist Church" (n.p., 1991).

32. Williamsburg Community Chapel, "Great Things He Hath Done" (n.p., n.d.).

33. Greensprings Chapel, "A Sketch of Greensprings Chapel" (n.p., 1992).

34. Williamsburg Mennonite Church, "Profile of Williamsburg Mennonite Church" (n.p., 1986).

35. Olive Branch Christian Church, A BRIEF HISTORY OF OLIVE BRANCH CHRISTIAN CHURCH (Norge, 1990); Olive Branch Church Cemetery Notebooks and Record Books (Norge, n.p.).

36. Williamsburg Christian Church, "From Out of the Past" (n.p., 1976).

37. Jamestown Presbyterian Church, "Jamestown Presbyterian Church" (Williamsburg, 1970).

38. St. Bede's Catholic Church, "A Profile of St. Bede's Church and Our Patrons" (Williamsburg, 1992); First Church of Christ, Scientist, "Historical Sketch" (n.p., n.d.).

Appendix A: James City County Quitrent Roll, 1704

(B.P.R.O., C.O. 5/1314 ff 413-414)

The individuals listed below owned or rented land in James City County, as its boundaries were defined in 1704. Their names have been alphabetized for the sake of convenience.
Abbitt, Francis: 100 acres

Adams, Anne: 150 acres
Adkinson, Henry: 250 acres
Adkinson, Thomas: 50 acres
Allen, Richard: 540 acres
Aperson, William: 80 acres
Argo, James: 200 acres
Armestone, Joshua: 50 acres

Bagby, Thomas: 180 acres
Baker, John: 100 acres
Ballard, Thomas: 100 acres
Ballard, William: 300 acres
Barnes, Francis: 200 acres
Barratt, William: 305 acres
Barron, Thomas: 100 acres
Bayley, William: 100 acres
Beckitt, Thomas: 60 acres
Benge, Robert: 60 acres
Bentley, John: 125 acres
Bess, Edmund: 75 acres
Bimms, Christopher: 300 acres
Bingley, James: 100 acres
Black, George: 200 acres
Blackley, William: 142 acres
Blankes, Henry: 650 acres
Blankitt, Henry: 100 acres
Boman, [no name]: 90 acres
Bonham, John: 50 acres
Bower, William: 50 acres
Brackitt, Thomas: 150 acres
Brand, Richard: 125 acres

Bray, James: 3,500 acres
Bray, David: 5,758 acres
Breeding, John: 100 acres
Broadnax, William: 1,683 acres
Brown, James: 250 acres
Browne, William: 1,070 acres
Bruer, Sackfield: 350 acres
Bryon, John: 100 acres
Burton, Ralph: 200 acres
Burwell, Lewis: 1,350 acres
Bush, John: 800 acres
Buxton, Samuell: 300 acres

Capell, Thomas: 200 acres
Cearley, William: 450 acres
Center, John: 100 acres
Charles, Philip: 200 acres
Clerk, Robert: 300 acres
Clerk, Sarah: 200 acres
Clerk, William: 1,100 acres
Cobbs, Ambrose: 350 acres
Cock, Jonathan: 250 acres
Cole, Richard: 80 acres
Cook, Richard: 75 acres
Cooper, Thomas: 60 acres
Cosby, Charles: 250 acres
Cowles, Thomas: 675 acres
Crawley, Robert: 460 acres
Cryer, George: 100 acres

Danzee, John and Jacob Coigan:
 4,111 acres
Davey, Francis: 778 acres
Davis, George: 50 acres
Deane, John: 150 acres
Deane, Thomas: 80 acres
Deane, Thomas: 150 acres
Deane, William: 100 acres
Doby, John: 300 acres
Dormar, John: 100 acres
Drummond, John: 700 acres
Drummond, William: 150 acres
Duckitt, Abraham: 290 acres
Duke, Henry Jr.: 50 acres
Duke, Henry Esq.: 2,986 acres
Duke, Thomas: 750 acres

Edmunds, Elizabeth: 175 acres
Eggleston, Joseph: 550 acres
Eglestone, Benjamin: 1,375 acres
Elerby, Elizabeth: 600 acres

Farthing, William: 50 acres
Fearecloth, Thomas: 277 acres
Fish, John: 100 acres
Flanders, Francis: 350 acres
Fouace, Stephen: 150 acres
Fox, William: 50 acres
Frayser, John: 250 acres
Freeman, George: 197 acres
Furrbush, William: 400 acres

Garey, Thomas: 60 acres
Geddes, [no name]: 476 acres
Gibson, Gilbey: 150 acres
Gill, John: 100 acre
Ginnings, Philip: 400 acres
Goodall, John: 400 acres
Goodman, John: 275 acres
Goodrich, Benjamin: 1,650 acres

Goodwin, Robert: 150 acres
Goss, Charles: 171 acres
Graves,. Joseph: 250 acres
Green, Thomas: 50 acres
Green, William: 100 acres
Greene, Thomas: 500 acres
Gregory, Nicholas: 50 acres
Grice, Aristotle: 700 acres
Guilsby, Thomas: 300 acres
Gwin, John: 100 acres

Hadley, Dyonitia: 100 acres
Haley, James: 310 acres
Hall, John: 50 acres
Hamner, Nicholas: 500 acres
Handcock, Robert: 300 acres
Harfield, Michael: 50 acres
Harris, William: 140 acres
Harrison, Benjamin Jr.: 100 acres
Harrison, William: 150 acres
Harvey, George: 1,425 acres
Hatfield, Richard: 100 acres
Hawkins, John: 200 acres
Henley, John: 100 acres
Henley, Leonard: 360 acres
Herd, Leph.: 100 acres
Higgins, John: 75 acres
Hill, Thomas: 210 acres
Hilliard, Jeremiah: 225 acres
Hilliard, John: 200 acres
Hitchcock, John: 100 acres
Hix, John: 115 acres
Hix, Joseph: 100 acres
Holiday, Thomas: 250 acres
Holoman, James: 150 acres
Hood, John: 250 acres
Hook, Mick: 260 acres
Hooker, Edward: 1,067 acres
Hopkins, John: 120 acres
Howard, John: 25 acres

Hubert, Matthew: 1,834 acres
Hudson, George: 100 acres
Hudson, Leonard: 100 acres
Hudson, William: 50 acres
Hughes, George: 250 acres
Hunt, William: 1,300 acres

Inch, John: 30 acres
Inglis, Mingo: 1,300 acres

Jackson, Elizabeth: 200 acres
Jackson, Richard: 150 acres
Jaquelin, Edward: 400 acres
Jeffrys, Mattthew: 100 acres
Jeffrys, Thomas: 60 acres
Jenings, Edmund Esq.: 200 acres
Johnson, Anthony: 100 acres
Johnson, John: 200 acres
Jone, Fred.: 300 acres
Jones, William: 50 acres
Jones, William: 150 acres
Jordan, John: 1,000 acres

Knewstarp, [no name]: 150 acres

Lattoon, John: 75 acres
Lawrence, Richard: 250 acres
Lidie, Robert: 500 acres
Lightfoot, John Esq.: 250 acres
Lightfoot, Philip: 1,650 acres
Lillingtone, Benjamin: 100 acres
Liney, William: 50 acres
Loftin, Corneles: 200 acres
Loftin, Corneles Jr.: 200 acres
Love, John: 100 acres
Ludwell, Philip Esq.: 6,626 acres
Lund, Thomas: 100 acres

Macklin, Wiliiam: 300 acres
Major, John: 100 acres

Mallard, Poynes: 100 acres
Manningaren, [no name]: 150 acres
Maples, Thomas: 300 acres
Marable, George: 135 acres
Marraw, Dennis: 30 acres
Marston, Thomas: 1,000 acres
Marston, William: 150 acres
Martin, Richard: 150 acres
Meekings, Thomas: 175 acres
Merryman, James: 300 acres
Mookins, Roger: 160 acres
Morecock, Thomas: 700 acres
Moris, David: 170 acres
Morris, Edward Jr.: 100 acres
Morris, James: 800 acres
Morris, John: 195 acres
Mountfort, Thomas: 600 acres
Muttlow, John: 170 acres
Myers, William Jr.: 100 acres

Nailer, William: 300 acres
Neshamah, Mary of the Blackwater:
    168 acres
Nicholls, Henry: 100 acres
Nicholson, John: 144 acres
Norrell [Norvell], Hugh: 328 acres

O'Mooney, Mary: 126 acres

Page, John: 1,700 acres
Page, Mary: 900 acres
Pall, William: 450 acres
Parish, Thomas: 100 acres
Parke, Daniel Esq.: 1,800 acres
Parker, Thomas: 1,650 acres
Pattison, Alexander: 100 acres
Pattison, Catherine: 150 acres
Pattisson, Thomas: 200 acres
Pearman, John: 200 acres
Pearman, William: 270 acres

Pendexter, Thomas: 550 acres
Peper, Stephen: 100 acres
Perkins, Charles: 320 acres
Philips, Edward: 100 acres
Philips, William: 300 acres
Phillips, John: 300 acres
Pigot [Piggott], Benjamin: 90 acres
Prince, George: 50 acres

Revis, William: 150 acres
Rhodes, Francis: 100 acres
Rhodes, Randall: 50 acres
Rovell, John: 50 acres
Russell, Samuell: 350 acres
Ryder, Mary: 350 acres

Sanders, John: 50 acres
Santo, Robert: 100 acres
Selvey, Jacob: 50 acres
Sewell, John: 75 acres
Shaley, John: 150 acres
Sharp, John: 800 acres
Sherman, Elizabeth: 500 acres
Sholtwater, Benjamin of York
   County: 300 acres
Short, John: 90 acres
Simes, William: 650 acres
Slade, William: 80 acres
Smallpage, Robert: 190 acres
Smith, Christopher: 450 acres
Rhodes, Francis: 100 acres
Smith, John: 114 acres
Soane, Henry: 750 acres
Sorrell, Mary: 500 acres
Sorrell, Thomas: 200 acres
Sprattley, John: 350 acres
Stafford, Mary: 210 acres
Sykes, Barnard: 1,012 acres

Thackson, James: 289 acres
Thomas, Hannah: 100 acres
Thomas, John: 250 acres
Thomas, William: 150 acres
Thomson, Henry: 150 acres
Thurston, John: 500 acres
Tinsley, Edward: 100 acres
Tinsley, Richard: 100 acres
Tomson, James: 100 acres
Tullett, John: 625 acres
Twine, Thomas: 100 acres
Tyery, William: 1,500 acres
Tyler, Henry: 730 acres

Udall, Matthew: 50 acres

Vaiding, Isaac: 300 acres
Vaughan, Henry: 1,900 acres
Verney, William: 50 acres

Walker, Alexander: 500 acres
Walker, Alexander Jr.: 2,025 acres
Walker, David: 150 acres
Walker, David: 100 acres
Warberton, Thomas: 190 acres
Ward, Edward: 150 acres
Ward, Henry: 150 acres
Ward, Robert: 800 acres
Ward, Thomas: 100 acres
Weathers, Thomas: 130 acres
Weldey, George: 317 acres
Weldon, Sarah: 100 acres
Whaley, Mary: 200 acres
Whitaker, William: 320 acres
Wilkins, Samuell: 170 acres
Wilkins, Thomas: 600 acres
Williams, Matthew: 75 acres
Williamson, John: 120 acres
Willson, John: 140 acres
Winter, Timothy: 250 acres

Appendix B: James City County Justices Through 1827

1702: Philip Lightfoot, Henry Duke, Benjamin Harrison, Philip Ludwell, Michael Sherman, James Bray, Thomas Cowles, Hugh Norvell, William Edwards, William Drummond, Thomas Mountfort, John Frasier, Dionisius Wright, John Geddis, Henry Soane Jr.

1710: David Bray, James Bray, George Marable, John Frayser, John Geddes, Henry Soane, William Broadnax, Alexander Walker, William Brown Jr., Frederick Jones, Mongo Ingles, Archibald Blair, James Duke, David Morce

1714: James Bray, John Frayser, Henry Soane Jr., William Brodnax, Edward Jaquelin, Frederick Jones, Mongo Ingles, Archibald Blair, James Duke, David Morce, Francis Lightfoot, William Marston.

1726: John Clayton, William Brodnax, Edward Jaquelin, Benjamin Weldon, David Bray, Lewis Burwell, Henry Cary, John Tyler, Henry Powers, Richard Hickman, Robert Goodrich, Joseph Eggleston

1729: John Netherland, David Bray, Lewis Burwell, Henry Powers, Robert Goodrich, Joseph Eggleston, Alexander Irwin, Joshua Fry, Samuel Cobbs, Lewis Holland, Francis Tyler, John Eaton

1731: Richard Booker, William Brodnax, William Marable, Willis Wilson, Michael Sherman, Lancelot Woodward, Joseph Marston

1734: Abraham Nicholas, William Prentis added

1736: Edward Barradell, Hudson Allen, Richard Taliaferro added

1737: Edward Barradell, Edward Jaquelin, Richard Booker, Lewis Burwell, Thos Bray, Phil. Ludwell, Henry Power, Robert Goodrich, John Eaton, Carter Burwell of the Quorum, William Marrable, Willis Wilson, Lancelot Woodward, Joseph Marston, Abraham Nicholas, William Prentis, Hudson Allen, Richard Taliaferro and James Bray

1738: Edmond Walker, Leonard Henley (replacing Richard Booker, who refused to act)

1740: John Graeme added

1752: Carter Burwell, Hudson Allen, Richard Taliaferro, Lewis Burwell, Leonard Henley, Benjamin Eggleston, Armistead Burwell, John Blair Jr, Edward Champion Travis, Julius King Burgidge, Joseph Morton, William Barrett

1767: John Randolph, Richard Taliaferro, Lewis Burwell, Philip Johnson Sr., Thruston James, Edward Champion Travis, Robert Carter Nicholas, John Tyler, Edward Ambler, Dudley Richardson, William Richardson, William Norvell, William Spratley, Edward Power, Benjamin Weldon, John Cooper, Charles Barham, Hudson Allen, Richardson Henley, Holdenby Dixon, Turner Henley, Joseph Eggleston

1772: John Randolph, Richard Taliaferro, Lewis Burwell, Philip Johnson, Robert Carter Nicholas, John Tyler, Dudley Richardson, William Norvell, William Spratley, Benjamin Weldon, Richard Taliaferro Jr., John Cooper, Haldenby Dixon, Joseph Eggleston, William Holt, Lewis Burwell Jr., Nathaniel Burwell, Champion Travis

1775: Robert Carter Nicholas, William Norvell, John Randolph, John Tyler

1776: Lewis Burwell, Richard Taliaferro added

1777: Charles Barham, William Trebell, William Hankins, Joseph Eggleston, Hudson Allen, Edward Power, William Barrett and Benjamin Warburton

1778: George Nicholas

1783: Robert Nicholson

1784: Samuel Griffin, Charles Barham, Dudley Digges, William Lee, Samuel Beall, Jno. Walker, Jno Browne, Jno Ambler, William Walker, William Wilkinson (the younger)

1788: Samuel Griffin, Jno Walker, Dudley Digges, William Norvell

1789: Robert Greenhowe, Robert H. Wates

1790: William Lee, Dudley Digges, John Fenton

1796: John Pierce

1801: William Norvell, Champion Travis, William Walker, Littleton Tazewell, William Ludwell Lee, William Allen, William Bush, Henley Tatlor, Robert Walker, John Pierce Jr., John Ambler, Josias Moody, Henley Taylor, William Lindsay Allen, Robert Walker, Baker Perkins

1809: Champion Travis, Littleton Tazewell, John Goddin, William L. Allen, William Bush, William P. Harris, William E. Bassett, Edward Ambler

1814: Littleton Tazewell, John Goddin, Baker Perkins, William E. Barrett, Archer Hankins, Allen Marston, John E. Browne, Carter Burwell

1825: Bennett Kirby, Thruston James, John Browne, John R. Pierce

1827: Burwell Bassett, Archer Hankins, John Warburton, Allen Marston, Richardson Henley, Thruston James, John R. Pierce, Edward Richardson, Francis Piggott, Robert P. Richardson

Appendix C: James City County Board of Supervisors

1887: Chairman D. S. Cowles, G. W. Geddy, R. E. Gatewood

1888: Chairman D. S. Cowles, G. W. Geddy, R. E. Gatewood

1889: Chairman D. S. Cowles, G. W. Geddy, R. E. Gatewood

1890: Chairman R. E. Gatewood, G. W. Geddy, William T. Tilledge

1891: Chairman R. E. Gatewood, G. W. Geddy, D. S. Cowles: Chairman (2nd) John W. Casey, R. P. Wright, A. H. Cranston

1892: Chairman John W. Casey, R. P. Wright, A. H. Cranston

1893: Chairman John F. Jones, D. S. Cowles, R. P. Wright

1894: Chairman John F. Jones, R. P. Wright, Whitaker Lee

1895: Chairman John F. Jones, W. B. Vaiden, A. S. Cowles

1896: Chairman W. B. Vaiden, A. S. Cowles, John A. Barnes

1897: Chairman W. B. Vaiden, A. S. Cowles, John A. Barnes

1898: Chairman W. B. Vaiden, A. S. Cowles, John A. Barnes

1899: Chairman W. B. Vaiden, A. S. Cowles, John A. Barnes, Arthur Denmead

1900: Chairman Arthur Denmead, John A. Barnes, R. B. Geddy

1901: Chairman Arthur Denmead, John A. Barnes, R. B. Geddy

1902: Chairman Arthur Denmead, John A. Barnes, R. B. Geddy

1903: Chairman Arthur Denmead, John A. Barnes, R. B. Geddy

1904: Chairman Dr. H. U. Stephenson, William Lee, J. R. Bush

1905: Chairman Dr. H. U. Stephenson, William Lee, J. R. Bush

1906: Chairman Dr. H. U. Stephenson, William Lee, J. R. Bush

1907: Chairman Dr. H. U. Stephenson, William Lee, J. R. Bush, C. C. Branch

1908: Chairman D. Warren Marston, William Lee, John A. Barnes

1908–1909: Chairman William Lee, John A. Barnes, D. Warren Marston

1910: Chairman William Lee, John A. Barnes, D. Warren Marston

1911: Chairman William Lee, John A. Barnes, D. Warren Marston

1912: Chairman J. B. Vaiden, A. J. Johnson, John A. Barnes

1913: Chairman J. B. Vaiden, A. J. Johnson, John A. Barnes

1914: Chairman J. B. Vaiden, A. J. Johnson, John A. Barnes

1915: Chairman J. B. Vaiden, A. J. Johnson, John A. Barnes

1916: Chairman J. B. Vaiden, A. J. Johnson, John A. Barnes

1917: Chairman J. B. Vaiden, A. J. Johnson, John A. Barnes

1918: Chairman J. B. Vaiden, A. J. Johnson, John A. Barnes

1919: Chairman J. B. Vaiden, L. J. Haley, John A. Barnes

1920: Chairman J. B. Vaiden, W. H. Cowles, A. J. Hall

1921: Chairman J. B. Vaiden, W. H. Cowles, A. J. Hall

1922: Chairman J. B. Vaiden, W. H. Cowles, A. J. Hall

1923: Chairman J. B. Vaiden, W. H. Cowles, A. J. Hall

1924: Chairman W. H. Cowles, J. B. Vaiden, A. J. Hall

1925: Chairman W. H. Cowles, J. B. Vaiden, A. J. Hall

1926: Chairman W. H. Cowles, J. B. Vaiden, A. J. Hall

1927: Chairman W. H. Cowles, J. B. Vaiden, A. J. Hall

1928: Chairman J. B. Vaiden, A. J. Hall, George A. Marston

1929: Chairman J. B. Vaiden, A. J. Hall, George A. Marston

1930: Chairman J. B. Vaiden, A. J. Hall, George A. Marston

1931: Chairman J. B. Vaiden, A. J. Hall, George A. Marston

1932: Chairman George A. Marston, J. B. Vaiden, P. H. Richardson

1933: Chairman George A. Marston, J. B. Vaiden, P. H. Richardson

1934: Chairman George A. Marston, J. B. Vaiden, P. H. Richardson

1935: Chairman George A. Marston, J. B. Vaiden, P. H. Richardson

1936: Chairman P. H. Richardson, J. B. Vaiden, H. E. Hailey

1937: Chairman P. H. Richardson, J. B. Vaiden, H. E. Hailey

1938: Chairman P. H. Richardson, J. B. Vaiden, H. E. Hailey

1939: Chairman P. H. Richardson, J. B. Vaiden, H. E. Hailey

1940: Chairman P. H. Richardson, J. B. Vaiden, H. E. Hailey

1941: Chairman P. H. Richardson, J. B. Vaiden, W. C. Martin

1942: Chairman P. H. Richardson, J. B. Vaiden, W. C. Martin

1943: Chairman P. H. Richardson, J. B. Vaiden, W. C. Martin

1944: Chairman J. B. Vaiden, P. H. Richardson, W. C. Martin

1945: Chairman J. B. Vaiden, P. H. Richardson, W. C. Martin

1946: Chairman W. C. Martin, P. H. Richardson, James E. Vaiden

1947: Chairman W. C. Martin, P. H. Richardson, James E. Vaiden

1948: Chairman W. C. Martin, P. H. Richardson, James E. Vaiden

1949–1951: Chairman W. C. Martin, P. H. Richardson, James E. Vaiden

1951–1952: Chairman W. C. Martin, A. B. Smith Jr., James E. Vaiden

1952–1953: Chairman James E. Vaiden, R. L. Moody, A. B. Smith Jr.

1954–1955: Chairman James E. Vaiden, Frank B. Anderson, R. M. Hazelwood Jr.

1956–1960: Chairman James E. Vaiden, E. D. Warburton, Frank B. Anderson

1960–1964: Chairman James E. Vaiden, E. D. Warburton, Charles W. Richards

1964: Chairman Charles W. Richards, Dr. Murray Loring, William F. Pettengill

1966: Chairman William F. Pettengill, Dr. Murray Loring, Fred Flanary

1967: Chairman Fred Flanary, William F. Pettengill, Dr. Murray Loring

1968: Chairman William F. Pettengill, Richard W. Coakley, Fred Flanary

1969: Chairman Fred Flanary, Richard W. Coakley, William F. Pettengill,Charles W. Richards

1970: Chairman Richard W. Coakley, Charles Quittmeyer, Abram Frink,William F. Pettengill, Charles W. Richards

1971: Chairman Charles Quittmeyer, Richard Coakley, Abram Frink, William F. Pettengill, Charles W. Richards

1972–1973: Chairman Abram Frink, Mayo W. Waltrip, Jack D. Edwards, John E. Donaldson, Stewart U. Taylor

1974: Chairman Jack D. Edwards, John E. Donaldson, Stewart U. Taylor, Abram Frink, Mayo W. Waltrip

1975: Chairman John E. Donaldson, Steward U. Taylor, Abram Frink, Mayo W. Waltrip, Jack D. Edwards

1976: Chairman Abram Frink, John E. Donaldson, Steward U. Taylor, Mayo W. Waltrip, Jack D. Edwards

1977: Chairman John E. Donaldson, David W. Ware Jr., Abram Frink, Stewart U. Taylor, Jack D. Edwards

1978: Chairman Jack D. Edwards, John E. Donaldson, David W. Ware Jr., Abram Frink, Stewart U. Taylor

1979: Chairman Stewart U. Taylor, Jack D. Edwards, John E. Donaldson, David W. Ware Jr., Abram Frink

1980–1981Chairman Jack D. Edwards, Stewart U. Taylor, Gilbert A. Bartlett, Perry M. DePue, Abram Frink

1982: Chairman Abram Frink, Thomas D. Mahone, Jack D. Edwards, Stewart U. Taylor, Perry M. DePue

1983: Chairman Perry M. DePue, Abram Frink, Thomas D. Mahone, Jack D. Edwards, Stewart U. Taylor

1984: Chairman Stewart U. Taylor, William F. Brown, Thomas D. Mahone, Jack D. Edwards, Perry m. DePue

1985: Chairman Jack D. Edwards, Stewart U. Taylor, William F. Brown, Thomas D. Mahone, Perry DePue

1986: Chairman William F. Brown, Jack D. Edwards, Stewart U. Taylor, Thomas D. Mahone, Perry M. DePue

1987: Chairman Jack D. Edwards, William F. Brown, Stewart U. Taylor, Thomas D. Mahone, Perry M. DePue

1988: Chairman Jack D. Edwards, Stewart U. Taylor, Thomas D. Mahone, Perry M. DePue, Thomas K. Norment Jr.

1989: Chairman Thomas D. Mahone, Jack D. Edwards, Stewart U. Taylor, Perry M. DePue, Thomas K. Norment Jr.

1990: Chairman Perry M. DePue, Judith N. Knudson, Jack D. Edwards, Stewart U. Taylor, Thomas K. Norment Jr.

1991: Chairman Thomas K. Norment Jr., Perry M. DePue, Judith N. Knudson, Jack D. Edwards, Stewart U. Taylor

1992: Chairman Jack D. Edwards, David L. Sisk, Perry M. DePue, Judith N. Knudson, Stewart U. Taylor

1993: Chairman Judith N. Knudson, Jack D. Edwards, David L. Sisk, Perry M. DePue, Stewart U. Taylor

1994: Chairman Perry M. DePue, Robert A. Magoon, Jack D. Edwards, David L. Sisk, Stewart U. Taylor

1995: Chairman Perry M. DePue, Robert A. Magoon, Jack D. Edwards, David L. Sisk, Stewart U. Taylor

1996: Chairman David L. Sisk, Robert A. Magoon, Jack D. Edwards, Stewart U. Taylor, Perry M. DePue

Appendix D: James City County Sheriffs Through 1994

1640: Robert Hutchinson, Raphael Joyner, undersheriff

1670: Thomas Ballard

1673–1674: Francis Kirkman

1676–1677: Theophilus Hone

1680: Edmund Jennings

1682: Samuel Weldon

1691: Henry Gauler

1692: Captain Benjamin Goodridge, George Marable

1693: Michael Sherman

1695: George Marable

1696: Edward Ross

1697: George Marable

1699: Henry Duke

1700: Thomas Cowles

1701: Thomas Mountfort

1702: Thomas Cowles

1704: Henry Soane Jr.

1706: David Bray, Henry Soane [Bray excused]

1707: John Geddes

1708: John Frayser

1709: John Frayser

1710–1711: Edward Jaquelin

1712–1713: Mongo Ingles

1714–1715: William Marston (Manson)

1716: Mongo Ingles

1717–1718: James Bray

1719–1720: James Duke

1721–1722: John Netherland

1723: Thomas Ravenscroft

1724–1725: Benjamin Weldon

1726–1727: Robert Goodrich

1728–1729: Henry Power

1730–1731: William Brown

1732–1733: Willis Wilson

1734: William Marable

1735: Joseph Marston

1737: Lancelot Woodward

1739: Hudson Allen

1741: Richard Taliaferro

1743–1744: Robert Goodrick

1745–1746: John Warburton

1747: William Parks

1749–1750: William Hocker (Hooker)

1751: John Blair, Jr.

1757: William Norvell

1767–1768: William Norvell

1769: William Spratley

1771: Benjamin Weldon

1777: Joseph Eggleston

1781: Edward Power

1783: William Bassett

1785: John Pierce

1786: Robert Andrews

1788: Samuel Griffin

1789: Dudley Digges

1790: Dudley Digges (deceased), William Lee

1790–1791: Wiliiam Lee

1792–1793: John Walker

1800: William Wilkerson

1801: William Coleman

1802: Littleton Tazewell
1804–1805: John Goddin
1806–1807: William Allen
1808–1809: William Warburton
1810: Champion Travis
1811: Henley Taylor
1813: William Allen
1814: Baker Perkins
1823–1824: John Warburton
1826–1827: Durro Spencer
1831: Bennett Kirby
1832: Richard Henley
1833: George Richardson
1834–1835: Archer Hankins
1836–1837: John Drice
1838: Durro Spencer

1840: Durro Spencer
1841: Michael Warren
1842: Joseph Gresham
1844: Joseph Gresham
1846: Bennett Kirby
1847–1848: Goodrich Durfey
1849: Henry Benskin Marshall
    Richardson
1888: E. Richards
1896–1904: Moses Harrel
1904–1916: Walker Ware
1916–1944: Louis Pendelton Trice
1944–1961: Vester Wayne Lovelace
1961–1983: A. M. Brenegan
1983–1994: Walter Dutton
1995–1996: Walter Dutton

Appendix E: James City County's Official Surveyors

1681-1699: John Soane
1702: James Minge
1714: Simon Jeffrys
1718: Christopher Jackson
1726: William Comrie
1728-1729: William Comrie
ca. 1770: William Goodall
1784: William Brown

Appendix F: James City's Burgesses and Delegates

Note: There are many gaps in the records from 1616 to 1642. Some of the individuals attributed to James City between 1642 & 1652 lived in what became Surry County. In 1776 the city of Williamsburg gained representation, whereas Jamestown and the College of William and Mary lost theirs.

1619: James City; Capt. William Powell, Ensign William Spence
   Martin's Hundred; John Boys, John Jackson
   Argall's Gift; Mr. Pawlett, Mr. Gourgaing

1623–1624: Richard Kingsmill, Edward Blaney

1629: George Menefie and Richard Kingsmill (Jamestown); Thomas Bagwell (Pasbehay); Richard Brewster (Neck O'Land); Theodore Moyse (Moses) and Thomas Doe (Archers Hope); John Utie and Richard Townsend (from Archer's Hope to Martin's Hundred); Thomas Kingston and Thomas Fawcett (Martin's Hundred)

1629–1630: Bridges Freeman (Pasbehay); John Southern and Robert Barrington (Jamestown Island); Richard Brewster (Neck O'Land); Theodore Moyses and Henry Coney (Archers Hope and the Glebe land); John Browning and Thomas Farley (from Archers Hope to Martin's Hundred); Robert Scotchmore and Thomas Fossett (Martin's Hundred)

1631–1632: John Southern and Thomas Crampe (Crump) (James City); Thomas Farley and Percival Wood (Archers Hope)

1632: Bridges Freeman (Chickahominy); John Jackson (Jamestown Island); John Corker (Pasbehay); Sergeant Thomas Crump (Neck O'Land); Roger Webster and Henry Coney (Glebe Land and Archers Hope); John Browning and John Wareham (Mounts Bay); Robert Scotchmore and Percival Wood (Martin's Hundred)

1632–1633: John Corker (Jamestown Island, Chickahominy and Pasbehay); Thomas Crump (Neck O'Land); Henry Coney (Archer's Hope and Glebe Land); Richard Brewster and John Wareham (Harrop to Martin's Hundred); David Mansfield and Robert Scotchmore (Martin's Hundred)

1641: Captain Robert Hutchinson, Francis Fowler, John White, Thomas Hill, Richard Richards, Ferdinand Franklin, Jeremie Clement, Thomas Follis, William Butler

1642–1643: Captain Robert Hutchinson, Rowland Sadler, Henry Filmer, Captain John Fludd, Stephen Webb, William Davis

1644: Captain Robert Hutchinson, Stephen Webb, Edward Travis, Thomas Loving, George Jordan, John Shepherd, Thomas Warren

1644–1645: Ambrose Harmer, Captain Robert Hutchinson, William Barrett, John Corker, Peter Ridley, George Stephens, John Rogers

1645: John Flood, Walter Chiles, Thomas Swann, Robert Weatherall, Ambrose Harmer, Thomas Warren, Peter Ridely, George Stephens

1646: Ambrose Harmer, Walter Chiles, Captain Robert Shepheard, George Jordayne, Thomas Loving, William Barrett

1647Captain Robert Hutchinson, Captain Bridges Freeman, Captain Robert Shepheard, George Jordan, William Davis, Peter Ridley

1649: Walter Chiles, Thomas Swann, William Barrett, George Read, William Whittaker, John Dunston

1652: Robert Wetherall, Lt. Col. John Fludd, Henry Soane, Daniel Mansill, George Stephens, William Whittakere

1652: Robert Wetherall, William Whittaker, Abraham Wattson, Henry Soane

1653: Col. Walter Chiles, William Whittaker, Herny Soane, Abraham Wattson

1654: Thomas Dipnall, Abraham Watson, William Whitaker, Henry Soane

1655–1656: Lt. Col. William Whittaker, Theophilus Hone, Col. John Flood, Robert Holt, Robert Ellyson

1657–1658: Henry Soane, Maj. Richard Webster, Thomas Loveinge, William Corker

1658–1659: Walter Chiles, Capt. William Whittacre, Capt. Thomas Foulke, Capt. Mathew Edloe

1659–1660: Henry Soane, Capt. Robert Ellison, Richard Ford, William Morley

1663: Capt. Robert Ellyson, Walter Chiles, Capt. Edward Ramsey

1666: Capt. Edward Ramsey, Thomas Ballard (James City County); Theophilus Hone (Jamestown)

1685: Col. Thomas Ballard

1688: Philip Ludwell, James Bray (James City County); William Sherwood (Jamestown)

1692–1693: Michael Sherman, Capt. Henry Duke (James City County); Capt. Miles Cary (Jamestown)

1696: Henry Duke, Miles Sherman (James City County); Philip Ludwell Jr. in place of William Sherwood, deceased (Jamestown)

1702: James Bray, George Marable, Robert Beverley (James City County and Jamestown)

1714: George Marable, Henry Soane Jr. (James City County); Edward Jaquelin (Jamestown)

1718: William Brodnax, George Marable (James City County); Archibald Blair (Jamestown)

1720–1722: Archibald Blair, John Clayton (James City County); William Brodnax (Jamestown)

1723: Archibald Blair, John Clayton (James City County); William Brodnax (Jamestown)

1726: Archibald Blair, John Clayton (James City County); William Brodnax (Jamestown)

1727–1728: Archibald Blair, John Clayton (James City County)

1736: William Marable, John Eaton (James City County); Lewis Burwell (Jamestown):

1738: William Marable, John Eaton (James City County); Lewis Burwell (Jamestown)

1740: William Marable, [John Eaton, deceased] (James City County); Lewis Burwell (Jamestown)

1742: Col. Lewis Burwell, Carter Burwell (James City County); Philiip Ludwell (Jamestown)

1744: Carter Burwell, Benjamin Waller [Lewis Burwell died during session] (James City County); Philip Ludwell (Jamestown)

1745: Carter Burwell, Benjamin Waller (James City County); Philip Ludwell (Jamestown)

1746: Benjamin Waller, Carter Burwell (James City County); Philip Ludwell (Jamestown)

1747: Benjamin Waller, Carter Burwell (James City County); Philip Ludwell (Jamestown)

1748: Benjamin Waller, Carter Burwell (James City County); Philip Ludwell (Jamestown)

1749: Benjamin Waller, Carter Burwell (James City County); Philip Ludwell (Jamestown)

1752: Benjamin Waller, Carter Burwell (James City County); Edward Champion Travis (Jamestown)

1753: Benjamin Waller, Carter Burwell (James City County); Edward Travis (Jamestown)

1754: Benjamin Waller, Carter Burwell (James City County); Edward Champion Travis (Jamestown)

1755: Benjamin Waller, Carter Burwell (James City County); Edward Champion Travis (Jamestown)

1756: Benjamin Waller, Joseph Morton (James City County); Edward Champion Travis (Jamestown)

1757: Benjamin Waller, Joseph Morton (James City County); Edward Champion Travis (Jamestown)

March 1758: Benjamin Waller, Joseph Morton (James City County); Edward Champion Travis (Jamestown)

September 1758: Benjamin Waller, Lewis Burwell (James City County); Edward Champion Travis (Jamestown), November 1758: Benjamin Waller, Lewis Burwell (James City County); Edward Champion Travis (Jamestown)

February 1759: Benjamin Waller, Lewis Burwell (James City County); Edward Champion Travis (Jamestown)

November 1759: Benjamin Waller, Lewis Burwell (James City County); John Ambler (Jamestown)

1760–1761: Benjamin Waller, Lewis Burwell (James City County); John Ambler (Jamestown)

1761: Lewis Burwell, Philip Johnson (James City County); Edward Champion Travis (Jamestown)

1762: Lewis Burwell, Philip Johnson (James City County); Edward Champion Travis (Jamestown)

1763: Lewis Burwell, Philip Johnson (James City County); Edward Champion Travis (Jamestown)

1764: Lewis Burwell, Philip Johnson (James City County); Edward Champion Travis (Jamestown)

May 1765: Lewis Burwell, Philip Johnson (James City County); Edward Champion Travis (Jamestown)

October 1765: Lewis Burwell, Robert Carter Nicholas (James City County); John Ambler (Jamestown)

1766: Lewis Burwell, Robert Carter Nicholas (James City County); Edward Ambler replaced John Ambler, dec. (Jamestown)

1767: Lewis Burwell, Robert Carter Nicholas (James City County); Edward Ambler (Jamestown)

1768: Lewis Burwell, Robert Carter Nicholas (James City County); Edward Ambler (Jamestown)

1769: Lewis Burwell, Robert Carter Nicholas (James City County); Champion Travis (Jamestown)

1770: Lewis Burwell, Robert Carter Nicholas (James City County); Champion Travis (Jamestown)

1771: Lewis Burwell, Robert Carter Nicholas (James City County); Champion Travis (Jamestown)

1772: Lewis Burwell, Robert Carter Nicholas (James City County); Champion Travis (Jamestown)

1773: Lewis Burwell, Robert Carter Nicholas (James City County); Champion Travis (Jamestown)

1774: Lewis Burwell, Robert Carter Nicholas (James City County); Champion Travis (Jamestown)

1775: Robert Carter Nicholas, William Norvell (James City County); Champion Travis (Jamestown)

1776: Robert Carter Nicholas, William Norvell (James City County); Champion Travis (Jamestown)

1777: Robert Carter Nicholas, William Norvell (James City County); Champion Travis (Jamestown)

1778: Robert Carter Nicholas, William Norvell (James City County); Champion Travis (Jamestown)

1779: Nathaniel Burwell, William Norvell

1780: James Innes, William Norvell

1781: James Innes, William Norvell,

October 1781–January 1782: Joseph Prentis, Champion Travis

1782: Nathaniel Burwell, Williiam Norvell

1783: William Norvell, William Nelson

1784–January 1785: William Walker, William Norvell

1786: William Walker, William Norvell

1787 : William Walker, William Norvell

1787–January 1788: William Norvell, John Pierce

1788: William Norvell, John Pierce

1789: William Norvell, John Pierce

1790: William Norvell, John Pierce

1791: William Norvell, John Pierce

1792: William Norvell, John Pierce

1793: John Ambler, John Pierce

1794: John Ambler, John Pierce

1795: John Ambler, William Browne

1796: John Pierce, John Allen

1797–January 1798: John Pierce, John Allen

1798–1799: John Allen, Littleton Tazewell

1799–1800: Littleton Waller Tazewell, William Lightfoot

1800–January 1801: Littleton Waller Tazewell, Champion Travis, William Lightfoot

1801: Littleton Waller Tazewell, William Lightfoot

1802: Littleton Waller Tazewell, William Lightfoot

1803: Littleton Waller Tazewell, William Lightfoot

1804: Littleton Waller Tazewell, William Lightfoot

1805: Littleton Waller Tazewell, William Lightfoot

1806: Littleton Waller Tazewell, William Lightfoot

1806–1807: William Lightfoot, Robert Greenhow

1808: William Lightfoot, Robert Greenhow

1809–1810: Littleton Tazewell, William E. Barrett

1811: Littleton Tazewell, William E. Barrett

1811–1812: Archer Hankins, Littleton Tazewell

1812–1813: Archer Hankins, William Barrett

1813–1814: Archer Hankins, William Tazewell

1815: Archer Hankins, William Tazewell

1815–1816: Archer Hankins, William Brown

1816–1817: Dabney Brown, Archer Hankins

1817–1818: Dabney Brown, Lewis C. Tyler

1818–1819: Lewis C. Tyler, Bennett Kirby

1819–1820: Burwell Bassett, Bennett Kirby

1820–1821: Burwell Bassett, Bennett Kirby

1821–1822: Bennett Kirby, John M. Gregory

1822–1823: Bennett Kirby, Richardson Henley

1824: Bennett Kirby, Richardson Henley

1825: Bennett Kirby, Richardson Henley

1825–1826: Richardson Henley, William F. Pierce

1826–1827: Richardson Henley, Bennett Kirby

1827–1828: Rascow Cole, Robert P. Richardson

1829: Rascow Cole, Robert P. Richardson

1830: Rascow Cole, Robert P. Richardson

1830–1831: James Semple Jr.

1831–1832: Robert Shield

1832–1833: John M. Gregory

1834: John M. Gregory

1835: John M. Gregory

1836: John M. Gregory

1836–1837: Robert McCandlish

1838: Robert McCandlish

1839: John Tyler

1839–1840: John M. Gregory

1841: John M. Gregory

1842–1843: Lemuel J. Bowden

1844: Lemuel J. Bowden

1845: Lemuel J. Bowden

1846: Lemuel J. Bowden

1846: William Howard

1847: William Howard

1848: William Howard

1849: William Howard

1849: George W. Southall

1850: George W. Southall

1851: George W. Southall

1852: John P. Pierce

1853: John P. Pierce (James City, Charles City and New Kent Counties)

1853–1854: Beverley P. Crump

1854: Beverley P. Crump

1855–1856: William Bush

1857: J. M. Wilcox

1858: J. M. Wilcox

1859: J. M. Wilcox

1860: J. M. Wilcox

1861: J. M. Wilcox

1861–1862: V. Vaiden

1862: V.Vaiden

1863: V. Vaiden

1863: Ira L. Bowles

1864: Ira L. Bowles

1865: Ira L. Bowles

1865: W. Martin

1866: W. Martin

1867: W. Martin

1869: F. S. Norton

1870: F. S. Norton

1871: F. S. Norton (James City County and Williamsburg)

1871: Robert Norton

1872: Robert Norton

1873: Robert Norton (James City and York Counties)

1874: Robert Norton

1874–1875: Robert Norton

1875: Sydney Smith

1876: Sydney Smith

1877: Sydney Smith, Robert Norton

1878: Robert Norton

1879–1880: Robert Norton (James City, Elizabeth City, Warwick, and York Counties, Williamsburg)

1881–1882: Robert Morton

1883–1884: Robert G. Griffin

1885–1887: Richard A. Wise (James City, Elizabeth City, Warwick, and York Counties)

1887–1888: J. H. Robinson

1889–1890: James A. Fields (James City, Elizabeth City, Warwick and York Counties, Williamsburg)

1891–1892: John H. Crafford

1893–1894: Robert W. Perkins (James City, New Kent, Charles City, York, and Warwick Counties, Williamsburg)

1895: Thomas T. Powell

1896: Thomas T. Powell

1897: Thomas T. Powell

1898: Thomas T. Powell

1899–1900: E. C. Madison (James City, New Kent, Charles City, York, and Warwick Counties, Williamsburg, Newport News)

1901: L. P. Stearnes

1902: L. P. Stearnes

1903: L. P. Stearnes

1904: A. J. Barnes (James City, New Kent, Charles City, Warwick and York Counties, Williamsburg)

1906: R. T. Gregory

1908: W. E. Goffigan

1910: H. U. Stephenson

1912: H. U. Stephenson

1914–1915: R. T. Gregory

1916: Norvell L. Henley

1918: Norvell L. Henley

1920: Norvell L. Henley

1922–1923: Norvell L. Henley

1924: Ashton Dovell

1926–1927: Ashton Dovell

1928: Ashton Dovell

1930: Ashton Dovell

1932–1933: Ashton Dovell

1934: Ashton Dovell

1936–1937: Ashton Dovell

1938: Ashton Dovell

1940: Ashton Dovell

1942: Paul Crockett

1944–1945: Paul Crockett

1946–1947: Paul Crockett

1948: Paul Crockett

1950: Paul Crockett

1952: Paul Crockett

1954: Russell M. Carneal

1956–1958: Russell M. Carneal

1959–1963: Russell M. Carneal

1964–1965: Russell M. Carneal

1966–1967: Russell M. Carneal

1968–1969: Russell M. Carneal

1970–1971: Russell M. Carneal

1972–1973: Robert Quinn

1974–1975: Robert Quinn

1976–1977: George Grayson

1978–1979: George Grayson

1980–1981: George Grayson

1982–1983: George Grayson

1984–1985: George Grayson

1986–1988: George Grayson

1988–1990: George Grayson

1990–1992: George Grayson

1992–1994: George Grayson

1994–1996: George Grayson

Appendix G: James City County School Superintendents Through 1952

1871–1881: James H. Allen

1882–1885: C. W. Taylor

1886–1896: James H. Allen

1897–1906: Peter T. Cowles

1907–1910: Hugh S. Bird

1911: Robert E. Henley, L. L. Martin (acting), M. J. Hoover

1912: M. J. Hoover, L. L. Martin, W. B. Coggin

1913: W. B. Coggin

1914–1919: Alvin C. Cooper

1920–1923: H. L. Harris

1924–1952: Clarence Jennings

1953–1964: Rawls Byrd

1964–1981: Henry Renz

1981–1989: John Oliver

1990–1994: Gayden Carruth

1995–1996: James Kent

Appendix H: The Clergy Of James City County's Colonial Parishes

James City Parish

Robert Hunt, 1607–1608
Richard Buck, 1610–ca.1624
Hawte Wyatt, before 1626
Francis Bolton, 1630
Thomas Hampton, 1640–1645
Philip Mallory, ca. 1658
Morgan Godwin, ca. 1667
Justinian Aylmer, 1671
Samuel Jones, 1671
James Wadding, 1672
John Clouch, ca. 1676
Rowland Jones, 1680
John Clayton, 1684–1686
James Blair, 1694–1710
James Worden, 1712
Peter Fontaine, 1716
Hugh Jones, before 1722
William LeNeve, 1722–1737
William Preston, ca. 1755
William Yates, 1759–1764
William Bland, 1767–1777
James Madison, 1777–1805

Harrop Parish

Extinct in 1658

Bruton Parish

Rowland Jones, 1674–1688
Samuel Eburne, 1688–1695
Cope D'Oyley, 1697–1702
Solomon Wheatley, 1702–1710
James Blair, 1710–1743
Thomas Dawson, 1743–1759
William Yates, 1759–1764
James Horrocks, 1764–1771
John Camm, 1771–1773
John Bracken 1773–1818

Blisland Parish

Daniel Taylor, 1721–1729
David Mossom, 1729
William LeNeve, 1729
Chicheley Thacker, 1730–1762
Price Davies, 1763–1786

Wilmington Parish

John Brunskil, 1724

Appendix I: James City County Records

Library of Virginia Inventory

Board of Supervisors Minutes:
September 1887 to 1908
Court Minutes: 1871–1882
Clerk's Guide to Sample Forms
for Certain Court Records,
undated
Chancery Execution Book:
1868–1916
Chancery Minutes: 1871–1873
Chancery Order Books:
1889–1903
Chancery Rules: 1872–1911
Execution Book: 1866–1916
Judgment Docket: 1865–1903
Law Execution Book: 1866–1916
Law Order Book: 1885
Circuit Court Minutes: 1866–1882
Circuit Court Order Book:
1879–1885
James City County and
Williamsburg Fiduciary Bond
Book: 1865–1908
James City County and
Williamsburg Plat Books:
1891–1918
Birth Register: 1866–1884
Death Register: 1864–1884
School Commissioners Records:
1819–1861
Tax Book: 1768–1769
Deed and Will Books: 1854–1861,
1865–1874
Land Tax Lists: 1782, on

Personal Property Tax Lists: 1782,
on
Agricultural Census Records:
1850–1880
Census Records: full run
Slave Schedules: 1850, 1860
Processioners Records:
1890–1891, 1903–1904
James City County/Williamsburg
Rolls of Registered Voters:
1900–1965
James City County/Williamsburg
Contracts for Personal Property:
1900–1918

Circuit Court's Office

Deed and will books, twentieth
century tax records, tax assessors
maps, plats, military induction
records, marriage records, death
records, order books and other
documents related to the modern
period are available in the Clerk's
Office.

Records Management Room
Government Complex

Microfilms of the Board of
Supervisors minutes are available
from September 10, 1887, on.

Appendix J: Rosters of the James City Cavalry and the Williamsburg Junior Guard

The James City Cavalry
(from the RICHMOND TIMES-DISPATCH, June 1, 1896)

Captains:
G. E. Geddy (dead); James H. Allen (wounded); L. W. Lane (wounded).

Lieutenants:
M. A. Meanley (dead); Andrew Hockaday; George E. Bush (dead); C. W. Hubbard (killed); J. F. Hubbard; E. M. Ware (wounded and prisoner, dead); J. W. Morecock (killed).

Sergeants:
G. E. Richardson (wounded, sabre-cut, prisoner); R. H. Whitaker (dead); J. T. James (dead); C. B. Ratcliffe (dead); M. R. Harrell (wounded); Felix Pierce (dead); R. G. Taylor; John Cowles (dead).

Corporals:
S. S. Hankins (prisoner); D. W. Spencer; G. A. Piggott (dead); C. W. Cowles (wounded, sabre-cut, prisoner, dead); G. W. Tyree; J. W. Manning (dead).

Privates:
Richard Apperson (unknown); G. W. Bacon; _____ Ball (unknown); J. H. Barnes (prisoner); Basil B. Bennett (unknown); [-] F. Blair (wounded); D. Frank Bowden; W. T. Bonwell (wounded); D. William Burke; N. H. Bush; G. R. H. B. Bush (prisoner); C. W. Coleman (dead); P. T. Cowles (prisoner); D. S. Coles; D. W. T. Coles; T. H. Davis; S. S. Edwards (dead); Sylvanus Edwards (dead); G. H. Enos (wounded); Jerry Garrett; Joe Garrett; Robert Garrett; F. W. Hammond (dead); T. W. Hankins (dead); Charles Hansford (ded); C. Harwood; John Hicks; Oliver Hockaday (dead); Gustavus Pope; J. W. Hubbard; G. W. James (wounded, dead); _____ Jeter (unknown); J. P. Johnson; B. A. Marston (dead); J. W. Marston; T. P. Marston; D. W. Marston; M. J. Martin (dead); M. Mattingly (dead); George Medansley (dead); _____ Moon; William Mountcastle; George Mountcastle; John Mountcastle; _____ Muir (killed); F.C. Newman (dead); Archer Pamplin (unknown); Sam. Pettit (killed); W. M. Pierce; H. D.

Piggott (dead); Hamilton Richardson (killed); Sydney Smith (dead); Tom Sparrow (unknown); R. M. Spencer (killed); G. W. Stewart (dead); W. M. Taylor; Cyrus Tyree (dead); W. B. Vaiden; Algernon Vaiden (dead); Vulosko Vaiden (prisoner, dead); Robert Warburton (dead); Southy Ward (unknown); H. B. Warren; Watkins Warren (unknown); Robert Watkins; R. C. Whitaker (dead); G. W. Whitaker, _____; R. C. Whitaker (dead); G. M. Whitaker; A. B. Willis (killed); Sam. Wooten (wounded); Tom Wynne (dead).

Promotions outside of the Company:
James H. Allen, lieutenant-colonel E. M. Ware, captain Dr. C. W. Coleman, surgeon Dr. Watkins Warren, surgeon Dr. R. H. Bush, surgeon

Roster of the Williamsburg Junior Guard
(from the VIRGINIA GAZETTE, June 24, 1899)

In 1862, when elections were held while the Company was bivouaced at Bottoms Bridge, some officers were changed.

Captains:
J. A. Henley (1861); Octavius Coke (1862),

Lieutenants:
W. H. E. Morecock (1861), H. M. Walker (1861), L. Henley (1861), R. P. Taylor (1862), J. H. Barlow (1862)

Sergeants:
Octavius Coke (1861), Parke Jones (1861), J. F. Bowry (1861), Richardson L. Henley (1861), W. T. Christian (1861)

Color Bearer:
W. T. Moss

Corporals:
A. J. Hofheimer, R. A. Bowry, W. W. Lee, W. H. Barlow

Privates:
J. H. Barlow Jr., T. J. Barlow, R. G. Barlow, G. O. Ball, J. V. Bidgood, W. Burke, R. Barham, W. Miles Cary, J. W. Clark, C. B. Coakley, R. Crandall, T. C. Carrington, G. W. Clowes, J. A. Davis, J. W. Davis, S. N. Deneufille, H. L. Dix, J. H. Dix, W. C. Durfey, W. F. Gilliam, W. G. Gatewood,

Benjamin Gilliam, R. J. Griffin, J. R. Harwood, J. M. Johnson, G. W. Jackson, H. T. Jones Jr., J. C. Lucas, W. H. Lee Jr., R. A. Liveley, E. H. Lively, R. C. Lawson, L. Lukehard, A. J. Lane, T. A. Moss, J. A. J. Moss, G. H. Mercer, H. V. Morris, H. A. Morris, J. W. Morris, F. P. Morrison, S. Maupin, D. R. Mahone, H. P. Moore, C. W. Mahone, J. H. Mahone, H. L. McCandlish, R. Owens, B. F. Piggott, J. T. Parham, B. H. Ratcliffe, J. Ratcliffe, C. H. Richardson, L. P. Slater, J. Simcoe, S. Simcoe, M. Spraggins, R. B. Shelburne, I. Smith, Talbot Sweeney, F. B. Sykes, L. Taylor, R. P. Taylor, W. Vaughan, T. H. Whiting, J. T. H. Wilkins, A. L. Williamson, J. M. Walthall, W. H. Yergy, E. M. Lee, J. B. Wilkins, A. W. Wilkins &c.

Markers:
B. W. Bowry, J. C. Maupin

As Company I, the Williamsburg Junior Guard was merged into the 32nd Virginia Regiment, Virginia Volunteers, with Colonel Edward Montague of Essex County as commander and Dr. James Semple of Hampton as regimental surgeon. The 32nd Regiment was organized by Colonel Benjamin S. Ewell in 1861. The regiment participated in the battles of Gettysburg and Yellow Tavern.

Selected Bibliography

Primary Sources

Published Material

Andrews, Charles, comp. NARRATIVES OF THE INSURRECTIONS, 1665–1690. New York: Charles Scribner's Sons, 1967.

Berkeley, William. A DISCOURSE AND VIEW OF VIRGINIA. London: no publisher listed, 1663.

Beverley, Robert. HISTORY OF THE PRESENT STATE OF VIRGINIA (1705), L. B. Wright, ed. Chapel Hill: University of North Carolina Press, 1947.

Bottom, Davis, comp. ACTS AND JOINT RESOLUTIONS PASSED BY THE GENERAL ASSEMBLY OF THE STATE OF VIRGINIA PASSED DURING THE SESSION OF 1906. Richmond: Commonwealth of Virginia, 1906.

_____. ACTS AND JOINT RESOLUTIONS PASSED BY THE GENERAL ASSEMBLY OF THE STATE OF VIRGINIA PASSED DURING THE SESSION OF 1908. Richmond: Commonwealth of Virginia, 1908.

_____. ACTS AND JOINT RESOLUTIONS PASSED BY THE GENERAL ASSEMBLY OF THE STATE OF VIRGINIA PASSED DURING THE SESSION OF 1912. Richmond: Commonwealth of Virginia, 1912.

_____. ACTS AND JOINT RESOLUTIONS PASSED BY THE GENERAL ASSEMBLY OF THE STATE OF VIRGINIA PASSED DURING THE SESSION OF 1914. Richmond: Commonwealth of Virginia, 1914.

_____. ACTS AND JOINT RESOLUTIONS PASSED BY THE GENERAL ASSEMBLY OF THE STATE OF VIRGINIA PASSED DURING THE SESSION OF 1916. Richmond: Commonwealth of Virginia, 1916.

_____. REGISTER OF THE GENERAL ASSEMBLY OF VIRGINIA, 1776–1918. Fourteenth Annual Report of the Library Board of the Virginia State Library, 1916–1917. Richmond: Commonwealth of Virginia, 1917.

_____. ACTS AND JOINT RESOLUTIONS PASSED BY THE GENERAL ASSEMBLY OF THE STATE OF VIRGINIA PASSED DURING THE SESSION OF 1918. Richmond: Commonwealth of Virginia, 1918.

_____. ACTS AND JOINT RESOLUTIONS PASSED BY THE GENERAL ASSEMBLY OF THE STATE OF VIRGINIA PASSED DURING THE SESSION OF 1920. Richmond: Commonwealth of Virginia, 1920.

Chamberlayne, C. G. THE VESTRY BOOK OF BLISLAND PARISH, NEW KENT AND JAMES CITY COUNTIES, VIRGINIA, 1721–1786. Richmond: Virginia State Library, 1935.

_____. "Acts of the General Assembly, January 6, 1639/40," WILLIAM AND MARY QUARTERLY, 2nd Ser., 4 (1924), 16–35.

_____. "Documents of Sir Francis Wyatt Governor, 1621–1626," WILLIAM AND MARY QUARTERLY, 2nd Ser., 7 (1927), 204–214.

_____. THE VESTRY BOOK OF ST. PETER'S PARISH. Richmond: Virginia State Library, 1937.

Church, Randolph W. VIRGINIA LEGISLATIVE PETITIONS. Richmond: Virginia State Library, 1984.

Clark, William Bell, ed. NAVAL DOCUMENTS OF THE AMERICAN REVOLUTION. 9 vols. Washington, D.C.: U. S. Government Printing Office, 1966.

DeVries, David. VOYAGES FROM HOLLAND TO AMERICA, LED 1632 TO 1644 BY DAVID PETERSON DEVRIES, Henry C. Murphy, trans. New York: no publisher listed, 1853.

Fisher, Daniel George. "Narrative of George Fisher," WILLIAM AND MARY QUARTERLY, 1st Ser., 17 (1908),165;

Fithian, Philip V. JOURNAL AND LETTERS OF PHILIP VICKERS FITHIAN, 1773–1774, Hunter D. Farish, ed. Williamsburg: Colonial Williamsburg Inc., 1965.

Flaherty, David H., ed. LAWES DIVINE, MORALL, AND MARTIALL, ETC. Charlottesville: University Press of Virginia, 1969.

Fontaine, John. THE JOURNAL OF JOHN FONTAINE, AN IRISH HUGUENOT SON IN SPAIN AND VIRGINIA, 1710–1719. Williamsburg: Colonial Williamsburg Foundation, 1972.

General Assembly of Virginia. ACTS OF THE GENERAL ASSEMBLY, 1825. Richmond: Commonwealth of Virginia, 1825.

Goode, James E., comp. ACTS AND JOINT RESOLUTIONS PASSED BY THE GENERAL ASSEMBLY OF THE STATE OF VIRGINIA PASSED DURING THE SESSION OF 1869–1870. Richmond: Commonwealth of Virginia, 1870.

Hamor, Ralph. A TRUE DISCOURSE OF THE PRESENT ESTATE OF VIRGINIA AND THE SUCCESSE OF THE AFFAIRES THERE TILL THE 18TH OF JUNE 1614. Richmond: Virginia State Library, 1957.

Harriot, Thomas. BRIEF AND TRUE REPORT OF THE NEW FOUND LAND OF VIRGINIA. New York: Dover Publications, 1972.

Harrower, John. THE JOURNAL OF JOHN HARROWER, AN INDENTURED SERVANT IN THE COLONY OF VIRGINIA, 1773–1776, Edward M. Riley, ed. Williamsburg: Colonial Williamsburg, 1963.

Hartwell, Henry et al. THE PRESENT STATE OF VIRGINIA AND THE COLLEGE [1697] BY HENRY HARTWELL, JAMES BLAIR AND EDWARD CHILTON. Princeton: Princeton University, 1940.

Hening, William W.,ed. THE STATUTES AT LARGE: BEING A COLLECTION OF ALL THE LAWS OF VIRGINIA. 13 vols. Richmond: Samuel Pleasants, 1809–1823.

Jameson, J. Franklin, comp. NARRATIVES OF NEW NETHERLANDS. New York: Barnes and Noble, Inc., 1967.

Jefferson, Thomas. NOTES ON THE STATE OF VIRGINIA, William Peden, ed. Chapel Hill: University of North Carolina Press, 1954.

Johnson, R. U. and C. C. Buel, comp. BATTLES AND LEADERS OF THE CIVIL WAR. 4 vols. New York: Castle Books, 1956.

Jones, Hugh. THE PRESENT STATE OF VIRGINIA. Chapel Hill: University of North Carolina Press, 1956.

Kimber, Edward. "Observations in Several Voyages and Travels in America, 1736," WILLIAM AND MARY QUARTERLY, 1st Ser., 15 (1907), 143–159; 215–252.

Kingsbury, Susan M., comp. RECORDS OF THE VIRGINIA COMPANY OF LONDON. 4 vols. Washington, D.C.: U. S. Government Printing Office, 1906–1935.

Latrobe, Benjamin. THE JOURNALS OF BENJAMIN HENRY LATROBE, 1799–1820, FROM PHILADELPHIA TO NEW ORLEANS, Edward C. Carter, II, ed. Vol. III. New Haven and London: Maryland Historical Society and Yale University Press, 1980.

Lee, William. LETTERS OF WILLIAM LEE. William C. Ford, ed. New York: Charles Scribner's Sons, 1967.

Lewis, Clifford M. et al. THE SPANISH JESUIT MISSION. Chapel Hill: University of North Carolina Press, 1953.

McIlwaine, H. R., ed. LEGISLATIVE JOURNALS OF THE COUNCIL OF COLONIAL VIRGINIA. 3 vols. Richmond: Virginia State Library, 1918.

_____. EXECUTIVE JOURNALS OF THE COUNCIL OF COLONIAL VIRGINIA. 5 vols. Richmond: Virginia State Library, 1925–1945.

_____. JOURNAL OF THE COUNCIL OF THE STATE OF VIRGINIA, 1776–1777. Richmond: Virginia State Library, 1931.

_____. MINUTES OF COUNCIL AND GENERAL COURT OF COLONIAL VIRGINIA. Richmond: The Library Board, 1934.

McIlwaine, H. R. et al, eds. JOURNALS OF THE HOUSE OF BURGESSES, 1619–1776. 13 vols. Richmond: Virginia State Library, 1905–1915.

Micou, A. R., comp. ACTS AND JOINT RESOLUTIONS PASSED BY THE GENERAL ASSEMBLY OF THE STATE OF VIRGINIA PASSED DURING ITS EXTRA SESSION OF 1887. Richmond: Commonwealth of Virginia, 1887.

Mumford, William, ed. REPORTS OF CASES ARGUED AND DETERMINED IN THE SUPREME COURT OF APPEALS OF VIRGINIA. 6 vols. Richmond: N. Pollard Printer, 1921.

O'Bannon, J. A., Comp. ACTS AND JOINT RESOLUTIONS PASSED BY THE GENERAL
ASSEMBLY OF THE STATE OF VIRGINIA PASSED DURING THE SESSION OF 1889–1890.
Richmond: Commonwealth of Virginia, 1890.

_____. ACTS AND JOINT RESOLUTIONS PASSED BY THE GENERAL ASSEMBLY OF THE
STATE OF VIRGINIA PASSED DURING THE SESSION OF 1893–1894. Richmond:
Commonwealth of Virginia, 1894.

_____. ACTS AND JOINT RESOLUTIONS PASSED BY THE GENERAL ASSEMBLY OF THE
STATE OF VIRGINIA PASSED DURING THE SESSION OF 1897–1898. Richmond:
Commonwealth of Virginia, 1898.

_____. ACTS AND JOINT RESOLUTIONS PASSED BY THE GENERAL ASSEMBLY OF THE
STATE OF VIRGINIA PASSED DURING THE SESSION OF 1899–1900. Richmond:
Commonwealth of Virginia, 1900.

_____. ACTS AND JOINT RESOLUTIONS PASSED BY THE GENERAL ASSEMBLY OF THE
STATE OF VIRGINIA PASSED DURING THE SESSION OF 1901. Richmond:
Commonwealth of Virginia, 1901.

_____. ACTS AND JOINT RESOLUTIONS PASSED BY THE GENERAL ASSEMBLY OF THE
STATE OF VIRGINIA PASSED DURING THE SESSION OF 1901–1902. Richmond:
Commonwealth of Virginia, 1902.

_____. ACTS AND JOINT RESOLUTIONS PASSED BY THE GENERAL ASSEMBLY OF THE
STATE OF VIRGINIA PASSED DURING THE SESSION OF 1902–1903–1904. Richmond:
Commonwealth of Virginia, 1904.

Palmer, William P., comp. CALENDAR OF VIRGINIA STATE PAPERS. 11 vols. New York:
Kraus Reprint, 1968.

Percy, George. "A Trewe Relacyon," VIRGINIA MAGAZINE OF HISTORY AND
BIOGRAPHY 4 (1922), 259–283.

_____. OBSERVATIONS GATHERED OUT OF A DISCOURSE OF THE PLANTATION OF THE
SOUTHERN COLONIE IN VIRGINIA BY THE ENGLISH, 1606. New York: AMS Press,
1965.

Pory, John. JOHN PORY, 1572–1636, THE LIFE AND LETTERS OF A MAN OF MANY
PARTS. Chapel Hill: University of North Carolina Press, 1977.

Randolph, Edmund. HISTORY OF VIRGINIA. Arthur H. Shaffer, ed. Charlottesville:
University Press of Virginia, 1970.

Rawson, E. K. et al., comp. OFFICIAL RECORDS OF THE UNION AND CONFEDERATE
NAVIES IN THE WAR OF THE REBELLION. Washington, D.C.: U. S. Government
Printing Office, 1898.

Rice, Howard C. trans. TRAVELS IN NORTH AMERICA IN THE YEARS 1780, 1781, AND
1782 BY THE MARQUIS CHASTELLEUX. Chapel Hill: University of North Carolina
Press, 1963.

Ritchie, William F., comp. ACTS OF THE GENERAL ASSEMBLY OF VIRGINIA PASSED IN 1855–1856. Richmond, Virginia General Assembly, 1856.

_____. ACTS AND JOINT RESOLUTIONS PASSED BY THE GENERAL ASSEMBLY OF THE STATE OF VIRGINIA PASSED DURING THE SESSION OF 1857–1858. Richmond: Commonwealth of Virginia, 1859.

_____. THE CODE OF VIRGINIA, 1860. Richmond: Dunnavent and Company, 1860.

_____. ACTS AND JOINT RESOLUTIONS PASSED BY THE GENERAL ASSEMBLY OF THE STATE OF VIRGINIA PASSED DURING THE SESSION OF 1861–1862. Richmond: Commonwealth of Virginia, 1862.

Rolfe, John. A TRUE RELATION OF THE STATE OF VIRGINIA LEFTE BY SIR THOMAS DALE KNIGHT IN MAY LAST 1616. Charlottesville: University Press of Virginia, 1957.

Salley, Alexander S., comp. NARRATIVES OF EARLY CAROLINA. New York: Barnes and Noble, 1911.

Schaffer, C. A., comp. ACTS AND JOINT RESOLUTIONS PASSED BY THE GENERAL ASSEMBLY OF THE STATE OF VIRGINIA PASSED DURING THE SESSION OF 1870–1871. Richmond: Commonwealth of Virginia, 1871.

Shelley, Fred. "The Journal of Ebenezer Hazard in Virginia, 1777," VIRGINIA MAGAZINE OF HISTORY AND BIOGRAPHY 62 (1954), 400–423.

Sheppherd, Samuel. THE STATUTES AT LARGE OF VIRGINIA. 3 vols. New York: AMS Press, 1970.

Simcoe, John G. A HISTORY OF THE OPERATIONS OF A PARTISAN CORPS CALLED THE QUEEN'S RANGERS. New York: Bartlett and Welford, 1844.

Smith, Annie L. THE QUITRENTS OF VIRGINIA. Gloucester County, Virginia: privately published, 1957.

Smith, John. TRAVELS AND WORKS OF CAPTAIN JOHN SMITH, PRESIDENT OF VIRGINIA AND ADMIRAL OF NEW ENGLAND, 1580–1631, Edward Arber, ed. 2 vols. Edinburgh: John Grant, 1910.

_____. TRAVELS AND WORKS OF CAPTAIN JOHN SMITH, PRESIDENT OF VIRGINIA AND ADMIRAL OF NEW ENGLAND, 1580–1631, Philip Barbour, ed. 3 vols. Chapel Hill: University of North Carolina Press, 1986.

Spotswood, Alexander. THE OFFICIAL LETTERS OF ALEXANDER SPOTSWOOD, R. A. Brock, ed. New York: AMS Press, 1973.

Stanard, William G., comp. "Instructions to Sir Francis Wyatt, January 1638/9," VIRGINIA MAGAZINE OF HISTORY AND BIOGRAPHY 11 (1904), 54–57.

_____. "Acts, Orders and Resolutions of the General Assembly of Virginia at Sessions of March 1643–1644," VIRGINIA MAGAZINE OF HISTORY AND BIOGRAPHY 23 (1915), 229–239,250– 254.

Story, Thomas. JOURNAL OF THE LIFE OF THOMAS STORY. London: no publisher listed, 1747.

Strachey, William. HISTORIE OF TRAVELL INTO VIRGINIA BRITANNIA, Louis B. Wright and Virginia Freund, eds. London: Hakluyt Society, 1953.

Tustin, Joseph P. trans., DIARY OF THE AMERICAN WAR, A HESSIAN JOURNAL: CAPTAIN JOHANN EWALD, FIELD JAGER CORPS. New Haven and London: Yale University Press, 1979.

Tyler, Lyon G., comp. NARRATIVES OF EARLY VIRGINIA. New York: Barnes and Noble, 1907.

Tyler, Lyon G., ed. "Diary of Miss Harriette Cary, Kept by Her from May 6, 1862 to July 24, 1862," TYLER'S QUARTERLY OF VIRGINIA HISTORY 9 (1928), 104–115.

U. S. Congress. THE REPORT OF THE JOINT COMMITTEE ON THE CONDUCT OF THE WAR, vol. 1. Washington, D.C.: U. S. Government Printing Office, 1863.

U. S. War Department (U.S.W.D.). THE WAR OF THE REBELLION: A COMPILATION OF THE OFFICIAL RECORDS OF THE UNION AND CONFEDERATE ARMIES. Robert N. Scott et al., comp. Washington, D.C.: U. S. Government Printing Office, 1891.

Virginia School Report. THE ANNUAL REPORT OF THE SUPERINTENDENT OF PUBLIC INSTRUCTION FOR THE YEAR ENDING JULY 31, 1885. R. U. Derr, Richmond: Superintendent of Public Printing, 1885.

_____. THE ANNUAL REPORT OF THE SUPERINTENDENT OF PUBLIC INSTRUCTION FOR THE YEAR ENDING JULY 31, 1908. Richmond: Superintendent of Public Printing, 1908.

Walker, Robert F., comp. ACTS AND JOINT RESOLUTIONS PASSED BY THE GENERAL ASSEMBLY OF THE STATE OF VIRGINIA PASSED DURING THE SESSION OF 1871–1872. Richmond: Commonwealth of Virginia, 1872.

Washington, George. THE WRITINGS OF GEORGE WASHINGTON FROM ORIGINAL MANUSCRIPT SOURCES, John C. Fitzpatrick, ed. Washington, D.C.: U. S. Government Printing Office, 1936.

West, George B. WHEN THE YANKEES CAME: CIVIL WAR AND RECONSTRUCTION ON THE VIRGINIA PENINSULA, Parke Rouse, Jr., ed. Richmond: Dietz Press, 1977.

Whitefield, George. GEORGE WHITEFIELD'S JOURNALS. Guildford, London: Billing and Sons, Ltd., 1960.

Winfree, Waverley K. THE LAWS OF VIRGINIA BEING A SUPPLEMENT TO HENING'S THE STATUTES AT LARGE, 1700–1750. Richmond: Virginia State Library, 1971.

Manuscripts

Ambler, Edward. Appraisal of Edward Ambler's estate, 1769. Transcript, Colonial Williamsburg Foundation Research Archives, Williamsburg.

Ambler, Eliza Jaquelin. Letter dated October 10, 1798. Microfilm, Colonial Williamsburg Foundation Research Archives, Williamsburg.

Ambler Family. John Ambler Papers, 1770–1860, James City, Louisa, Amherst, Henrico and Hanover Counties. Records of Antebellum Southern Plantations for the Revolution through the Civil War, Series E, Part 1. Microfilms, University of Virginia, Charlottesville.

Ambler, John Jaquelin. History of Ambler Family in Virginia, 1826. Microfilm on file at the Library of Virginia, Richmond.

_____. History of Ambler Family in Virginia, 1828. Alderman Library, University of Virginia, Charlottesville.

Ambler Manuscripts, 1636–1809. Originals, Library of Congress, Washington, D.C. Transcripts and microfilm, Colonial Williamsburg Foundation Research Archives, Williamsburg.

Ancteville, Chevalier de. Journal of the Chesapeake Campaign, 1781. Archives of the Navy No. B4–184. Transcript, Colonial Williamsburg Foundation Research Archives.

Anonymous. Passenger List of People to Virginia and Bermuda, [1620]. Ferrar Papers, Pepys Library, Cambridge University, Cambridge, England.

_____. The Sum total of all ye persons, cattle, corn, arms, houses and boats conteyned in the general muster of Virginia taken in ye beginning of March 1619 [1620]. Ferrar Papers, Pepys Library, Cambridge University, Cambridge, England.

_____. Number of People in Virginia; The number of Men in Virginia; Coppie of the totall sums of ye general muster of Virginia 1619 [1620]; The Sum of Cattle in Virginia. Ferrar Papers, Pepys Library, Cambridge University, Cambridge, England.

_____. Articles of Peace, [1680]. Virginia Records, 1606–1692, Papers of Thomas Jefferson, 8th Ser. 14:226–233. Microfilm, Colonial Williamsburg Foundation, Williamsburg.

Baker, Eliza. Memoirs of Williamsburg by Eliza Baker, born in Williamsburg, July 2, 1845. May 4, 1933, transcript. Colonial Williamsburg Foundation, Williamsburg.

Barraud, Dr. Philip. Letter to St. George Tucker, October 28, 1798. Transcript, Colonial Williamsburg Foundation Research Archives, Williamsburg.

Beaumont, Henry. Henry Beaumont Diary, September 6, 1817 to September [?], 1818. Transcript, Virginia Historical Society, Richmond.

Berkeley, William. April 18, 1663, letter to Lord ?. Egerton Manuscripts. Microfilm, Colonial Williamsburg Foundation Research Archives, Williamsburg.

British Public Records Office (B.P.R.O.). Colonial Office Papers, British Public Records Office, Kew, England, 1607–1781. Survey Reports and Microfilms, Colonial Williamsburg Foundation Research Archives, Williamsburg.

Bureau of Refugees. List of Confiscated Lands, 1862–1866. National Archives, Washington, D.C.

_____. Freedmen's Bureau Records, 1865–1867. Microfilm, National Archives, Washington, D.C.

Charles, John S. "Recollections," 1928. Transcript, Colonial Williamsburg Foundation, Williamsburg.

Clayton, John. Sketches of fences at Jamestown, 1685. Transcript, Colonial Williamsburg Foundation Research Archives, Williamsburg.

Cotter, John L. Notes on Nineteenth and Early Twentieth Century Jamestown as Reported by Mrs. H. L. Munger and Col. J. P. Barney, 1956. Jamestown Files, National Park Service Visitor Center, Jamestown.

Cronin, David E. The Vest Mansion, Its Historical and Romantic Associations as Confederate and Union Headquarters in the American Civil War, [1862–1865]. Transcript, Colonial Williamsburg Foundation, Williamsburg.

Custis, John Parke. Letter to George Washington, May 11, 1778. Microfilm, Virginia Historical Society, Richmond.

Eastern Lunatic Asylum Board of Directors. Minutes, 1869–1887; Annual Reports, 1869–1900. Colonial Williamsburg Foundation Research Archives, Williamsburg

Griesenauer, Paul M. The Reminiscences of Paul M. Griesenauer, 1956. Typescript, Colonial Williamsburg Foundation, Williamsburg.

Hall, Channing M. An Abstract of Title for Mr. Charles Norris Dozier, 1944. Original on file with Mrs. C. N. Dozier, Toano.

Harwood, Humphrey. Account Book, 1785. Colonial Williamsburg Foundation Research Archives, Williamsburg.

Hickory Neck Church. Bicentennial Celebration, October 28, 1934. Manuscript on file at Department of Special Collections, Swem Library, College of William and Mary, Williamsburg.

James City County Deeds, Wills, Orders, Legislative Petitions, Land Tax Lists, Personal Property Tax Lists, Agricultural Censuses, Censuses, Slave Schedules, Plats, 1745–1994. Various originals on file at the James City County Courthouse, Williamsburg, and the Library of Virginia, Richmond; microfilms, Colonial Williamsburg Foundation Research Archives, Williamsburg.

James City County School Commissioners. Abstracts of Petitions of School Commissioners and Abstracts of Accounts and Reports of School Commissioners, 1823–1860. Library of Virginia, Richmond.

James, Mrs. Lucy. Address given at Hickory Neck Church on October 28, 1934. Special Collections, Swem Library, College of William and Mary, Williamsburg.

Jeffreys, Herbert. Letter to the Rt. Honorable, June 11, 1677, Coventry Papers Vol 73, Bath 65, ff 64–65. Microfilm, Colonial Williamsburg Foundation, Williamsburg.

Jennings, John M. Address presented at Hickory Neck Church on October 28, 1934. Special Collections, Swem Library, College of William and Mary, Williamsburg.

Jones, Catesby ap Roger. May 3, 1861, letter to Captain H. N. Cocke. Virginia Historical Society, Richmond

_____. May 16, 1861, letter to Captain S. Barron. Virginia Historical Society, Richmond

_____. Report of Ordnance Experiments at Jamestown, October 12, 1861. Virginia Historical Society, Richmond

Kemp, Richard. Letter to Sir William and Sir John Berkeley, February 27, 1645. Clarendon Manuscript No. 24 ff 48–51. Bodeleian Library, Oxford University, Oxford.

King's Council. His Majesty's Council to Sir George Yeardley, December 18, 1618. Ferrar Papers, Pepsy Library, Cambridge University, Cambridge, England.

Lafayette, Marquis de. Certificate of services to Mr. Ludwell Lee, October 18, 1832. Microfilm, Colonial Williamsburg Foundation Research Archives, Williamsburg.

Lee, Victoria and Petricola. Williamsburg in 1861. Typescript, 1939, Colonial Williamsburg Foundation Research Archives, Williamsburg.

Lee Papers, 1638–1837. Manuscripts on file, Virginia Historical Society, Richmond.

Lee, William and Hannah Philippa. Deed of trust dated January 10, 1771, with Arthur Lee and Dr. Fleming Pinkston. Virginia Historical Society, Richmond.

Lovell, Mansfield. Account of Pedestrial Excursion, 1843. Huntington Library, San Marino, California.

Ludwell, Thomas. Letter to the Rt. Honorable, August 3, 1678. Coventry Papers 73, f 171. Microfilm, Colonial Williamsburg Foundation, Williamsburg.

Morris, Robert. Diary, January 14, 1845 through November 6, 1857. Virginia Historical Society, Richmond.

Olive Branch Church. Olive Branch Church Cemetery Notebooks and Record Books, 1833–1992. Olive Branch Christian Church, Norge.

Petersburg, City of. Hustings Court Will Book 1, 1795–1803. Microfilm, Library of Virginia, Richmond.

Public Service Claims 1776–1778. William Finnie's Accounts. Colonial Williamsburg Foundation, Williamsburg.

Rich, Sir Nathaniel. A Brief declaracon of Th'estate of the Plantacon in Virginia during the first twelve years, April–May 1623. Alderman Library, University of Virginia, Charlottesville.

_____. Rough draft of the charges presented to the Commissioners, July 12, 1623. Alderman Library, University of Virginia, Charlottesville.

Rolin, Mamie Bishop Letter to Georgie dated May 16, 1877. Virginia Historical Society, Richmond.

Smith, John et al. April 4, 1745 deed of John Smith and wife, Mary, and Martha Jaquelin, to Richard Ambler. New York Historical Society, New York.

Stirring, John. Letter to Mr. Ferrar, January 26, 1649/50. Ferrar Papers, Pepys Library, Cambridge University, Cambridge.

Strobia, John Henry. Diary, 1817. Virginia Historical Society, Richmond.

Sully, Robert. October 1854 letter to Lyman Draper. Wisconsin Historical Society, Madison, Wisconsin. Facsimiles of paintings and sketches on file at National Park Service Visitor Center, Jamestown.

Surry County Deeds, Orders, Wills, 1652–1700. Library of Virginia, Richmond.

U. S. Census Bureau. U. S. Census of Population for James City County, Williamsburg City, York County, 1910–1960. Typescript on file at James City County Historical Commission, Toano.

Virginia Land Office Patent Books 1623–1732. Microfilm on file at Library of Virginia, Richmond, and Colonial Williamsburg Foundation Research Archives, Williamsburg.

Virginia Navy Account Book and Papers, 1776–1784. Mariner's Museum, Newport News, Virginia.

Virginia Navy Board. Journal of the Navy Board, 1777. Mariner's Museum, Newport News, Virginia.

Virginia School Commissioners Abstracts of Accounts and Reports 1818–1863. 3 vols. Library of Virginia, Richmond.

_____. School Commissioners Reports 1823–1863. 3 vols. Library of Virginia, Richmond.

Williamsburg–James City County Tax Lists 1768–1769. Colonial Williamsburg Foundation Research Archives, Williamsburg.

Wynne, Thomas G. Farmer's Journal, 1861. Microfilm on file, Colonial Williamsburg Foundation, Williamsburg.

York County Deeds, Wills, Inventories, Legislative Petitions 1633–1839. Microfilms on file at Colonial Williamsburg Foundation Research Archives, Williamsburg.

Secondary Sources
Published Material

Allen, James H. "Our Confederate Column, the James City Cavalry." Letter to the editor of the RICHMOND DISPATCH, June 1, 1896. James City County Historical Commission files, Toano.

AMERICAN BEACON. AMERICAN BEACON, June 23, 1834, edition. Microfilm, Swem Library, College of William and Mary, Williamsburg.

American Medical Association. Report on the Number of Practitioners of Medicine in Virginia. TRANSACTIONS OF THE AMERICAN MEDICAL ASSOCIATION 1 (1847), 359–364.

American Petroleum Institute. POWER FARMING—A WAY OF LIFE. Undated booklet on file at James City County Historical Commission, Toano.

Andrews, K. R. "Christopher Newport of Limehouse, Mariner," WILLIAM AND MARY QUARTERLY, 3rd Ser., 11 (1954), 28–41.

Anonymous. "One Hundred Years of Agriculture." Undated clipping from unidentified newspaper on file at James City County Historical Commission, Toano.

_____. 1906 A Journal from Virginia beyond the Appalachian Mountains in September 1671. WILLIAM AND MARY QUARTERLY, 1st Ser., 15 (1906), 235.

Barbour, Philip. THE JAMESTOWN VOYAGES UNDER THE FIRST CHARTER, 1606–1609. 2 vols. Cambridge: University Press, 1969.

Barker, E. A., Jr. MAP OF JAMES RIVER AND VICINITY. Richmond: Virginia Historical Society, 1899.

Billings, Warren M. "The Growth of Political Institutions in Virginia from 1634 to 1676," WILLIAM AND MARY QUARTERLY, 3rd Ser., 31 (1974), 232–233.

_____. THE OLD DOMINION IN THE SEVENTEENTH CENTURY. Chapel Hill: University of North Carolina Press, 1975.

_____. JAMESTOWN AND THE FOUNDING OF THE NATION. Gettysburg, Pa: Thomas Publications, 1990.

Billings, Warren M. et al. COLONIAL VIRGINIA: A HISTORY. White Plains, N.Y.: KTO Press, 1986.

Boorstin, Daniel J. THE AMERICANS: THE COLONIAL EXPERIENCE. New York: Alfred A. Knoph and Random House, 1958.

Bowman, Jesse E. HISTORY, JAMES CITY AND JAMES RIVER BAPTIST CHURCHES. Williamsburg: The Trumpet Publishing Company, [ca. 1953].

Bradshaw, Nancy S., ed. TALES FROM JAMES CITY COUNTY, VIRGINIA, ORAL HISTORIES. Williamsburg: James City County Historical Commission, 1993.

Bradshaw, Nancy S. and Frances H. Hamilton. VELKOMMEN TIL NORGE. Williamsburg: Privately published, 1993.

Breeden, James O., ed. ADVICE AMONG MASTERS: THE IDEAL IN SLAVE MANAGEMENT IN THE OLD SOUTH. Westport, Conn.: Greenwood Press, 1980.

Breen, T. H. and Stephen Innes. MYNE OWNE GROUNDE. New York: Oxford University Press, 1980.

Brown, Alexander. THE GENESIS OF THE UNITED STATES. 2 vols. Boston and New York: Houghton, Mifflin and Company, 1890.

Bruce, Kathleen. "Virginian Agricultural Decline to 1860: A Fallacy," AGRICULTURAL HISTORY 6 (1932), 3–13.

Bruce, Philip A., ed. "Diary of Captain John Davis of the Pennsylvania Line," VIRGINIA MAGAZINE OF HISTORY AND BIOGRAPHY 1 (1894), 1–16.

_____. "Bacon's Rebellion," VIRGINIA MAGAZINE OF HISTORY AND BIOGRAPHY 1 (1894), 167–186.

_____. "Two Wills of the Seventeenth Century," VIRGINIA MAGAZINE OF HISTORY AND BIOGRAPHY 2 (1895), 174–175.

_____. "Culpeper's Report on Virginia in 1683," VIRGINIA MAGAZINE OF HISTORY AND BIOGRAPHY 3 (1896), 229.

_____. "Viewers of the Tobacco Crop," VIRGINIA MAGAZINE OF HISTORY AND BIOGRAPHY 5 (1897–1898), 119–123.

_____. "Vindication of Sir William Berkeley," VIRGINIA MAGAZINE OF HISTORY AND BIOGRAPHY 6 (189), 139–144.

Bruce, Philip A. SOCIAL LIFE IN VIRGINIA IN THE SEVENTEENTH CENTURY. Williamtown: Cornerhouse Publishers, 1907.

Burgess, Lewis W. VIRGINIA SOLDIERS OF 1776. Richmond: Richmond Press, Inc., 1929.

Bryan, John S. and E. G. Swem, eds. "Old Houses in James City County," WILLIAM AND MARY QUARTERLY, 2nd Ser., 14 (1937), 143–150.

Brydon, George M. VIRGINIA'S MOTHER CHURCH. Richmond: Whittet and Shepperson, 1947.

Brydon, George M., ed. "Virginia in 1726," VIRGINIA MAGAZINE OF HISTORY AND BIOGRAPHY 48 (1940), 141–153.

Buck, J. L. THE DEVELOPMENT OF PUBLIC SCHOOLS IN VIRGINIA, 1607–1952. Richmond: Virginia State Board of Education, 1952.

Bullock, Thomas K. SCHOOLS AND SCHOOLING IN EIGHTEENTH CENTURY VIRGINIA. Durham: Duke University, 1961.

Byrd, Rawls. HISTORY OF PUBLIC SCHOOLS IN WILLIAMSBURG. Williamsburg: Privately published, 1968.

Byrd, William. THE SECRET DIARY OF WILLIAM BYRD OF WESTOVER, 1709–1712, Louis B. Wright and Marion Tinling, eds. Richmond: Dietz Press, 1941.

Carrier, Lyman. AGRICULTURE IN VIRGINIA, 1607–1699. Charlottesville: University Press of Virginia, 1957.

Carson, Cary et al. Impermanent Architecture in the Southern American Colonies. WINTERTHUR PORTFOLIO 16 (1982), 135–196.

Carson, Jane. BACON'S REBELLION 1676–1976. Jamestown: Jamestown–Yorktown Foundation, 1976.

Catton, Bruce. THE AMERICAN HERITAGE PICTURE HISTORY OF THE CIVIL WAR. New York: American Heritage Publishing Co., 1960.

Chandler, J. A. C. et al., eds. "Journal of the Lt. Governor's Travels, Expeditions Undertaken for the Public Service of Virginia," WILLIAM AND MARY QUARTERLY, 2nd Ser., 3 (1923), 40–45.

_____. "George Wilson," WILLIAM AND MARY QUARTERLY 2nd Ser., 5 (1925), 266–267.

Cocke, Charles. DIOCESE OF SOUTHERN VIRGINIA. Richmond: Virginia State Library, 1964.

Clingan, Susan. THE HISTORY OF THE NAVAL WEAPONS STATION, YORKTOWN, VIRGINIA. Yorktown: Naval Weapons Station, 1961.

Colonial Williamsburg Foundation. WOLSTENHOLME TOWNE IN MARTIN'S HUNDRED AT CARTER'S GROVE. Undated pamphlet, Carter's Grove Museum, Grove.

_____. RESOURCE PROTECTION PROCESS FOR JAMES CITY, YORK COUNTY, WILLIAMSBURG AND POQUOSON, VIRGINIA, DRAFT REPORT II. Williamsburg: Colonial Williamsburg Foundation, 1985.

Commonwealth of Virginia Statistics. GENERAL BASIC DATA FOR COUNTY PROGRAM DEVELOPMENT, 1930–1960. James City County Historical Commission, Toano.

Cotter, John L. ARCHAEOLOGICAL EXCAVATIONS AT JAMESTOWN VIRGINIA. Washington, D.C.: National Park Service, 1958.

Craven, Wesley Frank. THE VIRGINIA COMPANY OF LONDON, 1606–1624. University Press of Virginia, Charlottesville, 1957.

_____. THE SOUTHERN COLONIES IN THE SEVENTEENTH CENTURY 1607–1689. Baton Rouge: Louisiana State University Press, 1970.

Dabney, Virginius. VIRGINIA. Charlottesville: University Press of Virginia, 1971.

Dauphine, Durand de. A HUGUENOT EXILE IN VIRGINIA: A BRIEF DESCRIPTION OF AMERICA WITH A LONGER ONE OF VIRGINIA AND MARYLAND, Gilbert Chinard, trans. Press of the Pioneers: New York, 1934.

Donald, David H. GONE FOR A SOLDIER: THE CIVIL WAR MEMOIRS OF PRIVATE ALFRED BELLARD. Boston: Little, Brown and Co., 1975.

Donnelly, Ralph W. "The Confederate Marines at Drewry's Bluff," VIRGINIA CAVALCADE 26 (1966), 42–47.

Dorsey, Susie. A HISTORY OF THE WILLIAMSBURG BAPTIST CHURCH, 1828–1978. Williamsburg: The Williamsburg Press, Inc., 1978.

Egloff, Keith and Deborah Woodward. FIRST PEOPLE: THE EARLY INDIANS OF VIRGINIA. Richmond: Virginia Department of Historic Resources, 1992.

Force, Peter, comp. TRACTS AND OTHER PAPERS, RELATING TO THE ORIGIN, SETTLEMENT AND PROGRESS OF THE COLONIES IN NORTH AMERICA. 4 vols. Gloucester, Mass.: Peter Smith, 1963.

Gaines, William H. "The Courthouses of James City County," VIRGINIA CAVALCADE Vol. 18 No. 4 (1969), 4–30.

Gee, Madeline. GROVE FESTIVAL: A BICENTENNIAL EVENT, JULY 31, 1976. Toano: James City County Historical Commission, 1976.

Godson, Susan H., et al. THE COLLEGE OF WILLIAM AND MARY: A HISTORY. Williamsburg: King and Queen Press, The Society of the Alumni, 1993.

Grace Baptist Church. THE HISTORY OF GRACE BAPTIST CHURCH, 1952–1986. Williamsburg: privately published, 1986.

Hakluyt, Richard. THE PRINCIPAL NAVIGATIONS, VOYAGES, TRAFFIQUES AND DISCOVERIES OF THE ENGLISH NATION. New York: August M. Kelley, 1969.

Hall, Jean P. et al. "Legislative Petitions from Virginia Counties with Significant Record Losses, No. 3, James City County," MAGAZINE OF VIRGINIA GENEALOGY 29 (1991), 154.

Hatch, Charles E. "Jamestown and the Revolution," WILLIAM AND MARY QUARTERLY, 2nd Ser., 22 (1942), 30–38.

_____. "The Affair Near Jamestown Island, July 6, 1781," VIRGINIA MAGAZINE OF HISTORY AND BIOGRAPHY 53 (1945), 170–196.

_____. THE FIRST SEVENTEEN YEARS: VIRGINIA, 1607–1624. Charlottesville: University Press of Virginia, 1957.

Heatwole, Cornelius J. A HISTORY OF EDUCATION IN VIRGINIA. New York: Macmillan Company, 1916.

Headley, Robert K., Jr. GENEALOGICAL ABSTRACTS FROM 18TH CENTURY VIRGINIA NEWSPAPERS. Baltimore: Genealogical Publishing Company, 1987.

Hotten, John C. ORIGINAL LISTS OF PERSONS OF QUALITY, 1600–1700. Baltimore: Genealogical Publishing Company, 1980.

Housing Partnerships, Inc. NEIGHBORS HELPING NEIGHBORS. Williamsburg: privately published, undated pamphlet.

Howe, Henry. HISTORICAL RECOLLECTIONS OF VIRGINIA. Charleston: E. Peters, 1845.

Hunter, Charles M. CIVILIAN CONSERVATION CORPS (C.C.C.) IN WILLIAMSBURG, 1933–1942. Williamsburg: Williamsburg Area Historical Society Historical Monograph No. 1, 1990.

Hunter, Robert R. Jr. PHASE I ARCHAEOLOGICAL SURVEY OF THE HUNT BROOKS, INC. DEVELOPMENT, JAMES CITY COUNTY, VIRGINIA. Williamsburg: privately printed, 1988.

Jarrett, Devereux. "The Life of the Rev. Devereux Jarrett," WILLIAM AND MARY QUARTERLY, 3rd Ser., 3 (1909), 346–393.

Jeffrey, Tina C. THE BIZARRE BAZAAR: THE STORY OF THE WILLIAMSBURG POTTERY. Williamsburg: Jeffrey Publishing Company, 1982.

Kale, Wilford. HARK UPON THE GALE. Norfolk: Donning Publishing Company, 1985.

Katz, William L. THE NEGRO IN VIRGINIA. New York: Arno Press and the New York Times, 1969.

Kukla, Jon. POLITICAL INSTITUTIONS IN VIRGINIA, 1619–1660. New York: Garland, 1985.

Lebsock, Suzanne. A SHARE OF HONOUR: VIRGINIA WOMEN 1600–1945. Charlottesville: Virginia Women's Cultural History Project, 1985.

Lederer, John. THE DISCOVERIES OF JOHN LEDERER, William P. Cummings, ed. Charlottesville, and Wachovia Historical Society, Winston–Salem, North Carolina: University of Virginia Press, 1958.

Leonard, Cynthia M., comp. THE GENERAL ASSEMBLY OF VIRGINIA, JULY 30, 1619 – JANUARY 11, 1978, A BICENTENNIAL REGISTER OF MEMBERS. Richmond: Virginia State Library Board, 1978.

Little, Lewis P. IMPRISONED PREACHERS AND RELIGIOUS LIBERTY IN VIRGINIA. Lynchburg: J. P. Bell Co., 1938.

Long, E. B. THE CIVIL WAR, DAY BY DAY, AN ALMANAC, 1861–1865. Garden City, N. J: Doubleday and Co., 1971.

Lossing, Benjamin. PICTORIAL FIELDBOOK OF THE AMERICAN REVOLUTION. 2 vols. New York: Harper and Brothers, 1851–1852.

Maddox, William A. THE FREE SCHOOL IDEA IN VIRGINIA BEFORE THE CIVIL WAR. New York: Columbia University Press, 1918.

Manerin, Louis H. "A Building . . . for the Preservation of the Public Records," VIRGINIA CAVALCADE Vol. 23 No. 1 (1974), 22–31.

Manerin, Louis and Clifford Dowdey. THE HISTORY OF HENRICO COUNTY. Charlottesville: University Press of Virginia, 1984.

Matica, Mildred. TALL TALES AND TRUE OF JAMES CITY COUNTY. Williamsburg: privately printed, 1976.

Maxwell, William, ed. "The Marquis de La Fayette's Movements and Operations in Virginia in 1781," VIRGINIA HISTORICAL REGISTER VI (1853), 200–205.

_____. "Jamestown," VIRGINIA HISTORICAL REGISTER 2 (1849), 138–139.

_____. "Original Letters," VIRGINIA HISTORICAL REGISTER 3 (1850), 25–29.

_____. "Lord Cornwallis's Movements and Operations in Virginia in 1781," VIRGINIA HISTORICAL REGISTER 6 (1853), 181–190.

McCartney, Martha W. "Seventeenth Century Apartheid: The Suppression and Containment of Indians in Tidewater Virginia," JOURNAL OF MIDDLE ATLANTIC ARCHAEOLOGY, Vol. 1 (October l985).

_____. "Cockacoeske, Queen of Pamunkey: Diplomat and Suzeraine," POWHATAN'S MANTLE: INDIANS IN THE COLONIAL SOUTHEAST, Peter H. Wood et al., eds. Lincoln and London: University of Nebraska Press, 1989

McClellan, George B. THE CIVIL WAR PAPERS OF GEORGE B. MCCLELLAN, Stephen W. Sears, ed. New York: Ticknor and Fields, 1989.

McDaid, Christopher et al. A PHASE I CULTURAL RESOURCE SURVEY OF THE UNDERGRADUATE HOUSING PROJECT, COLLEGE OF WILLIAM AND MARY, WILLIAMSBURG. Williamsburg: William and Mary Center for Archaeological Research, the College of William and Mary, 1991.

McDonald, Bradley M. et al. CAST DOWN YOUR BUCKET WHERE YOU ARE: AN ETHNOHISTORICAL STUDY OF THE AFRICAN–AMERICAN COMMUNITY ON THE LANDS OF THE YORKTOWN NAVAL WEAPONS STATION, 1865–1918. Norfolk: Atlantic Division, Naval Facilities Engineering Command, 1992.

McKnight, John L. "Comets," WILLIAM AND MARY (Summer 1985).

Meade, Bishop William. OLD CHURCHES, MINISTERS AND FAMILIES OF VIRGINIA. 2 vols. Baltimore:Genealogical Publishing Company, 1966.

Meyer, Virginia M. and John F. Dorman, eds. ADVENTURERS OF PURSE AND PERSON, 1607–1624/25. Richmond: Dietz Press, 1987.

Michie, P.S. GENERAL MCCLELLAN. New York: D. Appleton & Co., 1915.

Middleton, Arthur P. TOBACCO COAST: A MARITIME HISTORY OF THE CHESAPEAKE BAY IN THE COLONIAL ERA. Newport News: Mariner's Museum, 1953.

Miller, Francis I., ed. THE PHOTOGRAPHIC HISTORY OF THE CIVIL WAR. 10 vols. New York: Review of Reviews Co., 1911.

Minchinton, Walter et al., eds. VIRGINIA SLAVE–TRADE STATISTICS, 1698–1775. Richmond: Virginia State Library, 1984.

Moore, Frank, comp. SONGS AND BALLADS OF THE REVOLUTION. London: D. Appleton and Company, 1856.

_____. THE CIVIL WAR IN SONG AND STORY, 1860–1865. New York: P. F. Collier, Publisher, 1889.

Morgan, Edmund. AMERICAN SLAVERY, AMERICAN FREEDOM: THE ORDEAL OF COLONIAL VIRGINIA. New York: W. W. Norton, 1975.

Morgan, Philip D. "The Ethnic Heritage of James City County," WHERE AMERICA BEGAN: JAMES CITY COUNTY, 1634–1984. Williamsburg: James City County Board of Supervisors, 1984.

_____. BLACK EDUCATION IN JAMES CITY COUNTY, 1619–1985. Williamsburg: Williamsburg–James City County Public Schools and the Virginia Foundation for the Humanities, 1985.

Morrison, A. J. THE BEGINNING OF PUBLIC EDUCATION IN VIRGINIA, 1776–1815. Richmond: Superintendent of Public Printing, 1917.

Morton, Richard L. THE NEGRO IN VIRGINIA POLITICS, 1865–1902. Charlottesville: University Press of Virginia, 1919.

_____. COLONIAL VIRGINIA. Chapel Hill: University of North Carolina Press, 1956.

Nash, Gary B. RED, WHITE AND BLACK: THE PEOPLES OF EARLY AMERICA. Englewood Cliffs, N.J.: Prentice–Hall, Inc., 1974.

National Park Service. CONSERVING RICHMOND'S BATTLEFIELDS. Denver: National Park Service, 1990.

Netherton, Nan, et al. FAIRFAX COUNTY, VIRGINIA, A HISTORY. Fairfax: Fairfax County Board of Supervisors, 1992.

Neville, John D. BACON'S REBELLION. Richmond: Virginia State Library, 1976.

Noel–Hume, Ivor. 1775: ANOTHER PART OF THE FIELD. New York: Alfred A. Knoph, 1966.

_____. MARTIN'S HUNDRED. Charlottesville: University Press of Virginia, 1982.

NORFOLK AND PORTSMOUTH DAILY ADVERTISER. NORFOLK AND PORTSMOUTH DAILY ADVERTISER, June 26, 1834, edition. Microfilm, Swem Library, College of William and Mary, Williamsburg.

Nugent, Nell M. CAVALIERS AND PIONEERS: ABSTRACTS OF VIRGINIA LAND PATENTS AND GRANTS. 3 vols. Richmond: Dietz Press and Baltimore: Genealogical Publishing Company, 1969–1979.

O'Dell, Jeffrey M. CHESTERFIELD COUNTY: EARLY ARCHITECTURE AND HISTORY. Chesterfield: Chesterfield County Board of Supervisors, 1982.

Outlaw, Alain C. GOVERNOR'S LAND: ARCHAEOLOGY OF EARLY SEVENTEENTH CENTURY VIRGINIA SETTLEMENTS. Charlottesville: University Press of Virginia, 1990.

PENNSYLVANIA GAZETTE, 1774–1780. Synopses on file, Colonial Williamsburg Foundation Research Archives, Williamsburg.

Perry, William S., comp. HISTORICAL COLLECTIONS RELATING TO THE AMERICAN COLONIAL CHURCH. Vol. I, Virginia. New York: AMS Press, 1969.

Porter, Albert O. COUNTY GOVERNMENT IN VIRGINIA: A LEGISLATIVE HISTORY, 1607–1904. New York: Columbia University Press, 1947.

Purchas, Samuel, comp. HAKLUYTUS POSTHUMUS OR PURCHAS HIS PILGRIMES. Glasgow: Hakluyt Society, 1926.

Quinn, David B. ROANOKE VOYAGES, 1584–1590: DOCUMENTS TO ILLUSTRATE THE ENGLISH VOYAGES TO NORTH AMERICA. London: Hakluyt Society, 1955.

_____. ENGLAND AND THE DISCOVERY OF AMERICA, 1418–1620. New York: Hakluyt Society, 1973.

_____. NORTH AMERICA FROM EARLIEST DISCOVERY TO FIRST SETTLEMENT, THE NORSE VOYAGES TO 1612. New York: Hakluyt Society, 1977.

Rankin, Hugh F. THE AMERICAN REVOLUTION. New York: Capricorn Books, 1964.

Raschal, William M. E., ed. "The Jamestown Celebration of 1857," VIRGINIA MAGAZINE OF HISTORY AND BIOGRAPHY 66 (1958), 259–271.

Reese, George H. THE CORNWALLIS PAPERS: ABSTRACTS OF AMERICANA. Charlottesville: University Press of Virginia, 1970.

Reps, John W. TIDEWATER TOWNS IN COLONIAL VIRGINIA. Princeton: Princeton University, 1972.

Rice, Howard C. et al. THE AMERICAN CAMPAIGNS OF ROCHAMBEAU'S ARMY. 2 vols. Princeton: Princeton University, 1972.

RICHMOND DISPATCH. RICHMOND DISPATCH, May 25, 1822, edition. Transcription, Colonial National Historical Park, Jamestown.

RICHMOND NEWS LEADER. RICHMOND NEWS LEADER, Untitled article, July 27, 1938, edition. Microfilm, Swem Library, College of William and Mary, Williamsburg.

RICHMOND TIMES–DISPATCH. RICHMOND TIMES–DISPATCH, September 26, 1965, edition. Microfilm, Swem Library, College of William and Mary, Williamsburg.

Robinson, W. Stitt. MOTHER EARTH, LAND GRANTS IN VIRGINIA, 1607–1699. Charlottesville: University Press of Virginia, 1957.

Robertson, James I. CIVIL WAR VIRGINIA: BATTLEGROUND FOR A NATION. Charlottesville and London: University Press of Virginia, 1991

Rodenbough, Theodore F. THE PHOTOGRAPHIC HISTORY OF THE CIVIL WAR. 5 vols. Secaucus, N. J.: The Blue and Grey Press, 1987.

Rountree, Helen C. POCAHONTAS' PEOPLE: THE POWHATAN INDIANS OF VIRGINIA. Norman, Oklahoma: University of Oklahoma Press, 1990.

Rouse, Parke. "James City County's Records and Their Burning in 1865," WHERE AMERICA BEGAN: JAMES CITY COUNTY, 1634–1984. Williamsburg: James City County Board of Supervisors, 1984.

_____. "Virginia quakes have been no great shakes," DAILY PRESS. August 15, 1993, edition.

Ruffner, William H. et al. THE EDUCATIONAL JOURNAL OF VIRGINIA: ORIGIN OF THE EDUCATIONAL ASSOCIATION. 12 vols. Richmond: Educational Publishing House, 1871–1885.

Ruffin, Edmund. THE FARMER'S REGISTER 9 (1841), 710–711. Untitled excerpt, Virginia Department of Historic Resources, Richmond.

Russell, John H. THE FREE NEGRO IN VIRGINIA. New York: Dover Publications, Inc., 1969.

Sainsbury, William Noel et al., comp. CALENDAR OF STATE PAPERS, COLONIAL SERIES, AMERICA AND THE WEST INDIES. 22 vols. Vaduz: Kraus Reprint, 1964.

Saint–Mery, Moreau de. "Norfolk, Portsmouth and Gosport as seen by Moreau de Saint Mery in March, April and May 1794," VIRGINIA MAGAZINE OF HISTORY AND BIOGRAPHY 48 (1940), 263.

Salmond, John A. THE CIVILIAN CONSERVATION CORPS, 1933–1942: A NEW DEAL CASE STUDY. Durham: Duke University Press, 1967.

Sams, Conway. THE CONQUEST OF VIRGINIA, THE SECOND ATTEMPT. Norfolk: Keyser–Doherty Company, 1929.

Sauer, Carl O. SIXTEENTH CENTURY NORTH AMERICA. Berkeley: University of California Press, 1975.

Selby, John E. CHRONOLOGY OF VIRGINIA AND THE WAR OF INDEPENDENCE. Charlottesville: University Press of Virginia, 1973.

_____. REVOLUTION IN VIRGINIA: 1775–1783. Charlottesville: University Press of Virginia, 1988.

Selig, Robert A. Letter to David F. Riggs, March 18, 1993. National Park Service, Jamestown.

Shepperson, Archibald B. JOHN PARADISE AND LUCY LUDWELL OF LONDON AND WILLIAMSBURG. Richmond: Dietz Press, 1942.

Stanard, William G., ed. "Letters of Lafayette," VIRGINIA MAGAZINE OF HISTORY AND BIOGRAPHY 6 (1899), 55–59.

_____. "Notes and Queries: Management of Slaves in 1672 from the Records of Surry County," VIRGINIA MAGAZINE OF HISTORY AND BIOGRAPHY 7 (1900), 314–335.

_____. "Virginia Assembly of 1641: A List of Members and Some of the Acts," VIRGINIA MAGAZINE OF HISTORY AND BIOGRAPHY 9 (1902), 50–59.

_____. "Surrender of Virginia to the Parliamentary Commissioners, March 1651–1652," VIRGINIA MAGAZINE OF HISTORY AND BIOGRAPHY 11 (1904), 32–41.

_____. "Proceedings of the Virginia Historical Society," VIRGINIA MAGAZINE OF HISTORY AND BIOGRAPHY 14 (1907), iii–xxii.

_____. "Historical and Genealogical Notes and Queries," VIRGINIA MAGAZINE OF HISTORY AND BIOGRAPHY 16 (1908), 199–211.

_____. "The Randolph Manuscript," VIRGINIA MAGAZINE OF HISTORY AND BIOGRAPHY 17 (1909), 337–351.

_____. "Travis Family," WILLIAM AND MARY QUARTERLY, 1st Ser., 18 (1909), 141–145.

_____. "Virginia Legislative Papers," VIRGINIA MAGAZINE OF HISTORY AND BIOGRAPHY 18 (1910), 140–150.

_____. "Philip Ludwell to Edward Jenings, 1709, In Regard to a Negro Plot," VIRGINIA MAGAZINE OF HISTORY AND BIOGRAPHY 19 (1911), 250–254.

_____. "Miscellaneous Colonial Documents," VIRGINIA MAGAZINE OF HISTORY AND BIOGRAPHY 20 (1912), 23–32.

_____. "Historical Notes and Queries," VIRGINIA MAGAZINE OF HISTORY AND BIOGRAPHY 21 (1913), 319.

_____. "Virginia in 1677," Virginia Magazine of History and Biography 21 (1913), 370.

_____. "Appraisal of Estate of Philip Ludwell," Virginia Magazine of History and BiographyY 21 (1913), 395–416.

_____. "Virginia Gleanings in England," Virginia Magazine of History and Biography 13 (1915), 195–196.

_____. "Report of the Journey of Francis Louis Michel," Virginia Magazine of History and Biography 24 (1916), 1–43.

_____. "Letters of William Byrd, First," Virginia Magazine of History and Biography 26 (1918), 17–31.

_____. "Jones Papers," Virginia Magazine of History and Biography 26 (1918), 179.

_____. "Notes to Council Journals," Virginia Magazine of History and Biography 33 (1925), 183–193.

_____. "Proprietors of the Northern Neck," Virginia Magazine of History and Biography33 (1925), 352.

_____. "Draft for the Creation of a Bishoprick in Virginia," Virginia Magazine of History and Biography 36 (1928), 45–53.

_____. "Genealogy," Virginia Magazine of History and Biography 36 (1928), 7–101.

_____. "Some Notes on Green Spring," Virginia Magazine of History and Biography 37 (1929), 289.

Stanard, William G. and Mary. The Colonial Virginia Register. Baltimore: Genealogical Publishing Company, 1965.

Stephenson, Mary A. Carter's Grove Plantation: A History. Williamsburg: Colonial Williamsburg Foundation, 1964.

Stewart, Robert A. History Of The Virginia Navy. Richmond: Mitchell and Hotchkiss Printers, 1923.

Stryker, H. M. Thanks For The Memory. Williamsburg: privately published, undated.

Swem, E. G. "Some Notes on the Four Forms of the Oldest Buildings of William and Mary College," William And Mary Quarterly, 2nd Ser., 8 (1928), 217–307.

Tate, Thad W. The Negro In Eighteenth Century Williamsburg. Williamsburg: Colonial Williamsburg Foundation, 1965.

Tate, Thad and David Ammerman, eds. The Chesapeake in the Seventeenth Century. University of North Carolina Press, Chapel Hill, 1979.

Thatcher, James. MILITARY JOURNAL OF THE AMERICAN REVOLUTION. Hartford, Conn.: Hurlbut, William and Co., 1862.

Tindall, George B. AMERICA: A NARRATIVE HISTORY. New York and London: W. W. Norton and Company, 1984.

Travis, Robert J. THE TRAVIS (TRAVERS) FAMILY AND ITS ALLIES. Savannah, Ga.: privately published, 1954.

Trigger, Bruce G., ed. HANDBOOK OF NORTH AMERICAN INDIANS: NORTHEAST, Vol. 15. Washington, D.C.: Smithsonian Institution, 1978.

Trollope, Frances. DOMESTIC MANNERS OF AMERICANS. New York: Knoph, Inc., 1949.

Turner, Charles W. "Virginia Agricultural Reform, 1815–1860," AGRICULTURAL HISTORY 26 (1952), 80–89.

Tyler, Lyon G. THE CRADLE OF THE REPUBLIC. Richmond: The Hermitage Press, Inc., 1906.

_____. WILLIAMSBURG: THE OLD COLONIAL CAPITAL. Williamsburg: College of William and Mary, 1928.

Tyler, Lyon G., ed. "Ludwell Family," WILLIAM AND MARY QUARTERLY, 1st Ser., 1 (1893), 209–210.

_____. "Historical and Genealogical Notes," WILLIAM AND MARY QUARTERLY, 1st Ser., 4 (1895–1896), 65–69.

_____. "Personal Notices from the VIRGINIA GAZETTE," WILLIAM AND MARY QUARTERLY, 1st Ser., 5 (1896), 240–244.

_____. "Providence Forge," WILLIAM AND MARY QUARTERLY, 1st Ser., 5 (1896), 20–21.

_____. "The Armistead Family," WILLIAM AND MARY QUARTERLY, 1st Ser., 7 (1897–1898), 226–234.

_____. "Glimpses of Old College Life," WILLIAM AND MARY QUARTERLY, 1st Ser., 8 (1899–1900), 213–227.

_____. "Two Tragical Events: Schepps-togt von Anthony Chester in Virginia, gedaan in het jaar 1620," WILLIAM AND MARY QUARTERLY, 1st Ser., 9 (1900–1901), 203–214.

_____. "Jamestown Island in 1861," WILLIAM AND MARY QUARTERLY, 1st Ser., 10 (1901–1902), 38–39.

_____. "Historical and Genealogical Notes," WILLIAM AND MARY QUARTERLY, 1st Ser., 10 (1901–1902), 141–144.

_____. "Extracts From the Records of Surry County," WILLIAM AND MARY QUARTERLY, 1st Ser., 11 (1902), 79–87.

_____. "Historical and Genealogical Notes," WILLIAM AND MARY QUARTERLY 1st Ser., 16 (1907–1908), 139–142.

_____. "Williamsburg Caricature," TYLER'S QUARTERLY OF VIRGINIA HISTORY 3 (1921), 164–165.

_____. "The Burning of Green Spring," TYLER'S QUARTERLY OF VIRGINIA HISTORY 10 (1929), 176–177.

United Daughters of the Confederacy (U.D.C.). WILLIAMSBURG IN THE CIVIL WAR. Williamsburg: privately published, undated.

U. S. Department of Agriculture (U.S.D.A.). ABRIDGED LIST OF FEDERAL LAWS APPLICABLE TO AGRICULTURE, 1949. Booklet on file at James City County Historical Commission, Toano.

_____. "Status of Virginia Agriculture in 1870," REPORT OF THE COMMISSIONER OF AGRICULTURE, 1870. Washington, D.C.: U. S. Government Printing Office, 1870.

Van Schreeven, William J. THE CONVENTIONS AND CONSTITUTIONS OF VIRGINIA, 1776–1966. Richmond: Virginia State Library, 1967.

Van Schreeven, William J. et al. REVOLUTIONARY VIRGINIA: THE ROAD TO INDEPENDENCE. 8 vols. Charlottesville: University Press of Virginia, 1973–1979.

VIRGINIA GAZETTE, 1736–1996. Williamsburg, various publishers. Microfilm, facsimiles and originals on file, Colonial Williamsburg Foundation Research Archives, Williamsburg.

VIRGINIA GAZETTE. VIRGINIA GAZETTE DIRECTORY, [1898–1899]. Colonial Williamsburg Foundation Research Archives, Williamsburg.

VIRGINIA GAZETTE AND GENERAL ADVERTISER, 1784–1794. Richmond. Microfilm, facsimiles and originals on file, Colonial Williamsburg Foundation Research Archives, Williamsburg.

Virginia Education Association (V.E.A.). "School History of James City County," THE VIRGINIA JOURNAL OF EDUCATION 2 (1908–1909), 33–35.

_____. "School News: The Consolidated High School at Toano," THE VIRGINIA JOURNAL OF EDUCATION. 22 (1928), 439–442.

Wallis, Helen. RALEIGH AND ROANOKE. Raleigh: North Carolina Department of Archives and History, 1985.

Washburn, Wilcomb E. THE GOVERNOR AND THE REBEL: A HISTORY OF BACON'S REBELLION IN VIRGINIA. New York: W. W. Norton, 1972.

Weaver, Bettie W. Nineteenth Century Education in Western Chesterfield County. VIRGINIA CAVALCADE 25 (1975), 38–47.

Webb, Alexander S. THE PENINSULA: MCCLELLAN'S CAMPAIGN OF 1862. New York: Charles Scribner's Sons, 1881.

Wertenbaker, Thomas J., comp. THE PLANTERS OF COLONIAL VIRGINIA. Princeton: Princeton University Press, 1922.

Wiley, Bell I. EMBATTLED CONFEDERATES, AN ILLUSTRATED HISTORY OF SOUTHERNERS AT WAR. New York: Harper and Row, 1964.

Williams, Neville. "The Tribulations of John Bland, Merchant," VIRGINIA MAGAZINE OF HISTORY AND BIOGRAPHY 72 (1964), 19–41.

Williamsburg Reunion. WILLIAMSBURG REUNION, 1942 AND BEFORE; 1944 AND BEFORE; 1950 AND BEFORE. Williamsburg: privately printed, 1982–1990.

Yanich, Beverly. Changing Land Use Practices, 1634–1984. WHERE AMERICA BEGAN: JAMES CITY COUNTY, 1634–1984. Williamsburg: James City County Board of Supervisors, 1984.

Yetter, George H. WILLIAMSBURG BEFORE AND AFTER. Williamsburg: Colonial Williamsburg Foundation, 1988.

Yonge, Samuel H. THE SITE OF OLD JAMES TOWN, 1607–1698. Richmond: L. H. Jenkins, Inc., 1904.

Manuscripts

Barrow, Robert M. "Williamsburg and Norfolk: Municipal Government and Justice in Colonial Virginia," 1960. Master's thesis, History Department, College of William and Mary, Williamsburg.

Carson, Jane, comp. "We Were There: Descriptions of Williamsburg, 1699–1859," 1961. Typescript, Colonial Williamsburg Foundation, Williamsburg.

Chapman, Anne W. "Benjamin Stoddert Ewell: A Biography," 1984. Master's thesis, History Department, College of William and Mary, Williamsburg.

Chickahominy Baptist Church. "History of the Chickahominy Baptist Church," undated. Typescript on file with James City County Historical Commission, Toano.

Cook, Barbra M. "Sheriffs of James City Countie," 1994. Typescript, James City County Sheriff's Office, Williamsburg.

Davis, Emma Jo. "Mulberry Island and the Civil War, April 1861–May 1862," 1967. Fort Eustis Historical and Archaeological Association. Fort Eustis, Newport News.

Edwards, Edith. "Short History of St. Martin's Church, Williamsburg, Virginia," 1989. Typescript on file with James City County Historical Commission, Toano.

Faith Baptist Church. "History of Faith Baptist Church," 1991. Typescript on file with James City County Historical Commission, Toano.

First Church of Christ, Scientist. "First Church of Christ, Scientist, Historical Sketch," 1991. Typescript on file with James City County Historical Commission, Toano.

Fort Eustis Historical and Archaeological Association. "The History of Mulberry Island, Newport News, Virginia," undated. Typescript, Fort Eustis, Newport News.

Gibbs, Patricia A. and Linda H. Rowe. "The Public Hospital, 1766–1885 [Eastern State Hospital]," 1974. Manuscript, Colonial Williamsburg Foundation, Williamsburg.

Goodwin, Mary. "Kingsmill Plantation," 1972. Colonial Williamsburg Foundation, Williamsburg.

Greensprings Chapel. "A Sketch of Greensprings Chapel," 1992. Typescript on file with James City County Historical Commission, Toano.

Jamestown Presbyterian Church. "Jamestown Presbyterian Church," 1970. Manuscript, Virginia Department of Historic Resources, Richmond.

Kettenburg, Carol Ann. "The Battle of Williamsburg," 1980. Master's thesis, History Department, College of William and Mary, Williamsburg.

Majeske, Penelope K. "Your Obedient Servant: The United States Army in Virginia During Reconstruction," 1980. Dissertation, Wayne State University, Detroit.

McCartney, Martha W. "History of Green Spring Plantation, James City County, Virginia," 1990. Bush Construction Inc., Williamsburg.

McCartney, Martha W. and Margaret N. Weston. "The Friends of Skimino Meeting," 1973. Typescript on file at Virginia Department of Historic Resources, Richmond.

Mount Pleasant Baptist Church. "Mt. Pleasant Baptist Church: 92nd Anniversary," 1983. Typescript on file with James City County Historical Commission, Toano.

Mount Vernon Methodist Church. "Mount Vernon, 1887–1981, A Brief History," 1981. Manuscript on file with James City County Historical Commission, Toano.

New Zion Baptist Church. "New Zion Baptist Church History," 1985. Manuscript on file with James City County Historical Commission, Toano.

Norton, Mary. "A Brief History of Williamsburg United Methodist Church," 1991. Typescript on file with James City County Historical Commission, Toano.

Olive Branch Christian Church. "A Brief History of Olive Branch Christian Church," 1990. Booklet on file with James City County Historical Commission, Toano.

Our Savior's Evangelical Lutheran Church. "Our Savior's Evangelical Lutheran Church, Norge, Virginia," 1973. Manuscript on file with James City County Historical Commission, Toano.

Powers, Lou. "Owners of 'the Grove' from 1839 to 1906 (Thomas Wynne through Dr. E. G. Booth): A Preliminary Report on Carter's Grove in the Nineteenth Century," 1984. Report on file at Colonial Williamsburg Foundation, Williamsburg.

_____. "Owners of 'the Grove' from 1839 to 1906 (Thomas Wynne through Dr. E. G. Booth): A Report on Carter's Grove in the Nineteenth Century," 1987. Report on file at Colonial Williamsburg Foundation, Williamsburg.

Saint John Baptist Church. "Saint John Baptist Church: 105th Anniversary," 1983. Typescript on file with James City County Historical Commission, Toano.

Saint Bede's Catholic Church. "A Profile of St. Bede's Church and Our Patrons," 1992. Parish Bulletin on file at the James City County Historical Commission, Toano.

Schlotterbeck, John T. "Plantation and Farm: Social and Economic Change in Orange and Green Counties, Virginia, 1716–1860," 1980. Dissertation, Johns Hopkins University, Baltimore.

Shiloh Baptist Church. "Shiloh Baptist Church History: 1866–1989," 1989. Manuscript on file with James City County Historical Commission, Toano.

Slauson, E. M. "History of the Peninsula Dairy Association," undated. Typescript on file at James City County Historical Commission, Toano.

Smith Memorial Baptist Church. "A Decade of Dedication," 1966. Manuscript on file with James City County Historical Commission, Toano.

Suders, Steven D. "Summary history of the King's Way Church of Williamsburg," 1992. Typescript on file with James City County Historical Commission, Toano.

Tabernacle United Methodist Church. "Tabernacle Church Then and Now," 1991. Manuscript on file with James City County Historical Commission, Toano.

Virginia Department of Historic Resources. Historic American Buildings Survey Form No. 47–31, 1976. On file at Virginia Department of Historic Resources, Richmond.

_____. Windsor Castle National Register Nomination, 1987. On file at Virginia Department of Historic Resources, Richmond.

Walnut Hills Baptist Church. "Sanctuary Dedication, Walnut Hills Baptist Church, Williamsburg," 1987. Walnut Hills Baptist Church, Williamsburg.

Wellspring United Methodist Church. "Wellspring United Methodist Church: A History and a Future," 1992. Typescript on file with James City County Historical Commission, Toano.

Williamsburg Christian Church. "From Out of the Past," 1976. Typescript on file with James City County Historical Commission, Toano.

Williamsburg Christian Church. "Addendum to the History of Williamsburg Christian Church," 1992. Typescript on file with James City County Historical Commission, Toano.

Williamsburg Community Chapel. "Great Things He Hath Done," undated. Typescript on file with James City County Historical Commission, Toano.

Williamsburg–James City County Bicentennial Committee. "The Bicentennial in Williamsburg, James City County, Virginia," 1976. Manuscript on file, Williamsburg Regional Library, Williamsburg.

Williamsburg Mennonite Church. "Profile of Williamsburg Mennonite Church," 1986. Typescript on file with James City County Historical Commission, Toano.

Williamsburg Presbyterian Church. "History," 1992. Typescript on file with James City County Historical Commission, Toano.

York River Baptist Church. "History of York River Baptist Church," 1992. Typescript on file with James City County Historical Commission, Toano.

Cartographic Sources

Anonymous. "Militia A.D. 1780," 1780. Library of Congress, Washington, D.C.

_____. "Position of the Combined Army Under Command of Major General Marquis de la Fayette," 1781. Colonial Williamsburg Foundation, Williamsburg.

_____. "Map of Virginia Showing the Distribution of the Slave Population from the Census of 1860," 1860. National Archives, Washington, D.C.

Bache, A. D. "York River, Virginia, from Clay Bank to Mount Folly," 1857–1858. National Archives, Washington, D.C.

Berthier, Alexander. "Camp a Williamsburg le Septembre 7 miles de Archers hope," 1781. Colonial Williamsburg Foundation Research Archives, Williamsburg.

Berthier, Alexander et al. Untitled map, 1781–1782. Colonial Williamsburg Foundation Research Archives, Williamsburg.

Captaine, Major Michael. Untitled map, 1781. Colonial Williamsburg Foundation Research Archives, Williamsburg.

Colles, Christopher. "From Annapolis to Williamsburg," 1789. Colonial Williamsburg Foundation Research Archives, Williamsburg.

Desandrouin, Nicholas. "Plan du terein a la Rive Gauche de la Riviere de James," 1781. Library of Congress, Washington, D.C.

Dewitt, Samuel. "From Allens Ordinary Through Williamsburg to York," 1781. Colonial Williamsburg Foundation, Williamsburg.

Donn, John W. "James River from College Creek to Chichahominy River," 1873–1874. National Archives, Washington, D.C.

Gilmer, J. F. "Vicinity of Richmond and Part of the Peninsula," 1863–1867. Library of Congress and National Archives, Washington, D.C.

Hare, I. Knowles. "Hare's Map of the Vicinity of Richmond and the Peninsula Campaign," 1862. National Archives and Library of Congress, Washington, D.C.

Humphreys, A. A. "Yorktown to Williamsburg," 1862. National Archives and Library of Congress, Washington, D.C.

Simcoe, John G. "Rebels dislodged from Williamsburg landing," 1781. National Archives and Library of Congress, Washington, D.C.

_____. "Action at Spencer's Ordinary," 1781. National Archives and Library of Congress, Washington, D.C.

Smith, Captain John. "Virginia Discovered and Discribed [sic]," 1610. Library of Congress, Washington, D.C.

Soane, John. "Land for William Sherwood," 1681. Colonial Williamsburg Foundation Research Archives, Williamsburg.

_____. "Survey for Thomas Lord Culpeper," 1683. Colonial Williamsburg Foundation Research Archives, Williamsburg.

_____. "Plot of 660 acres for Christopher Wormeley," 1684. Colonial Williamsburg Foundation Research Archives, Williamsburg.

_____. "The plott of 76 acres of land survey'd for Henry Jenkins, 1690," 1690. Colonial Williamsburg Foundation Research Archives, Williamsburg.

Thompson, James. "Property of Champion Travis Esquire, Surveyed and Delineated the 20th of M[–]," undated [18th century]. Colonial Williamsburg Foundation Research Archives, Williamsburg.

Zuniga, Pedro de. "Chart of Virginia," 1608. Virginia Department of Historic Resources, Richmond.

Index

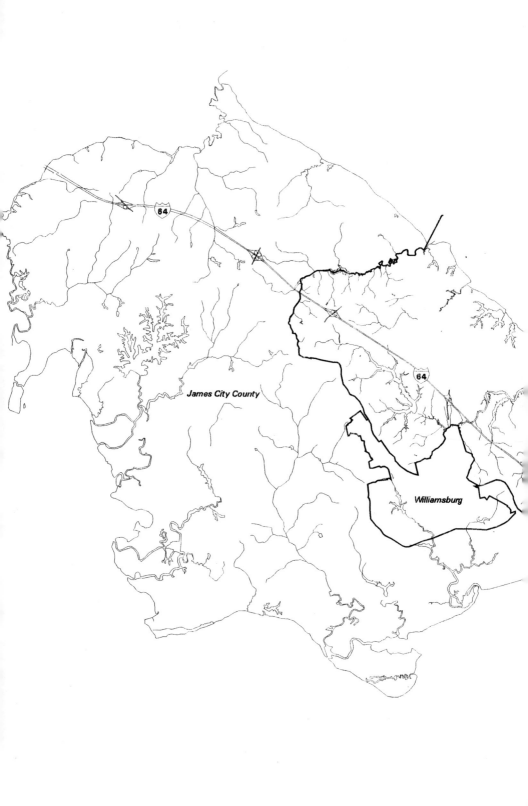